Post To Post

Book 2

(Walking in the Way)

By

Rayola Kelley

Hidden Manna Publications

Post To Post
Book 2
(Walking in the Way)

Copyright © 2022 by Rayola Kelley

ISBN: 978-0-9915261-8-5

Cover Design: Pam Wester

Printed in the USA

Except where otherwise indicated, all Scripture quotations in this book are taken from the King James Version of the Bible.

Hidden Manna Publications
PO Box 3572
Oldtown, ID 83822

Facebook:
https://www.facebook.com/HiddenMannaPublications/

CONTENTS

Introduction

This is the second book comprised of the Facebook posts I did over a period of three years. Both books address personal, national, and international events. It can show that even though life can prove to plod along, that by comparing the posts through the years it is obvious that life is a current that brings many subtle, as well as major changes with it.

The second book contains what I refer to as a different series that include such subjects as, "The Rock of My Salvation," "The Lord's Prayer," "The Christian Walk," and posts on the lives and happenings of men such as Adam, Abraham, Isaac, Moses, and Job. Unlike the first book that lays a type of groundwork, this book is meant to bring a realization of the steps of faith that are necessary in order to walk in the way of righteousness.

My prayer is that these posts will bring enlightenment to the spirit, and inspiration to the soul, and that as the reader allows each post to lead him or her on to the next post that it will become a means of encouragement, instruction, and enlargement of faith, vision, and purpose.

SEEKING GOD

*When men search for religious knowledge
instead of seeking to know God,
they end up embracing superstition and
ignorance about God.
(Rayola Kelley)*

What does it mean to seek? We are told in *Hebrews 11:6* that those who come to God must believe that he is, and that he is a rewarder of them that diligently seek him. Seeking when it comes to the kingdom of God proves to be a real discipline and it requires three responses—coming, believing, and diligently seeking.

There are many people looking for God, but they are not coming to Him. I know from experience you can look for God all you want and never find Him as long as you look for Him in the wrong places. This brings us to the inspiration that ensures us that we are looking in the right places and that is believing, but believing what?

I had a religious notion of God because we all have been born with a sense of who He is, but it was only from the premise of looking to and believing God for salvation in light of my sin and need for a Savior, I began to look in the right direction (upward) and the right place (the Bible) and for the right reason—to know God.

This brings me to the final aspect of seeking and that is being diligent in doing it. To be honest with you it was not until I was absolutely desperate and utterly hopeless that I diligently sought the Lord. I have learned that until I am at that point, I often simply seek relief and not deliverance because I am half-hearted about God really intervening outside of personal comfort zones.

The Bible is clear we must seek God if we are to live (*Amos 5:4*), for He is always faithful to reveal Himself to the truth seeker, but *Jeremiah 29:13* tells us how we are to seek Him, *"And ye shall seek me, and find me, when ye shall search for me with all your heart."*

What are you seeking for? Truth is becoming more and more a luxury in today's world. People are pursuing after substitutes instead of truth. They want experience that will supersede the Word of God, they desire the supernatural over the practical ways God often moves, they want fleshly worship that makes them feel good, and a reality that will fit their narrative.

Truth is often sacrificed on various altars to maintain delusion and wickedness. We are reminded that truth will affect people. It is a sharp sword that will penetrate the darkness of deception and wickedness, causing a reaction.

For some it will serve as a threat to their godless agendas and for others it will insult them because it brings a contrast to their wickedness. There are others who will become frightened by its reality because they cannot control it, and then there are those tender individuals who will be liberated by it because they choose to believe, love, and obey it.

Whether truth becomes a surgical knife of healing and restoration or a heartless weapon of chaos, judgment, or ruin, will be determined by the spirit in which it has been delivered and received.

Truth is truth, and the importance of the two virtues that must be present when speaking it are love and meekness. These virtues show the heart and attitude of truth. Love never rejoices in iniquity and meekness will always submit to truth and stand on it with a quiet confidence.

As I consider the reactions towards truth, I realize that people are not conditioned to allow the truth to challenge, shake, and offend them. The result for these individuals is that truth has lost its defining way as a light that brings clarity, its sharp ways as a sword to set the captive free from unseen chains, its blunt ways to awaken one's spirit, and its salty and bitter taste that can cause the soul to draw back from it, but once applied in the right way can heal wounds of the spirit and inflammation of the soul.

Today in the great darkness of deception, we believers need to become seekers and lovers of truth to walk through the darkness and be set free and healed of all that keeps our spirit from soaring in the currents of His Spirit and our soul firmly anchored to the Rock.

Desperate people are always looking for a lifeline to grab. Sadly, until people are desperate, they fail to realize they even need a lifeline. Before they find themselves in such a state, people for the most part see themselves as being sufficient, "good enough" to be immune from any real difficulties, capable of working out problems, skirting obstacles, avoiding pitfalls, and able to survive whatever comes at them.

Out of mercy and grace, God will begin to shake them in their self-sufficiency, push against their pinnacles of arrogance with the gale winds of the times, cause their faulty foundations to crack and split with the tests of the age, and turn upside down their different dependencies and notions to bring them tumbling down as they watch their strength being swallowed by some blackhole in the vast, empty universe of space.

I learned from past experiences that I usually do not seek God with everything in me until there is nothing left in me to wrestle, struggle, or control the present current. It is at that time I recognize that unless a lifeline is thrown my way, I will inevitably be pulled down by that current into the depths of utter despair and despondency. The mistake we make is we first look around us to see if some miraculous ship is coming to the rescue where someone will throw a lifeline to save us at the last minute.

It is when we realize there is no ship on the horizon, that we are apt to look up for the only truly glorious lifeline that has been cast down from above. Over 20 centuries ago, God provided a lifeline to pull us up from the miry swamp of this world and lift us out of the sinking mud of hopelessness, the decaying debris of vanity, and the quicksand of destruction. Even though we find ourselves taken down by the currents of time, we know that God's great lifeline can reach us.

King David admitted that even if he made his bed in hell God's presence would be with him. As believers we know who God's lifeline is, but how many of us are still trying to survive the currents and times of this age in our own strength instead of looking up, crying out to God and grabbing the lifeline of Jesus? How many of us are willing to simply concede that we need to hold onto that lifeline in the good, bad, and indifferent times to be lifted up from the doomed ship of this present world and placed in high places with our dear Savior and Lord? (See *Ephesians 2:6 & 7*.)

One of the people that serves as an example to me is the Samaritan who was healed of leprosy in *Luke 17:11-19*. This man was an outcast in different ways. First, he was a leper and these individuals lived outside of the city. Secondly, he was a Samaritan who lived outside of the acceptable Jewish religious system and was considered the worst of the lot by the Jewish people.

As he stood afar off with the other lepers in the village, and as Jesus came near, he along with the other nine began to cry out, "Jesus, Master have mercy on us." When it comes to seeking out Jesus, we must consider why.

These men stood outside of possessing any real quality of life. I don't know about you, but I came to Jesus because I was in a similar situation as the Samaritan. I was an outcast when it came to God, and my religion never addressed the matters of the heart and soul. I came to a place where I realized I stood afar off from God. Praise the Lord, Jesus did pass my way, heard my heart cry and called me, and as a result my life has never been the same.

There is an assumption on religious people's parts that all they need to do is say a small prayer here and there and everything should fall into place. However, when you studying the lives of people who were delivered or healed, many of them proved to be desperate because of the hopelessness of their situation. We see this in the case of the ten lepers in *Luke 17:11-19*.

After they cried out in desperation to Jesus, and He heard them, His instruction to them was to go to the priest to be declared cleaned. The Bible tells us that as they went to the priests, they were cleansed.

In other words, their encounter with and obedience to Jesus' instruction resulted in their healing. Many of us approach the Lord with needs, but how many of us approach Him to know and love Him? These men cried out to Jesus and received an instruction to go and confirm their healing, but how many gave thought to the One they encountered?

Out of the ten only one came back in an attitude of humility and gratitude. It is easy to act as if we deserve God's consideration by failing to be thankful to Him. Sadly, at the core of pride and selfishness is the same sin. It is call ingratitude.

Ingratitude will end in a person being presumptuous about a matter, especially when it comes to God's intervention. Presumption will end with mercy being abused, grace frustrated, love ignored, and disobedience covered up with half-hearted attempts to gain God's favor once again without choosing the way of faith and seeking with the whole heart to please, obey, and glorify God.

Do you wait for life, seek life, or experience life? Life is initially given to us. The Bible talks about how physical life is according to the will of man but our spiritual life is according to the will of God (*John 1:12-13*). It takes the combination of man and woman to ensure the life of its own kind, a life that is both a gift from God to mankind and part of His heritage.

Sadly, man and woman have decided to try and play God by choosing who will live by way of sacrifices through abortions and other occult practices. In a way, it may be a choice but not a right one. Every person has a right to have life and it is up to God, our creator how long our life is to be. Due to the fact man tries to play God in this arena shows how rebellious, foolish, and out of order he is, causing grave chaos, rotten fruits, and horrible consequences to bombard our homes and societies.

Today there are people who wait for life to fall on them; however, life is a current that flows where it will and eventually everyone gets caught up in it. For the believer, we are told to seek life so we can live or experience it. How do we seek life? We seek God who is the essence of life and we choose to get in the current of His Spirit to experience the life of Christ in us.

When it comes to seeking life, it means walking in the ways of righteousness as we desire to please God in all we do. As we walk in the way of life everlasting, we can expect to not only experience the power and blessings of this spiritual life, but we are assured of inheriting its promises.

Are you waiting for your life in Christ to fall on you? Such inaction shows unbelief towards God. The world offers each of us a vain lifestyle, but when it comes to lasting life, you must rise up and seek God so you can live, so you can experience the abundance of His gift of life.

Do you really want to be where the Lord is? I have asked myself this question many times. We want to think our devotion to the Lord would prove noble no matter what, our love for Him true and faithful regardless of circumstances, our faith genuine when nothing makes sense, and our complete hope based on Him when all seems hopeless. However, the darkness of times, the storms of life, and the challenges of character will reveal if our devotion is honorable, our love godly, our faith sustaining, and whether integrity of character is really present.

Before we can be where the Lord is, we must first count the cost of what it means to follow Him. Remember, Jesus' call to His disciples was "follow me." They had to walk away from the usual ways of maintaining life, familiar lifestyles, and cultural influences to embark on the unknown. The initial response for most would begin with a discussion or debate in the courtroom of the mind. Where am I going, why am I going, what will it do for me, how will I get there, and how long will it take? However, the Lord will never answer such questions because to follow Him we have to trust in Him that He will take us where we need to go because it is part of the preparation to finish the course as to fulfilling our calling and our destination for His glory.

The simple secret to any success in following Jesus is that we walk not by our fleshly, worldly understanding but according to faith directed toward the unseen Creator based on His Word and promises. I, for one, want to be where the Lord is, but am I willing to follow Him by faith. He will lead me into storms, but in the storms, I must discern if He is in the boat or walking on water. He may lead me to the wilderness away from the busyness of the world but will I trust Him to provide me with the necessary bread and water instead of looking back for the world's food and eventually running back into it because the suspense and worry of such matters is too much?

Perhaps He will lead me to the unpleasant fiery ovens that test my faith, or call me to follow Him up narrow paths that are often obscured by curves and clouds. At such times I must avoid falling into the temptation of procrastination and waiting until I can see beyond the crooked ways and the clouds, while losing focus of Him?

The real challenge in following Jesus is not where is He going but keeping my eye on Him. It is not about the why and what for, it is about trusting that the Lord has already taken care of every detail and all I have to do is follow Him to discover the life He has prepared for me.

SALVATION

God has weighed the whole world
in the balances and found it
wanting, and in Christ He provided
salvation for a wanting world
(R.A. Torrey)

When you hear the word "salvation," what does it mean to you? We need to remember that as Christians we have our own language, and sadly much of Christianity has become a subculture in the midst of many cultures.

Keep in mind, cultures point to cultivating people into a certain way of thinking and lifestyle. Language, food preferences, and dress are some of the things that set different cultures apart. Lifestyles point to the way people are civilized, but for believers Christianity is not a subculture with its certain lingos and lifestyles but it is **LIFE** itself.

Salvation has to do with being delivered from death to life. We need to be delivered from the influences of the world, the flesh, the devil, and, yes even aspects of our culture. Salvation implies Christ's life is in everyone who has believed the Gospel and received Jesus into their hearts.

According to missionary Paris Reidhead, there are four distinct tenses of salvation: the PERFECT tense of salvation is repentance. We must be ever ready to turn from, repent, and mortify our sinful old life to embrace a new life. The PAST tense of salvation is justification. Once we receive Christ, we stand justified as if we never sinned for we have been saved from the lasting influence of sin upon our life by the redemption of Jesus. The PRESENT tense of salvation is sanctification, for we are being presently saved from the workings of sin in our lives by the sanctifying work of the Holy Spirit.

The FUTURE tense of salvation is glorification with Jesus, which points to being saved from any future activities of sin on our lives. Are you walking in the perfect tense of salvation because you have experienced the past tense of salvation, while trusting in its present work of deliverance and looking forward to the future promise of realizing the fullness of redemption?

People are looking for some type of deliverance during these trying times. The truth is people have always looked for deliverance, but some had no idea that spiritual liberation is what their soul desires.

The reasons are clear for this dilemma. There are always those who do not see a need for deliverance because they either have survived past challenges and came out alright, or they are still toying with options to come out on top of a matter. There are those who convince themselves that if they just hold on for a little while longer, this insanity will go away and everything will return to "normal," but will it?

We are living in insane times that don't make sense and people are becoming more desperate to come out on the other end of it. We have been listening to the so-called "experts" about this problem for months and they are not offering any real hope except if we want to save our life, we must give up our quality of life and come under a type of oppression for the collective good of everyone else. However, what we are experiencing now is nothing new, and Ecclesiastes reminds us there is nothing new under the sun.

People may want deliverance but they really need to be saved not from the times, but from their own spiritual plight. Someone summarized the real issue of deliverance or I should say salvation when he stated that it is easy to get a person saved, but what is hard is getting him or her lost in the first place. In my own experience I have encountered the attitude that, "There is no way I can be all that bad."

It is like saying I am somewhat lost, but not really all that lost. It is for this reason that it takes the convicting power of the Spirit to penetrate the dark delusion of a person's spiritual state to reveal that he or she is totally lost due to the fallen state that operates in the darkness of sin and death. One must recognize he or she is lost before he or she can see the need for salvation and truly be saved according to God's plan of salvation.

The Apostle Paul was concerned that believers would get away from the simplicity of Christ, and what is the simplicity of Christ? He is the ONLY way to salvation. To the unsaved, we are not to preach or promote anything other than Christ and Him crucified.

As Christians we must be reminded that we are heirs of faith (not of certain denominations, laws, or practices), that identify us as the spiritual seed of Abraham, whose faith allowed him to see the day of Christ in the figure of his own son, Isaac while rejoicing as he looked for a city made by the hands of God.

It is that same gift of faith that Abraham possessed that allows us as believers to see who Jesus is and needs to be to us. The beauty about Jesus is that He allows us to look beyond this present world to see a future age that will cause our heart to rejoice, our spirit to soar, and our soul to come to rest in unseen promises.

Rayola Kelley

The Gospel is the power of God unto salvation. According to *1 Corinthians 15:1-4*, it has three main parts to it: Christ died for sin, He was buried, and He rose again three days later. This message seems simple enough, but if a person does not understand who Christ is and why He had to die for our sin, as well as the significance of His burial and resurrection, they will never see their need to embrace it. The only way a person sees the need to be saved is when they realize they are under a death sentence due to the fact we are all sinners in grave need of deliverance from the judgment that awaits us.

As stated, the preaching of the Gospel is to wake people up to their urgent, desperate plight so that they can turn from the darkness of their own sin and face the light and hope of Christ who took the place for each of us on a rugged cross. For Christians, the Gospel must never simply be whittled down to a mere word that is used without meaning, some doctrine that is referred to, or a sentimental idea; rather, we must see that we have indeed benefitted from the good news of Jesus Christ, and we need to urgently share it with others when given the opportunity.

It has always amazed me that we will share news that excites us, our good recipes, viable information, talk about decent shows, and etc. but how many of us remain quiet about the good news that has the power to determine a person's eternal destiny?

How important is it for Christians to be willing to share the "good news" of Jesus Christ? As believers we can take for granted the work of redemption that Jesus wrought on the cross for each of us.

I was saved out of a cult, but before my salvation experiences, I was on my way to hell without knowing it. There were Christians around me, but they remained silent. I realized I might have not been ready to hear the good news, but I clearly recall that no one shared the message of the cross of Christ with me during that time.

How important is it for each of us to fulfill our commission: it could mean the difference for one soul or many living in eternity with the Lord or in a Christ-less eternity of torment and utter spiritual ruin.

One of the words that I think has been discarded altogether is "gratitude." This word has been silenced with a vacuum that has been filled up to the very top with selfishness and vain imaginations. How does one gain gratitude? It is simple, we gain it by having some sense or semblance of the cost or value of something.

The greater the sacrifice made, the greater value is put on it, producing gratitude. When I was growing up, my parents did not have money, causing me to work for what I wanted, teaching me to appreciate and become responsible for what I earned. I went into the military to advance my education, and through the years worked hard to pay my debts, while realizing all I had was a matter of God's grace.

These simple experiences taught me to understand that nothing of value will ever be handed to me. If something is important enough to me, I must pay the price to obtain it so I can likewise enjoy it, and to properly enjoy it I must take responsibility for how I value it.

Experiences comes out of patience of enduring a matter and will produce hope in us because God is faithful to be with us and keep us during such a time.

It is clear that some of those who are caught up with the latest movements lack any gratitude for the country and the sacrifices of others. They do not value the freedom they now seem to be abusing and squandering, while being willing to take away the freedom of others. They rant over "injustices" while being tyrannical towards others; they want freedom from the law while falling into a cesspool of chaos that will eventually require some rules to prevent them from drowning or choking to death in utter insanity.

It is clear that because one group of people have not paid a price to be free, they are willing to deny others of their freedom. As Christians we know salvation is a free gift from God, but it cost God His best (His Son), and Jesus His all, (His life). The reason no man could obtain this salvation is because it is attached to a debt none of us could pay, but there is a cost once we receive salvation, and it begins with the word "if."

This word does not imply something optional, but a prerequisite to cause one to ponder if he or she is willing to pay a price to experience the fullness of salvation's bounties, and that is discipleship. "Deny self of your right to have life on your terms, pick up your cross of discipline and adjust your walk to the narrow path, and follow Jesus in obedience to discover the fullness of your spiritual inheritance." This simple call is a call to complete consecration.

THE ABCs OF
THE CHRISTIAN WALK

The Christian walk is associated
with every letter in every alphabet.
It covers it all by reaching heaven,
embraces all on earth and extends to
the deepest known parts. It is
eternal, glorious and in the end
INDESCRIBABLE!
(Rayola Kelley)

I often make reference to words that I meditate on, especially when I see them being misused, misconstrued, or overlooked. It is easy to change the intent of a word to fit propaganda and wicked agendas. As a writer, I love "words." They prove to be mightier than the sword when properly used, but for many people they have failed to recognize how words are cunningly used to affect their attitude towards a matter.

Take the word "meek" for example. In our language it means "weak," but in the Bible it means, "strength or rage under control." It is for this reason the word "meek" is used before "temperance" in the fruit of the Spirit. One must be under the control of the Spirit before they can exhibit true self-control (temperance).

Today, there are those who want to foolishly throw all restraints off of society that ensure that people's actions will be legally and morally

18

tempered towards each other to ensure order. To take away restraints where people are made responsible and accountable for dishonorable behavior will leave a vacuum in our society that will be filled with poisonous and nightmarish results.

We as believers must discern words, ideas, and claims in order to trace them back to their real source to properly discern the agenda behind it. This is necessary to ensure that we do not become sheep that are being led by some pied piper to the slaughtering pens. It is easy to discern words because they will reveal the intent or spirit behind a person while exposing their real attitude towards a matter. This is why Jesus warned people to beware of how they hear, because they can easily be conditioned into a deaf state where any constructive opposition and warning will not be heard, seduced into another reality that will be stirred up in a destructive way when challenged, and indoctrinated into a worldview that will rage against any reason that would dare shake their foundation with truth and consequences.

There are many voices in this world, but if we are Jesus' sheep, we will only be tuned into hearing His voice. His main voice is the Word of God, but to properly process His Word, we must love truth and allow His Spirit to reveal the intent as we discipline our walk to line up in obedience.

The more we temper our walk to the Word, the more we are brought under the control of the Spirit, and the clearer the voice of our Shepherd will become to us. Remember the warning of Jesus when He quoted Isaiah in *Matthew 13:13-16, "Therefore speak I to them in parables: because they seeing see not; and hearing they hear not, neither do they understand. And in them is fulfilled the prophecy of Esaias, which saith, By hearing ye shall hear, and shall not understand; and seeing ye shall see, and shall not perceive: For this people's heart is waxed gross, and their ears are dull of hearing, and their eyes they have closed; lest at any time they should see with their eyes, and hear with their ears, and should understand with their heart, and should be converted, and I should heal them. But blessed are your eyes, for they see: and your ears, for they hear."*

Most Christians know the ABCs of Christianity. We must ACKNOWLEDGE we are sinners, to intellectually ACCEPT that we are lost in sin and stand condemned. This is necessary if we are to come into AGREEMENT with God's evaluation that we are in need of a personal Savior; thereby, being BORN AGAIN by BELIEVING in our hearts and receiving it as so, that He has provided us with the only solution through His Son Jesus Christ.

We must then CONFESS Jesus is Lord. Confession is not just a verbal declaration. The Greek meaning of this word points to the concept of verbally declaring that you are entering into a binding contract, and what is the contract? When we confess Jesus is Lord, we are declaring He is our owner and we are His servant who will serve in His household *(1 Corinthians 6:20; 7:22-24)*.

In the Old Testament, there were two types of servants. There were those who were servants due to debts. They had to serve until their debt was paid or they were released from it, and the second type of servant was what they referred to as a bondservant. These were servants who indebted themselves the rest of their lives to serve their lord out of love.

In *Deuteronomy 15:15-17* we are told how such willing servants had an aul thrust through their ear to the door as identification that they would only hear their Lord and were committed for a lifetime to serve his household. Jesus paid a debt we could not pay to set us free from the tyrannical master of sin to give us freedom, but what does that freedom entail? Does it mean we can go live any old way, do our own thing, and decide how and when we are going to do the bidding of our Lord Jesus Christ? The answer is we were set free to choose who we are going to serve.

As servants we have no right outside of what our master ordains. The question is, are you a mere servant of Jesus deciding when and how you serve Him while holding on to the benefits of being part of His household or are you a bondservant serving Him out of love because He is worthy of your best service, your most honorable commitment, and all of your devotion.

Jesus said it best in *John 14:15* and *Luke 6:46, "If you love me, keep my commandments,"* and *"And why call ye me, Lord, Lord, and do not the things which I say?"*

Yesterday, I mentioned the ABCs of Christianity. When I first received Jesus into my life, I read a tract on the ABCs of Christianity that explains the necessary steps to salvation, and I was quite impressed with the simplicity of the message. But, as I began to mature in my faith, I recognized one of the problems with some Christians is they stop with the ABCs of salvation, failing to go on to spiritual maturity.

To such individuals, salvation is enough to get into heaven; therefore, there is no need to advance forward. However, the Bible does not present such a picture. The Apostle Paul instructs us to work out our salvation in fear and trembling in *Philippians 2:12*.

At salvation the life of Jesus has been freely imparted to us and now we are to work His life in us through faith and work it out through obedience, while walking according to it in our devotion and conduct. The more we work His life in us, the more we will become a reflection of Him in this world, verifying our testimony of Him as being true.

The question is, what is beyond acknowledging personal sin, believing Jesus died in our place to take our sin upon Himself, and confessing that He is Lord? We know the letter "d" follows "c," which immediately brings to mind the next step past salvation: *DISCIPLESHIP*.

The salvation of a soul is glorious, but it is not enough. We would never leave a helpless baby to defend for itself, but sadly how many baby Christians have been left to themselves to figure out much of Christianity, and in the process, they have been left floundering in cesspools of heresies, pigpens of worldly compromise and confusion, and prey to religious predators with their own agendas? Sadly, as believers we have often failed to make the necessary investment to ensure new Christians have every opportunity to grow in the knowledge of Jesus.

This brings us to true discipleship. Discipleship is about making a new believer a follower of Jesus Christ. So many times, we Christians

21

have a tendency to try to make converts according to our doctrine, or in our pious image, or in light of our religious causes and agendas. It is clear, our responsibility is to make new believers into true followers and students of their Lord and Savior, Jesus Christ.

We have been considering the ABCs of Christianity. We began with the simple foundation that leads us to the Rock of our salvation. As our foundation the Rock enables us to stand by FAITH when the storms of life challenge us. The storms reveal the character and resolution of our FAITH in order to enlarge and mature it for the next test that comes our way.

It is our faith in God that enables us to stand and our faithfulness in relationship to obedience to His Word that will allow us to climb higher on that Rock in the storms of life. The higher we climb on the Rock to get above the storm to gain His perspective, the more we discover that He is our refuge which we hide in and our high tower that lifts us above the storm.

As our high tower, we are allowed to encounter and feel the blessed wind of the Holy Spirit as He lifts us even higher so that we can indeed discover those heavenly places in Christ. Sadly, there are circumstances in life that fling us down to the very deep base of the Rock by grave losses and challenges. We discover all we can do is hold on to what we know is true about our Lord, cling in utter desperation to what seems hollow promises so that we do not lose our sanity, and cry out to God so we will not be consumed by the storms raging in our soul. I say all of this because our last letter was "d" for discipleship and now we have "f" for faith, but what happened to the "e" in our alphabet?

You can't skip a letter and expect anything constructive to make sense in any arena of life. Note the word that was used in the previous sentence, "EXPECT." This word is associated with the word "hope," which serves as a steady anchor to faith to keep one from being taken off course. We must live in EXPECTATION of God being true to His word to possess true and lasting hope, but there is another important word that begins with "e." It is the word "EARNESTLY."

We must EARNESTLY seek God in every aspect of our life with the expectation of being found by Him (*Jeremiah 29:13*). We are told to seek the Lord and we will live. Seeking something requires the expectation that what we are after is worthy of such consideration, and if it is worthy then we must earnestly pursue it until we find it.

Many people want to skip certain steps to claim faith without earnestly searching for God so they can know what it means to properly worship, serve, and bring glory to Him. The result of skipping over, or avoiding taking important steps in our faith walk, will end up with our faith becoming shipwrecked.

What does one expect when earnestly pursuing God? We have talked about acknowledging, believing, confessing, discipleship, expectation and earnestly seeking God by faith, but what is the purpose for this pursuit? This brings us to the next letter of our alphabet and that is "g" for "GOODNESS."

We are earnestly pursuing God to know and taste His goodness. For some people, God has become very small, often confined within some intellectual box of theology, adorned in some lifeless creed, and exalted on some pinnacle created by self-serving imagination, but the God of the Bible is real, living, and eternal. Man's attempt to bring God down to his limited understanding will simply strip Him of His glory in a person's mind, ending with that individual bowing before some idol of their own making.

God stands outside of all man's understanding. He does not operate in the same dimension as man, that of time, space, and physical material, and for man to try to put God, who operates in the dimension of eternity, within his fleshly, intellectual, and worldly dimension as a means to understand or control any narrative about Him, is foolish and dangerous. It is for this reason we are reminded that God's thoughts and ways are higher than our thoughts and ways (*Isaiah 55:8-9*).

There are many words that are used to describe God, and one of the words He uses is "goodness." God is good, but what does that mean? We all have our ideas, but to do God justice we need to understand it in light of His attributes. When you look up the word "good" in the Strong's Concordance it points to that which is beautiful, gracious, kind, loving, pleasant, precious, sweet, and well-favored. God is adorned in majestic beauty beyond all description. He is gracious towards us, kind in His desires, loving in His commitment, pleasant in His ways, precious because of His holiness, and sweet to taste because He is "GOOD."

It is clear that God is to be experienced in a personal relationship, but the only way we can experience Him is through Jesus Christ. Jesus is the face of God when it comes to His grace and love, the way of God when it comes to His kindness, the promise of God when it comes to the life of God, the standard of God when it comes to His holiness, the preciousness of God when it comes to His fragrance, and the hope of God when it comes to future glory.

The Apostle Paul summarized God's goodness in relationship to Jesus Christ in *2 Corinthians 9:15, "Thanks be unto God for his unspeakable gift."*

There are 26 letters in our alphabet and 22 in the Hebrew alphabet. You can use every letter of the alphabet to describe God and your walk with Him, and when you try to exhaust every word or phrase, you can only conclude that even if you could use every noun, verb, and adjective to try to describe our eternal God and the adventurous and abundant life we as believers have in Him, we would still come to a place of humble silence as we realize He is beyond comprehension and description.

There are times I am so overwhelmed by the revelation of God that I can't speak, while there are occasions where I have such a sense of His beauty and presence my voice breaks as I struggle to get the next word out to finish my thoughts or sentence. There are other times I experience the reality of God in the heights of His Spirit to realize that such an experience is too precious, too glorious to ever put into words.

Don't get me wrong, I walk and live in the valleys of humiliation in this world, but I try to live my life according to the next world and occasionally the two touch and when that happens, time stops, moments stand still, and what becomes real and true is what is eternal.

24

I say all of this because when there is silence and space even in our words and sentence, God fills them with something that is beyond description. And, what we discover at such times is that the eternal and the unseen is more real than the material world.

As believers we are to live in light of the next world to come, but never become so heavenly minded we cease be a realistic witness in this world. The truth is man is walking in this world according to some destination. In a sense, he is preparing to step through the door of the unseen into a different dimension, into eternity.

I have been using the alphabet to establish some simple truths about Christianity and my hope is other believers will sit down and write out their own vocabulary as to their Christian journey, and when you land on the letter "z," perhaps the word you will use is "zealous" unto good works, or "Zion," the city of the great King.

The last letter that was used was "g" for the "goodness" of God. God is good and His desire is to keep our feet on the narrow path so that when we come to the end of our journey in this life, we will step through the door to heaven and His glory and not off the edge of the abyss into hell.

What does your present walk and work reveal about your preparation for your future?

THE JOURNEY

Our very life must be held
not as a selfish possession
but as a sacred trust.
(A.B. Simpson)

It is easy to begin with salvation but I discovered my spiritual journey began long before I met Jesus. This is due to the fact that my journey before Christ and as a Christian has not always been focused in the right way or direction.

My initial religious journey began in the midst of false lights of religion that gave the impression of righteousness but lacked the power thereof. I realized that Satan, who presents himself as an angel of light, also endows his minions with the ability to present themselves as ministers of righteousness.

The more I became aware of the heavy burden of sin, I became desperate to discover the means of forgiveness, to be free of the great hopelessness I felt. I didn't realize it then, but the path I was on became a journey of discovering what life was all about and it led me to the way of forgiveness, the truth about deliverance, and the type of life I so desperately desired.

As a Christian, my journey took me up a narrow path that disciplined my steps, but also instilled in me the qualities to endure and reach places that brought growth and established character in me.

It is easy to settle into the easy chairs of the world after doing some religious duty. It is also comfortable to be arm-chair referees when it comes to others running the race, but as believers we must be willing to run our own race if we are going to possess the prize of Christ.

Life is an adventure that must be experienced. I often ask Christians if they are good mountain and rock climbers, canyon and cave explorers, and sailors on the high seas, seasoned enough to confront each challenge that buffets them on their journey through the world.

As a believer, we know God can move the mountain, but sometimes we must be willing to climb above our own perspectives to catch the currents of hope. When it comes to emotional canyons or caves, we sometimes must walk through them in order to walk out of them, knowing the Lord will not forsake us. And, when it comes to the tumultuous waves of life that can slam against our resolve, we can rest assured that the Lord is in the boat with us and at the right time, He will speak to the waves.

I have to admit, I have not always appreciated the hard places I have encountered in my faith walk, but hindsight reveals I would not trade those times for level plains and smooth waters that might be void of challenge. The problem with level plains and smooth waters is that they will cause one to lose his or her discerning edge as a watchman, as it is easy to slip into some level of sleep due to spiritual stagnation. It is for this reason Paul exhorted Christians to awake.

At such a point of slumber the Christian can become a Jonah who trusts everyone around him or her to keep the ship above water. The truth is the storms are here in America, shaking foundations, exposing corruption, and we as Christians must not remain content to stay in the hull of our religious boxes, holding onto some small rope of theology or a buoy of doctrine to keep us afloat if the ship goes down.

As believers we need not go down with any worldly, religious ship of the day; rather, we need to make sure we are clinging to the only true Rock of Ages Jesus, while standing on the unchanging foundation of God's truths, and looking up, knowing our redemption draws near.

As I look back at my experiences as a believer, I am amazed of how crooked my path has been even in the valleys, how many detours I took, how many walls I ran into, and how many closed doors I encountered. It took different types of experiences for me to realize that God was guiding my steps even though He had to make the crooked paths either straight or impossible to tread in order to guide me.

He allowed the detours, but was gracious enough to mark the end of them with cliffs or abysses, causing me to get back on track. He erected the walls to redirect my focus and sealed the wrong doors shut with a warning written on it, "DO NOT TRESPASS!"

I wish I could say that I became wise to each misdirected step, wrong course, and barricade that confronted me, but I had to walk away many times in great despair, disillusionment, or with a headache before I realized how merciful God was being to me. Since then, I have tried to watch for ripples that make me aware there is activity going on around me and to watch for the unexpected speed bumps that caution me to change momentum, visible bends that cause me to slow down in preparation, and discern diversions that could take me away from the main path.

Jesus is coming soon and time is short. As believers we do not have the time and luxury to make too many wrong turns. We need to make sure that our convictions are righteous and will hold us on course, sparing us from taking detours, while our mind is set on what is eternal to avoid becoming confused at the different crossroads. We need our map, God's Word in hand, our compass, the Holy Spirit to make sure we are pointed in the right direction, and our steps ever lining up to the ways of righteousness.

We must always be prepared to hold ourselves accountable to what is excellent in light of what is promised. We must not ignore the profane in the details, the wickedness in the practices, and the death and destructive evilness in the fruit. We must come out and be separate from the profane, stand against the wickedness, and flee from that which is associated with evil. We must be the light that shines in the darkness regardless of what is going on and for the lost who follow the light, they will discover that it reflects the solution to all matters concerning life and death, the Lord Jesus Christ.

My faith walk has allowed me to learn some important lessons, but one of them is nothing happens in my life by chance. On our recent trip, we hit a roadblock on a major highway due to an enormous rock slide comprised of a two-story tall boulder along with other boulders that were immense in size totally blocking the road.

We were forced to take a detour that allowed us to see the countryside from a different perspective. When it comes to spiritual construction, roadblocks, or detours, we must rest in the fact that either God is in control or become fearful and act as if He is subject to the times, whims, and events of this world.

I watch some Christians get caught up with the different tides flowing through the world and becoming fearful and wavering in their faith towards God. In the Christian life each hindrance or opposing encounter is of the utmost importance to us. Such hindrances are never meant to destroy us or prevent us from being about our Father's business.

In the spiritual construction zones of my life I have encountered, it has always been about me slowing down or even stopping because God needs to do some work in me. Spiritual construction zones are more about preparation than silly inconveniences that seem like a waste of time.

When it comes to spiritual roadblocks, they are meant to stop us and consider what route the Lord is opening up for us, trusting that He has good reason for it. Perhaps, it is to avoid some danger we are not aware of, and spiritual detours may be irritating, but it slows us down enough to enjoy that which was unseen before.

I have learned that spiritual construction is about preparation, but roadblocks and detours are a lot about timing. Because of God's timing, we missed a terrible landslide, and on our return a terrible car accident. If we believe God is in control, then we need to trust that the obstacles in our way have been put there or allowed by our Lord for a very good reason.

What serves as the essence of your life? Most people are after quantity which points to the tangible that is often gauged by lifestyle and not that which consists of life. The problem with lifestyle is that it is how we perceive we must live life to be happy. Sadly, some people are busy pursuing what is lifeless, causing much of their life to prove vain and insignificant as they chase after the next adventure, the next sensational event, and the next point of entertainment.

The Corona virus we now face, whether a hoax, exaggerated, or real, is clearly challenging our lifestyle, not just by halting all worldly pursuits, but by bringing us face to face with the possibility of death. I wonder how many people in light of this real life-and-death issue are discovering that their present life has no real substance and it leaves them feeling anxious and hollow. Jesus said it best in *Luke 12:15, "Take heed, and beware of covetousness: for a man's life consisteth not in the abundance of the things which he possesseth."*

Real life must be experienced as one walks or lives it out. Life can't be experienced until we realize is it a gift from God, and it cannot be walked out until we recognize the majority of the quality of our life is based on our relationship with God and with others. In people's pursuit to gain some type of life based on the world's ideas, they can easily miss the essence of real life.

It is only when the vanity of this world is measured against life and death issues such as an unseen virus that man has the opportunity to reflect on what is truly important. May this time serve as a valuable opportunity for every believer to examine and see what the essence of their life truly consists of.

We recently took a small journey. Some call it a vacation, but I call it a change of scenery. We need to occasionally get away from our normal environment to see if our present environment is becoming small and insipid because we live in small worlds when it comes to our particular realities.

I try to enlarge myself by reading books or expose myself to information that will NOT leave me comfortable in a swamp of ridiculousness or slowly sinking in some cesspool of the profane and deceitful. As believers, we must be willing to step outside of what is "normal," "comfortable," "convenient," and "narrow" to honestly examine the environment within, discern the environment without, and gauge the direction of our focus as to whether it is earthbound, being consumed by the world, or maintaining that upward tilt towards heaven.

On our trip we encountered construction, roadblocks, and a detour. We even got a bit turned around at one place and had to do some backtracking to get back on course. As Christians we sometimes forget we are simply passing through. Earth is not our destination but the place we are simply traveling through. As a result, we need to hold our involvement with this present life lightly, avoid being influenced by the world's ways, and avoid taking unnecessary detours that allow us to become totally lost in the insanity of our times.

The beauty about having our citizenship elsewhere is that we are not meant to stay where we're at because it is not our true home. As a result, we can keep our journey through this age in perspective as we learn the lessons of life in preparation of taking possession of our eternal inheritance. Meanwhile, we must get the most out of our walk.

Our journey here allows us to do some sightseeing, while maneuvering through different types of terrain that can be plagued by construction, roadblocks, or detours. We should avoid getting excited, irritated, and freak out when we encounter such obstacles by remembering it is God that directs our steps and not this world.

Saturday, I took a day off from technology to do spring work in the yard. There are always plenty of projects to do both in the house and outside of the house this time of year. It is a time of regeneration that reminds each of us we are part of a cycle of life. My heart is always to keep centered in what is important.

So many times, our priorities cause us to major in unnecessary activities and our agendas cause us to focus on dead-end activities. We live in a world that chokes out what is important with the insignificant and promises glowing results with that which is void of any life or substance.

Working out in the yard reminds me that since I am from the earth, I need to come back to it to remember I am but dust. It helps me to become grounded as I recognized how small of a footprint I will ultimately leave. Once I am gone, my footprint will quickly be lost when the dust is stirred up by the winds of changing times and cycles.

When I have looked around, I remembered God made all of the beauty I was beholding and that it is His blessing on a matter that ensures life and blessing. As I am reminded of God, I can't help but look up to the heavens above and remember that none of it can contain His presence and His power.

During these days in history, it is so important for believers to become and remain grounded in God's Word as they remember they are but dust, but that God knows their frame, holds their days in His hand, and that the work He desires to do in their soul is eternal. They must hold to the promise that the work He is doing through them, because of the great work of redemption, will become part of the great cloud of witnesses that will testify of God faithfulness, greatness, and power.

Many of us may have heard or grown up with the term, "Doing it in good faith." This concept pointed to the idea that whatever was verbally agreed upon would be carried out. To do something in good faith also meant you could trust the other party because they possessed the integrity to keep their agreements.

Sadly, since many people's word means nothing, we do not find this practice of "doing something in good faith." Now we have to have binding contracts that end up in court because someone fails to keep their end of the agreement. To do something in good faith points to another virtue and that is faithfulness.

Married couples take a vow of faithfulness. In good faith they are declaring that they will be faithful to their spouse until death parts them. In the Old Testament words spoken before witnesses in the gate made it a binding contract. This is why Jesus tells us our words will justify us in what we say and do or they will condemn us (*Matthew 5:33-37; 12:35-37*). In essence, our word will ultimately confirm or reveal whether our intention was sincere. If it wasn't, we have just committed a fraud upon the other person (*1 Thessalonians 4:3-6*).

Another word for "contract" is "covenant." When you look at the fruit of the Spirit, the word used to describe the attitude and conduct of a Christian is faithfulness. As Christians, we have entered into a binding contract with God. We are told that our witnesses on earth as to this contract are the Spirit, the Word of God (water-*Ephesians 5:26*), and the blood of Jesus (*1 John 5:6*).

Jesus' blood is what provided the way to enter into this contract, the Word lines out our part in this contract, and the Holy Spirit enables us to keep our end of it. The Bible also tells us that unless we are faithful with small matters, God will never entrust us with greater matters of His kingdom.

Due to our pride, it is natural to look to great things, but unless we learn to be faithful and take care of the small details, we will never be prepared to see the great things of heaven through to the end. As we talk about real faith, its natural byproduct is faithfulness to do what is right regardless of what confronts us along the way. We have a tendency to ignore small details, which can become a habit.

If you are not advancing in your Christian walk, examine to see if you ignored some small detail along the way, revealing either the presence of rebellion or unbelief.

THE ROCK OF MY SALVATION

It seems many Christians would rather put on their spiritual diapers of foolish expectation and suck on the pacifier of untested doctrine by standing on feelings and emotions instead of putting on their armor and standing on both the Rock (Jesus Christ) and the Word of God. (Rayola Kelley)

It is easy to become caught up with the "why's" of life, but the "why's" of life will eventually cause one to sink into the abyss of hopelessness. I have seen the small "why's" sink big ships because they will eventually allow doubts to flow like rushing water into our lives.

God will never answer the "why's" of a matter up front, but like the great patriarch Job, He will reveal Himself in a greater way in such dark times. I don't know about you, but I have had a lot of "why's" hit me at different times. The Lord never immediately answered my question, but if I decided to trust Him in spite of the question marks, He would reveal Himself to me in such a glorious way, that the "why's" receded into nothingness because what mattered in the end was the abiding reality of His faithfulness to never leave me nor forsake me when I am walking through such grave shadows and dark valleys.

It is easy for us to put too much emphasis on the "whys" to understand a matter to know that we are not some helpless corks on the ocean that is being tossed to and fro by something called "fate." I know personally that as a child of God the waves and storms in my life are directed by God and that I am not some cork on the ocean of life; rather, I am held by the anchor of joy to the Rock of Ages that cannot ever be moved by storms or waves.

As I allow the anchor of the joy of His salvation to hold me, I can encourage myself because I know that I will experience His mercy that is new every day, His grace that is ever flowing, and His protection that is flawless and complete.

The other night I was dreaming and I kept getting a message: "The Rock is your strength and if you abide in its shadow, you will have nothing to fear." I had that dream at least three times, leaving me with the same message. I don't remember most dreams but I knew the significance of the message.

How many of you have studied the "Rock" in Scripture? Some great passages about the Rock in Scripture can be found in *Deuteronomy 32; 1 Samuel 22, Psalm 18, 62,* and *78. 1 Samuel 2:2* states, *"There is none holy as the LORD: for there is none beside thee: neither is there any rock like our God."* Today we live in some pretty overwhelming times. We know that this time has been prophesied but it still proves to be a bit disconcerting watching what I consider a big wave of destruction pour through this country and the world, and it is not just because of a virus but because of the wicked, political agendas of tyrants and despots of our age.

I know that this great wave of destruction will hit, but those who stand on the Rock (foundation) will not be moved, those who cling to it as a cornerstone will watch the wave's power dissipate and move around it, those who hide in it will have complete assurance and safety from the destruction, and those who seek it will find salvation.

As believers we need to know everything that can be shaken will be shaken and only that which is founded on the Rock, lining up to it, and firmly hidden in it will survive the great wave that is rolling through the sea of humanity.

Are you holding to the true Rock of heaven?

One of my favorite studies to do is the one on the Rock. I usually start from the premise of *1 Corinthians 10*. In the first three verses it talks about the children of Israel's baptism through the sea and that they ate the same spiritual bread and then in verse 4 it tells us this, *"And did all drink the same spiritual drink: for they drank of that spiritual Rock that followed them: and that Rock was Christ."*

One of the Scriptures that presents a beautiful picture of this Rock is found in *Exodus 17:6*. It was at this time the children of Israel were murmuring in the wilderness about their lack of water while demanding Moses provide them with it. Moses cried out to the Lord and this is the instruction He gave him, *"Behold I will STAND before thee there upon the rock of Horeb; and thou shalt SMITE the rock, and there shall come water out of it, that the people may drink. And Moses did so in the sight of the elders of Israel."* (Emphases added.)

Notice, there are three things brought out about this Rock, two of which I emphasized. One is that the Lord would stand before His servant and the second is that Moses would smite the rock before the elders, and number three, water would come forth so that the people could drink. Is this not a beautiful picture of Jesus!

John 7:37-39 states this, *"In the last day, that great day of the feast, Jesus STOOD and cried saying, If any man thirst, let him come unto me and drink. He that believeth on me, as the scripture hath said, out of his belly shall flow rivers of living water. (But this spake he of the Spirit, which they that believe on him should receive for the Holy Ghost was not yet given; because that Jesus was not yet glorified."* (Emphasis added.)

Just like the rock of old had to be struck in front of witnesses before the water could come forth, Jesus had to be STRUCK by man, nailed to a cross for all to see, buried and rise again in a new glorified body before the Living Water of heaven, the Holy Spirit, could be sent and uncapped in man's spirit and come forth as rivers of Living Water to ensure eternal life for all of those who truly respond to Jesus' invitation by faith, and freely drink of the heavenly water.

Rayola Kelley

How many times have you sung that old hymn, "Rock of Ages"? Since my salvation, I have appreciated the concept of the "Rock" in hymns and Scriptures, but I remember the challenge I encountered that made me examine if the "Rock" was simply an assumption, a concept, or a reality. One particular scripture challenged me to question the type of attitude I had adopted towards the Rock.

Deuteronomy 32:15 says, *"But Jeshurun waxed fat, and kicked: thou art waxen fat, thou art grown thick, thou art covered with fatness; then he forsook God which made him, and lightly esteemed the Rock of his salvation."* The word "Jeshurun" in this case points to Israel during its happy and prosperous time, but the problem with man becoming satisfied in this world is that he begins to lightly "esteem" the Rock who made him.

I believe the abundance of America has caused some, even in the church, to lightly esteem the importance and significance of the Rock as the foundation, cornerstone, High Tower, and place of refuge in our Christian walk. It is easy to play religion, get emotionally caught up with the beat of the music, enjoy the potlucks, and become part of the church crowd, but where is the "Rock" in all of it?

The Rock can't be a mere stone that is simply added to our religious activities, tacked on to our religious duties to give some credibility to what we believe and know, or mixed in a pile of religious causes to perhaps add to some religious mosaic we are trying to create; rather, He must be exalted to a place of worship, He must be the center of all we do, the source of all we pursue, the inspiration behind all we offer, and our hiding place where we can know peace, rest, and safety from the storms of this age.

You will notice in some of my post my appreciation for the Rock. I have been challenged many times by my encounter with the Rock in Scripture and as a result I have one more question to ask, "How have you handled the Rock?"

When I was considering this question for myself, the first thing I had to determine is how big do I consider the Rock? Is it a pebble like Peter that can be fit into my life? Is it a stone that I can pick up and examine to see if it possesses the quality of something worthwhile? Is it a smooth stone that I might even pick up and see how many times I can skip it across my religious notions to see if it will do the job? Perhaps it's an ordinary rock where the individual may have noticed it contains some potential, but it is not what the person is seeking.

These examples may seem silly to some of you, but the truth of the matter, Jesus as the Rock, is not always considered in the light of His deity, His majesty, His power, and His glory. In some cases, He is simply there if He is needed, some tack Him on to their life when it is beneficial to do so, and others keep Him around for sentimental religious purposes, but such practices show those who have failed to see the eternal glory, power, and work of Jesus and have made Him small, keeping Him insignificant, and only consider Him for personal reasons.

Jesus as the Rock is all encompassing, all consuming, and all powerful. He is the eternal foundation of heaven, the great sustaining cornerstone to real religion, and is the only way to eternal truth and everlasting life. We as believers must make sure we never render Jesus small enough to fit our understanding, ordinary enough to fit into our religious terrain, and smooth enough that if we rub up against His truths, there will be no challenge or discomfort posed to our lives.

How does one respond to the Rock? In my last post I talked about those who can lightly esteem the Rock because we fail to regard it, but another key is how do we respond to the Rock? When in the wilderness, Moses struck it the first time to get water out of it and later was instructed to speak to it the second time to release the water.

Think about this for a moment. He was given two distinct instructions regarding the Rock. The Apostle Paul made reference to this Rock in *1 Corinthians 10:4, "And did all drink the same spiritual drink: for they drank of that spiritual Rock that followed them: and that Rock was Christ."* Jesus invited man to come to Him and partake of the Rivers of Living Water.

The question is why was Moses given two different instructions about the Rock? The first one where Moses struck it pointed to the Rock,

37

Jesus, being broken and His blood being spilled out on the cross. Jesus would be struck so the water of eternal life could come forth, but once the water came forth, the second instruction given to Moses revealed the access we now have as Christians. He was simply to speak to it the second time to release the water. "Speaking" points to our prayer life.

If you are a born-again Christian, it means you have come to Christ to receive the eternal water that was poured from the altar of the cross where Jesus' glorious sacrifice was offered. Now that you have access to the water of the Holy Spirit through Christ by faith, all you need to do is speak to the great Rock of heaven in prayer. We are told this in *Luke 11:13, "If ye then, being evil, know how to give good gifts unto your children: how much more shall your heavenly Father give the Holy Spirit to them that ask him?"*

Due to anger, Moses failed to speak to the rock and struck it twice. He was not allowed to enter into the Promised Land. How many of us fail to access the wonderful privileges and promises attached to the Rock of Ages because we fail to properly respond to it with pure love, sincere devotion, and child-like faith?

REPENTANCE, REDEMPTION & RECONCILIATION

*Broadly speaking, salvation was **planned** by the Father, **purchased** by the Son, and **processed** by the Holy Spirit. (Marvin Rosenthal)*

The message of repentance came first and was necessary to ensure the people would have to turn around to face their sins, and be forgiven in order to have the freedom to receive the king of the kingdom, Jesus Christ.

In *Revelation 3:20* we read where Jesus is standing at the door and knocking to be let in. We must remember this was in relationship to the churches that needed to repent, not unbelievers. I have wondered what was on the other side of the door, was it an empty chair where apparently Jesus wasn't even missed, or an empty space because there was no place that has been prepared for Him to sit awhile and commune?

This is true for us as believers. Has a space of worship been prepared and a place of communion been preserved just for Jesus? Remember it is Christ alone who can fill the space of our soul to overflowing abundance and satisfaction with His life and our spirit with His abiding presence

One of the attitudes believers must discern and change has to do with complacency towards the matters of God. Complacency slides into compromise and the call the person in this state will hear from your Lord is one of REPENTANCE. Like the Laodicean Church in *Revelation 3:14-19*, compromising Christians have a weak foundation, deluded opinions about their spiritual standing, and use worldly standards to grade themselves.

Jesus' warning and instructions to such individuals is that their faith must be tried by fire, their works consumed, and their eyes anointed so that they can see their spiritual nakedness and become zealous in true repentance. The one way we can discern complacency is to consider those who are paying a price to follow Jesus.

Persecution is a fire that separates the real sheep from the pretenders and prepares them to follow the Shepherd to Calvary. According to figures, in the 20th century alone there were more Christian martyrs than the first 2,000-years of church history, and the fear was that persecution would even surpass the number of martyrs in the 20th century within a few decades.

I don't know how many Christians are aware of these figures, but persecution has clearly escalated in just the last few decades throughout the world and it has taken root in this nation while much of the church simmers in a quasi-state that such persecution will not happen to them, while those awake are clearly seeing its ugly head rising up and taking aim in this nation.

Rayola Kelley

What should a believer's response be to such persecution? It should be that of Smyrna in *Revelation 2:8-10, "the devil shall cast some of you into prison that ye may be tried, and ye shall have tribulation…be thou FAITHFUL unto death, and I will give thee a crown of life."*

A few years back the Lord challenged me about my perspective of people. As believers we know that Jesus died for souls. Every person we know, encounter, and pass by is a soul that is heading towards heaven or hell. The concept that a soul would end in a place of separation and judgment is unbearable to consider, but regardless of how sad or unbearable it is, it does not change the truth of it.

There are three groups of people we encounter in our journey through the masses of humanity. There are those whom we know. I don't know about you, but God has given me such a love for their souls. Needless to say, I have done what I can to share my faith with them. However, In the past I had a tendency to avoid saying what I considered harsh truths and overlooked some unbecoming attitudes towards God to avoid driving them away from "all" religion.

There are acquaintances that I may know by sight, but for the most part I am oblivious to them as a person, and then there are those who are faceless but they stand on the sidelines as observers who are a bit judgmental, skeptical, and smug as they compare and judge others when it comes to God.

God sent His Son to reach out to souls, touch their lives, and die for them. As believers we are not here to reach the masses but to penetrate the souls of man. Every soul needs to realize they are heading towards eternity and if they are not heading towards God, they need to repent, turn from their destructive direction and face God about their lost state, their sinful ways, and their rebellious attitude and come into agreement with Him about their need to receive His great gift, the Lord Jesus Christ.

Yesterday, I mentioned three types of people. The Lord used them to reveal to me three distinct messages towards unbelievers. There are unbelievers who know about the truths of the Gospel but they dance around them. For one reason or the other they are not serious about God and feel they are either close enough that they can slide into heaven, or ride into it, because of some type of religious affiliation and experience. For such a person who is parleying with the devil, while playing in the pigpen of the world, the one word they need to hear is simple and clear, "REPENT!" These people need to turn from their wicked attitudes and ways and get truly saved.

For acquaintances, they may be acquainted with God, but they remain oblivious to the realities of God, and the message to them is apropos, "GOD IS LOST TO YOU AND YOU ARE LOST TO GOD." It is not that God does not know where they are spiritually, but in their oblivious state they see no need for salvation.

The message to the observer who continues to look for hypocrisy in others so they have an excuse to stay on the sidelines when it comes to the matters of God and their soul, the message is comprised of three words, "YOU ARE WRONG" Those who look for hypocrisy in others to avoid dealing with their own duplicity are further from heaven than those they are judging. To allow one hypocrite to become an excuse to reject the one true Savior of souls is not only plain wrong, but it identifies the individual as a fool.

Every soul is precious to the Lord, but it is only the soul who has turned in repentance to be redeemed by the blood of the Lamb that will find him or herself on the right side of eternity.

For the past couple of days, I talked about three groups of unbelievers: those who play around with religion when it serves their purpose as a means to keep God off their back, those who have no inclination or reality about God and their own wretched state, and those who excuse themselves from any religious commitment at the expense of those they deem to be "hypocrites." The Bible is clear about each group.

Those who hide behind forms of religion instead of truly repenting do so because they want life on their terms. They are rebellious, ungrateful, and do not want to give up their independence. Those who are clueless to God and their lost state have been blinded by the god of this age from seeing they are on the broad path that leads to destruction; and those who excuse their unbelief and skepticism towards God at the expense of hypocrisy are blinded by the board of pride in their eye (*2 Corinthians 4:3-6; Matthew 7:1-5*). They can't see that the unmerciful, indifferent judgment they level at others, has a boomerang effect. It will ultimately become their judgment.

The Gospel is the power of God unto salvation, and the question is what instrument or tools of the Gospel can be used to bring a reality check to each of these groups of people? With those who need to repent, the Holy Spirit needs to convict them of their sin, but they need to understand they are a sinner, separated from God, dead in their trespasses, and living in defiance of the Gospel that will either save them or be used to condemn them (*2 Thessalonians 1:8-9*).

To those who are lost, they need to hear the truth that they are lost souls, wandering in a barren wilderness, vulnerable to the predators of their age that will eventually bring their soul to utter ruin. And, to those who hide their arrogance behind judgmental smugness, they need a reality check that they are wrong, and one day their arrogance will be stripped away by the true Judge of the universe, while they will see that they are the ones who are spiritually dead, entombed by their own hypocrisy, firmly nailed in it by the same cruel arrogance that made them a judge and jury to others.

As Christians we must discern where sinners are and avail ourselves to the power of the Spirit, the truth of God's Word, and the clarity of our mission in this world. The Apostle Paul said it best in *Romans 10:14-15, "How then shall they call on him in whom they have not believed? And how shall they believe in him of whom they have not heard? and how shall they hear without a preacher? And how shall they preach, except they be sent? As it is written, How beautiful are the feet of them that preach the gospel of peace, and bring glad tidings of good things!"*

I have been thinking of valleys lately. I grew up in a place in Idaho that had a big valley called "Long Valley" running between mountains that were simply named West and East Mountains. Because there were a couple of valleys in our area, they appropriately called the county we were located in, "Valley County."

I have to admit I took for granted the beauty of the valley I lived in but through my travels, I have lived and traveled through many valleys. Some are beautiful and some are barren, but each valley has its own terrain that distinguishes it.

In the Bible there are valleys mentioned, and in a spiritual sense they represent valleys of humiliation because you must come off of the mountains of inspiration and revelation down to the valley. It is there in the valleys that we must walk out what we have encountered during our mountain-top experiences which always proves a bit humiliating.

Consider the valley of the shadow of death mentioned in *Psalm 23:4*. There is also another important valley, it is called the valley of Achor which means "valley of trouble" because it was where the disobedient, greedy Achan, along with his family and animals were stoned to death for bringing trouble on the whole nation of Israel in *Joshua 7*.

It is not unusual to encounter many troubling challenges in the valleys, but we must remember that God is in control and every challenge in a valley will become a door of hope. Consider what *Hosea 2:15* says about the valley of Achor, "*And I will give her her vineyards from thence, and the valley of Achor for a door of hope: and she shall sing there, as in the days of her youth, and as in the day when she came up out of the land of Egypt.*"

This was written to Israel, but the principle is there for us because we are traveling through the world (Egypt) and most of us encounter much trouble in this life and barrenness, but the Lord also promises us the door of hope—that of Jesus Christ and His redemption which promises us an abundant life.

What constitutes slavery? As I watched monuments of the past being recklessly destroyed by lawless and ignorant individuals that act as if it was nothing more than a party, I asked myself where is the reason and the sanity in all of it?

Rayola Kelley

We had a Civil War to address the issue of slavery, and now we have a cultural war to try redefine or wipe out our history. Past history is the teacher of wisdom, the present the student of ideas, and the future the witness that will bear record as to what is true. Take away the teacher and you end up with ignorance or indoctrination, pointing to the worst of history always being repeated as the future comes at the unsuspecting like a freight train.

As some of you know I love American history. To most people, the Civil War was about slavery, but even Abraham Lincoln refuted this in one of his speeches. Depending on what perspective you are considering in this time of history, there were three reasons that the Civil War occurred.

Keep in mind, for man to fight a war, the cause must be morally greater than himself and for that reason, he is willing to sacrifice all. For the union, it was the moral issue of slavery, but for many of the leaders in the Confederacy, it was a matter of state's sovereignty. The south saw slavery as more of a personal and economic matter, but what became of great concern for leaders such as Stonewall Jackson, who was a Christian and believed the fundamental principles of the Constitution, was that the states, (which voted on the issue of slavery according to individual conscience and majority) was in danger of losing their sovereignty to a central government.

The final reason for the war had to do with the central banking system in England that created the crisis over slavery so they could financially enslave America. It is said that is why Lincoln had money printed in the basement of the White House. History is not meant to be a judge and that is why it can teach us that a matter may be immoral at one point, but right in light of another point.

Today we are seeing a cultural war driven by a movement that expounds a murky justice and a lawless group of agitators that are backed by some of the most wicked power-players in the world, and we, the majority of the people, are caught in the middle of it. As a Christian, I refuse to be taken down into murky waters for "some" cause, intimidated by a bunch of lawless thugs, or become a pawn or victim to despots.

As believers we have a history that begins at the cross of Christ and will never change. We walk a fine line between being right, doing right and stepping into some swamp where nothing is clear. Even though the world does all it can to agitate us in some way to take a morbid, useless stand, we have a sure Rock that will cause us to keep centered if we remain anchored to it. As Jesus exhorted, "Keep looking up," for that is where our redemption comes from.

I often make reference to the white rock with a new name written on it. How important is a name? When it comes to the Bible, names are of the upmost importance. I don't know about you but I study the meaning of the names of people found in the Bible because they give me insight into the time or possible events taking place.

Keep in mind, Isaac was given his name by God, and the Lord changed Abraham, Sarah, and Jacob's names. And, we must not forget the craze over Jabez's name (sorrow/trouble), but his prayer showed he was not willing to accept the implications his name carried and in *1 Chronicles 4:10* he asked the Lord to reverse his plight and the Lord granted his request.

I like my earthly name and have become quite used to it for over six decades, but I realize that I will have a new name in the next world because of Jesus' redemption. Roman society used rocks in voting and in judicial matters. A black stone represented no or guilty and a white stone was yes or acquitted.

It is easy to understand why we will be given a white stone: it is because we stand justified in Christ. However, the name will be a mystery and my question is what will it speak of? Will my new name reveal certain things such as my relationship with Him and my level of service in His kingdom?

These are only speculations on my part, but I know there are two promises that I can encourage and challenge myself in, 1) Because of Christ's work on Calvary, I stand justified and 2) that if I am not going to accept the devastating implications of the present world, I must finish the course to receive a new name, a name that will be only known by Him and me, a name that will be personal and sweet.

The other day I talked about reconciliation. Christians tend to emphasize salvation, that glorious deliverance from the oppressive taskmaster of sin and the claims of death. This salvation costs God His best—His Son, and His Son Jesus Christ His all—His life.

Jesus not only gave up His life, but He gave up His sovereignty as God to take on the form of man in order to become subject to the Father's rule, submissive to the leading of the Spirit, and a true servant to man *(Philippians 2:5-8)*. In His humanity, Jesus became our example, and in His deity He was entrusted with all authority and power to heal as a great physician, as well as execute just judgment. In His humanity He represents man, and in His position as our High Priest He serves as our advocate, mediator, and intercessor to and before God, and as deity He reflects the fullness of God's glory to us.

The purpose for this incredible work has to do with reconciliation. Man lost his way in the garden, strayed from his Creator in the barren wilderness of the world, and became independent from God's rule as he made his own form of rule and government. Jesus came to reconcile man back into a relationship with his God.

This relationship with God is the only place that lost man with his wandering soul, his frayed nerves, and his tormented mind can be restored back to his high priestly calling to serve, worship, and bring glory to God. It is in a relationship with God that man can find his spirit revived, his soul at rest, his mind at peace, and his walk steady. It is only in a relationship with God through Jesus Christ that man can become fruitful as an instrument of righteousness, a vessel of glory, and an heir of all the promises of God.

THE REALITY
OF GOD

*When Jesus came as a Savior, he came
as a revelation of the mind of God,
because He was slain before the foundation
of the world. God provided a remedy
before the disease.
(Herbert Lockyer)*

I often make reference to the controversy and mystery of the God-Man, Christ Jesus. God becoming man can only be received at the point of faith. This unveiling of this mystery as a matter of truth to our spirits, can only be done by the Spirit of wisdom and revelation who will always lead us into the truth about Jesus (*John 16:13; Ephesians 1:17*).

The Old Testament is clear that the sacrifice of animals could cover sin, but as *Hebrews 10:2-22* points out, such sacrifices could not take sin away. The New Testament is clear that without intervention on God's part, man remains doomed in his sin, facing the wrath of God to come. It is hard for people to understand that only God can satisfy His Law by offering the sacrifice that pays the necessary penalty for our sin.

We are told in *Hebrews 10:5* that a body was prepared so that that a proper sacrifice could be offered that would address our sin for once and for all. When the fullness of time was come, God sent forth his Son, made of a woman, made under the law to redeem us, who were subject to the law, that we might receive the adoption that would identify us as His children. The result is that we would be no longer servants to sin, in bondage to the elements of the world, but we would be an heir of God through Christ (*Galatians 4:3-7*).

This plan of redemption was in place before the foundation of the world. The solution of our sin problem came from outside of man's will, the work of the flesh, and the world. This is important to remember.

As we look into the great darkness engulfing much of the world, we must always remember the problems in this world is the same—it comes down to sin and that the solution will always come outside of man, the

47

flesh, and the world. The solution will come from above and be manifested by the Spirit through Jesus Christ, the Son of the Living God.

Many people want God to prove Himself by entertaining or showing His power to do the impossible, but such individuals need to remember there were many people who witnessed the power of God in Jesus to do the miraculous, but they still refused to believe that He was sent to save mankind.

God does not, nor will He prove, He is God by getting on some pride trip and wielding His power around like some magician so people such as in the case of Herod during Jesus' trial will become impressed with Him. Such impressions at best will only last for a short season. Granted, the Lord might confirm a person's faith by doing the miraculous as He did in the second miracle He performed in Cana in *John 4:46-54* or to confirm the message of the Gospel as pointed out in *Mark 16:15-18*, but He will never use His power as a means to try to cause people to believe that He is who He is. He has clearly provided witnesses all around us that proclaim there is a God who is Creator, Ruler, and Judge of all.

Next time you want to see a miracle that confirms your faith, don't seek a sign; rather, look in the mirror. The sign Jesus left us was His death, burial and resurrection and if you have believed and received that sign as being the only way of salvation, you will see a living, walking miracle looking back at you.

I mentioned in the last post that there were a couple of things we need to remember about God's power. The first thing is that God does not use miracles to confirm His existence; rather, He uses them to confirm our faith towards Him or the message. The second thing you need to remember about God's power is that it is channeled or disciplined.

Power points to strength and ability, and it will find its strength in authority and its ability in integrity. Power that is not disciplined according to established authority and used to bring about honorable results is power that is being exploited and will cause chaos and destruction in the end.

The Bible is clear that God's power is disciplined through His Spirit and His goal is to bring about repentance to ensure redemption and reconciliation between Him and man. Salvation is the mighty work of God. We are told in *Matthew 28:18* that all power in heaven and earth was given to Jesus Christ, but as *Zechariah 4:6c* declares, *"Not by might, nor by power, but by my spirit, saith the LORD of hosts."*

One of the realities the Lord had to get deep in my spirit was that He was not an option, He was the SOLUTION. I have shared this many times with others in order to remind myself of this important fact.

In my initial walk of faith, it was a natural tendency for me to look to the world to figure out how to solve looming problems, while keeping the Lord as an option or after-thought. After all, the Lord gave me a brain and I needed to use it to figure a way around or through the situations that loomed before me.

Each time I applied my knowledge and logic to a matter, the situation would spin out of control, and it was only when I ran out of worldly options, I finally turned to the Lord to present my case in prayer. After various failed attempts on my part to resolve issues, the Lord eventually showed me that He was often my last resort when it came to seeking a solution and that when I did finally come to Him, it was out of desperation.

It was then that I realized I needed to train myself to first turn to Him, while forgetting the world altogether. After all, to look back to the world for a solution was like taking my hand off the plough and looking back to that which has no power or significance and already stood judged (*Luke 9:62*).

It has taken some real discipline on my part to change my tendency from looking within and around and to look up to seek the lasting solution of heaven.

Rayola Kelley

What do we do when it seems that circumstances are literally consuming us? There was a time that spiritually I felt I was in a 59' boat in the eye of a hurricane that was running out of diesel. This picture was realistic to me because in the navy I was a helmsman on a utility boat.

I was also a helmsman on the boat in the vision that was playing out in my spirit, and I felt if I could steer away from the impact of the storm that was barreling down on me that maybe I would survive it. I felt the Lord behind me and He instructed me to face the storm. I knew I would be consumed by it and taken down into the depths. I also knew what it all meant.

For months I had been running the race in my own strength and it appeared that the ministry I was part of was about to break forth, but instead of coming to fruition, the Lord was about to take it and me into the grave. I sat there in awe as I remembered what He said in *John 12:24, "Verily, verily, I say unto you, Except a corn of wheat fall into the ground and die, it abideth alone: but if it die, it bringeth forth much fruit."* The vision was overwhelming but the fact that the Lord wanted to bring forth much fruit in my life and the ministry that I was part of encouraged me.

As Christians we want a smooth ride to reach the heights of God, but I have discovered that before I can be lifted to such heights, God first must go deeper in me in order to bring forth greater fruit for His glory. I also knew that once again I must exercise my faith in trusting Him to bring forth the outcome He had ordained before the foundation of the world.

How would the Lord come to you? This may seem like an unusual question, but it is one that needs to be pondered. For example, He encountered Abraham with two angels before passing judgment on Sodom, knowing Abraham would serve as an intercessor. He met Moses in a burning bush, the children of Israel on Mount Sinai in the midst of darkness, lightning and thunder, and Joshua as Captain of the Lord's Host.

How would He appear and introduce Himself? He appeared to Abraham to call him away from country, kindred, and family to the

Promised Land. For Jacob He appeared as LORD (Jehovah) on top of a ladder connecting heaven and earth and introduced Himself as the God of Abraham and Isaac. For Moses and Joshua, He told them to take off their shoes because they were standing on holy ground before He gave them their marching orders, and He instructed Moses to introduce Him to the children of Israel as "I AM that I AM."

Years later Jesus introduced Himself as the "I am" and when you consider what He followed the "I am" with, you can begin to sense people's attitudes and needs. Jesus as the I am, came as the bread from heaven for the hungry, the giver of Living Water to the thirsty, the Great Physician to the hurting, and the loving, committed Shepherd to the lost and wondering sheep, and so forth. The introduction that summarizes it all is found in *John 8:58, "Verily, verily, I say unto you, Before Abraham was, I am."*

The reason we need to check out our attitude towards the Lord is we do not want Him to appear in darkness because of rebellion; rather, we want Him to appear to us to call us out of the darkness of our old ways. We must be willing to turn aside like Moses to meet with Him in whatever capacity He inserts Himself into our ordinary life in order to receive our orders, and like Joshua we must be willing to bow before Him and worship Him when He does introduce Himself.

The next time you enter a time of silence before the Lord, ask Him how He would come to you and from His answer it will give you insight of where you are with Him in your life before Him.

We need to discern where we stand in our relationship with God before we invite His presence among us. I remember once visiting a church where most of the activities were orchestrated by the pastor, whose main goal was to shake any extra money from the pockets of the congregation for an upcoming vacation.

Everyone was asked to stand facing the wall as if worshipping the actual building and ask for the Lord to come down in their midst (*Isaiah 64:1*). Needless to say, Jeannette and I were among the few who remained sitting in the pew, watching the fiasco in utter disbelief.

As the compliant sheep were standing, raising their hands and asking the Lord to come down in a powerful way, the Lord quietly spoke to my spirit and told me if He came down there would not be one left standing. I sensed some would be on their face crying out for mercy, but like the judgment on the deception of Ananias and Sapphira in *Acts 5*, some would be carried out of the building. It was obvious God was not pleased and it left me sober and shaken.

It is natural to want God's blessing on something, but when God comes down to meet with His people it is to do business with them. Whether it is to address sin, bring healing to a soul that has been wounded or left with taunting unresolved issues, comfort, direction, or etc., God desires to meet with each of us personally. Keep in mind, the fact that God comes down should be considered the greatest blessing, producing the uttermost satisfaction to a seeking soul and a lean spirit

The next time you ask the Lord to come down, make sure you are standing on holy ground, prepared to do business with Him to ensure right standing, right being, and right doing.

It is natural for all of us to want to fit into this world so we belong, but there is also a dichotomy present, and that is we also want to hold a special place, a place of adoration in someone's heart and life so we feel loved, recognized, needed, and appreciated. For some who have a realistic handle on things, they may have found this place in marriage, but for many this desire becomes tormenting because the feeling eludes them even in what would be considered close relationships.

They seek for that one person, relationship, or position to experience that feeling, thinking that once they find that place, they will finally feel special, completed, and satisfied in their life. The truth is God puts both desires in us, but we make the mistake of letting the world define what they will look like.

To fit into the world, it first requires you to sell your soul because the world can only love those who belong to it. When it comes to being that special person exalted to a distinct place where you become the sole consideration of someone else is not only unrealistic but idolatrous.

God put these two desires in us, knowing that a relationship with Him alone is the only way to revive our spirit and bring us to a place where we know we belong to that which is lasting. In fact, we are heirs with Jesus and belong to a heavenly family, body, priesthood, and kingdom.

God is love and only He can bestow love on us that is satisfying to the soul. Every time we look to something or someone outside of God to fill the vacuum in our soul or listlessness in the spirit, we are going to be set up to be greatly disappointed, disillusioned, and miserable.

The next time you feel the emptiness of vanity, the listlessness of focus and purpose, discern what the quality of your relationship is with the Lord. The Bible is clear, Jesus is our all in all, and to look, pursue, or desire the worldly and fleshly is to experience the emptiness of this present life, while missing the opportunity to discover the preparation and fullness of the life that has been promised to all of those who believe God and His Word.

GOD'S WORD

How do we get nourishment from God's Word?
We need to bite it—take a portion in. We need
to chew it—think about what it means. We need
to swallow it—make it part of our life. We need
to digest it. When we do, we are nourished
spiritually and the end result is spiritual growth.
(Anna Alden-Tirrill)

We are facing a new year. Realistically, the first day of the New Year points to just another day, but to me another day points to a new day; and, each year I approach a new day of a new year I take time to examine myself.

The Bible instructs us to do such an examination occasionally. We are to examine ourselves at Communion to see if we are in the right place with God and others to take of it (*1 Corinthians 11:28-29*). We are to examine to see if we are in the correct faith when it comes to Jesus

Rayola Kelley

Christ (*2 Corinthians 13:5*). The purpose of examining ourselves is to see if we are in a right spirit towards God and others.

As we walk through the world, we can develop improper attitudes, ignore unresolved issues, and justify or overlook our unchristian-like reactions towards others. It is up to us to make sure we let go of the past in order to properly face the present in the right spirit.

The Bible is clear we are in a race, and we are to set aside those sins that so easily beset us so we can run the race, and victoriously finish the course set before us (*Hebrews 12:1*). As the Bible tells us, each day presents its own challenges and I don't know about you but I don't need the baggage, the burdens, and the stuff from yesteryear to follow me into the present and hinder my walk, undermine my testimony, and rob me of my power to stand sure on my foundation in these dark days of testing, uncertainty, and chaos.

God's Word is truth and it absolute in what is so and unchangeable in what is right. It does not try to take the sharpness out of men's sin, the sorrow out of man's great losses, the bite away from the dogging hopeless reality of what is, and the harshness out of the reality of what will be. Regardless of truth being presented that shakes, pierces, cuts, and separates, it is what allows the glorious light of hope to penetrate souls.

When I become overwhelmed by the bazaar reality of this world and these times, I do not have far to run to come to a place of sanity, truth, light, life, and hope. I am constantly reminded that God is the only One who brings sanity to what is insane, makes sense out of what is senseless, and brings peace in the midst of the tumultuous lies of the present.

My goal is to invite each of you to come out from the insanity of this time and come to a place of rest and sit while you are refreshed once again by the knowledge that truth is out there and will prevail, sanity will one day reign, and our hope once again will be confirmed by what is eternal.

Jesus said of His Word that it was spirit and life. I have often meditated on what it means for the Word to impact my spirit and ensure the presence and growth of the life of Jesus in me.

I have been a Christian for over 40 years and I have discovered and rediscovered the impact of the Word on my spiritual growth. It has become wisdom to guide me, a source of hope to inspire me, healing balm to my eyes so I can see, meat to my spirit so I can mature, milk to my soul so I can be strengthened, sweetness to my taste, and salt to add flavor to my life.

The Word of God offers me a banquet table, but it is not enough to simply admire it. I must sit up to at the table and truly partake of it by believing it is God's Word and assimilating it through prayer and obedience because I do believe it is true and right.

The idea of DOING IT or doing what is right before God and towards others does not allow for procrastination or complacency. The reason for this is because everything a person has need of has been provided and there will be no excuse for not doing what is right. For example, the Lord has given us the power of His Spirit to walk out our lives in righteousness and the Word of God to show us the way of righteousness.

A good example of being provided with the necessary provision to carry out our Christian responsibilities can be found in the building of the first temple. King David wanted to build it but he was a man of war; therefore, the duty was passed down to his son Solomon, the man of peace. Even though David was not allowed to build the temple, it did not stop him from providing the materials for the temple before his death (1 Chronicles 22).

We are told David called Solomon and charged him to build the house for the LORD God of Israel. The aging king told his son that he needed to set his heart and soul to seek the Lord, arise and build the sanctuary of the Lord. In the discourse of David we learn what it takes to do right and it requires a heart determination and the initiative to arise and DO IT.

As believers we are temples of God, but to establish our lives in the Lord, we must build it upon the foundation of Jesus Christ to ensure its integrity. To build our lives on Christ means setting our heart to do so through obedience to the Word.

One of my favorite incidents to study in the Bible is found in *Genesis 26*. This is about Isaac, the son of promise, becoming a true spiritual heir to what was promised His father, Abraham.

The first thing I noticed in this incident is that there was a famine in the land. A physical famine often points to a spiritual famine. *Amos 8:11-12* tells us the famine that will exist in the end days will be hearing the words of the Lord. In fact, people will be wandering from sea to sea from the north even to the east, running to and fro to seek the word of the LORD; but let the last part of this Scripture bring sobriety to you, "AND SHALL NOT FIND IT."

I have to say it is very hard to find the truth in the great darkness that is now enfolding people's hearts and minds. Whether it is due to fear, unbelief, or the frantic, desperation of the people to hear or receive a word from the Lord, the famine clearly exists.

It is becoming more apparent because we have wolves in the pulpits openly expounding heresy, the promotion of watered-down gospels made palatable to a doomed world, but are powerless to save, and Bible versions that have been subtly stripped of various things such as authority (Jesus' deity), of substance (the call to holiness), of clarity (truth), of power (Holy Spirit's inspiration), and of righteousness (moral accountability), all of which makes it hard to find the truth and nothing but the truth.

The Bible clearly tells us all that love the truth will avoid being taken by the great delusion that will sweep the world in the end days. Do you love, want, and desire the truth more than any other reality including your own idea of what is true?

Yesterday, we talked about the famine of the Word of God described by *Amos 8:11-12*. It is important to notice how Amos describes the people, they are running to and fro to find some word, any word from the Lord. The truth is God's Word is available but it is found in His Written Word (the most reliable version being the KJV) that uses actual titles to identify Jesus' deity, His mission as the Messiah, and His work of redemption done in His humanity, and not generic pronouns that can be applied to anyone.

It clearly upholds the spirit and the foundational truths of all teachings, but sadly many people have not been prepared to delve into the deep things of God by reading (partaking of), studying (digging for treasures), and meditating (assimilating) on it. They have not been discipled at the feet of Jesus, while His Spirit takes from the abundant table of His Word to feed, nurture, and grow them up in the knowledge of the Son of God.

Rather, it seems many have been conditioned to run here and there, feeding on the fluff of positivity that leaves them temporarily satisfied and sucking on a bit of sugar water to keep them going as they take a bit of this Scripture because it makes them feel good, a piece of that wise saying because it inspires, or grab that spiritual thought because it does not take any real investment. God's Word is a full-meal-deal, but if we piecemeal it according to taste, preference, and our busy timing, we will find ourselves unnecessarily becoming part of the statistics of those who were thirsty and desperate but could never find the source of Living Water.

The Bible clearly warns us that the cares of this world along with the deceitfulness of riches will choke the Word of God from having its way in our life, causing one to become unfruitful in their life. What are the cares of the world?

We are in the world, but as believers the world is not our friend because we have no part of it nor do we belong to it. We must function within the world to live our present life, but we must not walk in the ways of the world because we will find ourselves as enemies of God.

Even though the world is an avenue in which we acquire what we have need of, we must realize that all things come from God and He is our true provider. We must look to Him for all provisions.

The world promises us happiness, wealth, success, and glory according to what will satisfy our flesh and pride, but to secure these pursuits, you must sell your soul and then expect whatever you managed to acquire from it to be pulled out of your grasp for one reason or the other.

The cares of this world mean we care for the world, and the world is a subtle but harsh taskmaster. Its light is nothing more than glitter that suddenly becomes dark once the light of attraction is gone. Behind the glitter is a graveyard of dead, decaying ruined lives and deeds of man's best and man's greatest, all lying in a dung hill.

The Bible is clear we are not to love the world; rather, we must come out and be separate from it. I have to admit I have to examine what my point of dependency is, is it the world or the author and finisher of my faith, Jesus Christ?

I feel I live in a surreal world, a world that doesn't make sense, and what I would consider to be the unimaginable and bazaar is more real than what I can see and understand. I wrestle with what is true and have to walk through a web of lies and intrigue to discern what is legitimate. I do not trust what I see, what I hear, and I hold my conclusions lightly. I put the probabilities of what might be true on the shelf to see what stands and falls in the end, and what is left standing I can actually trace back to a point where it was first brought out as a fact by some reliable source.

I learned a long time ago that the unseen affects our reality more than the seen. I must not hold too tightly to preferred narratives, or try to figure out the ending before walking through the pages of intrigue that allow me to see the legitimate clues and happenings that will lead me to a right conclusion.

What we see when it comes to the world is nothing more than an unrealistic image, a ruse to throw us off to what is happening, or a staged presentation that is trying to present a lie as being what is normal and acceptable.

As believers we must not let the upside-down world of perversion determine our reality, attitude, and truth. We must always come back to the one foundation of truth that can't be adjusted, that will stand, and ultimately expose any ruse that is trying to cover up darkness. That truth is Jesus Christ and the Word of God. We know that the only one we can believe a hundred percent of the time is God and the only truth is His Word, but it must be rightly divided.

I don't know about you but every day I need to be revived to advance forward in my spiritual life. It seems even more so because of the great darkness engulfing the world. It is only the light of Jesus that will penetrate, push aside, and set the boundaries for this darkness.

Jesus stated in *John 6:63* that the words He was speaking were spirit and life. The spirit represents the breath and flame of life. Man perceives if he has an intellectual understanding of a spiritual truth that it constitutes life, but without the oil of the Spirit and the flame of eternal life there will be no quickening of man's spirit. Besides the Holy Spirit who serves as the oil that allows the life of Jesus to be set aflame in every believer, there is also the trying flame of persecution.

The church will be presented without spot and wrinkle and we would all like to think that the church in America will be prepared by the Holy Spirit and not blatant persecution, but the Holy Spirit cannot work in any environment and heart without preparation. What type of preparation is needed?

In studying revivals where there was a true move of the Spirit, there is only one environment that brings revival and that is brokenness over sin, but there will not be any brokenness over sin unless sin is truly being addressed from the pulpits. In some pulpits we have cheerleaders and motivational speakers trying to make us feel good in our sin, inspire us to great heights without first taking care of the baggage of sin at the cross of Christ, and telling us that all will be alright because God loves us and wants us to be happy in spite of walking in sin.

The Bible is clear that if we abide in Jesus we will not openly, consciously walk in sin without true conviction and remorse that will eventually be followed by true repentance. The Word is clear that whosoever walks in sin has not seen or known Jesus because he or she will be of the devil. It goes on to say, *"Whosoever is born of God doth not commit sin; for his seed remaineth in him: and he cannot sin, because he is born of God" (1 John 3:6-9).*

I have often thought about the power of God's Word. We are told the Word of God is a powerful two-edged sword in *Hebrews 4:12.* In my infant years of being a Christian I zealously studied the Word to be able to debate or argue about the different Scriptural views. It is not wrong to know what you believe, for the Word instructs us to know what we are to believe so we can stand; but what I later discovered was my motive for studying the Word was a matter of conceit.

I did not approach to believe and apply it to my life. Unknowingly, I was adjusting the Word to my understanding instead of allowing the Word to align me to its eternal truths. My misguided pursuit brought me to a crisis of where joy was missing from my life. I realized that the Word was written to bring me joy, but the joy is not found in having an understanding of the written Word but in the joy of discovering the Living Word, Jesus Christ within its precious pages.

I am ever reminded that the written Word is a revelation of the Living Word.

God's Word comes in three forms, the written Word which is God's testimony, the Living Word (Jesus Christ), and through revelation of the Holy Spirit. In order to fall in love with the Living Word I must choose to love the written Word.

Like humanity that veiled the heavenly glory of Christ, He was also veiled in His written Word and it is the Holy Spirit who must reveal Him to our spirit to make Him truth and living. The Bible refers to this enigma as a great mystery of godliness, that in spite of the debates that surround the subject of this mystery, there is no controversy to it because faith comes by hearing and hearing by the Word of God when it comes to Jesus being revealed to our spirit in greater measure (*Romans 10:17*).

I approach all Scriptural matters to simply believe God's Word and receive them as truth like a child who has a pure trust towards God. And, what is this mystery that must be unveiled and confirmed to our spirit? According to the Apostle Paul in *1 Timothy 3:16, "God was manifest in the flesh, justified in the Spirit, seen of angels, preached unto the Gentiles, believed on in the world, received up into glory."*

My prayer is to always ask the Lord to unveil Himself in Scripture so that I can know and love Him more. Since I believe this is what is also in His heart, He will gloriously answer my prayer.

I realize through the years that the Bible must become many different things to me. As a new Christian I learned that it was food for my soul. As a child of God, I recognized it was my Father's loving way of laying out my inheritance to me, and as I started growing up spiritually, I realized it was God's personal diary to me about His love and plan for my life.

As one coming into greater spiritual maturity, I have learned I know less than when I started because God's Word is profound and eternal. It has allowed me to catch glimpses into its depth of wisdom, causing me to become overwhelmed. I have seen the heights of it truths that can take me above this age to know heavenly inspiration. It enlarges my vision beyond this world to see the end results and I have become humbled by it. But, what does it take for me to get the most out of it?

I am reminded constantly that I must approach it to believe it, kneel before my teacher the Lord, as I pray that my eyes be opened to its inspired and prophetic truths while asking for heavenly wisdom to handle it properly. Years ago, I was reminded it was up to me to sit at the banqueting table the Word prepares for me and become open as the Holy Spirit takes each truth and imparts it to me. We can talk about our love for the Word, but do we desire to partake of it and obey it more than pursue and possess the things of this world?

For the past couple of days, I have been having problems with Facebook and emails. It has taken a great deal of time for both to load up, and for someone like me who has much going on, such a problem is almost intolerable. I am sure some of you will relate when I tell you I have a terrible love/hate relationship with my computer and technology.

I appreciate that it proves efficient in many ways, but becomes confusing and overwhelming because it is in a constant flux of change that is used as a means to string people along with what is always being touted as "better." The question is, is it better or is it becoming more complicated in order to hide how much it is intruding into our privacy and disrupting our lives in unseen and destructive ways?

Technology appears to be the "big brother" among us, spying on us, conditioning us, and controlling the narrative in order to prepare us for a destructive reality. When I encounter problems with technology, I realize how dependent many of us are becoming on it for information, interaction, and connection. It is not that technology in itself is bad; rather, it comes down to how it is used.

As a Christian, I see it as a tool, but how many people see it as a reliable source when in reality it is an artificial means for some of the most wicked, sinister people to program the vulnerable and change the worldview of the unsuspecting, all to promote their wicked agendas?

As Christians we should not be confused by the darkness of our time because we only have one light to walk in, one truth to live by, and one sure hope that will prove to be so in the end—GOD'S WORD.

Yesterday, I mentioned my challenges with technology. When I consider how technology is being used today, I am so thankful there is only one source behind all truth, God. There is only one way to possess the truth, Jesus, and there is one way to test if a matter is the truth, the Word of God.

When we bring truth back to the person of Jesus, we realize it is UNCHANGEABLE, when we bring it back to the character of our righteous God, it will always prove RELIABLE, and when we bring it back to the complete counsel of God's Word, it is ABSOLUTE. After shutting my computer down a couple of times and letting it sit, both Facebook and my email started to work.

In these days expect to be overwhelmed, confused, and uncertain, but as believers we are planted on an immovable Rock, we have a sure record of what is true, and we have all of heaven that will back it up and confirm its authority. However, we need to keep in mind as believers that it serves us well when we shut down the outside influences of the world and wait before the Lord until we clearly hear His voice.

There are many sad statements in the Bible. For example, after the rich young ruler found out that in order for him to receive eternal life, he had to first let go of his idolatrous riches, we are told, *"But when the young man heard that saying, he went away sorrowful; for he had great possessions" (Matthew 19:22)*. Jesus made it very clear that a man's life consists not in the abundance of the things which he possesses.

Another very sad statement is found in *2 Timothy 4:10, "For Demas hath forsaken me, having loved this present world, and is departed unto Thessalonica."* The natural tendency for people is to debate whether Demas was even saved, but if you follow this man's involvement with Paul's ministry, it should cause Christians to stop, and ponder how can one, who was such an asset to a great man of God, forsake him to pursue what was vain and useless.

The Bible is clear about the pull of the world upon souls. We are born in it and the world knows how to entice the fallen flesh with false promises of happiness, ensnare the carnal intellect with arrogance that creates a false reality, seduce unabated affections that turn into inordinate lusts, choke out the Word of God thus, dulling people down towards the things of God, and ultimately making them slaves to the god of the world, Satan.

Now, when you consider the letter where Paul noted Demas' departure, while admitting he was also about to depart from this world, we know that he was facing his physical death. With this in mind we need to soberly examine the possibilities as to what happened to Demas.

The Bible tells us to come out and be separate from the world, but to get the world out of us requires our carnal minds to be transformed so our attitude towards it will change. In summary, the world must cease to not only be our solution we naturally turn to, but it must never become an option we keep on the back burner of unbelief just in case God fails us. We must apply the cross to the flesh so that we become crucified towards the world and the world towards us. After all, if we are dead to the world, we will not be tempted by it.

We must set our affections above and not on this earth to discipline our loyalties, pursuits, and passions and to avoid a divided heart, or idolatry. We must accept the fact that if we belong to the Lord, the world will hate us, and woe to anyone who is spoken well of by the world because of compromising with it. It is clear that as sojourners in the world, we may be walking through it, but we are leaving behind the influences of it as we walk towards our life in Christ. Each step will bring us higher, to the point we will begin to soar in the wind of the Holy Spirit. The question I ask myself is, "According to my thinking process, my devotion, and my fruit, 'Am I earthbound like Demas or am I heaven bound like Paul?'"

Yesterday I made reference to a man named Demas. In his last days on earth Paul sorrowfully talked about how Demas had forsaken him because of a love for the world and departed. Jesus is clear. Once you put your hand to the plow of Christian service in order to follow Him, you are not to look back to the world in longing, regret, or attraction. After all, heart longing comes down to fleshly desires, regrets to operating in fanciful possibilities and second guessing, and attractions can end in selfish pursuits. In fact, in my case the Lord ripped, tore, and purged me of my identification to the "old" life so that I would be prepared to walk in a life of service.

There are reasons people start out enthusiastic for God and eventually either abandon the things of God to pursue the world, slither away into the darkness of the world, or run back into it. For Demas it could be that he was following Paul and not Jesus. Even though he may have had one of the best teachers and examples of the Christian disciplines that lead to victory, he possibly kept the world as an option just in case the Christian life did not pan out for him.

To avoid being found a Demas we must sell out to the Lord. This requires us to deny self of life according to personal terms, notions, and dreams and become crucified to the world by nailing the flesh or old man to the cross, and following Jesus through the terrain of this world towards the glory He promised.

When people have divided loyalties, they will reveal a shallow devotion. As long as the world is kept as an option, God will not become a person's sole solution and focus. Instead of allowing his mind to be transformed, Demas could have maintained a worldly attitude, which would pervert his judgment about all things.

A worldly attitude will cause a person to wander around in a spiritual wilderness that seems to be void of life and will always prove hard on the flesh, indifferent to the pride, and an open grave that will eventually swallow everything up attached to the world. It often creates hopelessness for the wanderer.

The spiritual wanderers have a limited perspective because they can't see past this present world, but as Christians we know we are passing through this wilderness to the glorious promises of God. Sadly, those who are simply wanderers in the world are often waiting for the Christian life to somehow "fall" on them and make everything wonderful, but in due time such a notion reveals the folly of the human nature.

Those who follow Christ to have something fulfilled in their flesh according to their pride and way of thinking, will eventually see the Christian life as a reproach, allowing them to justify that which would allow their life to become a reproach to Christ. Whatever happened to Demas can happen to anyone if the Lord is not in the right place in our lives and the world is in the wrong place. I don't know about you, but I do not want to assume I could never be a Demas because I know myself too well. I allow the light of Christ to keep me honest about my character, my weaknesses, and my insipid pride.

It is in such a place that I am constantly reminded of my great need for God to preserve me and keep me on the right path, while holding me at times and sometimes carrying me during the difficult times until I am brought to a place where I am able to continue to follow Him in service while being guided by the light of His promises of greater glory

My challenge as a Christian is to make sure that I am properly handling His Word. Many years ago the Lord gave me a vision of what I had done to His Word in my attempt to understand it on my limited intellectual level instead of seeking to know Him. I had unknowingly dissected it and it was laying in pieces before me, lifeless and ineffective.

Clearly, I had rendered His Word useless. Upon my permission, the Lord began to form the sword once again and He stood there waiting for my permission to use it in a proper way. Upon my permission, He thrust it into me.

The lesson I learned is that unless I allow the sword to first dissect me and impact my life, I will not be able to properly impact other people's lives. My prayer is simple, "Lord use Your sword to reveal my heart to me, enabling me to properly discern if a matter is good or evil, and to clearly see You.

Remember what Job said after going through his terrible ordeal in *Job 42:5, "I have heard of thee by the hearing of the ear; but now mine eye seeth thee."* Oh, to see Jesus is the heart cry of a seeking heart, a thirsty soul, and a lean spirit.

Last night we had wind, rain, and lightning. The wind was alerting us of a coming storm, the rain followed and clearly left its mark on the terrain, and this morning the clouds hung on the mountains like curtains that would lift at any time revealing God's handiwork. But last night, it was as if God was speaking through the thunder and the sky was displaying its own fire-works in preparation of unveiling the miraculous works of

God within creation. Although the clouds created a type of subdued environment, the expectation that the best was on the horizon was present because we all know the sun will always break through.

The event reminded me of my walk with the Lord. The environment we are now in has caused many to become subdued with uncertainty, but the inspired Word of God has already warned the saints of the storms pending on the horizon.

Remember, God's Word is His voice and it still can be heard as long as the spirit is able to discern and the ears of faith are present to believe what is so. His thunder and lightning are necessary to cause people to heed the warnings in order to properly respond. Regardless of the intensity of the storm, the Holy Spirit will bring the waters to revive the spirit, renew the inner man, and bring expectation to the soul. Although the clouds of uncertainty shroud the future for many, as believers we know that the Sun of Righteousness will break through soon enough to reveal that God was in the midst of the storm doing a greater work on the terrains of men's souls.

THE CROSS

As we consider deliverance from sin,
we can see how we were delivered
from sin on the cross. We are presently
being delivered from sin by the
righteousness of Christ reigning
in us, and we will be delivered by
our hope in Christ. Obviously, our
deliverance from the slavery of sin through
Jesus' redemption will be complete.
(Rayola Kelley)

Jesus became sin for us so that we could be made into the righteousness of God (*2 Corinthians 5:21*). Jesus had to give up the glories of heaven, as well as His sovereignty to become a servant. He is our example as to what it means to be victorious. It involves self-denial and the way of the cross.

The Bible talks about denying ourselves to life on our terms and picking up the cross to daily mortify the influence of the old man in us. This is what lies at the core of the victorious Christian life.

As long as the old reigns, victory will elude us, and the more we choose the new and give way to it, the more we will taste the sweetness of victory in our personal lives. The struggle is that the world declares we have the right to have life on our terms in order to be happy, while the flesh demands such rights in order to be satisfied but each pursuit leaves people lean in their spirit and restless in their soul.

The world is temporary and the flesh stands judged and condemned. Neither the world nor the flesh can give or promise life, for real life only comes from God. Eternal life is a choice and the abundant life is the fruit of this life being lived out within Scriptural boundaries for the glory of God.

Today much to do is being put on how to preserve our present life in this world, esteem it to feel better about ourselves and life, and keep it because it is what we know, but the Bible is clear we are to die to the influence of the flesh as we become crucified to the attractions of this world so we can live a consecrated life for the glory of God.

Are you experiencing the abundance of the life of Jesus?

What side of the cross are you on? Have you ever noticed there are two sides to the cross of Christ? On one side the light is coming from the front of it, but it simply casts a shadow of the cross, but on the other side is the fullness of the light which highlights the reflection of God's love and heart.

We can get sentimental, zealous, and even silly when it comes to God and what we think He will do for us and what we think He should do for us. Granted, the cross of Christ is all about us. He died for us so we could be reconciled with God and have an eternal, abundant life, but beyond the born-again experience, the new life in us becomes a walk that is meant to fulfill our calling in Him, to make us His workmanship created unto good works for the sole purpose of bringing Him glory (*Ephesians 2:10*).

On one side of the cross is redemption, but when we are lifted up in identification to Jesus' eternal life, and we are translated from the kingdom of darkness into the kingdom of light, it becomes about a new life, a growing relationship, and calling in the Lord. This translation not only points to a new life, but it points to an eternal purpose.

From the baptism into His death in order for the newness of life to come forth, our life and walk should become about Jesus (*Romans 6:1-5*). The only way that Jesus Christ's life can be raised up in us is through communion, the only way it will be established in us is through obedience to His Word, and the only way we can ensure we are doing His bidding is prayer.

What does it mean to be on the wrong side of the cross? The cross of Christ serves as a spiritual line in the sand. On one side of it are simply shadows, but on the other side is the light. Many people are led to the cross out of some great quest or need, but they prefer to stand in its shadow. They may say they are a Christian because they have walked up to it and have intellectually agreed with its work of salvation, but they never come into the light of it because their sin would be exposed and they would not only have to own their sin and repent of it in order to come into complete agreement with the work of redemption. To come to the full light of the cross, they would have to embrace the reality, message, and work of the cross with their heart and become identified with Jesus in His death (to the old man) and in His burial (my sins now buried with Him) in order to be raised in newness of His life.

The wrong side of the cross means I will be able to hold on to certain rights of the old man as long as I remain in the shadow and still console myself that all is well with my soul, but on the right side of the cross I must become totally identified with Jesus, where the old truly begins to cease to influence and reign in my life and the new is established and unveiled as I begin to reflect the light of the life of Jesus more and more to a dark world.

Keep in mind, Jesus will not force His cross on you nor will He force you to carry a personal cross to constantly address the old man, but when you ask the Lord to have His way in your life, His way is the way of the cross, not just coming up to it but identifying with its work and picking up a personal one to ensure the work of the cross continues to bring death to the old so the new can be worked in the inner man.

The whole purpose of the work of the cross is to part the great darkness of sin upon man's soul with God's love. Through His act of sacrificial love on the cross, His mercy was made available to all who look to the work of Christ's redemption for deliverance from the great burdens that are upon their soul. It was God's mercy that erected an avenue of forgiveness and cleansing in which His grace could flow down to the broken sinner with the gift of life.

Upon receiving this great gift, the born-again believer can begin to walk out this life in greater measure by faith because they know that they have been reconciled back to God. Jesus did not die so we could live in sin with the idea we will be spared from deserved consequences: He died to take away sin with all of its claims upon our soul so we can discover His life in abundant measure.

Clearly, this life is a gift, but life involves interaction with our environment (communion and worship), investments to ensure its growth (faith and obedience), and expectation that inspires and ever advances us forward because we possess an unwavering hope that the best is yet to come.

THE LIGHT

Faith is a grace that sometimes shines
brightest in the dark night of desertion
(Thomas Watson)

Jesus asked the blind man this question in *Mark 10:51*, *"What wilt thou that I should do unto thee?"* It would seem that that problem was obvious, but the truth is that what really ails man is not always physical challenges but the spiritual condition of the soul.

I cannot imagine what it would be like to be blind, to never see the smile of a friend, the beauty of God's creation, or the changing pictures that God paints on the canvas of the sky. However, I know what it is like to be in spiritual darkness, groping for understanding in times of crisis, being swallowed by the dark clouds of depression, and being consumed by the storms of hopelessness that can rage in the soul.

At such times, Jesus will occasionally ask us questions to cause us to consider where we are and if we really want the responsibility that comes with heavenly intervention. The blind man's life would drastically change once his sight was given back to him and the question was, was he ready for the change.

Upon salvation, Jesus gave me the eyes of faith to see that my problem was sin and He was the only solution, but through the years He had to reveal other types of darkness that plagued my soul. He would ask me a question as a means of preparing me, "What would you really have me to do?" At such times I realize that He was illuminating a wrong attitude, practice, or detour. Each time He illuminated a matter, I realized that the real issue was not the obvious, but that which would hinder me from walking in the light that He would provide to bring me to a place of true healing and victory in Him.

The next time you ask the Lord for something like healing or deliverance, be still and see if He wants to ask you about the obvious to expose what really ails you in your walk with Him.

Our understanding of matters in the flesh will prove to be limited at best, inept in challenging times, and useless in spiritual darkness. Remember, our understanding serves as the light we walk in and Jesus warned us to beware of how we hear a matter. I try to keep this in mind every time I come to some conclusion.

I have learned unless a matter has been revealed to me by the Spirit of God, according to His Word of truth, and received as being so in my heart, which results in me walking in the light of it, a spiritual matter will remain hidden to me. I may understand something intellectually, but unless it becomes a revelation of the heart, I will never be able to live it.

Rayola Kelley

We are born with a carnal mind that can't mind the things of the Spirit of God. It can only understand earthly, worldly matters. This understanding is based on a limited reality, where thoughts easily enough digress into utter vanity, imagination becomes unrealistic and perverted, conclusions foolish, and the darkness of unbelief takes the mind captive.

As Christians, we are called children of light and the reason for this title is clear. We walk according to the light of Jesus' life in us by faith and we walk in relationship to the reality around us according to the Word of God. We also have the Spirit of God in us to discern the type of darkness upon us so we can properly maneuver through it, and we have the sharp truth of God that will penetrate all darkness with revelation that ends in clarity and greater understanding.

I am so thankful for the Light of the world. I have found myself in various types of darkness from depressing hopelessness to emotional destress, mental anguish, and sorrow of the soul. Each time I held on to what I knew about the Lord and waited for Him to part the darkness, He never failed to do so at the right time.

What kind of light are you walking in? Is it the darkness of sin and death, the gray shadows of worldly compromise, or the glorious transparent light of Jesus that, as in Paul's case, will first cause great darkness to the soul, but eventually it will remove all blinders so one can once again see the truth, stand on it, and, because of it, advance forward?

What are you doing with the light of Jesus? John told us that the life of Jesus is the light of men (*John 1:5*). Matthew 5:15 talks about putting it under a bushel, while *Mark 4:21* talks about putting it under a bed, and *Luke 8:16* makes reference to putting the light under a vessel and/or under a bed.

In considering this text, it was pointed out by Vance Havner that putting it under a bushel points to the business of the world. It is easy to allow the cares of the world to come in and dim our lights with idolatrous demands and useless activities that leave us empty. What about putting it under a bed?

The concept of putting it under a bed has to do with laziness. Spiritual laziness implies a lack of fervor, inclination, and commitment. Such laziness is expressed in complacency or lukewarmness towards God and spiritual matters. It is for this reason that Jesus stands outside of the door of such an individual's heart and knocks on the door to be let in for a time of reasoning, instruction, and fellowship.

The final one is a vessel. As a vessel of God, we must constantly stir up the fire of the Holy Spirit in us, as well as our gifts to ensure the effectiveness of service, and our devotion to avoid neglecting our life in Christ. We must not let a state of slumber overtake us, laziness to excuse away our obligations, and indifference to dull our ears and dim our eyesight of faith.

It is important to note we determine what we do with the light of Christ in us. We must remember it is to serve as a light in this dark world, a light that will penetrate the darkness, expose its wicked works, and become a reproof of warning and exhortation to those who are teetering between this present age and the glory to come.

It takes the light of God to penetrate every place where the darkness of sin, consequences, and ignorance resides. It is the light of God's truth that purges us of past accusations, heals us of those things that left indelible marks upon our soul, and restores our confidence and relationship with God where doubts towards His commitment taunted us.

I had to learn that the reason I covered any sin is because I was not willing to let the light expose the depth of its shame and when it came to unresolved matters left by consequences, my personal understanding could never serve as the bridge that leads to real healing and peace. And finally, I had to learn to trust the character of God in those things that appeared to be unfair, that always left me in a state of confusion towards His intention towards me and fear that in my case, He was not obligated to be fair and trustworthy.

My prayer is simple, "Lord turn on the light and let it penetrate any darkness in my being, purge the terrain of my soul, and transform wrong heart attitudes and thoughts towards You as a means to purify my walk before You."

God's Word possesses simple truths, as well as true life. We must live by it. After all, it is the light of His Word that will lead us out of darkness towards the light of the world. Jesus Christ. The problem is we often tempt the Lord to speak to us other than through His Word, or prove that He means what He says as a means to justify our selfish whims.

How often is it that we, in our arrogance, attempt to humble God by insisting He first bow before our insidious, selfish demands to prove something that is fleshly and fickle. The reality is it is not in our hearts to believe and we have already decided not to believe what is true.

At such a stage we are looking for entertainment, not truth. At such a point, we will never have the pure heart to truly see the Lord for Who He is. The Lord will never entertain us, but He will set us free with His unadulterated truth. I will and must choose the latter if I am to ensure that I never become barren in the knowledge of Jesus. (See *2 Peter 1:3-9*.)

One of the things we must be willing to lose is our personal understanding of eternal matters. We have a tendency to put God into an intellectual box and confine our beliefs to some emotional roller coaster that occasionally hits peaks of zealousness, but can easily descend into absolute despair. We possess ideas about ministry that are grandiose, but are void of any stamp of eternity on them. In essence, we operate from the highest places of earthly exaltation in our minds, but when compared to the heavenly, it is nothing more than a dot in the scheme of things.

We must realize that the heights we may reach in our carnal minds will not amount to anything more than a fanciful notion that will leave us disillusioned. It is for this reason our minds must be transformed by the renewing of the Spirit. This is the only way our minds will be able to embrace the spiritual truths of the eternal and gain a heavenly perspective.

In the past I had to let go of my earthly vision in the wilderness in order to gain the vision the Lord wanted me to possess. The problem of letting go of our earthly vision is that we will find ourselves in a spiritual darkness that will require us to trust the Lord to guide us through the night. However, we can rejoice in such darkness because the Lord's goal is to bring us to His light so we can walk in it.

Are you walking in the light of Jesus? Man walks according to three lights—natural light around him (sun/moon), the artificial light (man-made/understanding), and the light of God (Shekinah).

The natural light is what we function in as far this material world, but we walk through the present age (systems and philosophies) according to our understanding, while the light of God is veiled and must be revealed by revelation to our spirit by His Spirit. The importance of this heavenly light is it is the only way to take full advantage of Jesus' life in us and come into a place of true worship and communion with the Lord. This incredible light of God is complete. The fact that it comes from above into our understanding assures us that we are not bound to this age; rather, we are being prepared for the next.

The light from without of God's Word confirms in our souls that we do not walk in condemnation of the past, but in light of the resurrection power that will raise us up above the judgment that is already upon the world.

Finally, the true light of His life and Spirit from within our spirit brings an inner knowing that we are not groping in the present darkness, while walking according to a false light that blinds us to God's wrath. As Christians we must remember that we possess the true light of heaven and must walk in and according to it to become a reflection of true light in this world.

What does it mean to walk in the light of Christ? It means we are living His life and walking according to it. There are those who think that eternal life is in the future, but as believers, if we possess Jesus, we possess eternal life now, but it will be fully realized when we pass from this life to the next.

It is Jesus' eternal life in us that makes us heirs of salvation and also provides us with everything we have need of to ensure godliness (*2 Peter 1:3*). The Holy Spirit indwells us which means He is not only working Jesus' life into us but He is the source of our strength and wisdom necessary to walk out this life.

It has taken me a few years to realize that I do not work the life of Christ in me; rather, it is the Holy Spirit who does such a work. In my past attempts to somehow straighten myself out, I ended up wrestling with the Spirit instead of giving way to Him. I had to learn that my ideas of religion based on "good works" and God's works of righteousness are two different things altogether. I had to give up my ideas of what I thought my part was and simply trust the Lord to work in me His heavenly qualities.

When I start to become anxious over if I am doing things right, I remember *Philippians 1:6, "Being confident of this very thing, that he which hath begun a good work in you will perform it until the day of Jesus Christ."* God is doing the work in me and what is my responsibility? Not my will but Your will Lord, not my way but Your way, not according to my terms but according to Your Word, not based on my idea of righteousness, but based on Your work of righteousness.

The end product of such submission is genuine faith that can be accounted to me as acceptable righteousness by God.

We must always discern the darkness because there is darkness AROUND us, darkness UPON us, and the darkness ABOVE us. We must make sure the darkness AROUND us is due to the age we live in and not because we are not in the right place with the Lord. If the darkness is due to the age we are in, we need to realize it is an opportunity to allow our light within to shine in the darkness, and if it is because we have strayed, we need to repent and come back to center, God.

We need to know if the light UPON us is because God's sovereignty is at work or whether we are in a dark place because we have insisted on doing something our way and we have gotten off the narrow path. If the darkness is because God is doing a work, we must by faith allow the light of God's Word to guide us one step at a time through the darkness, but if we have insisted on our way, we need to turn around, face the light, and begin to once again line up to it.

If the darkness ABOVE us is of this age, then we must be content to wait upon God, knowing that He is refining the eyes of our faith so we can see the path before us. But, if it is because we have allowed the times we live in to bury us with its lies, silence us with fear, and enfold us in utter hopelessness, we need to stand up by faith, take the sword of God's Word and begin to withstand with truth, and continue to stand because we have no part in the darkness of the world.

In fact, we are like the children of Israel at the Red Sea, the darkness will part and we will walk in the way of victory to take possession of His promises.

In the past I have lost important papers and objects. I try to recall what to look for and I dig deep in my memory to consider the last place I actually saw it. When I can't find the desired object, I look at the most likely place I left it, usually in some of my piles of stuff that are sometimes stacked up for me to wade through and more than once file it in file 13, the trash container.

The problem with finding something is that things become lost in the shadows and appear differently then you last remembered them, or they become lost in stuff and hold no real distinction so that you can identify them. When I run out of options and become frantic, that is when I look up to the Lord, and ask Him to illuminate it to me so I can see it.

Up until that time I assumed I would find it, but discovered in my search, that I graduated to presumption that leaves me in complete despair. Once the Lord illuminates it, I realize it was located in the place I last absentmindedly left it.

I have found this true for my Christian walk. I sometimes leave Jesus behind because I am trying to keep up with the rat race around me and other times, He becomes shrouded in worldly activities and occasionally He loses distinction because I absentmindedly laid Him aside as I focused on other happenings that are demanding my attention.

When my focus is taken off of the Light of the world, everything eventually becomes dim and out of focus, causing me to realize I have lost sight of that which is the most important treasure I possess. The beauty about reconnecting to Jesus at such a time is that I don't need to find Him, I simply need to turn around in repentance to see that He is waiting for me to put my focus back on Him, knowing from that point on, the way will be illuminated for me as I follow Him.

The other day I talked about losing sight of Jesus. It simply means I have left Him behind. When you leave Jesus behind, it only requires you to stop and turn around to once again connect with Him because He is waiting for you to do so. But when it comes to a crisis of faith, it requires another type of search because you will find yourself in a thick, darkness that leaves you feeling lost, isolated, and hopeless.

The crisis becomes real because there is no light of understanding to guide you through the darkness, there is no fresh breeze to give you direction, and there is no sense of hope to inspire you. This experience is often referred to as "the dark night of the soul." As you try to stand on what you think you know, you buckle under the weight of the onslaught of what seems senseless, and as you take a step into the unknown, fear grips you because there is nothing to grab a hold of to prevent you from falling into some unseen abyss.

In such times the only thing you can do is hold onto what you know is true about God's character and trust that in the darkness He will never forsake you as He guides your steps and keeps you from slipping into the abyss.

"The dark night of the soul" has taught me that even though I am in darkness, God is the light and He knows how to preserve my soul. By taking steps of faith in confidence of His abiding care of my life and soul, I have always been brought through the darkness to once again feel the warmth and healing of His light upon my soul.

Each time I came out of the darkness, I did so with a greater awareness of God's faithfulness to keep me, His abiding care to watch over me, and His perpetual commitment to bring me out of it with my faith enlarged, a greater dependency on Him, and a deep gratefulness that He never leaves me nor forsakes me.

SPIRIT, LIBERTY, & GLORY

*I can see how it might be possible for
a man to look down upon earth and be
an atheist, but I cannot conceive how he
could look up into the heavens and say
there is no God.
(Abraham Lincoln)*

What voice do you listen for and to the most? Clearly, there are many voices clamoring for our attention in order to influence our attitude, preferences, and worldview. There are the contradictory voices of the world with its many causes, the inner voice of logic that seeks confirmation as to what it knows, the voices of others that must agree with us to ensure peace in our environment, and there is the voice of conscience that can stir up our worldview to unmercifully judge.

I have heard all of these voices and I realize I cannot trust any of them. There is only one voice in this world that is trustworthy and that is God's voice. Creation declares His glory, His recorded Word confirms His testimony, His true servants proclaim and teach His truths, and the Holy Spirit brings confirmation and life to what is true. However, to recognize and hear His voice we must be able to discern it, which requires us to know the Lord.

Rayola Kelley

Depending on our relationship with Him, will depend on how He speaks to us. To the lost it is a forlorn voice, "Adam where are you?" To the rebellious a stern voice of warning, to the seeking a sure voice that invites them to the Living Water, to the wounded a loving voice, and to His sheep a familiar voice. It is in the stillness of our spirit and the quietness of our soul that we can hear the still small voice of God's Spirit and what does Scripture say? "Hear what the Spirit is saying."

The Bible tells us to hear what the Spirit is saying. There are many voices vying for our attention to influence us; therefore, one of the great challenges of Christians is to fine-tune our spiritual ears to hear what heaven wants us to know.

Jesus told parables that could be easily understood by the physical ear, but if our spiritual ears are dull of hearing, understanding will elude us as the spiritual meaning remains a mystery (*Matthew 13:13-16*). The Spirit will not yell at you about a matter; rather, He will move upon you with gentle impressions about the deep matters of God, revealing a deeper revelation.

Now mind you a new revelation will never step outside of God's character, be contrary to the spirit and intent of God's complete counsel (His Word), or produce contrary fruits. The main responsibility of the Spirit is to lead you into all truth about Jesus who is the truth to ensure you are walking in the way that will lead you to real abundant life (*John 14:6; 16:13*).

Ephesians 1:17 tells us, *"That the God of our Lord Jesus Christ, the Father of glory, may give unto you the spirit of wisdom and revelation in the knowledge of him."* Therefore there are no new revelations outside the Word, but there will be a greater revelation of Jesus as the Holy Spirit unveils Him in greater measure in His Word.

I don't know about you but when the Spirit entrusts me with a greater revelation of Jesus, I am not only overwhelmed, but I am greatly encouraged in my faith as my love for Him grows.

In my last post, I spoke of hearing what the Spirit has to say. We have physical eyes and ears but we also have spiritual eyes and ears. These two entries give us the ability to interact with our environment.

We must have the eyes of faith that looks beyond this present world to trust in the promises of the next world that is yet to come if we are going to interact with God. We must have our spiritual ears fine-tuned to hear unfeigned truth that the Holy Spirit will speak and lead us to in order to keep us sharp and discerning in the days we live in.

Jesus warns as much in *Luke 8:18 "Take heed therefore how ye hear."* There is a lot of bad news flying around that can depress our souls, but we must remember that we determine how something we hear will affect and define us. We can succumb to the curtain of depression or we can step back and look up knowing that God still sits on the throne and He is sovereign over all matters that affect our life.

The personal question each of us has to answer is will we trust Him with our individual lives and the outcome, knowing that whatever is going on will in some way benefit our spiritual life and fine-tune our hearing and ability to see Him in greater ways.

I enjoy learning about eagles. In one book I read years ago it talked about how an eagle can live for many years. After all, as far as a bird goes, eagles are at the top of their chain and do not have to contend with enemies except for one main adversary: man.

Like all creatures, death works within the members of this great bird and because of age he hits a crisis. The crisis is that he cannot fly as high as he used to. Keep in mind, the eagle has to fly high enough to catch the air currents before he can soar. Apparently, when an eagle hits this crisis, he will stand on the end of some cleft in a mountainside, and literally fling himself against the side of the mountain.

Some believe that this procedure actually loosens some hindrances on the wing structure that keeps the bird from reaching the heights. Somehow the bird recognizes when the limitation no longer exists because it ceases flinging itself against the mountainside and begins to once again reach great heights.

According to the information I read, the eagle is able to soar higher than before. As believers, to encourage ourselves we sometimes need to quit accepting our present perspective and fling ourselves upon the great Rock of Ages, trusting that He will inspire or set us free to come higher in our understanding of Him, enabling us to be caught up by the wind of the Holy Spirit to see greater distances in the Spirit beyond this world to catch glimpses of the glory of the next.

I don't know about you but I do not want to settle for less in my spiritual life, but am I willing to be taken in depths of uncertainty to be lifted higher into the realm of His Spirit? As a new Christian I had the zeal of Superman, the grandiose vision of being some great evangelist that would impact many, and/or a committed missionary that was spilling my life out on a foreign mission field.

It took a few years for the romantic notions of greatness in regard to God's kingdom to fall to the wayside so that the Lord could reveal to me that greatness was not about being great in my own eyes or according to the world's estimation, but about becoming great as a lowly servant in His kingdom. From that point on I begin to make it my goal to be a faithful servant who would be able to stand before the Lord and hear those most important words, *"Well done thou good and faithful servant."*

One day a minister told me something that overwhelmed me. She said, "You desire to be commended as a faithful servant, but the Lord wants to call you friend." Jesus made reference to this friendship in *John 15:14-15*. He has chosen each one of us individually and He wants to be a true friend to each of us so that He can share the matters of His heart and kingdom with us.

As I meditated on the fact that the Lord wanted me to enter into a more intimate relationship with Him, I realized I first had to learn to be a faithful servant before I would prove to be a faithful friend that could be entrusted with the matters of His heart and kingdom. It was then that I learned an important lesson—we may be interested in position and placing in His kingdom but He is interested in positioning us close to His heart so that He can have a more intimate relationship with us.

The Bible speaks of the natural man and the spiritual man. The supernatural can make a person spiritualize things, religion may make individuals religious, and good works can make people appear pious enough, but the only thing that can make a person a spiritual person is the presence of the Holy Spirit residing in the individual.

The Holy Spirit is the One who empowers us as believers to walk out the Christian life in the barren wilderness and valleys of this present world. He is the One who transforms the soul in preparation for the next world yet to come.

The challenge for some Christians is that they try to hold onto the familiarity of this world, while grabbing at promises that they can fit into their religious activities. However, promises are not realized by picking and choosing them according to self-serving purposes, but as *Hebrews 6:11-12* reminds us, "*And we desire that every one of you do shew the same diligence to the full assurance of hope unto the end: That ye be not slothful, but followers of them who through faith and patience inherit the promises.*"

The Spirit empowers, faith endures, and prayer helps one cling to promises until they are not only realized in our lives but in the lives of others.

It is clear that I must give the Holy Spirit something to work with. The more I believe God's Word, assimilate it into my life as food, and walk it out in obedience, the more I give the Holy Spirit the means to bring His Word to remembrance when I am going through some storm, struggling in the midst of a battle, or when I need inspiration from above, and direction in confusing situations.

It is up to me to read and study God's Word in order to stand by faith because of it, withstand with its truth, and continue to stand on its many promises. I also know that humility puts my soul in the right state to receive what the Word has to say to me, prayer prepares my heart to receive what the Spirit wants me to understand from the Word, and worship will lift my spirit above the demands of this present world so that I can clearly see what the Word is saying.

I know the Word of God has to be more than a mental assent; it must be a heart revelation to bring about inner change so I can see Jesus Christ on every page and in every book of it.

In my early years as a Christian, I was very judgmental towards those who did not jump on my particular bandwagon. After all, I was very opinionated about what I thought was right, while looking down on those who called themselves Christians, but did not live up to my take on a matter, and becoming quite contrary with those who dared to disagree with me.

Praise God, He did not hold me to the same level as my judgmental opinions, my arrogant judgments, and my unloving ways. He in fact, gave me room to fail and allowed me to climb the heights of pinnacles to fall, letting me in the end be utterly broken before Him.

The brokenness is what allotted me the great freedom to finally gain His perspective about some things. It is natural to fight against being undone, proven wrong, and becoming broken, and yet there is great liberty when all three events happen.

Being undone before God's holiness puts things in perspective from a heavenly view, being wrong gave me the freedom to discover what was right, and becoming broken allowed me the freedom to turn around in repentance and seek God's forgiveness and restoration. It was in a humbled state God revealed His love, mercy, and grace in greater ways.

Our high opinion of ourselves will never like the great fall that will shatter it, our understanding will not appreciate being thrown up into the air to land in a state of confusion and darkness, and our pride hates being broken, but the experience is what liberates us from the greatest hindrances in our walk: OURSELVES.

As believers we serve a powerful God. The heavens declare His immense glory, the earth His incredible ability to bring about perfection in all He does, and weak man His design to do great exploits in order to reveal His glory to others. There are a couple of things we need to remember about the power of God.

The first thing we must remember is that we do not put our faith in what God can do, but in His character and Word. Faith comes by hearing, not seeing miracles, and it is obedient faith that allows us to walk in confidence towards God, allowing Him to miraculously confirm faith that has been properly directed towards Him.

The challenge people have is they want to understand God to alleviate the need to walk by faith. We must accept that in our limited state we can come to a certain understanding about God, but we will never comprehend Him, and if we could, He would cease to be God.

It is important to remember every time we set out to understand God in order to explain God, we will ultimately strip Him of His glory, not only in our minds, but in other people's minds as well. We are not here to explain God, but to proclaim Him and His works that He has done on behalf of man.

I was reading the other day about God's voice in *Psalm 29*. We know that God's Word is His written voice, testimony, or record that we must adhere to, and that the voice we are to listen for is the voice of the Holy Spirit. Whether it comes in pictures, gentle impressions, or a sense of strong conviction that feels like a burden or heavy hand, we must be able to discern His Spirit's voice. As Jesus stated, "Hear what the Spirit is saying," for He is the One who will lead us into all truth and reveal things we need to know about the days we live in (*John 16:13*).

The Holy Spirit will never yell at you and His way is that of gentle persuasion, but if there is ever an urgency to His voice it must not be ignored. I remember reading the story of an Englishman during WWII that kept getting an impression urging him to get out of bed and pray. After a couple of pressing nudges, he got up and as he was preparing to kneel in prayer an unexploded bomb came through his roof and landed on his bed where he had been laying seconds before. Needless to say, whatever He reveals must line up to the intent and truth of God's Word.

Psalm 29 reveals another aspect of God's voice. We are told the voice of God is upon many waters and one of the descriptions of Jesus' voice in *Revelation 1:15* is that his voice is as the sound of many waters. *Psalm 29* goes on to say His voice is powerful and full of majesty. Remember what *Hebrews 11:3* tells us that the worlds were framed by the Word of God.

No doubt, God spoke everything into being and it is obvious we could never in our present state begin to imagine the authority, power, and majesty of His voice. *Psalm 29* goes on to talk about God's voice breaking the cedars, shaking the wilderness as He did in Sinai, dividing the flames of fire, and ensuring nature takes its natural course.

Many people want to hear God's voice but unless they are obeying the voice of His Word and walking after the Spirit as He leads and guides, they will not be prepared to hear or recognize His voice when it comes in the form of revelation and judgment as in the case of *John 12:28-33*. If we do not tremble before His Word with its many warnings and admonitions, how can we stand before it when it sounds like the voice of many waters coming in all power?

We must be realistic about hearing God's voice. In a way, we hear it every day in creation, we can hear it when reading His Word, and since words can touch the soul, we can feel His Living Word when the Holy Spirit nudges us. The truth is, how we hear His literal voice, whether in love and gentleness or in judgment and wrath, depends on our response to His voice that is present in today's world.

What is the difference between God's presence and His glory? Man can stand in God's presence but he can't stand before Him in the fullness of His glory. God's presence among men is the Holy Spirit and He is symbolized in the wilderness by both the pillar in the day that leads and the fire at night that protects and comforts, while the glory of God is a burning, consuming fire that is represented by His transparent holiness and His consuming jealousy that will not allow or tolerate any sin or idol to stand beside Him or before Him in the hearts and minds of men.

God's presence comes down to inspire a proper response from man, while His glory must be shrouded before man dares to look at it to experience a greater revelation. For example, God's glory was shrouded by incense when the High Priest went into the Most Holy Place on the day of atonement. It was shrouded by darkness on Mount Sinai and clothed in humanity when it came to Jesus Christ.

We will sense the Lord's presence because it is able to be discerned, but we will only catch glimpses of His glory in times of worship. God's presence comes first to prepare man to look into His glory which has been manifested in His Son, but this only occurs when people like Moses in *Exodus 33:18* cry, *"I beseech thee, shew me thy glory."* This happens after man has been in the presence of God and he realizes there is so much more to discover, know, or experience about his eternal God.

At this point man's spirit is longing after more of God and will not be silent, and his soul is hungry and thirsty for a greater measure of the pure bread, meat, and waters of God. Moses was told that he could not see God's face and live; therefore, he was placed by the Lord upon a rock, and once placed in the cleft of it, the Lord would then cover him by His hand while He passed by. However, Moses could not look upon the face of God, only His back.

Keep in mind, Jesus is our foundation we are to stand on, the cleft in the Rock of Ages that we are hidden in, and because of redemption we are covered by His robe of righteousness. Unlike Moses, we do not have to settle for seeing the Lord's back; rather, we can choose to look into Jesus' wonderful face every time our longing spirit and hungry soul sincerely seek Him. As Jesus told Philip in *John 14:9, "Jesus saith unto him, Have I been so long time with you, and yet hast thou not known me, Philip? He that hath seen me hath seen the Father, and how sayest thou then, Shew us the Father?"* (See also *John 1:14*.)

The other day I asked what is the difference between God's presence and God's glory. We know as believers that the presence of God, His Spirit abides in us, but since He is the rivers of Living Water, we must be constantly filled up from above to ensure spiritual refreshing and cleansing to avoid stagnation in our spiritual life where we find ourselves becoming a barren wilderness.

It is God's Spirit that ensures edification of spirit and soul in the body of believers, otherwise nothing of eternal significance is ever accomplished. God's Spirit must be among us to ensure truth is handled properly and acceptable worship is preparing the saint for sweet communion with the Lord.

God's glory served as the light in the Most Holy Place. This transparent light of God exposes the great darkness of sin as it did on Mount Sinai, consumes the sacrifice and chaff on altars, blinds man so he can see the darkness of his own soul as in the case of Paul, and sanctifies that which has been dedicated to the Lord such as the Old Testament Tabernacle. The one thing that God's presence and glory have in common is that both can be withdrawn. David's request in *Psalm 51:11, "Cast me not away from thy presence: and take not thy holy spirit from me."*

The Holy Spirit is like a dove of Noah that is first sent to check out the condition of the terrain and will come back if there is no place to land, but God's glory moves according to the inner condition of the temple. It will come down to sanctify or lift to indicate judgment is upon the place.

I have been talking about God's presence and glory. In *1 Samuel 4* we read the story of the Philistines exerting God's judgment on the wicked priesthood when they defeated Israel, killed the High Priest Eli's wicked sons, and captured the Ark of the Covenant. The ark represented the presence of God among them as well as the trademark of His glory.

When Eli's daughter-in-law heard the bad news, she named the son that was born to her at that time, "Ichabod," which means, "the glory is departed from Israel."

In the mid-1980s, a woman came from South Africa to warn the American churches that the glory of the Lord was about to depart from many of them due to sin, idolatry, and unholy alliances. In fact, she implied that many church buildings would be left empty and some would be reduced to smoldering ashes, leaving the parishioners to mourn over the remains. As I listened to her, my main concern was not empty or burned church buildings; rather, how many Christians would even recognize that the glory of the Lord had departed from their congregations?

Today I see that warning coming true in various ways and as believers we must not mourn over buildings but over the state of the church, where the word "Ichabod" above the door would be an appropriate description of how the light of God's glory is no longer present in the place of worship.

THE FRUIT TEST

Virtue is not knowing of good and evil.
Rather, virtue is the doing of good
and not doing of evil.
(Lactantius)

You shall know them by their fruits. How many of us as believers have heard this term? I have, but in the process how many of us have become fruit inspectors? The question is what are we looking for when we consider fruit: quality or quantity?

What determines the quality of the fruit is size, color, smell, firmness, and taste. Size and color have to do with outward presentation, but we are told that we can't always trust what we see because our eyes serve as an avenue of temptation to stir up lust. We can smell it, but not all that is foul smells. We can touch it but it can defile us, and we can thump it and listen for a certain sound to see if it is worthy of consideration, but we are told to beware of how we hear a matter because our understanding of it may be limited and tainted. We can taste it, but we can't always discern if there is some type of poison present.

The key behind fruit is its source. If the source of the fruit is not healthy, the fruit will lack quality. A good tree produces good fruit and a bad tree produces bad fruit, and it is for this reason we are told to test the spirits behind a matter. Testing has to do with discerning a matter and as the days become more challenging, we better know how to discern or quickly ask for the means to properly inspect fruit.

This means we must ultimately discern what source any fruit comes from. In some cases, it is obvious that some fruit is bad, and yet how many people, including Christians, are willing to give it a pass because it appears there is some good in it? After all, look at the quantity and popularity behind it, but if it comes from a bad source, it will prove to be bad fruit.

Some believe that if we mix the best part of bad fruit with some good fruit, it will turn out alright. Such a mixture will prove to be poor at best and destructive at the most. There are those who figure we can handle or partake of terrible fruit because God will protect us, but we are instructed to come out and be separate from the unclean and not put God to such a foolish test.

The reason we must test the fruit in order to determine the source is because a little leaven, leavens the whole lump and we can't afford to have our spiritual ears dulled if we are going to hear the Spirit of God, our eyes shut if we are going to walk through this darkness, our taste buds rendered ineffective in determining what is good or bad our sinus clogged up so we can't smell what is foul, and our hands defiled so that we defile what we touch.

This brings us back to a simple question? Are you a good fruit inspector?

Yesterday, I talked about the fruit test. When we consider the fruit of the Spirit in *Galatians 5:22-23,* we must note the first ingredient is love. In fact, every ingredient in the fruit of the Spirit finds its origins in godly love.

Joy comes when our fellowship with the Lover of our soul, the Lord, is sweet, true, and pure (*1 Corinthians 13:6*), and peace follows because there is harmony in our inner man due to reconciliation with our Maker, for God so loved the world that He gave His only begotten Son on our behalf (*1 Corinthians 13:5, 7*).

If peace has taken residence in our soul, we have the basis to be longsuffering towards others, able to be gentle (kind), good (honorable), full of faith (selfless and obedient), meek (under control of the Spirit) and temperance (in control of the self-life) (*1 Corinthians 13:4, 6*). We are no longer subject to the Law of sin and death because we are living the life of Christ which leads us into the excellent ways of the Holy Spirit and righteousness (*Romans 8:2; Galatians 2:20*).

As the Apostle Paul stated in *Ephesians 5:9-10*, the fruit of the Spirit is in all goodness and righteousness and truth, proving what is acceptable to the Lord. The real test of our fruit is not realized during the good times, but when our character is being tested in the bad times.

Christians who truly possess the fruit of the Spirit will leave you with some distinct taste. Perhaps it might be the sweet taste of love, the salty taste of truth, the spicy taste of exhortation, and/or the calming taste of encouragement, but it will all be in line with bringing you to the glorious reality of Jesus and His truth and His will for the building up your lives in Christ. It might be to challenge you in your way and edify you in your Christian life, as a means to always ensure you are on the right path when it comes to finishing the course.

There is much debate going on about how to react to the challenges around us. Debate is not necessarily about truth or what is morally right, but about seeing who can talk over the other as a means to drown out controversial points or opposition, and, as we often witness, without always making a legitimate point, leaving one irritated, angry or completely confused.

Much of the debate going on in the world is propaganda that becomes a platform for many unsound, insane voices to hit our airwaves. That is why when you look up debate in the Bible it is classified as a fleshly activity because there is no debate when it comes to God's truth and ways. God's truths will stand in the end, and His ways will ultimately be proven to be right and perfect.

As Christians, we must avoid being part of the debate that makes one unstable because the rules can change in debates and making it unproductive because it leaves bitter fruits behind. Therefore, we need to make sure we are the pillars that are simply standing on what will prove to be true and right in the end. This means we can take control of the narrative for ourselves by making sure we are standing on the right side of eternity in every matter.

I spoke of the worthless practice of debate. My desire is to always discuss a matter as a means to challenge a person rather than debate it as a means to try to change their mind. I have learned that the Holy Spirit is the only one who is capable of changing a person's mind and He does so by transforming it to change the attitude behind a matter as well.

However, there are times I find myself debating but they are rare moments where I feel someone has stepped over a line when it comes to the real message of truth and I debate it for the sake of others who are present. This brings us back to the fact that people debate everything, and if important matters are settled in heaven, why must there be ongoing debate on earth, especially among Christians?

There are a few reasons debate exists, 1) difference over Scripture has to do with personal interpretations, 2) difference over politics has to do with preference such as in the case of political parties, as well as ideologies, 3) differences in societies have to do with cultural diversities and laws, and 4) differences in homes have to do with authority, individuality, and selfishness. We come back to how do we react to the incessant debates going on around us?

I don't know about you, but I want to stand on what is sure to avoid wasting my energy swatting at insignificant "gnats". I want to withstand by maintaining my authority in what is Scripturally sure, and continue to stand on what I know will remain standing when all else is shaken. I say this because it is time for Christians to step off the worldly merry-go-round of debates and come back to center as to the simplicity of Christ, the Gospel, and His truths.

As believers we need to realize we are citizens representing an unseen kingdom and every time we stand it must not be in relationship to this world, but in light of our high calling in Christ Jesus, which demands we become crucified to the world's influences and become true ambassadors in properly representing His kingdom to others.

I have been talking about the debates that often divide, causing dishonorable fruit in relationships. I have my own take on how to avoid wasting energy on the vain, useless exercises of debate. When it comes to Scriptures, I do all I can to stick with the reality of Christ and Him crucified because He is the only sure foundation, and I only tell people what I believe about a non-essential doctrine when asked, to avoid making it a moot cause that ends in some type of misunderstanding.

In relationship to politics, God is neither Republican nor Democrat, but He is holy which means I mainly vote based on the moral standing of a candidate in light of issues such as abortion, the sanctity of marriage and the family set forth by our Creator, and the need to maintain liberty that protects the rights of citizens for the sole purpose of worshiping God according to conscience and conviction without fear of persecution. My prayer is that the candidate is true to his or her convictions and has the character to stand when all hell comes against him or her while refusing to sell their soul.

When it comes to diversity due to culture, people can practice what they want in America, but if they are in this country, we have laws to ensure order in our culture and if individuals do not want to properly respect our laws and have no desire to become one who adds to the betterment of this nation, then my philosophy is that they need to go back to where they came from.

God established borders for a reason, and we do not need the wicked practices of other cultures to be forced down on us or added to our base practices that will produce greater political and moral erosion of our society. I keep in mind at all times my Christian convictions never end with politics, culture, or citizenship. I am here for one reason and that is to represent the kingdom of God to lost souls that need to see a way out of this present hopeless, insane world of endless debates.

What influences you the most? The influences in our life will develop the attitude we take on, the character that will be displayed, and the quality of conduct that comes out of our life. In other words, does our conduct and fruits line up to what we preach or proclaim or is it just show?

When we tear back the curtain of influences in our life, we will see that they are often based on what we prefer, which will determine what we pursue. The challenge for most people is to own who they are so they can be honest about their real master.

People who serve self are being influenced by the inherent, fallen nature of Adam and if they serve the world, they are serving the god of this world Satan. If the flesh is influencing you the most, then your spiritual life will be an inconsistent mess of emotional chaos, insecurities, and ongoing struggles where victory eludes you, and if the world is influencing you the most, you will become an indifferent, self-serving, and often deluded individual who is being set up for destruction.

As believers we are to only have one Master, Jesus Christ. Unlike the flesh which is a tormenting, insatiable taskmaster and Satan who is a cruel taskmaster, Jesus is a caring Lord, a committed master, a benevolent king, and a loving Shepherd. We need to remember that whatever, or whoever, becomes our master is what we prefer above all else.

May every Christian have one sole preference as to who will always and ultimately influence who they are: The Lord Jesus Christ.

Do you need to be set free? One of the great advantages of Christianity is true liberty. However, true liberty cannot come without a real dose of truth because truth is the only weapon that has sharp enough edges to cut away blinders, open festered wounds, and expose some tormenting aspect of our life that harbors anger, unforgiveness, bitterness, and skepticism.

As I have mentioned before, Christians can bop along on the assumption that all is well for them; that is, until something touches that one area that has remained in the basement or hidden away in a closet, bringing out some unbecoming human responses that can even surprise us. I learned long ago not to test myself according to what I know, what

I believe, what I stand for, or who I think I am. After all, such standards can easily leave me with a high opinion of myself. I test myself on the basis of the one thing that exposes the most about the state of my heart attitude and character, and that is my fruits.

Jesus stated you shall know people by their fruits. Most people think fruits are what you do, but fruit is more about how you respond towards a situation. It is your response towards a matter that will leave a taste in people's mouth. Up front, most of the time I want to react very human, but then I step away from the challenge and decide how to respond to it. Our approach or response to a matter is determined by our attitude towards it.

I have learned I need to take God's attitude about matters when it comes to my life. For example, He clearly states that others will know we are His disciples because we have love for one another. It is easy for my pride to take offense when I have been misunderstood or not properly recognized, and it is easy for my logic to justify any unloving reaction that may follow.

However, the Bible tells us the only right response comes from godly love which means it is tempered with meekness, ever benevolent, and ready to cover offense in order to show the proper response. This type of love is foremost interested in the person's well-being more than how it may personally affect our emotional state. Keep in mind, love is selfless, not selfish and it desires to respond in a becoming way that will not bring a reproach to Jesus or one's testimony.

PRAYER

Is prayer your steering wheel
or your spare tire?
(Corrie Ten Boom)

How many of you love to see God's grace work when it comes to answered prayers? Hopefully, we recognize that answered prayer is a matter of undeserved favor on God's part and that all He does is because it is consistent with His love, upholds His holiness, is in line with His will, and part of the working out of His greater plan.

I had to learn that I pray not to get my will done, but to discover His will to ensure that a matter can be brought to perfection for His glory. As a believer it is easy to take God's grace for granted, to somehow perceive that we are worthy of His consideration in our prayer life, merit His response to answer them, and deserve to be gratified because we think more highly of ourselves than we should.

Answered prayers have indeed brought excitement to my heart, but in my initial immaturity my prayers rarely ended with an attitude of gratitude due to the level of selfishness still present. Answered prayers have added to my testimony about God's power to miraculously intervene, His faithfulness to meet me, and His abiding care on my life, but recently I was reminded of a simple truth.

Years ago, I was challenged to adhere to the Bible by praying for laborers to be sent out to the harvest field. In the challenge the evangelist added, "And don't be surprised if you find out you are also an answered to that prayer." We know God answers prayers, and at times we are even aware that He uses others to become an answer to prayer, but we sometimes fail to see that in our expectation to see God move that perhaps we are also an answer to someone's else prayers.

Prayer is about availability, expectation, discernment, and identification. In prayer we want God available to hear and respond and in expectation we know that He has the means and the ways of answering it, but we must discern His will and make sure He is not calling us into a place of identification where we become a co-laborer with Him in the lives of others when it comes to answering their prayers.

As Christians, we need to remember that He blesses us so we can become an avenue in which others can be blessed. The truth is we can become an answer to someone's prayer, but the question is can we be entrusted to faithfully avail ourselves and willfully submit to become a real source of God's blessing in the life of such individuals who in our minds may not merit our consideration?

As American Christians we can be enthusiastic about various aspects of the Christian life even to the point that we can romanticize some of it such as in the case of prayer, complicating it or making it unrealistic. When we consider the "Lord's Prayer," we can begin to see a simple pattern that speaks of importance and order.

What is of foremost importance to the Lord is a right relationship with Him, followed by His kingdom being realized in the hearts of people. As people seek a relationship with Him and learn what is important to Him then they will be able to discover and know what is His "acceptable, good, and perfect will."

It is only as our life is lined up to the reality and will of God that we are able to understand and ask for our needs that will allow us to carry out His will. Once we line up our heart and will to the Father and put into perspective our needs, then we must examine our relationship with others. This is brought out in *Matthew 6:12, "And forgive us our debts as we forgive our debtors."*

If there is some type of sin in your life that has not been dealt with, you will find that you lack authority and power in your prayer life. It is clear that wrong attitudes towards others will prevent us from being taken seriously by heaven. As once pointed out, "The real test of our Christian life is not how we treat God in public, but how we regard others in the privacy of our mind and heart." The Bible is clear that if our relationship is to be right with God, we must be right with others.

The "Lord's Prayer" taught me our initial approach to the Lord is everything. This became more obvious as I studied the prayer lives of those in Scripture. These people knew who God was, knew what they were after, and as a result knew how to approach Him.

We can see this by how they would address the Lord. The different ways of addressing the Lord have been distinguished by how the name is printed out. For example, when you read "LORD," in the Old Testament, the Jewish people were calling Him Yahweh (Jehovah). Jehovah is in reference to God being a covenant keeping God.

When you read "Lord," they were referring to Him as "Adonai" which points to Him being owner and the One who possesses all things. When we see "God" (Elohim) it reminds us He is Creator, and when we see "GOD," He is "El" the Great "I AM," and just who is the I AM, I AM, all-inclusive the first and the last in all matters.

We should understand this approach because we come in the name of Jesus. Consider what Jesus said in *John 14:13-14, "And whatsoever ye shall asked in my name that will I do that the Father may be glorified in the Son. If ye shall ask any thing in my name, I will do it."*

First of all we see that we asked in His name to bring glory to the Father. What is Jesus' full name in many of the New Testament presentations? The Lord Jesus Christ. The word "the" points to singular, sole, or only, while the word "Lord" points to deity.

Jesus means "Yahweh saves" which reminds us of His mission to save us, and "Christ" identifies Him as the Messiah who was promised and anointed to bring healing to our souls. When I approach the Jesus of the Bible, I am approaching the one who is all sufficient and will ensure that my prayers and life lines up to that which is eternal, beneficial to heaven and for those on earth.

In the last post I made reference to approaching the Lord in a right way. Approach is everything. For example, how you approach a problem (or people) is going to determine the outcome. Problems arise when we approach someone based on our perspective. We assume that everyone will see it our way and we tend to forget that people have their own ideas and conclusions which will most likely prove to be "strange" to us.

Consider for a moment, would you approach a judge on the bench the same way you would an acquaintance? Would you approach a political leader the same way you would a family member? We have different approaches in light of who we are approaching. The question is how do we approach the Lord when there are pressing matters affronting our lives?

In the Old Testament you will see that many of the Jewish people addressed Him as "Yahweh," (LORD) which reveals that they were approaching Him on the basis of covenant. Covenant identifies God's people to His will and promises. It is a way of establishing a firm foundation to stand on as the saint asks the Lord to intercede according to His mercy and will.

As Christians, we are told to ask in Jesus' name and the reason for this is because it identifies us to an everlasting covenant that allows us to approach God on the basis of our spiritual inheritance and His promises.

The Lord has various names that identify Him to His work on our behalf, so the next time you approach God consider what you want to accomplish in your prayer closet and then approach Him accordingly.

One of the incidents that always causes me to stop and consider what is being said about prayer is found in *Luke 11:1, "And it came to pass, that as he was praying in a certain place, when he ceased, one of his disciples said unto him, Lord, teach us to pray as John also taught his disciples."*

It amazes me to consider how after these Jewish men had watched Jesus in prayer, they asked Him to teach them how to pray. No doubt they had seen the Pharisees in their outward show of praying in public places and being repetitious about it, but they could tell from observing Jesus in His prayer life there was something that was fundamentally missing from the prayers of the religious leaders they had observed. So what is the difference?

Jesus taught them what we call the "Lord's Prayer." As I studied this prayer, I realized that effective prayer begins with a right relationship. Notice Jesus' first words, "Our Father." If we have been born again into the kingdom of God then we are also adopted into the family of God. I don't know about you but my relationship with my earthly father gave me a right few had; in fact, I had the ear of my father at any time.

As I thought about the relationship between a father and a child, I realized that no formality is required but there must be that identification as a child of God before one can approach the Father who is in heaven.

Do you have such a relationship? If so, you have a right to approach the God of heaven at any time with your requests and concerns.

"Our Father which art in heaven..." (Matthew 6:9). Effective prayer begins with the right attitude and approach. What does it mean for God to be our Father?

For believers it means we have been adopted into a spiritual, heavenly household. We often relate this adoption process to the way adoption takes place in our culture. Perspective parents find the child they want to claim as their own and petitions the court to make it legal. According to H.A Ironside, adoption in the Roman culture during Paul's day was another matter altogether.

Apparently, every child born into the Roman Society was considered servants, not heirs. In other words, they had no rights; therefore, the one who was to become heir in the household was taken by the father to the court and officially adopted so that the child could receive his father's inheritance.

This puts a different light on every child of God's adoption. The truth is we all have the potential to be heirs of salvation, but because of Adam, we all have been born into the status of slaves to sin. It is upon believing the Gospel of Christ dying for sin, being buried and three days later rising again and receiving it as truth in our hearts that we are officially adopted into the family of God and the official seal of this official act is the Holy Spirit who identifies us to our inheritance. Since everyone has the potential to be a child of God, the real issue comes down to whether that adoption has officially taken place in the court of heaven.

As believers we must remember that Jesus died on the cross to secure a relationship for every believer with the God of the universe. This relationship gives us rights and an inheritance as children, privileges in our royal status as priests and kings, responsibilities as servants in His household, authority as His ambassadors, and armor as soldiers, and a seal (Holy Spirit) to identify us to each position in His kingdom.

When I consider these positions, I become overwhelmed because there is nothing lacking when it comes to my life in Christ. Consider for a moment that as priests and kings we must carry out a certain protocol (conduct), as servants we must carry out certain duties, as ambassadors we represent an eternal kingdom, and as soldiers we must march according to certain orders, but when it comes to being a child of God, we have the right to come to Him in the most personal, intimate way: prayer.

Prayer is about communication and to communicate we must be prepared to listen. How many of us pray expecting an answer? How many of us pray to find out what is important to the Lord?

As a child of God, I know that He hears me, but am I passed the selfish stage of immaturity to hear Him?

My level of spiritual maturity will determine what I will hear from the Father. As an infant in Christ, I had to learn His voice so that when I heard it, I would respond to Him. I remember a story of a missionary and his son in Africa. One day the small son joyfully ran ahead of his father. He suddenly heard his father's firm voice instructing him to hit the ground. The little boy immediately responded and fell to the ground. The father came running over to his son and quickly picked him up and rushed away with him.

As the little boy looked over the father's shoulder, he saw a big python snake occupying a tree that he had run under when his father had instructed him to hit the ground. If the little boy had not known the voice of the father and obeyed, he would have become the victim of the snake.

There are many voices in the world, but as children of God, we must learn the voice of the Lord so we can hear it in this world and respond to it to avoid the devices of the enemy and the destructive traps of the world.

Rayola Kelley

What does our next goal need to be when it comes to learning how to pray? As I stated in the last post, we must learn to hear the voice of the Lord. This brings us to the different witnesses that make visible declarations about the Lord. Creation testifies of the eternal power of the Godhead (*Romans 1:20*), the heavens His glory (*Psalms 19:1*), believers serve as His living epistles or letters (*2 Corinthians 3:2-3*), and His Written Word as His inspired, prophetic voice (*2 Timothy 3:16; 2 Peter 1:18-21*). It is also true that the Holy Spirit serves as a voice within our spirit, but the sure voice of God which will test and confirm whether He is speaking IS HIS WORD.

If something, whether it be doctrine, experience, or beliefs, do not line up to the spirit (intent) of God's full counsel, then it must be put on the shelf for more confirmation or discarded altogether. Keep in mind it takes the witness of two or three to confirm a matter (*1 John 5:6-13*).

The Written Word will always serve as one of the witnesses. God often uses His written Word to speak to me about a matter, allowing me to properly discern it. There are many warnings in Scriptures that in the last of the end days there will be many false claims, teachings, lying signs and wonders, seducing spirits, and false Christs.

There are four ways we must discern a matter, 1) Does it line up to the character of God, 2) Does it line up to context and intent of the Word, 3) Where or who will the emphasis of the teachings and messages ultimately lead you to, and 4) What fruits is it producing. I learned a long time ago that I had to give the Spirit something to work with by making sure I was properly engrafting the Word of God into my inner being so the Holy Spirit could bring it to mind at the right time in the right place.

Because of past religious experiences I had many assumptions about prayer. I initially saw it as a formal exercise. You had to be in the right place, somewhat in a pious frame of mind, and take on a certain physical posture before God would hear you. When I became a Christian, I realized that prayer was not an exercise, but it represented in a sense the very breath of a believer.

The Apostle Paul stated that we must pray without ceasing in *1 Thessalonians 5:17*. Even though our words take on sound, the sound

102

waves are carried by the air around us. As I considered Adam's relationship with his Creator, I realized that prayer was conversation which naturally occurred in a setting that encouraged such fellowship. For Adam it was a garden, but as I considered the two other men who walked with God, Enoch and Noah, I realized that they probably had to establish their own personal gardens in which they could walk with the Lord in sweet fellowship.

We all know that in the first garden sin broke that fellowship where conversation could not take place on the same level, and the sad result manifested itself in *Genesis 3:9, "And the LORD God called unto Adam, and said unto him, Where art thou?"* God's voice is still calling every man to once again commune with Him; and praise His Holy Name, we as believers know that Jesus came to restore that place of fellowship where we have heard His call and as a result we can once again walk with the Lord, converse with Him in our heart as prayer becomes the living, satisfying breath that fills our soul with new life and glorious expectation.

In the last post I mentioned how man walked with God, but there is one particular incident where God walked with man. The Apostle Paul put it this way in *Colossians 2:9, "For in him dwelleth all the fullness of the Godhead bodily."*

Over two thousand years ago God was clothed in the flesh, came by way of a virgin and a manger and grew into manhood to become the Lamb of God, to be a substitute for you and me on the altar of the cross. Think about it, man walked with God in the beginning, but in the case of Jesus, God walked with man.

In *Luke 24*, we have the case of the two men on their way to Emmaus, talking about the events around Jesus' crucifixion. They had heard that He had risen from the dead but it seemed like an idle tale. The account tells us Jesus drew near and went with them, but their eyes were closed to who He was. And, what did Jesus address? -- their confusion around the events.

I remember one incident where I was wrestling over matters concerning ministry and I sensed Jesus drew near to me to walk with me a bit and talk with me. You know what the conversation was about; it was about answering those questions on my heart that surrounded the matters of His kingdom. It may be hard to believe but there are rare times when the Lord wants to answer questions that are greatly besetting our spirit, and when we least expect it He will draw near to us.

Do you have such questions that only Jesus can make sense out of? Remember, He went out of His way to answer the question of the woman at the well about worship in *John 4*, and who knows? He might draw near to you to answer those heartfelt questions about Himself and His kingdom work.

The more I studied the concept of prayer, it became obvious to me that it was not to be some mere formal exercise that required me to put on some outward presentation like the Pharisees in Jesus' day, but that it was to bring me into a time of communion, of interaction with my God, with my heavenly Father.

For some people they bring the concept of "heavenly Father" down to the world's perception of it. The challenge with such scenario is that we can become silly, casual or flippant about it. I say this because in the "Lord's Prayer" the fact that our Father is identified to heaven and we are to hallow His name gives us insight into the attitude we are to have when approaching Him in prayer. It also reminds us of the third commandment which declares we are not to take the Lord's name in vain. In other words, we are to show a proper respect towards Him and who He is when we do approach Him.

I thought back to my relationship with my stepfather who actually raised me during very formative years. I had a very special relationship with him, but when I approached him to ask for something or to talk to him about a matter, I did so in an honorable way because I not only loved him, but I respected him. As long as I showed the proper respect to him, I actually was allowing him to give me his full attention with an open mind and heart.

The Lord wants to commune with us but there must be the proper honor and respect on our part to ensure a healthy relationship that will guarantee fruitful end results.

In the disciple's prayer, Jesus stated, *"Thy kingdom come."* A kingdom implies there is a king. We know that Jesus is the King of this unseen kingdom that resides in the heart of every believer.

When John the Baptist declared that the kingdom of God was near, he did so because the King of that kingdom, Jesus Christ, was about to start His ministry. The Lord Jesus Christ would make the kingdom of God real in the hearts of man. It was His way of establishing the kingdom of heaven on earth.

As believers we are part of the kingdom of heaven on earth but to carry out the work of heaven on earth, we must do the will of God. Doing the will of God means to consecrate our whole life by offering our bodies as living sacrifices. This is necessary if we are going to cease to be conformed to this present world and be transformed by the renewing of our minds so we can prove what is the acceptable, good, and perfect will of God (*Romans 12:1-2*). The key is that to ensure the will of God is done on earth it must first be done in our lives.

As to the sequence of the prayer Jesus taught His disciples in *Matthew 6*, He said, *"Thy kingdom come. Thy will be done in earth, as it is in heaven."* We know that it is God's heart to set up His kingdom in the heart of man. This is not only His heart, but His will. *James 4:3* speaks about people not having their prayers answered because they are asking amiss. I have had to realize my first prayers were very selfish, revealing my childish ways. At such times I was not treating God as a heavenly Father but more like a big "Sugar Daddy" or a "Santa Claus."

My prayers were all about God heaping on me what I thought I needed or wanted. I did not realize it then but I was missing the whole purpose of prayer. Prayer is not getting my will realized; rather, it is the means in which I seek out God to find out His will so that I can line up my prayers, my life, and my activities to His character and eternal plan.

The Apostle John said this in *1 John 5:14, "And this is the confidence that we have in him, that if we ask any thing according to his will, he heareth us."* Clearly, our goal in prayer should be to find out God's will. Prayers concerning selfish pursuits are a waste of breath and time. If we want our prayers to be effective then we need to come into line with God.

His first and foremost desire is to have a personal relationship of communion with those who love and desire to worship Him and His second desire is to see men saved. Communion with God will ensure authority in our prayer life and having the right focus in prayer will empower us to stand and properly intercede for others as part of the royal priesthood in the kingdom of God (*1 Peter 2:9*).

In my last post I talked about prayer being an avenue to seek God as to His will. Sadly, prayer is sometimes used to further personal kingdoms on earth rather than seeing God's kingdom advance in man's heart.

There are those who are seeking Paradise on earth rather than preparing for Paradise in the next age. "Paradise" is basically where the Lord is. It is true He made a garden for man in which He could commune with man, but man rebelled and the result is a wilderness, a world that outside of Christianity is void of communion with God.

My responsibility is to ask the Father to bring forth His kingdom and my part is to seek and know my part in His will and plan. I have had to ask myself, "What do your prayers say about you. Do they speak of maturity or are they revealing childish, selfish ways?"

Admittedly, God answered many of my prayers when I was new in Christ, but the longer I was a Christian, it seemed He became quiet while I became more frustrated and found myself floundering. It took a bit but I learned that maturity entailed having more sobering, serious conversations with the Lord. The more I understood what was important to the Lord, the more I could be entrusted with the matters of His kingdom.

Are you still wrestling with the Lord to try to get your way or have you learned to rest before the Lord with open ears to hear what is important to Him so you can be entrusted with that which entails life and death and eternity?

Do you have "tormenting wants," or have you done as Jesus did the night He was facing the cross, *"Not my will but thine be done."* Effective prayer is about gaining God's perspective that will take us above this present world to embrace the simplicity of heaven's message and work of redemption. I say this because needs represent simplicity while wants produce grave complications.

Clearly, the Lord promises to provide us with our needs, and in the prayer of *Matthew 6*, Jesus instructs the disciples to ask for their needs and step back to watch our Lord faithfully provide them. However, the big trap that "wants" bring with it is that we can wrongly judge God's fatherly care in our lives and His provision based on our wants.

We can deem Him an unloving God and father because He is not bowing down to our selfish demands. I can look back on my life and remember the times I have become obsessed over a matter that I felt was pertinent to my well-being. The more I thought about it the more my obsession escalated with torment because the lusts of the flesh were taking center stage.

This is the problem with wants, they tantalize our imagination as to what they will do or accomplish for us to the point we become obsessed with them. Obsession is tormenting and not of God. In fact, obsession is demonic in nature.

The challenge we have before us is to examine our motives and priorities. We can have the best intentions towards God, but if our motives are not pure and our priorities honorable and lining up to God's will, we will become what James warns us against, "A double minded man is unstable in all his ways" (James 1:8)

When we deal with the subject of wants, we have to consider how we look at blessings. There are material blessings and spiritual blessings. Sadly, like those at Laodicea in *Revelation 3:14-18*, many equate the status of their spiritual life to material blessings. However, we are told to compare the spiritual with the spiritual to see where we are in our walk with the Lord because the material blessings of this world are temporary and can do nothing to add to the inward quality of our spiritual life.

The Lord talks about spiritual blessings in *Ephesians 1:3*, *"Blessed be the God and Father of our Lord Jesus Christ, who hath blessed us with all spiritual blessings in heavenly places in Christ."* It is natural for the flesh to seek material blessings, but for the spiritual man he foremost seeks after the unseen blessings that will add to his spiritual life.

James 2:5 gives us this insight about what really enriches our spiritual life, *"Hearken, my beloved brethren, Hath not God chosen the poor of this world rich in faith, and heirs of the kingdom which he hath promised to them that love him?"* The Bible tells us that where our treasure is, is where the affections of our heart will be, and what we tend to pursue in prayer is also determined by where our affections rest.

We need to seek God for our needs, but to be rich in our prayer life we must seek after the unseen riches that are attached to our faith towards and in our great Provider.

One of the greatest hindrances to our prayer life is unforgiveness. People who refuse to forgive others find themselves becoming bitter and if the bitterness takes root, it will defile their attitudes and relationships with others. In some cases, it will turn into rage which is a type of insanity that takes over a person's reasoning.

We all know the scriptures on forgiving others, but I have met those who call themselves Christians who walk in unforgiveness towards others. They tout certain rights to not forgive, but the Bible does not afford anyone the right not to forgive. We are commanded to forgive and this forgiveness has nothing to do with the offender because our unforgiveness, bitterness, or rage does not hurt the culprit; rather, it hurts us. It causes us to shrivel up inside like a prune as we develop trigger points that can set off our anger, bitterness or rage at any time and any place.

We will find ourselves being taken captive by such emotions and to be set free we must repent of our own unforgiveness as we seek God's forgiveness and ask Him to heal our heart so we can truly forgive from it. True forgiveness is not a surface exercise, but it is something that can only come from a heart of godly love that desires to forgive the offender so it can show God's incredible grace when afforded the opportunity to do so.

It is important to understand what it means to forgive. Forgiveness has to do with someone who was offended, properly dealing with the offense and there are two meanings behind forgiveness. One meaning is "pardon."

God as the great judge is the only one who can pardon people. Jesus brought this out in *Mark 2:1-12*. When people ask God to forgive them for the offenses committed against His Law and covenant, they are asking Him to pardon them from paying the judgment leveled at them by His Law or covenant.

Breaking the Law and covenant is a sign of contempt towards God, and the sentence for breaking the Law is death and to break God's covenant is a point of rebellion that will cause offense and separation from God.

The second meaning is to "release" or "let go" of the offense. This meaning basically releases the one offended from seeing the culprit pay consequences for an offense. The Lord makes it clear that vengeance is God's alone. Since the Lord reserves the right as a just Judge to execute judgment on someone, we must release ourselves from seeing the person pay, which means we have to let go of our right to see what we would consider "justice" being executed.

Are you harboring any unforgiveness because you are waiting to see justice? If you are, remember God can only pardon you as you release others from the offenses they have committed against you.

The Apostle Peter states in *1 Peter 4:8* that love covers a multitude of sins (offenses). Many times offenses on our part often point to our pride or ego being hurt. Pride will never be satisfied with any type of judgment executed on the one who has offended it. This is why when people live to see justice done and actually may witness it, they are often left hollow in the end.

As believers we need to let offenses go by allowing the love of God to take the sting out of the offense and/or heal our hearts and memories if necessary, so that in the end we can show the same grace towards the offender as God has shown towards us.

Grace gives us the right to choose the more excellent way of stepping up and over matters that keep us from embracing the liberty that is available to those who choose to follow after the Spirit in attitude and practices.

It is natural to want to hold on to some type of offense but if we want an effective prayer life, there must not be one shred of unforgiveness present. We often hold on to offense to either remind ourselves of what happened in order to protect ourselves from it ever happening again or we try to take up the cause of justice until we see the person pay or finally understand what offense he or she has caused, but we are told that oftentimes people fail to see the offense they have committed.

Jesus on the cross revealed as much, *"Father, forgive them for they know not what they do."* Our anger and bitterness will never impact the offender, but such an environment will greatly affect us as it allows the root of bitterness to defile our perception and our relationship with others.

Bitterness often comes out of envy because we have failed to receive what we thought we should receive or we did not see a matter come to a proper fruition according to our sense of fairness. Life is not fair, but as believers, we must know that God is just and in due time He will righteously judge the offender and when He does, we must not rejoice at the plight of the offender, but humble ourselves before God as we realize He has shown us grace when He forgave us for the great offense our sinful condition committed against Him.

In my posts I have been talking about effective prayer which entails forgiveness. I don't know about you but in my prayer life I have to seek forgiveness because I have been un-Christlike in a matter or I have committed the sin of omission where I failed to do right in a situation (*James 4:17*).

We never must forget that forgiveness is a two-way street. God will forgive us as we forgive others. We must keep in mind God does not have to forgive us for the great offenses we have committed against Him. If we are honest with ourselves, we must admit that we have offended Him in many ways, but He chooses to forgive us because He wants to bring deliverance to our lives and open the door to communion.

Out of love He gave His Son to provide the way in which we can seek and obtain forgiveness even though there was a time we might have resisted or fought against His overtures to come to Him in our spiritual poverty. Before we can come to Him, we have to first realize our great need for Him. His example of forgiving us needs to be our example.

We must also choose to forgive from the heart to release ourselves of the great bondage that can occur in our life by choosing not to forgive. It is for this reason we are told not to let the sun go down on our anger and give place to the devil (*Ephesians 4:26- 27*). After all, unabated anger and bitterness are the fruits of the devil and they will graduate into a murderous attitude of being vindictive and vengeful.

I have been talking about effective prayer in light of true forgiveness. Some people struggle with forgiveness because they feel it requires them to become a doormat for reckless, inconsiderate people to continually walk on, walk over, and stomp into the ground. Forgiveness does not mean wo open ourselves up to the one who offended us.

John 2:24 tells us this about Jesus, *"But Jesus did not commit himself unto them, because he knew all men."* Jesus knew He could only trust so much to men and did not open Himself up to them. On the other hand, forgiveness does not mean we ignore the problem because real love will *"never rejoice in iniquity" (1 Corinthians 13:6).*

The reality is, we must confront sin when we become aware of it, but it will never be for our personal sake, but for the sake of the one in sin. *Matthew 18:15-17* clarifies what types of sin we must confront others about: Trespasses.

Trespasses have to do with trespassing the Lord's Law or covenant. Such a trespass must be brought to the light so the one who has committed it can repent and be restored into a relationship with the Lord. This shows us sin is serious but if we are offended because someone has hurt our pride, we are to allow love to cover such wrongdoings because godly love will take the sting out of the offense and allow us to release ourselves from seeing a person pay the consequences.

Let's face it, how many of us are willing to admit that someone has offended our pride? Granted, we want to treat such an offense as grievous, but we don't want to admit our pride has been hurt and yet it proves to be liberating when we do. The next time you feel offended, consider whether the Lord would be offended. God did not come to address that which offends us; rather, He came to address that which offended Him—SIN.

Forgiveness stands at the crux of salvation. There can be no salvation without forgiveness.

Jesus died on the cross to deal with the sins that greatly offended a holy God. We must confess those sins and ask for forgiveness before we can be reconciled to God. He cannot look on any sin without judging it, but if we have been born again with God's Spirit and the life of His Son is in us, we will find ourselves hid in Christ. When the Father looks at us, He will not see us in filthy rags rather He will see His Son with all of His wisdom, righteousness, sanctification, and redemption.

Love and forgiveness are not a feeling but a choice. I choose to love in a godly, honorable way and I choose to forgive, and that is why we are told to love our enemy, bless those who curse us, and pray for those who persecute us.

It is in such love we are able to manifest the same grace to others the Lord has shown us. We need to keep in mind as Christians that we have a ministry of reconciliation and not of judgment. As children of God, we are called to be peacemakers between God and lost man, and such reconciliation cannot occur without forgiveness (*Matthew 5:9, 44; 2 Corinthians 5:18-20*).

In the next aspect of the Lord's Prayer, Jesus instructed His disciples to ask the Father to not lead them into temptation. James 1:13 states, *"Let no man say when he is tempted, I am tempted of God for God cannot be tempted with evil, neither tempteth he any man."*

It is important to point out that the Lord will never tempt us to do evil, but He will test us. Temptation is directed at stirring up the lusts of our flesh while testing has to do with refining our faith. The Apostle Paul stated, *"Wherefore let him that thinketh he standeth take heed lest he fall. There hath no temptation taken you, but such as is common to man; but God is faithful, who will not suffer you to be tempted above that ye are able; but will with the temptation also make a way to escape, that ye many be able to bear it. Wherefore, my dearly beloved, flee from idolatry"* (*1 Corinthians 10:12-14*).

Pride will often set us up to fall into temptation because we think we can handle such a test in our own strength. However, to avoid falling into the trap, we must remember the flesh is weak and discern if we are being set up to ultimately bow down to the lusts of the flesh, thereby, finding ourselves in some type of transgression.

Unmortified flesh will prove to be a powerful idol and the only way to overcome it is to submit to God and obey His Word by fleeing all youthful lusts to follow after righteousness (*2 Timothy 2:22*).

It is always important to recognize moral weaknesses in ourselves and ask the Lord to keep us from the evil that would be too great to stand against.

Rayola Kelley

In my last post I talked about the flesh being weak. We have a tendency to become prideful in those areas where our flesh has no real attraction towards, giving us occasion to judge those who may be struggling with such weakness or falling into the temptations of them.

It is true we may possess certain fleshly appetites that are indifferent to the world's attractions, but such self-sufficiency is dangerous. The Bible warns us to instruct and consider others who are struggling with such matters in meekness. I know that if I confront matters in my flesh, weaknesses I never knew I had will suddenly appear, and if I failed to discern my dangerous sense of infallibility, I can easily enough fall into them.

We need to be honest about the weaknesses in our character and be ever aware that even though we may crucify the flesh daily, in the right situation, it can be easily resurrected by youthful lusts.

My prayer when it comes to weaknesses in my character is, "Lord, I know I am weak in this area, keep that which would tempt me to do such evil far from me."

The last part of "The Lord's Prayer," in *Matthew 6:13* is, *"For thine is the kingdom, and the power, and the glory, for ever. Amen."* Every time I end the prayer in this manner, I become overwhelmed because I am reminded of the purpose to all prayer—it is about the desire to see God's kingdom realized in others and that He has the power to bring it about in order to bring glory to Himself.

Jesus said of His kingdom that it was not of this world and we know those who believe in Him make up this spiritual kingdom. In fact, we serve as priests and kings of this kingdom according to *Revelation 1:6*.

As part of a priesthood, we are to stand in the gap and intercede and as kings we are reminded that we belong to a royal priesthood that identifies us to the King of kings. We are told we are citizens of this unseen kingdom and that we serve in the official capacity as ambassadors (*2 Corinthians 5:18-19*). In other words, we represent the interest of this unseen kingdom in this present world.

114

We are to be good-will ambassadors that carry good news. We are also diplomatic ambassadors that have a ministry of reconciliation to those seeking refuge, and we are to be ambassadors who will stand against anything that would threaten the advancement of this kingdom in hearts with God's Spirit and truth.

Today many people want to have a certain standing in this world to make a name for themselves or to make a difference. As ambassadors, we are in a position to make a difference, but we are not here to make our name known but to cause others to believe, know, and value the name which is a name that stands above all other names, THE LORD JESUS CHRIST.

Where will real prayer ultimately lead you? In the last post it was pointed out that the last part of "The Lord's Prayer" ends with reminding us of the three aspects of prayer and that it is to seek the reality and fullness of God's kingdom in our life and in the lives of others.

It is in prayer that the very power of God can be released to bring about His desired will in a matter, and finally the whole purpose of prayer is to bring glory to God, but where will it ultimately lead a person. We get insight into that aspect of prayer in *Revelation 4:4-11* and *5:11-14*. The ultimate goal of all prayer is to lead each of us into a real place of worship.

We all have our ideas of worship, and I remember when I became a new Christian, my idea of worship was three songs we sang in church, but needless to say I have learned worship is a heart attitude and a mindful activity, which requires preparation of the soul that allows the spirit to come into agreement with the Spirit of God in truth about who He is, what He has done, and what He wants to accomplish in and through our lives.

I am reminded that if my search is successful, it will lead me to God as well as lead God to me. I know according to *John 4:23* who the Father searches for, *"But the hour cometh, and now is, when the true worshippers shall worship the Father in spirit and in truth for the Father seeketh such to worship him."*

115

THE RIGHTS OF A CHILD

*Weak children of God pray only for themselves,
but persons growing in Christ understand how to
consul with love over what must
take place in the Kingdom
(Andrew Murray)*

We used to sing, "I am so glad I am a part of the family of God." In a past post, I made mention that we cannot assume we are children of God, we must make sure the right relationship is present. After all, we cannot declare we are part of the family of God unless we are born into it by the Spirit of God according to Water of His word and have the seal of the Holy Spirit in and upon our lives that identify us to our inheritance (*John 3:3, 5; Ephesians 1:11-14; 1 Peter 1:23*).

In the prayer, Jesus taught His disciples to pray, He instructed them to pray *"Thy kingdom come."* When John the Baptist was preaching in the wilderness of Judea, he made this statement, *"Repent ye: for the kingdom of heaven is at hand."* There are two terms used in relationship to this unseen kingdom: the kingdom of heaven and the kingdom of God.

Someone once stated the kingdom of heaven has to do with the work of salvation the Lord wants to do on earth in the lives of men, while the kingdom of God has to do with carrying out the will of God both in heaven and on earth.

Jesus told Pilate when He stood before him, "My kingdom is not of this world." As believers we have been born into an unseen kingdom. Because of our adoption, we are related to the king, which makes us royalty. We belong to the kingdom of God which becomes obvious when we do His will, but we are called to be ambassadors of Christ to continue to carry out heaven's work in this world in regard to our commission to preach the Gospel and make disciples of Christ.

I have mentioned my stepfather in different posts. It was the example of my relationship with him that taught me a great deal about my relationship with my Father in Heaven. I often stated, "I had three fathers, my biological father who gave me physical life, my stepfather who gave me identity, and my Heavenly Father who has given me both spiritual life and identity."

My stepfather definitely defined my person more than any other individual in the formative years of my life and it was in part due to my love and respect for him. He didn't have to take the responsibility to be a father to me, but he chose to, and he was a wonderful father. He passed away in 2015, four months after my mother passed away, but because of his commitment to be a father he left me a wonderful legacy of what it means for someone who had no real biological responsibility for a waif such as myself, but because of his relationship to my mother he made a heartfelt decision to be my father.

We need to remember it is because of Jesus' redemption on the cross that we can come to the Father, an act that also expresses His love for us and the grace He has extended to us.

It is clear that God wants to be our Father, and His desire to be our father has provided the right to come to Him as His child, but we as believers must recognize the great act of grace on His part and choose to love and respect Him in such a way it allows for a healthy, intimate relationship to take root and develop.

When my mother first married my stepfather, I asked him what I could call him. He asked me what I wanted to call him. There is only one word I wanted to call him and that was "Daddy." However, calling him, "Daddy," and having a relationship as father and child takes more than using the term.

There must be an investment from both parties for a father/child relationship to be established on an emotional level. This is true when it comes to our relationship with our Heavenly Father. *Romans 8:15 states, "For ye have not received the spirit of bondage again to fear; but ye have received the Spirit of adoption, whereby we cry, Abba, Father."*

We have been brought out from under the influence of the spirit of this present age in order to have the freedom to know what it means to be a child of God. God has provided that means through His Son; however, we must avoid hiding behind titles that may be able conjure up some emotional sentiment, but falls short of experiencing the relationship. We must develop that relationship with the Father in sweet communion. We must not only ask Him to be our Father, but we must learn what it means to be His loving and obedient child.

We can be assured that the heavenly Father wants to be our father, but what will it take to ensure we enter into the relationship with Him that will make Him our Father and maintain the integrity of the relationship?

I remember one day when I was meditating before the Lord. I was thinking about Jesus' baptism and I was reminded that it was there that the prophecy of *Psalm 2:7* was fulfilled when the Father introduced Jesus as being His Son.

Then it was as if the Holy Spirit dropped a scene and a question in my mind. I saw myself standing before Jesus in the court of heaven with the host of heaven looking on. The question was simple, "Based on your relationship with the Father, would He introduce you as His child?"

We cannot make assumptions about our relationship with the Father, we must make sure we are being established in a rapport with Him. Jesus made this statement when He was told his earthly family wanted to talk to Him in *Matthew 12:48b-50, "Who is my mother? And who are my brethren? And he stretched forth his hand toward his disciples, and said, Behold my mother and my brethren! For whosoever shall do the will of my Father which is in heaven, the same is my brother, and sister, and mother."* It is clear if we are to be introduced as a child by the Father, we must be interested in knowing His will and pleasing Him by obeying Him.

ATTITUDE

*It is impossible to keep our moral practices
sound and our inward attitude right while
our idea of God is erroneous or inadequate.
(A.W. Tozer)*

What is your attitude towards truth? We often quote *John 8:32* that truth will make us free. What many people fail to realize is for truth to make one free it has to cut through delusion, dissect and exposed all preferred lies, make a mockery out of fantasy, and expose the false light of darkness.

At such times truth can hurt, rip, and tear at everything one thought he or she understood about the matters of life. It is easy to say I want the truth and something altogether when it comes to walking it out. Jesus made it clear that truth will offend. Truth is a mirror that reveals the reality of something, good, bad, or ugly.

It is the knife that will go into the very soul of man and reveal the darkness of his own character. It is the sword that will cut all blinders off so that man can see the real carnage left behind by sin and actually be broken so he can humbly respond to it in repentance or become hardened by fear and indifference. It will not placate pride by trying to make peace with it, it will not water down the message so it will not offend, and it will not adjust to the wicked philosophies of the time in order to keep peace with the devil's systems. For truth to be effective it walks hand in hand with other Christian virtues.

For example, for truth to end in real worship the Holy Spirit must be present, and for it to be effective in confrontation it must be disciplined by meekness. For it to face what the harshness of reality really is, it must take hold of a matter with mercy, and to walk it out it in obedience it has to take the hand of faith. To ensure it ends in wisdom it must walk in the fear of the Lord and to stand with it in hand, lifted up as a weapon one must trust it, to withstand with it one must prefer it over all other realities, and to continue to stand with it, one must love it.

We often forget that truth is expressed in three forms: God's Word, what is so in present reality, and Jesus Christ. God's Word shows us the truth so we can stand on what is real by faith and the present reality is to wake us up to truth so we can be prepared to stand in light of hope. It is the fact that all hope, promises, and inheritance is found in the truth of who Christ is and what He did for us that we can continue to stand no matter what is happening around us.

This brings us to a simple fact, if you say you love Jesus, then you must love truth no matter how offensive it has been in the past, is presently today, or might be tomorrow to you, and if you do not love truth, you must not delude yourself by thinking you love the true Jesus of the Bible when in reality you are in love with a mere image you have conveniently conjured up in your imagination to fit into your controlled narrative and preferred reality.

I think one of the struggles for Christians is to come to terms with developing a right attitude towards this world. Being in this world, we are encouraged to pursue the vanity of this world instead of investing in that which has substance and meaning: The big one being our relationship with others, beginning with God.

Material things will never fill our lives, worldly accolades and accomplishments with never bring meaning to our lives, and getting and doing something our way will never bring happiness or satisfaction to us. In fact, we will be left with a hollowness in our spirit and a restlessness in our being.

The Christian walk of faith has allowed me to experience many different aspects of life without settling for the useless and selling my soul to gain the recognition of the temporary. I have been an adventurer that has discovered great spiritual heights of revelation and explored great depths where spiritual treasures abound. I am a journeyman that has been given an official title of "ambassador," but I have been provided with valuable tools to work in the harvest fields of the world, to feed the spiritually hungry and offer water to the thirsty soul, to bind up the wounded with the healing balm from above, and to offer a helping hand to anyone in a time of need.

Since I am called to be a servant of all, I am reminded I am a master to, or over, nothing, but I serve a Master who is all in all. I am a sojourner simply passing through this present world to reach another destination and meanwhile I must accept the fact that I do not fit in this world nor belong to it.

I will always be the odd-man out due to a restless soul that knows there is more yet to be discovered and possessed, but it will never be found in this world. I am a spiritual pilgrim that is in search of that which allows me to serve and worship my God in the way He is worthy of.

I must concede that like the great patriarch, Abraham, I am seeking for the city made by God, and will not be content until I enter His heavenly courts. As believers we must not think it wrong to be homesick, but we must never settle for just getting by in this world until our great homecoming. We need to continue to be faithful in occupying as we continue to run the race set before us.

I was watching gray clouds move across the sky this morning and realized that without the drama it brings to one's emotions that there would be no depth to creation. This is true for people as well.

We all prefer clear sunny days, but we need the drama of cloudy, rainy and snowy days to ensure that life advances forward in a meaningful and constructive way. That is why we are told that the sun shines on both the good and evil as well as the rain falls on the just and unjust (*Matthew 5:45*).

It is easy to identify the two contrasts when it comes to people's attitudes and approaches to life. You have the pessimist and the optimist. To the pessimist everything is a matter of suspicion, as they walk around under a cloud of hopelessness with a doomsday philosophy and a cynical view of life.

You have the optimist whose sees everything as having some silver lining in matters while maintaining an impractical view of life that all will turn out right in the end. Needless to say, this view is not realistic when brought down from the whimsical waves of fantasy and wishful thinking in light of reality.

We all prefer to be around the optimist who can leave us feeling hopeful and good about life, but eventually their notions become a source of irritation as we are confronted with the real matters of life and any attempt to realistically address them in their presence is never met with wisdom but with adverse effects of resentment and anger. After all, wisdom comes out of realistically facing and experiencing the different facets of life.

Even though we can see how the pessimist seems more realistic, we can't be exposed to their insipid reality for long without throwing our hands up in hopelessness and walking away in total despair.

As believers we are to be neither a pessimist whose attitude speaks of a wrong spirit for there is no hope to be found anywhere, or the optimist whose hope is based on a fantasy that has no substance to it. We have hope because we walk by faith towards the true God of heaven. We possess that which connects us to a heavenly inheritance with the silver lining of redemption and the red cord that identifies us to an everlasting covenant. As a result, we do not walk in despair regardless of the darkness because we possess the light of Jesus and we do not have to fear reality hitting us because we are founded on an immovable truth that will keep us standing secure on the Rock.

The question is when reality challenges our present understanding, which attitude do we lean towards?

The other day I mentioned the two contrasts when it comes to people's attitudes towards life. It is natural to initially lean towards being a pessimist or an optimist. However, there are two other attitudes that people can take on towards life. The first one is that of indifference.

Indifference is what happens when the pessimists can no longer stand their morbid reality, causing them to take on the attitude of indifference so they are not consumed by the onslaught of misery besetting them. When it comes to the optimists, they take on this attitude when their fragile view collides with reality in such a way that it reveals that the darkness of this world is all consuming and there is no light in any of it. Instead of having a total meltdown, these individuals will take on an indifferent attitude towards reality to hide their uncertainty, resentment, and anger. Although indifference points to a type of numbing taking place of the conscience, it does not prevent these individuals from having to taste the bitterness of life in different ways.

The final view has to do with a heavenly view of life. In Christendom we can see the first three attitudes even among those who call themselves Christians, but there are religious terms or beliefs attached to them to cover up the attitude. The optimists in Christianity are those who think they can control God and their reality by methods whether words or practices. Christians who operate from this premise want God's blessing to fall on them instead of walking by faith towards the promises that open up the way to experience blessings through obedience to His Word. They put their faith in what they do and not what the Lord has already secured at the cross for them.

The pessimists are usually legalistic, unloving, and judgmental. Their faith is in what they believe and not in the One who provided the way of salvation. When it comes to indifference in Christianity, it points to spiritual complacency towards the matters of God, which points out the crux of the problem when it comes to the first three attitudes: THAT OF UNBELIEF.

As believers we are told to look up to gain perspective, set our heart and affections on that which is heavenly and eternal, focus on the unseen promises of an everlasting life and a city made by the hands of God and walk by faith and obedience towards it. The reality is that we are optimistic in a way because we live in light of a heavenly expectation and even though we deal in reality, we do so in light of an eternal perspective that allows us to rise above the morbid reality of the present darkness.

As I have learned, truth lies between all extremes when it comes to reality and it is by loving and pursuing God's truth that our perspective will be heavenly, balanced, realistic, and sure.

One of the things that still shocks me is the propensity of people to ignore the practice of wickedness in light of some misconstrued loyalty. This propensity is so great that some believe if you put the right title on Satan, associate him to certain groups and ideologies that it makes him acceptable and one of the "good guys" in the crowd. In essence, people end up calling evil good and good evil.

As Christians, what should our attitude be towards any wicked practice and evil propensity? The Bible is clear. Love does not ignore iniquity and will stand against it, and righteous people will hate evil knowing what it does to the souls and fiber of a nation, shun the traps of wickedness, and walk in the path of what is right. The reality is that if we truly care about a person's soul, we will not let them merrily go to hell without warning him or her of the grave consequences of continuing on the broad path to utter destruction.

If you ask me why is our country in such a struggle? The struggle is not pollical, it is moral. As a nation we allowed ourselves to cast aside our moral compass that was clearly established on the holiness of a just God, on the immovable truth of His Word, and on the standard of righteousness. And, what have we replaced our moral compass with to pacify us as the nation's very soul became unrecognizable? sports, entertainment, fun, materialism, worldly degrees and etc. Any nation that allows its moral compass to be cast aside in the name of vain practices, worldly pursuits, and abusive rights will lose its way and find itself embroiled in one moral crisis after another.

The next question is, where is the church? The church loses its moral compass by compromising with the world, letting down the standard of righteousness, while watering down or adjusting the gospel to attract the world and not lost souls, ultimately erecting a "seeker friendly" environment where the world fits in nicely while the sheep flee because they cannot hear their Shepherd's voice.

Times have required many believers to gain sobriety as they fall on their knees, some in repentance, others in intercession, and some out of pure fear, acknowledging we are on the line as a nation. Whether the bullet misses us this time as a nation or not, we must avoid going back into a quasi-state of religion that is void of humility, gratitude, sacrifice, and selfless, consecrated devotion towards our Lord and Savior.

I don't know about you, but I have a sluggish body that holds onto everything. I learned that to keep it moving I must keep moving. This requires me to balance out physical activities in light of my busy, but not-so-active, life in front of the computer. As I move physically, my body gains more energy, I think less about such things as "food," and my attitude becomes lighter as I realize that I actually accomplished something for myself. When I ceased to look at exercise as a duty and considered it a small gift that I give myself, I am able to enjoy it more.

This is true for our spiritual life as well. Physical exercise profited the spiritual man little, but practicing godliness is how we as believers are to exercise the spiritual man. It is important to remember that giving in to the flesh causes us to become bored towards the matters of God, giving way to the world puts us in limbo towards our Christian walk, and giving in to the selfish life causes one to become indifferent towards the impressions of the Holy Spirit. Therefore, if I fail to follow after what is righteous, I can become sluggish and begin to cling to the things of the flesh, hold onto the things of the world, and slide into a lethargic state of indifference towards spiritual matters.

This is why I must stir myself up in regard to my spiritual life. The more I stand on the truth of the Word, the more I exercise my faith to go greater distances when the terrain becomes difficult, and when I continue to stand in my armor, I gain a greater knowledge of what it means to put on the life of Christ daily to ensure victory. We may be slack or unable to exercise our physical body, but there will never be a good reason to neglect our spiritual life.

Do you have the mind or attitude of Christ? *Philippians 2:5* tells me to have the mind or attitude of Christ. With a transformed heavenly perspective, I can soar on the wind of the Holy Spirit like an eagle above the earthly entanglements of this world to gain insight about the battles that rage in the spiritual realm.

I can stand on the cleft of my Rock, Jesus and see afar off to gain the wisdom I need to walk through this world by faith. I will be able to see the terrain below in order to identify tho ways of righteousness. I can learn to wait on the Lord above the influences of the age as He does a deeper work of sanctification in me to ensure greater perspective. And, finally from such heights I can enjoy the beauty of my redemption.

As Christians we must discipline our focus by looking up, knowing where our redemption is coming from, focusing our eyes on Jesus and becoming steadfast in our heart to follow Him, knowing He is the only One who will lead us away from the world, towards the paths of righteousness, and up to the clefts of excellency where we can gain glimpses into promises that are yet to come.

As *1 Corinthians 2:9* reminds us, *"But as it is written, Eye hath not see, nor ear heard, neither have entered into the heart of man, the things which God hath prepared for them that love him."*

DEVELOPING THE MIND

Heavenly wisdom may be ancient, or even
present before the beginning of time,
but it will never become obsolete,
useless, or outdated.
(Rayola Kelley)

Consider the things you remember. We remember those things that emotionally impact us the most, the things we flag as being important, or those things we think on the most. I have learned the only way I can discipline my imagination is by directing my affections heavenward, and the way I properly channel my emotions is by seeking what is Scripturally real and true; and the way I bring my memories into perspective is remember I have a select memory that is not trustworthy.

I have discovered that the Apostle Paul tells us in *Philippians 4:8* what to think on that ensures the right perspective in relationship to imagination, emotions, and memories, *"Finally, brethren, whatsoever things are true, whatsoever things ae just, whatsoever things are pure, whatsoever things are lovely, whatsoever things are of good report; if there be any virtue, and if there be any praise, think on these things."*

Many of us are familiar with this verse, but how many of us realize that the Apostle Paul is instructing us to think upon the Lord Jesus

Christ. He embodies all of these traits and when you put your mind on Christ, imagination is silenced, emotions are brought into balance and memories fade into the recesses of the mind.

Next time you are struggling with some aspect of your mind, remember—THINK ON JESUS.

In my last post I talked about what the Bible tells us to think on. The first thing we must think on is what is true. Jesus clearly said, "He was the truth." Many people may claim they want the truth, but many really only want to know what will fit into their idea of reality.

Reality for many Americans simply comes down to what will make them feel good about their present life, situation, or character. As a result, some consider truth too harsh and will look for a kinder presentation that will not challenge them. Some see truth as unbearable so they prefer to remain ignorant, while others shun truth because they prefer the fantasy they live in, and some rage against it because it never will adjust to their fickle, dark reality.

Truth is truth and there is no way one can approach the Lord without first of all preferring truth over any other reality. It is for this reason sin has been taken out of much preaching, hell is not mentioned for fear of insulting someone, and righteousness has been replaced with a gooey, worldly love that overlooks iniquity and tries to cover it up with wishful thinking that is nothing but Universalism, where everyone will be saved in the end.

However, the reality is not everyone wants to be saved because there are those who do not want anything to do with God. It takes one uncorrected degree for a plane to miss its destination and its takes one unchallenged lie to put us on the broad path of confusion, chaos, and destruction.

We must choose to love the truth because the essence and foundation of all truth is the Lord Jesus Christ.

Rayola Kelley

The next virtue we are to think on that follows what is true according to *Philippians 4:8* is that of honesty. I have met honest people but because they did not love the truth, they lacked integrity. If we do not start with truth, we will end up sliding into a lie no matter how honest we may be about life in general.

Truth ensures the integrity of something and without integrity an honest person will not always be an honorable person. There are people who take pride in being honest, but they do not have the integrity to do what is honorable. When you look up the word, "honest," in this text in the Strong's Concordance, it is associated with worship.

Clearly, our devotion, service, and actions must bring recognition and glory to the One who alone deserves worship. Obviously, the honorable actions of honesty point to righteousness being present in the person as to his or her right standing in the Lord, as well as standing before the Lord and doing right when it comes to others.

As Christians we must never settle for simply being honest about a matter, we must actually become honest people who are founded and standing on the truth of the Lord, believe His Word, and by faith honorably and humbly walk it out in obedience.

The next virtue we are to think on is the word "just." "Just" points to what is right, and all matters that are right will be executed according to justice. Justice is sound judgment that proves to be fair according to righteousness and pure in its motives to establish innocence or guilt.

Truth and honesty are the two pillars to ensure that justice is maintained and properly executed. When justice is missing in a society, oppression reigns while evil becomes good and that which is good is considered evil. Oppression in this type of environment produces hopelessness because it appears as righteousness does not matter, justice will not win out, the guilty will be given a pass, and the righteous sacrificed and silenced.

It is true justice is missing in many arenas of the world, but as Christians we must remember that in the end all will stand before the Judge of the Universe; therefore, it does not matter how unjust the world is around us; rather, what is important is that we strive for the excellent ways of justice as we weigh all matters between the pillars of truth and the respectable attitude and practices of honesty.

As we consider what we are to think on according to *Philippians 4:8*, we must realize that it will influence our attitude and the inward disposition of our soul. *Titus 1:15* confirms this, *"Unto the pure all things are pure, but unto them that are defiled and unbelieving is nothing pure; but even their mind and conscience is defiled."*

This brings me to the next virtue that we must think on: that which is pure. There can be no purity (innocence, chaste, clean, perfect) without truth, honesty, and justice. If people start from a lie, reality will be perverted, if they start from a dishonorable position their understanding will be that of darkness, and if they begin from the point of injustice everything will turn out wrong and prove to be destructive and condemning.

The Bible is clear that unless purity is present, everything will become warped including our "good" works. Consider what *Titus 1:16* says about those who are defiled, *"They profess that the know God; but in works they deny him, being abominable and disobedience, and unto every good work reprobate."*

We are told in *Matthew 5:8*, *"Blessed are the pure in heart; for they shall see God."* Our thought process must be brought to a pure state and that will only happen when we think on the only One who is pure through and through, Jesus Christ, *"Who did no sin, neither was guile found in his mouth"* (1 Peter 2:22).

The next virtue that must be present in our thinking according to *Philippians 4:8* is that which is lovely. The one word associated with "lovely" is "acceptable." We must think on that which is acceptable as far as the sentiments of heaven.

In order to think on that which is acceptable, we must come from a slate of purity, which requires us to direct our affections heavenward. Our thought process must not be defiled by that which takes on any type

129

of darkness or is driven into the extreme by lust. Sadly, we are being invaded by tremendous darkness coming from the demonic, immoral movies and books that are being presented, the evil agendas that are trying to normalize sin, and the wicked philosophies that are being propagated by a media that has become nothing more than a propaganda machine that borders on insanity.

It is hard to think on or imagine lovely matters when such darkness invades every aspect of life. Some people get to the point of wondering if there is anything that is really pure and lovely in this world. We can see aspects of such virtues in creation, but wherever man treads as to his imagination or where he puts his two cents worth in, he will often corrupt what is pure and lovely.

However, heaven has clearly presented to us that which is pure and lovely, the Lord Jesus Christ. If something in our thinking cannot show proper honor to the Lord and the life He has given to us and is calling us to, then we must consider it unacceptable to even give an audience to it.

The other aspect of heaven that is acceptable or lovely is doing God's will. Next time the ugliness of this world begins to encroach on your attitude and thinking, remember, thinking on the Lord Jesus Christ will bring all matters into the right perspective, ever adding a touch of loveliness to what is true, honest, just, and pure.

We are to think on that which is of a "good report." These two words have to do with something being reputable or well-spoken of. The Bible tells us to beware when the world speaks well of us, but the idea of "good report" in Scripture has to do with character and how one conducts the affairs of life more than reputation.

Clearly, Christians need to be Christ-like in every area of their life from speech to conduct and practices to ensure an honorable reputation. I can't tell you how many Christians I have known through the years who lost the respect of the community because of questionable business practices, moral inconsistencies, and their mode of speech. And, once a person loses respect, he or she ceases to be trustworthy and will lose credibility in every area of his or her life.

To have an honorable reputation means to be true to one's word, be honest in all transactions, being just to those we must deal with, pure in our conduct, and lovely in our attitude, even when it comes to not so lovely situations and people.

Once again, we are reminded that the Lord Jesus Christ had such a "good report," and God's Word reminds us that He is our example.

We are winding down on the different qualities that must influence and direct our thoughts in order to properly discipline our thought process. We know according to *2 Corinthians 10:3-5* that the strongholds that can plague us are located in our imagination, and it is for this reason we are instructed in *Hebrews 12:3, "For consider him that endured such contradiction of sinners against himself, lest ye be wearied and faint in your minds."*

It is only as we think on Jesus that we can bring every thought captive to the obedience of Christ. This brings us to the last part of *Philippians 4:8, "if there be any virtue, and if there be any praise, think on these things".*

Virtue is an interesting word because it points to something that will benefit you and lift your spirit up, causing a right attitude about something. How the matters of life affect us will be determined by the attitude in which we approach them.

It is hard to realize that our attitude harbors a prevailing mood that will clearly come out when things are not going right. This mood can be the epitome of selfishness which will prove to be unmanageable, undisciplined, unyielding, or unruly to those who have to contend with it. Such a mood can make us pigheaded (impenetrable), bullheaded (unreasonable), mule-headed (relentless-contrary), and hard headed (obtuse).

It is clear the things of life can cause us to react but we must always bring our thoughts under the Holy Spirit in order to channel our actions in a godly way, ensuring only that which is virtuous remains.

We have been considering what we are to think on according to *Philippians 4:8*. The test is whether our thoughts have any virtue to them that will ultimately produce praise. "Praise" in this Scripture points to something that is commendable and allows for such praise to be freely offered without hypocrisy.

When we consider what is commendable, we realize that we are to think on things that are worthy of respect, admirable because of being excellent, and splendid in estimation. There is only One who deserves such praise and that is the Almighty, a title ascribed to Jesus Christ in *Revelation 1:8*.

Hebrews 13:15-16 tells us that praise is the sacrifice of the lips and such a sacrifice not only acknowledges who God is but what He has done. Praise is what lifts the mind up towards God, causing the heart to come to a place of real worship and communion with the Lord.

The reason praise is associated with the mind is because we either make God small in our mind, stripping Him of His glory in our estimation of who He is, or our mind becomes enlarged and transformed by the reality of an All-Sufficient, eternal God as He is lifted above the present world as we consider the unseen, eternal dimension of Him being God Almighty.

The truth is, service and worship of God is based on our estimation of Him and like Eve did in the garden, the tendency of human nature is to humanize God to control our understanding of Him while somehow exalting man's intelligence and understanding to an even level with God so we can judge His Word and actions, pick and choose what we believe, and serve Him according to what serves us.

We need to beware that a mind that makes God small, is a mind that will eventually become reprobate, unable to retain any real knowledge of God (*Romans 1:28*).

Philippians 4:9 tells us, *"Those things, which ye have both learned, and received, and heard, and seen in me, do: and the God of peace shall be with you."* One of the things we must remember as Christians is that there is much we have to unlearn before we can learn a new way of doing something.

We have been conditioned by culture as to fleshly preferences and practices, indoctrinated by worldly influences to think a certain way, and corralled into boxes as to attitudes and conduct. It takes determination to unlearn the ways of the flesh and the world as a means to avoid trying to adjust or fit such matters into our spiritual life, thereby, defiling it.

We are told to come out and be separate from the world, to crucify the flesh, and have our minds transformed so we no longer are conformed to this world. The truth is I have been unlearning much that is associated with the "old man" in me through my Christian walk in order to relearn and properly process what is true and right. I have realized that there can't be any real conversion to the ways of righteousness until I let go of the old ways.

We are told in *Philippians 4:9* that those things we have received we must do to ensure that the God of peace will be with us. It is important to consider what the word "receive," means. It means "to get a hold of something."

We must beware of simply accepting spiritual truth on an intellectual level while failing to receive it as being so in our hearts. Truth is something that must be received by faith because it is not tangible like facts. We believe a matter is truth because the Bible tells us it is true.

Today much of Christianity has become weak because many settle for the intellectual agreement that something could be true, but they fail to institute it as truth in their own lives. Truth that fails to take hold in our hearts will never end in transforming the mind and producing everlasting life or liberty in the Spirit.

Philippians 4:9 tells us that those things which we have both learned, received, and heard, and seen we need to do and follow the example. Notice there is a process we must learn what is right in order to receive it as truth, but to learn, we must hear what is being taught.

The Bible is clear we must beware of how we hear a matter (*Luke 8:18*). We all have our own frame of reference that determines how we process information. We run information through what we understand and have experienced in our lives, but the problem is have we really learned the lesson that makes us wiser?

As far as our experience, it can't be applied to every situation because the variables can change. We must learn to hear what the Spirit is saying, while realizing that what we hear from the throne of God we will be responsible for in wisely applying it to our lives. God will not hold us responsible for what we don't understand and it is for this reason spiritual understanding eludes some.

God actually shows His mercy by hiding things from the eyes of those who think they are wise to spare them of greater judgment. Someone warned me, "Beware of what you ask for. If you ask for more wisdom, keep in mind that wisdom is knowledge put into practice and you will have to assimilate what you understand into your Christian life."

What I must ask myself is, "Am I practicing what I preach or am I expecting everyone to do what I say and not what I am doing in my hypocritical state?"

REMEMBRANCE

How much richer we would be if we
would refuse the books of the hour
and discover again the books of the ages
(Warren W. Wiersbe)

REMEMBER! This word may seem simple enough unless you are losing your memory. My father had Alzheimer's. As I watched him lose his ability to relate to the present and become lost in a confusing reality of what seemed like jumbled memories, I braced myself for that time when he would cease to remember me altogether, but he passed away before that happened.

As I thought about my father and the sharp mind he had before Alzheimer's, I began to realize how we take for granted our ability to remember. One of the commands in the Bible is to remember— remember who the Lord is, His Law, commandments, covenants, and promises.

There were various ways that the Lord established practices such as the Passover, to cause His people, Israel to remember their humble beginnings and His wondrous redemption. It was this example that showed me that I must choose to remember, and that I have a choice as to what I remember and how I remember it.

Sometimes the present can cause me to leave behind what I need to recall about my spiritual life and calling. At such times I have to step off the fast-moving train of the demands of this world and draw aside and remember who the Lord is in order to remind myself of my high calling, remember His commandments of love to discipline my walk in the ways of righteousness, remind myself of His covenant to be steadfast, and His promises to renew my hope. I have learned to do this so I can keep the present in perspective in light of the eternal. When it comes to remembering my walk in light of my Christian life, I asked the Lord to not let me forget who He is, who I am in Him, and the hope that is within me.

As I remember my father's life and the courage he displayed as he faced the terrible robber of memories and life head on, I have tried to erect a memorial each time to remind myself of the privilege and significance of remembering what is important and lasting, striving to keep the connection of my present life in Christ to the promised hope of the future.

What do you choose to remember? I have learned one thing about people, we have for the most part, select memories. Memories are those moments in our life that have left the greatest impact on our emotions. They are sometimes like moments frozen in time or short reels that play out the same way on the screen of our minds.

For me most of my memories are still pictures that come to the forefront because of something pricking my memory, reminding me of an event, a situation, or an incident. This brings me down to how some people handle memories.

Some live in the memories of the past and never advance forward in order to connect with the present. They bemoan what was based on sentiment or former glory producing a morbid reality. Some memories are locked away because of the darkness attached to them, but these memories often serve as skeletons in the closet that can haunt or taunt a person when they least expect it. Other memories become nightmares that torment the soul, and there are always a few that become points of accusation that causes a person to live in condemnation. For me, most memories prove to be entanglements to the past that sometimes cause me to look back in hopelessness because they could never be changed.

As Christians, we must keep in mind, our life in Christ is not behind us, our present life is in His hands and must be faithfully walked out in obedience, and our future has already been secured. This means our past can become a trap that can trip us up as to our present, but our present serves as our test and must be lived out according to future promises.

Memories can cause us to be like Lot's wife, looking back at what already is going up in smoke, while some hold to memories to give their life meaning, others use them as excuses for present failures, and some try to bury certain ones. I eventually learned that I can let memories define my present reality or I could define my present reality by using memories as stepping stones.

For instance, the Lord desires to heal those memories that broke my heart, He wants me to remember that memories of past repentant sins are under His blood to never be used against me, my regrets can become opportunities to learn valuable lessons, and my failures bridges to acquire wisdom. Memories are never meant to pull us back into the past, while defining our present life, but they can be used to develop character in us because of what we have learned from them.

Our past will always be and our present is what is, but the lessons of the past can become treasures that can shape our present walk and future in a positive way.

The other day I met a man who had lost his 26-year-old daughter. It was obvious that the sorrow was so great, he felt the need to do something, anything to try to make sense out of what seemed senseless to him. He decided to ride his motorcycle to the moon and back as a memorial to her. He even figured how far the moon is from the earth and according to his calculations he has traveled many miles but still has many more to travel.

He told us some of his adventures and how God has protected him, but as I listened to him, I wondered what he will feel once he accomplishes his feat. Keep in mind, this need to memorialize his daughter in some incredible feat is a driving force and reason for him to get up each day and face the unknown and challenge the odds with a type of recklessness that has cast all fears aside to continue down the road. However, at the end of the trail, her chair will be empty, his heart sad, his soul sorrowful, and the realization that it was his way of establishing a memorial for her after all.

We humans struggle with issues that seem so unfair, senseless, and too great to bear. We feel we must do something to avoid collapsing into a small puddle of despair because there is no way we can capture or memorialize something that seems confusing and vain, and any attempt to try to often proves extreme. The only hope I have when I come face to face with such inward struggle is that my Lord bear a cross for me, paid a debt I could not pay, and went to the grave on my behalf.

Today every time I take communion, I am reminded that the bread and the wine serve as a memorial of what Jesus did on my behalf and that a memorial is an earthly protocol, a point of personal remembrance. This memorial may remind me of my justification because of Jesus' death and helps me to take stock of my present walk in the path of righteousness, but it also reminds me that at the end of my course, resurrection will be my promise, eternal life my reality, heavenly inheritance my blessed lot, and bathing in the Lord's glory the joy of my salvation.

Rayola Kelley

I was thinking about the ability to remember something. Admittedly, I don't trust my memory. When I try to compare it to other people's memories about the same situation, they are all quite different. It does not mean that everyone is wrong about what they remember; rather, it just reveals that we remember things differently, based on the impact it makes on us.

It is true our imagination can at times stretch the truth of a matter into a great story or legend making it unbelievable or unrealistic, but when it digresses into a rumor, it becomes a complete lie. That is why I hold lightly to what I think I remember.

At my age I find myself digging deep in my various files of information to see if I can make some connection with people and incidents of my past to the present, and it is at such times I realize my analytical processes are unable to operate at "warp speed." In fact, I can remember small incidents of my past better than I can remember the present because there have been so many different experiences that have impacted my life between the days of innocence and youth, that the latter memories become a blur and any change causes some things to become unrecognizable.

It is also clear we do choose what we remember and how we remember, pointing to the fact that we have select memories. As I get older, I realize that "remembering" is a privilege and a priceless gift from God, but what are we to remember as believers?

As I realize how untrustworthy my memory is, I can only trust what is real, immovable, and unchangeable to ensure the integrity of what I remember. The only sure thing I can be sure of when I remember it—is the Word of God.

I was thinking of how the Lord commanded His people to "remember." They were to remember His Law, His Works, and His interventions in their life. If the law of love is written on the heart we will not forget and if His works have been intertwined with our testimony they will stand. If His interventions have caused us to be humbled, pliable vessels before Him, we will display and confirm that a matter is so.

The next time you look back to remember what the Lord has said, what He has promised, and what He has shown you for personal edification, be sure to thank Him for the memory.

TRUE CHRISTIANITY

*Labor hard, consume little,
give much—and all to Christ.
(Anthony Norris Groves)*

Do you possess the life of Jesus? It is dangerous to assume you are a believer because you are associated with some religious organization. It is presumptuous to hope you are a Christian because you have decency or sentimental notions towards religion, spirituality, and/or good works.

The word "Christian" is being loosely used today like a popular fad that anyone can become associated with by simply using the title of "Christian." True Christianity associates us with the Christ of the Bible and His life being in us. The ultimate evidence of this life is that we become Christ-like.

The Bible is clear we must be born again with the Spirit of the Living God to be a Christian. It is the Spirit who will impart the life of Christ in our inner man, as well as serve as a witness that we are saved (*John 3:3, 5*). Today there are those who are not sure of their salvation.

There are different reasons for this uncertainty: Satan lies to them because of their past making them feel unworthy of salvation, but none of us deserve to be saved, for we are saved by grace. The other reason is perhaps some simply have an intellectual understanding of salvation but have never been born again. Once again, I must stress what our Lord Jesus Christ emphasized, "You must be born again" to inherit the kingdom of God.

Do you have a new heart that leans towards and desires to please God? Do you have God's Spirit in you? If you do, you cannot continue to walk in any sin without the conviction of the Spirit. We must not assume or presume anything about our salvation; rather, we must know we are saved because we can know and we will know due to the witness in us (*1 John 5:6-13*).

139

What lies at the core of the Christian life? For some, Christianity seems complicated, outdated, and obsolete to confront the problems of the world. There are those who think Christianity is a matter of dos and don'ts. Others see it as a religious duty that they have to do on Sunday, and some simply add it on to their many worldly activities to soothe their religious conscience.

I have learned that what lies at the core of Christian living are simple decisions. Joel said as much in *Joel 3:14, "Multitudes, multitudes in the valley of decision: for the day of the LORD is near in the valley of decision."* Christianity is a life that must be walked out daily in the arena of the world. There are only two choices when it comes to living life: the right choice or the wrong choice. For Adam he chose the tree of knowledge of good and evil over the tree of life. In Lot's case he chose the valley of Sodom and Gomorrah over Abraham and the Promised Land. The two thieves next to Jesus had two choices--one chose to accuse and mock Jesus while the other chose to ask to be with Him in Paradise. In *Matthew 7:13-14*, we have the choices between the narrow path to life and the broad road to destruction.

We may not realize how many times we make a choice, but we need to remember that we are making decisions as to how we are walking out our lives in this world. We also need to note if we are taking the high road of excellence and godliness or if we are taking the low road of the flesh and the world. There can be a personal cost to take the high road, but taking the low road will leave your soul empty and dissatisfied as you head for destruction.

Psalm 119:105 gives us priceless insight in how faith enables us to walk out the Christian life, *"Thy word is a lamp unto my feet, and a light unto my path."* We talk about the importance of the Word of God, but how many of us value it in such a way that it transforms our life?

True faith comes by hearing and hearing the Word of God. How many of us expose ourselves to God's Word and assimilate it in our lives? We know it is food for the soul, inspiration to the spirit, and a sword to the enemy. It is water that cleanses, a hammer that knocks off the old life, and a fire that purges.

The Word of God is living, but how much of it is living in us, transforming our thinking, shaping our lives, and establishing our conduct? It is clear that the Word is our map but it only shows us the steps of obedience we are to take up front. Granted, it reveals great mysteries, encourages us with everlasting promises, and confirms the expectation of our hope, but we must believe it, walk in it, and obey it for it to have its way in our lives.

We need to get God's Word deep into our soul in order to give the Holy Spirit something to work with. We need to tremble before it, walk carefully in it, and urgently and soberly apply it to our lives. This is a very important lesson in light of *Amos 8:11, 12, "Behold, the days come saith the Lord GOD, that I will send a famine in the land, not a famine of bread, nor a thirst for water, but of hearing the words of the LORD: And they shall wander from sea to sea, and from the north even to the east, they shall run to and for to seek the word of the LORD, and shall not find it."*

I personally believe the famine is here and as believers we must seek to establish the pure Word of God as our foundation in order to give the Holy Spirit something to bring forth when we need it in order to stand.

What is Christianity to you? Is it an idea, a particular doctrine, a pious image, or a certain lifestyle? If Christianity is an idea, then I can outwardly conform to it and believe all is well. If it is a mere doctrine, I can somewhat reform my outward actions to appear as if I'm living it in order to feel good about my religion, while if it's an image I can perform according to the image and convince myself that I am what I am portraying, and if it is a lifestyle I can adopt the talk, adjust some of the walk and come out looking the part in order to fit.

However, note these are all outward adjustments to man's religious rulers, but when the Bible talks about Christianity, it uses words or concepts like translation, transformation, new creation, regeneration, and the renewal of the inner man. Christianity is not an idea, a mere doctrine, a religious image, or a lifestyle. Christianity is the "life of Christ in us." We are not trying to conform to some idea; rather, the Holy Spirit is trying to conform our inner man with the life of Christ to outwardly reflect Him.

There is a pure doctrine of Christ, but it is to enable us to understand it is not about reforming our outward actions, but doing the will of God to ensure righteous conduct. It is not an outward image of man's best; rather, it is the life of Christ being worked in our life so that we can take on His attitude and fulfill our highest potential in reflecting His image to the world.

Finally, Christianity is not some lifestyle that I adjust to, tack on in certain places or certain times; rather, it is the very life of Christ I live out, as I walk in who He is and what He has done for me. As we can see, Christianity is not a hat I change according to responsibilities, a label I attached to myself when it serves my purpose, or a point of representation that brings authority to empty, hypocritical claims. Paul talked about living, not his life out, but living the life of Christ out by faith.

Next time you hear the term, "Christianity," discern if there is any trace of the real life of Jesus present to verify such a claim

What does it mean to live the Christian life? You have to start with a very important fact and that is Christianity is a LIFE not simply a belief, theology, some religious affiliation, or a lifestyle. When we talk about what constitutes life, we need to concur there must be breath in order to interact with our environment, personality in which we express ourselves, experiences that causes us to identify with the world around us, and the need for relationships to ensure that the life that flows through us finds an avenue in which it continues to reproduce itself.

This brings us to the Christian life. To have this life, we must be born again with the very breath of God, His Spirit, so that we can actually interact with Him.

While growing up, the culture around us will determine how our personality will be defined and expressed, but we must recognize that Christianity is not another culture. Sadly, some of the visible church has made Christianity a subcultural practice within the various cultures of world. This subculture has taken on many worldly attitudes, which have caused the church to lose its effectiveness as it fails to remain distinct from the world.

The Apostle Paul was clear in *Galatians 2:20* that we, as believers, are to live the life of Christ in us, not our personal lives according to the desires of the flesh and the ways of the world. If we live the life of Christ, we will be reflecting His meek attitude and His ways of righteousness making us distinct in this world.

To have a growing testimony of the life of Christ, we must experience God's presence and glory in communion, service, and worship in a personal, intimate relationship with Him. When our relationship is right with the Lord, His life in us will reproduce itself in our relationship with those around us, our interaction with those we come in contact with and in our effectiveness when it comes to the work of His kingdom.

The question I have to ask myself is, "Am I living the life of Christ, or am I living my own life according to a religious culture that gives an appearance of righteousness but lacks the life and power of the breath of God—His Holy Spirit?"

When my Christian brothers and sisters asked me how I am doing, I always tell them I am running the race. Each day I get up and try to run the 100-yard dash to accomplish daily tasks while preparing for the ongoing marathon that requires me to run with the baton of the Gospel: MY COMMISSION AND MY CALLING until I can pass it off to another just before finishing the course.

The one thing I have noticed about saints like King David, they miserably failed before they crossed the finished line. Praise the Lord, King David wisely repented and did cross the line, but I have also been reading about some respected religious people of our time that looked like they were running the good race and at death would no doubt victoriously cross the line, but based on some of the information I have been reading, I fear some were not even close to the line of God's glory.

The Apostle Paul made it clear that we are running a race and we must set aside any type of sin that would beset our progress. We are not going to cross the line if we are still dragging the baggage of our past life, the graveclothes of religious attempts to win God's approval, abiding sins clinging to us, or pulling our worldly riches behind us. We must cast all such things aside if we are going to follow Jesus into glory.

The other aspect of running the race is that we can't be mere spectators; rather, we must be participants. There are too many in the grandstands watching to see who runs this race, waiting to see who wins, and speculating about who is properly running it. It is true that there are few runners on the field in worldly competitions where the best are competing, but when it comes to Christianity, we are all called to run the race.

Are you running the race or are you in the grandstands or sitting on the side line of despair because the course has become difficult? The reason I continue to run the race is because I know the end is in sight and the crown awaiting me is WORTH every point of struggle, failure, and challenge I have encountered along the way.

The problem with me is that I want to hold onto to bits of the self-life that have brought me comfort, but in the end, such attempts not only prove empty but have kept me from discovering that which is far better.

When we first moved into our present house, it required a lot of work because it had sat empty for a couple of years. There had been earlier attempts to landscape it, but it all fell into disarray because of the barren years. The grass was almost gone, the yard taken over by weeds and even though there had been work on it in the past, there was very little that could be salvaged. It was clear that we needed to possess the land but it would require hard work, which included taking the old grass up in the backyard in order to lay down new sod.

We managed to cut the old sod into various pieces so we could make way for the new sod. Our little dog, Bell, who we lost last February, begin to realize the limited amount of grass she had was being taken up, leaving her with nothing but dirt and rocks. Her solution was to claim the last piece of grass and so she laid on it so that she could save it for herself. Needless to say, her attempt was cute and understandable but not successful.

As believers we must beware of the small pieces of self-life that we are laying claim to because it represents some memory, personal comfort, and right. Bell soon discovered that by letting go of that small patch of grass, she received a whole new green lawn that gave her greater delight and freedom to run around in.

It is so easy in our Christian walk to limit our experiences of discovering greater pastures of God's blessings because we will not allow for the old to be rooted and taken out so that which is greater and productive can be established in our life by the Holy Spirit. The next time you think you can't possibly live or be happy without your small piece of the self-life, remember there is a whole new aspect of life that can't be discovered until you let go of that one small portion of it.

The other day, Jeannette and I were discussing Scriptures that seem to get very little attention. Granted, we like the promises—those scriptures that leave us feeling good, and concepts that allow us to nestle down into some spiritual chair that makes all seem right in our worlds, but there are other scriptures that reveal that there is no simply sliding by when it comes to our Christian Walk.

I like to visit these Scriptures because they remind me of simple principles that can be easily forgotten. One such scripture is found in *1 Thessalonians 5:22, "Abstain from all appearance of evil."* This instruction seems simple enough, but people's tendency is to test practices and conduct according to what has become acceptable and normal to society, such as fornication, where couples choose to simply live together without legally marrying. Granted, in the mind and heart of this couple they may be married to justify their actions, but when it comes to how others regard it, it fails the test of being a legitimate Christian witness.

One of the most important assets to our Christian life is our testimony. I know I have mentioned this many times that we are not here for ourselves to live life according to our terms; rather, we are here to be a living witness for Christ. Another word for "living witness," is "martyr."

145

Rayola Kelley

To be a living witness for Christ points to some type of martyrdom of what we sometimes consider to be normal, necessary, insignificant, and no one else's business. An effective testimony can reach any soul who is lost, wounded, hopeless, and feels doomed. For the lost, we can share how Jesus saved us, giving hope to their seeking heart as His light begins to part the darkness of their soul to warm their hearts. For the wounded we can relate how the Lord healed our wounded soul to bring restoration, to the hopeless how through Jesus, God provided the necessary consolation through His long-suffering, faithfulness, and great pity to resolve the impossible, and for the doomed how through Christ's redemption, there is forgiveness and reconciliation.

However, to ensure the integrity, the authority, and the credibility of our testimony, we must live what the Word of God established to be true and right. This is why we are told to abstain from ALL APPEARANCE of evil. For example, perhaps what a Christian is doing would not be considered evil to God, but if it becomes a stumbling block to others in their walk or wounds their soul, it is WRONG. It is for this reason we are to abstain even from that which would give an APPEARANCE of evil.

This may seem unfair to us, but if a disputed practice is that important to you or if we are willing to put another soul at risk, bring a reproach to Christ, and cause us to be considered nothing more than hypocrites that have "forked tongues," divided hearts, and an unsubmitted point of independence that needs to be exposed, addressed, and Scripturally dealt with, then we will find ourselves on the opposite side of God.

How many hats do you wear? I am not talking about responsibilities; rather I am talking about what motivates and determines your interaction with others. For example, there are Christians who wear a worldly hat when doing business. They adhere to the practices of the world and convince themselves that it is not personal when they fail to do something right in regards to another. After all, it is just business.

There are those who wear fleshly hats. In other words, they make decisions based on what will make them feel good. These people can do decent things but it is for their glory and not God's. There are also

146

emotional Christians who are looking for the emotional highs and the experiences that will cause them to fall short of their calling, while ultimately giving them a false security about where they are spiritually before the Lord. There are complacent Christians that simply get by in their religious activities to soothe any religious notions and there are religious Christians that operate strictly according to religious codes that lack life, love, and compassion.

The reality is that Christianity is not some hat one wears when it is Sunday and around certain people, Christianity is a life we are to continually walk out according to the complete counsel of God's Word. It is not a label that we proudly display; rather, believers are to be a living walking epistles and witnesses that display the heavenly life in attitude and action.

The purpose of living the life of Christ is so we become light in this dark world. As believers we are simply the reflectors that through our life, attitude, and actions, we reflect the light of Christ's life, which is in us, to others. When people see us, they must not see our best for they are filthy rags, and they must not walk away with an impression of our goodness for if it does not come from true godliness, it is nothing more than an empty façade. Finally, they must not walk away with a sense of our idea of Christianity but with the sense and reality of Jesus Christ.

Do not be mistaken, what makes our Christianity real, legitimate, and noteworthy to others, is that our present life lifts up Jesus in every interaction with others in all arenas, pointing to the solution to man's plight, and bringing glory to God.

Is Jesus' life an extension of your life or are you an extension of His life? Take time to think about this question. Yesterday I talked about hats. It is natural to change hats when it comes to responsibilities. As our responsibilities change, we adjust by putting on the right hat to calculate, figure out and ultimately meet the challenges and fulfill our obligations. The problem with changing hats is that much of what we do can become mechanical.

Rayola Kelley

As I stated yesterday, we often change hats when it comes to our Christian walk. We separate our Christian calling from other aspects of our life. For example, in business Jesus is put on the sidelines when conducting such affairs until He is needed to bless or multiply what is being done. In worldly interaction, He can become an addition when necessary or a point of credibility, in religion an excuse or a point of justification for inadequate or wrong attitudes and actions, and in personal pursuits He is someone who is conveniently fitted into desired or controlled activities. This is when Christians pick and choose what they believe concerning Christ and their vocation as a Christian. Needless to say, at such times Jesus becomes a mere extension of a person's life until He is tacked on in a time of need and crisis.

However, Jesus is the Vine, and as believers we must become an extension of His life. My heart is to be a natural extension of Christ. I want to be a branch that produces excellent fruit that points to Him, be a humble vessel that is effectively used by Him, and an instrument that He uses to bring deserved glory to Him. When people look at me, I pray they see Jesus. When they hear me, I want them to hear the voice of God's Spirit and Word, and when I touch them, I want them to experience His loving caring hands.

It is hard as believers to remember that we are not here to live our lives; rather, we are here to live the life of Christ, a life that becomes a sweet savor to God, a point of edification to other believers, a light in the darkness of the world to lost, seeking souls.

It is easy to hide behind doctrinal terms, dress ourselves up with pious platitudes, stand stiff-necked while teetering on a religious pinnacle of self-righteousness, and tout spiritual elitism over others because we believe a certain way to put forth a Christian impression. However, the real test for every believer will come down to the type of relationship they have with the Lord.

Salvation is about reconciliation with God through Jesus Christ and if there is no real evidence that such a relationship exists, then one must examine whether they have truly been born again. There are four groups of people when it comes down to a relationship with God.

There are those who have NO relationship with God. They have no problems touting their unbelief towards God, their mockery towards those who do believe, and their rage towards those who dare live it. There are those who claim they believe in the "Man upstairs." They have an emotional attachment to a CONCEPT of God that is very self-serving and one-dimensional. It is a concept that is neither challenging or realistic but it becomes a type of consolation to their religious conscience, and since they are "decent" enough or "not so bad," they operate according to "wishful thinking" that God will surely accept them.

The third group are those who are ASSOCIATED to religion in some way and see that their "particular association," "goodness" and "good works" as proof of their religious piousness and worth to God. They possess certain notions about God that seem right enough, but they at best have a limited understanding of the character and ways of God. Their idea of relationship with God is one-sided and is based on a merit system that will hopefully find their "goodness" balancing out the scales in the end so God will welcome them into heaven.

The final group are those who have an active, growing RELATIONSHIP with God. This relationship is evident because there is joy and peace in this person's life. Every aspect of their life points to this individual pursuing, desiring, and establishing an inner life of service, worship, and communion with God. They understand that the more they expose themselves to God in a relationship the more their life will become an expression of the spiritual, heavenly man that is being developed. The result is that they ultimately bring glory to God in their conduct and example, glorify the Lord in their works, and reflect the glory of the Lord Jesus Christ in their lives.

Is there any place in the Christian walk where complicity is condoned, encouraged, or allowed? To answer the question, all we need to consider are the other words that are associated with complicity. They are "lukewarmness," "complacency," and "indifference."

We need to be honest about this type of state because we live in a society where complicity is not only the norm but acceptable. When

149

complicity is accepted, what is real is adjusted and controlled to promote a lie. Integrity will be sacrificed in order for perversion to justify dishonorable actions. Such an environment strips and rejects true justice, allowing the unjust to avoid consequences and injustice to become oppressive to the law abiding. It is the covering that politicians hide behind as they swing according to bribes and self-serving agendas.

Complicity begins in the shadowy gray areas, but eventually will end in complete darkness. There are no grays or darkness in true Christianity. In fact, Christianity brings a contrast in any gray area by dissipating it and penetrates darkness with the light of truth. Believers are not to operate in any shades of gray; rather they are called to be distinct in this world in attitude, action, and conduct.

Christians are children of light and darkness has no part in their walk. For example, truth is absolute and unmoving, faith has one single focus towards pleasing the one true God and one goal to glorify Him, righteousness is expressed in doing right no matter what, godliness will show itself in honorable conduct, and hope will walk in expectation of possessing the eternal. If you are a complicit Christian, fearful of the times, faint of heart, complaining about the environment, vexed over the delusion, and shocked at the extent of wickedness, keep in mind that the gray of complicity allowed the darkness to take root and now we are seeing the full fruit of it.

It is time to repent of leaving your first love, Jesus, throw off the decaying gray garment of lukewarmness, humble yourself and in the sackcloth of mourning, ask the Lord to put the fire to the altar of your heart as you offer up your life as a living sacrifice for His glory and consecrate all you have toward doing His work and bidding.

As a zealous babe in Christ, I was very excited to begin my new spiritual adventure, but I ran into what I refer to as man's personal religious interpretations of what it means to be a Christian. You had to believe a certain way to belong, dress accordingly for others' sake so they will accept you as being legitimate, adhere to certain practices to fit in, and talk a certain way to be identified to the group.

I realized I had to have the right creed to ensure a sturdy foundation, but when it came to dressing a certain way, I felt it was a bit petty because God looks at the heart. I understood religion has its ordinances, but it was hard to say what really belonged to man and what was established by the Lord, and when it came to speaking "Christianese," that was simple enough to adopt, but I eventually found myself taking religious detours away from the simplicity of Christ.

It took a while, but I began to realize that the Christianity in America had become a subculture within cultures that promoted a certain lifestyle, instead of a life that needed to be walked out on a daily basis. I admit, initially I became lost in the formalities, methods, and surface religious presentations of others. In such a state I found that I had lost the joy of my salvation. It is at this point that I ceased from walking in the darkness of despair and turned around to see where I got off the narrow path.

God used those initial detours and confusion to bring me to a place of understanding that my Christian life was exactly that—it is mine to own and discover for myself. This life can only grow and develop as Christ is unveiled to you. I understood that I could not entrust my Christian walk to mere man's interpretation, and that the Lord had given me the Holy Spirit and His Word to discern and walk in the way He has prepared for me.

It is a walk of faith directed towards who God is and what His Word says that will cause me to walk in the ways of righteousness to discover the Lord in greater ways. After all, you can't discover the Lord outside of His holiness. If you stand confused, a bit skeptical, and overwhelmed by the endless debates in Christendom, cease from looking around, turn around and look up to the One who stands at the center of every aspect of the Christian life, and ask the Lord to clear away the confusion with His light of truth and reveal Himself to you.

It is clear that man can never walk in the middle of the road without meeting some kind of collision or on the fence without eventually falling off of it. In spiritual matters of life and death, heaven and hell, there is no middle ground. Granted, there are shades of confusing grays but they simply hide the darkness of compromise that is taking place.

When it comes to life and death, heaven and hell, it simply comes down to choices. As I stated in the past, inaction is action and indecision is a decision. It may not be blatant as to what the decision is and how the action will translate, but the fruit it will produce in the end will be of poor quality and will not be desired by anyone, such as in the case of the lukewarm Laodicean church in *Revelation 3*.

We see that as Cain went his way and built his city that man was digressing spiritually. Out of the environment came the likes of Lamech who was arrogant and welcomed killing. The problem with gray areas is that they leave a spiritual vacuum that must be filled in some way because it leaves people spiritually lean and frustrated. This brings me to the last verse in *Genesis 4:26, "And to Seth, to him also there was born a son; and he called his name Enos: then began men to call upon the name of the LORD."*

If you find yourself spiritually lean in these trying times, praise the Lord for it because He is being faithful to show you where you are, and then call upon His name in complete confidence that He will meet you in sweet communion and revive you with His Spirit.

Keep in mind that two of the examples Jesus left us were servitude and sacrifice. When we consider the two-sided coin of godly love, on one side would be the picture of the living sacrifice where a life of godly submission is being refined in the fire on the altar of consecration, setting forth the beautiful fragrance of the heavenly life being established through submission to the true work of God (*2 Corinthians 2:15-16*).

The other side of the coin is the cross of Christ where the ultimate sacrifice of the present life is being offered up in place of others, for the sake of what is right to ensure the glory of God. One sacrifice represented the perpetual living sacrifice that was for God's pleasure, the other one the sin offering where the old is dealt with in order to ensure the new is being established in righteousness.

This two-sided coin of love is what sets God's love apart. Many people perceive submission to be subordination. However, subordination has to do with being subordinate to someone's will, but godly submission has to do with giving way to what is right and honorable out of love. When it comes to honor, those who are often in a place of authority perceive they must be honored, their will must be carried out, and their whims satisfied, but godly love is about giving up the present life in preference of ensuring the quality of life for others in true service.

God's love is selfless and not selfish, benevolent and not tyrannical, leads by example and not with demands, is pure in motive, gentle in response to that which is vulnerable, and is ever ready to present the necessary sacrifice in preference of others in order to bring great pleasure to God's heart and glory to His wonderous works.

Jesus is clear that others would know we are His disciples because we have such love for one another.

I once had to asked myself why I wanted to be perfect and the answer was very telling, "I wanted to be perfect to cover up my imperfection." Imperfection speaks of missing the mark of our high calling and potential. It reminds us that we are not always right no matter how hard we try to be right, and that we are prone to make mistakes and missteps that may embarrass us.

There are times we even have to face the necessity of being broken at the place of our strength (pride) in true repentance in order to know reconciliation with God and restoration of our struggling spirit and tumultuous soul. As I said before, being human is a hard challenge because there are other words that begin with "h" that are attached to it when it comes to the Christian walk. The truth is that in our humanness, we must experience humiliation to come to a place of humility in order to be established in a state of holiness.

As Christians, our humanness is to remind us of our small beginnings that started with the cross of Christ, recognizing we were cringing beggars, spiritually bankrupted and in need of salvation. It was

RayolaKelley

at the cross that we met the perfect Jesus who was offered upon it for our imperfection of sin so we could be made in the righteousness of God. My humanness must give me a reality check that allows me to know that perfection is being worked in me, not by personal attempts, but by the Spirit of God as I submit to Him.

As the life of Jesus is being worked in me, my humanness is being overshadowed by the reflection of His life. The more my humanness is lost in the wondrous reality of Jesus, the greater His glory will be reflected from the mirror of my soul. Today is a day that instead of looking back at past failures in order to avoid traps, missed opportunities of yesterday, the worries of today, and the bleak possibilities in the future, we can come into rest, knowing He is the One who is doing the work in us, and is able to preserve our soul until He comes for us.

To me much of life is a juggling act. Through the years I have felt that the world is nothing more than a big circus where there are different acts going on all the time. As we know the world provides various entertainments but in reality, we must not forget that since the god of this world is Satan, it is also a big lion's den.

We are told in *Ephesians 4:1* that Christianity is a vocation, a calling, and through the years it has become obvious to me that to strive to maintain the integrity of my testimony I will become a spectacle to some. As I consider the Christian walk, I do not see myself part of the entertaining acts of the world; rather, I see myself on a tightrope that is over the lion's arena, trying to balance out my walk with godly love and all the Christian virtues as I carefully attain to gain the real prize of my high calling in Jesus Christ. There are some people who are hoping I fall among the lions because they want to see the destruction of my faith, but there are those who are also hoping I make it across so they can cheer me on to reach my ultimate potential and destination.

As Christians in this world, we are spectacles to those who think we are foolish to walk such a tightrope, to some we are living, walking epistles that speak of a love too great to describe, a faith that can't be understood by the world, and a hope that sees beyond the physical into the heavenly, while to heaven our lives are a sweet fragrance. We must avoid getting bogged down by vain activities, silly acts, and endless games of the world and strive to maintain our walk, knowing that below us is the net of the Spirit if we fall, the Word of God to push any lion back, the hand of God that will put our feet back on the narrow way once again, and the heavenly promises waiting before us to enfold us forever into the glory of the unseen and the eternal.

What does it mean to be a Christian? It seemed in my initial journey as a new believer that it was natural for others to define what it means to be a Christian. You have to believe a certain way, act according to some code or standard, and talk the talk by saying all the right things when asked certain questions or given opportunities.

As a new Christian it was simple enough to comply outwardly according to others' standards, but there was no inward transformation, which brought me to spiritual bankruptcy. The Bible refers to it as your faith becoming shipwrecked. Christianity is not some code you adjust to, not some religious affiliation that you become part of, and it is not some form of outward piousness. To reach our ultimate potential, we have to walk the walk of a Christian, not be a mere representative of Christ, but a reflection of Him.

Such a process entails the way of the cross which points to us becoming identified with Jesus in His death and burial in order to be raised up in the likeness of His life. Inward transformation is not outward compliance, performance, reforming, or conforming in order to express our best. Transformation is the inward working of the Holy Spirit that will be manifested in believers when they begin expressing God's best: the image of His Son, to a dark, skeptical, unbelieving world.

I made reference to transformation yesterday. As believers, we have been delivered from the power of darkness, and translated into the kingdom of God's dear Son. We all know about the process of a butterfly. It begins as a caterpillar. There are no similarities initially—that is between the caterpillar and the final product, the butterfly.

155

The caterpillar wraps itself up in a cocoon (grave) in submission to reach its ultimate potential, to come forth as a beautiful butterfly who will add its distinction of beauty to God's creation. We are told to not be conformed to this world but to be transformed by the renewing of the mind.

The key is that this transformation takes place away from prying eyes. Like the caterpillar, the miracle of transformation for the believer is done in obscure places. When we are first born again, the miracle of life takes place because the very life of Christ is implanted in us, but transformation can only take place when we become identified with Christ in His death and burial.

It is as we choose death to the old life that we become identified with Him in the grave where the old is left behind. It is at this point the real transformation can take place because it is from the grave that man can be raised in the newness of Christ's life, now capable of reflecting the beauty of the glory attached to His heavenly life.

I may have mentioned this in the past but there are two ways in which God delivers His people: from something or through something. To "deliver" someone means to save that individual from something. God does not merely deliver His people FROM something so they can go back to that which brings bondage and death, but He also delivers them TO something.

God saved Noah from the old world under judgment to a new world that had been purged by water. *Colossians 1:13* tells us, *"Who hath delivered us from the power of darkness and hath translated us into the kingdom of his dear son."* In Christ we have been delivered from death, but it is through Christ we are being brought forth as new creations.

To the Christian, Christ is his or her ark, for their life is hidden in Him and they are being delivered through this present age to be brought forth in the kingdom of God (*Colossians 3:3*). One of the Scriptures I love is found in *Genesis 7:17, "And the flood was forty days upon the earth; and the waters increased, and bare up the ark, and it was lifted up above the earth."*

Jesus put it best in *John 12:32, "And I, if I be lifted up from the earth, will draw all men unto me."* For Christians who have become identified with Jesus in His death, burial and resurrection, their lives are hid in Christ, and this identification also means they have been lifted up above this world into heavenly places so they will be spared from His wrath that is coming upon all children of disobedience.

In these dark, precarious times, we need to remember we may be here physically but spiritually we are observers who are simply passing through.

One of the many important lessons that we must learn from our journey through this world is that we must develop our own personal relationship with the Lord. We humans can complicate the simplicity of having a relationship with the Creator of the universe. We are told that unless we display the simplicity of a child to believe what he or she is told and have the child-like sincerity in approaching the Lord with awe and curiosity to learn the hidden secrets, we will miss discovering the essence of real life.

The one great secret of life is that it is a miracle, whether it be the presence of the physical or spiritual life, it is a miracle. We take our life for granted but if we don't realize that the life we know was given by God and that the life we can know entails a spiritual discovery we will miss the miracle of it.

Another secret about life, is that to discover what life can be we must step outside of what we know life to be. We see this in the case of Jacob. In order to find life, he had to leave his old life behind. It was on his journey to find a new life in *Genesis 28*, that he encountered the Lord.

Christianity is a search for life, but the difference between the world and Christianity is that the world offers a lifestyle, but it cannot offer real, lasting life. Christians know that the essence of life can only be found in the Lord, and if they do not discover that one great truth, they will fail to obtain the key that will turn the lock that will open the door to the life that the Lord has designed for them.

The question is simple, have you discovered and taken possession of that key?

Moses was delivered from a death sentence and raised in the courts of Pharaoh. It appeared that he had the beck and call of the world at his fingertips, but Moses knew who he was. He was a Hebrew.

Hebrew means to "cross over" as in a sense of Abraham crossing over the Euphrates River to sojourn in the Promised Land. It is also derived from the name "Eber," an ancestor of Abraham which means "beyond, on the other side." As we consider these meanings, we can begin to see how much of the believer's walk is about crossing over to the other side.

For us as believers, we must cross over from death to life, from darkness to light, from despair to hope, and from hopelessness to promise. The reason we must cross over is to become identified to what constitutes life in order to embrace our inheritance and God's promises.

Moses grew up in the courts of the world, but realized that he had a destiny that was beyond this world, a call that came from above, and a life that would require him to cross over from Egypt to be prepared in the wilderness in order to lead the children of Israel to the Promised Land.

It is important to point out, one can't lead people where he or she has never been.

THE CHRISTIAN WALK

Funny how so many church-goers sing,
"Standing on the Promises," when all they
do is sit on the premises.
(Jeannette Haley)

As I think about my Christian walk from the beginning until now, I sometimes follow what I refer to as the glorious design of God that has been laid out in the Bible. It began with the sweet conviction of sin by the Holy Spirit in my soul that actually started me on this incredible spiritual odyssey in the first place. Granted, such conviction may not be sweet at first, but it is designed to cause those with a searching heart and lean spirit to cease from looking into the darkness of utter hopelessness and turn in repentance to face the light of heaven.

I remember when I finally turned around out of desperation over my tormenting plight to face the wretchedness of my state that I found myself looking into the face of God's incredible love, a love that took all fear of judgment away so that I could look upon a brutal instrument, the cross. It became obvious that it was on the cross that God addressed my sin through the sacrifice of His Son. Since God's love made the fear of judgment flee, I could seek mercy, believing that my sin could be forgiven because it was laid upon the sacrifice of the precious Son of God.

Once I confessed my sin, God's mercy opened the way of His grace to bestow upon me what I clearly did not deserve, eternal life. As I realized I was spared from the great judgment I deserved by His mercy, and given something I did not deserve because of His grace, I knew I had the freedom to walk in and walk out this unseen life by faith.

Faith has led me to discover promises, experience blessings, and realize the hope in me, the life of Jesus, often putting such great expectation in my steps about the glorious future that awaits me. And, the closer I get to that future glory, the more settled my spirit has become and the more I become steadfast in my soul as to the course that I am to walk in order to finish the race set before me.

Who is defining you? I have ministered to many Christians through the years. I have identified two major trouble areas for many: 1) Their concept about God is incorrect because they have not been properly discipled, and 2) they do not know who they are in Christ.

In the Bible Studies I conduct, I often challenge the people to consider what it means for Christ to be **in** them, and what it means for them to be **in** Christ. I encourage them to read the epistles of the Apostle Paul and mark the small word "in,"

Rayola Kelley

This small so-called "unassuming" word that many overlook is a powerful word because it is all inclusive. There is nothing you can add to the fact that Christ is in you because He is all in all, and there is nothing that can be taken from your life in Him because you are being firmly established on who He is, placed in high places with Him to align your perspective, and hidden and identified in His death, burial and resurrection to ensure the great exchange of the old life with the new life (*1 Corinthians 3:11; Ephesians 2:6; Colossians 3:2; Romans 6*).

For many Christians, the people of the past are defining them, for others it is the high standards of family and religion, and there are those struggling with trying to bring the matters of their culture and Christianity together so they can function in both worlds. However, the only one who can define you according to your calling and potential is the Lord Jesus Christ.

The one thing I must constantly remind myself of is that I am not living my life; rather, I am living the life of Christ in me. The only way that I become more like Christ is to walk in His life through obedience to His Word, walk out His life by faith towards God, and to assure that His life of abundance grows and abounds in me. I must always be prepared to offer, share, and pour out His life to and in others. To choose His life I must choose the ways of righteousness and to walk out His life I must be an open vessel, and to share His life, I must be a willing instrument in His hands. Let's face it, our natural inclination is to watch out for self and our tendency is to make sure we come out in the right light when it comes to others.

Our selfishness wants to be honored rather than honor others. Our pride wants to be adored rather than show proper respect to others and because of our arrogance, we want to come out right regardless of whether we are in a right spirit, possessing a right attitude, and truly being honorable in our conduct towards others.

Christ showed us the way in which to walk. He became a humble servant to mankind in disposition, a sincere example of righteousness in His walk, and a loving sacrifice in His actions. If we are to be overcomers and victorious in this life, we must discipline and line our steps up to the ways, instructions and examples of Jesus.

What distinguishes you as a person the most? Glory has to do with that which distinguishes a person. It could be your winning smile, personality, or abilities. The Bible is clear there is only one God by nature and He is distinguished by who He is (*Galatians 4:8*).

There is no other being or creature that possesses the attributes of God. As a result, He shares His glory with no one (*1 Corinthians 1:31*).

What will distinguish believers among humanity? The world shines the light on abilities, but without character there is no substance. The flesh highlights good deeds, but good deeds do not determine whether a man is good (morally upright) or not. What will distinguish a person is the very life of Christ being manifested in his or her life.

The glory of Christ **IN** us will change our perception, our ways, and our countenance. The glory of Christ **THROUGH** us will reveal the liberty of the Spirit in our lives. It is the glory of Jesus that **REFLECTS OUTWARDLY** from our lives that will verify the truths written In the Bible. Such glory will declare that all such matters of the heavenly are indeed true, glorious, and eternal.

Do you live as a new creation in Christ? We are told in *Romans 3:23* that we all have sinned and fallen short of His glory. In other words, we fall short of reaching our potential which is to reflect Jesus to a lost world (*Romans 8:29*). The Apostle Paul speaks of believers being new creations in *2 Corinthians 5:17*, and that old things have passed away and all things become new. It is the life of Christ in us that identifies us to the life we are to live according to the Spirit.

Here is the great reality of being in Christ. When God looks down on us, He sees His Son and not a doomed sinner who will be found guilty by the Law that demands the sentence of death be carried out. As believers we allow the life of Christ to be worked in us by the Holy Spirit to fulfill our highest calling and potential in His kingdom.

The more Jesus' life is worked in us the more we will reflect the light of Christ's life to the world. Keep in mind, because of sin we all start out like cracked mirrors. The light we reflect from our souls will be fragmented, tainted, and blackened, but when we come to Christ, we are given a new heart and revived with the Spirit of God.

It is the Spirit of God who begins to put our lives back together by establishing the life of Christ in us. The question is how much are you giving way to the work of the Holy Spirit in your life? Are you warring and resisting the work of the Holy Spirit by holding onto any part of the old life? If you are, know that your life and testimony will be inconsistent and will hinder you in coming to the fullness of your calling and potential in Christ.

Once we understand we are in Christ, what does Christ need to become to us? We must choose who we serve. We cannot have one foot in the world to try to get the most out of it and one foot in religion in an attempt to keep good standing with heaven to avoid hell. Jesus is clear that we can only serve one master at a time.

Something or someone will rule in our lives because we are all born into slavery because of sin. We are subject to the world's demands and constantly tempted to bow down to the lusts of the flesh in order do the bidding of the god of this world (Satan), that is until we change our master.

Romans 10:9 states, *"That if thou shalt confess with thy mouth the Lord Jesus, and shalt believe in thine heart that God hath raised him from the dead, thou shalt be saved."* It is clear we must believe in our heart the Gospel message, but we must acknowledge that Jesus is Lord, our personal Lord.

"Lord" in this text points to "Adonai," which means "owner." Scripture is very clear that we have been bought with a price and that we do not belong to ourselves. It is important to remember kings have subjects, but Lords have servants. As Christians we are not here to be subject to this world or serve ourselves, we are here to serve in the spiritual household of Jesus.

He is the One who bought us with His blood and should be calling the shots in our life. We have been given instructions (God's Word) as well as examples of how to conduct ourselves (Jesus in His humanity), and the authority (Holy Spirit) to carry out our responsibilities in this glorious household. The problem is some servants reject being servants because they are half-hearted towards their duty and their Lord, but if we love Jesus, we will graduate from being mere servants who are half-hearted in our service towards Him and become bondmen who commit the rest of our lives to serving and pleasing Him. (See *Deuteronomy 15:12-17*.)

It is important to remember that every knee will bow and every tongue will confess that Jesus Christ is Lord (*Philippians 2:9-11*). As Christians we have accepted this fact in our mind, but we must resolve it in our heart to avoid being ashamed of shabby service on judgment day.

Is the life of Jesus establishing godly characteristics in you? The Apostle Paul stated in *1 Corinthians 1:30*, "*But of him are ye in Christ Jesus, who of God is made unto us wisdom, and righteousness, and sanctification, and redemption.*"

Consider these four virtues: wisdom has to do with the mind, righteousness with the attitude of our heart, sanctification with our life, and redemption with our state. Wisdom determines how we think, righteousness comes down to what we must know to be true in our hearts, sanctification is the inward working of holiness and the outward working of godliness, and redemption identifies us to our spiritual inheritance. In a sense these four matters represent a total work of Christ in our lives.

Godly wisdom comes from above transforming the mind, righteousness come from outside of us (from His Word) but develops a right heart attitude within if we obey it by faith, sanctification is a work that is done within by the Spirit to establish us in our outer walk in this world, and redemption marks us for our future life. The problem is we piece meal Jesus. We take a bit of this understanding from experiences to try to make sense of a matter without looking up, we use a scriptural promise to make aspects of our life okay while ignoring fruit that points to inconsistencies in our lives, as well as a piece of decency to stamp our life with some type of approval to avoid facing other things that may not be so great, and adopt some wishful thinking to shore up our state of affairs that may be plaguing us with a sense of failure.

We need to keep in mind if we desire wisdom, we need to look up and ask for it and if we desire righteousness, we need to believe what the Word says and act on it. If we long for sanctification (cleansing) we need to humble ourselves before the Lord and ask Him to forgive, cleanse, and to restore us in a complete relationship with Him. If we need to know something is complete, we need to stand on the complete work of redemption, and as Jesus declared on the cross, "It is finished."

There is nothing more I can do to add onto His glorious work and no matter what I do, it will remain so; therefore, I need to simply come to a place of rest in my life in Christ through genuine faith towards Him."

Is Jesus your source of wisdom? If Christ is in us, we have all wisdom available to us. There are many different ideas of wisdom being promoted, but there are a couple of characteristics that set godly wisdom apart from the common sense secured by daily experience, the intellectual knowledge of this present world, and unrealistic worldly philosophies that sound great but never work.

The basis of all true wisdom comes down to knowledge that has been put into practice and actually works in a constructive way. Such wisdom reveals that it is based on truth. When truth is present, godly principles can be applied that will manifest the virtues described in *James 3:17, "But the wisdom that is from above is first pure, then peaceable, gentle, and easy to be intreated, full of mercy and good fruits, without partiality, and without hypocrisy."*

The second aspect of wisdom is that it recognizes the proper order and authority of something. For the Christian, this recognition comes down to the attitude known as the "fear of the Lord." *Psalm 111:10* tells us the fear of the Lord is the beginning of wisdom.

Godly wisdom reveals discipline that is often displayed in discretion and expresses itself by doing what is honorable. Those who fear the Lord above all do not want to displease Him because they love Him. They recognize the Lord's supreme authority over them and will avoid being foolish about their godly responsibilities, silly towards His Word, and will develop a hatred for sin that ruins lives, destroys relationships, and ends in destruction of souls.

Godly wisdom is greatly missing in today's world and as a result, a certain insanity--a fanaticism--is filling the vacancy that has been left. As Christians we need to keep in mind where our wisdom comes from and ask for it while seeking it in His Word, with the main goal of applying what is true through obedience. Faithfully applying what we know is true will develop a type of discretion that ensures that all of our conduct and actions will be honorable.

Are you displaying the righteousness of Christ? Righteousness is often associated with the idea of "goodness." There are various forms of righteousness on display.

There is self-righteousness that is based on personal goodness. There is piousness that is based on a religious presentation of maintaining certain ordinances, and there is a worldly presentation that is sentimental in its ability to make a person feel good about what he or she is doing in regard to the ails of the world. As you can see, each type of righteousness finds its origin in man, but the Bible is clear there is none righteous, no not one (*Romans 3:10*).

Righteousness to God is not just a matter of us trying to be or do "good." When it comes to God, "goodness" has to do with moral integrity, while righteousness has to do with a person's standing before Him. Keep in mind when the rich young ruler called Jesus, "Good Master" in *Matthew 19:16* the Lord clearly stated, *"Why callest thou me good? There is none good but one, that is, God."* In short, moral integrity does not originate with man nor can it be found in him in his unregenerate state.

We each must recognize as Christians that righteousness in our lives is truly a work of grace on God's part. If we are in Christ, we have right standing IN God. God sees His Son; therefore, we are not subject to His wrath. When we believe God about a matter we will have right standing BEFORE God, giving us the means to approach Him in service with our sacrifices and He will receive them in good faith and count it for righteousness. Finally, the last type of righteousness is when we DO right where others are concerned out of obedience to His Word, the Lord will reckon such actions as being righteous.

As you can see, there is no acceptable righteousness to be found in any of us, but if we understand how righteousness is imputed to us as believers, we can trust our position in Him, have assurance in our life before Him, and be confident that our worship, whether it comes in the form of service or sacrifice, will be accepted as being righteous, approved of and received by Him as being so.

Are you being made in the righteousness of God? The Apostle Paul stated that Jesus became sin for us so that we could be made in the righteousness of God (*2 Corinthians 5:21*). As I stated yesterday, righteousness is about having right standing in Christ because no righteousness can be found in an unregenerate man.

Since we are all born in Adam, we have a bent towards justifying sin or casting the blame for its destructive fruits on others, as well as bowing to fleshly desires and becoming entangled with the world's vanity (*Romans 5:12*). It is important to realize that giving way to the work of righteousness is the only way to change the bent being directed towards self and the world.

In Christ we have right standing, but we must choose the way of righteousness to change our habit from leaning naturally towards the things of this world towards the things of God (*2 Timothy 2:22*).

To do this we must go against the natural grain of how we used to do things and line up to the more excellent way of doing something which is based on the Word of God. Once we choose the excellent way over the base way, the bent will begin to change. Granted, it takes everything in us sometimes to choose and walk in the most excellent

166

way. The flesh will cry foul and the logic of the world will try to convince us that it is not necessary to take such radical measures or that we are becoming too fanatical, but the truth is, changing our natural preferences will take radical actions on our part to ensure that we are not just reforming the outside, but we are actually giving the Holy Spirit liberty to transform our inner man to take on the likeness of Jesus Christ.

The more we line up to the excellent ways of righteousness, the more integrity will be established in our inner man ensuring that our conduct and actions will be honorable. *Psalm 1:3* describes such a person in this way, *"And he shall be like a tree planted by the rivers of water that bringeth forth his fruit in his season: his leaf also shall not wither; and whatsoever he doeth shall prosper."*

Are you submitting to the work of sanctification? It is hard for Christians to understand sanctification, because very few elaborate on the holiness of God in the religious world. Scripture is clear that without holiness we will not see the Lord.

The Word commands us that since God is holy we need to be holy (*Hebrews 12:14; 1 Peter 1:15-16*). In order to understand what holiness is we must consider it from God's perspective.

Holiness is purity and this purity manifests itself as a type of fire that will either purify or consume (*Hebrews 12:29*). There is no darkness, inconsistencies, compromise, or underlying motives in God's intentions, words, promises, works, and ways. Keep in mind, Satan attacked God's intentions when he challenged Eve with this statement in *Genesis 3:4b-5, "Ye shall not surely die: For God doeth know that in the day ye eat thereof, then your eyes shall be opened, and ye shall be as gods, knowing good and evil."*

Holiness means "set apart." Believers are to be "set apart" from worldly and freshly influence on their lives in order to be set apart to God for His use (*2 Peter 2:19-22*). Clearly there is no holiness in man apart from God and a person must be placed in Christ upon salvation, giving him a status of a "saint."

We are born sinners because of Adam, but in Christ our status is changed to being "saints." The question is simple, are you living like a sinner or are you pressing forward to obtain Christ so His life can set you apart as a saint?

There are two types of holiness where man is concerned: they are consecration and sanctification. One points to man doing what he needs to do in order to be set apart to be made alive unto God, while the other one points to the Holy Spirit setting a person apart to be made fit for the kingdom's work that will bring glory to God.

Consecration is our part and is the act of being "set apart." This act involves a complete separation from the profane (world & flesh) in order to offer our bodies as living sacrifices to do the will of God (*Romans 12:1-2*). It requires the believer to daily put off the old man so the new man can be properly worked in him or her.

The second type of holiness is the actual work of sanctification and it is the Holy Spirit who does this work in the inner man (*1 Peter 1:2*). Sanctification points to cleansing with water and produces the work of regeneration (*Ephesians 4:22-24; Titus 3:5*).

Clearly, in Christ each believer has the status of the saint, but each of us must be diligent to consecrate every aspect of our lives for God's glory as we submit to the sanctifying work of the Spirit to continually bring forth the new man in us.

DISCERNMENT

*Discernment is about classifying
between such things as a duck and a goose
in order to make a proper judgment call.
To discern you must know what you are
looking for before you can discern what
you are looking at.
(Rayola Kelley)*

Many Christians wrestle with how to discern a matter. As believers, we can no longer afford to hope, wish, or somehow slide by this issue. To stand in these days we must properly know how to discern the signs and times we are living in.

To discern the signs, we must know what we are looking at when it comes to events, especially where Israel is concerned, and to discern the times, we must understand what we are looking for according to Scripture. In discernment, signs often are the visible manifestation to awaken and alert us to discern the spirit behind something, watch for the type of fruits it is bound to produce, prepare for the shaking that may occur, and pray to properly interpret what we are observing, while times allow us to follow certain patterns in order to see where something is leading us in relationship to our attitudes and relationship with God and the fruits it will ultimately produce in lives and ministries.

It is important to point out that true discernment is not a mental calculation that ends in some intellectual judgment; rather, it is the ability to sense the unseen. In intellectual judgment, we will come to conclusions that bring us what we perceive to be clarity, while in discernment there is no real clarity; rather, there is a knowing in the spirit that something is not what it seems to be and we must now discern the unseen spirit that is in operation and the environment that it will ultimately produce.

If you have allowed others to cause you to put your discernment on some shelf so you will not be judged as being "judgmental," it is time to take it off the shelf, dust it off, and start exercising it. If you lack discernment, ask the Lord to give it to you so you can properly stand in this present darkness while preparing yourself against its deception and destruction, as well as warning others about it.

There are people who, without the weather channel, know how to discern a storm is coming even when they can't see one on the horizon. In nature, the environment actually prepares for storms as it braces itself to withstand the winds that will shake, rip, and destroy all that is in its path.

Nature's preparations often serve as signs or warnings for those who are discerning or those who detect there is trouble on the horizon. Jesus talked about the religious people discerning the seasons as far as the cycles of earth, but not the prophetic times they were living in. The reason religious people are not discerning the prophetic times they are living in is because they are not looking for them or they are too busy establishing a religious kingdom on this earth instead of preparing their hearts to pursue the God of heaven. They also are not allowing their minds to be transformed and enlarged by the Spirit to discern outside the box of worldly facts, acceptable beliefs, pet causes, and religious notions.

It is important to discern the times we live in, in order to prepare for what is coming. In spite of the numerous signs around us, I fear too many are convinced that they will be spared of facing the storm and are sitting in the hull of self-delusion instead of preparing for the storm. Granted, I hope I am spared from the trying, challenging winds of such storms, but Jesus' instruction to His followers was that they were to be watchmen, aware of the signs, ready to face the storm and prepared to withstand it.

As a Christian I understand that I belong to an unseen kingdom. My responsibility is to be a light to a seeking soul that points them towards the One who will satisfy the wandering restlessness in their inner being, as well as become a source of comfort and hope to a wounded soul who needs the touch of healing from heaven, a strong voice of warning to the rebellious soul, and a clear voice as to the times we live in.

The Lord gave us the "spiritual weather almanac," the Bible, that informs us of the signs we need to beware of in order to sound the proper warnings so that God's people can prepare for the storm. However, to properly discern the times we are in, we must note the political and international environment around us. We know that there is a great war going on between the kingdom of darkness and the kingdom of light. However, storms in the spiritual realm point to testing and judgment, and it is important to remember that before a tornado hits, there is often an eerie silence that settles on the environment. We can see a similar scenario when it comes to hurricanes.

People know they are in the eye of a hurricane, when all becomes calm and silent, but what often follows are even stronger winds. There is another silence that is recorded in Scripture and that is found in *Revelation 8:1*. It occurs in heaven when the seventh seal is open before the trumpet and bowl judgments. Discernment is necessary to ensure we are ready for the storms, but silence in storms tell us to brace ourselves even more for the winds will prove to be greater. As a nation we have been politically and spiritually experiencing some tough storms, but what will we hear next, the wind or the silence?

Yesterday I asked what will we hear next, the wind or the silence? We have definitely been witnessing various winds of shaking pointing to judgment passing through our land. We must remember that after the great winds, eerie silence can follow. What do we do when everything becomes eerily quiet?

It is natural to try to logic what is amiss and second guess what is going on, but the truth is silence often points to more intense winds of testing and separation. As Christians we must be prepared for the storms so that we can stand on the Rock in the winds of judgment, but in silence we must brace ourselves.

Silence for the believer points to a time of waiting in order to hear, but not for the winds. When it comes to spiritual silence, we need to realize the next move to be made will be God's move. When God is about to do something, it requires silence. At such times we are not listening for the winds, but like Elijah in *1 Kings 19:11-14*, we must wait for the small still voice of God's Spirit to speak.

The silence allows us to get our spiritual bearings, calm our spirit, and reined in our fray souls in order to hear what God wants to tell us. We must wait in patience until God speaks, and stay in place until God tells us what to do. As we wait and brace ourselves in silence, seek His face, asked Him for wisdom, revelation, and authority, we can be assured that we are in a great place of safety. And, regardless of the intensity of the winds around us, we will not be moved because we are truly hid in God. We can be assured that He will calm the winds when it is time, as well as fight on our behalf against the demonic powers, the oppressive giants and Pharaohs of our age, and the armies of hell to secure true victory for His people, ever bringing praise and glory to Him.

What are you protecting? It is interesting how we strive to protect something. For example, some are trying to protect their family, but for Christians sometimes family can be the point of hindrance when it comes to serving the Lord, mocking when it comes to standing for the Lord, and a point of temptation to stop them from realizing the fullness of their calling and ministry.

Perhaps you are protecting your reputation, which is attached to credibility and authority. Proverbs tell us our reputation is of the upmost importance, but we must remember that Jesus became of no reputation to identify with us and we must keep in mind the world will slander us in an attempt to destroy any good reputation.

Maybe you are protecting your heart from being broken. We must guard our heart from becoming unforgiving, bitter, and hateful, but there is no way of keeping it from being broken. Betrayal, hopelessness, and sorrow can break the heart, but we must remember Jesus' heart was broken on the cross over man's spiritual plight, and that as the great physician He is the one who is able to heal the broken heart.

Maybe, you are trying to protect some ministry, and such a goal may appear noble but not honorable. Ministry is not to be an entity unto itself.

It is a simple tool, avenue, and means to minister to souls. When you balance out ministry with even one soul, the wellbeing of the soul is far more important than the reputation of some ministry.

We need to discern what we are protecting to ensure we are hitting the mark that God has set forth in His Word. If you sense you are protecting something, ask the Lord what it is. It could be the Lord is waiting for you to seek Him out so He can set you free, heal you, and cause you to realize your true calling and your highest potential.

Yesterday I asked whether you are protecting something. The next question is why are you protecting that particular aspect of your life? It is important to discern what and why we are guarding something because it will reveal certain things about our spirit and heart.

The Word tells us that it is the pure in heart that see God. When it comes to purity of heart, it is speaking of pure motives, agendas, and priorities. If your motive is not the love of God, your agenda to glorify God, and your priority to ensure He, along with His Word, are being lifted up in the right spirit and in truth, then the heart will prove to be very untrustworthy.

If the heart motive is wrong, it means the person is in the wrong spirit, if the agenda is wrong it means that the heart is operating in some form of perversion of truth, and if the priority is wrong, then the heart will prove to be divided and idolatrous. Many people perceive that what they are protecting is noble, responsible, and logical, but when you get them down to the real reason for their point of protection, you find they are often just protecting themselves.

For instance, we sometimes protect family to avoid personal shame, regret, and guilt. When it comes to reputation, people are often protecting fragile egos, insecurities, and rejection. If we are protecting ministry, we may think it is to protect God's work, but it is often to cover up sin, heresy, or deviant practices, which will make us partakers of wickedness because the Bible is clear all such matters must be brought to the light with the hope of restoring the one in error.

As for the heart, we are trying to avoid being vulnerable which can result in our heart becoming cold and hardened so it can't be broken, making our wills unyielding, our minds unreasonable, and our necks stiff.

The question is, how can we make sure our heart is pure and remains so? The first thing is we must remember that upon being born again we were given a new heart which possesses the right Spirit. The Spirit will write on our heart the things of God in order to change the bent of our attitude, reveal the quality of our character, and cause the light to shine on those things that would defile our tender heart, profane our testimony, and cause us to walk in the darkness of unbelief.

There are four reasons people will sell their soul to the world: health, wealth, power, and peace. Satan told the Lord in *Job 2:4-5* that all one has to do to cause a man to curse God is give skin for skin because he will he give all he has to maintain his life.

Due to the global health crisis that is causing much debate as to the legitimacy of the information that is coming out about it, we can see how health can cause fearful people to sell their soul and turn on each other. The rich young ruler walked away from possessing eternal life because he was wealthy with the riches of the world and was not willing to give them up for unseen heavenly riches.

Many desire power to control, but as Abraham Lincoln pointed out absolute power corrupts absolutely. Keep in mind wealth and abusive power are both associated with greed, which the Bible refers to as idolatrous.

Finally, people desire peace so they can simply live their lives. However, in a world where man learns to war, he is in constant conflict with one another and often within himself, and as *James 4:4* states is an enemy of God. The world can't and will never know true peace. Granted, it can create a false sense of peace, but such a façade will crumble in due time.

It is important to remember that a future leader will appear to bring a solution of peace to the whole world, giving men a false sense of peace that will be disrupted by sudden destruction (*1 Thessalonians 5:2-*

6). As a Christian, I must discern what means the most to me in this present life.

When health is an issue, as a believer, do I believe I am immortal until God calls me home? When wealth is a pursuit, have I become a spiritual beggar because the things of the world define and possess me instead of me pressing forward to attain the real prize of heaven by faith, Jesus Christ? As for power, is it so I can be in control of my life or come under the control of the Holy Spirit so that I can obtain, walk in and walk out the eternal life within me? And as for peace, there is only one Prince of Peace, Jesus Christ. He is Prince of Peace because He brought reconciliation between God and man. Without reconciliation with God, there will be no true peace to be found. I am not talking about peace in this world, but a peace that is within and will remain regardless of the conflict and tribulation taking place around us

One of the challenges of a Christian is to properly discern what is going on. We are told in *Ephesians 6* that we are not fighting against flesh and blood but the unseen realm. How many of us find ourselves fighting or ducking the so-called friendly fire of those who are supposed to be on the same side as we are?

Discernment has nothing to do with circumstances, intellectual understanding, or personal feelings and convictions. It has to do with the spirit that is operating behind and through something. I say this because Satan can come as an angel of light and will magnify the deadly fruit he is offering as being desirable and beautiful to cover the wicked agendas and the evil intent of what is behind it. The devil wants us to partake of it in order to plant the deadly seeds into the soil of our heart to bring doubt, division, and death.

One of the first ways we can begin to discern a matter is to consider what is being magnified to us. Keep in mind there is always some promise of life, happiness, or enlightenment attached to what is being presented, but the Holy Spirit's main responsibility is to always lead each of us to Jesus. It is the point of what is being magnified and promised that you can discern if Jesus is being presented as the only source of real life, the only place where happiness can be secured, and the end of all truth as to what is real and right. With this in mind, consider where your causes, battles, and convictions are leading you to make sure you are not settling for the shifting sand of this world, but that you are standing on the Rock of heaven.

What do you consider when you are making judgment calls about a matter? We are called to discern between good and evil. Good points to that which always proves moral, honorable, and righteous in the end, while evil points to a state that can come across as light, but in the end is only capable of producing the worst type of fruit.

As believers we must never partake of, embrace, or condone evil in any arena. The problem is that some people stop at titles, labels, or degrees, others at affiliations and associations, and some with how something sounds or makes them feel. Judgments that stop with such surface, fleshly evaluations are based on assumptions or presumptions that such sources can always be trusted when in reality the fruits they produce are lacking in any real substance, are disappointing and temporary when tested, and prove miserable at best and foul at worst.

As I watch events unfold in our nation, I ask myself how did Americans allow such a state of corruption to take root in our nation? In other words, how could we let so many self-serving wolves into the halls of Congress, as well as in state and local governments? Some might say are you not being a bit harsh, insensitive, and even cynical? The present fruits clearly show that not only corruption exists but it has existed long enough to become foul, filling an unseen cup that demands God's attention and judgment. And, what is the visible fruit of this corruption? chaos, tyranny, death, and utter destruction.

We live in very troubling and despairing times, but we need to take heart because before God can address a matter its fruit must come to full fruition. As a just God, He will bring a matter that is in darkness to the light to expose it just before He judges it. The corruption of evil is certainly being exposed in our institutions, but before we fall into great despair as we watch evil revel in its insanity while declaring victory, we must remember that the darkest time the world experienced was when

Jesus was on the cross where our sins were being judged. It seemed that evil had won; that is, until three days later when Christ arose from the grave, showing that He had secured the keys of hell and death to claim His rightful place as Victor.

How often do you discern the premise of your frame of reference? I am quite opinionated which can make me sound like an authority in a matter, as well as caught up with what I think I know which can make me feel like an expert. However, through the years I have continually discovered that I am not all-knowing and that I may know in part about matters, but I know very little of anything and I see "through a glass darkly" which means my perception is not only limited, but cloudy which perverts what I do see and understand.

Due to the fact that I have embarrassed myself and revealed my ineptness in always being "wise" through the years, I have been forced to discern just what I do know and understand. There are philosophies and different theologies that have influenced how I judge things which ends with me operating in assumptions and with a critical spirit.

There are facts that bring me to a general area of understanding something, but if they serve as an end and not an open door to explore beyond what I understand, I can become obstinate towards other facts that may not fit into what I do perceive. This reality serves to remind me I really do know only in part.

I have those sentimental notions that cause me to feel strongly about something, but strong feelings do not make something so, and then I have wishful thinking that something is a certain way when in reality wishing something does not make it so either.

I struggle to keep matters in perspective because I know I can sound like the ultimate authority in a matter that will ultimately reveal my ignorance and my arrogance, fight on and over some mountain of knowledge that will prove useless to my real calling, and end up looking foolish or proving to be a hypocrite because I have to be right or come out on top in all debates to keep people from seeing how little I do know or how insecure I am about what I do know.

There is only one way that I can learn the matters of God and that is by seeking Him in humility. There is only one way that I can be assured of facts and that is to make sure they line up to the complete counsel of God's Word, and there is only one way that I can be confident that I am not standing on the shifting sand of foolishness and that is by faith walking out what I know is pure and true.

HOPE & PROMISES

*Nothing that is worth doing can be achieved
in our lifetime; therefore, we must be saved by hope.
Nothing which is true, or beautiful, or good makes complete
sense in any immediate context or history; therefore,
we must be saved by faith. Nothing we do, however virtuous,
can be accomplished alone; therefore, we are saved by love.
No virtuous act is quite as virtuous from the standpoint
of our friend or foe as it is from our standpoint.
Therefore, we must be saved by the
final form of love which is forgiveness.*
(Reinhold Niebuhr)

God never forgets a promise. I remember the Lord showed me I was to write a book. This revelation changed the whole course of my life. I availed myself to obey, but the problem was I had many issues when it came to writing. I struggled with various handicaps, (and, I might add, still do), but I knew what the Lord showed me.

To make a long story short I hit one challenge after another, encountered various valleys of despair, and at times I just wanted to give up, but then I remembered the Lord enables those whom He calls, and as a result, I kept encouraging myself in what I knew was true about the Lord, ever pushing forward.

On May 8, 1995, I held the book in my hand, 18 years after the initial vision and calling. As I look back on those 18 years, I realize that there were nine years of personal preparation and nine years of a gestation period before the information could be brought forth. The end product revealed that it was His doing, His grace, and His faithfulness.

On that same night, the publishers had a book signing for me. I had to present the book to the group of people who would be in attendance. I asked the Lord what He wanted me to share. I will never forget what He showed me. He wanted me to tell them: "HE IS FAITHFUL."

Many people believe that if God calls you to do something that He will make the way smooth for them, but the opposite is true. Consider God's promise to Abraham at age 75 that He would give him a son. It happened 25 years later when he was a 100.

We have Jacob who was away from home for over 20 years after encountering Jehovah at Bethel and just before meeting his brother Esau, he endured a great wrestling match. There was Joseph who went through various trials for years, some believe 17 years before his vision was brought to fruition. There was also Moses, David, and even Jesus who spent His first 30 years in obscurity.

It is hard to understand that God must first prepare us before He can entrust us with our calling or a promise. I say all of this because God is the one who will faithfully bring a matter to fruition, but we must first of all determine what the Lord has put in our heart concerning our calling and work in His kingdom. We must then avail ourselves to Him by giving Him permission to have His way.

The next step after that is we must faithfully occupy, which means being faithful with what is before us as our spirit remains quiet before Him and our soul remains confident that He will bring it about in His perfect timing.

One of the Scriptures that many use is *Psalm 37:4, "Delight thyself also in the LORD, and he shall give thee the desires of thine heart."* This is an incredible promise, but most promises have a condition that must be met before a person can realize the promise.

Most people in this Scripture emphasize the desires of the heart, and fail to focus in on the condition. And, what is the condition? We must first delight ourselves in the LORD. "Delight" in this Scripture means to become soft, delicate, or pliable before the Lord.

Clearly, we must become pliable before Him so that He can reveal His desires to us, and out of love and joy those desires will become the desires of our heart. The greatest delight we should take in regard to the kingdom of God is not that we GET OUR WILL done; rather, that GOD'S WILL IS BEING DONE.

When you study the word "delight" in Scripture you will find that the obedience and righteousness of His people is what the Lord delights in, and His heart is that we share in that delight by making His desires our personal desires.

I try to take note of how the LORD introduces Himself such as in the case of *Genesis 15:1*. Meeting the Lord in such a way can always be a bit overwhelming and unnerving. There may be months or years of silence from Him, but as in the case of Abram, He suddenly stepped on the scene, inserted Himself into a time of preparation of Abram for the fruition of a future promise. He told the patriarch not to fear and then He gave a personal insight into Himself by starting the introduction, "I am."

We all know the significance of the Lord beginning with those two words. To Moses, He said, "I AM THAT I AM." "I AM" a name that points to not only who He is presently but who He has always been and will continue to be. He is involved in all past matters, is situating present events, and will bring forth future promises according to who HE IS. He is the same today as He was yesterday and will be tomorrow. There is no beginning and end to Him and when all is said and done, He is who He is, He is the great "I AM."

It is important to note that when the Lord uses these two words, He is ready to follow them up with some revelation about Himself that will bring greater perspective, enabling the person to receive the promise.

The next time you read or hear the Lord start with "I am," take note because it will be followed by some insight, He wants you to understand about Him as a means to enlarge your faith to receive.

There were two-and-one half tribes of Israel that chose to stay on the other side of the Jordan River after all the tribes claimed their inheritance. Remember, the Jordan was one of the boundaries of the Promised Land. The tribes of Reuben, Gad, and one half the tribe of Manasseh were sent away by Joshua to possess their requested land on the other side of the Jordan.

These tribes chose this land because it offered great pastures for their flocks. No one could fault them for wanting the best, but these tribes were susceptible to being attacked first by the enemies of Israel without being able to expect any assistance from the other tribes.

This can be true for what I call carnal Christians who try to hold onto the best of the world while still claiming their spiritual identification to the Lord and their spiritual inheritance. Such people can run in and out or religious activities while trying to remain as close to the promises of God as they can without having to give up all of the world. Christians need to be reminded that the more they are in the world and the world is in them the more susceptible they are to being attacked and defeated by the enemy of their souls.

As believers, we can always find hope when we reside by faith and obedience within the boundaries of what God has promised us

In my last post I spoke of the two and a half tribes that were on the other side of the Jordan River, separated from the actual Promised Land. In order to be identified to the rest of Israel and the Promised Land, the two and a half tribes built an altar that would be referred to as "Ed" *(Joshua 22:10-34)*. "Ed" means witness.

This gesture almost created a war before the tribes of Reuben, Gad, and Manasseh assured the other tribes it was not an idolatrous or pagan act; rather it was a way that they could establish a witness that they were part of Israel and heirs of the inheritance. It is important to realize that God has established such a witness in this world.

Even though this great witness is an equalizer of all who stand before it, it has caused many misunderstandings and even great conflict and division; and, what is this witness: the cross of Christ. It is referred to as an altar in *Hebrews 13:10-12*, and it stood outside the gate of promise and peace. It identifies believers to the kingdom God and their inheritance. It clearly looms between the light and darkness and will bring a great separation in mankind.

This witness will eventually bring condemnation to those who refuse its refuge, but for those who have come into the light of it and embraced it, there is identification to an inheritance, promises and hope that points us to that which is eternal, glorious, and beyond all description.

I have been watching the pansies outside of our sliding door. After cold temperatures of 27-degree weather and freezing fog I expected them to succumb to the harsh elements, but each morning they are still there to greet me with their vivid colors. Their simple beauty and unique design clearly speak of the Creator's artistic ability that graces His creation.

Here is a small flower compared to others that proves to be hardy in tough situations, withstands in harsh elements, and continues to point upwards even in a sagging state. The tenacity of this flower has caused me to pause and examine my spiritual life. It is true that these pansies are somewhat protected by the house and the eaves but it is also obvious that they are not going to give way to the elements without a fight.

As I consider the days we live in, the temperature is freezing with indifference, cold with the hateful attitude of the tumultuous times, and overwhelming to those who are shocked by the type of spiritual weather that is enfolding the whole world. As a saint, it matters little how small we are in the scheme of things because we know, love, and serve the Almighty God who is not in the slightest rocked by any of it.

We may feel the coldness of the world, the freezing fog of man's heart, and the tenacles of darkness enfolding us, but we are hid in God's refuge, Jesus Christ. We may feel the sinister darkness trying to grab at our soul to bring us down into the pit of utter despair, but we are firmly held in the palm of God's hand.

As I admired the pansies, I was reminded that in the garden of God, I am one of His flowers and it doesn't matter whether I fade in this world, for it is inevitable I will, but what is important is as long as I have the life, strength, and hope of Christ, I am able to stand and put forth heavenly beauty in and through the coldest temperatures this age can throw my way.

What or who have you put your hope upon? Hope can fly through the air on the fragile branches of wishful thinking, or bob on shadowy waves on the bated hope that everything will eventually turn out right, or soar on the heavenly currents of expectation towards unseen promises. The problem with pseudo hope is that it has no real foundation, a net of safety to catch a failing soul, or a sure place to land.

Today the false hope is waning from fear, struggling in the midst of hopeless situations, and finds no place of rest in grave darkness. It is obvious that some are looking in the wrong places for it, but for others they are trying to look up, but the darkness is so thick upon their soul that despair seems to be the only place they can lay their head upon without be taken under by the great undercurrent of depression.

What can a soul do when the branches of wishful thinking are no more, the shadowy waves have hit the shores of reality, while hope can't be found anywhere, and the promises can't be seen in the distance? One of the examples that I love to study when times get dark is a young man who in the darkest times purposed in his heart to do what was right before the Lord.

This man was of royalty and had been taken captive from his royal family and palace to serve in the palace of an enemy. He could have become angry with God and life, but instead he set his heart to do what was right over a small matter, but that small way was a beginning to prepare him to stand by trusting the Lord to work out the details when his life was being threatened, withstand with faith towards God when he was put in a lion's den, and continue to stand as a witness of God's abiding faithfulness when all seemed hopeless.

This man of God chose the food of a servant instead of the rich food of a king. As others cowered and trembled before the threat of death, he bowed and prayed. As some catered to the ego of those in power, he humbled himself before God only to be exalted as a beacon of light of the truth and placed in great places of leadership.

The key to this man started with that one choice to purpose in his heart to do it right no matter what, but each right choice ultimately produced in him an excellent spirit that caused him to stand distinct in times of great testing. This man's hope was in God, his faith towards God rested on it and his life before God stayed the course of righteousness. The man's name was Daniel. (See *Daniel 1:8* and *6:3-4*.)

Where do we put our trust when times are uncertain? Trust is a very interesting word, because, in a way, to have trust points to something that must be earned or proven trustworthy. To give trust without some form of credibility present would be unwise or it reveals that a person is gullible, too trusting, and immature to discern.

The reason many become skeptics is because the testing or discerning of trust has been skipped over, allowing a person to direct their hope towards the wrong source or person. This brings us to what often sets a person up to become a skeptic.

If you trace the steps of a skeptic when it comes to the matters of God kingdom, they jump over establishing the trust factor to swing on the limbs of expectation. Expectation points to hope which can be deferred when integrity is missing, misdirected when a false narrative is in operation, and depressing when it collides with reality.

It is important to note "trust" is a matter of faith that is directed towards what is true, right, and real, while worldly expectation is based on what one expects to SEE and fleshly hope is based on what one desires to HEAR. God's Word is clear, we cannot trust what we see or understand about a matter because we can only know in part.

Jesus warned us to beware of HOW we hear something because it will determine how we handle it or measure it out. As believers we have been given the Spirit who allows us to see beyond this world, the ears of faith to believe a matter when it lines up to God's truth, and discernment to see if what we hear, see, and taste can pass the smell test as to its real quality.

THE CHURCH

*When it comes to testing the effectiveness
of preaching, evangelical leader of the Anglican
Church, Charles Simeon presented these
criteria, "Does it humble the sinner? Does it
exalt the Savior? Does it promote holiness?"*

Jesus said of His kingdom, which is made up of the church, that it was not of this world and the Word shows us that souls, not land, are the true legacy of this kingdom, faith is the real riches of it, and His glory the final target.

God's church as a light and witness in this world, is to serve as a mirror that sets the standard of truth, righteousness, and morality in every home, society, and nation, and a church that fails to hold itself to this excellent standard will eventually reap the sad fruits of it as every part of society digresses into a cesspool of corruption and decadence.

To once again gain our authority to stand, we as believers must first humble ourselves and repent, knowing that without inward cleansing and preparation to stand before a holy God, there will be no outward advancement to reclaim that which truly belongs to our eternal inheritance and spiritual legacy.

It is natural to talk about the one solution for the church that would change the environment that now exists in this dark world. We hear this word "much" and it is "revival." I have read different books about revival, but how many people who are calling for it, stop to realize that revival first of all identifies the problem, and what is the problem?

To "revive" something means it is either asleep, in a dangerous comatose state, or it is dead. Many people think "revival" is for the unsaved, but revival is a word directed at a church, congregation, or Christians who have bocome inactive, indifferent, lukewarm, or asleep at the helm. It is directed at those who may be religious and rigid but are lifeless because they lack the real Spirit of heaven.

In my studies I learned that the book of Joel was calling the people of Israel to set up an environment in which revival could take place. Notice, revival can't just simply take place because religious people want it or are calling for it. Joel called for a "sweeping revival" *(Joel 2:16),"* a "weeping revival *(Joel 1:13),"* and a "reaping revival" *(Joel 2:18-32).*

What does it take to have a sweeping revival? It takes the movement and power of the Spirit of God upon the people to wake them up in order to bring them to a repentant and broken state of weeping over their sins, the sins of the church, and the sins of the nation.

Once God's people have been brought to a point to true repentance, reconciliation, and a place of restoration with God, then the reaping revival where fruit such as lost souls can be brought into the fold takes place. The reality is until the church is prepared to embrace lost, wounded souls, they can't be trusted with reaping a revival. The next time you hear the word, "revival," stop and examine what it would really mean to see a revival. I actually witnessed a mini revival and I can tell you right now it was the complete work of God's Spirit, but He had to first prepare the instruments and vessels that would be used to pour out His life into thirsty, seeking souls.

The next time you hear this word or are about to speak it, take the time and examine why there is a call for it and realize that the only thing between an alive, fruitful church or an ineffective and powerless church, is the presence, moving, and power of the Holy Spirit.

Isaiah 57:15 states, *"For thus saith the high and lofty One that inhabiteth eternity, whose name is Holy; I dwell in the high and holy place, with him also that is of a contrite and humble spirit, to revive the spirit of the humble, and to revive the heart of the contrite ones"*

I mentioned the word, "revival" yesterday. It is easy to sound grand when using the right terminology when the situation obviously calls for a certain solution, but talk is cheap. If revival is to occur, we must speak of or teach on the condition where revival can occur. To me the scripture in Isaiah pretty well lays out what is necessary to ensure revival.

The first thing we must note is that God must be in His rightful place in hearts, in congregations and in the Church for revival to occur. He must be lifted up as the only true God, worshipped in such a way that when all is said and done silence enfolds the environment as the awe of His glory fills a person's spirit and the wonder of His presence the soul, while humility begins to clothed the inner man, brokenness shakes and shatters any pinnacles of the self-life, and the altar of the heart is rendered into contrition before Him.

The truth is we have made God small by bringing Him down to our understanding, dissecting His Word to fit our comprehension and interpretation, and making Jesus a "good" guy that is here to do our bidding, placate our whims, and adjust to our cultural arrogance.

Revival will never happen until, like Isaiah in *chapter 6*, we see Him high and lifted up as the train of His glorious garments fills the temple of our inner being.

We are the products of the age we live in. Each age has its subtle ways of humanizing God in the minds of people. It is easy to see that in minds and presentations, God has been rendered into a mere pronoun that has no real absolutes to His character. He has been stripped of His deity in order to fudge the decisiveness of His holiness that will ultimately prove to be a consuming fire to anything that belongs to the kingdom of darkness, the flesh, and the world.

He has been demoted to worldly positions and titles such as being related to a CEO, sentimental presentations such as the "big man upstairs," and various others terms that ultimately embraces Universalism where everyone will be saved in the end. And, since there is no real distinction concerning God and salvation, the narrowness of the path to life, and the terrible judgment of wrath yet to come on all unbelievers has been broadened. Heaven is no longer a place of unadulterated worship of God, but has simply been redefined as another earth on steroids where everyone will continue to party and enjoy their favorite pastime, such as fishing, while remaining indifferent and aloof from spiritual matters.

Revival will begin with the contrast of the true God being lifted up by those who are awake to who He is, and His people coming out and being separate from all perversion of the present age. This separation allows them to become the lights that reflect His glory, instruments that speak His message, and vessels that possess the true life and fragrance of the Son of God, Jesus Christ, that will be imparted to others.

There is much talk about unity today, but in some cases, it is not about godly unity but going with the flow and not challenging or disrupting the wicked agendas of the powers of the present darkness to live in some quasi state of peace.

People think that unity means peace, but unity in God's kingdom really means having the same spirit, coming into agreement with what is honorable, necessary, and right, as well as possessing the same biblical convictions, and being on the same page as to what is going on and what needs to be done.

People want peace at any cost, but peace that is void of true agreement will prove to be tyrannical, false, mocking, and tormenting. Why are people willing to accept a false peace instead of fleeing from that which is contrary to true unity? The answer sometimes comes down to people wanting to settle back on their worldly laurels without worrying about the tidal wave of judgment that is heading for every shoreline of the world. They do not want to face that every foundation is about to be shaken and every way challenged. They do not want to have to stir themselves up to stand for that which may not be popular before men, withstand with truth that exposes the darkness to see the hatred, rage, and agendas of man, and continue to stand when all seems against them.

However, if we are to stand on the right side of eternity, we must agree with God's evaluation of a matter, side with truth no matter the cost, and do what is honorable no matter how ridiculous it may seem to others. To be overcomers of this present world, we must come out and be separate from the world's attitudes, ways, and practices. The way to true spiritual victory is the narrow way of the cross, the hard way of self-denial, and a foreign way because it often ends in sacrificing what is considered normal to our way of thinking, acceptable to the world, and popular with those who set the trends, and control the indoctrination and propaganda of the world.

The Bible is clear that the world's goal is to wipe out the light of God and it is obvious that, like the seven churches in *Revelation 2-3*, the church can be undermined in various ways. It can be robbed of its passion (love), rendered ineffective by unholy agreements, seduced into spiritual fornication, and experience hindrances and persecution to wear down the resolve and patience of the soul.

The key for those churches whose testimony has been or is being dulled-down by some sin or unholy mixture, is that they must repent; to the persecuted, they must continue to be faithful until the end; and to those who patience has been or is being worn thin, to remain steadfast to their calling until God moves.

When people speak of great revival in our country, I tell them there will be none until God's people become truly broken over sin, not just the sins of the nation, but personal sin and the sins of the church. The problem is, how many pastors are truly calling out the sins in their congregations so the Holy Spirit can bring strong conviction to hearts?

The church appears, in many cases, to have lost its way and its passion is gone because it has been lulled asleep by the world, and rendered lifeless because the Spirit of God has lifted. There are three "Rs" that I have heard through the years.

My co-laborer and I have been referred to as being RADICAL because we will not budge from the issue of sin, consecration, and commission, and yet compared to those of the early church we are not even close to being on fire and consecrated like many of them were in order to advance the kingdom of God.

Those who are radical will bring about a REVOLUTION among the ranks of soldiers in the battlefields and the workers in the harvest field.

Revolution has to do with enlarging people's vision and calling. The final word is REVIVAL.

There can't be radicals who inspire revolution among the ranks until the church has been revived with the fire of the Holy Spirit to once again stir up the passion for lost souls, along with the desire to be broken vessels. It is only as broken vessels that the life of Jesus can be poured out and imparted to others for the glory of God.

FEAR OF THE LORD

Give me a hundred men who love God
with all their hearts, and fear nothing
but sin, and I will move the world.
(John Wesley)

The Lord is always willing to contend with man, and if man is willing to be reasoned with, he will see the wisdom of God and the error of his own ways. This fact became obvious in the case of Cain.

Cain was angry because God accepted Abel's offering while rejecting his offering. The reason for it is because Abel offered what God required and Cain offered what he considered to be his best. The fact that God did not accept Cain's best proves that God can only reckon those things as being righteous that He sets forth as being acceptable to Him.

Cain wanted to show his best in his offering but when rejected, revealed the essence of his character in the form of jealousy. He took his anger out towards his brother Abel because he dared to bring the acceptable sacrifice, killing him out of jealousy.

It is interesting to point out that before Cain murdered his brother, the Lord contended with him. The Lord asked why was he angry, why had his countenance fallen. Clearly, the Lord was trying to make Cain aware of his flawed character and the dangerous precipice he was teetering on.

Isaiah 1:18 is very clear that the Lord wants to reason with us about our sin so that we can be cleansed from it. However, to be reasoned with we must give up our right to be right when we are wrong before the

Lord. The Bible is clear that God's ways and thoughts are higher than ours and God will never be lowered to our ways; therefore, we need to come into agreement with the Lord about what is right and choose it as the excellent, and only way to walk in.

If you could make one request, what would it be: worldly riches, fame, success, peace, or happiness? The world seems to offer various options to secure our heart desires but most will turn out to be dead ends marked with the sign, "Disillusionment."

There was a king who was given an opportunity to make such a request. But, instead of asking for the obvious, he asked for wisdom. His name was Solomon. Since Solomon asked for wisdom, he was entrusted with everything else.

The opposite of wisdom is foolishness, silliness, and indiscretion. The truth is, without wisdom we will not know how to properly handle other gifts, abilities, or worldly possessions.

Today, in a world that seems to be going mad, wisdom would prove to be a priceless gem, but how many desire or would value it? This brings us to an important aspect of wisdom—that it comes from God (*James 1:17; 3:13-18*). *James 1:5: "If any of you lack wisdom let him ask of God, that giveth to all men liberally, and upbraided not; and it shall be given him."*

We need to put a great value on wisdom in order to seek it and obtain it to walk through the insanity of this present age. The next time you hit confusion about a matter and even if you think you know, make it a habit to look up and seek the wisdom from above. The results will prove to be rewarding and satisfying.

In *Proverbs 23:4* we are told to cease from our own wisdom. Just as Paul warned, we are living in precarious times. Watching the news can be a bit overwhelming and frightening as we can clearly see there are freight trains of judgment coming at this nation due to its rejection of God.

This rejection of God is for the purpose of replacing the moral fiber of this country with wicked agendas that are destroying everything that is sacred and honorable. In Samuel's day the people wanted a king, but their idea of king had to do with appearance more than character and ability.

God gave them the king they wanted by the name of Saul. We are told in *1 Samuel 10:9* that God even had to give Saul another heart because it was not within his heart to be king.

Man logics a matter according to his ideas of how something will make him feel or what it should look like in order to fit some imaginary standard and comfort zone. Saul may have fit the people of Israel's surface qualifications but God's wisdom was clearly missing in their choice, proving that in reality man prefers his ways over God's ways because he perceives he is able to control a matter.

In Saul's case political matters got out of hand because Saul failed to choose the wise ways of God. Man must remember that he will always choose the world's way of doing and thinking, and the result is that he will also end up drinking the bitter cup of it.

In an existence where man is reigning in selfishness and arrogance, you will find people enclosed in small worlds where they major in minors and minor in majors. Jesus described this concept as swatting at a gnat while swallowing a camel.

Such individuals ultimately miss the real issue of a matter and sometimes come out looking clueless, revealing that they are lacking in their ability to separate and discern what is true. In small worlds, man's opinions are law, feelings their gauge in which they measure a matter, their biases are considered righteous judgments, their philosophies the truth, their doctrines the gospel, and their presumptuous conclusions the ultimate reality.

When we consider what we call the church in America, we must realize the size of our world will depend on how much our mind has been transformed by the Holy Spirit. We can easily step over into fleshly worship that becomes unholy and unacceptable to God or we can step into the pious role where we can't and will not be moved outside of our programs that are considered proper and ensure what we consider propriety in our services, regardless of whether they are in truth and anointed.

The problem is that in both cases the Holy Spirit is missing. In fleshly worship He will not be present, or if He was, He lifted without anyone discerning it. When it comes to stoic piousness, the sweet moving of the Spirit is shut down, kept out, and at times rejected. Yet, without the Holy Spirit, there is no real worship and there will be no unveiling of God's truths that make preaching or teaching sharp enough to awaken the spirit, alive enough to cause the soul to respond to gentle impressions, inspirational enough to look up, and life-changing enough that a person walks away renewed in the inner man.

As believers, we must not allow ourselves to become double-minded by settling for fleshly or stoic religious environments, but we must give God permission to shake us from our comfort zones, root us out of religious piousness, awaken our spirits to see beyond this world, and cause such a hunger and thirst in our soul that we will rise up, and with diligence pursue the things of God.

As we watch our nation reeling from the shaking, the testing, and the frontal attacks being leveled at everything that has been regarded as sacred, we must remember a couple of things: 1) the events we see were prophesied over 2,000 years ago; 2) the world has always lay in great darkness, 3) God's people are called to be the light of hope in such dark times, and 4) that the gates of hell will not prevail against the church. Another important upside about such darkness is that it never leaves any shades of grey where the half-hearted can slither in when light hits them to hide their real spiritual condition and slither out when the darkness abounds so they can be about their worldly deeds.

Today the church needs to get its bearings by coming back to its real roots of redemption, its true calling of holiness and separation, its commission to preach the gospel and make disciples of Jesus, in light of its real hope, which is Christ in us the hope of glory. We need to be like Abraham and gain the spiritual insight of faith that reminds us that what we are really looking for is that city that is not of this world, but made with the blessed hands of God. We need to become like the prophets of old and the first apostles who no longer fit in the world and prove to be restless in their souls, never landing in their spirit on the things that would defile their calling.

Some saints lost their physical eyesight, but were never hindered because they walked by a heavenly eyesight that saw beyond the darkness of this world to catch glimpses of the glory of the next. We need to be like David who would not allow uncircumcised lips to speak amiss about his God without challenging the giant to see who would be left standing in the end, knowing that the Lord would fight the battle and prove victorious.

We must never let the bullying, bad tidings, tyrannical oppression, and the onslaught of slanderous accusations of what appears to be giants standing before us stop us from pressing forward in confidence while reaching up in assurance that the victory has already been won. Keep in mind, God is waiting for the ordinary "shepherds" of this land to stand up to the giants of this world, whether in prayer, in the political arenas, in the churches, schools, and etc. so that He can exalt those of ordinary status to extraordinary heights by showing Himself mighty in and through them.

There is an historical event that involved a king of a particular city that might have some significance for this day. His grandfather had established an empire, his father was trying to enlarge it in foreign places with his army, and he had been named king over the empire's capital city.

This city was considered one of the seven wonders of the world. It was populated, surrounded by thick walls, and no doubt assumed safe from the army camped outside of its walls. This novice king had benefitted from the great leadership of his fathers and was entrusted with much, but he had a couple of problems, he was void of character and full of pride.

Even though the enemy was outside of the camp he presumed that they would be safe until his father's army came and rescued their prized city. He decided to throw a big party. Part of the custom was to bring out all the idols from the nations their army had captured and subdued. As they paraded the idols out, no doubt the party-goers ramped up their cheers and declarations. Parties have a way of doing that. However, there was one nation whose God forbade images, but they had the vessels of the temple of this God.

The king had the vessels brought forth and as they began to defile the sacred vessels with profane wine, a hand appeared out of nowhere and the finger of the hand was used as a pen to write out a message that was of another language. It was amazing how subdued that king and the party goers became. What did this message mean? There was none present to interpret it, but his mother told him of a prophet that interpreted the dreams and visions that her father had as king.

The man by the name of Daniel was summoned and promised great position and rewards, but he was not interested in it. He read the message after giving the arrogant young man a very important history lesson. The message went like this "God has numbered your kingdom and finished it. You have been weighed in the balances and are found wanting and your kingdom has been divided and given to the Medes and the Persians." That night the enemy made a way into the city and it fell within the hour, and the king was killed.

The name of the king was Belshazzar and the city was Babylon (Daniel 5). We need to keep in mind God numbers our days, as well as the days of the wicked. He weighs all things in a just balance. On one side is His holy Law and on the other side are the books kept of every deed done in darkness, every evil thought, every idle word, and every wicked scheme. As soon as the king's doings were weighed, they were found wanting, in other words a great deficit was present that required complete judgment.

As Christians, we are hid in Christ and subject to the Law of the Spirit of life in Christ Jesus, and when we are weighed in the balance it is Christ who stands on the other side of the balance of God's Law. Since Christ satisfied God's holy Law on the cross, we stand justified and not condemned for He is the end of the law for righteousness to everyone who believes (Romans 8:2; 10:4). The question is are your deeds standing exposed on the just balance of God before His holy Law that will proclaim your guilt, or are you hid in Christ because you believe?

JOY, GRACE, & PEACE

Truth will always make demands, and grace
will always be there to meet them.
(Watchman Nee)

The Bible talks about lifting up holy hands to the Lord (*1 Timothy 2:8*). I am the type of person who wants to understand why I do what I do. The reason for this is because I want to make sure my attitude lines up to the real intent behind my practices when it comes to my spiritual life, and that I am able to receive whatever blessing or promise that is bestowed on me by God's grace.

I remember asking someone as to what the significance was of raising my hands in worship. The person told me it was a show of surrender. I could see where complete surrender is necessary for true worship to take place. However, the Lord took it upon Himself to answer my question in such a simple but profound way.

I had watched one of my friends that I worked with walk out of a store with her two-year old son. He went one way as she went the other way. She had to chase him down so she could take his hand and lead him. I remember laughing to myself, thinking, a child will be a child.

A couple of days later I was working with her in the office. We were up in a loft and her husband brought the little boy up the stairs to see his mother. I recall the scene as if it was yesterday. The young boy let go of his father's hand and reached up as he ran to his mother who automatically reached down to pick him up. It was at that moment, the Lord spoke to my heart, "Rayola, that is the reason you lift up holy hands to Me, because when you do, I will, as a loving Father who will automatically reach down and pick you up."

Even as I write this I am overcome with great awe and humility, knowing that the Lord rejoices in picking up His children that run to Him in excitement while reaching up in expectation to be lifted up in sweet communion.

It seems two of the most misunderstood, abused, and misused attributes of God are love and grace. Often people bring God's love down to a fleshy concept that has Him overlooking moral indiscretions and renders His grace into some flimsy covering that covers up man's worst practices. It is true God made His love available by providing the solution to man's sinful plight, but it is redemption that addressed it.

God's grace does not cover up the wrong practices of man; rather, upon the born-again experience, the gift of the Holy Spirit begins the transforming work that empowers man to overcome that which is wrong, while grace provides the avenue of freedom and victory to walk in the ways of righteousness to obtain and secure His promises by faith.

Love is committed to see the best for man while grace is the face, (Jesus Christ), of what God is able to do on behalf of man to bring about the best in His life. The truth is God is holy and can't and won't tolerate sin. He loved mankind and could do nothing less than provide a means of reconciliation to bring man back into a relationship with Him. He extended grace to mankind so that man could be saved **from** His miserable lot in life, not saved **in** it.

The truth is we want life on our terms, to do what we want to do, and live as we want to without any consequences. It is because of this fierce independence of the self-life that we are ever tempted in times of moral indiscretion, indifferent attitudes and unbecoming conduct that we console ourselves with a fleshly concept of God's love and hide behind a false idea of grace.

The conflict arises when our conscience pricks us that God's holiness will not allow His love to rejoice in iniquity and that grace can be frustrated when man adds his personal attempts of being righteous or shows a casual attitude that God's grace will abound and cover up foul moods and wrong practices. As the Apostle Paul would say, "God forbid that man should give way to such foolishness." I, for one, am so thankful that God opened my eyes to see the cross of Christ and by His

Spirit drew me with a child-like faith to embrace it as my solution to my sin problem.

It was at the cross I experienced the real, sacrificial love of God. I am humbled and awed that in spite of my past indiscretions God's grace flowed down to me, met me in my hopeless state, and flooded me with the assurance that His Spirit will lead me into the path of righteousness and the ways of victory to discover spiritual blessings and obtain incredible promises.

Many people improperly equate happiness with joy. *Psalm 144:15b* states, *"...happy is that people, whose God is the LORD."* Unless happiness is associated with God and a right attitude towards our life in God, it will prove to be a fleshly feeling that will flit around in a temporary state of euphoria, only to be shot down by the challenges of life, causing it to either whimper in self-pity or rage against what is perceived to be a terrible disruption and injustice.

When it comes to joy, it is an inward state, as well as part of the fruit of the Spirit that produces a response. As part of humanity, it is natural to seek happiness, but as Christians, our real goal should be to develop the state of joy. To possess a state of joy is to have an anchor in our soul that keeps us steady because it holds us to that which is eternal, Jesus Christ, even in times of great challenge and distress.

Nehemiah 8:10 tells us the joy of the Lord is our strength. The source behind this strength is found in three arenas. John the Baptist admitted his joy was fulfilled as he decreased so Jesus could increase (*John 3:29*). We can only establish and know true joy the more Jesus becomes a reality in our lives.

Another area is prayer. God desires to answer our prayers in order to bring joy to us, but we must pray according to His character and will to release a constant flow of such joy into our spirits (*John 16:24; 1 John 5:14*).

The third arena of joy is found in believing His Word. Jesus stated, "These things have I spoken unto you, that my joy might remain in you, and that your joy might be full." (See also *John 17:13* and *1 John 1:4*.) I was a helmsman in the Navy, and sailors understood the importance of an anchor because without it in times of distress and storms, a ship and its crew would be at the mercy of waves. To me decreasing is the same as releasing the anchor, prayer is like throwing the anchor, and the Bible is the chain that connects the anchor of our Christian life to the immovable Rock.

As these times try our faith, we need to know that if that anchor of joy is missing, we will find ourselves at the mercy of circumstances instead of holding steady and firm to the Rock.

Joy is a state that is founded in love and is able to produce the glorious fruit of peace in our souls. Clearly, our joy is not based on circumstances and environment; therefore, it is not fickle like sentiment, fleeting like fleshly happiness, and unstable like the waves of uncertainty.

Joy is a glorious anchor that goes deep into our soul to hold us to what is eternal. I so much appreciate the joy from above. I have not always immediately reached down into the depths of troubled waters with my faith to lay hold of the Rock, but the heaviness in my soul eventually required me to quit dragging the bottom of wishful thinking and take hold of the promises of God in order to become anchored to the Rock.

The Apostle Paul was under house arrest when he wrote, *"Rejoice in the Lord always: and again I say, Rejoice" (Philippians 4:4)*. Paul explained the reason he could rejoice was because he kept his heart and mind on Christ, while learning to be content in whatever state he was in, knowing that Christ was the source who strengthened him, along with trusting that God would supply his needs according to His riches in glory by Christ Jesus (*Philippians 4:7, 11, 13, 19*).

As Christians we should not get caught up with the many bad tidings of the world; rather, we need to take hold of the Rock so that we can rejoiced in who our God is, as well as stand confident knowing that our needs are already met in Christ Jesus, our Lord and Savior.

Rayola Kelley

THE WORLD

God never gives back the world to the
Christian, in the same sense that he requires
a convicted sinner to give it up. He requires
*us to give up the **ownership** of everything*
to him so that we shall never again for
*a moment consider it as **our own.***
(Charles Finney)

How big is your world? Through the years I have encountered four different worlds. The first world I had to come face to face with was, and will always remain, very small.

This world can be insipid, depressing, ridiculous, full of self-pity and excuses, and prove to be downright insane. And, what comprises this world? SELF. I spent the first years totally wrapped up in self. Self never wanted to accept the intrusion of other worlds; therefore, it learned to play games in order to try to manipulate other people as a means to get them to fit into, or adjust to, my particular reality that often was void of any real purity. When I became a Christian, I had to learn to nail self to the cross in order to connect to what was really happening around me.

The second world I encountered were OTHER people's reality. I was a bit surprised at how other people viewed life, reacted to different things that challenged their philosophies and beliefs, and how they faced crises. Some individuals proved to be as selfish as myself, while others possessed fragile realities that caused them to display various meltdowns when challenged even in small ways as a means to avoid all unpleasant realities.

There were those who became hard in their attitudes and possessed a steel resolve due to the fact that they were going to survive and come out on top no matter what, and then there were strong people who, regardless of the challenges of life, remained tender in heart and uncompromising in character. I had to admit, the selfish irritated me, and the fragile made me want to run the other way to avoid the ongoing emotional tidal waves that would catch me up into an immature reality. I felt intimidated and suspicious of those who always had to come out on top, but I respected those who maintained an inner integrity that would not let them be any less than who they were.

As a Christian, I had to remind myself that Jesus died for every person in order to redeem their soul and that the reason I was not taken to heaven upon my salvation experience was because I was here to reach out to OTHERS with the Gospel that is the power of God unto salvation. If I was to effectively minister to others, I had to first get past myself, and like Jesus become identified to their plight in order to enter in with them so that I could offer His life. We must never stop at self and we must allow others to remind us that we are not the only duck in the pond, so get over self and learn to embrace what is, so you can possess the best of what can be.

Do you know the smallest world that actually exists among us? Granted there are various dimensions that exist that require us to use a microscope or a telescope to see them, but there is a visible world that is so small, insignificant, and insipid that is prevalent today, and that is the world of I, me, and myself.

I realize I have this statement turned around but I believe everything in the self-centered life begins with the "I," making everything in its small environment incorrect. The big part of the "I" in man is that he is a s"I"nner who is often blinded to his need to be saved from h"I"mself, and the small part of this world is nothing more than the small insipid voice that constantly resonates with the declaration, "What about ME?"

The "me" which must be the center of all things in this world creates the narrow maze of selfishness and emptiness that keeps such individuals hitting the same wall of frustration, disillusionment, and anger. And, there is that last aspect of this small world that implies that all must begin with "me" and end with "myself" as being the most important person in the world.

The "I" declares it must be first to know it is important, the "me" insists it must be regarded as being worthy of every bit of consideration it seeks to keep it pacified, and the ego of "myself" demands it must ultimately be exalted to ensure that all is well, keeping this small world from colliding or disrupting other worlds. The problem with stopping with "I" is that I can't see past it and when others placate "me" to keep me quiet, I become a prudish snob, and when "myself" is all that ends up counting in my world, my ego becomes a monster that others must keep at bay with a wall of self-preservation, the chair of resentment, and the whip of truth or anger.

I remember when I discovered "I" was a sinner and realized how great a failure I was, but it was in that failure, I found Jesus who came to save "me" from "myself". As the Lord exposed the narrowness and foolishness of my world, I realized how the "me" kept me from seeing how narrow my understanding and perspective was about God and life.

I found the darkness of my reality enfolding me in fear, self-pity, and despair. It was then I came to the end of "myself" to recognize the emptiness and hopelessness of it all, and that is when I begin to cry out to the Lord in desperation. I was so thankful for constantly being reminded that the one way to take the sole focus of "I" away, was by looking beyond it to the cross of Christ. It was in submission to God's Word and will that the walls of "me" came down and it was by accepting the call to true discipleship that all that was associated with "myself" was cast to the side to pursue, discover, and know what is truly important, worthy of all consideration and excellent, the Lord Jesus Christ.

The Bible is clear we must deny the self-life of its right to exist, and Paul made it clear that it is a daily process to mortify it. One of the tests we challenge people with is see how long they can go through the day without bringing the attention back to themselves or thinking about self. It amazes some people to find out that most of their concerns come back to self, centers on self, and will insist self is acknowledged in some way.

Yesterday I spoke about the small world of the self-life. I don't know about you, but every time I tried to make "I" first in a matter I came out looking small and when I tried to manipulate others to consider "me" I often came away feeling deflated, rejected, and a failure, and when I have been so full of "myself" I often walked away feeling embarrassed and foolish. This is the world of "me, myself, and I."

The problem for most of us is that it is natural for our self-centered worlds to begin with "me" and for that reason it is hard for our worlds to embrace the concept that beyond the self-life is a greater life, outside of the "me syndrome" is that which will satisfy, and the narrow pinnacles created by the "I" problem always ends with the downward slide into the empty cauldron of the "myself trap" of dark nothingness.

Through the years I found that if I stepped back from the "I" problem to ascend the narrow path up the mountain to gain God's perspective, that is when I realized that in the scheme of things God is everything and I am nothing. To get past me, I had to make it about others, caring, ministering, entering in with those in need without condition, personal agendas, or getting some insatiable need met, and in doing so I discovered greater treasures. I began to see that there are people who are hurting more than I, have greater sorrows than me, and are fighting to not drown in the pool of self-pity, discouragement, and depression.

As I entered in with the plight of others, I found what true character looked like, how genuine faith simply stood on the Rock of Ages, and real meaning and purpose could only be realized outside of "me, myself, and I." It is when I left the "I" behind, silenced the "me" by applying the cross, and flinging myself to the side in order to follow Jesus did I find the freedom to begin to discover the heights of His Spirit, the depths of God's love and grace, the width of His pity and compassion, and the beauty of His presence in praise, and the satisfying sweetness in worship of and communion with Him.

We must always begin with the Lord in prayer, meditation of His Word, and in setting our faces in the right direction, and if we fail to start out with Him, we BETTER end with Him if we are to be overcomers in this world. As the saying goes, "More of me, less of God; less of me, more of God; none of me, ALL of God."

I spoke about the four worlds man lives in, or experience along the way. The first world is SELF, small, insipid, and delusional. Once you come to the end of self, you encounter utter hopelessness.

The second world is the reality of OTHERS which can prove to be confusing, at times neurotic, shifting, fragile, and sometimes insane. The third world is the WORLD itself.

This world is comprised of godless systems, the light of fading glitter, and false promises that leave a person empty and disillusioned about life. The main reason for emptiness is that all things attached to the world are temporary. It has no real substance and ultimately will leave a person empty and despairing because plans are often snatched away, their footprints that are being left in the sands of time will disappear within a short time after they are gone, and the pinnacle of success simply leaves them teetering in confusion, fear, and uncertainty because there is nowhere to go but down.

The highly pursued labels and degrees of the world will come to mean nothing in the end and the prized trophies will become tarnished and stored away in some attic or container becoming non-essential. This is the reality of the world whose systems are ruled by Satan, and for this reason we must come out and be separate in order to become part of the REAL WORLD where truth reigns, holiness is man's state of mind, righteousness his garment, godliness his walk, and worship his very life and breath.

The real and lasting world is the kingdom of God. It is eternal and sure, as well as invisible to the naked eye, but glorious to the eyes of faith. And, how do we make this world our world? As believers we know it begins with seeing our lost state, looking to God our maker to reveal, identify, and confirm His solution: Jesus Christ.

It is upon receiving Christ as Lord and Savior that we will be lifted from the judgment upon this present world into heavenly places as self is crucified, and others stand equal before the cross in need of a Savior. Once we are born into the kingdom of God, we must make sure our reliance is not on Satan's systems, our affections are not influenced by self but are on things above, and our heart is not divided by worldly allegiances, but single in devotion. We must set our mind on what is eternal and avoid pursuing the temporary, while our service proves honorable as His servants. We must always choose the excellent way, and our worship must also prove to be acceptable because it is done in the right Spirit, lining up to the truth of Jesus Christ.

Stuff, stuff, and more stuff! Jesus stated that our lives do not consist of the things we possess, but it seems that the things we have collected often possess us. In fact, like Saul of old, people hide among their stuff (*1 Samuel 10:22*).

The biggest challenge for me is to get rid of stuff. I personally don't like too much stuff, but when your life consists of three women with personal needs, a ministry, an artist (Jeannette), a massage therapist (me), and a school teacher (Carrie) under one roof, it is easy to collect things. Even our little Chihuahua, Tucker, has a tub of "personal items."

You can become confused because you don't know what you might need and you do not want to waste money or time in getting something new. You must weigh matters and sort the old familiar that you often resort too because you are comfortable, the non-essentials, and the necessary into proper piles to rid yourself of things that cling to you. You must separate the sentimental objects from what is NEEDED, and the non-essentials from what is NEEDFUL.

As I consider my spiritual life, I realize this is also true. We are often buried by worldly demands that need to be identified according to what must be considered in light of right priorities and we need to separate from wrong attachments that we are comfortable with to recognize what we have need of to ensure necessary changes. We have heavy, confusing burdens that weigh us down from making spiritual advancements and sins that easily beset us because they cling to us. For a good house cleaning to be successful, whether in the physical or spiritual realms, we must be ready to examine what possesses us. The Apostle Paul had it right when he stated in Philippians 3, that he counted the things of this world as dung while focusing on and pressing forward in gaining Christ who is eternal.

For the past week we have been building a patio. It is rewarding to be part of something constructive that you can see taking shape. Praise

Rayola Kelley

God for those who know how to design something, lay it out, and properly instruct inexperienced helpers to get it done.

Today, it seems that people have lost their way, many in light of the virus. I heard about a young boy who committed suicide because his active life was suddenly brought to a halt by this virus. Without any outlets in which to emotionally, intellectually, and perhaps spiritually to talk about or express his confusion, frustration, and hopelessness, he chose the way of hopelessness and depression: death.

This tragedy is being played out in various arenas. In a world that presents itself as one's only hope to happiness, success, and purpose, it is hard to realize that man was created with a purpose. It is also hard for man to see beyond this present age to know that the time here is about preparing for what is yet to come. I am so thankful that I know who designed me and He put within me the Master Craftsman, the Holy Spirit, who is able to bring forth the design of my life, the very image of Christ.

This design is what will bring honor and glory to the Creator. He has given me an emotional outlet through praise, an intellectual outlet through His Word, and a spiritual avenue in which to discover the hope of the next world through worship and service. Sometimes I need to take my eyes off the hopelessness of this world that is playing out across this nation in various ways and look up to keep in perspective that regardless of age, no one is long for this world.

The first man, Adam, was made for a garden of fellowship not for a dying world where man now constantly tastes the different bitterness of its darkness: that of sorrow, loss, and death. As believers, we are not of this world, belong to it, or destined to sink with it into a cesspool of despair and destruction.

It is natural for all of us to want to fit into this world so we belong, but there is also a dichotomy present, and that is we also want to hold a special place, a place of adoration in someone's heart and life so we feel loved, recognized, needed, and appreciated. For some who have a realistic handle on things, they may have found this place in marriage, but for many this desire becomes tormenting because the feeling eludes them even in what would be considered close relationships. They seek for that one person, relationship, or position to experience that feeling, thinking that once they find that place, they will finally feel special, completed, and satisfied in their life.

The truth is God puts both desires in us, but we make the mistake of letting the world define what they will look like. To fit into the world, it first requires you to sell your soul because the world can only love those who belong to it. When it comes to being that special person exalted to a distinct place where you become the sole consideration of someone else is not only unrealistic but idolatrous.

God put these two desires in us, knowing that a relationship with Him alone is the only way to revive our spirit and bring us to a place where we know we belong to that which is lasting. In fact, we are heirs with Jesus and belong to a heavenly family, body, priesthood, and kingdom. God is love and only He can bestow love on us that is satisfying to the soul. Every time we look to something or someone outside of God to fill the vacuum in our soul or listlessness in the spirit, we are going to be set up to be greatly disappointed, disillusioned, and miserable.

The next time you feel the emptiness of vanity, and the listlessness of focus and purpose, discern what the quality of your relationship is with the Lord. The Bible is clear, Jesus is our all in all, and to look, pursue, or desire the worldly and fleshly is to experience the emptiness of this present life, while missing the opportunity to discover the preparation and fullness of the life that has been promised to all of those who believe God and His Word.

I was recently talking to a friend in Georgia when she asked me if we had snow. This friend loves snow and I asked her why. She stated that snow reminds her of Isaiah 1:18, "Come now, and let us reason together, saith the LORD: though your sins be as scarlet, they shall be as white as snow; though they be red like crimson, they shall be as wool."

Rayola Kelley

The flesh profanes, the pigpen of the world perverts, and Satan with his great spiderweb of deception ensnares to destroy. It is impossible to walk through this world of Satan's demonic systems and not be dulled down in some way by their wicked ways. Sometimes we are so dulled down, we don't realize how far off the mark of God's ways we have strayed.

It is for this reason that the Lord must reason with us about where we are spiritually. This is why King David asked the Lord to search and try his heart and reveal his thoughts and if there was any wicked way in him to lead him back into the way of what is everlasting (*Psalm 139:23-24*).

I don't know about you, but after walking through the pigpen of this world, I know that occasionally I need a good cleansing because the abhorrent ways of the world cling to me, making my spirit lean and my soul restless. I sometimes feel the great heavy burden of its filth around me as described in *Romans 8:22* that all creation groans and travails in pain under the great weight of sin, that at times my soul becomes overwhelmed with despair as I cry out to God to be able to feel the freedom from such grave oppression.

As believers we can take courage and rejoice because we have a fountain we can come to for cleansing, an oasis in the wilderness that will never run dry no matter how barren the soul becomes, and a place of rest where the water will be provided to revive the spirit once again to soar above the hopeless, dying ways of this world.

The beauty of these sources is that repentance points us in a heavenly direction, the eyes of faith allow us to see Jesus and His redemption, and hope takes flight on the wings of expectation that washing and partaking of the source will take away that which weighs us down, causing our souls to feel the lightness only purity can bring and our spirit the liberty to once again regain great heights in the Spirit.

CARNALITY

*Change usually comes when it hurts so much
that you have to change, when you learn
so much that you want to change, and
when you receive so much that
you welcome change.
(Unknown)*

One of the big challenges for Christians is something called carnality. Carnality comes down to a worldly attitude that has not been transformed by the renewing of the mind. It speaks of Christian immaturity where some of the garments of the world's ways still cling to the Christian, causing inconsistencies in their walk, testimony, and response.

Carnality will not keep Christians out of heaven, but it will keep them from a deep walk that speaks of a consecrated life. A good picture of how carnality works can best be described by a Facebook post I once saw. There was a guy standing at the end of a pier with a swimsuit and cap on. You expected him to dive in, but instead he ran across the surface as fast as he could to the opposite pier. You then realize he was running on ice.

Carnal Christians are surface Christians. They may talk the talk and speak about the deeper life in Christ, but they are best described by the late chaplain of the Senate, Peter Marshall as dressing up in deep sea diving gear to only end up in the bathtub.

The one thing I have learned is if you want to come higher in God, you must be willing to let Him go deeper in you as you go deeper in your life with Him. The height you reach in your understanding of God is determined by how deep you have dived into His Word to discover Him in His glory.

Talk is cheap. It is not enough to talk about coming higher in the Lord unless you are preparing to get out of the bathtub, walk past the kiddie pool, avoid stopping at the water front, and instead head straight for the deep part of the ocean where you catch glimpses into the vastness of

His eternal character. It is those glimpses in who He is that will transform the mind.

Yesterday, I made reference to carnality. Sadly, our society has conditioned us to demand and pursue instant everything when it comes to our appetites. Our culture has substituted the idea of integrity with arrogance that mocks it, fear that shuns it, and ideology that rages against it and refers to it as evil. Clearly this wicked agenda of Satan's systems of the world is to rid each age and each generation of God, silence believers, and put out the light of heaven. As a result, many people have a semblance of life, but there is no quality to it.

Sadly, some in the church have adopted the same carnal attitude towards life. They prefer the pacifier of good sayings, declarations, and cheers as a replacement for the Word of God, the milk of doctrine to the sustaining Bread of heaven, and milk toast instead of the meat of the Word. The problem with such an attitude is that people expect all things to be handed to them without toiling and sacrificing for it to quickly come to them without difficulty, and to always leave them feeling good in their unproductive state.

They want the picture without connecting the dots, the revelation without being prepared to properly handle it, and a productive life without cultivating it. The fruits of such a diet are listlessness in spirit, indifference in the soul towards the things of God, a lifeless religion, inept testimony, and an unproductive life in Christ.

The Word is clear that we must study it to show ourselves approved, workmen that need not be ashamed to stand for its truth in order to avoid feeling utter shame when we stand before the Living Word, Jesus Christ on that great day of reckoning. Christians must cease from settling for tidbits of wisdom, little morsels of religion, sugary sayings, and sit up to the great banquet table of God's Word and ask the Holy Spirit to impart the right nourishment to grow them up in their life of Christ. They must have the goal of ensuring the milk is pure, the bread is properly assimilated through obedience, and learn how to chew the meat of the Word so they can discern the will of God for their lives and bring glory to Him.

Every believer must remember it is the Holy Spirit who takes God's Word and cleanses us with it, but He also uses it as a hammer to form us into the image of Christ, and the fire to purge and light the spark of life in us to shine in darkness.

I have been talking about carnality. The problem for the Christian is that you can't mix carnality with holy living without defiling it. In other words, carnality in any arena of a Christian's life points to an unholy mixture that will spiritually dull a person down, making them complacent towards God and His Word. Eventually it will bring such Christians to crossroads, where they will have to choose a master: the present world which is under the god of the age, Satan, where a person will find themselves in a barren wilderness of drudgery or the creator of the world, Jesus Christ, where they will discover the abundant life.

God's goal is to separate each of us with His various tools such as trials, adversities and sorrow. He uses them to separate us from the flimsy fig leaves of lame excuses for an inept, powerless life, the decaying rags of lifeless dead works, and the heavy robe of self-righteous piousness to ensure we possess the life of Christ as we put on His life daily to walk in the light of it.

Life is meant to be experienced and that means the good with the bad, the joy with sorrow, and the anguish with hope. We often times have to step outside of what we are used to, risk what we can't control, and trust what we know is true in order to experience all aspects of life before we can know what constitutes real life, enjoy the simple things, recognize what is important, value what is often overlooked, and be inspired by what we often take for granted.

I ask myself, am I living life or trying to just get by until something better comes along. Picking from the world and choosing certain aspects of the Christian life to try to have the best of both worlds results in having the worst of the world and missing the best of Christianity.

We only have one life to live and the only way we are going to survive this present world is to know that we have an eternal destiny and that it is not about getting by until something better comes along. It is about possessing as much of the heavenly and eternal life we can so that when we enter glory, it will be as natural to us as entering a familiar room in our home.

There are fruits to carnality and in *1 Corinthians 3,* the Apostle Paul takes on this state. There were schisms because the people identified with those who baptized them to validate childish elitism and cliques, rather than to the one who saved them, Jesus. They valued the intelligence of man more than the revelation of God.

They could easily become caught up with the vanity of the fading glory of the flesh and the world instead of preparing for the glory of the next. They were self-sufficient, making them deficient in discerning what was of God. They ignored sin in their midst and were instructed to address it, and separate it out from among the congregation until there was true repentance. They aired their disputes in the public courts of the world instead of humbling themselves to seek out godly counsel to maintain their Christian witness.

These carnal Christians were surface in their devotion, causing them to become judgmental in their attitude and show indifference to needs among the brethren. They upheld lifeless customs instead of maintaining the true spirit of the Christian life. They went after what they perceived would exalt them in the church, instead of seeking ways in which they could truly serve the church. The main problem with carnality is that it is man-centered and not Christ centered.

Even though we are called out of the world, carnal Christians have not left the ways of the world, allowing them to operate in the ways of the flesh. The flesh is doomed and the world stands judged and we have been called to count this life as dung and to come out from the world so that we can be spared of tasting the judgment that is upon it. As believers we need to remember the world is our enemy, not our friend and it has nothing of substance to offer us, but requires us to pay with our very souls. There is only one solution when it comes to carnality and that is, we need to repent, face God and ask Him to give us the compelling desire to let all carnality fall to the wayside so that we can begin to grow up in the knowledge of Jesus Christ.

It took more than a few years for God to reveal the level of my pride. I have to admit, I was shocked to see how it infiltrated every nook and cranny of the "old man" that was ever ready to be resurrected from the grave, and memorialized as it was once again nailed to the cross to keep it from taking center stage of attraction to avoid giving it some type of consideration or audience as to its importance. Pride was the springboard to wrong attitudes, the throne upon which the self-life sits, the wretched prejudice behind my opinions, the blinding bias in my judgments, and the arrogant pinnacle to any superiority and conclusions I dearly held too.

It is for this reason God's Word warns each Christian to avoid being an expert because in the end we will be found to be a fool, thinking more highly of ourselves than we should, and when we fall into the trap of thinking we are standing, we need to know we are about to fall (*Romans 12:3; 1 Corinthians 10:12; Galatian 6:3*). The only way I keep myself from falling into the prideful traps of my flesh and the world is to remember that God's presentation of truth is simple and that instead of embracing it with child-like faith, it is easy to fall into one of the prideful traps to understand and control the narrative of it so I can look wise and clever, ultimately complicating it.

That is why Paul told the bickering Corinthians who were standing on their arrogance, fighting over neutral ground of the non-essential, and choosing sides against each other over a moot point that he wanted to know nothing among them except Christ and Him crucified (*1 Corinthians 2:2*). I learned my great challenge is not to get it right and make sure everyone agrees with me, but to make sure I am right before the Lord in my attitude, holding to what is pure and important to Him, and making sure the ground I am standing on is upheld by the immovable Rock of Ages.

Don't get me wrong, as long as I am in this body, humility is a route I must choose to keep pride from gaining its place of importance in my life. I must say the activity of nailing the old to my personal cross is a daily occurrence, but choosing the route of humility is one I must choose when it comes to lining up to the will of God and simply choosing the ways of righteousness. This route includes being willing to be wrong, especially when you were of a wrong spirit, giving up the right to be right to avoid being wrong where you have to actually humble yourself before those who you have demanded your way with, admit it, and possibly even repent of it while being broken over the fact that your prideful knowledge and reputation was exalted over the things of God.

Too many times platforms such as Facebook become a place where Christians quibble over non-essential points and personal agendas and the world takes note of it and mocks us. That is why I try to keep focus on Jesus' words in *John 12:32, "And I, if I be lifted up from the earth, will draw all men unto me."*

What kind of person are you? There are four types of men in this world, the worldly man like Cain, the fleshly man like Ishmael, the earthly man like Esau, or the spiritual man like the man, Christ Jesus. The difference between these men comes down to their preference.

Cain preferred to live life on his terms, according to his own code and he became angry and murderous when challenged by a righteous man. Some can be like Ishmael, a son of bondage to the ways of the flesh who is fierce and knows nothing but war. Such a person will mock that which is attached to the Promised Son.

Then there is Esau who would be recognized as a man's man, but he sold his birthright because he did not value it. Finally, you have Jesus whose main emphasis was doing the Father's will, His focus was the cross, and His preference was what was righteous and excellent.

As you study these different men, you realize the first three can have an appearance of being religious, but they know nothing of Spirit and truth. For example, Cain offered a sacrifice that spoke of his best, but his heart was far from God. Ishmael was a son of a righteous man but his relationship was fleshly, his preferences pagan, and his inheritance associated with the age he lived in. Esau showed remorse, but could not find a place of repentance because his was a worldly sorrow that was void of brokenness over his indifference to the matters of God.

In a world where these three types of carnal, worldly individuals seem plenteous, even among the religious, as believers we must strive to become the spiritual man, who walks in the Spirit, values our spiritual inheritance above all else, chooses the ways of righteousness, is indifferent to the world, and only cares about pleasing our God.

We are told in *2 Corinthians 2:11* that we are not ignorant of the devices of Satan. We know that lies (robbers), slanders or accusations (killers), and murders (destruction) are well-known devices he uses, but there is another device that is very effective in robbing us of authority in the world, killing our credibility as a saint before others and murdering our witness as a believer, and that is DIVISION.

Jesus was clear, a house divided against itself will fall. The Apostle Paul rebuked the church at Corinth for the members' schisms over fleshy (carnal) issues. He told them that it was clear they were still on milk (doctrine) and had failed to develop the teeth for meat (God's will) (*1 Corinthians 3:1-3,* refer to *John 4:34; Hebrews 5:11-14*). What can we learn from the Corinthians when it comes to division?

At the core of schisms is always some elitism where a person or a group perceives they are better, correct, and have a corner on a matter over the others who are being classified as stupid, inferior, lower class, substandard, and dispensable. If they are stupid, the truth is beyond them, if they are inferior, they are incapable of getting it, if they are a lower class, they do not deserve it, if they are substandard, they will never obtain it, and if they are dispensable, they can be cast aside without any consideration for their person, feelings, or significance they might play in the scheme of things.

At the core of elitism is pride that is competitive, jealous, self-righteous, judgmental, indifferent, and treacherous. Since it is carnal it is petty such as in the case of the Corinthians. Their division was based on who influenced them in their faith: Apollo or Paul.

Paul reminded them that they were both ministers of the Lord Jesus Christ. He also told them that he may have planted the seeds of life among them and Apollo had watered them, but it is God who gave the increase. The truth is that most division among Christians is not caused by the sharp sword of the truth, but by disagreement over non-essential doctrine that may affect one's attitude, causing a superior attitude to arise, possibly opening a door to a wrong spirit, but such doctrine can't save anyone. Doctrine does not save, only the person of Jesus Christ and that is why pure doctrine will always point people back to Jesus.

Division is not only carnal and petty, but it is unprofitable. The fruits from it are miserable and it becomes clear in due time, no one benefits from it because it plants seeds of discord among the brethren which God hates. In Christ we are one and the place of true unity for every believer is the Holy Spirit and the point of truth is Jesus. His cross reveals we are all in the same boat because of sin, His redemption reminds us we are all bought with the same price which points out there is no partiality, and what is inferior is exalted to the same footing, what is considered lower is brought higher, what is substandard is perfected by the Spirit, and what is considered dispensable is reminded of God's great love for all at the cross, and that the great Shepherd Jesus always goes after that one lost sheep.

JUDGMENT

No word is God's final word. Judgment,
far from being absolute, is conditional.
A change in man's conduct brings about
a change in God's judgment.
(Abraham J. Heschel)

When we study Israel in the Old Testament, we can see that God was rarely sought when the people were looking for a deliverer from oppressive government. Sadly, in their desperation to be delivered, they came into unholy agreements with pagan nations who might deliver them from one oppressor, only to bring them under their oppression. During the final siege on Jerusalem in 586 BC, the Jewish leadership turned back to their former oppressors, Egypt, to deliver them from Babylon. Keep in mind, the oppressor is the one who decides who will be in leadership, which is nothing but a puppet government that must carry out their wishes.

God, out of mercy, will judge the nation first to humble the people and separate the remnant, but if the leadership continues down the same wicked path of doing business as usual, the next judgment will be on the leadership. Just before Jerusalem fell to the Babylonian army the third and final time, the prophet Jeremiah came to King Zedekiah and instructed him what to do to avoid utter defeat and destruction. Even though Zedekiah knew the prophet was right, he chose to take his chances, knowing it meant the total destruction of Jerusalem. And, why was he willing to sacrifice his country, citizens, and city?

Imagine, the decision of one leader brought down a kingdom and for what reason? It was because Zedekiah feared the disapproval of the Jewish leadership more than God. When God shakes and judges a nation, the hearts of the leaders will be tested and exposed. The foolish wicked will plan and scheme to hold on to their darkness, the weak and fearful will give way to the bullying of tyranny, and the half-hearted will try to make a deal, often leaving, if any, a few brave souls to stand against the wicked tide.

Remember, it only takes the right decision of one brave leader to ensure mercy and deliverance of a people. Is the major part of the leadership of our nation about to be judged? If so, it will be completely purged by God, and whosoever remains on the sinking ship will go down with it. The final results of such purging are best described after the destruction of Jerusalem, *"every one that passeth thereby shall be astonished, and wag his head" (Jeremiah 18:16).*

The subject of judgment is hard for some to face because there is confusion about it. Judgment comes down to separation from something to something. Judgment entails testing the quality of something to reveal what is true, just, and right. This is why believers are told to do righteous judgment *(John 7:24).*

There are three major judgments mentioned in Scripture. Judgment begins with the house of God and each believer's works will be tested by fire to see if they are pure gold, refined silver, or precious stone or if they are of inferior quality due to a profane mixture of the flesh and the world. Profane works will be consumed by fire *(1 Peter 4:17,18; 1 Corinthians 3:11-15).* Even though such works may be consumed, the person will still get into heaven, but he or she will be void of any rewards and will have nothing to offer back to our Lord for His glory.

The second type of judgment will be that of the nations *(Matthew 25:31-46).* The great test for the nations will come down to how they treated the Lord's brethren, Israel and it will be at that time that the nations will be separated as a Shepherd would separate His real sheep from independent, wild goats, whose destiny will be damnation.

The third judgment is the Great White Throne Judgment *(Revelation 20:11-15).* This is where every unredeemed sinner, wicked, and evil person's dark deeds will be brought to the light as an indictment to their utter guilt before our Holy God. It is at this time the person will be cast into the Lake of fire along with death and hell.

There are three tools that God uses to judge: consequences, chastisement, and wrath. Consequences are designed to bring a person to a point of decision as to the way he or she is going to choose to walk in. In other words, there will be no one straddling the fence or walking in the middle of the road to try to maintain the best of this present world and heaven.

Chastisement is for God's people so they will partake of holiness, and God's wrath has always, and continues, to abide upon all children of disobedience. God uses consequences to shake, chastisement to humble, and wrath to put an end to evil schemes. I believe that America is now paying consequences for allowing the One who blessed this country to be cast aside. I also perceive that the lukewarm church is beginning to taste God's chastisement for failing to be the light, but I also sense that God's wrath is about to fall on certain groups of people and areas for their wicked ways and evil schemes.

Judgment is happening in everyone's life and the wise thing to do is to discern whether we are being separated from this world in light of gaining a greater resurrection in the next, or are we paying consequences for foolishness, or God forbid, are we abiding under His wrath because we are nothing but tools of Satan?

I spoke of chastisement yesterday. There is also another side to chastisement and it is silence. When a Christian shows utter contempt towards God's holy standard by knowingly, willingly fornicating themselves in some way, while deluding themselves that God will certainly understand and they will ask for forgiveness later, God will become silent.

This silence either means the person is not really a child of God and is being turned over to complete delusion, blinded to the ruin that awaits them, or that God has turned them over to the severity of the consequences that will bring them to the point of utter destruction as a means to save their soul.

The REALITY of judgment is that God is a consuming fire, and that is why the Bible states that it is a fearful thing to fall into the hands of the living God. As Christians our life is hidden in Christ. We may pay consequences, but we will never have to pay the great debt for our sin, that of spiritual death and separation from God. Instead of judgment, God has offered each of us mercy that comes by way of pardon by offering His Son up in our place.

There are times He will chastise us and even though it causes bitterness and anguish for a short time, it brings us such glorious joy and hope as we realize we are indeed His children. As far as God's consuming fire, it points to His wrath.

In Christ we are placed above this wrath, which means we will be spared from it. As believers, we must not be casual, flippant, or ignorant about God's judgment. We must recognize that the only safe place is being hidden in Him, walking in His Spirit, and adhering to His perfect ways.

When it comes to making correct judgment calls about something, what do you rely on the most? Some people rely on analytical deductions, others on how something makes them feel, some on logic, and others facts. Clearly, to those who use such measures they can't see how they could be wrong in their final conclusions or analysis. It is for this reason the Bible tell us the ways of a man seem clean to him because he has done all he can to come up with the right conclusions.

The problem does not necessarily rest with the particular mode one operates in to come to some type of understanding, but rather from the premise, or the spirit, in which they begin. If one does not start in the right spirit from the premise of truth, deductions will prove to be inadequate and stifled, feelings unstable and perverted, logic self-serving and foolish, and facts unreliable and presumptuous.

I, for one, desire truth, but I know that often my present, undesired reality is the only way to face and embrace truth, and that most likely my pride will end up being insulted, my flesh resentful, and my inclination ready to run in the opposite direction. Our present reality can be earth-shaking but it is meant to wake us out of comfort zones, from a comatose state of indifference, and a complacent attitude towards spiritual matters. It is only in a humbled spirit that my premise will begin to line up to the truth of a matter so that I can properly face the present reality and take steps of faith to overcome personal obstacles in order to be victorious in my walk.

Our judgment calls mean nothing if we do not start in the right spirit from the premise of truth that will be upheld by God's Word. We must be careful not to take ourselves to serious while soberly discerning the spirit and testing the conclusion.

As we seek to make proper judgment calls, we have to realize that we see through a dark premise that can taint, pervert, and defile what we see, hear, and understand. It is the sharpness of truth that cuts away the blinders from off the soul, the penetration of truth that awakens the spirit, and the clarity of truth that will enable us to walk in the right way.

I have learned that I can't discern the truth of a matter until I am honest about my present reality, my thoughts, feelings, opinions, and the happenings around me. It is natural to ignore, resent, rage against, and mock unpleasant realities, but such responses point to being a captive to the darkness and not a child of the light.

As a Christian, I am a child of the light and I must walk in it by faith if I am going to come to a place of freedom. However, love walks hand and hand with faith and I must choose with all of my heart to love the truth, the righteous ways, and the loving, caring, sacrificial heart of God towards the seeking, lost, and hurting souls of this present world.

What sources do you rely on to interpret what you hear and what you see? Jesus warned that we must beware of how we hear a matter because it could become a point of judgment.

How many of you realize that you are determining how you perceive, understand, and assimilate information, whether it is secular or spiritual? How many of you are aware that you can interpret information based on feelings, opinions, attitudes, and the predominate mood of the day? Are such gauges reliable? The answer is no.

Feelings are unstable like the waves on the ocean, opinions can be indifferent to what is really going on, attitudes can be influenced by some type of bias, and foul moods point to a wrong spirit. Either of the four premises mentioned point to a person mishandling the truth in a destructive way.

God has made truth available in His Word to bring clarity and to take away the incessant arguments and debates that man often gets into over non-essential beliefs, causes, and agendas, but the problem rests with the fact that man determines whether he is going to accept God's truth as being so, adjust it to fit into his narrative, or discard it altogether?

Truth serves as a line in the sand of time. It will always be what it is, and in the end, it will be standing when all other narratives will be bought to utter ruin. We are coming up to what is considered a possible turning point in our nation. It is called an election, and please, I am not looking to start a debate. What you believe and what you vote for is between you and your conscience.

The Bible tells us to stand for what is true, right and pure, and it you think about it, an election is the one place where we can take a stand for what we know is right. As a Christian I can't wear different hats. For example, I can't lay my Christianity aside in order to support someone or something that is blatantly contrary to God, His Scriptures, and His ways. Whether it is in the pew, the pulpit, the streets, or the ballot box, my stands must remain the same or I will find a hypocrite staring back at me when I look into the mirror.

I want to encourage each Christian to take a stand, but when you do, check out your loyalty. Is your loyalty to what you think is so, what you feel is so, what you desire to be so, what you insist on being so, or is it towards God and His truth?

Recently I asked if we as a nation were ready to be shaken by the events around us. No doubt we are in the midst of great shaking. In such times people will become fearful, indifferent, and angry as they look around to point a finger at someone instead of holding on to what is true and look up to the One who is the solution.

From past experiences, I've learned that it is after all misdirected hope lies shattered in the shallow ground of doubts and insecurity that our real Hope, the Lord Jesus steps on the scene and brings forth what He has declared. Meanwhile the great shaking goes on and people must come to terms with what they really believe.

Recently, I was asked how are we to respond to the wicked. I dealt with some of this yesterday because there can be confusion. Jesus said we are to pray for our enemy, but what enemy? We have personal enemies, civil enemies, and national enemies. Personal enemies are those individuals who have personally offended us. Jesus' response to such enemies was, "Forgive them for they know what they do." Clearly, these enemies rarely realize that they offend us because as humans we can be quite touchy or clueless. This is when the love of God covers a multitude of such offenses and allows us to become peacemakers that regard the well-being of our enemies as of the utmost importance to God; thereby, allowing us to be sensitive as to how we are to respond: intercession or ministry.

The next enemy I want to consider are the lawless that rebel against society. Whether it is stealing, killing, or destroying, they prove offensive to the quality of life. In some cases, their offenses may not directly touch us but eventually they can cause a collapse of society. Our response is if the lawless have touched our lives personally, we must forgive them and pray that God keeps our attitude right towards such an individual in order to be sensitive to how the Lord might direct us in ministry.

As a body, we must pray for their souls as we avail ourselves to be a source of ministry whether it is through an organization or personal involvements. Our goal is to expose these individuals to the Gospel for the salvation of their souls.

The third enemy are those in high places. Do we pray for such enemies and if so how? Let me respond by asking, can we pray that God blesses Satan? These individuals are often the tools of Satan. We can't pray that God blesses such an enemy, but as soldiers we can pray that if any be heirs of salvation among them that they be turned over to Satan for the salvation of their souls, but if not, that God exposes their schemes, scatters them, and nullifies their wicked ways, so in the end God will be glorified. It is clear we need to not only know how to use the sword of God, His Word, but how to use the place of authority, and our prayer life, in order to be effective in our intercession.

SERVICE AND WORSHIP

When it comes to the world we live in,
greatness is always born out of the ordinary.
It never begins from that which is already
considered great to the world, but from that
which is considered foolish, base, and despised.
It is from this premise that real greatness is realized.
(Rayola Kelley)

What is in a name? I have been playing along with the game on Facebook that takes your name and tells you things about yourself. I could probably figure some things out about people simply based on their Facebook page because we tend to emphasize those things that touch our heartstrings, post the posts that agree with our opinions, causes, and agendas, as well as will reveal our interests, along with the type of sense of humor we may have. Granted, there are people who have Facebook to keep up with family and friends, but such post shows what these individuals' value.

As most know, I have an unusual name and I have only been aware of a couple of others who have the same name. The question is, does our name define who we are or the character we establish? For the most part what really defines the impression we leave behind will be our character. Granted, the mention of our name may remind others of our person, but the impression people will remember will be based on our character.

In the Bible, names were significant because they may have described an event, or served as a message, warning, or witness. And, we must not forget there are those who feel they need to live up to the reputation of some name whether it is family, favorite sport team, or a hero. However, when it comes to the Lord Jesus Christ, His very name identifies who He is. He is The (one and only) Lord (Adonai—owner) Jesus (Jehovah is our salvation) Christ (the Messiah, the Promised One, the Anointed One).

Jesus was anointed to bring salvation to mankind by the way of redemption and in doing so bought us with a price and now serves as our owner. His name should not only cause our heart to rejoice, but cause our knees to bow in humble adoration as we look up to offer the sacrifice of praise with our lips. When was the last time you allowed His name to bring you to the place of real worship where you communed with Him with sweet adoration?

Our prayer and worship will be determined by the type of relationship we have with the Lord and how we perceive Him. For example, the caliber of worship will come down to how small or big we view God. The more we understand the majesty of God, the more we are apt to worship the Lord in such a way that He is able to receive it.

Many people think too small of God and their worship is either fleshly hype, casually flimsy or childish with silly notions. They bring God down to either some sentimental level or to an intellectual notion that lacks dimension.

There are two ways in which true worship is established. The first one is through brokenness, where man is brought down to the depths of his own depravity and the second one being that of the sacrifice of praise. The first time I experienced real worship in my life was at a point of great brokenness. It was only as I was reduced to bits and pieces by my wretchedness that I was able to look up and begin to see how great God was.

It was then that I realized the bigger I become in my own eyes the smaller God becomes in my sight. It is only when I am out of the way that I can begin to realize the greatness and majesty of God. The beauty of true worship is that it will bring one to the great heights of God, causing the spirit to soar in adoration and the soul to be overwhelmed with awe, while freeing the lips to offer up the sacrifice of praise.

Have you ever thought about what it means to worship? The Old Testament describes four types of worshippers in *Exodus 33*. The tent of meeting (before the tabernacle was constructed) was moved outside of the camp because of Israel's idolatry. The presence of the Lord came down on the tent and it was at that time that these four groups of worshippers were identified.

The first group can be found *in Exodus 33:10, "And all the people saw the cloudy pillar stand at the tabernacle door; and all the people rose up and worshipped, every man in his tent door."* Real worshippers want to be where the presence of God is, but note these individuals were content to stand afar off at their tent door and bow down.

God deserves worship, but real worship requires a heart response where one comes out and separates themselves from their regular duties in order to give God the attention and devotion He deserves. I am sure you might know a few people who on Sunday are still back at their "tent" in their heart and are simply going through the motions until they can resume their ordinary lives.

May we not be named among them who fail to come into God's presence to truly worship Him in Spirit and truth.

In the last post I talked about four types of worshippers. It is the tendency to look around during times of worship to see how others are doing it or whether others are failing to do it. The reality is that it is none of our business whether certain individuals are worshipping or not, but it would serve us well to identify the true worshippers to learn from their example even though we know all real worship is a matter of the heart.

When I studied *Exodus 33*, the Lord graciously illuminated four types of worshippers for my benefit. The first one stood at the tent doors and worshipped, but real worship can only occur when we are actually standing in the presence of the Lord, which brings us to the second type of worshipper. The second group is found in *Exodus 33:7, "And Moses took the tabernacle, and pitched it without the camp, off from the camp and called it the Tabernacle of the congregation. And it came to pass, that every one which sought the LORD went out unto the tabernacle of the congregation, which was without the camp."*

The second group are those seeking the Lord. They will follow the true worshipper to the place of worship. Such people are prepared to meet the Lord, and this must be true of everyone who desires to worship the Lord in the right way. They must come out and be separate from the worldly demands and influences as they separate themselves to honor the Lord with their heart.

The third group of worshippers are represented by one man. He was a servant to Moses. He was the only person who followed Moses up to the mountain. Granted, he could not go all the way with Moses but he waited there for Moses until the leader came down from the top of the mount *(Exodus 24:12-13)*. His name was Joshua.

It tells us that even after the presence of the Lord had lifted from the tent of congregation that the son of Nun, a young man, departed **not** out of the tabernacle *(Exodus 33:11)*. It is important to point out that

Joshua's desire to always draw as near to the Lord as he could not only showed his heart towards Jehovah, as in the case of being a faithful servant to Moses, but it also highlighted his calling and preparation to be the military leader that led the children of Israel into the Promised Land.

If a believer's calling is to be realized they must be quick to draw near to the Lord as much as possible because it is in that drawing that a person is prepared to walk into his or her calling. True worshippers understand that worship must be evident in all they do including their service to the Lord. Therefore, they are always drawing near to the Lord to ensure they are as close as they can be to what the Lord is doing, and what He desires to do through His servants.

Jesus Christ is our Joshua and He has prepared the way for each of us to realize our high calling in our service to Him, but we must always be rising up out of normal activities to ever draw near to Him in spite of what others are doing and what is going on around us.

I have been writing about the four types of worshippers. The fourth group of worshippers is represented by Moses *(Exodus 33:11)*.

Worship can be compared with the three compartments of the Old Testament Tabernacle. The first group that stood afar off are those who remain outside of the gate of the tabernacle. They may be looking in and observing, but they never enter through the gate to come to the place of true worship.

The second group is represented by the outer court. They enter into the gate but they have come as far as the first altar of burnt offering but they have not yet entered into the door of service to prepare for worship. Joshua represents those who enter through the door into the Holy Place to avail themselves to serve the Lord in preparation to worship Him.

The final group points to Moses and they enter through the veil into the Most Holy Place to talk to the Lord face to face in sweet communion. Moses' encounter with the Lord shows us it is an individual experience. The collective group will not enter into this place together; rather, it is up to each individual to come to a place of worship and communion with the Lord.

Moses experienced the presence of the Lord and even spoke to Him as face to face, but it was not enough for him, he desired to see God's glory. We are told in *John 4:23* that the Father seeks those who will worship Him in Spirit and truth.

The question is where does my personal worship place me as far as these four groups? I know the second group is seeking to worship and the third is drawing near to worship, but I want to be a Moses who enters into that sweet place of worship and communion with the Lord.

When I consider the purpose and reason for my life, I sense awe reaching up from my spirit. When I was a junior in high school, I sensed I had some type of destiny. I didn't know what it was, but I knew that if my life was going to make sense that I had to discover what it was.

After high school, I tried to calculate what my destiny was and attempted to bring it about with utter defeat. It was only after I became a born-again believer of Jesus Christ that I realized that my destiny was not attached to the present world but to that which is eternal. However, I had to rid myself of hindering, worldly and even religious notions before I could begin to understand my purpose.

I first had to walk through some trials and tribulations, and it was through personal struggles that I began to understand my real destiny: I had to know God through Jesus Christ. It was knowing God that helped me to realize that my real destiny was to bring glory to God in everything I do.

The problem I encountered is that we humans are so earth-bound, and because of it we must develop an inward life of praise and worship to bring such glory to our Creator. It is true, praise that sets the mind free to embrace the majesty of God in greater ways is real worship that allows one to see the heart of God. We must see His heart so that we can know what will please Him, and it is only those things that God can find pleasure in that serve as points of real worship of Him that will truly bring glory to Him.

As believers we must discern who or what we are worshipping. Jesus made it clear to the Samaritan woman she did not know who she worshipped *(John 4:22)*. The problem is if we do not really know the God of the Bible, we end up worshipping an image of Him that we have created in our mind.

Wherever ignorance reigns concerning God, it is natural to fill in the blanks with religious notions about God. We can even be quite sentimental about the image we have erected and become emotional as we become worked up over our devotion to the image, but we are not worshipping the true God in Spirit and truth.

We must never be casual about our worship. We must not be content with the idea that if religion is present, sentiment can be stirred up, and emotions can reach a certain hype that we are worshipping the Lord. As stated, we may be worshipping the image, the idea, or the feeling, but we are failing to worship the one, true God which ends up becoming idolatrous.

It is important to discern if we are worshipping the true God or paying homage to something that has been erected by an imagination that has been running amiss because of ignorance.

The Samaritan woman at the well in *John 4* asked a very important question that was a matter of her heart. She was clearly a sinner that was most likely being shunned by the community that had made her a subject of gossip when they gathered at the well for water. However, this woman had a question that Jesus had come to answer. He met her in the heat of the day when she alone would draw near to the well.

Even though her lifestyle revealed her fallen condition and unacceptable actions, she still possessed a question that was of the utmost importance to those who want to really worship the Lord. Her question was where should one worship, at Jerusalem like the Jews or at Mount Gerizim like her people.

Jesus made it clear that the place does not matter, but the spirit in which it is done and whether it leads to the true God does. It is a tendency for man to worship the Lord from a fleshly premise, but the Lord is clear that the flesh must not be present and that the Holy Spirit is the only means in which a person can properly offer worship that will be acceptable to the Lord.

The story of the Samaritan woman always amazes me. She was honest about her sin, receptive to Jesus' words, and displayed a child-like faith. The reason I say this is because she perceived Jesus was a true prophet because of what He revealed about her lifestyle, but she also believed something else. Consider what she said, *"I know that Messias cometh, which is called Christ: when he is come, he will tell us all things" (John 4:25).*

Since she perceived that Jesus was a true prophet, she felt the liberty to ask Him a question about worship, but she also believed the Messiah was coming and He would answer all questions. Think about the implication. She believed in the Messiah and the One who stood before her she perceived to be a prophet. She knew that both could answer her question, but she knew that the Messiah would answer all of her questions.

People claim Jesus remained silent about who He was, but consider what He said to this woman, "I that speak unto thee am he." In other words, He claimed He was the Messiah. Did this woman believe she was standing before the Messiah?

Her response might answer the question, she left off what she was doing and became an evangelist that went to the city to the men and made this statement, *"Come, see a man, which told me all things that ever I did: is not this the Christ?"*

The Samaritan woman shows us that the Lord not only wants to answer the questions of the heart, but He is the only one who really can.

Are you choosing better things? Being in a physical body and living in this world can confuse our desires, appetites, and priorities, complicating our choices. The world can easily redirect our desires for the things of heaven, causing us to look for and pursue temporary things according to the world's propaganda. Sadly, the change can be so subtle that we don't even recognize it until the world leaves us empty and our walk leads us into one dead end after another, leaving us in despair and disillusioned.

This brings us back to choosing better things. In *Luke 10:38-42* we read about two examples: Martha and Mary. Martha was a servant at heart and was willing to serve Jesus in a physical, practical way. Where she ran into problems was when she began to judge Mary's response to Jesus. We must remember some are called to immediate service and some are being prepared to serve. Martha's service was necessary, while Mary's service was yet to come.

Practical service allows for future service, but present service must never become a judge of those who are being prepared. Mary was being prepared to anoint Jesus for His burial, and for Jesus to put matters in perspective for the anxious Martha who was judging Mary according to worldly notions, He stated this about Mary, *"But one thing is needful and Mary hath chosen that good part, which shall not be taken away from her."*

Practical service is necessary, but when it comes to future service, it is needful for the person to be prepared in order to ensure that when the time comes the servant will be able to properly fulfill his or her calling.

In the last post, I spoke of practical, needful service and of those being prepared for service. Some served at tables while others sat at the table in preparation to serve in another capacity. As for Mary she was being prepared to anoint Jesus for His burial. It would cost her personally.

Remember Mary became a target for Judas Iscariot to criticize and some Bible scholars suggest the oil she poured on Jesus to anoint Him, was for her own burial. It is important to note the place where Mary was prepared for this time; where she appealed to the Lord after her brother's death, and where she ultimately ended up serving Jesus—at His feet (*Luke 10:39; John 11:32; 12:3*).

The main purpose of service is to exalt Jesus. Whether it is a Martha preferring Jesus' basic needs over her needs, or a Mary falling at His feet and anointing Him, all true service will bring honor and glory to the Lord. If we are desiring the spotlight of recognition for some act, we will find ourselves touching His glory and losing the blessing.

It is important to understand practical service to Jesus requires faithfulness, but prepared service requires communion. Mary was prepared for service at the feet of Jesus, seeking Him in humility and listening to Him in preparation of being at the right place at the right time to ensure His will was carried out.

Are you in need of preparation for a time such as this? If so, preparation will be done at the communion table in humility with a prayerful attitude.

What is the inspiration behind your service to God and your worship of Him? It is natural to want to serve God on our terms and worship Him according to our sentimental notions about Him. But, as the Apostle Paul's writing recently reminded me, the things of God are spiritual, and due to our inherent state passed down from Adam, we are carnal, sold under sin until we taste the liberation of Jesus' redemption.

God is Spirit and truth. He does not operate on any carnal, fleshly level. He is not beholden to any law, man, or principle. Granted, He will never step outside of who He is and He will keep all of His promises, but He is not bound by the earthly, accountable to the fleshly, or subject to sentimental whims and notions of man.

Sadly, man is always trying to bring God down to the carnal level in order to comprehend His ways, control His doings, and understand His thinking to manipulate the narrative. Man refuses to simply believe what the Word says, willingly submit to what is godly, and choose that which is righteous and excellent.

As Christians we abide in a fleshly abode that can be bombarded by various temptations and we are in a world that is an enemy of God, but we are called to be a spiritual man. There is only one point of identification when it comes to the spiritual man and that is the Holy Spirit in us. It matters little how pious, religious or decent we are, without the Holy Spirit, we still remain earthbound, enslaved to the carnal and the temporary, and self-righteous at best in our futile attempts to be righteous and good.

How many of you wondered how could God ever use you? I remember asking God how could He consider me in my failure, use me in my pathetic state, and put up with me in my selfish mode. It is not unusual to look from the outside at the men and women of God, while secretly coveting their life that speaks of courage, overcoming, and victory. It is easy to fail as believers to see that we have examples of ordinary men becoming part of something extraordinary.

We judge their feats by events; rather, than recognize that they were mere individuals who decided to simply trust their sovereign God Almighty. When it came to David, he recognized that the battle belonged to the Lord and Daniel knew to seek God first before resorting to the state of fear after being threatened with death for something beyond His control. Like Elisha, he gave up the ordinary to follow after the extraordinary and ended up receiving a double mantle of Elijah when it came to his calling. In spite of losing it all, Job held on to his faith towards God and his integrity. When you consider the list in *1 Corinthians 1:23-31* as to who God uses and why, you realize that the only thing that would disqualify any of us from being used is that we dare perceive ourselves of having something of value to add to the Lord's work.

In my initial years as a Christian, I was arrogant enough to try to offer the Lord something and it turned out, for the most part, to be useless. It was after I faced the extent of myself as a fallen creature that I realized I had nothing to offer.

The more I faced the emptiness of the self-life, the more available I became as a vessel and instrument of God to be used by Him. I am a mere vessel, normal at best, cracked at worst but since I possess the fragrance of Christ's life, I am a sanctified vessel ready to be used for His glory. I am a tarnished instrument, but once the Master picks me up, beautiful music can come from my life that will prove to be a sweet sacrifice to Him. The truth I learned is that I had to quit looking to self for worth, and look up to the One who alone is worthy of all praise, knowing that every good gift that is acceptable to God and beneficial to others comes from the Father above (*James 1:17*).

As stated in my last post, I struggled with being a "good" Christian. It was only in a state of humility that I could accept the fact that after reading the qualifications of *1 Corinthians 1:23-29*, I was a good candidate for God to actually use. It is natural for us to start out our Christian life thinking we know what it means to be Christian, which often comes down to our concept of religion, but the Bible is clear that the wisdom that comes from the fleshly arena will perceive the wisdom from above as being foolish.

Heavenly wisdom can make us a spectacle to the world because it rests on what is unseen and what proves to be mysterious at times, and beyond comprehension at other times. It is normal to strive for some type of personal excellency or perfection in our strength when it comes to being a Christian, but such perfection can never come out of self-effort, because self-effort is not based on child-like faith that simply enters through the entrance of the person, work, and ministry of Christ by faith in order to walk out the Christian life through obedience to His Word.

In our flesh we want to appear noble about what we do for the Lord, but such nobility puts a spotlight on us instead of the one who is worthy of all exaltation, and He will not share His glory with another. We often complicate our Christian life by trying to overcompensate for our failures, climb above our pathetic state with our own merits, and silence our selfishness with good works but all such things still point back to our best, which God's Word describes as filthy rags in *Isaiah 64:6*.

Paul discovered that the Way, Jesus Christ, was the true light to wisdom and truth, that in weakness God's grace was what proved to be sufficient in all things, and that the simplicity of Christ and His gospel were not based as the world implied and although despised by the world, led to real salvation.

Paul understood the real essence of wisdom was Jesus who was/is the Word. He knew that Jesus was the summary of all righteousness to those who truly hunger and thirst for it, the place of sanctification for the spiritual sojourner, and the fullness of redemption for the spiritual pilgrim who will not be content until they reach their ultimate destination.

In the past, I asked three questions where Satan was concerned. What is his main target? As pointed out in a previous post, it is man's faith. The second question I asked is what is he after? Satan's main target is man's faith because without undermining or stripping man of genuine faith towards God, he will not succeed in obtaining what he is after from you and me. And, just what is he after? He is after WORSHIP.

The devil wants to be honored, adored, obeyed, and preferred. It is not important how he is worshipped, directly as done in the occult, witchcraft and covens, or indirectly as in idolatry, cult practices, and through such tactics as fear, obsession, and possession. It is important to point out something about worship. It is the arrogance of pride of both Satan and man that desires worship, but since neither deserve it, it becomes a pinnacle that is prized and strived for but once it is reached, it ends up being hollow.

All worship that is not directed at God is idolatrous or perverted worship. Perversion in any arena leaves behind delusion, frustration, emptiness, disillusionment, and desperation. In order to be worshiped, Satan has to gain some inroad into man's soul to take him captive. As he did in the Garden of Eden, with our first parents, he continues to use one of the three arenas of the world *(1 John 2:15-17)*.

There are three avenues that Satan used to gain inroads into our souls. One I have already mentioned is pride, but the other two are the flesh and the eyes. To give in to the flesh is to lust after something, ultimately MAKING it god, to give in to the pride is to BOW before a tyrannical god, but to give way to the eyes is to EXALT something as god.

Jesus was tempted in the wilderness the same way as Eve was in the garden, but He overcame Satan in all three areas. In the area of the flesh, He established that the Word of God was the source and sustainer of His life, not the world. When it came to pride, Jesus stated that He would not give in to what I refer to as an idolatrous, childish dare (the ways of pride) by having God prove He is who He is because HE IS GOD.

Let's just consider the last temptation because it reveals the ultimate goal of all temptation. Satan took Jesus to a high mountain and shewed Him the glory of all of his worldly kingdoms and take note of what Satan said, "All of these things will I give thee, if thou will fall down and worship me." In other words, sell your soul and bow down and worship me and I will give you the false glitter, the temporary glory of my kingdoms that are already doomed. And, what was Jesus' reply, *"Get thee hence, Satan for it is written, Thou shall worship the Lord thy God, and him only shalt thou serve" (Matthew 4:10).*

I have asked three questions and two of them have been answered. The first question is what is Satan's main target and the answer is man's FAITH. The second question is what is he after, WORSHIP, and the final question is what is his ultimate goal? The answer is to wipe out anyone who dares to REFLECT the glory of God.

It is important to remember what man was created for: to reflect God's glory in creation. Mankind was to serve as the crowning glory of God. The concept of being such a crown points to true worship that will honor God in His holiness, stand in awe of His majesty, be humbled by His greatness, be overwhelmed by His power, and be consumed by His love. This is the essence of every saint's high calling.

Each of us have been called to be part of and serve as God's holy priesthood in this world. We are to be reflectors of the life of His Son in order to serve as living letters and examples as to the excellent ways of His righteousness. We are part of a holy nation that does not belong to this world, will not fit in the ways of this world, and will never be confused by where our loyalty rests.

As believers it takes believing faith to receive this reality as our true calling, obedient faith to walk in such a calling, and an abiding faith to truly rest in the promises of it regardless of the chaos and destruction taking place around us. I have made reference to this Scripture, but let us consider it again, *"And they overcame him (the devil) by the blood of the Lamb, and by the word of their testimony, and they loved not their lives unto the death" (Revelation 12:11).*

It is important to realize how each aspect of a victorious Christian life is clearly laid out in this Scripture. The blood of the Lamb points to God's great love and commitment to redeem us and make us a part of an everlasting covenant. We have been bought with a price and we do not belong to ourselves and it is in this knowledge we have authority to STAND against all false claims upon our lives.

It is because of redemption we now have a personal testimony of Christ that cannot be refuted by the world. This testimony is living and growing as we grow in Christ, thereby, reflecting His glory, allowing us to WITHSTAND the devices of the enemy.

Since all belongs to Christ, we continually offer up our bodies to be living sacrifices for His glory. As martyrs, (witnesses) we are walking towards our demise in the present world in order to gain the glory of the unseen. It is our continual offering of this present life by faith that allows us to CONTINUE TO STAND in light of the promises of the next world.

A few days back I spoke of lifting up Jesus. I realize that those who minister the truths of God on public platforms are reaching out to certain types of people. For instance, there are the evangelists who are trying to reach the lost and stir up any sleeping Christian. There are teachers who are trying to challenge and disciple those who want to grow in their knowledge of Jesus, there are watchmen who are establishing the only foundation that will withstand the test of the storms of this age, and there are those who are trying to establish an indelible witness of the person and work of Jesus.

When studying the different ministries of people in the Bible, you begin to realize the warnings of Isaiah's for our time will probably fall on dull ears; and due to worldly conditioning and seductive indoctrination that the Pauls of our time will express frustration because many refuse to spiritually grow up and graduate from the milk stage to the meat; and those who are Jude will forever contend for the faith that was first delivered to the saints because of the incessant pet doctrines that are promoted along with New Age methods, worldly gospels, and heresies.

I could go on and on, but we must realize the multi-faceted work of the body of believers when it comes to establishing pure doctrine, a sure foundation, and unfeigned faith in the pig pen of the world. And what constitutes pure doctrine? Jesus stated in *John 7:16-17*, *"My doctrine is not mine, but his that sent me. If any man will do his will, he shall know of the doctrine, whether it be of God, or whether I speak of myself. He that speaketh of himself seeketh his own glory: the same is true, and no unrighteousness is in him."* In fact, you can find the six principal doctrines of Christ in *Hebrews 6:1-2* and if your pet doctrine does not fall within these six principal doctrines that will always bring you back to the real, simplicity of the work, goal, and purpose of redemption, it is a non-essential doctrine that lacks authority and significance.

When it comes to the foundation, you are either standing on shifting sand of the world or the Rock of ages Jesus Christ (*1 Corinthians 3:11*). As for unfeigned faith, *2 Corinthians 13:5* instructs us to, *"Examine yourselves, whether ye be in the faith; prove your own selves. Know ye not your own selves, how that Jesus Christ is in you, except ye be reprobates."*

The true Gospel is about Christ and Him crucified, the emphasis is Christ's redemption, and the true agenda must be to see God glorified as His will is truly carried out according to the complete counsel of His Word.

CHARACTER

What is left standing when
all has been shaken: **TRUTH.**
What is left standing when all
has been tested: **UNFEIGNED FAITH.**
What is left stand when all
has failed: **GODLY CHARACTER.**
(Rayola Kelley)

One of the interesting principles found in Scripture is that the first will be last and the last first. I realize there are a few ways you can look at it. For instance, what starts out to be first can end up last and what ends up last can be brought forth in a powerful way as being first.

To me this principle reminds me that the counterfeit is often presented first, followed by the one who would be chosen. The first one will be called, but it is usually the second one that will be chosen to fulfill a mission. We see this principle in operation between the first man Adam and the second man, Jesus. We also see it between Cain and Abel and Ishmael and Isaac, and Saul and David.

Even though the children of Israel were first called, the church now stands chosen because of Jesus' redemption. It seems that the first comes across too good to be true. For Adam, he had the potential of reflecting God, but Jesus was the manifestation of deity in human form. Cain had the markings of quite a man of the world, but Abel proved to be the man of God. Esau was the man of the earth, but when the Lord changed Jacob's name to Israel, he became a man that was exalted as a prince among men. Saul was man's choice, but David was God's choice.

We must understand the contrast between the called one and the chosen one. We have met a lot who were called, but we have to step back and wait for God to illuminate those who are chosen. It is a good principle to remember when you are trying to discern what is real and what is an image that has the presentation "down pat," but who fails to walk in the excellent ways of God.

239

It is vital to consider what our preferences say about our character. Preferences are tied into the way we have allowed ourselves to be conditioned. Notice how I noted the words, "allowed ourselves."

When we are young it is natural to be conditioned by family because we assume they know what is best and right, and when we become older (teenagers), we are often conditioned by peers who either put pressure on us in some way to comply or standards on us in order to fit in.

When we become adults, we often fall into the category of presuming that our ideas, logic, or way of doing things are right, but the truth is we must see what is influencing our preferences. Is the flesh influencing our preferences which will naturally cause us to make our choices based on lusts? Is the world influencing our preferences, and if so, will such an influence cause us to make choices about how to get the best out of the world by beating it at its own game without falling into its traps and quagmire? If man's religion influences us the most, it will naturally be more about presenting the right image, while hiding behind a religious garb of self-righteousness to hide the fact that we don't possess the true goods of heaven.

I have allowed myself to be conditioned by all of these things at one time or the other, and the flesh left me a hypocrite, the world caused me to know the emptiness of vanity, and man's religion allowed me to delude myself about my real spiritual condition. It was after I realized I determine who I allow myself to become, I took the reins of my life back from all sources and started to expose myself to the reality of God.

I allowed the Spirit to put His finger on the worldly, the Word of God to expose the insidious side of the flesh, and truth about Jesus to challenge my religion. A good way to know what you prefer is to check out the fruits of your life for they will reveal what is not only conditioning you, but the real character of your preferences.

How easy is it to change one's way of doing something? It depends on what part of your character needs to change. For example, if your concepts need to change it takes undoing what you know with the Word of God and relearning to overcome unbecoming habits or what has become familiar to you to ensure righteousness.

To relearn what seemed so right at one time, but is proving to be ineffective at the present, can be very challenging because it takes consistent discipline until all imagination and thought processes are lined up to Christ and His Word. If it is behavior, you must change your attitude about something but for an attitude to change you must see that it is adverse to what is honorable, destructive to your goals, and ruinous to your testimony.

Changing behavior involves genuine repentance that only occurs when one turns from what was and finally turns to gain God's perspective and come into agreement with Him that a matter is unacceptable to Him, wicked in light of His plan, and evil in the fruits it produces; therefore, it must become completely unacceptable to you. To change your natural response to something, you must be willing to see the wrong behind it regardless of how you feel about it. You must choose to see the carnality in it, and/or the vanity to it, realizing there is no substance to be found in any of it.

The truth is we hate change. What we are used to, and may even complain about, we unknowingly trust that it will never fail us, and what we are familiar with, we may be bored with it, but we can turn on "autopilot" and breeze through without any disturbance. As for changing focus and direction from what is known to the unknown, we can't stop with fear; rather, we must step back and look up with faith towards the One who promises us that He will direct our steps and lift us above it.

Years ago, there was a message given to our fellowship that was clear to those present, "Come higher in Me or you will be consumed by the grave darkness coming upon the world." The "higher in God" means choosing the high road of excellence in all matters, the narrow path of righteousness, the divine ways of godliness, and the attitude of Christ. My prayer is, Lord do not let me drop the ball by allowing Your warnings to fall to the wayside, while selfishly resorting to the base way of the flesh, foolishly broadening the narrow path with excuses, and being willing to stop on the plateaus of compromise because the way is becoming harder and harder for the flesh to maintain its pose and the world to hold on my affections.

It is interesting observing people during these days of testing, and note that it is a time of testing for the whole world. I have a saying, "the bottom is the bottom," but one never knows when a person will hit it. They might hit other sources and not the bottom.

For example, some bounce back because something catches them along the way, and others find their fall is broken so they don't feel the complete impact when they hit the bottom, and there are those who are determined to not let their fall impact them no matter what transpires. What I have learned about people hitting the bottom is that for this particular experience to be constructive, the inward environment of their character must be prepared to be broken, the circumstances have to be right to ensure the abrupt landing is effective, and the loss has to be correct to bring an awareness of crisis.

It would be nice to avoid the bottom, but for most of us that is the only experience that will make us look up; otherwise, we try to beat the odds, figure our way around or out of circumstances, and resolve that we are not going to let the things of this life get us down. It is natural for people to look everywhere but upwards for a solution towards the Lord.

It is important to realize the purpose for testing is to show us our need for the Lord, reveal our true character, and that we are not in control of our life. The impact is meant to wake us up to what is going on, the breaking is to prepare us to properly respond to the touch of our Master, and the purpose for this experience is so the Lord can have His way in our lives.

As we face this time of testing, let us first of all ask the Lord to have His way no matter what it takes. The next thing we need to do is expect something to happen to bring us to a place of breaking where the proper response, whether it is repentance, humility, or preparedness to face greater testing. And, when the breaking happens, we must let it be so by being willing to submit to it.

Finally, we must always come to the place where we become unwilling to submit to the "norm," the "regular," or "how it was" before we hit bottom. As Christians, the testing experience is to cause us to press forward, while looking up as we focus on the finish line of possessing future glory.

FIGHTING THE GOOD FIGHT

God never wastes anything in our lives.
He uses our challenges to enlarge us to receive more;
our wounds to make us more compassionate;
our failures to make us more realistic,
and our defeats to make us victorious.
In other words, all the hard lessons
from the past can be made into priceless treasures
that strengthen us for each new day and challenge.
(Rayola Kelley)

Ecclesiastes 3:1 and 8 tells us there is a season for all things from war to peace. As we consider the seasons we are in right now, what must we do and what must be our strategy? One of the statements I have heard that is associated with the times we live in is "Brace yourself."

"Brace yourself" is not a call to battle but a call to stand. When I heard this term, I was reminded of being at the ocean when waves were rushing in. To withstand waves, you must prepare yourself to face them head on. If you are not properly prepared for waves, they will knock you down and dangerous riptides will pull you out into deep water. I actually had this happen to me when I was in the Navy serving in Hawaii.

I was standing a distance away from where the last wave receded on the shoreline. I assumed I was out of reach of any incoming waves, but all of a sudden, I found myself being pulled down by a riptide. I remember my body being literally enfolded by a force that was pulling me quickly out to dangerous and deadly waters. One of my friends saw what was happening to me and managed to quickly position his body to stop the rolling motion of mine. That day four young girls' lives were claimed by that same riptide.

The water may look a bit choppy in this world. It may be beautiful to some because of angry waves crashing against the shoreline; and frightening to others because the waves are a bit contentious; but the real danger is underneath the surface that is able to catch those unaware who are not reading the signs of the times. The present waters are precarious; therefore, never underestimate the riptides that are lurking beneath the surface of the present waters that are working to take the unsuspecting out into the waters of judgment.

As Christians we must cease from assuming that the time we are living in is not going to test or affect our lives. We must not presume that we can merrily continue on in our normal or worldly lives and ways while ignoring how many souls are being pulled out by the present riptides into destructive waters.

In order to avoid being cast about in the ocean of present events, we as believers, must by faith honestly face the waves that are coming at us with great force, take a firm stand on who and what we know to be true; that is, our Lord Jesus Christ, and as each wave is about to hit us, we must be ready to lean into them by faith. At this point, we must trust that the Lord is the One who is positioned in front of us, thereby, serving as our breaker against all such forces, while keeping us from being pulled out by the riptides of this world.

Some of you might be asking why must we be prepared to stand instead of fight? The answer is simple, everything that can be shaken by our Lord is being shaken and everything that is not firmly on the Rock will collapse and be taken out by the current tides. During such times the character of our faith will be tested, the dross of our flawed character will come to the top, leaving that which is refined on the bottom in order to be retrieved by the Holy Spirit and shaped as an instrument that God can use for such a time as this.

Standing, for the soldier points to being at attention, ready to march into battle upon command, but until the order comes, we must brace ourselves by simply standing while facing the tidal waves of this time.

As I delve below the surface of the things happening in our world, it becomes very obvious that Satan is the god of this world and that there is a spiritual battle going on of such proportions that it would cause the weak-minded to faint, the whimsical to hide in a dark corner of despair, the gullible to panic, and the wishful thinker to be rendered into a puddle of hopelessness. Let me state, it does not take much delving to become informed and absolutely vexed and repulsed at what has been going on for years.

It seems some Christians are living in a dull state of denial, the comatose state of indifference, the ignorant state of wishful thinking, or the gullible state where all tides are capable of taking them away from the Rock of truth, the shorelines of reality, and the stability of the unmovable ground of the Word of God.

The Bible is clear that people perish who lack knowledge. Ignorance of God's Word makes one a fool in all matters, and to remain ignorant of what is true will prove to be one's downfall, and to insist on ignorance, points to utter destruction. It is true that as a society we have been conditioned to our present state of being asleep or living in denial as to what is going on, but as soldiers of the cross, we have to become seasoned soldiers in order to recognize the ways of our different enemies and how to best combat them if we are to be overcomers and victorious.

As believers, we have enemies on three fronts, our homes (flesh), our societies (world), and the unseen realm (Satan and his kingdom). We can't claim ignorance about the enemies' devices because the Bible reveals that the attractions of the world stir up our fleshly lusts and affections, and that the systems of world want to entangle us into its vain affairs to rob us of our spiritual edge and testimony, and that Satan wants to seduce and indoctrinate us into an insane reality that is nothing more than a lie. Nor can we declare we never knew because the present enemy of this time brags about his plans and tactics on social media.

We must honestly face the fact that we can't avoid the battle because it is a bit too much for a tender conscience when God's Word has already given each of us our marching orders, the armor, and the means to walk through such conflicts and advance forward. The tactics we must use are clear, deny self of rights to partake of this world, apply the cross to the flesh, and follow Jesus. The problem with trying to avoid the spiritual conflict is it will eventually come to your community and then your home and by that time one is not prepared to defend the territory.

The Bible does not tell us as soldiers that it is up to us to win the war, but like David we are to stand in the Lord's might, withstand with His authority, and continue to stand because victory is always close at hand.

$$\rightthreetimes \kappa \longrightarrow \psi$$

I am sure you have noticed the mess our world is in. We can point our fingers at what we think the source of the problem is but in reality, this mess proves one thing, and that is man can't get it right because he is in a sinful, fallen condition and refuses to do right because he lacks real life (Jesus), divine vision (inspiration), integrity (moral authority), and heavenly power (the Holy Spirit).

Perhaps, he is fearful because of the idea of losing his present life, deluded by the rampant lies and propaganda of our times, intimidated by the bullies and tyrants of our age, overwhelmed by the injustice of despots who are in leadership, or despairing because many in key positions have sold their souls for the crumbs of money, while grabbing for abusive power that will ultimately oppress the masses and destroy them. It is clear that man wants his own way causing him to throw off wisdom and all moral restraints as he pursues the delusional idea that he can create an utopia for himself on earth without God and righteousness.

The Bible is clear that man will face judgment and his wicked ways will set him up to meet with destruction. However, man chooses not to believe the unchanging truth of God because he wants to call the shots, and every time he does, he makes an absolute mess of it, ending in failure, disillusionment, and complete ruin.

It appears we will actually see some of the wicked brought down-- not for our enjoyment--but for our example that as judge who holds all of the books, everyone will stand before the Lord and give an account of their life, their works, and their ways. As Christians, we will not be judged for our ways for they are under the blood, and our works may be burned up if they are not based on love of God, but our fruits will be revealed to show us the extent of how much we allowed the life of Christ to be worked in us. After all, in ourselves we have nothing to offer back to the Lord and it is only in Christ that we stand, we walk, and we become the reflection of His glory.

As believers we might be in this world, but we do not belong to it. We have been bought with the price of Jesus' precious blood and we have a different legacy that leads us by way of an old rugged cross back to a relationship with God. We have been given a seal that identifies us to the heavenly, and a life that is eternal and complete.

In Christ we are separated from the mess, empowered to endure trials, and lifted above the wrath that abides on the world. In Christ darkness becomes light, despair hope, and fear an opportunity to choose genuine faith to walk through the darkness and finish the course.

As we watch the world heading towards the abyss of destruction, let us choose to stand on the sure foundation of Christ, be true and obedient to God's Word and steadfast in our vision of our destination as we advance forward on the narrow path of righteousness to cross the finish line into eternity. We must become like a good soldier, our armor in place as we prepare to fight the good fight of our faith, withstanding the dark forces that are clearly at work in this world, and whose goal is to keep us from reaching the far unseen shores of unending, magnificent glory.

It is obvious we are in a war. The other day I talked about the concept of "bracing ourselves," which points to our need to stand and face what is coming. The reason we must often stand before we fight is because there is no other position in which we can effectively meet the enemy.

Before a soldier can advance forward, they first are given the command, "ATTENTION." This command requires them to take a standing position in expectation of waiting for further instructions. The stance of attention is a real point of discipline for every soldier. This pose ensures that the soldier is not only ready to march or advance forward, but that he is prepared to hear the command.

Jesus is clear, we as believers, must be prepared to hear what the Spirit is saying. Keep in mind, victory depends on leaders knowing or anticipating the enemy's next move and the soldier understanding the type of enemy and devices that will be used against him. Our commander knows the plans of the enemy, but as His soldiers in the present chaos, are we able to discern the enemy and recognize his devices?

The Apostle Paul tells us we must not be ignorant of the devices of Satan, and yet how many of us are being stopped right now by the enemy because we have not been properly trained to discern his presence, recognize his methods, withstand his attacks, and move forward to victory. The one frustration I sense from many believers is that they know our nation is under attack, our communities are under siege, our homes are in chaos, our churches teetering, and our lives in disarray, but they do not know what to do about it.

The real challenge for any soldier comes down to being ready to go into battle. Readiness of this nature cannot happen unless there is proper training of how to use the gear, but there is something else of the utmost importance to a soldier. A good soldier is also trained to listen for the command from their leader, hear it with clarity, and respond in good faith with unquestionable obedience.

What does it mean to stand? There are three reasons we physically stand, 1) to make our presence known, 2) when waiting in line, and 3) in preparation to move forward. In the military there were three reasons for standing: 1) to acknowledge the presence of one in authority, 2) to stand at attention as a means to wait for direction, and 3) in preparation to march.

We are told in *Ephesians 6:11-13*, as soldiers of the cross to stand in order to withstand and to continue to stand regardless of what is before us. The type of standing when it comes to the Christian life has to do with inner character. Character is determined by whether we are established according to our holy calling, have developed integrity of heart, and have truly been converted to righteousness.

Upright character is forged through doing what is right out of faith and simple obedience regardless of the personal moods, hindrances, obstacles, or circumstances. The important aspect about standing is being prepared to stand. Good character is forged in challenges and hardship when an individual is willing to go against the current in order to do what is right.

The great reason soldiers are defeated is that they are not alert, standing, and prepared to march forward to hold the line of great conflict that is taking place over strategic points. For the Christian soldier, it is over truth that confirms all orders, instructs in the right ways, and maintains the ground of righteousness.

There are different reasons people stand, and for the most part such standing has nothing to do with doing what is right and honorable. Some stand to speak their mind and others stand to become part of the crowd, while some may temporarily withstand to impress others of their intentions, but few continue to stand because they lack moral courage, integrity, and conviction.

In fact, I fear some Christians are not prepared to stand because they have been told to be silent when it comes to truth, sit when it comes to standing against what is wicked, and never give in to the evil current as a means to get along and appear "Christian." Clearly, the Bible says differently and we must wisely know when to stand in the Lord's authority, and wait for instructions from our real Commander and Chief before we march off in the power of the Spirit to confront the enemy.

However, we need to keep in mind, we can't stand unless we are first established on the right foundation, Jesus Christ, and we can't withstand unless we are in line with the cornerstone of the truth of His Word and example, and we can't continue to stand unless we have the sure conviction of our faith to endure to the end.

FAITH

*For faith to produce a greater quality of character
in the believer, it must, in a sense, be conceived
in the darkness of uncertainty, birthed in sorrow,
and brought forth to maturity in pain, despair,
and hopelessness.
(Rayola Kelley)*

The Bible tells us we are to walk by faith and not by sight *(2 Corinthians 5:7)*. The concept of "walking" points to "living our life by faith" towards God and according to His Word, and not by what we understand, think, feel, or see as far as the present age we live in.

The Christian walk seemed simple enough to me at the beginning of my new birth experience, but then it turned into an enigma that I wrestled with until I realized that there are different stages of the Christian walk to ensure spiritual growth. For me it started out being zealous for the Lord, but then I understood that I lacked real substance.

The second phase was what I refer to as the breaking, preparation period. I had to be knocked off of the high thinking pinnacle I was on to be broken at the point of my self-righteousness and self-sufficiency that was based on personal conclusions, to actually be prepared to be used by God. I have to admit, in the first phase I was flying high on the limbs of self-importance only to collide with the reality that it was all being done in my own strength.

The third stage was learning of Him. I knew about Jesus, knew of Him, but I did not know Him. How can you grow in love with someone you don't know? How can you effectively serve or worship the Lord unless you know Him realizing that the quality of service and worship will be determined by such knowledge? The fourth stage was the call to discipleship and the fifth to the consecrated life.

You can't sell out to Christ until you deny your old life and crucify your old ways. The life of the disciple is about doing an exchange, while ever shedding the old, to continually put on the "new man." It is only as one is set free from the claims of the old that a believer can truly offer their complete life as a living sacrifice to God. At this stage one is able to discern what is the acceptable, good, and perfect will of God.

It is easy to ask what faith is, but sometimes the best way to answer a question is by pointing out what it is not to bring a contrast. Faith is not wishful thinking, which is nothing more than whimsical hope or unsubstantiated hope. Faith is based on what is real, (God), and what has already been established as a matter of truth and righteousness, (His Word).

It is not a method where you do certain things or all the right things to somehow make God obligated to do something that is of the upmost importance to your way of thinking and doing. As Christians, we do not wish God does something; rather, we can confidently believe it is already so if God has declared it.

God is never obligated to do something for us; but since God is grace, He willingly does things for our benefit, according to His will and plan, ever bringing glory to Himself. It was/is God's grace that provides an avenue in which faith can be effectively exercised, producing lasting fruits. That is why we are saved BY grace THROUGH faith *(Ephesians. 2:8)*.

Grace is God's part and faith is our response, for God is the only One who can save us, and He provided the way of Christ's sacrifice on the altar of the cross as a means of redeeming our souls. It is what is done by faith that a matter is reckoned or counted for righteousness by God, which provides a way in which God's grace is able to reign through righteousness *(Romans. 4:2-3; 5:21)*.

It is for this reason we are told that whatsoever is not a matter of faith is considered sin and that is why it is impossible to please God without faith *(Romans 14:23; Hebrews 11:6)*. It is not a matter of claiming a promise of God until He fulfills it; rather it is believing God for the promise while walking in light of it.

As a believer, God's promises are part of my inheritance, but it is only as I faithfully walk out my life in Christ that I can possess my inheritance *(Hebrews 6:12)*. In fact, it will not be until I realize the fullness of my redemption that I will even begin to realize the great spiritual blessings or riches attached to my inheritance *(Eph. 1:3-9).*

It is for this reason *James 2:5* talks about us being rich, not in worldly possessions, but in faith. In *2 Corinthians 8:9, "For ye know the grace of our Lord Jesus Christ, that though he was rich, yet for our sakes he became poor, that ye through his poverty MIGHT be rich."* (Emphasis added.)

Yesterday I wrote about faith. There are many people who try to describe what faith is and how it works. Through the years there have been many books about faith. In these books the authors give the impression they are now "experts" on how to corner faith and use it to basically get their way with God. Since they think they have discovered the secret, the method, or practices to get God to respond, they want to now share it with the rest of us.

There is no one method that will activate genuine faith because it is based on simple child-like trust. A child never questions or debates what they are told by their parents, they simply believe it is so because their parents told them so. This is true for every believer. I believe a matter is so because my Father in heaven has revealed it to me by His Spirit and/or through His Word.

Everyone has their own faith walk and have discovered different treasures of truth and wisdom along the way. It is not faith in itself that makes us rich; rather, it is the walk of faith that allows us to discover that what we have been told by God is indeed true, precious, and eternal. Every discovery enlarges our faith, but what makes us rich in faith is that the discoveries simply confirm what we have already chosen to believe about the character and work of God.

Every Christian has the opportunity of being rich in faith, but not everyone cares to walk the walk of faith to discover those precious treasures that will make them rich towards the Lord. That is why yesterday in *2 Corinthians 8:9,* I emphasized the word "might" be rich. This word does not denote a sure thing; rather, it puts forth a question mark to cause the reader to recognize there is some type of choice or condition involved to truly become rich in their life in Christ.

Jesus said to the disciples after He calmed the contrary winds in *Matthew 8:26*, *"O ye of little faith."* It is natural to look at the circumstances and it is easy to foolishly judge God when it appears He is asleep or silent, but such conclusions come out of unbelief.

Life brings many contrary winds with it. Some winds are fierce and threaten to sink you, others are contrary causing irritations and fear, and there are those sweet breezes that can bring us into safe harbors. Life reveals three very important facts, 1) we need God, 2) you aren't Him, and 3) nothing makes sense but God. The winds of life show us we are small and we do not have the power to change the intensity or course of the winds as many blow us out to seas of uncertainties or rush us headlong onto rocks of destruction.

As believers we have many promises that the Lord will never leave or forsake us, but we must quit looking at the waves and choose to trust the character of God and His abiding care towards us. God is sovereign and if He allows terrible winds in our life, it is to either enlarge our faith and/or our testimony. God never wastes a wave and we must never let it sink us but we need to learn to ride each one out trusting God with the glorious outcome.

One of the illustrations I have heard in relationship to unbelief has to do with Peter, the time he walked on water and sunk. We have a tendency to pick on Peter for sinking in the water, but what was the real test when it came to that situation?

Faith cannot be enlarged unless it is tested. Was Peter's faith being tested on the water or was the test of his faith having to do with getting out of the boat? I have asked myself this question many times.

To me, my walk of faith has taught me that Peter's real test was not walking on water but getting out of the boat. Peter wanted to come to Jesus but he dared not until the Lord invited him. Out of the twelve men, he was the only one who risked walking on the water to meet Christ in the storm.

253

It takes faith to meet Jesus in any storm. Granted the waves caused him to take his eyes off of Jesus and he sunk, but what a powerful illustration we have been given. We can't walk on water unless we step out of the boat we are in so that we can meet Jesus in the storm, and if we take our eyes off of Him for a second and put it on the circumstances, we will sink.

I know my faith will wane when I put my eyes on circumstances and as I feel myself going down into the waves of despair, my faith has taught me to look up for my deliverance. I can tell you from experience my initial test of faith was when I realized I had to get out of the boat if I was going to meet and experience Christ in the storms of life. There are times I have sunk into the waves because I was looking at the circumstances, but I also knew that all I had to do was look up while reaching up and He would be there to take my hand.

⋇⋎⟶⤝

We often use Jesus' disciple Thomas, as an example of one who doubted. How many times have you heard, "Now don't be like Thomas and doubt what God said?" Doubting for most Christians has nothing to do with what God said; rather, it has to do with whether God personally showed them something.

Through the years I have sensed God giving me insight about personal matters or revealing certain things that I have asked Him about. For instance, when I sensed we were supposed to relocate, I would prepare for it, but the door to do so remained closed even after much preparation was made. I would begin to doubt whether I really received it from the Lord, interpreted it properly, or wondered if it was something I imagined because I wanted to see it happen. I would eventually come to rest between the pillar of faith that trusted God to be God in all matters and the pillar of truth that if it was so, the Lord would bring it forth at the right time confirming it was from Him.

⋇⋎⟶⤝

What was the source of Thomas' doubting Jesus' resurrection? Thomas' problem was not a matter of doubt but skepticism, which is nothing more than unbelief. Thomas is an interesting person to study. At one point he was willing to die for the Lord in *John 11:16*, but when it was the darkest hour when true faith can rise out of utter despair and shine the brightest by grabbing hold of the promise of resurrection, he would not believe that Jesus rose from the grave, even though the other disciples proclaimed it.

What was Thomas' response when he was told that they saw Jesus in *John 20:25? "Except I shall see in his hands the print of the nails, and put my finger into the print the nails, and thrust my hand into his side, I WILL not believe."* (Emphasis added.) The problem at this point is that since Thomas was skeptical about what Jesus said, he was unwilling to believe any words without Jesus proving first that He was who He claimed to be.

Remember what Jesus said in *Matthew 4:7* to the devil when he challenged Him to prove He was who He said He was, *"It is written again, Thou shalt not tempt the Lord thy God."* For a person like Thomas, skepticism comes out of a sense of betrayal that something did not happen in the way they thought it should; therefore, nothing is true and everything will prove to be a sick joke or mockery.

When Jesus appeared to Thomas and the disciples, Jesus instructed Thomas to check out the marks in his hands and side, as he ceased to be faithless, and believe. That is when Thomas acknowledged what was true, "My Lord and my God."

However, Jesus said something of the upmost importance to all skeptics, "Thomas because thou hast seen me, thou has believed: blessed are they that have not seen, and yet have believed." True faith never seeks to have God prove He is God to believe His words; rather, genuine faith rests on the fact He is God and that whatever He says is true and will be so. In the end, it is faith that allows us to see what is true. This is why faith comes from hearing and hearing from the Word of God *(Romans 10:17)*.

Yesterday I talked about Thomas's skepticism. For a Christian who possesses genuine faith, doubting a matter never has to do with God's

255

character or Word, but one's understanding and interpretation of a matter. It is natural to try to fit what God tells us into our understanding and timeframe.

Take the times we live in. How many interpretations have you heard about the prophetic events that are to take place? In many cases, man has taken the events and put them within some type of timeframe where we will see certain events and not others. Let me state, until a matter is proven as being so, such interpretations are nothing more than man's theory. Granted, each theory has the Scriptures nicely fitted into each presentation to give credence to what they perceive could be nothing but the truth, but this is so with every other theory, including evolution.

The question is how much of these presentations are based on personal interpretation and how much of it has been inspired by the Holy Spirit and will prove to be so in the end? The problem with trying to figure out God's timeframe is that God does not work within certain periods. When the right or approved time comes for God to bring forth a matter, it is never according to man's timing, interpretation, and logical presentation.

The truth is, man thinks within a certain box, but God never operates within any such boxes. God sees a matter from the beginning to the end and ultimately will fulfill His Word according to His will to ensure He receives the glory. He is not limited by the present time, nor is He obliged to confirm man's interpretation of a scriptural matter to prove He is God. God often shakes such interpretations, revealing that man is relying on his interpretation of a matter instead of holding his understanding lightly until God proves that it is correct. If man insists on his box of interpretation instead of humbly conceding that God will fulfill His every word, but rarely according to personal interpretation, he can become a total skeptic towards God.

The problem is that those who hold to the same unreliable interpretation can find themselves falling into the same ditch. I have held to theological and doctrinal boxes in the past, only to have them lay shattered before me. It was then that I realized that God was showing me much mercy because I never wanted to miss what He was doing. Once my boxes were shattered, I was able to go back to what He said about such matters and actually witness what He was doing.

When we box ourselves in, it is easy to miss what God is doing and fail to discern where we are as to God's prophetic timeline. We are living in exciting times and I don't know about you, but I do not want to miss what God is doing.

One of the questions that I must ask myself is how much conviction do I possess when it comes to God and His truth. Believing has three different stages which you can follow in *John 8:30-47*. They are believing God's Word where there is agreement, believing God, and believing in Him. Intellectually we can agree with aspects of God's Word, but if we do not believe God based on who He is, we will strip the complete counsel of God's Word of its absolute authority, while picking and choosing what we decide to agree with as to what is truth.

Since we don't believe God, we won't believe what the Word says about Him. To believe God we must possess the same spirit that ensures agreement with Him. This agreement brings a witness to our spirit that His Word is true in every area. If we do not believe God, then we will fail to believe in Him; thereby, we will be unable to put our reliance on Him and walk in child-like faith towards the life He has for us.

The first type of belief can lack the right spirit and those who do not move beyond this will often become hard towards truth that does not fit their particular narrative. The second type of belief lacks revelation that brings life to the Word and those who remain on this level can become rigid and judgmental which sets them up to eventually become offended by the truth. The third one will lack heart conviction, causing the person to often lose heart in service and commitment to finish the course.

As I deal with Christians, I have encountered all three of these levels. When we begin our spiritual journey, it is because we believe what we are told about our need to be saved which is outlined in Scripture, but if we do not graduate to believing God is who He is as the Bible declares, we will live an uncertain, powerless life before Him. Without heart conviction, we will prove to be fickle and inconsistent in our Christian walk.

Paul talked about always coming to the knowledge of Jesus, not theology, doctrine, or religious pursuits. We need to approach God's Word to believe whatever it says in order to grow in the knowledge of Christ and in the conviction of our heart that all it says is absolutely true.

Through the years I have been asked by believers what does God expect from them in times of personal struggles, great conflicts, and intense wrestling matches. It is easy to say, "Trust Him," at such times, even though these two words constitute truth, this type of statement comes across as an indifferent platitude. What most Christians fail to realize is that faith does not spare us of challenges in our life; rather, it enables us to walk through the conflict.

The walk of faith is what advances us forward, knowing the real battle belongs to the Lord. It prepares, enlarges, and seasons us to face our enemies, while holding onto the invisible knowing we are preserved by the eternal. Although words such as trust, assurance, confidence, persuasion, and believing are used to describe faith, for many the word "faith" creates more sentiment than a foundation of conviction and expectation that our real hope will be realized at the end of our journey.

This brings me back to our part as far as faith. Faith is a walk and within that walk I must choose to be faithful to what I know is true, right, and acceptable to the Lord. Faith requires me "in good faith" to trust what God says, while being assured in the end I will not be disappointed in putting my total reliance on Him. As I walk in confidence of His promises, I am constantly being persuaded that all obedience to His Word is my reasonable service in light of believing that His Word is true, as well as following the leading of His Spirit, the inspiration and teacher of all truth, to guide and lead me to a greater revelation of the great I AM. It is in the greater revelation of Christ, the author and finisher of my faith, that I become more established in my faith.

My faith walk has been comprised of many small steps of faithful obedience to what was before me. Each step often led me into the unknown, while preparing me to trust Him in the darkness that He has ordained on this path for me. In the end, the steps of faithfulness led me to my calling, refined my testimony, defined my gifts, and enlarged my heavenly vision of the Lord.

As believers, why are we here? Are we here to simply live life according to preferred creeds, religions, and realities or are we here for the glory of God? In immature zealousness, we can declare that we are willing to go all the way for God no matter what it costs us, but such zealousness is like a flash in the pan, here one moment and gone the next.

We can possess a sentiment that can be stirred up by a certain environment, but it proves to be fleeting once the environment is no longer. We can have certain passion that will see its intention as honorable, but once the fiery passion is gone, it is like a match stick that flames up but quickly fizzles out. This is the way of the flesh, but real faith is enduring. It is what keeps us putting one foot in front of the other as we walk in dark places, knowing God will not let us slip. Its obedient ways to the Word of God are what disciplines us as we walk the narrow paths of righteousness, and it is what stands at the end of our faith that keeps us focused enough to run the course, to gain the prize. And what is the prize, some promise?

The prize is Christ and realizing the fulfillment of our high calling, which is to reflect His glory in this dark world. So many people's focus is wrong because it is on a promise and not on the Promiser. As a believer, we know we have the promise of eternal life and we are to walk by faith according to that life in us to inherit the promises attached to it. However, we also need to realize the life in us belongs to the One who promised it and that our goal must remain simple like the Apostle Paul, we must do all we have to attain that which would ensure, above all else, that we GAIN Christ.

In my walk of faith one of the things I have discovered is that BELIEVING WHAT God says allows me to trust what He says as being true, while BELIEVING GOD creates an assurance in me that nothing is happening that His hand or approval is not upon, and BELIEVING IN GOD allows my spirit to soar on the waves of inspiration because HE IS GOD.

We sometimes take for granted that God is God, but we can never experience inspiration until we understand HE IS GOD. This means there is nothing before Him, beside Him, or can be accomplished outside of Him.

When we can receive this fact into our spirit then we will find inspiration all around us, knowing that God is "El," the great "I AM THAT I AM;" the One who will bring about His promises, covenants, and plans. He is ever present and His creation shows us His artistic abilities, His heavens His vastness, and mankind His design to be glorified in creation. The more inspiration lifts me up towards the heavenlies, the more I will take on the beauty, the light, and the greatness of heaven, the Lord Jesus Christ

Do you have romantic notions about the faith walk? Your faith walk has to do with trusting the Lord in whatever situation you are in. Do you truly rely on Him to provide what is necessary or rely on your abilities? Do you try to figure out how to solve a matter of you looking up confessing your inability to handle anything without His intervention?

Most of us start out with romantic notions about faith. These notions are void of the reality that pure faith is a tried faith. I had such romantic notions and the first thing the Lord had to do when I stepped out in faith was to knock the silly notions out of the way so that I could realistically face the looming mountains before me. I never realized that the faith walk sometimes required me to become a mountain climber.

A faith walk is just that—a walk, and you have to walk through the terrain that is before you. Some of the terrain is flat, while some may be valleys, canyons, and mountains. Regardless of what was before me, I had to trust Him to take my hand in order to discipline my steps. I discovered the terrain before me was designed by Him to test my faith to enlarge it, but as I have pointed out in past posts I was constantly faced with the same reality: I had no faith until the Lord met me in my need as I sought Him and He gave me the measure of faith to step into the foreboding, unknown darkness that stood before me.

Life happens and it brings challenges your way that will always give you a reality check that you are not in control and you can't change what is before you. Faith is not developed as we swing from the limbs of silly expectations; rather, it is developed in the fiery ovens of testing, the deep trenches of inner personal struggles, the dark canyons of despair, and overwhelming mountains of challenges that will ever require us to look up and fling ourselves on Him.

RIGHTEOUSNESS & OBEDIENCE

Righteousness is not a concept
of some religious life, it entails
standing (positionally), being in the way
(the life I am living), and doing (that which
is honorable to others and acceptable
to God.
(Rayola Kelley)

What does it mean to hunger after righteousness? We must come into line with what is right before God and then diligently follow after it with great zeal to possess the fruits of it. One of the ways we will be able to discern our level of commitment to follow after righteousness is to consider our attitude towards the Word of God. After all, the Word of God proves profitable in establishing sound doctrine, reproof, and correction for instruction in righteousness.

It all comes down to how the Word of God tastes to you. Is it bitter because it is cutting across the grain of your present reality? If so, you should humble yourself and seek the course the Lord has set for you. Is it salty to you because the truth of God's Word has set you free? Then continue to walk in obedience to it to come to greater places of liberty in service and worship. Is it sweet to you, which means you have a tender heart towards the Lord? Then learn to truly enjoy Him even more so in times of worship and communion. Does His Word leave you lean in spirit? Then realize you are in a spiritual wilderness and you need to rise up and seek Him with your whole heart. Does His Word leave you spiritually dry? Then know you may have a divided heart towards Him, and the Holy Spirit will be missing in your worship and service because unbelief is present and you need to repent of it. Is the Word boring to you? then you need to recognize that you are half-hearted towards the things of God because you have not fully consecrated your life to Him.

Once you have discerned your attitude towards the Word of God and respond accordingly, you can begin to discern true righteousness so that you can follow after it with everything within you.

Jesus, when sharing the parable of the sower and the seed, made this statement in *Matthew 13:15, "For this people's heart is waxed gross, and their ears are dull of hearing, and their eyes they have closed; lest at any time they should see with their eyes and hear with their ears, and should understand with their heart, and should be converted, and I should heal them."*

Clearly our heart condition determines if and how we hear a matter and we must be prepared to be converted to the ways of righteousness to ensure that the healing balm of the Spirit maintains the integrity of both our spiritual hearing and seeing. I encourage myself in knowing that I have to be truthful of how God's truth affects my heart attitude towards Him.

Jesus stated that truth will offend because it can prove to be sharp when it cuts away blinders so we can see. Even though truth may rattle my cage, disrupt my perception of things, and throw me into chaos about what is real, it will also set me free to truly receive the matters of God in the right spirit. It is upon receiving the truth, that I am healed and converted.

Conversion is not a one-time event. We must be constantly converted from the profane influences of the flesh and the perverted ways of the world to the righteousness of God in order for our minds to become less conformed to this world and more transformed. It is in clarity of mind that I can see beyond the present and encourage myself in the eternal.

A word that is often overlooked, ignored or misunderstood is "conversion." There are those believers that treat this word as being a one-time event which happens upon being "born again." However, real conversion is an ongoing process. A person must be constantly converted in order to see a matter through. In essence, they must find reason to be converted to something because true "conversion" is not a matter of sentiment, but deep-seated conviction.

People who are sentimentally caught up with a matter will soon enough fizzle out and wait for the next sentimental wave to come along to once again stir them up into an emotional zeal that will allow them to ride high on the crest of the latest popular cause. When it comes to a real conversion, a person will eventually become completely sold out to what becomes a matter of the heart. For the people of the world, which includes heretical religions, that often means they must be indoctrinated into the darkness of it, but the problem with such a conversion to lies is that they lack truth and/or moral substance. And without substance, such a conversion will lead people down a path of delusion, insanity, and destruction. This type of individual may be sincere and sold out, but their foundation is faulty and will collapse underneath them when shaken.

When it comes to Christianity, we are initially converted with child-like faith towards God's evaluation of our sinful plight and His provision of salvation, Jesus Christ. However, the next step in conversion entails righteousness. We must be constantly converted to the ways of righteousness and that can only occur when we become a true disciple of Jesus.

As Jesus' disciples we will believe His Word as being truth, walk according to His instructions and examples, and follow Him into a life of service and worship that lines up to the will of God.

Have you been converted to the ways of righteousness? The Bible is clear that those who are not converted will not enter into the kingdom of heaven. I believe conversion is what is missing from the salvation message that is presently being presented in churches.

Rayola Kelley

Many hear the message, "Accept Jesus and you will be saved," but such a presentation is weak. The Bible is clear that one must repent to be saved. Repentance is turning away from the old in order to face the reality of a matter. True repentance will cause you to receive the solution in your heart as being so, which brings you into agreement with God about the issue, but real repentance will also result in true conversion towards righteousness.

Conversion is not a one-time experience; it must happen every day by way of believers making a decision to do what is right in a situation because the Bible says so. At the core of conversion is a transformed mind. It is where the mind has completely been changed about a subject, producing a right heart attitude.

I have been thinking about conversion. To me it appears that there are those who are sentimental towards Jesus, while some are loyal to certain teachers, doctrines, and/or church affiliations, while others simply tack Jesus on to give their half-hearted religion some credibility. However, when it comes down to whether they have been converted, that quickly becomes a matter of debate because the fruit being produced in their lives and relationship with others clearly lacks substance.

Some believe conversion is a one-time event, but the truth is because of our spiritual state, we must be constantly converted to ensure our minds are being transformed and our spirit renewed daily. This brings us to how does conversion happen? It begins with real repentance, where one turns away from what is wrong in order to come into agreement with what is true.

Conversion of the mind takes place when a person by faith truly agrees that a matter is so and he or she is going to make it so in his or her life. What are we being converted to—the righteousness of God. The mind must be converted to be transformed, allowing the heart attitude to come into compliance with God and His Word.

Through the years I have had to be constantly converted to the things of righteousness. It begins with a choice to believe the Word of God in a matter as being true. Such belief allows me the confidence to

264

assimilate it into my walk. As I walk it out, it is confirmed as being so which establishes my heart in the ways of righteousness, lining up my attitude concerning the matter to God's attitude.

It is important to point out, unless one possesses the same attitude towards a matter as God does, taking away all doubt and debate about it, he or she has not been truly converted. I often examine my attitude about something in light of the Spirit and truth of Scripture to see if I have been truly converted in that area.

It is easy to get caught up with who is right and who is wrong. When the Bible speaks about contrast it refers to good and evil, dark and light, and the righteous and the wicked, but when it comes down to mankind, it is what is right and what is wrong or fair and unfair. The problem is we define what we consider to be right based on our own ideas.

The book of Judges best described it as man doing what he thinks was right in his own eyes and yet Jesus said the light we may be personally following could very well be darkness. When we look at everything based on whether it seems right, feels right, and leaves us with a sense of well-being, we can't see how we possibly could ever be wrong. But the problem is, whosoever fails to line up to our way of thinking and doing, will be judged as being wrong.

In essence, when a person is the final authority as to what is right, it allows them to fudge the lines of what is good, making it evil, create some kind of shadow to take away any real stark contrast to allow for compromise, and redefining what is just in order to make something that is right, very wrong.

Behind the ideas of personal rightness is the iniquity of pride. It is amazing how personal pride will draw a line in the sand to bring contrast according to its terms, arrogance will lift a flag declaring its superiority, haughtiness will claim it is the king of the hill, and conceit will smugly tout it knows what it is talking about and all should come into subordination by giving way to that which is superior, submitting to that which is obvious, and coming into allegiance to that which has been exalted.

Even though the principle of right and wrong is in the Bible, the main goal of God's Word is to bring people to a state of holiness, for without holiness no person will see the Lord. Holiness is not a matter of being on the right or wrong side of the matter. Holiness is about having a right standing before the Lord as far as relationship, walking in light of His truth, and making sure we are standing on the right side of eternity with the one who is perfect in all of His ways, absolute in truth, and immovable as to what is right.

The next time you want to take issue with what you think is right or wrong, avoid creating some hill with the backhoe of pride that would prove vain and foolish to your Christian testimony. Make sure you are standing on the side of the Lord when it comes to what is acceptable to Him, with Him when it comes to righteousness, and for Him when it comes to truth.

In the past I have been attacked by passionate people over the issue of salvation. If I speak of obedience, they adamantly remind me that we are saved by grace. If I speak of doing good works, I am told you can't earn your salvation. When I speak of the Lordship of Jesus I have been accused of advocating a different Gospel. I shake my head at such times because I am not talking about such matters in relationship to salvation but in light of my Christian walk.

You see, I am already saved, and obedience, good works, and the Lordship have nothing to do with getting saved, it has to do with that which accompanies salvation. I am not saved by being obedient; but because I am saved, I DESIRE to be obedient to the Lord, which means believing His Word is true and being obedient to it as a matter of reasonable service.

It is true, as a Christian I believe in "good works" but not as a means to earn "brownie points" to save myself; rather, I understand I am saved UNTO good works, works that were ordained by God for me to do. As to the matter of what some refer to as "Lordship salvation," which for some points to a requirement that must be met to be saved, the Bible is clear in *Romans 10:9* and *10*, "*That if thou confess with thy mouth the Lord Jesus and shalt believe in thine heart that God hath raised him from the dead, thou shalt be saved, For with the heart man believeth unto righteousness; and with the mouth confession is made unto salvation."*

The concept of "Lord" is not promoting another Gospel; rather, it is establishing Jesus' ownership and authority over and in your life. His authority allows you to stand before your enemies who can't encroach into your life without Jesus' permission and restraints.

Yesterday I mentioned the significance of Jesus' Lordship in our lives. When I talk about the Lordship of Jesus, it is not because it is a matter of salvation; rather, it is acknowledging that Jesus is who He says He is. He is Lord (Adonai—Owner, Headship, Ruler) Jesus (Jehovah is our salvation) and He has bought me with the price of His blood and I am to be His SERVANT. By confessing who He is I am declaring that I have entered into a binding contract as His servant.

I do not see such service as a requirement to be saved but as a privilege, an opportunity to choose a benevolent Lord who went to great lengths to buy me back from being a slave to the flesh, a servant of the world, and a sick minion of Satan. It is important to note that man is born into slavery and that he will be a servant to some master, and it is only through the redemption of Jesus that a man has been given liberty to decide who he will serve.

It is because I am saved, that I have chosen to consecrate my life and serve the Lord Jesus Christ. If godly obedience, good works, and Lordship are stumbling blocks to some, I fear it is to their loss, but to me they are precious steps that are leading me to glory. They simply confirm what I already believe, and what I already know, "I once was lost, but now I am saved."

I am sure we can all agree we live in a time of great darkness. The darkness we are witnessing can be depressing, unnerving, and overwhelming but I must say this, "Stark darkness is better than the foggy grays that are void of any real contrast."

Sadly, I must admit for years I have seen the foggy grays in this nation in every arena including the visible church, and it has caused a leanness in my spirit. Without distinct contrast, people do not have to face what is so and honestly address it. They can ignorantly and happily dance in and out of some silly reality, while hiding their lack of commitment towards God or hypocrisy behind their so-called "goodness," "decency" or "religious piousness".

The grays allow people to hide in dark shadows while doing their own thing as they venture into the lighter shadows of fleshly independence, worldly compromise, a surface religious devotion, and self-righteous judgment. Even though Jesus made reference that darkness is a form of light, many people do not realize that darkness exposes much about a person's spirit (motives), character (moral convictions), and preferences.

The darkness tells me more about a man's real convictions than the light, because a man can always put some mask on in the light, but he can't hide the darkness of his own soul when darkness is all about him. Consider how people react to darkness.

For example, there are people who rage against such darkness, while some rage in it, and others use it as a cover to carry out their wicked deeds. As a Christian, what is my responsibility in the darkness?

As a true heir of faith, I must never settle for the gray shadows of compromise, vanity, and masks of hypocrisy if I am going to honestly face the darkness. I must walk in the true light of this world which is in the truth of Jesus Christ, knowing that the more I walk in light of His life by faith, the greater the light of His life will shine in me and through me. I must choose the way of righteousness according to His Word, which will put a light on what is wicked and reveal the path before me.

Regardless of how much the present darkness tries to consume the light in me, I can be sure that it will never be extinguished and when my race is completed here, another torch carrier will pick up the baton of His light and carry it. What are you doing about the darkness engulfing the world and what is the darkness revealing about your life in Christ, your devotion to Him, and your attitude towards His truth?

Yesterday I talked about the spiritual gray environments that people often operate in. There is no distinction or contrast in such an environment and without contrast there is no discernment, and if there is no discernment, righteous judgment will be illusive.

For the last week we have been in such a physical environment. Due to the fires, a dingy grey smoky sky greets us every day. We have not seen the mountains since this blanket of smoke moved in and there are times, we can't even see our shed. Even though the sun is trying to break through the smoky covering, it becomes fragmented by the filter that has laid claim to the countryside. The emotional toll this type of environment places on people can't really be seen or calculated, but it stifles initiative, causes depression, and since we can't open the windows, it can cause feelings of claustrophobia.

The greys in life represent normalcy, compromise, and an attitude of simply getting by while settling for less. However, the Christian life is about walking in the light of Christ, while exposing and reproving the works and ways of darkness in order to avoid the greys of compromise. We must never settle for what the world considers normal, accept less to get along in this life, and bump along until the greys of life part.

As Christians we are called to be a light that will stand out regardless of how grey or dark it is. We must not cover the light of Christ in darkness with fear, hide the light in darker shadows of unbelief, and blend in even in the light of day. We must allow the light of Christ to shine through us, allowing it to point to the true light of the world. We must accept that part of our high calling that calls for us to walk in the ways of righteousness to ensure that the distinction of excellence of Christ stands out regardless of the environment around us.

We need to discern where we stand in our relationship with God before we invite His presence among us. I remember once visiting a church where most of the activities were orchestrated by the pastor, whose main goal was to shake any extra money from the pockets of the congregation for an upcoming vacation.

Everyone was asked to stand facing the wall as if worshipping the actual building and ask for the Lord to come down in their midst (*Isaiah 64:1*). Needless to say, Jeannette and I were among the few who remained sitting in the pew, watching the fiasco in utter disbelief.

As the compliant sheep were standing, raising their hands and asking the Lord to come down in a powerful way, the Lord quietly spoke to my spirit and told me if He came down there would not be one left standing. I sensed some would be on their face crying out for mercy, but like the judgment on the deception of Ananias and Sapphira in *Acts 5*, some would be carried out of the building.

It was obvious God was not pleased and it left me sober and shaken. It is natural to want God's blessing on something, but when God comes down to meet with His people it is to do business with them. Whether it is to address sin, bring healing to a soul that has been wounded or left with taunting unresolved issues, comfort, direction, or etc, God desires to meet with each of us personally. Keep in mind, the fact that God comes down should be considered the greatest blessing, producing the uttermost satisfaction to a seeking soul and a lean spirit

The next time you ask the Lord to come down, make sure you are standing on holy ground, prepared to do business with Him to ensure right standing, right being, and right doing.

ISSUES OF THE HEART

*The battle that rages today is not for the head,
but for the heart. It is not the head of man
that must be enlightened. It is the heart
that must be circumcised by the sword of
God's Word before it can rightly perceive
and embrace truth, thereby, enlarging man's
ability to properly understand and
receive spiritual matters.*
(Rayola Kelley)

I have wondered why a Judas Iscariot could turn on Jesus. He walked with Him, witnessed His miracles, and observed His merciful ministry of compassion, but betrayed Him with a kiss of friendship. I know there were a couple of things that happened. One, he was humiliated in public when Mary anointed Jesus for His burial and he tried to cover up his thievery intentions by declaring that the expensive anointing oil being poured on Jesus could have been sold and the money given to the poor (*Matthew 26:1-16*).

Imagine, Jesus who is worthy to receive the best was upstaged by a thief who wanted to appear noble at the expense of sincere ministry in order to hide his real agendas. Jesus said this, *"Verily I say unto you, Wheresoever this gospel shall be preached in the whole world, there shall also this that this woman hath done, be told for a memorial of her"* (Matthew 26:13)

We are told after this incident Judas went to the priests to make a deal with them about betraying Jesus. The woman's action established a memorial because they pointed to His death, burial and resurrection. Keep in mind, Jesus admitted that she was anointing or preparing His body for His burial which pointed to His death but it also pointed to His resurrection.

Remember, that the ladies on the first day of the week came to His tomb to prepare His body, but He had already risen from the grave. The woman left a memorial and Judas left a bad example. It is easy to try to nobly hide wrong agendas because they are embarrassing, but ultimately any attempt to appear noble at the expense of what is genuine will set the person up for a fall.

One of the lessons that Judas' example teaches me is that it does not matter how close you are to Jesus in His teachings, examples, and influences, you can still walk away from Him and even betray Him if your whole heart is not towards Him as your Lord and Savior.

I mentioned heart conviction in the past. So much of our Christian faith is debated, maintained and lived out in our mind and can fall short of it becoming a matter of our heart. We may surround our mental understanding about spiritual matters with Scripture, religious causes, and good deeds and activities, but when challenged by the fierce storms and winds of the age, we can end up fainting in our minds.

We need to remember there are three avenues in which the world can greatly influence us. There are the lust of the flesh where our desires and our emotions can be taken captive, the pride of life where our intellect can be manipulated by the attitudes and base, heretical teachings and philosophies of the world, and the lust of the eyes where the attractions of the world can entice our affections to pursue the various proverbial carrots of its many illusive promises of happiness and success. It is easy to fall into these traps, and the only way we can avoid them is by examining our heart motives in relationship to our pursuits, emphases, priorities, and agendas.

After all, our flesh can convince us that our emphases are normal, but only the Spirit and God's Word show us whether they are honorable. Our intellect can tell us our priorities are understandable, but only God can reveal if they are acceptable and in line with His will. Our eyes can convince us that our pursuits are innocent enough, but only the Lord can show us if they will take us by way of that which ultimately profanes our calling and witness.

The Bible is clear that we must choose to believe His Word is His reality in our heart to establish it as truth. For truth to become an immovable pillar, we must walk it out in obedience and assurance that our faith towards God will always be confirmed in the end.

Heart conviction establishes the spirit, anchors the soul, and disciplines the mind. However, the key about heart conviction is that it must be founded, grounded, centered, and in line with the person and work of Jesus Christ. Our mental understanding will end in darkness, our emotions will become frayed, our strength fading, our causes hollow, and our deeds empty if they are not grounded on and in the Lord Jesus Christ.

The Bible is full of examples, good and bad and what I call the in-between. When you consider what governs people's responses towards God, it all comes back to the heart condition.

The heart is the soil of our lives and determines the fruits. *Proverbs 4:23* tells us to keep our heart with all diligence for out of it come the issues of life. This becomes obvious when you study the kings.

The Bible usually tells you their heart condition as a means to explain their fruits and actions. How many of you know Solomon asked the Lord to give him an understanding heart so that he could discern between good and bad and God gave him a largeness of heart, but later his heart was turned away by idolatry and judgment was pronounced on him (*1 Kings 3:9; 4:29; 11:4-14*).

Rehoboam, the son of Solomon, did evil before the Lord because he was not prepared in his heart to seek the Lord (*2 Chronicles 12:14*). Abijam's heart was not perfect or pure before the Lord and he walked in the sins of his father, Rehoboam (*1 Kings 15:3*).

As you study these kings, some sought the Lord early because they had a tender heart towards Him, but because they failed to keep their heart with all diligence, like Solomon their hearts were turned away by idolatrous, worldly pursuits, the arrogance of power, or wrong influences.

We know the bad heart is the hard heart but the in-betweens include the stony heart that is still full of the rocks of the self-life and produces half-hearted results and disappointing fruits. There is the worldly heart that is a divided heart due to divided loyalties and caring too much about the things of the world that produce a poor quality of fruit. And, the final heart is the open heart, tender towards God, sensitive towards the Spirit, faithful in service, and a lover of all that is true, pure, and right.

It is easy, in our Christian life, to start out with zeal towards the Lord, but zeal without heart will leave a person spiritually shipwrecked. To properly discern our heart, all we need to do is examine the fruits that are obvious in our attitudes and relationships with others.

What is your main emphasis? This question may seem simple enough but the reality for many of us is that we really do not know what our emphasis is. We assume it is noteworthy and responsible, but for the most part we never really think about it. However, a good test in coming to terms with the identity of our present emphasis is what do we talk about the most?

Whatever becomes the main topic in conversation is where our emphasis lies. Granted, emphasis can change according to events and challenges, but if the emphasis is truly a matter of the heart and the focus of one's pursuit, it will remain consistent. Through the years my emphasis has been attached to that which is earthly, selfish, religious, and demanding such as family, events, people, church, doctrine, and problems. These emphases may seem normal and noteworthy, but are they honorable and profitable to others? Do they leave those who get caught up with them in an indifferent mood or edified?

The problem with the wrong emphases is that they can become like whirlpools that snag us in them while floating through the drudgery of life or when struggling to get through dangerous rapids, taking us down into murky waters that are void of life. These whirlpools will eventually spit out the lifeless but they leave no trace of one's victory over struggles, of an overcoming testimony, or evidence of an eternal impact. It is important as believers to make sure our emphasis always leads back to the Rock of Jesus, holds to the pillars of His truths, and remain firm in light of promises to come.

What is your priority? If you are like me I have assumed much about my character. I felt as long as my goals were right that I would finish the course. It took a few years for me to understand what it meant to be a double-minded person who found that instead of being steadfast in my Christian walk, I would often become unstable in my ways.

What I learned is if my agendas and priorities do not line up to my goal, I will find myself taking my eye off the goal and becoming unstable in the ways I walk and becoming lost as to the finish line. I eventually learned that my agendas affected my motives as to why I did something and my priorities influenced my intentions as to what I would pursue. This caused me to consider the acceptable motives and priorities that would line up to righteous goals.

My motive had to be out of a love for God to ensure service to Him, and a love towards others because God's love makes the salvation of souls and bringing them into His fold His sole agenda. My intention had to be that everything I did was for the glory of God. If God is not ultimately glorified in a matter, I have failed to fulfill my high calling.

As I came to terms with my agendas and priorities, I realize I could no longer assume my character was lining up to righteousness; rather, I had to discern my agendas and priorities to make sure I was operating in a right spirit, confirming and reinforcing righteous goals in relationship to the kingdom of God.

What is your goal? When I first became a Christian, I was zealous towards God, but the Apostle Paul best described me in *Romans 10:2, 2, "For I bear them record that they have a zeal of God, but not according to knowledge. For they being ignorant of God's righteousness, and going about to establish their own righteousness, having not submitted themselves unto the righteousness of God."* Needless to say my zealous ideas fell flat in my initial Christian years.

I had to realize that it was not as much a matter of doing religious things as it was of having right standing in the Lord. Righteousness has three aspects to it. The first begins with believing. We must choose to believe the Lord about such matters as sin, repentance, confession, and salvation that leads to the "born again" experience that puts you in right standing with the Lord.

The next stage of righteousness has to do with being converted to righteousness. To be converted to righteousness entails mixing faith with action that results in obedience to what has been established as being right in God's Word.

The final level of righteousness is godliness. Godliness is exercising the ways of righteousness in practical ways. Can your attitudes, conduct, and practices be traced back to God and His Word, confirming that you are exercising godliness?

I always appreciated how the parable of the Sower and the Seed summarized the four heart conditions, but to see how they manifest themselves I study the kings of Israel. In the past I talked about the heart in relationship to the kings.

It has always interested me that God gave us the examples in the Old Testament as to the ways of something such as righteousness and wickedness and good and evil, while the teaching and summary of it can be found in the New Testament. There are a couple of kings that always cause me to pause because they started out on the right footing but missed the mark of their high calling.

The one king I always cheered on was a man whose heart was lifted up in the ways of God. He sought the Lord and walked in His commandments and took down the high place of idols. He even witnessed a miraculous defeat of his enemies. However, because of some assumption or misdirected notion, he joined himself with Ahaziah, King of Israel who did wickedly, ending with disaster even for his descendants, tarnishing his legacy. His name was Jehoshaphat (*2 Chronicles 17-20*).

Another king started out doing right in the sight of the Lord, but there was important information that was added. He did right as long as the priest Jehoiada was there to influence him (*2 Chronicles 24:2*). His name was Joash, and without godly influence he went into grave idolatry and in the end his own servants killed him and he was not even buried in the sepulchers of the kings.

There was another king who did right before the Lord, brought great victory and reformation to Judah after the temple doors had been shut by his father, but in his later years his heart was lifted up in pride. He did humble himself when he realized the wrath of God was upon him along with Judah and Jerusalem, and as a result stayed God's wrath until after his death. His name was Hezekiah (*2 Chronicles 29-32:25-26*).

As I study these lives, I can see where Jehoshaphat failed to seek God about coming into alliance with a wicked king, while Joash did not establish his own life in the Lord, thereby failing to possess faith and character. And, when it came to Hezekiah he had a hard time accepting God's will, ushering him into a quasi-state that saw the birth of a very wicked king and his heart being lifted up in such a way that God's wrath was upon him.

Obviously, we need to avoid any assumption about our walk with the Lord and seek His will. We must surround ourselves with godly influences and never settle on what we had in God, but shore up what we do possess as we especially guard our hearts when we become weary with the battle, overwhelmed with the challenges, and surrounded by confusing voices

As Christians we can't be half way about anything and think we will somehow be successful in our walk. Perhaps in the world we can slide by but in the kingdom of God there is no simply getting by. If we fail to go forward in our walk, we will find ourselves digressing.

Christians who are half way are half-hearted towards God. Christians who are half-hearted about their spiritual life remind me of Ephraim in *Hosea 7:8* who was considered an unturned cake, burnt on one side and doughy on the other. Such Christians will find themselves half-baked when it comes to the things of this present age and their Christian life.

For example, they can have a zeal towards the things of the world and even make what appears to look noble as their cause, but when it comes to Christianity, they are somewhat doughy. They have an inconsistency that is unattractive and will be spit out by those who try to partake of it.

Clearly, we must not be half way in any aspect of our Christianity because Christ will spit us out and people will keep their distance because there is nothing desirable about our testimony, attitude, practices, and ways. The Bible tells us we must consecrate ourselves, which means we must come out and be separate from the world so we can present our bodies/lives as a living sacrifice to the Lord so He can do with it as He will.

SPIRITUAL SEASONS

There is no riding to heaven in a chariot;
the rough way must be trodden;
mountains must be climbed, rivers must be forded,
dragons must be fought, giants must be slain,
difficulties must be overcome,
and great trials must be borne.
(Anonymous)

What season are we in according to the Word of God? Tuesday night and Wednesday morning, we had a wind advisory for good reason. There is nothing like the force of wind ripping through our area that can blow trees down as if they are mere toothpicks. At such times we expect outages.

For us, it usually is our Internet and water, but for others it is electricity, and sure enough, the communities close to us were without electricity. Sometime during the night, as the wind pounded against our house, threatening to fling anything not nailed down to a different location, I asked the Lord if I should get up and fill buckets with water for our toilet just in case of an outage, but I had the assurance it was going to be alright.

Our electricity went out but came back on by the time we got up to face the day. Our only casualty was our Internet and I am not sure when everyone will have the opportunity to read this post. However, when I saw the lights blinking, I filled buckets with water as a precaution.

For most of us, we expect certain weather to challenge the countryside at different times of the year. If you are like me, I watch the sky and educate myself by checking the weather report to be ready for the unexpected. Even though we do not know when the storms are coming, we prepare for them by preparing for the season that has come upon us.

Jesus spoke of seasons as a means to prepare people to discern the sky, watch for the storm clouds, and prepare for the unexpected. We must never assume the storms will not hit us or presume we will remain untouched by the storms of life. We must be prepared to stand, withstand, and endure to the end.

How important is it to understand the season we are in? As pointed out, it is vital if we are going to be prepared for the storms that are coming. When bad weather approaches, we are ready within seconds to adjust for the possible challenges it may bring. I say all of this because as Christians we should know what season we are now in based on prophecies and the signs of coming storms. It is important to discern the season as a means to prepare for what the days ahead may bring us.

Preparing for the season causes us to watch for the signs, and the signs give us an indication of what we must do to face the day as we live in expectation of what might come. The reason I am saying this is because some people have the cart before the horse. They are looking for the hour, while failing to prepare according to the season so they can face the days ahead to ensure they are ready for the hour of expectation when it finally comes.

The problem with interpreting signs according to an unknown hour is that people see no need to prepare themselves to face the challenges of the day. Jesus was clear when it came to His coming that we were to observe the season through preparations, and discern the signs of the days in order to act accordingly. This was to ensure that we would be ready for that unknown hour of expectancy when He comes again.

Another problem with interpretating everything according to the unknown hour of expectancy is that if the day brings something that one is not prepared to face, a person can end up sliding into the darkness of skepticism, despair, and unbelief. Our hope is not in the hour of expectation, but in the event when the expectation of the promise is realized as the eastern sky parts and Jesus comes for His chaste, expectant bride.

Rayola Kelley

One of the questions I ask myself is what has God put in my heart? For example, has He put a question in my heart that only he can answer? Has He put a prayer in my heart that only He can bring to fruition, or has He called me to something that at the time I knew would have to wait because of my present situation? Has He given me a vision or promise that has not been fulfilled? Perhaps I have even forgotten it because it seemed so long ago.

God never forgets such matters because He has put them there for the right season, but we must choose to guard them, knowing that when the time is right, we will be stirred up to remember what He has given us and we in turn will remind Him. Keep in mind, He does not forget what He has declared and ordained, but it requires faith towards Him to believe it is so as we wait for the right season.

The woman at the well in *John 4* had great confidence that when the Messiah came He would answer all of her questions, and do you know what He did? He answered a question that was at the forefront of her heart and what was the question about? WORSHIP!

We must discern what God has put in our heart, but once we do we must stand in confidence that since it is so in heaven, it will be so on earth. It is in such confidence that we can encourage ourselves that what God has put forth, will in the right time be brought forth for His glory.

One of the wonders of watching a season change is that it seems as if the present season does all it can to hold on before giving way to the next season. Although spring has not officially started, there seems to be a battle going on between winter and spring. This battle causes the weather to always be up in the air and unpredictable.

There can be 60-degree weather one day and snow the next. You can have a nice breeze refreshing your soul on a Wednesday and on Thursday a cold wind that sends shivers through every area of your being. As I watch this battle going on, I am reminded that Christ promises every born-again believer new life, but how many of us are still being pulled, tantalized, or entrapped in certain areas by the old life.

It seems at times as if we are mere puppets being dangled by unseen lines. Our heart is to go one way, but our mind wonders off into the wastelands of vanity, our emotions swing from the heights of fragile limbs of fantasy, and our desires are tossed to and fro by unpredictable waves that seem to be heading right into dangerous currents and storms.

I have been a Christian since 1976 and the one thing I have learned is that dying to the claims of the old-man on me is a daily and sometime minute-by-minute process that I must choose to do. When it comes to the mind, it is not enough to change it here and there, it must be completely transformed by disciplining every thought and bringing each one into captivity in obedience to Christ. This is the only way I can let the mind of Christ become my mind, ensuring a right attitude towards a matter.

When it comes to emotions, they must not determine reality; rather, they must give way to the truth of God's Words to be brought into proper order and submission of the Spirit, and when it comes to desires, they must be discerned and those that are of the flesh must be mortified and those of God, must come into line with His will, His timing, and His plan.

As a believer, I must keep in mind that I needed to be saved from the old so that I could live out the new life of Christ in me. The Bible is clear there will be a battle between the old and new, but it must be one where the old becomes weaker as it loses rights, its claims are silenced more and more, and its power nullified, signifying that the old life has and continues to be overcome by the new creation that is being worked in and out of my life by the Holy Spirit.

Today I woke up to encounter something that brings expectation to my soul. It is the fog that is caused by the autumn season. We live a mile from the Pend Oreille River. Due to the colder temperature of the atmosphere colliding with the warmer temperature of the water and wet ground, we have this curtain that forms and begins to slowly blanket the countryside.

There is a big difference between a smokey covering and the curtain of autumn fog that enfolds the terrain. First of all, the color is different. A smokey covering is a brownish gray that lies heavily upon the landscape, while the autumn fog is simply a damp, almost transparent gray. It reminds me of a curtain that is constantly moving because the Director of all creation is about to part it with the light of day.

This is where the expectation comes in, once the light parts the fog, it highlights different fall colors that will serve as backdrop to life that is all about us. Sometimes there are dramatic skies where clouds set the mood and blue sky that reminds me that what we see is the work of heaven. The autumn fog points to a humbling but inspiring truth.

We are all clothed with humanity through which we attempt to peer into the ways and works of eternity, but we do so through shadows and fog. However, as children of God we can walk in expectancy because the light of Christ, the unveiling of His Spirit, and the revelation of His Word parts the curtain, revealing the sovereign working and care of God. We know that we only know in part and that the mysterious aspects of God's sovereignty are shrouded, but they will not remain as so.

The problem is we must wait for the light of truth to part the grays but we can do so in expectancy knowing that the light is there and at the right time it will part that curtain and we will catch glimpses of the glorious work of God on our behalf, as well as in the lives of others. Such work always proves refreshing, inspirational, and glorious.

Fall is a season of preparation. Today we hear a lot about the spiritual season we are in, in relationship to Jesus' coming. But as believers, we must be discerning as to our response to this time. It's easy to ask if one is ready, but I have learned that the real question that needs to be asked is "What does it mean to be ready?"

To some people, the idea of readiness is vague or they bring it into the material word as far as physical preparation. However, how can you plan physically when you really don't know what is going to happen in your particular area? Do you prepare for a flood or a fire? Perhaps you will lose electrical power or find yourself hiding in some corner because of gangs of rioters, looters, and thugs causing mayhem around you. Don't get me wrong, I believe in preparing as much as we can, but I also know the Bible warns about planning too far ahead, and that we must be careful about storing up worldly goods, because they can easily be destroyed.

When it comes to challenging days for Christians it is about spiritual preparation. This brings us to another question we must explore. How can we prepare for something unless we understand what we are waiting or looking for? As believers we should all be looking for the same event. I have known this event as "The Blessed Hope."

In the past when I have talked about this subject, people are more caught up with the signs that will surround this great hope instead of the actual event itself. In fact, the debates are endless over what we will see or not see before we actually see the source of our hope, Jesus Christ, part the clouds. Sadly, like all fleshly exercises the fruit of this debate has produced skepticism.

I remember after constantly hearing all sides of the debate as to the signs we will see or not see, I went to the Lord and asked Him who was right. I remember He spoke very clearly to me, "All you need to know is I AM coming back."

As believers we must not prepare ourselves according to signs but according to the fact that our precious Lord and Savior is coming back for the second time, and He is coming back for a chaste church, an adorned bride, a prepared people that are looking upward for their redemption and not caught up with unprofitable debates that have no power to save or prepare people to stand, withstand, and continue to stand in the precarious season that is upon them.

We had our first snow storm and guess what? The pansies I mentioned awhile back are still with us, only now they are triumphantly peering through snow. I am still amazed at how the pansies have survived the 21-degree weather, the wind storms, and now the snow storms.

Even after drooping over their containers, their happy little faces with diverse colors continue to rise up above all that is thrown at them to receive the warmth of the sunrays, while appearing to joyfully sending forth praise. Once again, these tough little flowers remind me it is not the size that ensures endurance; rather, it is the strength of the heart, the conviction towards living life to its fullness, and the joy of realizing each day is a gift from God.

It is not unusual to go through challenging times and I believe we are living in the times of sorrows which point to loss that will bring anguish to the spirit and despair to the soul. Jesus stated that in the world there will be much tribulation but do not fear for He has overcome the world, and we know that since we are born again and placed in Him, we will overcome the world by our faith towards Him (*John 16:33; 1 John 5:4*).

Regardless of the darkness of the age, the storms of our time, and the cold hearts of our day, we can endure to the end as we peer through it all with joy because we have been given glorious promises that will not be fully realized until we pass from this present age into the next.

We must cease trying to see through the darkness to understand it for it is too great, but we must look up towards the light. We must not let the winds of judgment blow us off course, the cold hearts cause us to fear and faint, and the storms to bury us under the weight of hopelessness. Like the pansies, we must be ever prepared to grab hold of the eternal life in us as we give thanks for it and look up towards our Creator with the sacrifice of praise on our lips as we glory in the warmth of His love, mercy, and grace.

As we embark further into this controversial season of Christmas, I was meditating on what we as believers need to focus on. Every day we should be naturally celebrating Jesus. It should not be points of celebration during certain times of the year that we acknowledge aspects of our faith, although it is beneficial that we have times to highlight events such as His death, burial, and resurrection, but a daily recognition of who He is (praise), what He has done for us (thankfulness), and the hope and promises we have available to us in Him (worship).

As I consider what we are supposed to be highlighting during this season, I realize there are two distinct truths we need to keep center. The first one is that God became man. He came by way of a virgin, took on the disposition of a servant as He was clothed in humanity. Attached to this great revelation is the fact that the Father gave His Son in this fashion and sent Him forth in order to redeem us. We can get awestruck by His miraculous conception, become sentimental over His birth, and overwhelmed by the reception He received, but the reality is that as a babe born in a manger, He came with a mission that entailed sacrifice and death and a ministry that would revolutionize the way man would walk out his life before God.

At such times we are reminded that God has done His part when it comes to salvation, but what is our part? This season reminds me that my part, which never changes, is to seek Him. Before I can seek Him, I must be led through ordinary activities to the place where I could experience His birth in my spirit and His wonder in my soul in order to come to a place of real dedication and worship.

It is true that the shepherds had to have that incredible encounter with the angelic host in the midst of normalcy, but they remind me that once the revelation of Christ comes, regardless of the time or season, I must rise up out of normalcy and seek Him even in the midst of worldly activities. The wise men remind me that I must seek Him in spite of the signs, times, and controversies of my age. I must not get caught up with the debates of what is acceptable to others or what has been ordained by the religions of the day; rather, I must personally seek Him with my whole heart for myself so I can discover Him, know Him, and develop those places and times that are not marked by man's calendar and traditions, but by personal experiences.

It is those intimate experiences with the Lord that have highlighted places of preparation where I experienced the extraordinary in the midst of normalcy, received heavenly revelation in spite of man's traditions, and spiritual growth in the midst of great darkness, debate, and controversy of the age.

PREPARATION

Earth allows preparation for eternity,
eternity possesses the expectation
of unhindered glory, and glory reminds us
of the glorious face of glory: Jesus Christ
(Rayola Kelley)

The other day when we had the wind storm, we felt we missed the bullet because our power and water remained on. It was a blessing, but yesterday, as we would say, "the bullet found us after all." Some damaged transformer blew two fuses and destroyed our community water pump, and now our whole subdivision is without water and at present there appears to be no one around who is qualified or willing do the necessary work to resolve it.

Water is necessary for life, maintenance, and well-being. We often take it for granted until we are without it and then we begin to appreciate what it adds to our life. As believers we have the rivers of Living Water the Holy Spirit, but how many are in a spiritual drought and don't even realize it? According to *Amos 8:11-12*, the drought has to do with the Word of God. We may have many Bibles, but how much of the truth has been contaminated by heresy, preventing the hearers from seeing where they are spiritually while they slowly faint away because the pure water of the Word is missing.

Water cleanses and I like my showers, but how many are content to be dirty from within. It is said of the religious leaders of Jesus' day, they were like cups that appeared clean on the outside, but were dirty inside. The Apostle Paul described it this way, "Having a form of godliness, but denying the power thereof."

As believers we can assume much because of love, take much for granted due to grace, and unknowingly avoid getting "too wet" with religious conviction, too deep in a life of consecration, too short on vision, and too casual about commitment. To demand mental cleansing involves agreement with what is true, repentance of what is wrong and transformation of the heart attitude.

To insist on inner cleansing entails examination of present status, repentance of spiritual indifference, and confession of missing the mark. To be spiritually cleansed takes the transparent, holy light of God and the purifying fire of the Holy Spirit to reveal what is unclean in our lives, purge us of what is corrupt, and restore what can be sanctified and dedicated to the Lord.

My present unpleasant ordeal with the lack of physical water is temporary, but the rivers of Living Water is what is preparing each of us to stand in the midst of corruption, to withstand with living truth, and to possess the very promises of eternity. Going without outward cleansing will not kill a person, but being void of inward cleansing will bring an individual to a complete state of ruin.

Jesus is coming and the question is are you simply waiting around for the blessed hope to happen or are you preparing in expectation of His coming? We prepare according to who is coming; therefore, who are we expecting?

We are expecting royalty, the King of kings, and will we not put forth our greatest effort in every way to prepare for such an auspicious visitation? The owner of our household is coming back, do we not properly prepare His residence as if He never left? The righteous Judge is coming and we must make sure our record has been truly cleansed by the blood of the Lamb, and our Bridegroom is coming, and we must be fit to meet Him as His chaste bride.

It is clear we are living in prophetic times, and that as believers we are to live in expectation of our Lord coming. However, when it comes to hope there are two important virtues that must be present. One is expectation, but the other is faith. Expectation speaks of waiting, but faith speaks of preparing. Genuine faith will never simply wait for something to happen; rather, faith entails being active in preparation, moving forward in anticipation, and focusing on faithfully and victoriously crossing the finish line.

When Jesus spoke of His coming, He laid out that we must be watchmen who anticipate His coming at any moment, spiritually prepare to be ready to meet Him when He does come, and sober enough to know we must not assume we will be ready without the proper preparation, presume that we will suddenly be able to get ready when He does come, and ever prayerful about being counted worthy when He does come.

We all are aware of the parable of the ten virgins in *Matthew 25:1-13*. They were all waiting for the bridegroom, but only five were prepared to enter into the wedding chamber when the bridegroom came for them. I am living in great expectation of Jesus' coming because it is my blessed hope, but I am also occupying until He comes because the harvest is being prepared for the Lord of the harvest, the kingdom is being made ready for the King, and every bit of my debt caused by sin must be written off through repentance and confession to ensure I stand justified before the Judge. And finally, the church has to be prepared by the oil of the Holy Spirit and clothed in the white, sanctifying linens of righteousness for the Bridegroom to claim her and take her into His chambers.

What attracts you to Jesus? Jesus mentioned the different points of attraction. For His hometown, He was the hometown boy they were familiar with, but when challenged to recognize that He was the Messiah, they went into unbelief and anger.

Some were attracted to Jesus because of what He could do for them in the physical realm. For instance, some followed Him because He fed them bread and fish and when Jesus failed to serve their purpose, they departed from Him, seeking out some other source. The problem with these people is that they are prone to sell their soul to the world.

The next type of attraction that Jesus made reference to was the fact that many followed Him to see signs and wonders. Signs and wonders were a form of entertainment and as long as He performed, this group continue to be impressed with Him, but when he failed to save Himself from the ordeal of the cross, they mocked Him. Jesus said of this group that they represented a wicked generation.

There were those who followed Jesus because that is who the crowd of His day was seeking, and who doesn't want to be part of the world's crowd as a means to fit in? But the problem with such people, like the crowd of Jesus day, is that they can turn around and yell for one's crucifixion.

There were those who had an inclination towards Jesus, recognized the truth of His teachings, and even followed Him. However, when the cost of following Jesus leaves a person confused, troubled, and afraid, they can be separated into one of three groups: those who depart and cease from following Him; those who will betray Him, and those who deny Him.

As a believer we know that the time of separation is a time of testing and for those like Peter who have a heart for God, it will prove to be a time of sifting, breaking, and humbling in order to know forgiveness, find comfort, and experience restoration in order to comfort others. The purpose for such restoration is that when a disciple of Jesus hears the voice of his master, he will be prepared to respond in the right spirit and attitude. And, what will the Master asked of him? "Do you really love me, then feed my lambs, feed my sheep, feed my flock."

Yesterday I asked what attracts you to Jesus. It is not unusual for people to be attracted to what is popular, what feeds the flesh, what placates the pride, what allows them to fit in, or what will serve their particular pursuits. The truth is that to be attracted to Jesus in the right way means being attracted to who He is.

There is only one Lord Jesus Christ and the world is forever presenting counterfeits to seduce man into serving Satan, the flesh is trying to cover its perversion with religious garb to maintain its hold on man to prevent him from consecrating himself totally in following the Lord, and pride adjusts its images and plays the game to come out as more religious and noble than God to receive exaltation and worship. Each counterfeit, wrong pursuit, and misdirected worship leads people away from the true Jesus. Even what we consider to be noble, best, and proper can easily fall short of what is honorable, right, and excellent.

I remember dealing with an individual whose main desire was to be a person of the Word and was able to quote Scripture after Scripture, especially when it came to certain pet doctrines. Sadly, this person fell short of morally obeying the Word and had lost much credibility with those who knew what was going on in their life. As I wrestled with the noble goal of this person, whose fruit lacked real quality and their testimony had become a source of reproach to those who knew the situation, the Lord reminded me there is a difference between being a person of His Word and a man or woman of God, and it comes down to pursuit.

James 1:21-27 tells us we must be doers of the Word, not simply hearers of it. It is clear that for the aforementioned individual, the pursuit was the knowledge of God's Word, but the correct pursuit for any believer is to know God. There is only one means of attraction to the one and only Lord Jesus Christ and that is the Holy Spirit.

The Holy Spirit will lead one to the truth and a greater revelation of Christ. This causes a saint to grow in love with Jesus, as they walk in fellowship with Him, while developing an intimate friendship with Him, ultimately bringing them into a place of sweet communion and worship.

We are in the mode of preparation for a big snow storm to hit us that will last for the next couple of days. We have canceled our Friday night fellowship and are filling various pans with water, including the bathtub, in case the electricity to our water system goes off in our subdivision. The problem with this storm is not only the eight to twelves inches of snow that is predicted to fall, but the wind.

The snow may prove to be heavy but the wind is what can blow down the trees, disrupting our service, causing whiteouts and drifts as well as hiding slick spots on the roadways. As we are preparing for the worst, I had to ponder how many of us in Christianity are spiritually preparing for the days we live in.

We have all the evidence on the horizon that Jesus' prophetic warnings concerning the end of this age are upon us as grave storm clouds are gathering, and in some cases they have already arrived. It's easy to talk about Jesus coming and walk around waving flags and declaring victory, but Jesus clearly stated that the nations of the world would experience grave birth pangs before His appearance and that it would cause men's hearts to grow cold.

Such a concept should cause us to take time out of our daily routines and examine if we are really ready for this blessed event. We need to seriously take the necessary measures to be spiritually prepared, while ensuring our hearts are, and remain, tender towards the Lord in spite of the great darkness engulfing this world. We must learn to be sober watchmen so we are not caught off guard when the storms hit us. *Luke 21:36* gives us three instructions that I have put into caps as to what it means for us to be ready, *"WATCH ye therefore, and PRAY ALWAYS, that ye may be accounted worthy to escape all these things that shall come to pass, and TO STAND before the Son of man."* Clearly, we must have a sober attitude towards the precarious times we live in, as well as pray that we may be accounted worthy to escape it so we can stand without shame before the Son of Man when He does come."

The Bible describes the end days as being precarious. We are living in such times which brings us to an important point and that is will we, as believers, take this opportunity to be part of the solution or will we become part of the problem? Will we take this time to be visible witnesses of the unseen reality (Jesus) and promises of heaven (the eternal and abundant life) or will we be rendered into a puddle that will be taken with the waves of fear or indifference that are the natural responses of the unbridled flesh and the world.

As I watch current events, I see the world acting as expected, people rushing out of fear and panic to selfishly preserve their life. I even understand it because it is the only life they possess and have ever known. Sadly, it is temporary, fragile, and eventually will succumb to death, and it is natural for them to do everything to avoid their demise.

The reason our witness as believers can stand distinct at this time is because our former life is no longer, it is crucified and left in the wilderness, and the life we now possess is eternal. This season will pass, but meanwhile we need to test our faith by our personal responses to this event. I think it is wise for every person to have supplies on hand for such a crisis so they can avoid being taken with the wave of fear and trampled under by its indifference. However, the most important question is are we prepared to personally stand because our faith is founded on our real Provider and Protector, withstand the temptation to be taken away by the tidal wave of panic because we are anchored in Jesus, and continue to stand because we are not of this world and our life is found in the author of Life who is also the finisher of our faith.

THE DAYS WE LIVE IN

Casual Christianity leads
to causalities.
(Pastor Phil Skoog)

We are living in precarious days. Have you ever noticed the emphasis that is invading our society? It is on the supernatural. The supernatural includes such things as spiritualism (communicating with the dead), the New Age (yoking with spirits to gain enlightenment), and the occult (practicing witchcraft). Sadly, some of the beliefs and practices have made inroads into the Christian church.

Satan, the father of lies knows all he has to do is repackage his lies according to the popular fads or the terminology of the age. The problem is that many Christians do not prove ministries or ministers because they do not know how to discern the spirits, ask the right questions, and recognize the fruit. They accept up front a person who can say all the right things, but Jesus clearly stated we will know people by their fruit and not by their speech.

For example, every erroneous belief has a different take on Jesus than the one set forth in Scripture. Jesus is simply one of the way-showers or He is a created being rather than the Creator (*John 1:1-3; Colossians 1:15-18*). The Apostle Paul put it best when describing Jesus in *1 Timothy 3:16, "And without controversy great is the mystery of godliness: God was manifest in the flesh, justified in the Spirit, seen of angels, preached unto the Gentiles, believe on in the world, received up into glory."*

In the Old Testament Jesus was the mystery hidden in shadows, but in the New Testament He is God manifested in the flesh, confirmed by the Spirit, witnessed by the angels, preached to the Gentiles, believed as being the Promised One, and received up into glory in a new glorified body and will one day come back for His church.

Are you ready for Him to come back?

Vance Havner made this statement, "We live in a day of resignation, not to the inevitable, but to the inexcusable and unjustifiable. In the international realm we are resigned to communism with our policy of appeasement, compromise, and peaceful coexistence in hopeless toleration of what should have been isolated and quarantined like smallpox."

There are clearly those who are more concerned about the communistic philosophy of "Political Correctness," instead of being correct in attitude about life, truth, and lawful conduct. There are those who, regardless of personal health issues, are more concerned about compliance with unconstitutional mandates than showing any regard or compassion for those who are vulnerable. Rather than stand against the bullies, the despots, and the tyrants of our time, many have simply resigned and given way to the insane, unjust, and cruel ways of these people in order to simply get along. The problem with getting along with the "infidels" is that eventually resignation will turn into complete surrender to evil.

In the Old Testament walls and gates kept out the enemies, but if the walls were breached and the gates burned, there was no other recourse except to fight to the end, surrender to complete slavery, or become like cornered sheep who will be led to the slaughter. As Christians, we are never told to stand down when it comes to truth and righteousness; therefore, we must never become resigned to accept wickedness in the name of love and peace, ignore iniquity in the name of Christian kindness, or tolerate the evil currents of this time by consoling ourselves that it is God's will, timing, and way.

God has made it clear that we are to stand against the wicked forces of our day. We must keep in mind that we are in a spiritual battle, and the enemy seems to surround us from many different fronts, but we must know the victory is ours, but it requires us to stand, put on our armor, and lift up our sword.

If you have resigned yourself to the "fate," of today, you need to turn around and face God and ask Him for a new vision and to re-assign you to a different post. As servants of the Lord, we must fulfill our obligations no matter what, as runners we must not quit because of the hardness of the terrain, as ambassadors we must not shirk our high calling, and as soldiers we must not abandon our present post, cast aside our armor and lay down our sword in surrender.

Finally, we must not go AWOL to find some small corner or cave to hide in because the battle is intense and fear is reigning. We must know and trust that in every battle, God is our shield, our side guard, and the watcher of our back, and He will never leave us totally to the hands of the ruthless, the despots, and the wicked to do with us as they will.

Yesterday a great wind storm smashed against our house, alerting me that there was an unexpected weather event intruding into my world. The first thing I did was run to the opposite end of the house to see how my flags and the flag pole were weathering the strong winds. Needless to say, the flags were more than waving in the wind and the flagpole was doing everything to withstand the affront leveled against it. In the wind and rain we rescued the flags and pole.

To us the wind was unexpected, but apparently there were warnings going out on the weather channel but we rarely watch TV during the day. Jeannette had noticed the black clouds, but you don't know what to expect or prepare for—rain, wind, sleet, or a combination of all three.

I was reminded of how important warning signs are, but how many of us are tuned into the right channel to hear the warnings? We all know we are living in prophetic times, but how many of us are listening for the warning signs? We have to be tuned into God's Spirit, studying His Word to keep ourselves up to date with the times we are living in, and being realistic that storms are coming, and watching for their approach.

The Bible is clear that if we are spiritually awake, we will not be caught off-guard no matter how great, intense, and fierce the stormy winds of our time may become. Since we are awake, we will be prepared to stand the affront, while maintaining our testimony, and continuing to withstand them.

The windstorm yesterday reminded me that I really can't afford to be caught off guard, spiritually speaking, for there is too much on the line that can be uprooted in my life, taken by the winds into judgment, and unrecoverable because the hour is late and will prevent me from seeing both the damage and the means to recover what has become lost in the ominous winds of this time.

In these dark days, we believers need to know how to encourage ourselves in the Lord. However, it requires me to "remember." The Bible instructs God's people to remember who He is, what He has done, and what He has established as being so.

The first thing I remind myself is that I am simply passing through because I am a citizen of heaven. This world has no claims on me and will not have the final say over my destination.

The second fact I remind myself is God is in control. He knows what is going on in this world and He may have permitted things to happen, but it is for the sole purpose of judging it.

The third thing I remind myself of is that the battle belongs to the Lord and all I have to do is make sure I am on the right side. Granted, I can't be like the paralyzed army of Saul because of a giant, but if I have been provided with the means to stand against the giant with the right tool and use it at the right time, I will actually allow God to show Himself mighty on my behalf.

We make God too small in our understanding, our strength too great in our mind, and remain ignorant and inept when it comes to our weapons. There are two major weapons I use when it comes to spiritual battles. I use God's Word to prepare myself to stand and prayer (intercession) to stand in the gap for others. I must remember that the battle that is going on is spiritual and no soldier of the cross will be able to stand or advance forward to victory unless they know how to properly utilize both weapons.

Another fact I choose to remember is that I am dead to this present world. I once heard it was said of Christians in Communist countries, "How can you kill someone who is already dead?" Today fear is driving many people into an insipid paranoia. They are afraid of losing their life, of paying some type of consequences, and of being betrayed etc, etc, and etc. Fear is the opposite of faith and becomes oppressive to all who submit to its demonic, tyrannical control (*2 Timothy 1:7*). In fear, people may keep their physical life for a short time, but they will lose any quality to it.

As believers we know who numbers our days and it is not the world. We also have the assurance that if we are dead to this world, we know this world has no power to control, oppress, and influence us. We need to keep in mind that we are to be led by the Spirit and as a result we have liberty to advance forward in any darkness by faith, and we have the agreement with heaven that all will be worked out for our good.

Finally, I always remind myself that no one can do anything against the truth but for it (*2 Corinthians 13:8*). Regardless of how much lies and injustice seem to be winning, God's truth is what is going to be left standing in the end. His truth is the absolute standard of heaven and it never changes, adjusts, and it can't be manipulated. It is eternal and sure. My responsibility is to be established on it so I can't be moved by fear and the world's lies, and standing for it when darkness is trying to silence it and snuff out its light.

In the past I talked about what or who are you loyal to. Loyalty operates in different arenas. There is blind loyalty that occurs when one allows passion or sentiment towards something to rule in the arena of ignorance. Such individuals often end up following crowds, fads, and popular philosophies. The Bible is clear that people of this caliber will perish for lack of knowledge.

There is a loyalty that can prove to be idolatrous. Idolatry in any arena points to something being perverted to such an extent that it has become abnormal. This misconstrued loyalty is driven by unabated affections, personal causes, fleshly preferences, and worldly agendas. The main thing that props up this type of loyalty is that instead of seeing that there is really a perversion occurring, these individuals see their loyalty as being honorable, noteworthy, and trustworthy.

The third loyalty has to do with that which is excellent. Loyalty to something that is not worthy of consideration is unwise, allegiance to something that is fleshly and worldly is vain, faithfulness to something that is wicked is foolishness, and devotion to something that is not divine, moral, and righteous is spiritual suicide.

It is clear if we are to survive these times by standing as the Bible instructs, our loyalty can't be fickle, divided, or misdirected.

As Christians we know where our loyalty needs to be towards: The Lord Jesus Christ. We know where our allegiance must stand—on truth. We understand that our faithfulness must be towards what is right and that our complete devotion is firmly planted on the Rock of Ages. I watch various divisions take place between people, including Christians, as individuals often throw reason out the door as they take sides concerning different issues, and once they are planted on their particular side, they are often quick to pick up rocks and throw terrible insults, judgements, and innuendoes at the other side.

Some people stand on their side based on what they are against, and others for what they are for, but how many are simply standing for what is true, right, and acceptable to God? I have learned as long as I stand on the Rock, I stand neither as a judge who throw insults at the other side, a jury that sits in judgment based on whether others see it my way or not, or a spectator that becomes an arm-chair quarterback that knows exactly how everyone should play the game to avoid being considered inept losers.

I have learned that as long as I stand on the Rock, I may see different people come and go depending on their loyalties, callings, and the issues at hand, but it does not matter to me who stands with me or against me because the Rock of Ages never moves from what is true.

My responsibility is not to get others to agree with truth, that is the Holy Spirit's job; rather, my responsibility is to be a living Witness of Jesus, with a written record of what is true on my heart while being a walking epistle of God's salvation that He has shown through sacrificial love, endless grace, and mercies and compassions that are new every day.

THE HIGH CALLING

Naturally, most of us want to avoid the fires of tribulation.
Our flesh desires the promises without the price; however,
if the Spirit leads us, there will be fiery trials on the
"sanctification road". May we follow where He leads
in complete faith and trust.
(Rayola Kelley)

Through the years I have thought about the word "potential." We all have potential but whether we use the tools, talents, and opportunities to reach our potential is another story altogether. When I was in high school, I sensed I had some type of destiny, but I had no clue as to what it was. In time I learned that to understand destiny, one had to come to terms with potential.

Potential gives us an idea as to what our destiny is and what to aim for in order to ensure we reach it. There are a few things I learned about potential: 1) people will never be satisfied with their life or happy in and with themselves until they understand what it is and strive to reach it; 2) True potential requires character that will endure the challenges and obstacles until potential is reached; 3) Nothing makes sense in this life unless we reach our potential, which allows us to view our life from incredible heights. After all, potential never points to digression but progression. 4), And, the final lesson I learned is that our potential can only be realized when we find our life in Christ.

Every creation must function according to the design put forth by its creator. However, the only creation that truly goes haywire is man. He was designed to reflect the glory of God but how many of us are fulfilling our potential? We have been given the tools of God's Spirit and Word that are designed to form the life of Jesus in us, but how many ignore or quench the work of the Spirit, while neglecting and mishandling the Word? We have been given talents to enable us to fulfill our high calling, but we squander them because we have no real vision that lifts us above the insipid world of self and the wicked philosophies, pursuits, and ways of the present age? Finally, how many opportunities did we miss because they didn't fit our theological understanding, and when open to us we were not in the right mood or feeling to pursue them.

To reach our potential of truly reflecting Christ in this dark world, we must be willing to go through the purifying fires in order to come out with the heavenly reflection of Jesus Christ. The cost may be great but the benefits of reaching such heights in the Lord are priceless.

One of the most alarming aspects of fallen man is his attitude towards truth. He wants to adjust it to his reality, ignore it if it does not serve his ideas, mock it if it reveals him to be a hypocrite, and rage against it when it proves him to be a liar. It is clear in man's fallen condition, he has a hard time with truth, but yet truth will remain standing in the end to judge each of us no matter how man wants to stamp it out.

In the days of Judges, outside of the Torah, there was no real standard of truth and since there was no king like the rest of the pagan nations around them, the people of Israel did what they thought was right in their own eyes *(Judges 21:25)*. Sadly, this is what the world is clamoring for in the name of political correctness, but the harsh reality is that without one distinct moral standard of truth there is no place that man can be called to accountability.

Granted, man has been given an inward knowledge of God and righteousness but this conscience in many has either been seared by lies and indoctrination, ignored because it is not self-serving, or logicalized away because it does not adjust or fit to lustful pursuits. The children of Israel were called to lift up the standard of righteousness in the midst of the idolatrous and pagan beliefs and practices around them, but instead they succumbed to them.

The question is how much is the church lifting up the standard of truth and righteousness according to their high calling and how much is it sliding into the cesspool of what it was called to come out of and be separate from?

As a Christian I am aware of my personal challenges with the inherent disposition of Adam in me and that I must apply the cross daily to gain any headways in this world. As a citizen of this nation, I have watched fleshly exercises, worldly entertainment, and vain pursuit of fleshly happiness numb many to the spiritual digression taking place in every arena, while some, including myself, constantly struggle to come out and be separate from it. And, as part of the body of Christ, I have watched some being taken captive by wolves, others growing dull to spiritual matters, and some becoming indifferent to the great commission of the church, while a blanket of spiritual despair causes many to battle hopelessness and isolation because they feel like Elijah among wicked leaders, false prophets, and idolatrous people.

However, the Bible reminds me that such times are for a season. We need to know the season we are in and I believe that it is in a time like that of John the Baptist, that the church's voice ceases to be weak among the insane times of political correctness and woke, and becomes clear and firm as it calls for true repentance.

As in the days of Gideon, the real soldiers need to step up and be separated for the battle, like Isaiah the church needs to ask for the people's lips to be purged, and like Jeremiah it needs to cry over sins, while taking up the example of Elijah and asking God's fire to fall on its altars. It needs to recognize it was never meant to fit in the world and like Elisha burn the bridges to the old in order to be consecrated to be endowed with a new mantle of anointing so that even in the grave its very remains will cause one to rise from the dead.

This is the high calling of God's people. In extraordinary times, we as believers, are not being called to be super spiritual, but to allow God to raise us up with His power to meet the challenges with assurance that no matter what happens on the battlefields or in the harvest fields, God will leave His mark on hearts, add souls to His church, take possession of what is His, and come out the Victor.

What is your calling? As believers, we have the same two-fold commission—to preach the Gospel (the death burial and resurrection of Christ that addresses all aspects of our sin) and to make disciples of CHRIST, not converts to a particular belief, denomination, or popular leader.

To function as a body, we have different callings in which we are to carry out the commission. To carry out our commission we are entrusted with certain abilities or giftings of the Holy Spirit to ensure success and fulfillment. It is not unusual for Christians to sense their calling, but the problem is they make two mistakes, they define it according to worldly understanding and they set out to bring it about in their own strength. Both scenarios will meet with utter failure.

A good example is Moses. He had a sense that he was to somehow help his people and when he saw a Hebrew brother being harassed by an Egyptian, he took matters into his own hands and killed the Egyptian. Instead of his action exalting him in the eyes of his people, it ended up driving him into the wilderness for forty years.

Just because we have a calling, we must not assume that we understand what it will entail and presume that it is up to us to bring it about. The truth is God has His own ways and He has His own timing. Meanwhile, we must learn to wait upon the Lord for His timing, while being faithful to occupy in obedient faith in preparation for when the Lord finally calls us forth to carry out our high calling established before the foundation of the world.

Are you a holy temple? When you consider the Old Testament temple, inner defilement of idolatry eventually brought judgment upon the people of Israel and ultimately left the temple building in complete ruin along with their religious feasts and rituals. The more we ignore the encroachment of self into the activities of our souls and let the world come in and influence our thinking and conduct, the more our life will fall into disarray.

The temple of our body must be like the temple of old. It was separated from the world by walls (of protection from enemies from without) and gates (of preservation of the integrity of inner activities). The priests dealt with their sin at the Altar of Burnt Offering by offering the necessary sacrifices (the cross of Christ to us) and washing at the laver (the Word of God to us), where they cleaned themselves to enter into the Holy Place to minister before the Lord.

The Bible is clear, we must crucify the self-life and separate ourselves from this present age to make sure that our consecrated lives are not defiled from without or from within. This is the only way we can ensure that our temples do not come under some kind of judgment leaving our lives in ruins.

Is there any unholy agreement in your life? The Apostle Paul talks about unacceptable unions in *1 Corinthians 6:17-19, "But he that is joined unto the Lord is one spirit. Flee fornication. Every sin that a man doeth is without the body; but he that committeth fornication sinneth against his own body. What? know ye not that your body is the temple of the Holy Ghost which is in you which ye have of God, and ye are not your own?"*

We do not belong to ourselves for we have been bought with a price and have no real say over our lives. As temples we are places where God's glory resides and we are to reflect it in our attitudes, lives, and actions. Since we have the Holy Spirit in us, there can be no spiritual agreement with someone who is of a wrong spirit.

To try to come into agreement with a wrong spirit will cause a person to spiritually fornicate him or herself defiling his or her temple. It is for this reason that the Apostle Paul points out in *2 Corinthians 6:16, 17, "And what agreement hath the temple of God with idols? For ye are the temple of the Living God; as God hath said, I will dwell in them, and walk in them; and I will be their God, and they shall be my people. Wherefore come out from among them, and be ye separate, saith the Lord, and touch not the unclean thing; and I will receive you."*

We are not to wallow in the pig pens of the world, play footsy with idols, and use our bodies to come into unholy agreement, whether physically or spiritually. We must remind ourselves that we are to be holy temples, living lives set apart, standing as beautiful witnesses of God's glory, and being separate from worldly attitudes, idolatrous conduct, and selfish actions.

Revelation 12:11 states, *"And they overcame him (devil) by the blood of the Lamb, and by the word of their testimony; and they loved not their lives unto the death."* (Parenthesis added.) Testimony points to witness and another word for witness is "martyr." What kind of witness do you want to leave behind?

Enoch left a living, ongoing testimony behind for he was taken by the Lord, but there are other witnesses we must consider in order to answer the question. In the life of Cain and Abel we have an example of the two types of witnesses. One witness cried because the consequences of his sin was too great to bear, and he became a fugitive to God, while *Hebrews 11:4* speaks of the witness of Abel, whose blood cried from the earth, leaving a greater and lasting witness for those who follow by faith.

The key is people will only leave two types of witness behind, that which dissipates or that which has a touch of eternal significance that becomes part of the great cloud of witnesses as it follows a saint into eternal glory. Cain ended up wandering the world as a vagabond and establishing the first, ungodly city ruled by man due to his separation from God, while Abel's life, sacrifice, and blood continues to serve as a testimony for the saints of every subsequent generation.

As Christians we must consider what type of testimony we are establishing because so many religious people are establishing a witness of dead religion that will fall when the storms of life challenge their faulty foundations. As Christians we are to be living epistles that have the very words of life written on our hearts, ingrained in our minds, and established in our lives.

People will naturally read and examine whether our witness is true by how we live (*2 Corinthians 3:2-4*). We need to keep in mind, our witness has been established by the death of Jesus. We are marked by His blood which identifies us to His redemption and covenant. His life in us reminds us He is not a dead Savior, but a Living Lord who sits on the right hand of the Father as our High Priest and Intercessor. The question is how distinct and impactful is our witness before the unseen realm of angels and demons and to a dying world of lost souls?

TIME

Jesus is the ladder that connects
the work of heaven with the matters
of earth.
(Rayola Kelley)

God's timing is everything. I know I am impatient to do each project, whether of an earthly, worldly nature or of a spiritual one so that I can go onto another project. I have lists to mark off and plans to complete; therefore, I am never bored, left without purpose, or lost due to the endless vanity of activities. I want to do what the Bible tells me to do and that is redeem the time because the days are evil.

As I get older, I become increasingly aware that my time to finish the course, fight the fight, and keep the faith is becoming narrower and narrower in scope. My challenge remains the same, to be faithful with what is in front of me but I must prioritize my activities. I begin with God.

Lately it has been with prayer. In the past, I first meditated on Scripture giving Him an opportunity to talk to me by way of inspiration, instruction, and revelation and as He lays a matter on my heart to pray for. However, we are living in dark times. Jesus spoke of the night coming when no man can work. Such darkness is upon many of us and the question is what are we to do? There is only one thing we can do in this waiting time and that is to intercede.

Author Jerry Sittser said it best, "The quickest way for anyone to reach the sun and the light of day is not to run west, chasing after the setting sun, but to head east, plunging into the darkness until one comes to the sunrise." We must turn and face the present darkness to avoid surrendering in fear to hopelessness. We must avoid trying to outrun it by holding onto foolish notions and realities of denial, or give way to the anger and bitterness of it; rather, we need to know that it calls for, as well as affords each of us as God's people, an opportunity to truly intercede. Instead of looking for a way around this darkness, I challenge every believer to look up to the light and pray their way through this time while seeking God's heart, will, and way for their life.

As we approach the New Year, we must decide if we want to look forward by making new resolutions or whether we look forward based on the glorious promises of God. I like to make resolutions but they have to do with what I would like to see happen, but if I consider my present life in light of my final destination, I can properly put what is important to God in proper perspective in order to line up personal agendas and priorities to that which is eternal.

A new year in God's timetable points to the reality that time is short and when you are my age you have already hit many peaks, and even though one may see other mountains in front, the personal strength to climb those mountains has been ebbed away by time.

In my Christian journey, I have had to learn to be a mountain climber because God does not move all of the mountains out of the way. I am not an expert mountain climber but I have gained some wisdom along the way to learn that I must first redeem the time before I try scaling another mountain without first seeking out the Lord as to my approach, the mission and the destination.

This year, as believers instead of making resolutions, let us rededicate ourselves to our real mission according to our high calling and our eternal destination.

As we embark onto a new year and into a new decade, we need to make sure that there is nothing in the way of running the race set before us. As I get older I am less patient and recently I realized that I don't have the time to be patient because I am only promised today, nor do I have the energy to be easy-going about things I used to be or possess the resolve to pull myself back from becoming impatient when I see time and energy being wasted.

Keep in mind, I am not talking about waiting on the Lord; rather, I am talking about redeeming the time. In the past, time got away from me because I felt I had more time. I could afford to be more easy-going because I figured I had the strength to work it out or work around it in the end. However, I found out time is easily wasted in such cases, energy can quickly flow out like the tides and one's resolve must be standing on what is possible and necessary to be firmly grounded.

The example of the priests of the Old Testament reminds me of a very important principle. They wore white linens underneath their robes, and the white linens represented righteousness. Not only did the priests not stand in their own righteousness before God, but the linens kept them from sweating, pointing to the fact that all service to God was not a matter of man's personal work or attempts.

As Christians, we stand in the righteousness of Jesus and the real work has been done on our behalf. We are to carry the burden of His love and come under His yoke when it comes to carrying out His work. When I start "sweating" in any point of my service to the Lord, I realize that I have added to my burden in some way, or when I find myself wrestling with the yoke, I am now trying to accomplish something in my own strength my way.

God's burden keeps my perspective and heart attitude right before Him while His yoke for me keeps me in step with His timing and ways. Are you "sweating" as you enter into this New Year? If so, you are wasting time by carrying a burden He has not given you, or you are under a yoke that will keep you from accomplishing the tasks set before you.

When was the last time you walked down memory lane? As I have shared with my friends, being on Facebook has made me feel like a Rip Van Winkle who was asleep for twenty years and woke up to a different world. I have reconnected with some friends I have not seen or talked to for over 30 years.

It is obvious we have traveled different paths. The common denominator for many of us is our past, and there are memories to awaken what was, but one discovers a big gap between the past and the present, and quickly realizes that memories alone will not bridge such a gap.

As I was meditating on this fact, I can remember when I allowed time to pass between me and the Lord. Granted, I was busy with religious things but I let some dust collect on my personal time with Him, causing leanness in my spirit. My relationship with the Lord has taught me that healthy relationships require people to grow together. There must be the constant establishing and maintaining of common ground in which a relationship can take root and grow.

God has made the necessary investment in His relationship with me through the sacrifice of Jesus. I have the common ground of redemption in which I can meet Him and even though dust occasionally settles on my time with Him, I remember that all I need to do is go back to where I left the Lord in my business, remembering He is always the I AM (the past and the future comes together in Him), who is ever present to welcome me back into sweet communion with Him. The Lord not only proves to be a faithful, enduring friend, but our relationship together proves to be a timeless friendship.

We humans are creatures of time. God made us that way when He established time, which according to the Bible, it was on the fourth day of creation He made the two great lights, one that would rule the day and the other one would rule the night. They would essentially mark time with seasons, days, and years.

It is amazing that He began with the evening and not the morning and we know that the Jews count their day from evening to evening and we Gentiles count it from sunrise to sunrise. If the first day of the week is Sunday, then time was inserted into creation on what we consider to be Wednesday. Up until that time, everything was being created within the dimension of eternity where there is no time, no moments, minutes, hours, days, months, and years.

People ask, "What came first, the chicken of the egg?" The answer is simple, the chicken because God created everything in its mature state to ensure that it would be able to reproduce after its own kind, including man. When you study why God inserted time into creation you begin to realize it is to protect and preserve mankind.

We can look at our own time and see the great corruption of man causing homes to spin out of control, societies to take a nosedive into a cesspool of wickedness, our nation gasping for breath as it is being drowned by the onslaught of pure corruption and evil, and we are told that there will be a time when earth will wobble like a drunkard.

The truth is time puts a limitation on generations because they often become wicked, lives cut short because the days are evil and will consume them, and on corruption with judgment and wrath. This is why we are told to redeem the time we have. We need to remember that our life is define by timing that God ordains, controls, and uses to control the seasons of our lives. And, as one of my favorite songs reminds me, "I am here for such a time as this." May I redeem the time, be true to the life given to me, and remain faithful to my high calling.

I have mentioned how we are creatures of time. Time can be many things to us: a teacher when it comes to the past, a nemesis when it comes to productivity, and a friend when it comes to experiencing the different aspects of life. I recently shared with a precious soul how memories are found in the moments, opportunities in the minutes, and accomplishments in the days, otherwise months become a blur and years a passing fancy or disillusionment where vague shadows will dissipate with time.

Since we are creatures subject to time, we often try to understand the days we live in according to our limited understanding and worldly calculations instead of understanding God must insert Himself into time to interact with us in the fleshly arena. Such interaction is sometimes referred to as "the day of visitation."

Since God is not subject to our time, what determines when He does insert Himself into history, in the midst of humanity? It comes down to when He brings all the events prophesied together in order to bring forth "the fullness of the time." This was true for Jesus' entrance into the world, *"But when the fulness of the time was come, God sent forth his Son, made of a woman, made under the law To redeem them that were under the law, that we might receive the adoption of sons"* (Galatians 4:4-5).

The key word is "fullness." All prophesied events must converge at the right time (environment) to ensure that all things will be fulfilled according to His Word. You can see this as you study the events surrounding both Jesus' conception and birth. As to our need to know the exact timing of Christ's birth, most agree He was miraculously conceived in December and was born in September during the feast of Trumpets. After all, heaven announced His birth. As the Lamb of God, He came to not only atone for the sins of the people (Day of Atonement) but to tabernacle among them (Feast of Tabernacles).

In our limited understanding there is no way we will know when everything has come together for Him to fulfill His plan. A good example of that are the days we live in. *Romans 11:25* talks about blinding the Jewish nation until the fullness of the Gentiles is accomplished and *Ephesians 1:10* states, *"That in the dispensation of the fulness of times he might gather together in one all things in Christ, both which are in heaven, and which are on earth; even in him."*

We can't know the exact time when all events in the right environment are all aligned for Him to fulfill His plan, but we should not be ignorant of the season, the day, and the time we are living in because God's Word lays it out. However, we must avoid trying to interpret the time according to our theology and fit events into our timeframe, which will cause debate and confusion. It is vital that we pay attention to the signs to discern the times, but above all else we need to seek the Lord to show us by His Spirit what we need to know about the days in which we live in, in order to prepare and brace ourselves for the storm that may come our way.

We are told in the Word of God to redeem the time because the days are evil. We need to walk uprightly and not as fools, but be wise as to the days we live in as we seek to understand and do the will of the Lord. We must avoid being filled with the ways of the world, but be filled with the Holy Spirit so we can walk in power and authority *(Ephesians 5:15-17)*.

Wicked people seek to be the master of the innocent and lords over the righteous. They want to oppress the people into service to them. If they can't control certain individuals, they will try to seduce them into their warped reality in order to destroy them. Ultimately, the evil will rage against those who refuse to bow their neck before their wickedness.

We are living in evil days, and as unbelievers prepare to go back to their former lives after this virus passes, we as believers need to realize this is our opportunity to examine what we are doing with our time and make sure that the bent of our character is not towards this world, but towards obeying the Lord. We need to let the light of Christ's life in us shine as we walk in righteousness, respond according to godliness, and avail ourselves to know and do the will of God at all times.

What does it mean to redeem the time? Redeeming has to do with buying back or ransoming what has been unjustly taken. So much robs us of time and if our time is being robbed, so is our energy and possible accomplishments.

Time is a gift and according to Scripture our life is like the grass and flowers, here one day and fading the next and eventually will be no more. Therefore, we need to identify the culprits that would rob us of our precious time.

One of the biggest culprits is wasting time on that which is vain and useless. Many times, we justify this culprit because we are tired or we have earned the right to do as we please with our time regardless of how silly, foolish, and vain our activities might be. Wasted time often reveals how selfish our priorities are and that we are procrastinators and lazy when it comes to what is eternal.

It is easy to put off eternal matters until tomorrow, but like our life, the tomorrows fade into today and cease to be. To avoid wasting time, we must daily seek the face of God and find out what is important to Him, and once it is clear we MUST DO IT.

We are living in interesting times. As believers we look back and see a cross where our history and future have come together to influence our present. For Christians, history speaks of justification, the present points to the ongoing work of sanctification, and the future points to glorification, but meanwhile we live in a world where history is being eerily repeated, prophesy is being fulfilled, and the present events are reminding us we are living in precarious times.

It is hard to keep the present in perspective. Many want to opt out by creating a false reality, while ignoring the present reality, or to rage against it because it cannot be controlled. Clearly, we are living in exciting times, but trying times that will overwhelm the soul if a person is not firmly planted on Jesus, standing according to His Word, and living in expectation of the promises that are yet to come.

As a Christian I couldn't handle the reality of this present world without clinging to the eternal, immovable truth of God. I would utterly become hopeless and skeptical if I thought the present life was all there was to life. As a Christian I look back to remember I do not belong to this world, I consider the present in light of future promises and the future in light of being glorified with the One who so loved me and captured my heart.

As Christians we must not let our focus settle on this world, but we must continue to look up, knowing that this world is a testing, preparation ground for each of us. Paul described what awaits us in this fashion in *1 Corinthians 2:9, "But as it is written, Eye hath not seen, nor ear heard, neither have entered into the heart of man, the things which God hath prepared for them that love him."*

Rayola Kelley

I've been thinking a lot about time recently because it is my goal to complete all of my projects, and I struggle with pushing through the different demands of the day so I can make the time to wrap them up. I am the type that never wants to leave anything undone.

When I was in the military and within a few months of fulfilling my enlistment, I earned the prized title: short-timer. Those who were counting down years and months envied the short-timer, but for the short-timer the days until their enlistment was completed seemed like an eternity. It was as if everything was moving in slow-motion. However, the day for my release came in a surprising way.

The problem was I was counting the hours and not the days. Hours have a way of inching their way towards the next hour but they never seem as if they are going to cross the finish line. However, when everything settles, the day seems to escalate into high speed as it moves us into the next day with lightning speed. It is then that we realize we didn't have enough waking hours in the day to complete our goals.

It is for this reason time is not always a great gauge unless you consider it in light of eternity. Time plus eternity equals a realistic gauge that can create a proper perspective. What is a day to eternity? According to 2 Peter 3:8 one day with the Lord is as a thousand years and a thousand years as one day. In other words, we can't calculate or fathom eternity in light of our days.

When it comes to eternity, the shadows of the past come together with the working of the present as the reality of the future comes into focus. The past is "so be it," the present is "amen," and the future is "for it is so." When it comes to suffering, we are told in light of eternity it will be considered as a light affliction that works a far greater glory in us.

In light of a certain day such as our physical death or Jesus coming, we will not know the hour of it, but we will experience the promise of the abundant life as we enter the presence of God to abide with Him forever. As to the minute, something will happen, we must be prepared to hear our Shepherd and bridegroom's invitation in order to follow Him whether it is up a different path, through a different door, or into a different dimension. And, when it comes to the moment, the corruptible will give way to the incorruptible in the twinkling of an eye.

312

The one thing I realize is that in light of eternity every saint is a short-timer and we must redeem the days, be prepared to hear His call any minute and know that in a moment everything could be changed for us.

VESSELS AND INSTRUMENTS

*God can take an insignificant branch like Abraham
and produce fruit a thousand-fold.
He can take a small branch like David
and produce a strong nation. He also took an
unlikely branch in the form of His Son,
and provided salvation for all who will believe.
(Rayola Kelley)*

When considering new year, it would be a good time to reflect on the past year, consider the present year to make sure we are on course and prepared to run the necessary race in light of that which is eternal. When I reflect on the past year, I ask myself if I am carrying any regrets forward, feel bad because of missed opportunities, or wish I had redeemed the time better.

I do this examination in order to repent and become wiser with the present. It is important to tie up any possible loose ends still left dangling that Satan could possibly use as a whip against me. When I consider my present, I do it in light of the future. The way I consider my future in relationship to disciplining my steps is according to the epitaph I would like to leave behind.

Although I am very much alive, as a believer, I am aware I am walking towards my demise. I ask myself what type of witness do I want to leave behind in relationship to my character, life, and convictions as a Christian. Granted, it only matters how God sees us and epitaphs are written by those left behind. But we must acknowledge that such inscriptions are engraved on hearts according to the type of investment we make in those relationships.

When I first started this little practice, my epitaph was quite elaborate revealing the high opinion of myself. It became quite clear that my arrogance wanted to still be recognized and exalted. Through the years as I became more aware of how wretched I was and how God's mercy had reached me in my despair, His grace had provided the way for my salvation, and His hope raised me up in a new life, I was knocked off my pinnacle and brought down to face the reality that it is and always will be God's work that endures.

I am nothing more than a mere clay vessel that has no significance outside of the life of Christ I possess, a simple, worn instrument that has no worth or beauty unless in the master's hand, and a vulnerable worm in the scheme of things. It was at that time I adopted another epitaph that I read about that was left on a wooden grave marker. This marker had only one word carved on it: "Forgiven."

I eventually graduated from the one word, "forgiven" to two words, "faithful servant." I must admit, I have moved on to three words and they are words that I hope will, in the end, serve as the epitaph I leave behind. They are, "FRIEND OF GOD."

Do you possess the real prize of heaven? Vessels may be useful for certain activities, in which they may be used to advertise and attract people to their contents, but we need to keep in mind at all times that it all comes down to what is on the inside. Granted there are vessels that are simply for show, but in God's kingdom it is about the contents that His people possess.

In this world where it is all about image, we must make sure we do not fall into the trap of being simply an advertising board with the name of "Christian" printed on it. Our outer life should tastefully advertise and attract people, but not to us. People need to initially be attracted by our countenance or actions, stirring up enough interest for them to check out the contents. Once an interested party is exposed to the "contents" of Christ, it must/will cease to be about the vessel as it recedes into insignificance.

John the Baptist put it best, "I must decrease so He (Jesus) can increase." As vessels of God, we must remember we are filled from above by the hand of God with the life of Jesus. We know that this filling involves the Spirit of God who identifies us to the value of the contents within and serves as a seal that it has the very endorsement of heaven behind it.

What are you saying about the Potter? There is quite the process a clay vessel must endure in order to be brought forth as an honorable, useable vessel to God. One of the interesting facts about the vessels in Japan is that the potters have two celebrations. The first one involves all the potters.

They have to work 24/7 around the clock when the vessels are in the ovens to make sure that the temperature is kept at the right degree. Once they are finished with the process, they celebrate together along with many of those of the community. This reminds me of the celebration of heaven over one sinner coming to repentance mentioned in *Luke 15:3-10*.

The second ceremony occurs once the oven is cooled. It is at this time that the potter invites those close to him to a very private ceremony. He goes into the oven to bring each piece out one by one so that the individual piece will speak of his gift and ability to create masterpieces.

As believers we need to keep in mind that heaven has already rejoiced over our salvation, but now the world must clearly see our great Potter's ability to bring us forth as His masterpieces, and not only for the purpose for others to admire His great skill, but to bring honor to Him as our Creator, God, and Redeemer.

What kind of vessel are you? The Apostle Paul made this statement in *2 Timothy 2:20, "But in a great house there are not only vessels of gold and of silver, but also of wood and of earth; and some to honour, and some to dishonor."*

When I come to statements like this I pause and ask myself tough questions. For example, when it comes to this Scripture, I consider what kind of vessel am I? I would like to be gold or silver that when put in the fire will be more so refined, but am I a vessel of wood that can be rendered in ashes by the fire of judgment (separation) or a clay vessel that in the end will not withstand the heat of trials and tribulations and break into many pieces? The next question I must ask, "Am I a vessel that will bring honor to my Lord or am I a vessel that my Lord will eventually render judgment upon?

In my Christian life I have hid behind certain aspects of Christianity that allowed me to live in assumptions about my Christian life without truly examining the fruits that were being produced. There is a tendency to overlook or downplay Scriptures that remind Christians that they are called to live according to a level of excellence when it comes to character and conduct.

So what determines the quality of our lives as vessels of God? The answer is simple: it comes down to our heart condition. Is our heart pliable and sensitive to the Lord so that we can be made a prized vessel, used in honorable ways to bring glory to our Potter?

What kind of vessel am I? The Apostle Paul relates how believers are nothing more than mere earthen vessels that possess a treasure within (*2 Corinthians 4:7*). Earthen vessels point to clay vessels, and every believer knows the treasure is the life of Jesus.

There are many vessels out there such as glass, aluminum, plastic, etc., but we are not to be just any vessel that can be used once and cast aside or even recycled, we are to be a clay vessel. From the information I have read about this subject, clay covers 75% of the earth, which makes it available, but what sets clay apart is the process and what it will be used for once finished.

In Japan pottery making is a real art and the stages the potters take the clay through include weathering it (keeping it out in the elements from anywhere from 2 to 5 years), water (putting it in a vat of water to step on it and separate it from impurities), pounding (the potter works it until it is ready to be shaped—an expert potter goes by touch and feel of the clay), the wheel (shaping and forming it for a particular use) and then the ovens.

I have found myself experiencing this process, except my weathering process took seven years, the water process took five years, the pounding process three years and I have been in and out of the ovens for the last 27 years. Through it all I have been aware that the Lord was, and is continuing to work on me and will do so until He brings me home.

As a clay vessel have you considered where you are in the process of being made a vessel fit for His use? Adam's body was made from the dust of the earth and since we all are made up of water, as a result all of our bodies will return back to the dust of the earth. I am sure we all can agree there is no shortage of humans in this world, but what makes each of us distinct?

Our Master Potter, the Lord knows what kind of process to take us through in order to bring us forth as a vessel fit for His use. Just like the clay being prepared by a skilled potter, the Lord is preparing each of us as He forms and shapes us into a unique vessel for His use. The question is, am I allowing Him to prepare me or must I be left in the weather longer? Am I allowing the water of the Spirit to separate me from impurities or am I insisting on holding on to that which is profane? Do I submit to Him working on and in my life so that I can be put on His wheel and formed into the vessel He has designed me to be?

Clay must become pliable in the hands of the Potter and I have learned from my process, regardless of what it takes and how long it takes, being made into His vessel to carry, advance, and offer the treasure of heaven to others is well worth the process.

Have you been in the ovens? Yesterday I made reference to the process clay goes through to become a vessel of use. Clay vessels can be broken down at any point and made into clay to be reshaped by the potter; that is, until they are put in the ovens. It is the fires of the ovens that finally establishes the vessel. We know it is the fiery trials of our faith that firmly establishes us in Christ (*1 Peter 1:5-9*).

A potter can put certain clay vessels on a shelf with the intent of making them better or reshaping them for a greater purpose. Some of us have felt like we have been put on the shelf, but if so it is because

Rayola Kelley

God has a greater plan for us and must reshape us to be made more useful. However, once shaped, then we must be established in our calling and in the work the Lord has for us.

This only happens when we are placed in the ovens. According to the information about vessels made in Japan, each vessel had to go through two firings. They would individually be placed in the oven by the potter. Keep in mind, one oven in Okinawa, Japan held thousands of vessels and each vessel had to be placed in a certain spot of the oven depending on how hot the oven became.

It is important to remember that when the Lord is establishing us in our faith and high calling that He has personally placed us in the oven at the right place to receive the correct heat, in order to bring us forth as a vessel made for His use. Is that not why we are here, to be vessels of honor for His glory and use?

As a vessel, will we trust the potter to bring us to our potential? We all have such great potential in God's kingdom, but we must trust the potter with the outcome.

One of the things that fascinated me was that there were only a couple of washes that were used by the Japanese potters to color the vessel, but the potter never knew what it would look like because the clay and the heat would determine the final hue. I am sure that the potters wondered if the particular wash would reveal a glorious design that would prove pleasing to the eye of all who looked upon it.

Out great Potter knows as His vessels how we are going to come out of the ovens, but we need to remember our attitude towards the Lord and the process He is taking us through will determine what pattern is set forth in our lives. Paul's process made him aware that he was setting forth a pattern for others to follow (*1 Timothy 1:15, 16*).

May we come forth as prized vessels that reveal our Potter's handiwork to establish a visible pattern of the work of Christ in our lives for the world, and those following in our footsteps to observe the Lord's mastery, and bring glory to Him!

Have you considered yourself a vessel? There are four types of vessels. There is the full vessel that can't receive, an empty vessel that is for show, a cracked vessel, and an open vessel. As believers we must be an open vessel to receive, knowing that the heavenly contents are meant to be poured out for the benefit of others.

There is a difference between a cracked vessel and a broken vessel. A cracked vessel represents someone who has been broken by some type of circumstance and has attempted to put themselves back together, causing inconsistencies in their lives. However, as Christians we experience brokenness at times and the reason for it is because God wants to put us back together as a vessel for His use, open to receive the contents He has for us, and to be used to pour it in others.

The vessel that is empty of any contents may be good for show, but for the Christian realm it points to a vessel that is described in *2 Timothy 3:5, "Having a form of godliness, but denying the power thereof; from such turn away."*

Once again we are reminded it is the contents in us that stipulate our value and if a person is empty of the Spirit of God, he or she may be self-righteous outwardly but lack any heavenly power. The vessel that is full represents those who are full of their self-life.

The question will always come back to the contents we possess within.

Are you full of the right contents? I mentioned four types of vessels yesterday. One of the vessels is the vessel that is full of the self-life. There is an important truth found in *Matthew 9:16-17,* that speaks to this very subject, *"No man putteth a piece of new cloth into an old garment, for that which is put in to fill it up taketh from the garment and the rent is made worse. Neither do men put new wine into old bottles: else the bottles break, and the wine runneth out, and the bottles perish: but they put new wine into new bottles, and both are preserved."*

As vessels of God, we must be emptied of the self-life to be filled with the life from above. However, the process often entails being broken before we can be rid of the defilement that comes with the old, and be prepared to be filled with the new.

In *Leviticus 11:32-33*, we are told a wooden, skin, or bronze vessels corrupted by something such as a dead body could be washed, but an earthen (clay) vessel had to be broken. Brokenness has occurred in my life many times. This brokenness happened because of sin or a corrupt area being exposed in my life. Such brokenness produces humility and repentance.

The truth of the matter is we must be broken because of our former corrupt life and our lives must be put back together by the Lord to ensure we become a vessel fit for His use.

Are we a show vessel or a useable vessel? Outward religion with its different rituals allows us to become mere show vessels, but our worth is based on whether we have been made fit for the Master's use. In essence, do we possess the prize and fragrance of heaven?

We can be the most incredible show vessel on display in this world, but if we do not possess the right contents within, Jesus will not be able to claim us as His own when we stand before Him. We cannot afford to be mere show vessels that bring recognition to ourselves; we must possess the oil of the Spirit.

We all have read the parable of the ten virgins in *Matthew 25*, five were wise because they had the necessary oil to identify them when the bridegroom came for them, but there were five foolish virgins who lacked the necessary oil and had to go purchase some at the last minute and missed the bridegroom.

We must beware of what we are working towards—to give the impression of being Christian or are we living the life of Christ because He is in us and as our great Potter, we are in His hands being used by Him?

What does it mean to be a vessel of God? For me it has proved to be very liberating and given me the opportunity to be who I am, letting God use me the way He wants to regardless of the biases or prejudices attached to my person, status, or gender.

The type of vessel the Lord uses is not based on man's ideas or standards as to what is acceptable and worthy of consideration. Even Samuel made the mistake of stopping at the outer appearance in *1 Samuel 16:7, "But the LORD said unto Samuel, Look not on his countenance, or on the height of his stature; because I have refused him: for the LORD seeth not as man seeth; for man looketh on the outward appearance, but the LORD looketh on the heart."*

So many times we limit ourselves by the fact we judge the vessel and not the contents, or are limited by a certain stigma that has been attached to a particular vessel. In fact, the Lord has shown me that the very things that people judge me for that was and is beyond my control such as gender, status, etc. serves as the test of their own character.

Through my walk with the Lord, He has used these boards in people's eyes to guide my steps. I have learned to trust that God is not limited by other people's hang-ups; rather, He uses them as an opportunity to show His obedient servants how He is still able to carry out His will.

I must remind myself that God's church and kingdom is His work, all I have to do is surrender myself as His vessel. As believers, we are formed and prepared to be used by the Lord in constructive ways, but if we refuse to give way to our Potter, He also can use us in such a way that we can bring judgment down on ourselves.

The Apostle Paul in *Romans 9:20-21* made this statement, *"Nay but O man, who art thou that repliest against God? Shall the thing formed say to him that formed it, Why hast thou made me thus? Hath not the potter power over the clay, of the same lump to make one vessel unto honour, and another unto dishonor?"*

As a vessel what am I being used for? Vessels carry various things. For us we carry the life or light of Jesus. Jesus posed this interesting statement in *Matthew 5:14-16, "Ye are the light of the world. A city that is set on a hill cannot be hid. Neither do men light a candle, and put it*

under a bushel, but on a candlestick; and it giveth light unto all that are in the house. Let your light so shine before men, that they may see your good works, and glorify your father which is in heaven."

The life of Christ must be shining from our life and our works must bring glory to the Father; therefore, we must avoid dulling down this light with compromise and worldliness. We must also realize for this light to shine brighter we might have to occasionally be broken (brought to a state of humility) to ensure victory in overwhelming challenges.

Consider Gideon's great victory in *Judges 7*. The Lord fought the battle but Gideon's army of 300 had to put lamps in empty pitchers and break them as they blew the trumpet of victory.

We are part of the army of God, but we must make sure we are not entangled into the affairs of the world, hiding our light under compromise, and live in expectancy to be broken occasionally to ensure our light will glow brighter in dark times to shine on God's work and intervention on our behalf

As a vessel do you emit the fragrance of Christ? The Apostle Paul made this statement in *2 Corinthians 2:15-16, "For we are unto God a sweet savour of Christ, in them that are saved, and in them that perish: to the one we are the savour of death unto death; and to the other the savior of life unto life. And who is sufficient for these things?"*

As a vessel we carry the very life of Jesus in us. This life will emit a beautiful fragrance. Keep in mind when they offered some of the sacrifices in the Old Testament, they poured frankincense on them and when the fire was put to the sacrifice it even caused the fragrance of the frankincense to become richer. This fragrance is what went up to God as an acceptable sweet savour.

The Apostle Paul beseeched us in *Romans 12:1* to offer our bodies as a living sacrifice, and just like the contents in Mary's vessel in *John 12:3* of ointment of spikenard, once we do make such an offering, the fragrance that will be emitted from our lives will be the fragrance of Jesus. This fragrance will point to death to those who refuse to receive Jesus Christ, but for those who possess Him, it will prove sweet to their souls.

It is important to point out that the life that is associated to this world must first be offered up to ensure the fire is put to the life of Christ in us. It is the sanctifying fire of the Holy Spirit that will make the life of Jesus smell even sweeter to heaven.

Each person must make sure he or she is born again and if the person is, he or she needs to present his or her body on the altar to be rid of the old in order for the fire to bring forth the life of Christ in greater measure.

Is the content in your vessel being poured out into the lives of others? I talked about how as believers we possess the very fragrance of the life of Christ. It is the heart of the Lord to pour His life into others. This is why we must at all times be an open vessel where the Master is not only pouring out the contents but pouring in more.

If we are a closed vessel, holding on to the treasure within, it will become stagnant and lose its fragrance. It is like the parable in *Matthew 25:14-30* of the unprofitable servant who buried one talent because he did not see how it would benefit him personally to invest it for the One who entrusted him with it. As vessels we need to remember it is not for us to keep the treasure, but to share it, to pour it out into other people's lives, emptying ourselves in expectation of receiving more.

I remember a time that the Lord was gracious to pour into my life nuggets of wisdom. On the day I received the nugget at His banqueting table I would look for someone who I could share it with, knowing that the Lord would entrust me with more. Keep in mind it was not noble of me that I shared such matters; rather it was quite selfish because I knew He would pour more into me.

Jesus lays out this principle in *Luke 16:10-11, "He that is faithful in that which is least is faithful also in much: and he that is unjust in the least is unjust also in the much. If therefore ye have not been faithful in the unrighteous mammon who will commit to your trust the true riches?"*

Rayola Kelley

What type of instrument are you? The Apostle Paul made this statement in *Romans 6:13*, *"Neither yield ye your members as instruments of unrighteousness unto sin; but yield yourselves unto God, as those that are alive from the dead, and your members as instruments of righteousness."* Christians are vessels that carry the life of Christ, but they are also instruments to be used by God.

Whether it is an instrument that plays beautiful music, a brush that creates some masterpiece, or a tool that forms a necessary object, we are to serve as some type of instrument to be used by God in the matters of righteousness. The challenge for most Christians is that unlike an inanimate object, we have a will and must choose to yield our whole selves to the Lord to be used. This means every member of our body, from our mind, eyes, hands, feet, heart, and voice must be yielded for one purpose that God will use us in the ways of righteousness.

So many times I have been reminded that my life is the "glove," but God wants to put His hand in my life and direct all that I do. This is also true when it comes to me being His instrument.

Are you an instrument yielded to the hand of God or are you an instrument that Satan can pick up during your fleshly activities or worldly pursuits and use for unrighteousness?

Are you a fined-tune instrument? Instruments are crafted and formed. They must be shaped to carry out a function. Consider a musical instrument, a saw, a chisel, or even a simple baton that is used by the conductor to lead the orchestra.

Vessels may differ in their shape, but instruments are diverse in their function. Imagine a musical instrument that is prized by the masters because of how it was made by its creator. All masters look for the right instrument that will reveal their talent or ability to create music, beauty, or bring forth their creation.

There are many instruments that the artist can get by with but real masters want the best to create the best. This is true for the Lord. He is not looking for just any instrument to get by with; rather, He is looking for an instrument that has been created and mastered by Him so that when He uses it, it will speak of His incredible ability and bring glory to Him.

What kind of instruments (people) are you watching when it comes to your relationship with the Master? Most of the time all we can see is hypocrisy that either allows us to justify taking a lower road concerning our own faith walk or excusing our unbelief by walking away from God.

The Bible talks about a great cloud of witnesses that bring us an excellent example of what the Christian walk looks like. So what are you looking at or identifying with? We have instruments like the Demas's who run back to the world, while many fail to see the Joshua's that have come as far as they dare as a means to personally experience God.

We see the Aaron's of religion erecting the golden calves of idolatry in the sanctuaries of churches, and not the Noah's who are hidden in the ark of Christ. We see the children of Israel dancing around the altars of idols but do not see the seven thousand who have never bowed their knees to the idols of their present age.

Like Jonah who was asleep in the hull of indifference while the storm raged above, we see those who are asleep in the pews of churches as the darkness of the present age slams against the doors of complacency, but we do not see the ones who are hidden in the secret chambers of communion or the obscure caves of God's abiding protection.

It is easy to look at the instruments that are just getting by or failing to be used by God, but the question is what kind of instrument are we when it comes to being used in God's kingdom, and among His people, in the harvest field of the world?

We are told in *Hebrews 6:12, "That ye be not slothful, but followers of them who through faith and patience inherit the promises."*

What instrument will God use on you to bring you forth as His instrument? God uses various instruments in the lives of His people to bring us forth as His creation. The Bible tells us in *2 Corinthians 5:17* that we are all new creations and the old has passed away. It is true that upon our born-again experience we have received a new heart and spirit, which points to a new inward disposition, but we need to keep in mind that at such times we are a pliable instrument that is ready to be shaped and formed by the Master.

This means our process has just begun as to what God wants to do with us and how He will fit us into His kingdom's work. In many cases we are not aware of the work He is doing in us and other times we become quite aware that He is going deeper in us.

We need to remember one of God's most effective tools is His Word. We are told that it cleanses us as it prepares us to become part of the bride of Christ, but it is also a hammer that is intended to knock a lot of personal notions out of our thinking, and an ongoing fire that illuminates and purges what remains of selfishness, as well as the sword that penetrates down to wrong motives, exposing them while circumcising the intents of the heart *(Ephesians 5:26; Jeremiah 23:29; Hebrews 4:12).*

Do you compare yourself to other instruments? The Apostle Paul made this statement in *2 Corinthians 10:12, "For we dare not make ourselves of the number, or compare ourselves with some that commend themselves; but they measuring themselves by themselves and comparing themselves among themselves, are not wise."*

For example, some Christians judge others by the cross they carry. However, there is nothing noble in a cross, no matter how big, or what it is made of, or our how shiny. A cross is an instrument of death to the life associated with this world and has been specially formed to have its way in a person's life.

It is also easy for us to judge other Christians who are in their process, without realizing we are actually judging the work God is doing in them like Job's companions did to him. We all must go through a process to be made useful to the Lord and we do not have the right to judge His method or tool according to the process He using in our lives.

Perhaps, He is using a chisel of trial on one person, an onslaught of personal problems to hammer and shape another, a chainsaw to cut away unnecessary baggage in the life of someone, or a knife to whittle down a person's resolve to be shaped a certain way. The test is never according to our personal experiences, but whether the person comes out reflecting Jesus Christ.

The Bible warns we will be judged in the same manner we judge others, ever keeping in mind that God is doing the work in His people.

As an instrument, what are you proclaiming? As a vessel, Christians carry the truth, Jesus, but as an instrument we are to proclaim the truth.

Hebrews 4:12 tells us the Word of God is a sharp, two-edged sword able to cut through and cut deep into the target. Due to the father of lies, Satan, the world is shrouded in lies. Whether it is a form of seduction into a false reality, indoctrination to hide wicked agendas of destruction, or propaganda that twists the truth to influence attitude, it is all a house of cards standing on shifting sand that one day will collapse as the waves of judgment hits against the shoreline.

The problem today is that many are not conditioned to embrace the truth and there are those in the Church who have failed to choose to love the truth. Which brings us to the crux of the problem, many are unprepared to hear the truth and when it slams against their present reality.

These individuals become like the disciples of Jesus when they felt what Jesus said was too hard to receive. As a result, we are told, *"From that time many of his disciples went back, and walked no more with him"* (John 6:66).

Truth will never change and to try to override it with another reality, simply means you have left the truth to buy a delusion, and when it finally rocks what you understand, you, like the disciples of old could very well walk away from the truth in disillusionment.

Are we an instrument that values truth above all other realities? Clearly, the attitude we adopt towards truth will determine whether we will humble ourselves before it to receive it as being so or rage against it.

Truth will eventually fly against everything we hold dear or think is the "Gospel" truth of a matter. We forget that truth is eternal and we may catch glimpses of it along the way that will change how we look at a matter, but we will never be able to know ALL the truth. Granted, we can know "THE TRUTH" Jesus Christ and as a result possess all truth, but in our limited state, we cannot possibly know all truth because that would require an eternal perspective.

As a result, we must expect truth to challenge our limited understanding, insult our arrogance, shake our foundation, and cut deep into our way of thinking. The problem is that the greatest bondage in man comes down to how he thinks. This is brought out in *2 Corinthians 10:3-5*.

The Bible talks about strongholds, and the Apostle Paul clearly points out strongholds are found in our way of thinking. Our thought process is where the greatest bondage occurs and only the truth can set us free. Sadly, since it is easy to perceive that the points of bondage is actually what we consider enlightenment, we can become quite reluctant to let such lies go and exchange them for liberating truth that will require us to humble ourselves. We fail to take responsibility for our lack of love for truth, and repent that we preferred a lie that served our narrative over the truth. However, once we embrace the truth, we can be assured that our minds will be transformed by it, allowing us to soar in the heights of who THE TRUTH really is.

NUGGETS

That which is priceless comes with a price.
Obviously, it takes tribulation to purify, refine,
and fine-tune God's people to possess the
priceless life of Christ. Therefore, how can
Christians believe there will be no challenges
in discovering the fullness of God in their lives?
(Rayola Kelley)

How many nuggets have you picked up along the way? As Christians we have within our possession a gold mine (God's Word), rivers of Living Water that possess great wealth (the Holy Spirit), gems shrouded in the darkness of this world (godly wisdom), and veins of heavenly promises that will never be fully mined in this world. I have had to asked myself if I have such treasures available to me, why am I living like a spiritual pauper, becoming anemic in my spirit, dried up in my pursuits, caught up with the insanity of this hopeless world, being buried by vanity, and suffering under some oppressive burden put on me by this age?

The answer comes down to what I value, because what I value is what I will pursue. Jesus made mention of this in the Sermon on the Mount, *"For where your treasure is, there will your heart be also" (Matthew 6:21).* This is a simple truth, but it is easy to miss when we put more value on what we do than who we are.

Who we are is based on the type of relationship we have with the Lord. The issues of life are a matter of our heart condition, and for this reason we are instructed to love the Lord with all of our heart and in order to do that we must guard our heart against any idol, keep it open for the light of examination to expose any wicked way in us, and set our affections on things above to avoid divided loyalties.

Keep in mind, there are only four heart conditions and they are the hard heart that is closed to God, a stony heart that is fickle towards God, a worldly heart that is divided when it comes to God, and an open heart that is receptive towards the Lord. We all want to believe we have an open heart, but sometimes we need to consider our attitude about life, our present pursuits, and our fruits to determine if our heart is truly open, receptive, and pure before the Lord.

My faith walk has allowed me to discover precious nuggets of truth along the way. There are a few things I have learned about God's kingdom that I would like to share with you beginning with this one, *"The more you know about God the less you know."*

I started out believing there is a God because it is within every man's conscience to know there is a creator behind all that we see. With this knowledge there is also a sense that this God is morally good because He is holy. As I got involved with religion, I assumed I understood who He was, and as I became more opinionated about my religious beliefs,

I graduated to making many presumptions about Him. It was only after I fell from the height of the pinnacle of arrogance that I discovered I knew nothing about God.

Assumptions are faulty foundations and presumptions are those things that glue the assumptions together, but such a foundation is being established on the shifting sands that will not sustain a person once the shaking begins, making it obvious that these foundations are destined to collapse in due time (*Matthew 7:24-27*).

Through the years I have become more and more aware that the more I understand about God, the more I realize I don't know about Him. He is eternal and we occasionally get glimpses of Him, but these glimpses are like drops in a great vast ocean that puts our smallness in perspective to God's greatness. My personal prayer is that the more I learn about God, the humbler I become before Him.

It is only in true humility that earthly, fleshly limitations part, allowing us to see glimpses of Him in His glory.

Another nugget I have learned that is constantly being reinforced is, *"It is not your faithfulness towards God that keeps you; rather, it is God's faithfulness that preserves you."* Through the years I have failed the Lord. Such failure was due to being too busy with the matters of this life, being caught up with the challenges of the world, or being neglectful in my spiritual walk.

Keep in mind, my heart is to always to be faithful, true, and upright before the Lord, but my earth-bound, self-centered, worldly-oriented humanity confuses the matter as to what is important, revealing that I am not always faithful to my Lord, occasionally robbing me of blessings and victories in my spiritual life.

The Apostle Paul points to the simple truth in *2 Timothy 2:13* that where we are void in faith towards God and the matters of His kingdom, He remains faithful. The things I have done in God's kingdom are not a matter of my devotion, stamina, and determination but because He has kept me, while giving me that measure of faith to continue to move forward as His Spirit empowers me to see a matter through to the end.

I can clearly declare that my accomplishments and projects completed is due to God's abiding and sustaining faithfulness in my life. If you want a special blessing for today read about God's great faithfulness in *Psalm 89*.

Yesterday I talked about the precious nugget of God's faithfulness. I have always been aware of God's faithfulness, but the significance of it took center stage in my life at the publishing of my first book. The stages of getting a book published is a trying experience because it goes through a type of birthing process.

There is always the conception of it where it takes root in the mind and heart, then the preparation and development of it in writing it, the maturing of it in editing it, and the presentation of it in publishing it. Many know this story but the conception of my first book happened back in 1977 and it was finally published 18 years later.

Looking back, I can see that the first nine years had to do with preparing me and the last nine years was the "gestation" period for the book. Let me say this, bringing forth my different books has never been a matter of months, but entailed years and I can do nothing more than accredit all to the Lord.

The publishers of my first book set up a book signing for me. Needless to say, I was asked to speak. As I waited on the Lord to show me how I was to promote my book, He quietly spoke to me, "Tell them I AM faithful." At that moment, I was overwhelmed by His presence in the room. I knew that the birthing of that book was all God's doing, from its conception to its completion because He was faithful to do so.

Every important point of spiritual growth and accomplishment in my life is because of God's faithfulness and it is because of His Spirit in me that I am faithful to Him. It is easy to become frantic over a timing of a spiritual matter, desperate in seeing something accomplished, and hopeless that it will ever happen, but I have come to realize it is in the faith journey that we are allowed to see something come to fruition that unveils, not only the faithfulness of God to us, but just how personal He is with each of us.

Truly, all glory, along with the wondrous fruit that comes out of His abiding faithfulness in our lives, goes to the Lord.

Another important nugget I have acquired in my spiritual journey is, "Do not receive from the enemy what does not belong to you, and only own and take responsibility for what does belong to you." However, we have to discern wrong spirits in order to resist their lies. Jesus told John and James in *Luke* 9, that they did not know what spirit they were of when they wanted to call fire down on the Samaritans.

It sometimes takes brutal honesty on our part to properly examine the spirit we might be operating in because we can bring a reproach to our testimony. I've developed a means to test and discern my own spirit in order to distinguish if I am operating according to my natural spirit or being pushed by the spirit of this world (Satan).

It is also vital that we also discern what we receive and what we take responsibility for. We have a tendency to receive the lies of Satan, while refusing to take responsibility for our own moral deviation in a matter by playing the blame game or hiding behind excuses.

It is easy to discern what is what. Satan's lies are the darts that come from without that cause us to look within resulting in confusion and condemnation. That which is the product of our own moral deviation will cause an inner struggle between the flesh and the Spirit to occur.

The flesh wants to justify why it is missing the mark of righteousness and the Spirit wants to bring conviction to us that will lead to repentance to ensure we walk in the ways of righteousness. The right spirit in me will cause me to be unsettled in my spirit when there is a wrong spirit present and I need to take authority over the spirit of the world and repent by honestly owning my own moral deviation, whether it is in my attitude, my words, or my conduct.

Living in uncertain times makes you realize that everything is filtered by the god of the age, Satan, through his world systems in one way or the other, and that truth is a nugget you must dig for. It is like having to sift through tons of material to find that one priceless nugget that brings a matter into clarity, but how many have the initiative, the desire, and the wherewithal to tackle a mountain of lies with a mere shovel, and then sift through the shovel full of propaganda with meticulous discernment by using the magnifying glass of God's Word?

Many people accept living within the different levels and filters of compromising gray for various reasons: 1) they do not love the truth, 2) they prefer their own filters of reality, 3) delusion serves their agenda, and 4) they don't care what truth is because it will simply challenge or hinder them from doing what they want to do.

Truth is contrary to the natural man. It will stand opposite of lies, skepticism, ignorance, and fear. It will cut through the grays with clarity, sharply penetrate darkness with its light, shake and insult indifference, and expose the shady terrain of man's soul. The reason I mentioned the filters is because the filters of the world have created a great darkness to enfold many into its ugly reality, creating a false light that simply hides the destruction behind it.

Right now, the light of truth is penetrating the darkness of these filters, and what it ultimately exposes will completely astonish many as to the depth of corruption that exists. Remember the Bible warns that all done in darkness will be declared from the rooftops. This penetration is presently creating a gray cloud of confusion. It is at this point many people will become afraid, muddled, and lost as to what to believe and trust. As believers, we know who to trust, the Truth, Jesus Christ, as we stand still to see what God is going to do.

We must not be deceived by the darkness, moved by the grays, or paralyzed by the depth of corruption. We must counteract darkness with God's Word, take time to examine our attitude towards the truth by examining ourselves to see if we have any filters that pervert what is true, and remember to look up, because our redemption is coming from above and not from this world.

LEGACY

*The reality of greatness will be based on
the type of witness it will leave behind. Often
such a legacy of greatness is riddled
with what appears to be failure. However, it
is in times of what appears to be utter faillure,
that the forging of character takes place.
True character is what lasting
legacies are made of.
(Rayola Kelley)*

As we edge our way towards a new year, we must consider our past in light of valuable lessons, our present in lieu of eternity, and our future in regard to the type of legacy we want to leave behind. As I consider the past year, I want to know if I have gained any hindsight, and when it comes to the present how can I apply the wisdom of hindsight to my present Christian walk in order to ensure the spiritual legacy that I hope to leave behind.

The problem with being in this world is that we can live too much in the temporary happenings of it rather than disciplining our walk as we consider all matters in light of eternity. The saints that went before us became part of the greater cloud of witnesses of *Hebrews 11* and *12:1*. They did not look back at whether they were leaving prints in the sands of the world; rather, they looked forward into eternity in order to obtain a better resurrection.

Every new year reminds me that I have been allotted another day and that in light of the present darkness, I need to properly redeem the time in preparation for eternity. We are all bound to this earth by physical bodies, but we are called to be spiritual people in spite of the earthly hold on us.

To be spiritual people we must become strangers to the present world as we become more heavenly minded, while becoming steadfast in our heart towards God and bent on finishing the race as we increasingly become strangers in this world, while being more consumed by the glory of the promised world to come.

One of the people I often pause to consider in my studies is a woman by the name of Achsah. She was the wife of the first judge of Israel, Othniel and the daughter of Caleb. Othniel won her as a bride by taking certain territory.

Clearly, this woman was surrounded by two great men. One day she came to her father to ask him to enlarge her inheritance. He had already given her the south land but she wanted the springs of water as well, and Caleb ended up giving her both the upper and nether springs (*Joshua 15:17-20*).

This may seem insignificant, but to me she represents me. As a believer, I already have an inheritance but I have a wonderful Father in heaven who instructs me to ask and He will give me more of the Holy Spirit, the river of Living Waters. I am part of a living body that has been fought for and bought by Jesus on the cross of Calvary and one day He will step on the scene as Judge of all.

What Achsah teaches me by her example is that I must not be willing to settle for less when I know my Father has it within His heart to give me more. Too many of us quickly settle for less because we fail to come to our Father in confidence to obtain a greater inheritance. The reason for this is because our vision is often overshadowed by the world which can cause us to lack any inward desire to ask for, pursue and inherit the unseen blessings of heaven.

When I get rid of stuff, I start to think about legacy. It is not unusual for people to want to leave some legacy behind them. This is one of the reasons we collect things that have memories attached to them, valuable possessions, or some point of heritage and history that will remind us of those who went before us and the price they paid to prepare the way.

Whether it is land, heirlooms, possessions, or mementoes it is our way to leave our mark, a type of footprint in this world. All you have to do is walk into a cemetery and realize that the problem with such legacies is that they are like footprints in the sand that are there one moment but as soon as the winds of time blow in and there is a change of guard with a new generation, the only thing left is some name left on stone. It is at such times I realize the legacies of the world are useless.

Visions, dreams, and sacrifice that established past legacies are often sold, squandered, or cast aside by those who are void of the same vision, have no real dreams, and have no understanding of the cost and sacrifice of a real legacy. As Christians we all have the same legacy. It is a spiritual legacy that points to a spiritual inheritance envisioned in the heart of the Father, seen by those with eyes to see beyond this world, left as part of a living witness, and a sacrifice on a cross that opened the door to untold riches.

What does it mean to inherit the promises of God? The first thing we must recognize is that we have this inheritance available to us because of Jesus' death on the cross. It was made clear that the testator (Jesus) had to first die before the inheritance could be made available (*Hebrews 9:15-17*).

The second thing is we must be identified to it as being a rightful heir. This means we must be born again and officially sealed with the Spirit of God to be identified as a child of God.

The third thing we must do is value our inheritance. If we think our inheritance is not that important, we are not going to be in the position to claim it. Joshua told the seven tribes in *Joshua 18:8* that had not yet claimed their inheritance to walk it out. We often fail to see what we have in Christ because we fail to walk out the life we have in Him by faith.

The more we walk out our Christian life, the more we begin to value it, and the more we value it, the more we are apt to possess it.

The question we must ask ourselves, is "What must I do to obtain my spiritual inheritance?" Some Christians may become content that they have been entrusted with the right to claim an inheritance, but how many are really benefitting from their inheritance? The Bible is clear, the inheritance we as believers have been entrusted with has been secured by Christ, and we claim it when we believe in our heart that Jesus died in our place to pay a necessary debt for our sin, and confess He is Lord, but now we must possess our inheritance (*Romans 10:9-10*).

There were seven tribes of Israel who failed to enter the Promised Land to possess their portion of the inheritance. There are different New Testament books that are considered counterparts of Old Testament books. For example, Leviticus and Hebrews complement each other, as well as Proverbs and James. When it comes to Joshua and inheriting the Promised Land, the counterpart book in the New Testament is Ephesians. Check it out.

Paul's letter explains our spiritual inheritance, how it operates and what it will take to possess it. I can tell you that to possess our inheritance we must first value it or we will settle for being in the entrance of salvation, while failing to enter in and discover its many benefits.

Like the seven tribes that Joshua told to walk through the land and describe it in order to realized what they were inheriting, we likewise need to walk out our inheritance. And, once we get a true glimpse of our inheritance, we will begin to value it enough to finally rise up and possess it.

I have to admit, I wonder how many Christians need to rise up out of the gate of salvation and truly walk in obedience towards God's promises in order to discover what they have in Christ in order to value it above this world enough to possess it.

One of the subjects that causes me to rejoice is the one about refuge cities. There were only six located throughout the 12 tribes (Joshua 20). These refuge cities had a distinct purpose. They were for those who accidentally killed someone and by faith these people would seek out the promise of refuge in the ordained city.

They would flee to the city closest to them and the family could not take revenge on them. However, it also had to be determined by the elders if the person had committed man-slaughter or murder, for the Law left no refuge for one who took a life in anger.

337

These refuge cities were for the stranger or pilgrim who were passing through. In other words, they were not to harbor people who were fleeing bad circumstances or looking for free handouts because the land was the inheritance of the Israelites. The manslayer was to stay in the city until the death of the High Priest and then he could go home and reclaim his inheritance.

The beauty of these refuge cities pointed to our refuge, Jesus Christ. Keep in mind that Jesus is our High Priest and upon His death the believer could find pardon and claim his spiritual inheritance. The Lord is the place where the man-slaughterer who is fleeing death, the stranger (alien) of God, and the spiritual pilgrim seeking a city not made by the hands of man can come and find protection, rest, directions, and restoration.

I don't know about you, but every time I think about Jesus and what I have in Him, I rejoice over the place my faithful God provided for me in my Redeemer.

When I ponder how easy it is to pursue the inheritance of this world, I also consider the idea of legacy. Legacy points to some type of inheritance or memorial that one leaves behind. In a way the power or impact of legacy is determined by the name and reputation one leaves behind. Sometimes legends are born out of such legacies.

Consider the type of lifestyle and reputation Jesus had that led Him to the cross to be treated as a common criminal. Clearly, the world's idea of inheritance and legacy is upside down in light of the cross of Jesus. Jesus had no place to lay His head, His physical beauty was stripped from Him by the indifference and hatred of those who mocked and beat Him, and eventually He was left naked before the world as He hung on the cross.

Jesus died to obtain a spiritual inheritance for us. Obviously, what we need to value to spiritually survive the onslaught of the vanity of our present age is to pursue, maintain, and value our relationship with God. It is in a relationship with God that He can pass down the lasting legacy of the inheritance that was secured on the cross by His only begotten Son.

It is the last day of the year, and at this time, I often talk about leaving an inscription behind that would describe one's life. When I think about epitaphs, the next thing that I think about is my name being inscribed on some object.

It is natural to want to leave some legacy behind, but the only thing that will possibly be left behind beyond memories is our name being inscribed on some memorial or family tree. The world's way of establishing memorials of a life once lived is on paper that can burn, through history books that can be manipulated, plaques that can tarnish and rust, grave markers that can be worn down by time, and sometimes statues that can be thrown down. However, when it comes to the Bible our names can be written on three different sources.

The first one is the Book of Life, but we are told that if we do not choose God's way of salvation that our name can be blotted out of that book. This is why I believe everyone born starts out with their name in the Book of Life, but what they do with Jesus will determine if it remains so.

Many people hope or assume their name will be in the Book of Life when they depart this world, but there is only one way to ensure that it is, and that is by receiving God's provision of Jesus Christ. Jesus' blood identifies us to an everlasting covenant, the Holy Spirit seals us to it, and genuine faith receives and ingrains its promise in the heart and soul.

The world values names on memorials and government values names on documents, but I am sure all will agree that the most important place for our name to be is in the Book of life. There is another place where a name can be written.

The next element our name can be written on always leads me back to the incident in *John 8* where the woman was caught in adultery. Jesus was writing something in the dust of the earth and the debate to the possibilities are interesting, but I believe that a scripture the religious leaders would've known about and most likely quoted during the Feast of Tabernacles due to its water ceremonies that are observed during its seven days of celebration, can be found in *Jeremiah 17:13, "O LORD, the hope of Israel, all that forsake thee shall be ashamed, and they that depart from me shall be WRITTEN IN THE EARTH, because they have forsaken the LORD, the fountain of living waters."* (Emphasis added.)

If Jesus was writing the name of these religious accusers in the earth, they would have understood that it points to their name be trampled under by feet while the winds of judgment take away all remembrance of them. We must keep in mind that everything that is of the flesh and the world will be trampled under and rendered into dust, and whether or not it is taken away with the winds of judgment brings us back to what we do with the Lord Jesus Christ.

Names are important to God because where they are written will determine one's citizenship and destination. We definitely want our name written in the right book and not written on something that will cease to be.

There is another place where our name must be written, and that is on a very important stone that is described in Revelation. However, it will not be the name we now have, but a new name. *Revelation 2:17* says, *"He that hath an ear, let him hear what the Spirit saith unto the churches; To him that overcometh will I give to eat of the hidden manna, and will give him a white stone, and in the stone a new name written, which no man knoweth saving he that receiveth it."*

Clearly, the new name will be based on our Christian walk and our relationship with the Lord. Perhaps obtaining a new name is not all that important to some, and even though I have assurance my name is written in the Book of Life, I believe that the life I live here will determine the new name I receive on that glorious day, revealing the quality of the relationship I established with the Lord.

Before this year ends, make sure your name has been clearly established in eternity.

What will the Christian find at the end of securing his or her inheritance in the Lord? *Peace.* Today many people are looking for peace, but in a world where man learns to war, where corruption is reigning, and the tyranny of a few is tolerated and preferred by the elite, innocence is exploited, righteousness is mocked, and the pure are offered up on the various altars of selfishness, wicked ways, and evil agendas, there will be no peace.

An important question is how can there be peace when Satan is the ruler of this age? After Isaac established a relationship with the Lord and took ownership of his inheritance and Abraham's legacy in *Genesis 26*, his enemies came to him to make peace.

The Bible tells us that the Lord can make peace even with our enemies, but that peace can't occur until we are at peace with Him. For example, our family relationship to God makes us peacemakers in *Matthew 5:9* because we are to be ministers of reconciliation according to *2 Corinthians 5:18-20.* The Gospel is associated with peace in the armor in *Ephesians 6:15*; the walk of faith allows us to enter into rest according to Hebrews 3:18-19, and the last title accredited to Jesus in *Isaiah 9:6* is Prince of Peace.

The greatest wars are usually within our own souls. Jesus said it best in *John 14:27, "Peace I leave with you, my peace I give unto you: not as the world giveth, give I unto you. Let not your heart be troubled, neither let it be afraid."* To have peace we are told our mind must be on the Lord, and we are not to allow trouble to beset us. We must know and choose to trust He overcame the world and opened the way up for us to be overcomers.

Finally, to avoid being swallowed by fear, we must put our complete faith in who He is.

HOLIDAYS

*Christianity should be a celebration of life
but as **Steve Quayle** pointed out on his video,
Christianity began as a personal relationship
with Christ. When it went to Athens, it became
a philosophy. When it went to Rome, it became
an organization. When it went to Europe, it
became a culture. When it came to America,
it became a business.*

This last week has been interesting. Without water for four days and having our windows replaced for two days proved interesting. The two events temporarily crossed paths so those who were replacing our windows did not have to experience the full extent of the challenging restroom situation.

For us things seem to happen around holidays because many of our past crisis occurred around some holiday where we found ourselves in the midst of solving a matter rather than celebrating the day, even if it is a somber celebration such as Memorial Day. We often look at celebrations as a day to party, but each celebration is to serve as a type of memorial of an event, remembering some great feat, incredible service, or certain individuals.

Memorial Day is about sacrifice, remembering those who made sacrifices for our country, for our benefit, and for something bigger than all of us—freedom, honor, dignity, and life. There are three types of sacrifice: there is the offering of our bodies for what we often consider a worthy purpose, the crucifying of our flesh in order to ensure that instead of pursuing an empty lifestyle, we are actually seeking after that which constitutes life, and the sacrifice of our life in order to discover and be set free to discover life.

We see these three sacrifices in Christ. He offered His body as the Lamb of God, His flesh (sweat) was poured out in the Garden of Gethsemane as He submitted Himself to the will of the Father, and His life, which is found in the blood was poured out on the cross so we could have life. In His body, He became the perfect sacrifice, in His flesh He became a prepared sacrifice, and when His life-blood was being poured out, He became the acceptable sacrifice.

When it comes to offering our body, it is our reasonable service, the offering of our flesh to be crucified is necessary in order to become a prepared sacrifice, and the offering of our life is what will make us an acceptable sacrifice that God can receive for His use and glory. In a sense "offering" is the least we can do, but "sacrifice" requires us to go on to that which is excellent and greater.

Whenever the terms "offering" and "sacrifice" are used, remember that which is of great value has cost others in the past and unless we are willing to do our reasonable service by picking up the torch of sacrifice and paying it forward, future generations are doomed because there is no real price being put on that which is worthy to possess, inspiring them to offer up their very lives to ensure it for others. Remember, sacrifice is about and for the benefit of others, and never about ourselves. That, my friend, is why it is referred to as a "sacrifice."

It is Memorial Day. This day is to remember those who have sacrificed their lives to ensure we can live in freedom. Growing up in America can cause us to take our freedoms for granted. Freedom hinges on rights. We have the right to life, liberty and the pursuit of happiness (property).

Without life, we have no need of liberty and without the liberty to pursue the quality of life we desire there is no real initiative to strive for that which is excellent. It is easy to lose sight of why freedom is so precious when taken for granted by those who have failed to understand that anything that is worth having is worth fighting for and even dying for, and real freedom is one of those priceless gems we must possess.

The problem for many Americans is that the real purpose freedom was sought in the first place came down to people's desire to have the freedom to worship God according to their conscience. This is the real purpose of true freedom. It is not so man can get ahead financially or do his own thing; rather, it is because man must be given the freedom to choose to live for God without persecution, stand for God without being silenced, and worship God without being hindered. It is for this reason rights come from God and not government. Our Creator wants man to have the freedom to choose that which is moral, excellent, and eternal.

Two thousand years ago a memorial was established on an old rugged cross. A body was broken and blood shed so that man could have life that allotted him freedom to look up to receive the gift of life, to stand up with the inspiration to gain vision beyond this world, advance forward with the initiative to seek great heights, and hope that becomes the wings that are caught up by the unseen wind to reach one's potential.

Rights can't be taken, but they can be exchanged for something that promises some type of bondage. Let it never be said of any Christian that we exchanged our freedom and life in Christ to taste the bitter bondage of this present world as a means to maintain some sick peace with it or keep our fleshly lifestyle intact.

Today is the last day of the Memorial Day Weekend. Many did the best to get the most out of their weekend, but for the loved ones, families, and friends who lost a soldier on the front lines due to some international conflict, it is the time to once again grapple with the emotional fallout that comes with such losses. The questions are, was a precious life cut short because of the evil tyranny of others, was the cause worthy of their lives, and will the present sorrow that is quietly screaming in utter despair in their hearts make the cost prove too great and unfair for them in the end?

People love to celebrate, but we must not forget that at such times as these it is not a celebration for those who understand when sacrifices are made for the benefit of others, the ones left behind must pick up the pieces of their lives and somehow continue on. They must face the empty chair that will never be filled, the hollow area of their lives that at times taunts them, and the pain in their hearts that may lessen with years but will never really go away.

Meanwhile, they desperately hold to memories that may be fading with time. In fact, this is true in the case of every lost loved one and for this reason we are told to rejoice with those who rejoice and weep with those who are weeping. It was the Lord that established the concept of memorials. Even though heaven looks at the death of a saint as a time of great liberation, it is mankind who emotionally struggles with such grave losses even in spite of great hope for those who believe the promise of eternal life that comes through Christ; and we, as servants of the Most High, must be sensitive towards others who are mourning or grappling with such grievous losses.

Losses can embitter or enrich our lives, and for Christians it is to become part of their testimony so that they can become a source of consolation to others who are experiencing like loss. We must remember that God can only entrust certain losses to certain saints. He knows whether a sweetness will eventually emerge from the loss that will serve as a healing balm to others, as well as a fragrance that will reach the throne of heaven as a sacrifice to Him.

As believers we can take comfort that God established ways in which He acknowledged the inner struggle brought on by great loss. There were altars that served as memorials, times of national grieving so that the nation of Israel could soberly move on, days set aside for somber reflection, and ordinances established so following generations would never forget the prices others paid as they look forward.

It is easy to celebrate when we have not been personally touched by any real loss and sacrifice and another story all together when we have tasted the depths such losses plunge us into. No memorial will take away the pain of loss, no day set aside will match the loss, no tradition will ever satisfy it, and no practice will ever pay the type of tribute to even do it justice, but we must keep in mind such pauses are a time of reflection and remembrance of what was, so that what can be can come to fruition.

On the night Jesus was betrayed He established an ordinance to pause and remember that He not only came, He would die, and be buried, but He would rise again and is coming back. He was facing the cross and it would bring great darkness to the struggling, despairing souls of His followers, but in due time the light of resurrection would resurrect their hope, and in the end when their journey was completed, the culmination of their earthy sorrows would be consumed by the promise of the great celebration of the marriage supper of the Lamb. Meanwhile, the sorrow is real, but the pause to remember is a small gesture on our part that may prove to be a tiny drop of healing balm to lessen the pain of those who are still trying to pick up the pieces left behind by the sacrifice that continues to be perpetual for them.

Memorial weekend has passed but the real Memorial Day would be this Friday, the 31st of May; that is, if man was not so caught up with three-day weekends. To change a day such as Memorial Day to be part of the weekend in a way demeans the reason behind it. Instead of remaining a separate, unique day it becomes something that is fitted into man's activities, causing some to forget what the day is all about.

Memorials are a record to remind us of those who have gone before us, who prepared a better way for us, and left an example behind that was worth distinguishing as sacrificial and excellent. The only ones in our society who fit such qualifications are those who do service on our behalf such our military women and men, as well as the police and firemen.

We see the importance of memorials when considering that God also set up different memorials for the children of Israel to pass on from generation to generation, beginning with His name, "I AM THAT I AM" (*Exodus 3:14-15*). Moses set up an altar as a memorial and called it "Jehovah Nissi" or "Jehovah our banner" (*Exodus 17:13-16*). Stones with the name of the children of Israel were worn by the priests and the blowing of trumpets were to serve as memorials as well. And what about Christians?

Every time we have communion, we are remembering, recalling, taking note of the great sacrifice of Jesus. We are looking back at what was accomplished on the cross, while taking time to examine our lives while we look forward to Him coming again (*1 Corinthians 11:23-31*). We stand justified because of God's great sacrifice, but we are ever being prepared in the household of our Lord to walk in a life of excellent service in His kingdom while looking for His coming in the future as King of kings.

Every time we take communion it should be an opportunity to remember Jesus' sacrifice on our behalf and it would seem that taking one day out of the year as a nation to recognize the sacrifice of those who serve our country would be the least we could do, but instead we have allowed this day to be swallowed up by man's insistence to have a three-day weekend.

The beauty about memorials is that they are meant to be personal, and we should not only remember Jesus' sacrifice every day, but the great sacrifice of men and women, along with their families' great sacrifices, that have allowed us to live it up on our three-day weekends.

Those who know me, know that I had unique experiences with three fathers. My biological father gave me life, but was not very much a part of it after a divorce when I was nine. From the age of ten I had a wonderful step-father who God hand-picked to step into my life at a very vulnerable time. I met this man for the first time on June 22, 1965, the very day he married my mother.

It is a day I will never forget because it serves as a lasting memorial. At the grand age of ten, I found myself traveling on a bus to an unknown mountain community, and my first impression of my new home was overwhelming due to its beauty. The stranger who was about to become my father, greeted us with an enthusiasm that made me immediately feel comfortable around him. His round face was highlighted by wire rim glasses that allowed the twinkle of zest and adventure to freely dance in his brown eyes. The twinkle in his eyes were reinforced by the slight mischievousness that was clearly present in his smile.

My mother had met him in the hospital she worked at due to a sawmill accident where his leg was broken. They had only known each other for two weeks on the day they took their marriage vows, and obviously, their courtship was far from a whirlwind romance; rather, it was more about two brave people who were willing to risk it all to make a commitment that would serve as a foundation in marriage, establish a family that had been previously broken, and endure the challenges of life up to their deaths that were a little over four months apart, and a few months short of celebrating their 50th wedding anniversary.

On that most memorable day, he met us on crutches. A friend had driven him in his car to pick us up, but what defined the new adventure we were embarking on was his determination to take on a challenge of a new family and make it a time of discovery for all of us. It was my step-father that gave me more insight into the commitment of my Heavenly Father through his example.

My step-father was not responsible for my brother and I, but he willingly took it when he married my mother. He was not our biological father, but he chose to become our father who supported us at every turn in our lives. He was our willing provider and even though unable to give us what we always wanted, he was always willing, and if need be, sacrificial to provide what we needed.

So much of my present identity, character, and understanding of my relationship with my Heavenly Father who gave His Son so I could have life, identity, and all I have need of has been shaped by my relationship with my step-father.

I want to wish the fathers out there "Happy Father's Day" and remind them that regardless of how they may be overlooked for their provision in this world, their honorable and sacrificial examples are what will leave a lasting legacy in the hearts and minds of their children.

Yesterday I saw such a blasphemous mockery on the news—drag queens reading to our children in the public library. These drag queens flaunted their bodies in front of the cameras, and I couldn't tell you what they were flaunting because it was all an illusion, a front, and a terrible perversion, especially since they have not been endowed by our Creator with womanhood.

Today we may ask, where are the men since some are trying to be women? I don't know about you, but I appreciate the men in my life who are secure about their manhood, love God, and desire to be an example to younger men and a strong guide to their daughters, whether biological or spiritual.

What I am about to share with you, I have shared often, including at my stepfather's funeral, and since it is Father's Day I will share it again. I had three fathers in my life, my biological father, my step-father, and my Heavenly Father. Although absent much of my life, I am thankful to my biological father because he gave me my life. However, it was my stepfather who gave me my identity at a very crucial time of my life, but I am thankful most of all that it is my Heavenly Father who has given me both life (eternal) and identity. My biological father showed me the harsh side of life, my stepfather revealed the great adventure of life, and my Heavenly Father unveiled the real hope that can be found in life.

Today I am realistic about life because of my biological father, but I know how to embrace its lessons due to my stepfather, while living in expectation of the promises of my hope being fulfilled because of my Heavenly Father. I am thankful to each of my fathers for bringing balance to my life and I am thankful for every man who understands the great legacy and responsibility that has been entrusted to them as men.

To the men who take their manhood seriously, honor their Creator with sobriety and right living, love their wives and value their children enough to invest in them spiritually and emotionally—this day is yours and thank you for being true to your legacy, and may God continue to strengthen you to stand against the attack leveled at righteousness, the sanctity of marriage between one man and one woman, and the family.

As we celebrate the 4th of July, we need to remember the heroes that have paid a price for our freedom, while remembering as believers we are called to be soldiers. The question is are we or have we become seasoned soldiers on the front lines?

I was told a story about a woman sitting on her deck when she heard a commotion. Before her eyes she watched a procession beginning with her small hysterical dog running as fast as it could, followed by wild turkeys running at high speed and behind them was her small grandson with his toy bow and arrow in hand. Such a sight would bring laughter to anyone witnessing it, but I had to wonder as I considered my position as a soldier in the army of the Lord whether my armor appeared paper-like and did my weapon appear as if it was just a toy to my enemy.

We must not forget that our founding fathers did not enter into the establishment of this country lightly. They all had to count the cost, and in some cases, it cost them dearly from land, homes, family members, and even their own lives. It is true they had fireworks, but it came from guns and the people assembled, but it was to fight and stand.

It is easy for Christians to talk about the armor of God, but we have the armor because we are in a war and we are called to endure as good soldiers the fight before us. It is also true we must count the cost and realize that what we are battling for is greater than us.

As soldiers, we have been given all we need to fight the battles before us, but have we become seasoned enough that we can properly utilize our armor and weapons, or do our declarations and poses prove to be nothing more than child-play to the enemy of our souls?

We just celebrated the 4th of July. It is interesting to see how people celebrate. Some actually understand what the holiday is all about and soberly take time to consider the reason we celebrate the day. There are others who couldn't care less about the reason for the holiday but they are opportunists who want to be part of the festivities, and there are those who see every holiday as a time to act silly or foolish.

As I consider the different celebrations in the Bible, I recognize that a day of celebration points to time of actually showing appreciation as one celebrated the life and blessings of God. In fact, it was a day to celebrate the reality of God.

It is important as Christians to realize we celebrate the quality of something, not the quantity. We celebrate out of an attitude of appreciation towards what we have, what we have been given, and what we have been entrusted with because of the sacrifice of others that have prepared the way for such celebrations. Let it never be said of us that we mindlessly, selfishly, and foolishly partake of the things God has blessed us with spiritually and in regard to this nation's freedom without first realizing what it cost.

As Christians, we know our life and spiritual liberty cost God His Son and Jesus His life so we could have eternal life and the liberty to pursue it, and as far as this nation, the freedom and blessings we enjoy have cost untold lives. May we take time to soberly, and humbly bow before God and thank Him, not only for His provision of Jesus Christ but for allowing us to live in a country that has afforded us the freedom to pursue a life in Him and to experience quality of life in the midst of great abundance.

The 4th of July holiday is now over and those who live in light of such holidays have probably emotionally crash landed on the runway of every-day drudgery. Their only hope is that Labor Day is coming.

I understand what it means to live in excitement in relationship to certain days. I've even had expectations what such days may bring me and I would start counting down to that particular celebration, to only end up being disillusioned by it. The problem with living in light of certain days is you can miss the blessings and opportunities that can be found in each new day.

As Christians, we need to remember every day is a gift that we can celebrate in relationship to Christ's redemption and God's blessings. This attitude allows us to appreciate the present instead of clinging to the future that is never certain. It is true as believers we live in expectation because of a great hope that has been promised to us—the blessed coming of our Lord. It is true I personally strive to conduct many of my daily activities in light of this glorious hope, but I also know I need to be a good steward occupying in the present to be faithful with what is in front of me in preparation to be spiritually prepared for the future.

The question for each Christian is where have they placed their expectation? If you follow your expectation to the source, you will also find that is also the source of your hope.

We are within a few days of an election. I am sure most people are set on who and what they are voting for. Some see it as the most important

351

election of our time. The question is "Is not each election the most important election?"

I have been involved in politics over five decades. I was growing up in the 60s when we were taught in school how to respond if we were ever nuked by Russia. I remember the warning of the Soviet Leader in the late 50s, "That they would take America without a shot." What they did was infiltrate our colleges with one goal: to indoctrinate our impressionable young people into their religion: Communism.

This oppressive religion from hell was promoted through different avenues such as Liberalism, that moved to throw out any absolutes or moral restraints, along with family traditions, and humanism that taught man, he was not created by God with a high calling to reflect the image of the heavenly; rather, he was no different than the beasts, and in some cases valued less.

Like the father of lies these individuals serve Satan, as they caused the young people to believe an outright lie. The problem is the rebellious radicals of the 60s became the professors, activists, and leaders of the day, and without any challenge or oversight, they have greatly influenced the present generation that Communism is the way to go. Now these radical, angry people, who have no history to gauge anything with, and who have become lost in a vacuum of the grave darkness of foolishness and ignorance, are demanding America go their way or they will bring this country down to nothing.

What these indoctrinated people do not realize is they are considered useful idiots by their indifferent oppressors and that these "elite masters" have no qualms in letting them be sacrificed for their sick little kingdoms. The truth is, Communism has not, nor will it ever be a successful government, religion, or ideology.

Communism is a culture of death and is nothing more than a parasite that must gobble up other societies, countries, and nations to survive economically, and when there is nothing more to gobble up, it will totally collapse in on itself. I watched it happen to Russia in the 1980s.

What is at stake this election is the soul of this nation. America was not founded on Communism but it was based on an incredible experiment, where man for the most part, would be allowed to governed himself. The criteria in this experiment, was that for man to successfully govern himself, he must be moral in his conduct, just in his dealings, possess integrity when it comes to his word, and hold himself to an excellent bar.

For man to meet these criteria, God, not man must be the center and source of what is true, acceptable, and right. There are many different religions, ideologies, and philosophies that are vying to be the ultimate overseer of the one-world government for Satan, but I know that in the end there is only going to be one leader, His name is the Lord Jesus Christ, and there is going to be one government, the one He will be overseeing.

Tomorrow is election day. Some voices of debate will cease, while others might escalate. Elections in this country are meant to settle political debates in a civil manner, but for those who will not accept what is to be the will of the people, they will try to exert their will by using or building other platforms to silence any who dare think contrary to them.

The tyrannical despots who can't accept the will of others prove to be the most oppressed, miserable individuals around and they must make you as miserable as they are because they can't stand true liberty, respect any moral restraint, accept just judgments, and listen to sane discussions. These people tolerate elections, but if it does not go their way, they will do what they can to subdue the opposing side and make them so beholden to them (as they exact a type of wicked vengeance on them) that they will never dare oppose them again. After all, they have already warned others with intimidation and now they will pay.

Sadly, this is what I have been hearing for months and witnessed during the former administration when agencies were used to oppress and make the opposing side pay. As a believer, I ask myself what kind of society do I want to live in? Will I come under the despot to avoid vengeance or do I realize that to let a despot rule means I will have no real quality of life; therefore, I have nothing of value left to lose, so I will count the cost and stand for what is right.

Jesus said it best when He stated that to gain the world, means you will lose your soul. In the past, it did not cost Americans to have opposing political opinions or to vote, but now it does and the question is, "Will we give up our religious freedom in order to have some sick semblance of life while we drink the bitter dregs of demonic oppression?"

As a Christian in America, I have enjoyed the many blessings God and this nation has afforded me, but if I have to give up my religious liberty to maintain some semblance of it while drinking from the bitter oppressive cups of tyrannical oppression, I would rather not be here, knowing that the best still awaits me. As a believer, I have a sure election established in the courts of heaven. I have an inner liberty that can be surrendered to a despot (if I choose), but never taken away from me, and I have a confidence that if I am standing on what is true, standing for what is right, and standing in light of what is eternal that in the end truth will be left standing, judgment will silence the evil, righteousness will overcome the wicked, and the meek will inherit the earth.

Yesterday I watched democracy at work by volunteering at our local voting place. I appreciated the procedures that were required to ensure that a person' vote was properly counted and protected from any tampering and fraud. As I watch the world become worse day by day, clearly spiraling towards a final climatic event that will take place in Israel, I have to admit I am becoming more and more homesick for heaven.

Each day it becomes clear that I don't belong here. In many ways I have never fit into this world. I was always a square peg that some tried to pound into a round hole without any success. I am also a person who will not simply comply to get along with others. As I watch prophetic events come together, I am reminded that the world will become more frightening. God will let Satan make his final play as many godless powers try to push every nation towards globalism or the one-world government. In some ways, it is going to appear that they have succeeded, but like in the case of the tower of Babel, God will throw a wrench into it at the last moment and wreck their plans.

Meanwhile, things will, and are, going to happen regardless of who is influencing the dynamics playing out on a national and international scene. It is interesting to watch how people respond to the days we live in. Some who understand what is going on can go into utter despair, while others become completely deluded about it and live in denial as to what is taking place. You have those who comply to get along with the vipers, the wolves, and the raging lions, and others who are holding on to a thin line of wishful thinking that it is just temporary and everything will go back to "normal."

The reality is that it will not really go back to "normal," because right now some events are happening in the world that point to an unseen, unstoppable current. The kingdom of darkness is clearly clashing with the kingdom of light. The kingdom of darkness never plays fair, while some in the kingdom of light never utilize all they have in Christ to overcome and be victorious. I have no doubt that God will use these trying times to test, purge, refine, and prepare the church in America for His coming, but the question is what are you preparing for?

We are about to celebrate a very important day: Thanksgiving. But what is Thanksgiving? To some it is a big feast with family and friends and for others it is also a day of tradition with the Macy's parade and football.

Growing up, I have experienced all of these aspects of Thanksgiving, but as I have grown older, I have realized that Thanksgiving is a day that serves as a memorial to remind us of the blessings from above.

We know that every good gift comes from above and is a matter of God's grace. Like the offering of old, thanksgiving should be offered up to the Lord and poured out in adoring worship as it becomes the wings to lift up praise for all past and present blessings, as we look forward to the promised blessings to come.

True thanksgiving has a way of purifying the lips, lining up the attitude with gratitude, and ushering one right into the will of God. We are told, *"In every thing give thanks: for this is the will of God in Christ Jesus concerning you" (1 Thessalonians 5:18).*

There are things we might not be thankful for because of the devastation it leaves behind, but true thanksgiving will ultimately serve as that silver lining in every dark cloud and dark day because what we can be thankful for is that whatever the loss, storm, or challenge we encounter, we do not have to go it alone.

The Lord sits on the throne of sovereignty and is aware of us and our situation. He will either take our hand to guide us through the challenge, carry us through the devastation, or hide us in the storm.

Today we celebrate Thanksgiving. The Bible speaks much about this subject. Being thankful is an attitude, declaring thankfulness is a form of praise, and offering it up to God is a type of sacrifice. It is for this reason, giving thanks is the will of God.

I have thought much about thankfulness. Being a somewhat spoiled American, I have often thought in the past that I deserved to taste of the good things of life, had a right to be a recipient of abundant blessings we have enjoyed in America, and saw myself as being an exception to the rule when it came to experiencing any real challenging adversity. Needless to say, the more spoiled a person insists on being, the greater the heart attitude of ingratitude will be present along with the miserable temperament it will produce.

God had to lead me to my personal cross many times where I became crucified to silly, worldly notions, before I realized that life affords many tastes, one of them being bitterness, and that I deserve hell not blessings that were a matter of God's grace. I was also not an exception to anything, and that in the scheme of things I was nothing but a vulnerable worm, whose best was filthy rags that belonged in the garbage dump of the world.

True thanksgiving is not based on what we have or the circumstances and environment we are in, but on the awareness that all that is valuable, lasting, and truly benefits our life comes from above. *James 1:17 brings this out, "Every good gift and every perfect gift is from above, and cometh down from the Father of lights, with whom is no variableness, neither shadow of turning."*

As believers, we may not be excited about our present situation, but we can look up, knowing that what we have need of, our Lord provides daily, what we presently possess, which includes our life and family and friends, are blessings and gifts bestowed on us by the love of God, and what we have waiting for us is far greater glory than we can imagine.

At Thanksgiving it is natural to look at what we have, but as believers our life consists of so much more than worldly possessions. Let us get beyond the temporary, and count what we spiritually possess, and rejoice in the great hope that has been secured for us. As a final note, the one glorious fruit that that true thanksgiving brings forth is wonderment.

Wonderment is a child-like quality where the small things brings joy to the heart, the surprising things end in awe in the soul, and the sweet things produce satisfying pleasure in the spirit. I pray today during this Thanksgiving celebration that the sacrifice of true thanksgiving takes hold of your heart, and as you look upward towards the One who never changes to thank Him, that you develop the wings of praise to take flight and reach into the heavenlies that will bring glorious wonderment to your soul.

I heard a song the other night that had to do with the celebration of lights known as "Hannukah." Most of you know the story of this celebration where the great defilement of the temple by Antiochus Epiphanes occurred when he erected an idol in it and sacrificed a pig on the altar.

After the Maccabees (priests) cleansed the temple, they set about dedicating the temple by lighting the Menorah in the Holy Place but they only had enough oil for one day. It is important to note that one of the main responsibilities of the priests in the Holy Place was to keep that candlestick lit at all times. They had to keep the wick free of debris and the oil flowing to ensure the flame would continue to glow. The light represented the eternal light of God that must be kept burning in His temple.

As the story goes, the fire continued for eight days without any oil to keep it burning, until they could receive the appropriate supply for it. It was a miracle that the Jews celebrate today.

As believers we are the temple of God. The fact that we are born again represents an incredible miracle. The eternal flame in us is the gift and promise of the Holy Spirit who is the free-flowing oil from above. However, as priests of our temples we must keep our light from being snuffed out by the debris of the old man, the perversion of the world, and the darkness of Satan. We must keep our altars free of unholy sacrifices and strange fire. Like the temple of old, I realize there are times I do need to rededicate my temple to the Lord after cleansing it to make sure that I have not unknowingly erected an idol, allowed the defilement of the world to come in, and the self-life to lay claim to that which has truly been dedicated to Him.

As we come near to Hannukah, let us remember as believers that we possess the light of the world (the life of Jesus) and the oil of the Holy Spirit; therefore, let our prayer be that our wick of devotion is never dimmed, dulled, or put out by the elements of the world in our temples and that the eternal light of God will penetrate the great darkness with the hope of life, the joy of salvation, and the promises of eternal glory secured on the cross by our Great High Priest, Jesus Christ.

When I take offense for something, I have learned to ask myself why am I offended? We would all like to think we take offense for that which is honorable and worthwhile. For example, we take offense for what we consider to be the truth to a matter, but truth needs no defense. Rather, truth will cause offense to fragile realities and we are to stand on it not defend it. Like John and James *in Luke 9:49-50*, we may try to take offense for Jesus, but His honor does not need to be defended because He is truth and serves as our foundation.

We can take offense for non-essential beliefs that have no power to change or save a person, but in the end all such emphasis proved to be unprofitable for everyone involved. This brings me to the thought, why is there conflict over certain matters that speak of personal conviction as to whether we celebrate a certain holiday? Is it a matter of truth or is it a preference? Is it a salvation issue or is a matter of interpretation based on personal understanding?

Some people give the impression that the real message that is attached to religious celebrations such as Christmas is nullified because it does not fit within facts, finds its origins in paganism, and for that reason, the only recourse is to sulk off into some corner, offended with others who do not harbor the same convictions.

My goal is to always seek Christ in a matter, as a means to look for opportunities to lift Him up in a proper way. It is important to remember that Christ did insert Himself into history, walked among mankind and used the practices of that day, (often presented in parables) to challenge and teach the people. God used the political factions to carry out the judgment on sin and in the greatest time of darkness, Jesus was lifted up to draw all people to Himself.

As long as Christ is lifted up in glory, the message is unadulterated, and people are challenged to stop and consider a truth, God can use it to draw, convict and save a seeking soul.

As we enter into this particular season, I cringe because I know the same old debate will raise its head and start all over again about whether Christians should acknowledge or celebrate certain holidays such as Christmas. Such unprofitable debates cause unnecessary division, sometimes making believers a spectacle to others when they air it in front of the world, bringing a possible reproach on the Gospel.

In such division, offense is bound to rise out of feelings of being judged over a matter that cannot save and will not change a heart or mind. It is an argument that in all reality is not profitable, and as a result serves either a band wagon to stand on or a cause for others to forge ahead in a crusade. In fact, this very matter was brought out months ago by one of the people attending the Bible Study I conduct.

She took on an attitude of superiority as she implied if anyone of us dared to disagree with her about this subject, we were wrong! I was aware that she possessed a strong conviction of what she believes and I don't begrudge her for her conclusion, but personal conviction leads to debates because there is always another side. For me I have long ago learned that no matter how strong a person feels about his or her convictions, when the other side is presented, it usually ends in a stalemate because both sides have their reasons for their convictions and they can easily enough present powerful arguments.

The problem is that when a conviction becomes a truth in the mind of the person, the other side has no credibility and needs to be disregarded without any real discussion. In a sense, this type of individual tries to become the Holy Spirit in trying to influence how a person must think or believe for their Christianity to be considered legitimate.

It was obvious this individual was interested in dictating to people based on her conclusions, and it was clear she was not interested in discussing or reasoning with others about any contrary points of view. It is important to keep in mind when one has to actually step outside of a subject and insert his or her point of view about something else, that person will be out of order, and when he or she makes such a fleshly move, the flow of the Spirit will stop and it will rob others and bring personal offense.

As Christians we need to keep in mind we are not instructed to defend or give reasons for our views; rather we are told in *1 Peter 3:15* to be able to give a reason for the hope in us, and what is the hope, *"To whom God would make known what is the riches of the glory of this mystery among the Gentiles; which is Christ in you, the hope of glory"* (Colossians 1:27).

During this season, we can get caught up with the various debates of the Christmas celebration legitimacy, but the real issue comes back to who is Jesus to you? It is always easy to identify with the humanity of Jesus as we become sentimental about a baby in a manger, but we must remember that in the spring time we become emotional about the sacrifice of Christ on the cross during His ordeal at Calvary. On Sunday we can see our church activities as a means to do our religious duty for the week or get our weekly "fix," while the rest of the week we can tack Him on to those things that we want to give credibility to as we maintain the right to do our own thing on our terms.

The Apostle Paul in *1 Timothy 3:16* refers to the truth and work of Jesus as being both a controversy and a mystery, but what is so controversial and mysterious about Jesus' coming? These two matters rest in who He is, specifically in light of His incarnation. The great mystery is that God became man, which was and continues to cause a great point of controversy.

Even though God made it clear that nothing is impossible to Him, man continually looks to his mind to understand the unseen, the unexplainable, and the eternal, especially in the case of the mystery of God becoming man, and every time he does, he goes into unbelief and will come under an anti-Christ spirit. However, the Bible is clear that we are to approach the Bible to believe what it says rather than debate, adjust, and profane it by bringing it down to our base level of understanding.

Jesus in His humanity became our example of the ways of righteousness, the sacrificial Lamb of God, and now sits on the right-hand of Majesty serving as the High Priest, but because Jesus is God, He served as the expressed image of God in bodily form, and as the sacrifice He did not just cover our sins with the shedding of His blood, but He took them away.

It was the power of His deity that brought healing to mankind's body and soul, and raised Him from the grave to be victorious over death, taking away the dominion of hell and death from Satan. It is because Jesus is God in the flesh that He is able to become all in all to us.

Sadly, this mystery still remains a mystery to many. Make sure you are not on the wrong side of this controversy. This mystery can only be revealed by the Holy Spirit at the point of child-like faith for those who seek a greater revelation of His incarnation and not an explanation for it.

I have learned as a Christian to carefully choose my battles. The older you get the more you realize you can't waste time and energy on that which would prove to be unprofitable. I have been writing about the debates Christians have over such matters as whether or not we are to celebrate Christmas, and I even understand why some have a problem with it.

Most would agree Christ was born in the fall which would invalidate believers celebrating His birthday at this time, but I must admit I don't really see people celebrating His birth in the fall either. However, I understand that according to some Eastern cultures, they celebrate one's birthday on the day of his or her conception. If we westerners believed life began at conception, I wonder how many abortions would have been averted?

Consider for a moment if Jesus was born in the fall, He could have been miraculously conceived towards the end of December; therefore, it would be legitimate for people to celebrate His birth according to the Eastern perspective. This brings me to the reality of Christmas. Why do we consider this time at all? It is because God Incarnate came into this world. Jesus was inserted into history as a baby in a manger in preparation to be offered up as the sinless Lamb of God. It is because of Christ's birth we celebrate another event: Resurrection Sunday.

We all want to be on the "right side" when it comes to spiritual matters, but we must take note that when John and James passionately took offense for Jesus towards the Samaritans' lack of response to Him in *Luke 9:53-55*, He told them they were of a wrong spirit. When the disciples complained about someone (in *Luke 9:49-50*) who was not part of their group, and who was casting out devils, Jesus told them *"Forbid him not: for he that is not against us is for us."*

There was also the incident in *John 21:21-22* where Peter asked the Lord what was He going to do with one of the disciples, Jesus stated, *"If I will that he tarry till I come, what is that to thee? Follow thou me."* We can't forget Paul who had people preaching the Gospel out of contention in *Philippians 1:16-18*, but he rejoiced because Christ was being preached.

It is true that the world emphasizes commercialism and religion tradition at this time of the year, but as Christians we are called to emphasize who Christ is and what He did on our behalf at all times. As *Isaiah 9:6* prophesied, *"For unto us a child is born, unto us a son is given."* John reminds us of the significance of Jesus coming in *John 1:14, "And the Word (Jesus) was made flesh, and dwelt among us."*

As Christians we can be passionate about what we think is right and still be in a wrong spirit. We can believe we can be critical of those who are not on board with us, while forgetting that we all serve the same Lord and belong to the same kingdom, and we might become busybodies as to how God is dealing with or using others, and be reproved and instructed to be about the business that is before us. Paul summarized it best when he addressed the contentious Corinthians in *1 Corinthians 2:2, "For I determined not to know any thing among you, save Jesus Christ, and him crucified."*

Today I want to wish my friends a special day. For many, this time and season is a sorrowful one. It marks or magnifies times of losses and tragedy, times of mourning and not celebration. I realize that not everyone celebrates this particular day as being anything other than another day that in some cases reminds them of past painful events or even a time of great abuses and indulgence where man seems to be sucked into a vacuum of commercialism, despair, and insanity, but as believers we can take time to celebrate in our hearts that Jesus Christ came into this world.

He was God's gift to the world and He was miraculously inserted into history as a babe, a Son sent by the Father who became the Lamb that would take away the sin of the world. The fact that God clothed Himself in humanity in order to come into this world where He would experience all we do in our human state—joys, sorrows, losses, betrayals, and even physical death, everything except sin, is what also allows Him to serve as our High Priest, who not only saved us to the uttermost but now serves as the only High Priest who stands between God and man, ever making intercession for us.

As a believer I am daily aware of God's gift, ever conscious of how in His humanity, Jesus gave up the glories of heaven to become identified with me in my hopeless plight. I can agree with the angels when I think upon the great announcement of heaven around His entrance, *"Glory to God in the highest, and on earth peace, good will toward men."*

The reality is, every day our God deserves to be glorified. We know that if Jesus reigns in the heart there is peace on earth, and where He is Lord there will be good will between others. Every day I celebrate different aspects of my Jesus coming into this world. I am reminded at different times of the glory, the hope, and peace when I take time to allow the joy of my salvation to take hold of me and I can find such comfort when I take time to remember, *"For God so loved the world that He gave His only begotten Son, that whosoever believeth in him should not perish, but have everlasting life."*

Have a blessed day in the Lord.

ADAM

*People who are half-hearted towards
their spiritual inheritance are in danger
of losing all of their future blessings
and promises.
(Rayola Kelley)*

The first promise found in *Genesis 3:15* was given because of the entrance of sin into the world because of rebellion. Eve was deceived and found in transgression, while Adam was not (*1 Timothy 2:13-14*). Adam and Eve reveal the two ways sin enters.

Eve was beguiled, seduced by the serpent and fell into his trap, while Adam knew full well what he was doing and knowingly walked into Satan's trap. *Job 31:33* actually reveals that Adam's rebellion was a matter of iniquity or a moral flaw.

We are told by Job, *"If I covered my transgressions as Adam, by hiding mine iniquity in my bosom."* Adam was toying with transgression or the breaking of the covenant before he actually partook of the deadly fruit, and when he finally rebelled, he tried to cover his transgression; thereby hiding his iniquity by blaming God and Eve (*Genesis 3:12*).

Hosea 6:7 revealed that Adam's rebellion was a treacherous act on his part. Man, either falls into sin because of some type of ignorance or he knowingly walks into it, but one must keep in mind that sin works from some platform of deception, whether a person is being deceived to his or her actions, or trying to deceive self and others when the individual begins to pay the consequences for his or her actions.

Sin must be dealt with, but it is often hidden under some cloak of deception instead of brought to the light in sincere repentance, thereby, allowing its seeds to bring forth spiritual death. The Bible is clear that we inherit our fallen condition from Adam, and it is in the first Adam we all die, but it is because of the redemption of the second Adam, the promised seed of woman, Jesus Christ that we can live.

It is time to stop the ridiculous deceptive debates about sin and it is time for each of us to take responsibility for the sin that individually besets us so that it can be put under the blood of Christ and put away forever in the grave of forgetfulness.

One of the things that brings sobriety to my spirit is the type of questions the Lord sometimes asks individuals or the simple one-liners that are given to cast some type of shadow. A good example of a question is found in *Genesis 3:9*.

We are told in *Genesis 3:8* that the first couple heard the voice of the LORD God walking in the garden in the cool of the day but the couple had hidden themselves from the presence of the Lord. Now here is the question, "*And the LORD God called unto Adam, and said unto him, Where art thou?*"

Due to the first man's rebellious action, most people hide themselves under some type of darkness from God's presence to cover their transgressions with fig-leaves of excuses while hiding their iniquity under some cloak of good-works, personal decency, or religion. And what is the Lord doing? He is asking a simple question, "Man, where are you?"

It is not that the Lord does not know where a person is, it is because the person needs to be awakened to where he or she is. Due to sin, people have become lost to God and God has become lost to them. Man hides from the light of God, unwilling to be exposed in his plight, and preferring his darkness of separation from Him.

When comparing themselves to the evilness of the world, people tend to think they are not all that bad. They hide their moral deviation under a cloak of self-delusion that there is some good in them that can be salvaged, but *Isaiah 64:6* is clear that man's best is filthy rags and that according to *Romans 7:18* there is no good thing in the flesh that can be salvaged or will qualify one to inherit the kingdom of God.

In the last post I talked about how the Bible contains questions or one-liners that should cause us to pause and consider the implications attached to them. One of the one-liners I often pause at when I read it is found in *Genesis 3:21, "Unto Adam also and to his wife did the LORD God make coats of skins, and clothed them."* This is a powerful verse because there are three powerful pictures in this one verse.

The first one is that the first man tried to clothe himself, but it was not acceptable to the Lord. Man is always trying to construct some type of garb that will attempt to hide him from the light of God, but it can't cover his spiritual state before the Lord. Jesus stated in *John 15:22* that Jesus came to take away the cloak that hides sins.

The second fact we must note is that God took the necessary measure to clothe them. Only God can address and cover man's spiritual state of being naked and undone before Him.

The third aspect of this Scripture casts a powerful shadow and that it would cost an innocent animal's life in order to cover them. This points to God addressing our sin with the offering of His own Son, the Passover Lamb.

The blood of the Old Testament sacrifice atoned for or covered man's sins so he could approach God, but the blood of the New Testament sacrifice took the sins away resulting in reconciliation with God. When we are born-again, we are placed in Jesus and we are clothed in His wisdom, righteousness, sanctification, and redemption.

One of the challenges we humans have, is to avoid the "blame game." We see this blame game with Adam when he blamed both God and Eve for his personal actions. I had someone tell me that they did not mind being blamed for something they were not guilty of, but to quietly accept the responsibility for something they were guilty of was a different matter altogether.

To quietly take the blame for someone's error seems like a "noble gesture," but to be confronted about something that reveals personal guilt and shame often causes offense within the person, at which time the individual tries to turn the table, making someone else guilty. In fact, this is where the guilty start to transfer their guilt to another so they can slide by possible consequences, while cowardly letting someone else take the blame. In fact, such actions are considered shrewd and not wicked, but they clearly show a lack integrity.

However, these reactions are indicative of how pride works. Pride must come out looking noble, right, or as the misunderstood, suffering victim, but it can never accept any real wrong. Whether pride is hiding jealousy, high opinions, rights, or some type of fear about failure, rejection, incompetence, or losing control, it will not allow the examining light of truth to shine on it long without putting the spotlight on someone else so it can once again run to the shadows and hide behind some façade of innocence and fake nobility.

As a believer we must own who we are if we are going to face the light of God, take responsibility for who we are becoming if we are going to truly repent, and become responsible for who we are allowing ourselves to become if we are going to overcome the flesh, the world, and the devil.

As truth, God can't meet us in any other state but brokenness, show mercy unless true repentance is present, and allow His grace to flow unless we are humble enough to owe up for our wrongs, confess our miserable prideful state, and seek true reconciliation with Him.

We live in a society that is oriented towards works. My grandparents and parents were hard workers. Even though I had great examples, I still had to learn and develop my own work ethics. Adam was given responsibility to dress and keep the Garden of Eden. It is amazing when you consider these two words, they point to service and protection.

For Adam, it was not to keep the garden free of weeds, thistles, and thorns for there was none until after sin, but it was clear that he was to serve the Creator in the way that would bring glory to Him and protect the environment to ensure their fellowship.

To be able to work hard and enjoy the fruit of your labors is a privilege that should not be taken lightly. People in Socialist and Communist countries have learned this the hard way. They have given up their rights to excel in order to be equal in receiving the same free handouts that trickle down to nothing except oppression, leanness, poverty, and absolute despair.

However, when it comes to our spiritual lives the work of redemption has been completed on the cross by Jesus, and the work of sanctification is being done in us by the Holy Spirit in order to ensure glorification. It is natural for us as Christians to try to do our part in His kingdom to bring the Gospel to lost souls, change hearts and minds, and set people free which brings me to the next nugget of truth, "It is not your work that impacts and lasts in someone's life, rather, it is His work."

It is important to know our part. We are to be submissive to the leading of His Spirit in a willingness to be separated unto our callings and used by Him, obedient to the truth of His Word, and a living witness of His life. This reveals an openness of heart and mind, but the other thing we need to go back to are the simple responsibilities given to the first man in the Garden of Eden. We need to dress our lives with service to our Creator for His glory and protect and guard against anything that could threaten our fellowship with Him to ensure that we share in His glory. If it is not God's work in us, it will not transform us and if it is not God's work in others, it will never be eternal.

ENOCH

If God is to move among His people,
man must not be an observer, but
a humble participant in His Work.
(Rayola Kelley)

The statement in the Bible that causes me to stop and consider a man and his life is found in *Genesis 5:22, "And Enoch walked with God."* Think about what this one line is saying. Granted, it seems a simple statement, but it is one of the most loaded Scriptures in the Bible.

I am told that even in a fallen state, living in a cursed world, that there was a man who walked with God. Keep in mind, Enoch lived before the Law and before the Holy Spirit was given as a gift and promise to believers for the dispensation of grace. He did not have the tools we have to understand what it would mean to walk with God, yet he did. He had a close relationship with God. He fellowshipped with Him not in a garden but in the barren wilderness of this world. We know that he walked on this earth for 365 years, relatively a short time compared to his son Methuselah who lived to be 969 years old.

Even though Enoch did not live as long as others, he must have had a glorious life. It does not matter how long you live, what is important is how you live. Enoch discovered the secret to real life and reached such pinnacles with the Lord that his epitaph is recorded in the Bible, *"And Enoch walked with God: and he was not: for God took him."* Enoch had to be so consumed by the reality of God that this present world could no longer hold him; therefore, God took him.

My hope is that I will be so consumed by the reality of God at the end of my journey that when He comes to take me, the hold of this world will completely dissipate and I will truly feel at home in His glory.

I have often pondered what it means to walk with God like Enoch. Surely it means having an intimate relationship with the Lord. It implies walking in step with Him in the garden of fellowship, not just occasionally but

369

daily. In fact, it would mean that Enoch walked more with God than he related or interacted with the age he lived in.

For Enoch to walk with the Lord in such a way that he "ceased to be" in this world "for God took him" tells us that his life in God became his all-consuming reality. To me it speaks of the possibility that Enoch was so caught up with God's glory that the present world could no longer hold him.

I have always wanted to have such a walk with God, not because I want to appear "super spiritual" but because I want the world to lose its claims on me so that His glory can take hold of me in a greater measure. We must be able to discern our walk so we can identify those who are walking with the Lord as well.

The real measuring stick is how much of our life is being consumed by the reality of God right now.

Enoch walked with God and what a testimony he left behind him for us to ponder. To walk with anyone points to a relationship of intimacy. The Old Testament records the relationship that existed between God and Enoch, but it is the New Testament in *Jude 14-15* that shows us the result of that walk. Enoch was given prophetic vision to see into the future.

The important reality of Enoch's walk is that his eyes of faith were enlarged to see future events. It matters little what we know about God if we fail to have the eyes of faith to see Him in greater ways. It is as our vision of Him is enlarged that we begin to see beyond this world to that which is coming. We can see by Enoch's example that God does not give just anyone such prophetic insights; rather, He gives it to those who have developed an intimate relationship with Him.

For those who seek to operate in the prophetic to try to get a handle on the events of the day, they must first learn to walk with God in the normal activities of life while looking into the heavenly. The more a person walks in such places with God, the more their eyes of faith will be enlarged to see into the future.

To seek the prophetic, we must first desire an intimate relationship with the Lord as we seek His reality and truth about all matters.

Remember, Abraham was given many promises, but ultimately what his portion became was God Himself, and what he sought was the city made by God.

ABRAHAM

As you follow Abraham, you will see a man
that matured in his faith. His faith started
out as a mustard seed, was made simple
in its purity through obedience, and
materialized in a friendship with God.
(Rayola Kelley)

There are so many shadows, types (examples) and patterns in the Bible *(Hebrews 8:5)*. Veiled in the Old Testament are shadows that are cast by heavenly light as a means to prepare pure hearts to discern and recognize the real thing.

There are types to identify what has been declared as being so and patterns that allow us to follow them to fruition and find prophecies and promises completed. *Genesis 14:18-19* casts a powerful shadow that we as believers have witnessed the glory of. We see Melchizedek king of Salem and High priest of the Most High God meet Abram after his great victory to rescue Lot.

It is interesting to see what he brought with him. He brought bread and wine. We know that in the government established by God over the children of Israel that there would never be a person who would serve as both High Priest and King due to the lineages. Kings would come from Judah's line and priests from Levi's descendants.

However, this High Priest and King of Salem held both offices, and his appointment as priest was not a matter of ancestry but of God calling and ordaining him as such. We are told that every priest had to be taken from among men to be an effective intercessor (Hebrews 5:1).

The Gospel of *Matthew 1* identifies Jesus to His office as King, but the genealogy found in *Luke 3* reveals His priestly lineage that takes Him back to God. The beauty of it is that like Melchizedek of old, our Melchizedek also brought us bread by way of His body becoming a sacrifice and wine, which represented His blood, to establish an everlasting covenant with the Most High God.

Abraham had been given a lot of promises from God about his descendants that he would never really see come to fruition, yet he believed that everything God promised would come true. *Hebrews 11:13* put it this way, *"These all died in faith, not having received the promises, but having seen them afar off, and were persuaded of them and embraced them, and confessed that they were strangers and pilgrims on the earth."*

The first thing I want you to note in this Scripture is that these individuals saw the fruition of these promises in the future. This ability to see reveals that they were walking by faith according to the promises that were given. Faith allows us to see that a promise is always "Amen, so be it because God declares it as being; therefore, it is so."

Abraham believed the promises but *Hebrews 11:10* tells us this, *"For he looked for a city which hath foundations, whose builder and maker is God."* Abraham believed the promises of God but what he was walking towards was the city where God resided.

We are not meant to reside on the earth but we were created and formed to abide with God forever. The present world is our preparation for this eternal city, but such preparation requires us to be strangers in attitude towards the world and pilgrims in disposition, ever restless to seek out and find the place where we can freely worship and serve our God.

Abraham approached the Lord as an intercessor in *Genesis 18*, but it is important to consider how the Lord appeared to Abraham and came to him. We see in *Genesis 18:1* that the LORD (Jehovah, Yahweh) appeared unto him. "LORD" points to the Lord appearing to Abraham on the basis of covenant.

If you read on the Lord not only reaffirms His covenant with Abraham but promises Isaac would be born. But consider how Abraham addresses him after bowing himself towards the ground in *18:3*, "My Lord." The presentation of "Lord" in this Scripture points to Him as Adon (Adonai) owner and possessor of all things.

Covenant is the ground in which we can approach Jehovah, but when we make a matter personal, we approach Him as our owner, the one who is responsible over the matters of the household we are part of. Later Abraham would intercede to LORD (Yahweh) on behalf of Sodom and Gomorrah.

Like Abraham, we approach the Lord on the basis of covenant established by His shed blood on the cross, but we do it knowing that Jesus is also our owner and overseer of our lives. As children of God, we have the grounds to approach the One who owns us and is responsible for all those who are in His spiritual household (*Hebrew 3:3-6*).

One of the chapters in the Bible that often causes me to stop and ponder is *Genesis 13*. This is where Lot separates from Abram. The Bible tells us the land could not hold the two men, causing strife between their herdsman.

It was Abram that went to Lot and stated that the strife needed to cease and he gave Lot the first choice. Lot lifted up his eyes and beheld all the plain of Jordan. He noticed how well watered it was and chose in essence the world that was represented by Sodom, Gomorrah, and Zoar.

Lot left Abram with land that did not hold the same attraction. In fact, it was probably unattractive to the natural eye. What did Lot leave his uncle? The Promised, the Chosen Land of Jehovah. Lot went to the plains to dwell in the world but what did the Lord instruct Abram to do? Here is one of those Scriptures that says much, *"Arise, walk through the land in the length of it and in the breadth of it; for I will give it unto thee"* *(Genesis 13:17)*.

While Lot was dwelling in the world and being conditioned by it, Abram was told to arise and walk out his inheritance and wherever he walked in the land, it would become part of His inheritance. This is true for us as Christians.

We are not meant to dwell in this world but to walk out our spiritual inheritance through obedience that is motivated by our faith towards the Lord. The beauty about walking out our spiritual inheritance is that it will condition and prepare us for our heavenly inheritance and destination. The question is simple, "Are you walking out your spiritual inheritance?"

When it comes to the Lord introducing Himself as the "I AM," in Scripture, believers in their finite state need to remember for God there is no time or space. He either inserts Himself into time or He fills all space with His glory.

Over 20 centuries ago, a Man by the name of Jesus often used the two words "I am," to bring greater insight about Himself to the hearer. Someone counted the use of these two words in the Gospel of John, declaring that he had counted it being used 35 times as an introduction.

In *John 8:58*, Jesus said this, "*Verily, verily, I say unto you, Before Abraham was, I am.*" The people who heard Jesus say this understood what He was saying and picked up stones to kill Him, but He passed through their midst. Jesus will always present Himself in a new light to enlarge our understanding, but if we refuse to accept it, He will pass through our midst leaving us in a state of unbelief.

It is clear that if the Lord introduces Himself, it is because it will be followed by a greater revelation. The hearer will either receive the truth by faith or reject the truth and go into unbelief. Abram in *Genesis 15:1* was prepared to receive the revelation. As the I AM, the Lord wanted Abram to know that He was His shield and reward.

To me one of the incredible miracles of God is that a small seed can produce great life. Consider the conception of a child and how a person who begins as the size of a period in the womb of his or her mother develops into a person who has the potential to reflect the very glory of

God. Take the seed of God's Word, the Gospel, and realize once it takes root in a person's heart it can produce eternal life.

Sometimes we overlook the small seeds and their potential to produce life, missing not only the blessing of God but the work of God. God had promised Abraham the Promised Land, but did you know a seed was planted there first? That seed was the result of death, but it identified the children of Israel to the Promised Land.

The land was bought by Abraham from the Gentile who owned it and in it was planted a very precious seed to Abraham and important seeds followed which showed the faith of Abraham, Isaac, and Jacob. The seed I am talking about was the death of Sarah and she was planted in a burial place close to Hebron (*Genesis 23*).

In that place Abraham, Isaac and Rebekah, and Jacob and Leah were also planted. In that burial place were seeds that would produce an inheritance for Israel. This should not surprise us because there was a seed planted in a tomb, the life of Jesus, and it was raised up three days later to become the first fruits of a New Creation, securing an eternal inheritance for those who believe.

ISAAC

Fainting is more apt to occur in the valleys of daily drudgery than on the pinnacles of public performance. The real test of our faith will always be in the dark valleys where we cannot perceive God's presence. It is there we question our calling, our capabilities, and our commitment.
(Jeannette Haley)

I mentioned the situation with Isaac, Abraham's son in *Genesis 26*. The first thing we are told is that there was a famine in the land and the question is simple, was there a spiritual famine in Isaac's life?

The first thing I noticed is that God was blessing him for his father Abraham's sake. It struck me that Isaac did not have a real personal relationship with God. He was clearly in the shadow of his father's legacy, holding onto his "shirttail" when it came to the covenants, and trying to possess something he was not prepared to receive.

As believers we know that we are saved by grace, but we sometimes need to take a step further beyond that truth and realize we are saved for the sake of Christ and what He did on the cross for us (*John 16:23-26; 17:2, 6-26*). We receive nothing outside of Christ.

The covenant we enjoy was made possible by Jesus' blood, the forgiveness because He became the place of propitiation for us, our faith because He is the author and finisher of it, and our hope is because His life is in us, and Christ in us is the hope of glory. It is important to realize that depending on the type of relationship we have with Christ will determine how much the Lord intercedes on behalf of others for our sake.

This is why having a right relationship and upright life before the Lord gives authority and power to each of us as believers to stand in the gap for others when it comes to intercession and prayer. Only eternity will reveal how much the Lord has done for others for the SAKE of His people.

Isaac is an interesting man to study and there is no chapter like *Genesis 26* that gives us some insight into him. Unlike his father who went to Egypt, Isaac obeyed God's command to not go down to Egypt during the famine and to dwell in the land the Lord instructed him to reside in. The Lord also told him if he did what He commanded that He would perform what He had promised to Abraham, who had kept His commandments, statutes, and laws. In other words, it was up to Isaac to obtain the promises made to Abraham for himself.

Since Isaac obeyed, one would think it would be clear sailing for him, but in reality, God's commands will serve as a great test to those who are immature in their faith walk. It can seem easy enough to obey God up front assuming that it will ensure blessings and keep God off of one's back, but the test that follows obedience comes down to exposing one's motive for obeying.

The motive behind true faith when it comes to obedience is simple, it is the right, honorable thing to do; therefore, I will do it out of love for God. Notice how such a motive is void of self. That which is honorable maintains integrity in a matter, and that which is right will prove to be

376

acceptable to God because it requires self to be sacrificed up front (*Romans 12:1-2*).

Did Isaac obey God because it was the right thing to do? The only way to expose motive is to test character and conviction. You must have good character to stand against something that is challenging to your faith and threatening your testimony, and strong conviction to maintain moral uprightness. When Isaac was tested as to his character and moral conviction, like his father before him, he lied and failed the test. It had to do with Rebekah being his wife.

He knew she was beautiful and would be desired by the leader of the country; therefore, he told her to tell the powers that be that she was his sister. However, the leader found out and called Isaac to give an account of his lie that could have brought great reproach on him, his household, and his people. Isaac's answer was quite telling, "Lest I die for her." It was clear Isaac was watching out for number one and willing to sacrifice his wife and others to maintain his life.

I am so glad that my Lord Jesus Christ did not have the same attitude as Isaac. He would have never thought it worthwhile to give up the glories of heaven, nor would He have seen the need to go to the cross and allow Himself to be offered as the Lamb of God to die on our behalf, so we who believe, could have eternal life.

Genesis 26 shows Isaac's challenges to come to the place where he could be identified to the earthy inheritance and the spiritual legacy of his father Abraham. Isaac was the promised son but like the Promised Son of God, he had to obtain the inheritance for himself.

In *Genesis 26*, we see the famine, Isaac's obedience and testing, but now we are about to see the separation that usually comes as a result of conflict. No one could share in Isaac's inheritance including Ishmael. As a result, we constantly see a separation occurring in the lives of God's people such as in the case of Abraham and Lot. However, for Isaac it would be a separation from the people of the land.

These people represented the fleshly and the worldly. The fleshly will become jealous and mocking towards those who are people of promise and the world will become suspicious and resentful of them. These attitudes become open doors in which conflict will come in, causing a separation between the promised seed of God and the seed of Adam. This conflict centered over water.

Abraham had dug wells to sustain his herds and these wells were part of Isaac's inheritance, but those of the world will always try to stop up that which belongs to those who are heirs of faith to control or drive them away, or they will claim and take ownership of that which rightfully belongs to God's people to oppress.

There are two battles over wells recorded in *Genesis 26* which reminds us of the two fronts that some of the greatest battles take place at, and it is interesting to see how Isaac responded to both of them. We need to remember that the flesh wars against the spirit. There is contention at the point of flesh and quarrelsome strife at the point of pride when it comes to advancing forward in our Christian walk. Did Isaac take on the fleshly opposition because it was a matter of principle, and did he try to subdue pride because he had rights to the wells? The answer is no. He put down all desire to get in the pigpen with the fleshly and walked away from the temptation to come out on top of the prideful, thereby, depriving all arrogance of any real audience and credence.

The Bible is clear we must flee all youthful lust and humble ourselves before what is right to be overcomers of all that is attached to this earthly life. We must not get in the pigpen of the world to claim what is ours because we will come out smelling like the world and we must not try to be the king of some hill to prove a point because we will end up falling into a destructive trap.

May we heed *2 Corinthians 6:17-18, "Wherefore come out from among them and be ye separate, saith the Lord, and touch not the unclean thing; and I will receive you, And will be a Father unto you, and ye shall be my sons and daughters, saith the Lord Almighty."*

The incident concerning Isaac in *Genesis 26* contains many valuable examples. It is important to keep in mind that water in Scripture also represents the Holy Spirit. In the incidents of the wells, Isaac was not in the wrong, but the flesh (the herdsmen of the Philistine land) was opposing him from partaking of the refreshing qualities of life-giving water. This conflict happened over two wells, both revealing the jealousies of the flesh and the obstinance of pride.

When the battle of the flesh rages against the things of God, it keeps a person from coming to a place of simply partaking of what the Lord has for him or her. Isaac removed himself from both conflicts and dug a third well but this time there was no opposition and he called the well "Rehoboth."

Rehoboth implies being brought to an enlarged place or given more room or space. This may not seem significant except when you compare it to *Psalm 118:5, "I called upon the LORD in distress: the LORD answered me, and set me in a large place."* There must be a place without inner conflict before one can enjoy the liberty of the Spirit.

We can make the mistake of trying to battle it out with the flesh instead of mortifying it to ensure we are able to come to that place in the Spirit that we have the liberty to soar in the heights of praise, serve the Lord with gladness, and worship in His Spirit while lining up to His glorious truths about who He is and what He has done on our behalf.

One of the interesting subjects in the Bible to me is the concept of the "large place." The Lord used the incident with Isaac in *Genesis 26* to highlight the "large place" to me.

Isaac was associated with the promise given to his father, Abraham, but he was not personally identified to it. It is natural for each of us to begin in the shadow of another's faith, but we must go on in our Christian walk for our own faith to be perfected.

When you consider Isaac, he was first separated from the people of the land, but then he encountered opposition as he traveled from one well to another well to find a place of rest. The question is where can you find rest when what you encounter is nothing but conflict? Isaac came to another place called, "Rehoboth," and dug a well. Abraham had orchestrated the digging of the other wells, but Isaac was behind establishing this well. In other words, he was beginning to take ownership.

As pointed out the name of the well means a "broad place" and the significance of coming to such a place is that there was no conflict. As long as one is in the middle of conflict there is no liberty to move forward in their spiritual journey. It is for this reason we must avoid battles that would take us away from the course we are on. After all, faith is about being steadfast in our walk towards God to obtain the promises.

What does a broad place mean in relationship to our spiritual walk? *Psalm 118:5 gives us the answer, "I called upon the LORD in distress: the LORD answered me and set me in a large place."* A large place signifies deliverance and what does it mean for Christians?

When you consider *Isaiah 12:3,* and *John 4:14,* wells point to Jesus, but the water that comes forth points to the Holy Spirit. Consider what *2 Corinthians 2:17, says "Now the Lord is that Spirit: and where the Spirit of the Lord is, there is liberty."*

In *Genesis 26,* Isaac came to a broad place where he had the freedom to dig a well without opposition and to get his bearings. When you are a sojourner and stranger in the land, you must always come to a broad place to have the liberty to seek direction and perspective.

It is important to realize that one's status of simply passing through will not let you stay at such a place for long. It is a rest stop so that you can figure out where you are and the direction you must travel. In today's world some Christians' "broad places" have become "comfort zones" where they fail to move on spiritually to obtain their promises.

Remember, obtaining the fulness of promises are ever before us and we must remain pilgrims in hearts, sojourners in this age, and strangers to the world to inherit them. We must not be content to simply experience freedom in the Spirit, we must walk in that freedom according to the Spirit's leading. Case in point, Isaac did not stay at "Rehoboth," he went on to a place call Beersheba. Beersheba means "well of the oath."

It was here that Abraham made a covenant with the Philistine leader of the land that there would be peace among him and their descendants, and to confirm it, Abraham gave the leader sheep and oxen but he set seven ewes aside to serve as a witness to the oath (*Genesis 21:22-34*).

It is important to realize that at such times the Lord will always lead you to the place of covenant in order to remind you of what has been already established and what has been promised. It is at this place that spiritual sojourners can lay claim to the promise for themselves, while having their vision enlarged to embrace that promise by faith.

Isaac in *Genesis 26* reveals the Christian walk. As believers, we begin in the shadow of the cross of Christ, where we have been somewhat humbled and broken by sin. It is a glorious place, but we are not to stay there, we must now walk out our life in Christ by faith to obtain all the promises attached to it.

We sometimes take detours in our walk, but we will always end up at the place of covenant. Isaac came to a place of covenant and guess what happened? The Lord appeared to him. It is important to note what the Lord does when He appears because it will set the tone. When the Lord appeared to Isaac in *Genesis 26:2-3* it was to instruct him not to go down to Egypt during the famine, and if he obeyed Him, He would bless him and bring forth the promises He had made to his father, Abraham. Clearly, the Lord was doing it for Abraham's sake.

However, in this appearance in *Genesis 26:24,* He appears to him at the place of the covenant and introduces Himself to him. Think about this for a moment. When you study God's encounter with His saints, it is not unusual for Him to introduce Himself. And, how did He introduce Himself to Isaac, *"I am the God of Abraham thy father."* When God is about to do something new in one's life or make a matter personal, He will introduce Himself. Even though the Lord was still making His appearance for the sake of Abraham to reestablish the promise with Isaac, it was clear that His introduction was personal and it was to become personal to Isaac.

As Christians it is about relationship and I know that during my journey there are different times that the Lord has personally introduced Himself to me to enlarge my understanding, to transform my attitude, to change my direction, and to expand my vision. How about you?

In the Gospel of John, He constantly introduced Himself and it usually began with two words, "I am." Are you walking in some darkness? Jesus will introduce Himself as the light. Are you hungry? He will introduce Himself as the Bread of life. Are you thirsty? He will invite you to partake of His Water. And, are you lost? He will seek you out as the "Good Shepherd." Jesus is our all in all and He will meet us right where we are, but are we ready for Him to insert Himself in our reality at the place of covenant, and enlarge our understanding of Him in order to establish us in a more intimate relationship with Him?

The example of Isaac in *Genesis 26* reveals that one must be free of personal inner conflict to come to a large place to get his or her spiritual bearings. Once believers get their bearings, then they can be led to the next place, the place of covenant.

After Rehoboth, Isaac went to Beersheba. Beersheba was a place where Abraham had made a covenant of peace with the ruler (Abimelech) of the Philistines and Phichol the chief captain, and sealed it with seven lambs that were also to signify that he had dug the well at that location (*Genesis 21:22-34*). "Beersheba" means "well of oath" or "well of seven."

It was at Beersheba that same night that the LORD appeared to Isaac and said, *"I am the God of Abraham thy father, fear not, for I am with thee, and will bless thee, and multiply thy seed for my servant Abraham's sake."* The Lord reaffirmed His covenant with Abraham to Isaac.

It is important to point out that Isaac had not made the Lord his God. Granted, the Lord was Abraham's God and God was honoring the covenant He made with Abraham, but it was time for Isaac to make the LORD his God so that he would become identified with the covenant as the LORD's servant.

Everything God does on our behalf is for the sake of His Son, Jesus Christ, but there must become a time when we are identified to the New Testament covenant because we have believed God about salvation and received the Lord Jesus Christ into our hearts as Lord and Savior.

After Isaac encountered the Lord at the place of covenant and the Lord reaffirmed the covenant to Isaac, Isaac's response contains a sermon in itself. We read it in *Genesis 26:25, "And he builded an altar there, and called upon the name of the LORD and pitched his tent there; and there Isaac's servants digged a well."* What is the significance of Isaac building an altar?

We must ask if this is his first altar that was constructed by him. We know that Abraham built altars, but it does not appear that Isaac was much into this type of activity. After all, it is easy to ride into God's blessing off the shirttails of others, but the reality is that if a person is going to come into a covenant for him or herself, the individual must construct his or her own altar.

There were four types of altars in use in the Old Testament: an altar where sacrifice for sins were offered, an altar establishing a memorial to remember who or what God did, an altar that served as a witness, and an altar where a person would call upon the name of the Lord.

For believers we have two altars. The first one is the cross of Christ where our sin was dealt with and we call upon the name of the Lord, and the second altar is our hearts where we establish a memorial to commemorate our consecration of service and erect a living witness of our faith.

The question is, have you come to the first altar and if you have, are you erecting the altar of your heart in preparation of ever meeting the Lord at the place of covenant because of what Jesus did on the cross for you?

The second response of Isaac in *Genesis 26:25* after he build an altar was to call upon the name of the LORD. Why would a person call upon the name of the Lord unless they wanted to meet with Him and secure a personal life in Him?

When I call upon the name of the Lord it is to draw near to Him in order to be delivered in some way, seek Him out for mercy in regard to my present plight in order to be a recipient of His grace, to approach

Him with a request, or to meet with Him in communion and worship. Calling on the name of the Lord is not just an Old Testament practice. We have this promise in *Romans 10:13, "For whosoever shall call upon the name of the Lord shall be saved."*

In *Romans 10:13*, calling upon the name of the Lord is in relationship to salvation. Every believer has called upon His name of the Lord to be saved from their spiritual plight and the promise that is associated with it is eternal life and the blessings are that of grace and communion.

The third thing Isaac did in *Genesis 26:25* was to pitch a tent. This action may not be significant to us, but pitching a tent points to abiding. Isaac was going to abide at Beersheba, and why would a sojourner abide? He would abide until the pressing matter was resolved.

For you and me this means waiting on the Lord to see what He wants us to understand or until a matter is resolved and clarity is finally brought to it. It was clear that Isaac was not willing to move from the place of covenant until he was released to do so.

We don't know what this release would look like, but for me it is a lifting of a burden, a matter brought to completion, or an actual release from the Lord that it is time to move on. This brings believers to an important challenge and that is as sojourners in this age, we must discern those times that we are simply to abide before the Lord and wait upon His answer, approval, or marching orders. We need to be in step with the Lord at all times, ever disciplined by His yoke, and that can mean waiting.

Sometimes we sit before Him until we meet with Him and other times we stand before Him waiting for marching orders, and there are times we simply abide in Him until He moves. The Apostle John gives us this insight on abiding in *1 John 2:6, "He that saith he abideth in him, ought himself also so to walk, even as he walked."* It is important to point out that waiting is one of the disciplines of faith that prepares one to walk in obedience when the right time presents itself.

The fourth thing Isaac did in *Genesis 26:25* was to have his servants dig another well. Perhaps it was the same well Abraham had previous established, but nevertheless to abide, one needs to have a water source.

Jesus invited all those who were thirsty to come to Him by faith and He would give them Living Water. The truth is the source of our Living Water is found at the place of covenant, Jesus Christ. In a sense Jesus is the well, and the Spirit of God, the rivers of Living Water. However, we must come to the well (Jesus) to receive this water.

It is Jesus who uncaps the rivers of Living Water in our very spirits, reviving them so that the water can flow through our souls refreshing the inner man. *Isaiah 12:2-3 states, "Behold, God is my salvation; I will trust, and not be afraid; for the LORD JEHOVAH is my strength and my song; he also is become my salvation. Therefore, with joy shall ye draw water out of the wells of salvation."*

Have you accepted the Lord's invitation to come to Him to quench your spiritual thirst?

In *Genesis 26*, we see the Lord introducing Himself to Isaac as the God of Abraham. This may not seem significant for some, but the reality is that the Lord was blessing Isaac for the sake of Abraham. To those who have a relationship with the Lord it is humbling to realize that God benefits others because of our prayers on our behalf. However, there comes a time that a person must establish their own relationship with the Lord and for Isaac at Beersheba, it was his time.

That is why his actions in *Genesis 26:25* are so important. It was his way of establishing his own relationship and identity with the Lord. We know that out of it came peace with his enemies. Until we have reconciliation with the Lord there will be no peace, but that reconciliation comes when we establish a relationship with the Lord.

Consider the incident with Jacob, Isaac's son. He was on his way to his uncle's when the Lord inserted Himself into Jacob's journey at a place called Luz (separation) that Jacob renamed Bethel (Place of God). It is interesting to see how the Lord introduced Himself in *Genesis 28:13,*

"And, behold, the LORD stood above it, and said, I am the LORD God of Abraham thy father, and the God of Isaac..."

It is clear that Isaac made the LORD God of his father, Abraham, his God.

We have been following Isaac on his journey in *Genesis 26* to come to a place where what was promised to Abraham, becomes his promise as well. The Bible is clear we must obtain and inherit the promises of God for ourselves. It is true they have been secured by and in a covenant for us to claim, but we must possess them.

For Abraham and seven tribes of Israel, they were told to walk out their inheritance (*Genesis 13:14-17; Joshua 18:2-8*). The New Testament is clear that we are to walk out our inheritance. It is through the faith walk and by faith we inherit the promises of God.

Isaac was brought to a place of covenant where the Lord introduced Himself to him. God will make Himself personal to us and for Christians He becomes personal in Jesus Christ. The more we know about Christ, the more we know Christ, and the greater revelation of Him we possess, the more personal the truth of God becomes to us and the more we will grow in a relationship with Him.

When it comes to God establishing a matter in one's life, it must be a new, complete work. The Apostle Paul refers to the work as becoming a new creation where the old is put aside as the new is unveiled in our lives. As believers, we can't lay claim to the garment of salvation or someone else's oil of the Holy Spirit, nor can we think that any old religious garment will pass the inspection of God on judgment day. God will look for the evidence of His New Testament covenant in our lives and what is that evidence? He can see the reflection, or the image, of His Son's life, attitude, and ways in us.

We have been considering our Christian walk in light of Isaac's experiences in *Genesis 26*. Christianity is not some religion where you nail down theology; rather, it is about walking out what is true in order to gain what is eternal. It is for this reason we are told we walk by faith and not by sight (understanding).

Let's face it, if Christianity was simply about getting some creed right, we would never have to worry about living it. However, when we are divorced from practicing what we believe, we become nothing more than hypocrites.

Christianity is about allowing what you believe to be tested and refined by walking it out in obedience to God and His Word. Isaac came to a place of covenant where God introduced Himself to him. What was Isaac's response to his encounter with the LORD? *Genesis 26:25* tells us he responded in four ways: he built an altar, called upon the name of the LORD, pitched a tent, and had his servants dig a new well. I want you to consider what these four responses mean.

Isaac's altar marked a meeting place of sacrifice, memorial, witness, and intention. It was clear that Isaac's intention was to finally claim the promise given Abraham for himself. The second thing he did was call upon the name of the Lord to resolve the matter. We are told if we call upon the name of the Lord, we shall be saved. He pitched a tent which shows he was willing to dwell there (wait upon the Lord) until he had secured it for himself, and finally the digging of the new well pointed to the fact that for him to secure it for himself, he had to make a personal investment. The question is, did Isaac secure the promise for himself? The answer is found in how the Lord introduced himself to Isaac son's Jacob at Bethel in *Genesis 28:13, "I am the LORD God of Abraham thy father, and the God of Isaac..."*

The question I sometimes ask is if God introduced Himself to some family member of mine would He say, "I am the God of Rayola?"

JACOB

We all start out like Jacob, a mere supplanter,
but God intends to turn us into kings and
priests who even the ungodly seek
blessings from.
(Rayola Kelley)

How many of you have become good wrestlers in the kingdom of God? I can't tell you how many times I have wrestled before the Lord about different matters. Some of my wrestling matches remind me of Jacob's struggle at Peniel in *Genesis 32:24-30* with the heavenly being, who was clearly identified as being God (or Jesus) in His pre-incarnate state.

It was after the match that his name was changed from Jacob (supplanter) to Israel (the prince that prevails with God). As I considered Jacob, I realized that he endured the long match because he believed there was a blessing to be had.

Someone once said there is a difference between wrestling WITH God and wrestling BEFORE God. The first one you are likely to get your hip knocked out of joint, where in the case of the latter you are apt to get the results with your hip in place. What was the wrestling match all about?

Jude 3 gives us this insight, "*Beloved, when I gave all diligence to write unto you of the common salvation, it was needful for me to write unto you, and exhort you that ye should earnestly CONTEND FOR THE FAITH which was once delivered unto the saints.*" (Emphasis added).

"Contend" in this Scripture means to wrestle. Most wrestling matches in the spiritual realm is not about pressing against God to receive a blessing; rather, it is about getting our fears, doubts, and areas of unbelief out of the way so we can let God be God, trust Him to be God, and have assurance that in the end we will not be ashamed for putting our confidence in Him.

It is also interesting to note in *Revelation 2:17*, each overcomer will also receive a new name, written on a white rock that will only be known between them and the Lord. It makes me wonder if the many wrestling matches I have had during my faith walk will determine the name I receive in the end.

Because God keeps His promises, like Isaac his father, Jacob was blessed for the sake of Abraham. God's encounter with him at Bethel caused Jacob to make a vow before the Lord. *Genesis 28:20-21* tells us what the vow was, *"And Jacob vowed a vow saying, If God will be with me, and will keep me in this way that I go, and will give me bread to eat, and raiment to put on, So that I come again to my father's house in peace; then shall the LORD be my God."*

Jacob realized that he needed to make the Lord his God, but first he had to finish the journey before him and return back to his father before he could make the Lord God his God. It is important to realize that Jacob was simply asking the Lord to be God in his present plight, show Himself in his future well-being, and bring him back to the land of promise in peace and he would then make Him God of his life.

It may seem like a tall order from man's perspective but it wasn't from God's perspective. You can see how the Lord kept, maintained, and blessed Jacob through his 20 years with his uncle. But it also is interesting to note what Jacob did, he sought the Lord's wisdom and did right by his uncle. It is clear that Jacob believed enough in his grandfather's God to act according to genuine faith.

It is interesting to consider what Jacob did after his encounter with the Lord in *Genesis 28:18.* He rose up early in the morning and took a stone that he had used as a pillow and set it up as a memorial, and poured oil upon the top of it. We may not consider his actions of importance but they foreshadow the need for us to establish a pillar as a memorial each morning in our lives as well.

Our pillar needs to become a place of rest as well as a point of establishing something of the utmost importance. The oil points to anointing, foreshadowing the need for our pillar to be anointed from above. His actions cast a powerful image, for Jacob foreshadows Jesus Christ.

The Lord is our place of rest, but He had to be lifted up from the earth by a cross, as well as anointed from above with the oil of the Holy Spirit to become a standing, lasting memorial for each believer. This is to remind each of us to line up to a cornerstone by faith, to be established on a sure foundation through obedience, and to walk in light of the promise of the heavenly.

JOSEPH

Joseph's life reiterates that greatness
in God's kingdom often rises out of the ashes
of rejection, slavery, oppression,
and brokenness.
(Rayola Kelley)

One of the interesting lives to study in the Bible is Joseph. We can all appreciate the man he became in the midst of challenging times but it is important to follow Joseph's progress.

We see that Joseph was given a vision of a future reality when he was a teenager. As Joseph learned, visions from above may take years for them to come to fruition. Visions often give us a stake we can remember, but it takes obedient steps of being faithful with what you know is right before you will even see such visions come true.

Consider Joseph's process. He was sold into slavery as a teenager because of jealousy, put into prison because he would not compromise, and forgotten until the right time. Joseph had to be around 40 before he witnessed this vision coming true.

It is hard to say if he thought much of that vision until it came to fruition, but you can see that through his life, he made the right choices and each time he made the right choices, God showed him favor until he was prepared to become the second in leadership to the Pharaoh.

The question is, has God given you a vision? If He has, you must make sure you do not become discouraged and walk away from the process, knowing in due time God will bring it about at the right time.

Meanwhile, the key is being faithful with what is right in front of you. Each step of faithfulness will lead you to the fulfillment of a heavenly vision.

Joseph was a unique man and an incredible representative. It is said that there are 130 parallels between his life and the life of Jesus. As a result, Joseph is considered the Messianic patriarch.

One of the aspects of Joseph's story is that of redemption. Silver represents redemption and the silver cup that was put in Benjamin's sack to bring a type of accusation against him puts a light on a past event and foreshadows a future event. We know that Benjamin was innocent as far as the silver cup, but so was Joseph when he was sold into slavery and Jesus when He was betrayed.

Benjamin was brought before Joseph the representative of Egypt and Jesus before the Sanhedrin and the Roman authorities. However, another interesting figure steps in on behalf of Benjamin and that was Judah.

If Judah had only been honorable on behalf of Joseph before he was sold into slavery, he would have not willingly participated in the wicked act. It is clear that Judah had been through a process and was willing to take Benjamin's place as a slave. Judah's actions brought Joseph to tears and he would reveal himself to his brethren.

We know on the cross that Jesus took our place and as a result, redeemed us. The problem is that we often take for granted what Jesus did on our behalf. He was without guilt, but became guilty so that we could stand justified instead of condemned.

No doubt Benjamin appreciated Judah's willingness to become a slave in his place, but it also set up the occasion for Joseph to reveal himself. The more we rejoice over Christ's redemption, the more He will be unveiled to us in the light of His wondrous grace.

I so appreciate what Paul said in *Ephesians 2:7, "That in the ages to come he might shew the exceeding riches of his grace in his kindness toward us through Christ Jesus."*

One of the Scriptures that I often fall back on is what Joseph said to his fearful brothers after the death of their father, *"Fear not: for am I in the place of God? But as for you, ye thought evil against me, but God meant it unto good, to bring to pass, as it is this day, to save much people alive"* (Genesis 50:19-20).

Consider the faith of Joseph. He was sold into slavery that took him down what seemed to be a dark, impossible path of despair and hopelessness. At the time Joseph probably struggled with the "whys" of it, but through it he established and maintained his moral character so that God could show him grace. It was hindsight that gave Joseph the insight as to the "whys."

Faith does not walk according to hindsight; rather, it chooses to trust the sovereignty of God when nothing seems to make sense to work out a matter for His purpose that in the end will benefit His people. There are many times I have not understood something when I was walking through it. My only real choice, as a believer, was to believe by putting my faith in God and trusting Him.

It was hindsight that allowed me to see God's wondrous hand in all of it causing thanksgiving to rise up for His abiding work of grace in my life.

MOSES

*Moses' life reveals how God's calling
carries us through the shadow of death,
delivers us from oppression, prepares
us in the wilderness, and brings us forth
to stand sure in the different world
courts of the Pharaohs.
(Rayola Kelley)*

The story of Moses is interesting and inspiring. Here was a man who was destined to die because he was a male in the midst of grave slavery, yet the Lord had a calling on his life. Clearly, Moses' mother received wisdom from above to know what to do with this special child.

She made an ark for him which represented a type of burial. However, this burial was not a physical one but a spiritual one, where a child born in slavery would come forth to be raised in the courts of Pharaoh.

This is true for every Christian. Born in slavery to sin, we have a death sentence hanging over us and it is only by becoming identified in the provided ark of the death, burial, and resurrection of Christ that we can be brought into the courts of heaven to be adopted into a heavenly family, a royal priesthood, and a holy nation.

We are indeed a blessed people with such hope and promise.

God has a time for everything. Many people who have a calling on their lives mistakenly think that God is going to bring it about quickly, but example after example shows us this is not a correct assumption. There must be a time of preparation.

Moses had a sense of his calling when he took offense for his Hebrew brother and killed an Egyptian to deliver the slave from his oppressor. However, it was not the right timing for Moses to be a deliverer, and the deliverance would involve all of Israel and not just one man. Moses' action was premature and his real destiny would be realized in the future after preparation in the wilderness for forty years.

Many times, God must cause us to end up in the wilderness to prepare us for our calling. At such a time He defines our true destiny by enlarging our vision in line with the excellency attached to our high calling. God will never fling His people into the unknown without first preparing and enabling them to walk through their age to fulfill their potential.

It is easy after having some type of mountaintop experience with God to feel infallible or empowered to do the impossible, but we must come down to the valleys and walk out the mountaintop revelation in the valleys where shadows can cause confusion, drudgery can end in apathy, and the struggles and challenges can become overwhelming.

393

Take Moses for example; he was called to a mountain to receive the law of God and had to bring it down to the wilderness in order to instruct people, and then the people had to commit to it and work it out by walking it out in the barren place.

The truth of the matter is we are not meant to live on the mountain of spiritual experiences. Such experiences may cause the spirit to soar but as long as the body is subject to this world, the soul will experience that great rush from the mountaintop of experiences to the depressing valleys below.

It is on the mountaintops where we may receive revelations, but revelations are not to be admired but to be walked out. It is as the person walks out the revelations that transformation takes place in the soul area, developing the ability to see beyond this present age in order to walk according to the next world to come.

Faith enables our spiritual eyes to look beyond this world to see the possibilities of the next world, but prayer often allows us to grab a hold of the promises of God that become stepping stones that allow us to advance into the great chasms of the unknown, leading us to our ultimate destination.

The theme that came up in my Bible reading this morning was the concept of "taking something in a light manner." When Moses was on Mount Sinai, the Lord told him to go down and charge the people and warn the priests to adhere to the instructions of not touching the mount. God's concern was that they would break beyond the barriers to simply gaze and many would perish as in the case of the men in 1 Samuel 6:19-20 who looked into the ark and perished (*Exodus 19:21-22*).

1 Samuel 2:30 talks about those who despise Him will be lightly esteemed, and *Isaiah 17:10* talks about the people not being mindful of the Rock of their strength. Our attitude towards the Lord will determine how we approach Him.

It was obviously the people of Israel were about to break through to simply gaze on what was going on at Sinai. God ways and doings do not make up some side show for the curious to simply gaze at it. Those who lightly esteem God because they want to do their own bidding will

394

be lightly esteemed by God when it comes to their prayers. And those who pay no mind to God because they are mindful of the things of the flesh and the things of the world will miss it all.

People have a tendency to insert God into their way of thinking—how they see themselves, regard their life, and what is important to them, but God's ways and thoughts are higher (*Isaiah 55:8-9*). For example, there are those who only want to look at God through a fleshly love and a worldly tolerance and when challenged in their thinking they ask how can God be so harsh and unfeeling towards faults and failures. It is not that God is harsh and unfeeling, it is that He is holy and can't look at sin without judging it, give sin a pass without betraying His character, or allow sin because it separates man from Him.

Today many people are talking about the need for revival, but the key is how are we approaching God? God is a loving Father, but He is also an angry God when it comes to the wicked and sin. When my earthly father was unhappy, I did not flippantly approach him by assuming love will overlook the problem, but I humbly and carefully approached him because of the need for grace and reconciliation.

We need God to move on our behalf as a people, a church, and a nation, but our need to examine our attitude to ensure we are sober and humble towards Him is vital and it must begin with those who call upon the name of the Lord.

Yesterday, I talked about approaching God. This subject may not seem like an important subject but the children of Israel realized that, for the most part, they had to approach the Lord through Moses based on the covenant. Yes, God loved, chose, and exalted them as a nation, but they could not approach Him from any perspective except by mediation and covenant because outside of both, there was no expectation and authority from either party about a matter.

Many fail to realize that we approach God at the place of mediation and covenant. It is the place of the cross of Christ where, as the Lamb of God, Jesus would become High Priest in the courts of heaven after the shedding His blood provided a better covenant and way for us.

The challenge people have today when it comes to approaching God is that He is usually presented in one dimension. Is our response a generic one that is based on limited understanding, notions, and assumptions about God or is it one who needs to meet with Him to do business as far as His kingdom, souls, and will?

Is He simply all love to us, or do we keep in mind He is also holy, and when it comes to an unregenerate sinner, holiness declares that without salvation a sinner will fall into the hands of an angry God? However, if a sinner seeks forgiveness at the cross of Christ, they will experience the love of God that expresses itself in mercy, forgiveness and salvation, and they will be exalted to a status of a child of God and a saint.

We also make God all about grace, but He is also a God of judgment that is a consuming fire. The Bible is clear that to seek the grace that saves, we must ask for mercy that opens the door with faith to enter into the place of grace. We must be aware of our status when we approach God.

Are we approaching Him as a seeker of His intervention or as a child who seeks to sit in the presence of the Father? For those seeking intervention, we begin from the point of humility and mercy; and for those who seek to sit in His presence, we begin from humility as we offer the sacrifice of praise that will lift us into His presence to commune with Him in an attitude of worship.

One of the great aspects of Moses' life is that he teaches us a lot about the presence of God. In his first encounter with the Lord, it entailed a burning bush that was not being consumed. Moses had to turn aside from regular activities to consider the unusual event taking place in the mundane wilderness.

To meet with the Lord, we must often turn aside from the normal to encounter the presence of the extraordinary. We must remember that if the Lord inserts Himself into our ordinary activities that our day will prove to be anything but normal.

The other aspect of the Lord inserting Himself into normalcy is to bring some type of change in our direction, whether it is to redefine our calling, instruct us, or create a certain attitude in us. It is meant to bring some type of change in our life.

Next time you sense the presence of the Lord, make sure you turn aside to meet Him.

Moses turned aside to see a burning bush and encountered the presence of God. The question is how do you approach the Lord? God's instruction to Moses was to take off his shoes for he was standing on holy ground.

The first thing we must acknowledge if we encounter the Lord's presence is that we are standing on holy ground. The concept of God's holiness should cause us to realize our approach should involve a separation from the world, a realignment of our focus from the normal to stand before the extraordinary, and allow the awe of it all to create humility in us.

The problem with people is that they can become quite casual in their approach to God without recognizing His holiness. If one's attitude is not right towards God, then his or her approach will miss the reason for God's insertion and visitation in a matter.

God's strength is always revealed in and through our weaknesses and the Apostle Paul added that the Lord's grace becomes our point of sufficiency in all matters.

In the wilderness, Moses was brought to a state of uncertainty and when God steps on the scene, such an individual feels unworthy and inept. It may be hard to believe, but this is the type of state that prepares us to be used by the Lord.

Clearly, Moses' youthful zeal gave way to the recognition of weakness in the wilderness. His former status and abilities seemed to have given way to the normalcy of life as a shepherd. He did not feel he could speak properly and fulfill God's call but the reality was that Moses may have not felt prepared, but he had been prepared.

His greatest concern was that he felt he could not carry out God's plan. He had learned the great lesson that a state of weakness is the only place God can show His strength and His might through his people. The Apostle Paul concurred when he stated, *"For ye see your calling, brethren, how that not many wise men after the flesh, not many mighty, not many noble, are called: But God hath chosen the foolish things of the world to confound the wise; and God hath chosen the weak things of the world to confound the things which are mighty"* (1 Corinthians 1:26-27).

When Moses encountered the Lord in the burning bush, he was given his marching orders. He was to go to Pharaoh and tell him to let God's people go so that they could worship Him.

As believers we all have our marching orders because, in a sense, we received it upon salvation. We are to go into the world and share the "good news" with everyone who will hear. In other words, we are all called to be evangelists.

I have two other co-laborers I work with in the harvest field and we all carry out this commission differently. When Jeannette had the full use of her voice, she was spontaneous in recognizing opportunities to share the Gospel, often with complete strangers.

The second co-laborer is Carrie, and since she has a beautiful singing voice, she shares it in song and music, and for me I am a one-on-one person who likes to look for the opportunity in personal encounters that would allow me to share the wondrous message of Jesus and His salvation. The reason I am sharing this is because we must find our particular way of sharing our testimony of Christ with others, knowing that there is no right or wrong way and that in the end, the Father must draw the person, the Holy Spirit must convict the conscience, and the Son will save a soul if a person truly accepts His invitation to come to Him to partake of the rivers of Living Water.

Moses' initial reaction towards the Lord calling him, revealed that he was looking at himself in light of carrying out his calling and not at God. It is natural for us to consider our calling in light of our strengths and abilities, and if there is any shred of self-sufficiency left in us, we have the tendency to try to figure out how we are going to accomplish the feat.

The Lord must often make us feel inept by using circumstances to reveal our inability to carrying out a mission. Every servant must learn that what God ordains, He will also equip His servant with the ability to carry it out. It is God's strength and doing and not man. If a matter is not God's doing, it will not last nor will it have any real impact.

One of the things that has always fascinated me about Moses is that he was not initially called to the wilderness but to the mountain to serve the Lord (*Exodus 3:12*). We know it is at Mount Sinai that Moses received the Law that established a covenant between the Lord and the Jewish people.

Moses had to wait before the Lord to receive the instructions, and the first time around he had to leave the presence of God because the people were committing idolatry. When he witnessed what they were doing, he threw the stone tablets to the ground breaking them, symbolizing how the people had already broken the first three commandments.

I have stated this before, mountain top experiences are glorious because it is there on the mountain that we often receive revelation, but we must bring such revelation to the wildernesses and valleys of this world and walk them out to become a living witness of our experiences with the Lord.

Too often, we make our experiences into some formula or method but our relationship with the Lord can't be captured and made into a "recipe" that will work the same way every time. We must be discerning enough to recognize the times and environment, sensitive to the Spirit to know when to move, tender enough to hear His voice, and open enough to follow Him wherever He leads, and where will He lead? He will lead us to places of communion, service, and worship.

Many people note that Moses saw the Promised Land from a distance, but never made it into the Promised Land, but that was not true. Moses did enter into the Promised Land during the incident on the Mount of Transfiguration.

It is important to point out that Moses points to the first covenant, the Law. As a shepherd prepared in the wilderness, Moses could not bring the people into the Promised Land because it required a military leader. As Christians we know that the Law was to be a schoolmaster that pointed us to Christ, our Joshua.

In his physical body Moses saw the Promised Land from a distance and likewise we see the fulfillment of the promises of God in the future as well. What will bring us into any promises of God is faith exercised towards Him.

It is faith that has the eyes to see into the future and the ears to hear the voice of the Spirit as He leads and guides us through this age into the glory of the next.

There is one important aspect that I want to bring out about Moses. The glory we emit from our countenance will depend on who or what we expose ourselves to the most. Moses was never content to settle for encountering the Lord's presence, he wanted to see His glory. Of course, he could not look into God's full glory and live; therefore, he was taken to a rock and hid in the cleft of it.

The Lord used His hand to cover Moses as he passed by in all of His glory. The Lord stressed that Moses could not see His face, but he would see His back parts. Moses' encounter with God's glory is what he reflected when he came down from the mountain.

The problem is that man in his unprepared state could not look at Moses' face because he was reflecting the backside of God's glory (*Exodus 34:29*). As Christians we are to reflect the glory of the Lord Jesus Christ. Like Jesus, His glory was covered by flesh so man could look upon Him, and our flesh allows man to be able to see Jesus' glory without fear of death and judgment.

In the last post I talked about the type of glory we reflect and that it is determined by what glory we expose ourselves to the most. If we expose ourselves to the world's glory, we will discover it is temporary because it has no real substance behind it. If we walk in the personal glory of self, it will prove to be vain and fading. If we expose ourselves to the false glory of man-centered and inspired religion, we will find that it is a false light that hides much darkness behind it but will crumble in the light of truth and judgment.

Moses' exposure to the glory of God caused him to reflect the glory of the first ministration which was the Law. The Law could only reveal sin but had no way for man to be pardoned or justified before it. Its glory was that of God's holiness, thereby, proving to be overwhelming to the people of Israel who stood undone and guilty before it.

The second ministration came by way of Christ. Man could look into its face and find forgiveness and grace. In fact, we are told in *2 Corinthians 3:14, "But their minds were blinded: for until this day remaineth the same vail untaken away in the reading of the old testament; which vail is done away in Christ."*

The first ministration put a veil of darkness upon man's mind and heart because he stood condemned, but the Lord Jesus Christ takes that veil away from those who come under His ministration of grace. The more we expose ourselves to Jesus' glory in His Word, prayer, and fellowship, the more we will reflect His glory.

The Apostle Paul put it this way, *"Now the Lord is that Spirit: and where the Spirit of the Lord is, there is liberty. But we all, with open face beholding as in a glass the glory of the Lord, are changed into the same image from glory to glory, even as by the Spirit of the Lord."*

What glory are you reflecting the most in your life?

JOB

*Job is the type of man who could never rest in
the church, or in the scriptures, for he needs
living reality. The man who rests in creed
is apt to be a coward. The whole point of vital
Christianity is not the refusal to face things,
but a matter of personal relationship, and it
is the kind of thing that Job went through
which brings a man to this issue.*
(Oswald Chambers)

When I need to encourage myself during trying times, I read *Psalms* or think about *Job*. Job is a man who lost his children, his servants, his possessions, and his quality of life, only to be falsely accused by those who called themselves his friends. His life was at its lowest, but he always managed to land on the runway of faith.

When you land on the runway of faith, you are able to look up. What many people don't realize is faith is a CHOICE. I stress this often because some people think faith is a feeling, something you must conjure up out of nothing. However, faith does not find its source in nothing, but in the character of God. Job could not understand his plight, but He could choose to trust what He knew about God. This is so for those who believe upon the Lord Jesus Christ.

There is so much about life that seems unfair, which causes confusion to our sense of fairness. However, the quality and promise of life is not based on our life in this world, but on the world yet to come. Faith is based on hope that operates in expectation that since God has declared a matter as being so, it is so and will prove to be so in the end, but sometimes to cause faith to soar above the circumstances of the present world we must look up and cling to the Rock of Ages, Jesus Christ.

Regardless of how bad present circumstances present themselves, we can by faith make the same claim as Job, *"Though he slay me, yet will I trust in him: but I will maintain mine own ways before him" (Job 13:15).*

The book of Job is the book that reveals the great debate, and what is this debate—does God allow bad things to happen to good people? In this great debate it is not unusual for people to be right about God but wrong about what He is doing behind the scenes. They judge a matter by circumstances instead of properly discerning the spirit and environment.

In such judgment they adjust the circumstances to fit their understanding of God and as a result can wrongly judge the person who is wrestling with the darkness that surrounds him or her. There are different types of darkness. There is the darkness of the night, the darkness of sin, the darkness caused by ignorance, and the dark night of the soul where a person finds him or herself engulfed in terrible circumstances that do not make sense.

This person has examined every aspect of his or her life and activities to make sure that the heavy hand of God is not behind the events taking place in his or her life. It is clear there are faults in each of our characters, but even in this these individuals cannot find any real conviction.

The dark night of the soul is the hardest darkness for the saint to contend with and the only way such an individual can find any consolation is to know God is sovereign, in control and that He is allowing it for a reason. It is true that the reason is usually hidden, but as believers we do not find encouragement in understanding something but in knowing that our God has the best in mind for us and that in due time the darkness upon the soul will part, revealing a new and glorious revelation about the Lord.

Job in his plight made some powerful statements. One of the statements he made was, *"Naked came I out of my mother's womb, and naked shall I return thither: the LORD gave, and the LORD hath taken away; blessed*

be the name of the LORD" (Job 1:21). Man is part of an ongoing cycle that entails life and death. He enters this world naked and leaves it in the same manner, undone and void of any real possessions.

At the end of life, the only thing man will own is his character, and his character will often decide what type of legacy he leaves behind. It will reveal whether he sold his soul to the devil or consecrated it for the glory of God, along with who he served: sin or God, and what he prepared for in light of eternity: heaven or hell.

Due to Job having integrity (character) he was a man who could face the harsh reality of things and decide how it was going to affect him. Either a person will give way to a morbid attitude or he will determine in what attitude he will respond to a matter. Job chose the latter, and as a result he could encourage himself by knowing that it is the Lord who gives us what we have and therefore, it is the Lord who has the right to take it away. But regardless of what is happening in our reality, the Lord is worthy to be blessed at all times.

The only way we can get beyond the morbid reality is to center on the reality of God, who deserves all blessings, honor, and glory regardless of what is going on in our worlds.

The two great challenges of man when in trials is to maintain his faith and integrity. Interestingly, these two virtues walk hand in hand. You can't have enduring faith without integrity, and integrity will lack substance without hope that is based on what will always prove to be true in the end.

Hope is the expectation in faith that allows it to trust in the unseen to bring about a matter as promised. It is for this reason that Job's wife asked him a simple question in *Job 2:9, "Dost thou still retain thine integrity? curse God, and die."*

Job's wife understood that if Job would give up his integrity that his faith would fall apart, but as long as Job refused to deny what he knew was true, he would hold onto God. There are believers who have a zeal about faith, but lack personal integrity and as a result they find themselves losing heart when trials come their way.

Job could not rejoice in his circumstances, but as long as he remained true to his integrity, he held onto what was true about God, and he could choose to remember, look up, and put wings of expectation to his faith so that in the end, God would prove to be God, the Almighty, who ultimately works all things out according to His will and glory.

When Job's wife told him to let go of his integrity, curse God and die, he made this statement *Job 2:10, "Thou speakest as one of the foolish women speaketh. What? shall we receive good at the hand of God, and shall we not receive evil?"*

A lot of people put Job's wife down, but we need to remember she lost her children, her possessions, and from all appearances her husband. Clearly, she was speaking out of great sorrow and anger, while probably trying to corral the bitterness that was taking root. Job challenged her perspective.

It is hard to be reasonable in such an overwhelming time, but it is clear that Job understood the crux of the matter. God blesses, but He also allows great sorrows to come our way. Such sorrows usually come out of some type of loss. In fact, when we are hurting, we can speak out of spite, when angry we can speak out of bitterness, and when miserable we can speak out of foolishness. Job stopped her by reminding her in essence that the sun shines on the just and unjust and the rain falls on the just and unjust alike.

Life happens and it can bring the most unexpected events our way, but we must remember that God never moves from who He is and that He is sovereign and has the final say over the events that will come our way.

One of the most liberating aspects about being a Christian is realizing we are but clay. God has to take us through a process before He can make us into a vessel fit for his use. Job understood that he was but clay. Consider what *Job 10:8-9* states, *"Thine hands have made me and fashioned me together round about; yet thou dost destroy me.*

Remember, I beseech thee, that thou hast made me as the clay; and wilt thou bring me into dust again?"

Job was wresting with something that did not make sense. He understood that he was but clay and could be returned to dust, but he also knew that the Lord had fashioned him and would not destroy what He had fashioned without good reason. He even stated in *Job 10:7a, "Thou knowest that I am not wicked."*

The question is why would the Lord allow an honorable vessel to be destroyed? The truth is the Lord knows how much heat a vessel can take before breaking. Job was no exception, but Job knew the Potter and recognized he had to trust the sovereignty of the potter. Hence comes this statement, *"But he knoweth the way that I take: when he hath tried me, I shall come forth as gold" (Job 23:10).*

One of the challenges in Christianity is accepting our humanness and the struggle it causes when we are confronted with the unseen, interrupting challenges of life. The book of Job clearly reveals the struggles that center around being human.

Many people use Christianity as a label that bears unrealistic standards of perfection that never allows for the struggle that takes place due to our humanness. The Lord knows our frame and has pity on us because we are all humans living in a dying world, limited by a finite mind, and wrestling with being spiritual when we have to contend with the fleshly and physical. I don't know about you, but I do not receive the accusation and judgment from the unbelievers that when my human flaws show, they can imply I am not being Christian; therefore, they do not have to take my testimony seriously. Clearly, such individuals are looking for a reason to not believe.

Christianity identifies me to my master, Jesus Christ who is leading me into a glorious life. The Christian experience is not a matter of trying to be something in my own power; rather, it is about the life of Christ being worked in me so that I can reflect Him to the rest of the world. This reflection is not made obvious when things are going my way or when I am not living up to perfection as seen by others but when the fire is being put to the character of my faith will I come out choosing to trust God while still maintaining my testimony of Him and the integrity of my moral character.

This reality has made me realize the real test is not about my flaws in my humanness, but holding onto God because of my faith in Him. It is for this reason that Job made this declaration, *"Though he slay me, yet will I trust in him: but I will maintain mine own ways before him" (Job 13:15)*.

In the book of Job, we are faced with the reality of the struggle of the human spirit, the test of the human soul, and the limitation of the human body. We are clearly told in *1 Thessalonians 5:23* that we are made up of spirit, soul, and body. We must be born again in the spirit, while our soul must be transformed by the Holy Spirit so that we can reflect the glory of our Lord in our outward countenance.

Job understood that because of his circumstances that his spirit was experiencing great anguish and his soul was tasting the bitterness of loss, despair, and depression. He also understood how his flesh was simply the shell that housed the inner man. He made this statement, *"Thou hast clothed me with skin and flesh, and has fenced me with bones and sinews. Thou hast granted me life and favour, and thy visitation hath preserved my spirit" (Job 10:10-13)*.

The Apostle Paul stated that our outer man is perishing, but our inner man is renewed daily. Job clearly understood that his outer shell was temporary but that the Lord had granted him grace to walk in the world and had preserved his spirit.

We need to remember that one day our body will fall to the way side, allowing our spirit to lift and setting our soul free from the entanglements of this world in order to experience the complete revelation of grace of the next age to come. As believers we must walk according to the promises yet to come and never the present circumstances of the age we are now passing through.

Rayola Kelley

After losing his children, his possessions, and his health, Job had become a vulnerable man emotionally, but not a weak man because he still had his integrity. The problem with being vulnerable is the sharks and vultures began to circle one's resolve. After all, if a person is vulnerable, it would seem reasonable that he or she is also weak.

When a person is down, it does not mean he or she is out, but the tendency of people is to assume that such a state implies not only weakness but compromise and sin. At such times some people will become experts as to what your problem is and how to solve it, others will become judges that also will serve as juries as to your guilt and punishment, and there are always those who will become observers who take the ques from others to justify their judgmental attitudes.

When people are emotionally wading through a trying time such as Job, they need room to walk through the upheaval and not be kicked and knocked down even more so by the opinions of those who have exalted themselves in a superior position in order to step on the person's neck to bring him or her into compliance to their arrogant narrative.

As Christians we have the example of Jesus. He took on humanity to enter in with our plight. He showed mercy not judgment, love not indifferent opinions, and pity because He understood man's vulnerable frame. Likewise, we are to be merciful and not judgmental; silent instead of being an unfeeling counselor, and gracious knowing that like circumstances could fall on us as well.

We need to keep in mind, man's challenges are not just his personal test, but our test which gives our Christianity the opportunity to shine in such dark, distressing times.

Job understood man's frame. He stated that man is born of a woman and his days are few and full of trouble. He added that man will come forth like a flower that will be cut down, causing his life to flee like a shadow and cease to be (*Job 14:1-2*).

The big challenge of man is to connect the fact that he will live forever but not in his present state. It is hard for man to consider the matter of physical death. He has the will to live, but he can't imagine this present life ending while residing in a physical body in spite of the fact that death is working in it.

It is clear that we must consider what perspective we live in, the fleshy one or the eternal one. I don't know about you but I try to live my life in light of eternity, not this present troubled world. I know that the present age will pass, but eternity will always be and my choice is simple enough. I choose to live in light of eternity to secure my spiritual inheritance and lasting heritage in heaven. How about you?

Job teaches us that it is the trying times of life that will reveal the quality of our relationships with others. Job had considered his companions good friends, but in his greatest time of testing, his friends became his accusers, and in *Job 16* he talks about how his friends made him weary, tore him down with their wrath, and scorned him. Clearly, instead of comforting him, they were judging him. Instead of showing mercy, they proved to be cruel and treacherous.

I learned long ago that other people's testing often becomes the test of my own character. How will I react with something that will test my endurance, challenge my theology, and ruffle my sense of right and wrong? After all, as Christians we can talk about love but prove to be indifferent and cruel to things that may prove to be inconvenient for us. We talk about compassion, but prove to be very judgmental to that which makes us feel nervous and uncertain. We can talk about grace, but be the last to show any tolerance towards that which offends us.

Let's face it, when we are down and out, we do not want people to knock us down even more; rather, we desire them to encourage us, yet how many of us, when we have the opportunity to encourage those who find themselves in trying times, judge instead of encourage?

Job encountered the cruel, unbending judgment of others. It is natural to want encouragement when we are facing personal challenges but how many of us are willing and prepared to afford others of such compassion?

If something makes us nervous, we automatically deem that there must be something wrong. If something has made us jealous in the past about a certain person, we begin to justify it when that same individual is vulnerable and shows weakness, avoiding facing the real jealousy in our own character. If something makes us feel uncertain about our own character, we become a judge in order to exalt ourselves above the other person and situation, making everything inferior. Such an inferior state of another individual will justify our cruel judgment while covering over the flaws in our own level of integrity. If we fear something because we do not understand it or control it, we choose to hide behind a type of smugness that allows us to ignore such a matter because we deem that the person is paying the consequences for his or her wrongs.

Whether we like it or not, this is the way of human nature, but the Lord was clear, that we will be known by godly love and godly love is compassionate, avoids being judgmental, and is ready to enter in with others in their plight. After all, Jesus became man so He could enter into our plight, address it in love and offered Himself as the supreme sacrifice to take away our sins, bringing reconciliation between God and us.

Job went through a trial of inner conflict. When we go through tough times, if we are believers, we always look within to make sure that God's hand is not heavy on us because of some sin, attitude, or habit that is unbecoming to our Christian walk. Even though the Bible does not say that there was such an inner conflict for Job, I believe the defense that he gave to his companions proved that he considered all matters before the debate occurred.

It was clear that Job had established his case about his own standing before the Lord. Because we have the Bible, we know what the great battle in and around Job consisted of, but, he did not understand why he was in such a great struggle. However, he did know one thing and that was it was not due to sin.

Job was in his struggle because of his testimony before heaven and the kingdom of darkness. And, what was the testimony that came from God? *"There was a man in the land of Uz, whose name was Job; and that man was perfect and upright, and one that feared God, and* eschewed evil" *(Job 1:1).* We know according to *Revelation 12:11* that one of the tools to overcome Satan is the word of a person's testimony.

Job was walking through the valley of the shadow of death. His breath mocked him, he was unrecognizable by those who knew him, and his body was dying. His nights were filled with great darkness, his days with dark shadows of uncertainty, the path before him was shrouded, and his future black.

King David spoke of this valley long after Job walked through it, but David knew that his great Shepherd would comfort him and he made this declaration in *Psalm 23:5-6, "Thou preparest a table before me in the presence of mine enemies: thou anointest my head with oil; my cup runneth over. Surely goodness and mercy shall follow me all the days of my life: and I will dwell in the house of the LORD for ever."*

What did Job know and decide to cling too in his deep, dark valley, *"For I know that my redeemer liveth and that he shall stand at the latter day upon the earth: And though after my skin worms destroy this body, yet in my flesh shall I see God: Whom I shall see for myself, and mine eyes shall behold, and not another; though my reins be consumed within me" (Job 19:25-27).*

In this age of darkness, we must remember to cling to the One who is immovable in all of His righteous ways.

Job 23:16 states, *"For God maketh my heart soft, and the Almighty troubleth me."* It is hard for a believer to know the Lord is the one who makes our heart soft towards Him and then He allows circumstances to come that troubles the soul. It is difficult for us to realize that God must establish our hearts.

Hearts that have not been established can cease to be soft towards God when tested, becoming hard with bitterness and skepticism. I learned a long time ago that the Lord knows what I can endure and He will only allow that which would enlarge me to come my way. I have learned that an established heart is a heart that is soft, submissive and receptive, making it pliable and ready to say, *"Not my will but your will be done."*

The problem is that those who do not understand the ways of God will not accept such testing. They resent such inconvenience and fail to see that the Lord is trying to prepare them to stand with a steadfast heart in the darkness of great testing and challenges that life will bring their way. Remember, when we ask God to have His way, we are asking Him to have His way with our heart attitude about Him, and before Him.

As I consider Job, I wonder how in such trying times he could hang on to what He knew about God. It appeared that God was against Job and Job wrestled with the "whys" to his circumstances but he never let the present circumstances cause him to throw his hands up in the air and tell God to take a big hike because his faith in Him appeared to be a farce.

We often think that God is willing to do everything to prove to us His intention from bowing down to our whims, performing according to our standards, and proving He is God, and that He loves us by giving us our way. The truth is God will not bow down to our whims, that would be idolatry. He will not perform according to our standards because His ways are higher than our ways. As to His love, He has already proven it by sending His Son into the world to die for us, and in the case of proving He is who He is, He would be giving way to a foolish test.

We may not understand why God allows the circumstances into our life, but we can be assured that our faith is being tested and that we will remain true to what is true—the Lord Jesus Christ. And, what is the reward for our faith? *Romans 9:33* states, *"As it is written, Behold, I lay in Sion a stumblingstone and rock of offence: and whosoever believeth on him SHALL NOT BE ASHAMED."* (Emphasis added.)

In Job's contention with his companions, he asked an important question, *"How hast thou helped him that is without power? How savest thou the arm that hath no strength? How hast thou counselled him that hath no wisdom? And how hast thou plentifully declared the thing as it is?" (Job 26:2-3)*

It is easy to believe that we are experts in a matter. After all, we have looked at it from every angle and in our minds, there is no way we can be wrong in our conclusion or our counsel. The truth is we only know in part and the part we do not know is the part that will not only trip us up in our conclusions, but it will prove us wrong and judgmental in the end.

We must hold our conclusions lightly so we can let go of them to grasp what is true. We must realize platitudes make us sound indifferent and experiences only have a 50% of being applicable. We must learn to discern our opinions from what is fact, our platitudes from what is reality, and our experiences as to whether they are pertinent to the situation.

Job knew his friends thought themselves quite wise in their conclusions, but they were dead wrong. He stated in *Job 24:1* that nothing is hidden from the Almighty who knows all matters from the beginning to the end, and consider the Apostle Paul's instruction in *Romans 12:3, "For I say, through the grace given unto me, to every man that is among you, not to think of himself more highly than he ought to think; but to think soberly, according as God hath deal to every man the measure of faith."*

We are to walk by faith, and genuine faith has a discerning quality that can see past this world into the unseen one, and not a judgmental one that is based on intellectual conclusions.

Job contains one of the longest parables in the Bible. It begins in *Job 28* and ends in *Job 31*. Parables are based on culture and will bring some type of contrast that has been touched by the mystery and sovereignty of an unseen Hand. One might wonder why Job spoke on wisdom, because true wisdom comes from the Lord and only can be developed when one is walking in righteousness.

In *Job 28:28*, he made this statement, *"And unto man he said, Behold, the fear of the Lord, that is wisdom: and to depart from evil is understanding."* Wisdom has a healthy fear in avoiding displeasing God.

It will choose the way of righteousness and it will depart from evil because it recognizes the consequences.

The opposite of wisdom is foolishness. Man is born with foolishness bound in his heart and it takes faith towards God and obedience to His Word to walk through and out of foolishness. Integrity is what you will replace foolishness with, and Job had integrity.

We need God's wisdom. We are told to ask Him for His wisdom but we cannot develop it unless we deny self and walk in the ways of righteousness. Foolishness will end in failure and despair, but wisdom will lead us back to the reality of God, and shine a light on what is sane, realistic, trustworthy, and enduring, causing real hope to rise up in our souls.

When you consider the parable about wisdom in the book of Job, you begin to realize that Job's explanation of wisdom was not just a matter of inspiration but one of experience. In order for Job to write about one's search for wisdom, he had to experience it firsthand. For Job to be the type of man that was described and pointed out by God, he had to have wisdom that he had searched out and discovered in his walk before the Lord. He even brings this out in *Job 28:20-21, "Whence then cometh wisdom? And where is the place of understanding? Seeing it is hid from the eyes of all living, and kept close from the fowls of the air."*

Think about what he is saying. True wisdom cannot be seen with the physical eye and even though the fowls of the air have a different perspective, it is not close to them. It is clear that the wisdom we need cannot be found in the physical world we live in and obtained from a higher perspective, and yet how many seek wisdom through intellectual pursuits and vain experiences to no avail?

The inspiration, encouragement, and knowledge of wisdom we humans need comes from above—it comes from God. We are told in *1 Corinthians 1:30, "But of him are ye in Christ Jesus, who of God is made unto us WISDOM, and righteousness, and sanctification, and redemption."* (Emphasis added.)

When we consider Job's spiritual journey during his ordeal, we often get caught up with the debate instead of the results. God never allows us to go through a test of faith that is not intended to work in us lasting results.

Job's journey not only required him to exercise the faith he had towards the Lord, but it was enlarged. The martyred missionary, James Elliot, made this statement about Job, "*Job is a lesson in acceptance, not blind resignation but of believing acceptance, that what God does is well done.*" Peter tells us that at the end of the trying of our faith is salvation or deliverance (*1 Peter 1:9*).

Job was clearly delivered from his ordeal by God but what blessing did Job receive because of it? HE SAW THE LORD. Job stated, "*I have heard of thee by the hearing of the ear: but now mine eye seeth thee*" (*Job 42:5*).

The testing of our faith refines us through purifying fires, and as Jesus stated, "*Blessed are the pure in heart for they shall see God*" (*Matthew 5:8*). No one enjoys the long dark night of the soul where the refining fires of faith are burning and purging, but when it is all done and the light once again returns, the conclusion is the same, "It was worth it to see God, because He is worth my best and my all, knowing confidently that He does all things well."

The Old Testament Patriarch, Job, had nowhere to run to get away from the circumstances that were burying him. Not only was he confronted with overwhelming losses, his friends were falsely accusing him of having some hidden sin in his life. When he stated that even if God slayed him, he would trust Him and maintain his ways before him, he was establishing that he knew he could stand before the Lord and give an account of his life without fear.

Clearly, Job knew what his life was before God and had probably already asked the Lord to turn on the search light to expose any sin, any moral deviation, or any destructive root that would cause him to be at odds with his Creator, and that would open him up to His judgment. Job's plight was not due to judgment; rather, it was a testing of his faith, which would prove that God had a man that would maintain his faith towards Him in the most trying times.

If Job was incapable of passing the test, God would have not allowed Satan to sift him in such a manner (*1 Corinthians 10:13*). Each time Job was challenged by his accusers, you hear him struggling with the facts of the circumstances, but at the end of each debate Job encourages himself in the God he knew and believed and made wonderful statements such as *Job 19:25-27, "For I know that my redeemer liveth, and that he shall stand at the latter day upon the earth: And though after my skin worms destroy this body, yet in my flesh shall I see God: Whom I shall see for myself, and mine eyes shall behold and not another; though my reins be consumed within me."*

Job was truly a man of faith. Unfeigned faith allows us to endure the testing of our faith. Peter talks about this test in *1 Peter 1:5-9*. In these Scriptures, we are told we are kept by the power of God through faith unto salvation and that we can greatly rejoice because the heaviness of our temptations will only last for a season. We are also told in *1 Peter 1:7, "That the trial of your faith being much more precious than of gold that perisheth, though it be tried with fire, might be found unto praise and honour and glory at the appearing of Jesus Christ."*

Job's faith was being tried by an intense fire that could easily have consumed him, but he made this incredible declaration in *Job 23:10, "But he knoweth the way that I take: when he hath tried me, I shall come forth as gold."* Job did not understand what his ordeal was about but as a man of faith he realized that the character of his faith was being tested, and since he knew where to rest his faith, he would actually be brought forth as gold.

When the Lord has tested the character of my faith, I could sense that it was about to be consumed in the intense heat, but then I would look up in faith and begin to see a reflection in the fiery test. The reflection was that of Jesus Christ.

A pastor who used to mine gold explained to me that when the gold is being separated from its many impurities by fire that the overseer has to keep a diligent eye on the temperature of the heat because past a certain degree the gold can be totally consumed. It is clear by the example of Job that when the Lord allows our faith to go into the fiery ovens that He knows how intense the heat can be without destroying us.

God is faithful to keep the fiery test of our faith from becoming too hot for us to withstand. This should be a point of encouragement to each of us. Granted, our flesh hates the fire because it will lose its power in our life and our soul wants to avoid it even though it will be refined in the fires while our spirit is purified, but to establish an enduring faith, the fires are necessary.

We do not have to embrace the fires, but when they come, we must look up, knowing that only God can oversee the process in order to bring us forth as precious gems that one day He will wear in His crown.

The book of Job has become an encouraging book to me. It is easy to get caught up with the debate that went on between Job and his companions, and understanding the debate is valuable because it is going on today when it comes to trying circumstances.

It is natural to assume if a person is going through it that there must be some sin in their life, but Job's story warns us that the unseen world greatly affects our lives, and unless we properly discern it, we will end up wrongly judging matters, bringing possible judgment on ourselves.

We must be careful not to take our conclusions too seriously about matters of heaven and the heart and remember it is what God says about a matter that is not only important, but it is final. We know how God looked at Job from *Job 1:1*, but there is another Scripture found in *Ezekiel 14:14, "Though these three men, Noah, Daniel, and Job, were in it, they should deliver but their own souls by their righteousness, saith the Lord GOD."*

The Lord spoke this around the time when Jerusalem would be attacked the third time by the Babylonian army and completely destroyed. He clearly pointed out that only the three men named would be delivered from the pending destruction because of their righteousness.

It is important to point out that these men's righteousness was based on their faith and obedience before the Lord. If we have right standing with the Lord we can encourage ourselves regardless of what is going on, and be assured that the Lord will deliver us when the time comes.

When I read the three Scriptures in *Ezekiel 14* about the three men who would have been delivered from the pending judgment that would come upon Jerusalem, I wondered why Noah, Daniel, and Job were mentioned, versus Abraham, Moses, and David. As I meditated on these three men, I was reminded that as believers we must overcome the world, the flesh, and the devil.

As I considered Noah, I realized by faith he overcame the world, when in fear of the Lord he obediently built an ark, while Daniel by faith purposed in his heart not to give into the flesh by partaking of the rich lifestyle of Babylon, and Job by faith endured great testing to overcome Satan's attacks and accusations. *Revelation 21:7* reminds us, *"He that overcometh shall inherit all things; and I will be his God, and he shall be my son."*

It is clear that as believers we must be overcomers and we can encourage ourselves in knowing the victory is at hand, but we must overcome the enemies of our soul, for the Lord has given us Christ (our ark) to overcome the world, the cross to overcome the flesh, and the armor of God to overcome Satan.

Faith towards God is the only foundation that will remain intact when you find yourself fainting in the circumstances. All we need to do is consider Job. Many people state that Job's problem was that he feared losing everything from his family, dignity, and reputation, but who among us would not feel such fears when we think about losing someone or something of great importance to us.

The main issue with Job is that God pointed him out to Satan as being one-of-a-kind who was perfect, upright, one who feared Him, and hated evil. It is important to realize that Satan was trying to wipe out Job's testimony, but Job held onto God and with patience he endured that grave testing of his faith. Granted, he wrestled before the Lord as to the whys and debated with his companions, but he continued to stand on what He knew about God and his commitment to Him.

Job clearly made incredible statements that revealed that even in the testing of his faith it was coming forth as pure gold. For example, there was one statement he made when his wife asked him why he insisted on holding onto his integrity before the Lord and told him to curse God and die. His response was, *"Thou speakest as one of the foolish women speaketh. What? shall we receive good at the hand of God, and shall we not receive evil?"* Scripture goes on to say, *"In all this did not Job sin with his lips" (Job 2:11).*

We must not weigh matters according to circumstances when our faith is being sorely tested, but decide to encourage ourselves in our faith by remembering who God is, while trusting Him that He will bring us through to the end.

SAMUEL

Samuel's life teaches that
God can speak to us at any
age, use us powerfully when we are
tender in age, and raise us up
to be a powerful instrument in His hand.
(Rayola Kelley)

Most of us know the story of Samuel. His mother Hannah was in such distress because she was barren. To women in her day, this felt like a punishment too great to bear. The truth is, women of that time saw their value as women in ensuring the future of God's lineage (children) and the survival of the Jewish people.

Could you imagine what Hannah and Elizabeth, John the Baptist's mother, would think of how our children are aborted and killed outright in the name of so-called "rights" that are used in most cases to cover up immoral conduct? As I considered Hannah, I was struck that God allowed her to become desperate so that she would dedicate her firstborn to Him.

God knew the character of Hannah and that she could be entrusted with being brought to an emotional impoverishment in order to commit her first fruits to Him for His use and service as a type of bargain or vow. Samuel, who was a prophet and the last judge of Israel, was the product of that bargain.

Most believers know the story of Samuel in *1 Samuel 3* when he first heard the voice of the Lord. The first thing we need to recognize is that in those days the Word of the LORD was precious because there was no open vision. As *Proverbs 29:18* reminds us, where there is no vision, the people will perish.

The second thing we must note is that the physical blindness of the priest, Eli, and the light going out in the Holy Place were symbolic of the spiritual darkness that had ascended on the priesthood due to sin. Sin will always cause the shadows of compromise to descend on one as darkness eventually takes the person captive.

The third thing is that Samuel was a child simply ministering in the tabernacle. This shows us God can speak to whosoever He will. Samuel did not know the voice of God, but he was about to learn to discern it.

Sadly, we have allowed our children to play and be entertained during church instead of learning what it means to serve in God's glorious kingdom. We have not encouraged them to listen for, or hear the voice of the Lord, and it could be because the adults have not been trained to listen either.

As in the days of Samuel, there seems to be very little open vision that awakens those who are asleep, and who knows, the Lord could very well have spoken to and through another Samuel to penetrate the present darkness with His truth. However, the question remains, "Will the people hear, humble themselves, heed, and submit to it with all their heart?"

One of the statements about Samuel that has always stood out to me is found in *1 Samuel 3:19, "And Samuel grew, and the LORD was with hm, and did let none of his words fall to the ground."* The more you value what God says, the more you must value what you say.

Today it is hard to find people who are true to their word. Their word can be easily forgotten when the mood is not present to seriously set it before their face. Any promise can be cast aside when the emotional sentiment is not there to cheer it on. In some cases, there are those who throw a few crumbs in an attempt to silence their guilt that they either lied about their intention or were bearing false witness. Ultimately, they failed to follow through on what they promised, ensuring they would see a matter through to the end.

Such people may start out with the right intention but there is no real conviction to see something through to the end, and therefore this person's words are found to be false, their promises untrustworthy, and in the end such a person will lose all credibility with those who dared to put stock in what they declared.

The problem is if our words mean nothing to those around us, speaking God's Word will have no meaning or authority either. The words we speak must be law to us just as the Word of God must become the unchangeable law that governs our attitude and moral conduct.

I love the example we have in *1 Samuel 3* about the Lord speaking to a young innocent boy who was simply serving in the tabernacle and never imagined that Yahweh would ever take note of him. After all, he was insignificant in the scheme of things. He was a young boy and not the priest. He was a vessel that carried out the wishes of the priest and not the one in the position of authority and yet he was the one God spoke to.

We often make the mistake of thinking that God gauges a person the same way the world does. The world judges according to decrees, intelligence, position, money, and the power of a person, but God does not look at any of these criteria. He is looking at the mainspring of where all the issues of life find their basis, determines attitudes, and the quality of our fruits (*Proverbs 4:23; 23:7*).

Clearly, God doesn't use someone based on the standards and bias of this world but on the heart condition of a person. Is the heart tender towards God, open to His truth, humble before His ways, and genuine and submissive when the person says, "Not my will Lord, but Your will be done?"

The young boy Samuel heard God speak to him in *1 Samuel 3*. He called him by name which means He personalizes His encounter with people. Samuel did not know the Lord's voice, but he was about to be introduced to Him. Hearing God's voice should be our greatest desire.

Whatever the Lord says is backed up by unchanging deity, along with heaven and all power to confirm and bring forth a matter. But, have you ever met someone who walks around and constantly states, "The Lord told me this or that?"

God does speak to people, and He has spoken to me occasionally. It comes more as an impression about something or in prayer He may bring a truth or a matter to my mind. However, God's main voice is His Word, and whatever is spoken to me in times of communion and prayer, must and will always line up to His Written Word.

I often find people who run here and there to find a word from the Lord, have failed to hear His voice in His Word. Hearing the voice of God is more about following the Lord into our life with Him and then claiming a corner on some spiritual insight. Consider what Jesus stated, *"My sheep know my voice"* (*John 10:3-5*).

We must learn God's voice according to His Word so that if we do hear a voice, we are able to discern if it is God's voice, and if it is, follow and obey it.

Most people would never imagine God talking to the young boy Samuel, but God uses unlikely instruments, while the world uses those who fit its narrative and looks a certain part and has some kind of talent or degrees that will impress those of the world. In fact, those of the world are looking for some savior among the academia (science), heroes among sports and cartoon figures, and insight or inspiration from motivational speakers.

Don't get me wrong, I have no problem with looking for some individual who inspires us, but as Christians we must avoid getting caught up with the false images and presentations of the world that must be propped up in some way. We must realize that they are temporary and fantasy at best, and at worse, leaving us disappointed.

The reason I so appreciate the people God uses is because they are human and will never have to be rendered or presented as some unrealistic cartoon character that is made bigger than life by computerized techniques. The people God uses are ordinary people who become extraordinary because He imputes them with His wisdom and power to accomplish a task or to complete a matter.

There are people I admire because they wisely use their gifts, there are others that serve as an example to me because of their exemplary character and faithfulness, and there are those whom I allow to influence me because they have a right spirit, but my real and only hero is Jesus Christ.

He never has to be propped up and dressed in some cartoon outfit to have save my soul, inspire me to excellence, enable me to take courage to face the impossible, and trust in the miraculous, because Jesus Christ is God Incarnate.

Samuel lived during some critical times. In *1 Samuel 4*, we are told he had to witness the judgment that was pronounced on the priest Eli and his family being executed, leaving Eli and his sons dead and the ark of the covenant taken by the uncircumcised Philistines. Eli heard that his sons were dead but what brought the greatest destress to him was what happened to the ark, and the old priest had to know that the corrupt priesthood was mainly to blame for God allowing the ark to be taken.

The ark represented the presence of God in the midst of the people, but it was taken by the enemy, leaving them without any witness of

God's presence and protection. A grandson was born to the wife of one of Eli's dead sons when this event happened and she named the child, "Ichabod" which means "The glory is departed from Israel."

I admit this story always unnerves me. The people of Israel had a physical representation of God's presence, but we as believers have the Holy Spirit, and when the Holy Spirit withdraws His presence from some matter, He does it quietly. I often wonder how many Christians and churches are losing the spiritual battles because they have failed to discern that the presence of God is not in it.

We are living in critical times and we will not be able to stand, fight, or advance forward without God's presence leading and pushing back the enemy to allow us to advance forward in victory.

KING DAVID

*King David started out an insignificant
shepherd boy, graduated to what we
would refer to as a "Rock Star," and became
a hero, but fell at the height of his popularity.
And even though he never reached the
same status in the world again, he did make
it across the finish line. David reminds
us it is God that takes the insignificant person,
and as Daniel 12:3 states, will make him
shine as the brightness of the firmament
in his age and as a star in the next one to come.
(Rayola Kelley)*

When I desire to encourage myself, I sometimes consider the examples of King David. You can see that he went through many difficult times, a few due to his own doing, but many challenges came because he had a distinct calling on his life that caused jealousy on the part of people such as Saul.

Divisions of this type cause others to take sides for and against a person, and as for David, it forced him to be on the run. David wrote many of the *Psalms* and you can see his approach to these challenges in the book of the same name, and the attitude he took on to overcome.

However, to overcome you first must learn how to encourage yourself in the Lord.

Consider the first *Psalm*. The first thing we must note is that David made reference to how a man is blessed and ends it comparing it to those who are ungodly who will stand in judgment. How can a man be blessed in challenges unless he knows he is NOT walking in the counsel of the ungodly, or STANDING in the way of sinners or SITTING in the seat of the scornful? Clearly, the environment and company you expose yourself to will determine your attitude and whether you can rightfully encourage yourself in the Lord.

We need to make sure we are standing on the side of the Lord and not pitted against Him to ensure the battle has already been determined and won.

In *1 Samuel 18:5* we are told, *"And David went out whithersoever Saul sent him and behaved himself wisely."* To me this revealed much about David's character. The Christian life is all about discipline of the inner life in order to reflect the reality of godliness in our outer conduct.

The one thing we must keep in mind is that when we exercise godliness it is pointing to a disciplined life that reveals the influence and work of God and His ways on us. The Bible tells us what we must do in every aspect of our life to ensure godliness. We must deny self and apply the cross to the fleshly life to make sure we do not become a castaway, one of the concerns Paul voiced in *1 Corinthians 9:27*.

We must be moderate in our lifestyle, modest in our presentation, meek in our spirit, and temperate in our soul to ensure our testimony is not compromised. The concept of "let" is a form of discipline.

We must let the mind of Christ be worked in us to learn contentment in all states and allow the Spirit of God to transform and renew our inner man to ensure we become His workman that will bring glory to Him. To stay on the straight and narrow path we must always choose the way of excellence to obtain that which is superior, give way to that which is worthy of all consideration in light of eternity, and insist on personal obedience to His Word to ensure that we as Jesus' followers have the authority to stand and the power of heaven behind us to overcome.

We are told in *1 Samuel 30:6* that David encouraged himself in the Lord. Mind you he had just found out that the Amalekites had invaded, smitten and burned his city Ziklag and taken his family along with the families of his soldiers into captivity. He was faced with great obstacles of personal loss and dealing with the despair of his men, yet he encouraged himself in the Lord.

My question is how did he do it? We talk about the saints of old with a certain awe but they were ordinary people just like you and me. What made them extraordinary is that they had a relationship with the living God whose norm was the impossible. How did David encourage himself in the Lord, he had to take stock not in his abilities or circumstances but in the God he believed and trusted in.

It is only the God of the impossible that takes what is and changes it to speak of the impossible. The first thing David did to encourage himself was to go to the Lord and seek out His mind in the matter. I learned from this future king's example that the Lord wants to encourage us, but we must first encourage ourselves in Him before we can be invigorated by Him to once again face the overwhelming obstacles of life.

At such times of encouragement, we can stand up and advance forward in assurance that the Lord will go before us as He strengthens us and works to bring forth His perfect will and purpose in our life.

David encouraged himself in the Lord in *1 Samuel 30:6*. Was it easy for him to do so as he faced what seemed like overwhelming odds? He had lost his family and home, and the distraught soldiers were even threatening to take their grief out on him. I don't know about you, but I would want to crawl in a corner and melt into a pool of self-pity.

To encourage ourselves means to "take courage" and when we face overwhelming challenges the first thing we need to do is turn aside from the harsh reality of a matter and seek the Lord with all of our heart regardless of how broken it is over our loss, fearful because of circumstances, and fainting because of hopelessness.

Jesus said in *John 16:33, "These things I have spoken unto you, that in me ye might have peace. In the world ye shall have tribulation: but be of good cheer: I have overcome the world."* Our precious Jesus is encouraging us to find our courage in knowing that He has already overcome the world and that even in the midst of challenges, we can have peace that passes all understanding.

One of the many things that can rob us of our peace and confidence in God are our enemies. We have the enemy of the flesh within that will tempt us in the wrong way pitting us against God. There is the world around us which brings us under the god of this age, Satan, and Satan (operating in the spiritual realm) who wants to take ownership of our souls and receive worship. Finally, there are those of mankind that can become our enemies.

Although David wrestled with the flesh, the world, and Satan, he also had to confront many enemies who chased after him or would betray him. In *Psalm 2*, he admits that the heathen rage because they imagine vain things. Many of our enemies imagine vain things about our intention, our motives, our desires, and our goals. Out of such times comes false accusations, slander, and treats as they try to bully us into subjection to their reality.

One of the greatest types of encouragement is when we realize that most battles are spiritual and that God is the one who defeated all enemies at the cross of Christ. However, when we encounter Goliath, we must stand on truth, when we face an army we must withstand with our shield of faith, and when we feel the enemy bearing down on us, we must remember that the greatest battle of all was fought over our soul and was won at the cross of Jesus.

We are a redeemed people who have a citizenship in an everlasting kingdom, an eternal inheritance, and promises that are so or will be made so in the end.

THE PROPHETS

*God sent His prophets of old
to point us forward, and sent
His Son to fulfill what has been
declared in the past, and now
the Son sends us forth to point
upward to what is yet to come.
(Rayola Kelley)*

I don't know about you but I love studying the Old Testament. My main goal is to see Jesus in events, Scriptures, and types such as the tabernacle. The New Testament is the unfolding revelation of Jesus Christ, but the Old Testament is the presentation of Christ in types, shadows, and patterns in the lives of such people as Joseph, Moses, and David so that when He came the first time, He could be properly discerned.

Although Jesus is shrouded in the Old Testament, He did make an appearance in it as the Word, the actual and sometimes visible expression of God. In *John 5:37*, Jesus made this statement, *"And the Father himself, which hath sent me, hath borne witness of me. Ye have NEITHER HEARD HIS VOICE AT ANY TIME, NOR SEEN HIS SHAPE."* (Emphasis added.)

We know that in line with the prophetic, the Father did introduce Jesus as His Son at His baptism and on the Mount of Transfiguration, and He spoke a third time in *John 12:28-30,* but the people described it as thunder or that it was a voice of an angel. The question is whose voice did Moses hear when it came to the burning bush in *Exodus 3:14-16*?

God introduced Himself as the great "I AM." How many times did Jesus declare, "I am?" It is important to point out that no one has seen the shape of the Father and yet the Lord appeared to Abraham in *Genesis 18* with two angels, to Jacob in *Genesis* 28 as LORD standing at the top of the ladder that connected earth to heaven, to the elders in *Exodus 24:9-11*, to Joshua as the captain of the Lord's host in *Joshua 5*; and one of my favorites did not take place on earth but heaven. This happened in *Isaiah 6*, where the Lord was sitting on the throne, high and lifted up and his train filled the temple.

There are a couple of things I look for to make sure that it was not some mere messenger or angel. The first thing is worship. No angel from God would receive worship from man, only God is worthy of such adoration. The second thing I look for is if a sacrifice was offered and received. God is the only one who can receive sacrifice, which entailed fire coming from heaven to receive it. The third thing I consider are the people's attitude.

For Abraham it was humility and servitude, for Jacob it was dread, for Moses and Joshua, they took off their shoes in order to stand, for the elders they communed, and for Isaiah he acknowledged he was unclean and that his lips needed to be purged. Keep in mind shoes were removed because they represent defilement due to the fact that man must walk through this world.

The next time you take a journey through the Old Testament, ask the Lord to reveal Himself to you. It is not enough that we read His words, hear His Spirit occasionally, but we MUST SEE JESUS to continue to grow in the knowledge of who He is

Another Old Testament saint that is interesting to study is Noah. His name means "rest." Imagine the days he lived in. According to Jesus the last generation will also be living as in the days of Noah. Everything may seem normal, but we know according to the Word of God that if there was any "normalcy" it was that the people were exceedingly wicked.

Their imagination was continually evil and *Job 22:15-18* speaks about the attitude of the people before the flood and states in the last two verses, "Which said unto God, Depart from us: and what can the Almighty do for them? Yet he filled their houses with good things: but the counsel of the wicked is far from me."

We know that God showed Noah the judgment to come upon the whole earth, but He also instructed him to build an ark. In times like Noah, warning will come first, followed by the judgment of separation, and then God's wrath will come if there is no repentance. The point of judgment for the people was an ark. It revealed that man has a choice, and he can choose to believe the message and example of a righteous man or continue to live as usual in a wicked world as he scoffs at the warnings.

In today's world, we have sorrow compassing us, our spirits being quenched, and our hope teetering on some precipice but we need to remember that an ark has been established among us. His name is Jesus and if man believes the warnings of what is to come, he will flee to the ark and enter into the place of safety and rest. We must remember that in spite of the days we live in, we have a sure place of rest, but we must build our lives upon it and line it up to His instructions in order to be prepared to enter into it by faith.

There are many types or shadows in the story of Noah. Only eight people entered into the ark because of the faith of one man. We enter our ark, because of the work of redemption of one man.

2 Peter 2:5 tells us that Noah was a preacher of righteousness, but the Man we follow into our place of safety is the essence of all righteousness. As I have stated, our ark is Jesus and just as in the parable of the ten virgins, when the invitation goes out from the bridegroom, we must be prepared to enter into the place of union, safety, and rest before the door is shut by the Lord for good (*Genesis 7:16*).

There is also the dove, a type of the Holy Spirit sent forth by Noah (representing the Father) from the ark, Jesus to find an undefiled place (His people) to abide upon and within. There is another type that involves the ark. This is found in *Genesis 7:17*. It is where the ark was lifted up above the great judgment of the waters. In *John 12:32*, Jesus was lifted up on the cross above the judgments of man and hell so that He could draw men to Himself as the Lamb of God who would take away our sin.

As believers, we are hid in Christ our ark, and we were drawn to His great work of redemption. He was lifted above the wrath abiding on this world, causing the work of His cross to be a great dividing point between darkness and light, life and death, and hope and curses. However, it takes faith to enter this ark. It is not enough to come up to the entrance and consider entering in, by faith one must enter in because it was decreed by God that today is the day of salvation.

You can stand outside of it and debate the legitimacy of it, the timing and wisdom of it, as well as the reasoning, and events for the need to enter in at this time, but if you do not enter in, you will miss the place of deliverance altogether because of unbelief. We as believers need to cease with the incessant debates of our time and make sure we believe God's Word of warnings, instructions, and inspirations by entering all of the way into our ark by faith. We must prepare for the spiritual night so that when His call and light penetrate it, we will hear and be lifted up by the Spirit to meet with Him in the air

If you are walking according to unfeigned faith, know you will be brought to a crisis to experience fiery trials. The trials of our faith are to enlarge it by making Jesus more precious to each of us.

We often get caught up with the debates of life, but for Christians in such trials it usually is about choosing the way of faith where we direct our trust towards God, put our confidence in His sovereignty, and our assurance in His character and promises. The crisis that faith will bring you to is never fun, but it proves to be glorious because you begin to realize how faithful the Lord is to deliver you through such times.

There are two types of deliverance: we are delivered from something such as the claims of spiritual death on our souls to be delivered or saved unto eternal life. Then there is the deliverance through something. For those who have been brought to the crisis by their faith walk, it involves being delivered through the trials.

Consider Noah, he was delivered through the flood, and likewise God's people will be delivered through the fiery testing of their faith. Such deliverance may appear as if it will never come, but at such times we must encourage ourselves that our Lord will deliver us into His glorious light to see His faithfulness and hand in it.

How would the Lord come to you? This may seem like an unusual question, but it is one that needs to be pondered. For example, He encountered Abraham with two angels before passing judgment on Sodom knowing Abraham would serve as an intercessor. He met Moses in a burning bush, the children of Israel on Mount Sinai in the midst of darkness, lightning and thunder, and Joshua as Captain of the Lord's Host. With these examples in mind, how would He appear and introduce Himself?

He appeared to Abraham to call him away from country, kindred, and family to the Promised Land. For Jacob He appeared as LORD on top of a ladder connecting heaven and earth and introduced Himself as the God of Abraham and Isaac. For Moses and Joshua, He told them to take off their shoes because they were standing on holy ground before He gave them their marching orders, and He instructed Moses to introduce Him to the children of Israel as "I AM that I AM."

Years later Jesus introduced Himself as the "I am" and when you consider what He followed the "I am" with, you can begin to sense people's attitudes and needs. Jesus as the I am, came as the bread from heaven for the hungry, the giver of Living Water to the thirsty, the Great Physician to the hurting, and the loving, committed Shepherd to the lost and wondering sheep, and so forth. The introduction that summarizes it all is found in *John 8:58, "Verily, verily, I say unto you, Before Abraham was, I am."*

The reason we need to check out our attitude towards the Lord is we do not want Him to appear in darkness because of rebellion; rather, we want Him to appear to us to call us out of the darkness of our old ways. We must be willing to turn aside like Moses to meet with Him in whatever capacity He inserts Himself into our ordinary life in order to receive our orders, and like Joshua we must be willing to bow before Him and worship Him when He does introduce Himself.

The next time you enter a time of silence before the Lord, ask Him how He would come to you and from His answer it will give you insight of where you are with Him in your life before Him.

The one team I enjoy studying is Moses and Joshua. Moses represented the deliverer who, as a shepherd, would lead God's sheep, Israel, out of bondage through the wilderness, while Joshua pointed to the conqueror who would lead the children of Israel through battles and into the Promised Land. One was used to bring forth the first covenant, the Law while the other would point to a future covenant of grace that was yet to come. One brought the children of Israel up to the Promised Land, while the other led them into the Promised Land. One represented the Law that reveals man's great need for salvation, while the other one went before the children of Israel to ensure that they entered into the place of deliverance, blessing, and abundance.

Moses ultimately failed to lead the people into the Promised Land, but his example points to the fact that the Law could bring people up to the precipice of salvation, but could never secure salvation or a new life. We know according to *Galatians 3:24*, the law was meant to be a schoolmaster that points to Jesus. Since Moses was a shepherd and not a warrior, he was not called or equipped to militarily lead the people into battles in order to possess the land. Joshua was a soldier, but before he became a leader of the people, he served as Moses' servant. He was with Moses on the mount when he received the law, stayed behind at the entrance of the tabernacle after Moses departed because the presence of God had come down (*Exodus 24:12-14; 33:11*). Joshua was ever so close to Moses in preparation to fulfill his calling.

To reach our potential in the kingdom of God we must be to our great Shepherd as Joshua was to his shepherd Moses. We must ever be close to Him so we can hear His voice and follow Him as we are prepared to lead others to Him in a victorious fashion.

Moses was told to encourage Joshua because the mantle of leadership would be passed down to him (*Deuteronomy 3:28*). Moses, the shepherd, led the children of Israel through the wilderness for 40 years, but Joshua, the military leader would lead them into the Promised Land that would have to be militarily subdued.

For Christians Moses represented the old leadership of the Law, while Joshua (in Greek his name would be Jesus) represented the new covenant bought and paid for by our Joshua, the Lord Jesus Christ. The old could only point to the promise of the new, but it would be the leadership of the new that would fulfill the promise of the old.

The question is how under the new can we enter into the promises of God? We need to learn to encourage ourselves because the Christian life is about being delivered through the barren wilderness of sin and death up to the doorway of life by Jesus' redemption. But we must enter through that doorway to follow Jesus, our Shepherd in order to experience all the promises that are attached to the new life.

As in every adventure through the unknown terrains of this world there will be obstacles that we must overcome before ultimately inheriting all of God's promises, but we must remember who is ever going before us, pushing back the enemy while securing the terrains of our souls. Let us take courage by remembering the greatest battle was already won at Calvary and that the promises of heaven are ours to inherit.

I was talking about the team of Moses and Joshua. Most probably know that Joshua's name in Greek is "Jesus," which means "Jehovah saves" or "Jehovah is our salvation." We are told Jesus was the Lawgiver, but He was also the only One who could fulfill its judgments.

We know that Moses failed to sanctify God in the eyes of the people, but this was to cause us to recognize that the Law could not establish people in true righteousness. Moses came first with the Law, and Joshua came second with the means to fulfill the mission. Jesus came first as the great Shepherd to lead the way through the barren wilderness of sin and death and will come back as the victorious lion of Judah, the King of kings, and the Judge of all.

Moses' failure did not keep him out of the land, for he entered it when he appeared on the Mount of Transfiguration with Elijah and Jesus, but in light of Jesus, he pointed to the fact the first ministration of the Law would give way to the work of redemption, while Elijah represented that all prophecies about Jesus pronounced by the prophets would be

434

brought to fruition in Him. Remember, Jesus is the end of the Law for righteousness unto all who believe (*Romans 10:4*).

Joshua opened up the way for the children of Israel to come into the Promised Land, just as Jesus opened the way for all the heirs of salvation to come into the fullness of promises. It is true that the first, Moses, became the last to receive the promises attached to the first covenant, but if such individuals are truly heirs of salvation, by faith they will enter into them because Jesus first came as the Shepherd of His sheep and the Savior of all mankind to prepare the way for those who follow by faith.

The other day I was reading about Elijah and Elisha. Elijah represented the power of His prophetic office but Elisha pointed to the cost, the insight, and the determination to receive and walk in the authority and power of such an office. It was obvious that God knew Elijah and Elijah knew God and that he had been prepared in obscurity before he ever hit the scene to pronounce judgments on the likes of Ahab and Jezebel.

When it came to Elisha in *1 Kings 19*, Elijah simply cast his mantle upon him and Elisha went back, kissed his parents good buy and took the yoke of the oxen he had been plowing with, killed them and gave the meat to the people to eat. Clearly, Elisha had been chosen by God and was prepared to say farewell to his old life in order to follow Elijah into a new one as a means to impart that which would prove eternal to hungry souls.

As I was reading the incident surrounding Elijah's translation, I took note of some important facts. The first one is that Elisha and those from the school of the prophets knew Elijah would be translated and yet it was only Elisha who stayed as close as he could to Elijah, whether it was to benefit from it such as in the case of receiving a double portion of his spirit or being a witness of a wondrous miracle.

This is true for Christians as well. Due to the Bible, we know what we have in Christ, but how many of us are willing to leave the familiarity of our old life and religion, the comfort of pews, and rock the boat of normalcy to truly follow Jesus into a life that proves to be extraordinary where the miraculous is the norm?

It is to point out there may have been a school of prophets but they remain nameless while Elijah and Elisha were counted among the few that tread beyond this world to be called, prepared, translated into glory, and entrusted with more of a heavenly calling.

Yesterday I made reference to Elijah and Elisha. There were four places these prophets encountered before Elijah was translated. They started at Gilgal, and went by way of Bethel, Jericho, and the Jordan River. Gilgal means "rolling." This is where the Israelites rolled off the old (manna) of heaven in order to partake from the abundance of the Promised Land but it also later became a place of great idolatry.

Bethel means "house of God." This is where Jacob witnessed the Lord standing at the top of the ladder, but it later was polluted by an altar erected to an idol. We all know the story of Jericho, which means "place of fragrance." It was the first place conquered by the children of Israel after entering into the Promised Land, but it also proved to be a great place of temptation for a man named Achan, ending in defeat for Israel because sin was among them.

It was at Jordan that Elijah was finally translated but that was not before he had first parted its waters. What can we learn from this journey as to the example of Elisha? Elisha could have stopped at Gilgal which served as a mere entrance, but he knew he must enter through Gilgal and leave the old ways behind if he was to be entrusted with more.

He could have settled for staying at the House of God and mingling among the prophets and the religious activities, but a mere replicate of something is a poor substitute for what is real. He could pause to smell the fragrance of what represented victory, but such victory is a beginning of the spiritual journey not the end of it. He could have let Jordan become a boundary to how far he would go in his life before God, but he knew where God called him, He would part the waters of all hindrances.

Jesus' call to follow Him can prove to be a physical journey but the reality is, it is a spiritual journey of the soul that will go by different places where the real spiritual pilgrim will never simply settle for crumbs, stale bread, and empty activities. In summation, the Elisha's will not be content until they receive that portion that ensures they will triumphantly finish the journey for the glory of God.

Other books by Rayola Kelley:

Hidden Manna
Battle for the Soul
Stories of the Heart
Transforming Love & Beyond
The Great Debate

Volume One: Establishing Our Life in Christ
My Words are Spirit and Life
The Anatomy of Sin
The Principles of the Abundant Life
The Place of Covenant
Unmasking the Cult Mentality

Volume Two: Putting on the Life of Christ
He Actually Thought It Not Robbery
Revelation of the Cross
In Search of Real Faith
Think on These Things
Follow the Pattern

Volume Three: Developing a Godly Environment
Godly Discipline
Prayer and Worship
Don't Touch That Dial
Face of Thankfulness
ABC's of Christianity

Volume Four: Issues of the Heart
Hidden Manna (Revised)
Bring Down the Sacred Cows
The Manual for the Single Christian Life
Parents are People Too

Volume Five: Challenging the Christian Life
The Issues of Life
Presentation of the Gospel
For the Purpose of Edification
Whatever Happened to the Church?
Women's Place in the Kingdom of God

www.ingramcontent.com/pod-product-compliance
Lightning Source LLC
Chambersburg PA
CBHW060236100426
42742CB00011B/1543

This book is dedicated to Avatar Meher Baba

For Austin, Caleb, Gus, Meg and Frances June Darnell.
Also for my brothers, family and the Baba community.

Brian Darnell
May, 2020

Light and lofty

The linnet bird touts
its high wire wisdom

without contention, knowing
not enough to be consequential.

A statement of conditions –
not a song of complaint or praise.

Brilliant, this moment of sunlight
in the glen on its warm,

feathered, bird-boned back,
a smidgen of bliss

far as the breeze will carry.
How light and lofty

to be inconsequential,
above all, in God's corner

singing in, of and for the blue sky
and the wide green world

not one qualified, discordant,
contestable note.

O child of God, trade in your intuitive discernment
for the clean abandonment of not-knowing.

An ocean away

I've been to India many times.
I've never quite felt at ease there.

It's the oppressive, ubiquitous unfamiliarity –
ever a stranger in a foreign milieu,

an ocean away from home. These days,
holed up in my hometown, homestead,

habitat, my own planet and (gross) plane,
I'm also ever slightly ill-at-ease,

every familiar thing now drenched
in a foreign light, heard in a disquieting way,

smelt and tasted seasoned with dust and ash.
Ill-at-ease in my own skin, my head and heart.

I've listened to You and told myself
so many times I've come to believe it

beyond any intentional, intellectual concept,
down to my very bones –

this world is not my home.
This world is not my home.

O child of God, don't rest until you
get back to where you started.

The nature of stars

A sky full of stars and the magi looking
eastward to an extraordinary flare

moving contrary to fixed patterns,
to all known predictions,

contrary to the nature of stars.
They follow it pell-mell –

blazing sun, freezing nights –
in a burdensome gallop,

destination unknown. It doesn't matter –
they are chasing the cosmic,

leaving behind the earth.
And the great mysteries of heaven

come down to greet them, those wise men,
to intermingle and lay on hands,

no longer ashen remnants,
distant trackers and observers

but burning, existential participants
in the ancient, great fires of creation.

O child of God, chase after truth;
let nothing stand in your way.

The scent of a peach

A ripe peach is on a wooden table.
Rather than reach for it, I write poetry

on its virtue, beauty and succulence;
safer, more enduring than the true peach

in this unreliable realm –
(I find it's never there when I reach for it).

I'm back again in my bare cell, empty-handed.
This poetry is not much like a peach –

not within a country mile;
a very rough approximation

yet it's imbued with the scent of a peach
with which I must content myself.

A ripe peach on a wooden table
and I have thrown my life away

in pursuit of it and its presumed reward;
swallowed every tale; followed the wildest rumors;

written down my confessions for all to see.
I have trusted You, my Lord,

in complete ignorance for the truth
of the long-trumpeted, promised perfect peach.

O child of God, keep your faith confidential
and pray for Meher not to let you down.

A grass hut

God has no boundaries.
Make Him the hub (said my Lord)

and He will someday also
become the periphery.

Walk with Him this immediate realm,
at some point you'll enter the other –

you'll lose your own boundaries.
God tolerates (apparently) for the sake of illusion,

our claims of authority, the iron pins
by which we stake out our properties.

Only on rare occasions does He trespass –
a revelation, a vision, an inexplicable synchronicity.

But God has no boundaries. That is the sobering truth,
the great fear to which we all must attend –

utter vulnerability and ultimate non-existence.
Like an elephant entering a grass hut

(if He has a mind to) – no locks, barricades; no walls,
no appeals to our sovereignty will keep or contain Him

as He invades and supplants,
obliterates the structures of our beings.

O child of God, Meher did often avow –
we are not we but One.

The unfolding answer

A man of deep faith, just as a man
without faith, asks nothing of God.

Life itself to such a man
is the unfolding answer to all prayers.

Pain, fright is there – but not anxiety;
loss but not grief;

failure without disappointment;
solitude without loneliness;

death (we are told) without termination.
Perched on the tip of the bow,

a man of faith is serenely poised
to receive, to pass along

only what he's given; responsible
for nothing but vigilance and acquiescence.

He gets the big picture, the ocean view,
recognizes the nuances, though as yet,

is unable to grasp the details.
Less than a hair's breadth (the Masters say),

separates heaven from earth –
it requires an unhanding,

an atrophy of judgment,
a relinquishment of presumption.

O child of God, life itself to a man of faith
is the unfolding answer to all prayers.

Cross yourself

Cross yourself – routinely
(in whatever form customary) –

puja, zikr, mea culpa; yarmulke,
psalter, kusti, damru, suf.

Don't look for trouble; let it find you –
keep it between the shoulders,

o good neighbor. You'll find dear enough,
familiar faces around the corner,

down the street, in need of heartiness
and a gentle hand. Cross yourself –

quietly, discreetly; apply deeper wisdom,
a farther vision, visceral caution.

Keep your balance to help
balance the world around you.

Cross yourself, o traitorous one,
and you may find after so long a time

crossing yourself befriends the Friend –
befriends the One, befriends your true Self.

O child of God, give only advice gingerly
gleaned from the words of the Master.

Chortle

Somewhere between a chuckle and a snort –
this word invented by Lewis Carroll.

No one quite sure of the wordsmith's
original intended meaning and pronunciation.

(He let the word speak for itself),
it's precise nomenclature

in the common vernacular
summarily up for grabs.

Creation began
with the invention of a Word

(perhaps, an immortal chortle)
entering into the vernacular

and no one's quite sure now
of its original meaning and intent . . .

as endlessly in a cacophony of fear and desire
we assert, opine, question and debate,

while the Wordsmith looks on,
lips pursed behind an upraised finger

in ambiguous silence,
letting the Word speak for Itself.

O child of God, Meher said, 'Life is a jest' –
surely worthy of a chuckle and a snort.

In the thick

The nearer you get to God,
the more you take Him for granted.

God becomes a necessary routine –
soap to skin, food to belly,

the hours allotted for sleep.
Daily we remember God –

to give Him His due
until one day we are shown

He's due everything, every moment.
Then, life becomes a prayer.

You take it for granted God is there
because it's *His* life, *His* due

and where else would God be
but deep in the thick of His own Self?

O child of God, make Him the center
until He becomes the everything.

Orb of the heart

When the center of the sky was earth,
the movements of planets and stars

seemed erratic; calculations difficult and complex.
The sun took over and flights clicked

more easily into predictable patterns.
And when the center of the sky

became a distant, conjectured,
long-ago point of origin, the earth,

stars and planets began to interact
in calculable and precise ways,

parts of an infinite, well-oiled machine.
As long as that blue, stone cold

orb of the heart is taken to be
the center of the universe,

every outward movement,
every body spinning beyond it

will be judged as erratic and arbitrary,
inexplicable and incalculable.

O child of God, the truth makes things
o-so-much-more simple and clear.

Just another route

You and I are on a first name basis.
I've grown up with this intimacy –

praying as a child each night
for You to take and keep my soul,

allaying with Your name
my fear of death and harm.

Yesterday, I heard part of a speech
by a famous crusading atheist.

He's made God the center of his life.
No one gets around You.

Everything is a part of Your work.
Every sin, every blasphemy, every ignorance

as well as every revelation and act of compassion
brings us closer to You.

O child of God, running from the Everything
is just another route into His arms.

God's gift

Enjoy this moment God has made
knowing full well

you have no right to joy –
not having earned it,

not owning it nor having created it.
It's a momentary gift you can never possess,

slipping invariably through your fingers.
Endure the suffering moments, too, God gives,

knowing you do not own suffering
and have not earned it. Knowing it too shall pass.

We pray for joy while the teachings
emphasize the efficacy of suffering.

But God gives neither joy nor pain; God's gift is life –
the undivided experience and awareness of it –

the ecstasy and horror, beauty and bitterness,
pride and grief, the gentility and brutality of it all.

O child of God, to accept the gift of God,
accept the total, eternal ownership of the Giver.

The truth of illusion

Moths circle the lamp, hover
and hurtle, attracted to the flame

but also driven from the midst
of their dark surroundings.

You reach God
when you come to the end of yourself.

You get wise. It's the truth of illusion
that shatters, that jades;

the truth of illusion that bores, sates,
disheartens, disenchants.

You rush toward God when God
outshines His surroundings.

When the dark has gobbled you up –
bones and blood.

You rush and flail
and hurl yourself toward the light

when you see there's nothing
in the darkness worth living for.

O child of God, turn from illusion
toward the way, the truth, the light.

Apparently, fearless

Rumi likened the soul to a bird's beating wings,
propelled toward God by (love's) expansion

and (fear's) inevitable, subsequent contraction;
a thrust and recovering – fear and repugnance,

joy and inspiration and back again in pursuit
of truth and beauty and the leave-taking gamble

of the solitary perch of nestled desire and pleasure,
our final approach being, apparently, fearless –

of a gliding, unalloyed posture, wings stretched to their limit,
braced and unbending, our flight's path and pattern

determined solely by the play of winds, from beak
to feather beyond our efforts, desire and control.

O child of God, abandon fear and soar
into the holy, awaiting firmament.

An emphatic breach

In the pouring rain, the old man said,
I do not get wet and one day,

not as theory or concept
but, in a clear, emphatic breach,

I answered, of course, of course.
Somewhere from a dry, rustling field

where he stood and spoke,
the words reached me

over thirty years but more –
over centuries and continents,

oceans and dynasties –
a crack of the door,

the stones of the temple
and the lush gardens behind the walls;

the crumbling old myths.
The earth shook, dislodged a stone,

the shift of an ancient foundation
upon which everything I am

and seem to be, everything
I know and seem to know, rests.

O child of God, the flowers of the garden
unfold strictly according to God's schedule.

Unhook your soul

The creature is tethered. It tugs the chain taut.
It barks and snarls, scuffles and whines.

It lunges toward freedom. It goes 'round and 'round.
For an Enlightened Soul or life itself

to free the creature, it must be persuaded or gain
the strength and wisdom over the years

to slacken the tether, move toward the axis
so that it might be unhooked at the critical point.

Liberation (apparently) comes not from struggle
but from retreat and acquiescence.

O child of God, let the creature recede
so that Love might unhook your soul.

Zero

Life is a dream, said my Lord.
I was glad to ponder on such.

Twenty odd years later, I heard Him
phrase it in an different way –

O lover, you are dreaming Me!
I am, said my Lord, whatever the dreamer

takes Me to be, dependent upon their karma –
God to some, fraud to others,

a photograph, a name in passing,
an anonymous cipher in the human throng.

Then, also a dream, I replied, is what You are saying.
Everything is zero, said my Lord. Zero into zero –

it all equals zero. I'm at sea, I said.
Not yet, He replied, but you're getting there.

In order to drown, you have to let go
of everything that holds you up.

O child of God, the child is a dream;
God is a dream; this idea, this poem also a dream.

Paper dolls

Our lives are spent cutting out paper dolls –
the piecemeal extracted from the whole.

Our hearts set, gazes fixed
upon various relative, handsome,

scissored and brightly-colored figures
we prop up and manage;

with whom we play act for our own exculpation,
amusement and gratification

while discarding the ravaged sheets
from which they are cut, the origin

and background, field and root,
never to humbly let things lie

unhanded and dormant in their contextual truth
but take up our scissors, our scissors,

again and again, to wreak havoc
upon this paper-thin, flimsy, fluttering world.

O child of God, how improbable and illusory
is the human predicament and personality.

Love Itself

Everyone is a Baba lover.
Most don't know the phrase

or use the name. Those who do,
even the ones who consider Him

mad or a fraud, self-indulgent, evil,
love Him and serve Him

in their own limited and inimitable way –
can't we imagine this?

Can't we grant Him this much?
Everyone loves God, don't they?

Even those who've given up
or never knew or profess not to believe.

What else can love be (and from whence)?
What other object can love be for

in hearts that long, the force
that propels all life, all humanity

towards beauty, mercy, perfection, bliss?
Towards an ultimate quenching of loneliness?

What else can that love be for ... but for God?
The ineliminable and ubiquitous God and for Love Itself.

O child of God, everyone is a Baba lover,
each in his own limited and inimitable way.

On love's behalf

The Godman lives on love's behalf
and thereby couples the disparities

of flesh and spirit, truth and self.
A lifetime of service and repair,

the epitome of mercy, the Godman
appears on love's behalf

and as is His habit, never looks back,
never looks up from His task.

Arrives, survives and departs on love's behalf,
relying upon the resounding chords

of love's lilting, everlasting, ultimate
presence and essence to carry the day,

to preserve and persevere, to convey
His holy mission and message

to every hungry cell and soul, every being
in God's vast and illusory repertoire.

O child of God, liberation involves the lover,
also, living at last only on love's behalf.

A two-cent remark

Have faith in nothing of this world, said the old man,
except the efficacy of having faith in nothing.

When were you ever invited by God
to make a choice, conjecture,

display a preference, submit a two-cent remark
regarding His most holy and only apparent gift?

Out of ignorance comes our assumptions,
self-assurances, our unauthorized permissions

(in spite of ceaseless clues to the contrary),
to change any of the whole inviolate order

of things laid bare by our Creator
from the beginning of time,

for our own limited, fleeting comfort,
convenience, elucidation and desire.

O child of God, from whence comes
the notion the world is yours to change?

Various apples

We desire in our human love
only the best for the various

apples of our eyes,
our clutched-to-the-breast beloveds.

Our love's great failing –
the truth that we know not exactly

what *is* best and what constitutes
further entanglement on a field

so sad and vast as time and creation;
what is pure and what is tainted

from hearts sorely cleaved and teeming;
sorely cleaved and teeming.

Love Divine, on the contrary, said my Lord,
is not originated but bestowed (divinely);

wants nothing, has no center, no motive,
no standpoint, no hub, beginning in the light

of non-existence and never venturing
into the shadowy realms of the illusory self.

O child of God, wish your loved ones the best.
You are so very far removed from Love Divine.

A smidgen of God

To know a smidgen of God, step backward;
out of life; overlooking and through illusion,

adopting theoretically His holy hidden agenda.
To disappear into God, move forward

and toward, dropping your sword,
blending imperceptively into illusion

with staunch conviction of flimsy death,
shallow grave and your own sort of eternity.

Move like a winged bird,
not track nor trace to scratch

the empty sky, by turning your back
upon yourself (so suggest the scriptures) –

not to alter, grow or evolve but to *die*
taking the whole universe down with you;

dying with Jesus, Baba, Buddha,
dying so you may join them

beyond the impairments of time, space,
tangibility and individuality.

O child of God, surrender involves courage,
desperation and a feckless disregard of self.

Utility pole

A Cop-R-toxed or creosote pine pole,
lopped forty feet tall, slightly tapered,

branches shorn from the functional bole,
cross beams notched and bolted, spikes

for the climb set eighteen inches on center.
Die before you die, the mystics say.

When I imagine throwing my life away
on such a rumored glory,

there's always something to it to hold onto,
an essential sovereignty over which

I dare not presume authority, clutching
the utile pole, gloved hands,

thick boots glued to the spikes.
Thinking to climb to the top

where the real work begins.
More than a fear of death

or an instinct for survival –
a primordial knowledge, an inchoate awareness

keeps me clinging unquestioningly
to this separate, individual awareness and existence.

O child of God, surrender is not a life tossed away
but returned to its original owner.

Even to ask

Prayer is the start of detente,
a tête-à-tête, a turning away

from the cheap, the shoddy;
away from the opportunist, the scoundrel within,

drawing nearer to the purity of the Source.
But, comes the day, o petitioner,

when any request or suggestion
is a grave faux pas,

an attempted undermining,
a sundering of faith.

Even to ask for virtue or liberation;
even to ask for the sake of others.

Even to ask . . . is a violation
of the most delicate, flyweight,

prayerful and paper-thin arrangements
between illusion and Truth,

lover and God;
separating the rare truly faithful

from the scheming, frightened,
manipulative crowd.

O child of God, your intended destination?
You can't get there from here.

Appomattox

I die daily, said Paul.
Dynamic is the process,

suggested Eruch, surrender chosen freely,
repeatedly at every critical juncture.

Yes, but surely eventually strung
like an endless rosary beyond

the clutches of time and self.
A seamless union, a tightly clasped fetter;

acquiescence trussed up
and delivered entire.

I want to surrender like Lee at Appomattox,
stripped of rank and authority,

at the mercy of forces I have long opposed,
my world in dissolution and ruin, broken sword,

blood and smoke, silence, cessation,
the last battle, last death over,

a reuniting, the cleansing wind above
unfurling our common flag.

O child of God, you want this war to be done;
to rest in the arms of peace.

Impartiality

He preferred His juice lukewarm;
a glass of water, even an occasional

soda pop – room temperature.
And windows tightly shut

in the most sweltering weather. O lovers!
This should make us weep hot tears –

these small preferences,
for the delicately broken

human being who held them
and Who in the large,

went about the business of service,
sacrifice and surrender, without a thought

to self or pleasure, comfort or ease,
placing Himself under His own weighty thumb,

meeting His own austere requirements –
the Epitome of servitude and mastery.

One with karma, without waver,
equivocation, preference or doubt.

O child of God, true humility is found
in the impartiality of the great Godman.

The rose thorny lane

Stop and smell the roses, the pundits say
but shall we keep God waiting

down the rose thorny lane another day?
With death approaching from behind,

ever overtaking us among its dusty, fragrant shadows,
this path we've tread countless times –

and are we not yet sated
by its alluring splendor and bouquet?

Praise the Creator not creation;
enjoy and savor its showy riches

from the safe and lofty lap
of His holy, immaculate perspective.

Fly to His arms, then wander up the lane
hand in hand, with all the time in the world.

O child of God, remind yourself of Mehera's labor
in the gently scented gardens of Meherazad.

The matter of Love

You replaced First Cause by Original Whim,
karma's tripwire rendered moot

where only Love matters (saith my Lord)!
Birds made of sky, fish of ocean, songs of silence,

trees of clay like Adam the walking tree
or the walking Fish, the tree-bearing Jesus

stumbling up Calvary Who became
the Silent Master on the Hill,

revivifying every bird feather, tree leaf, song note,
fish scales luminous, iridescent, transparent

with the One and only sacred, vibrant
and ubiquitous matter of Love.

O child of God, your words are birds escaping
through an broken-barred window in the holiness.

Love comes first

Love overflowing;
love enough for everyone.

Jesus feeding the multitudes
loaves and fishes –

love enough for everyone,
plenty left over, and still yet more.

You showed me such a love once.
You filled my basket. Overflowing.

I should have spent the rest of my life
hovering near that love – undistracted,

plumbing its depths, bringing it to the surface,
ladling it out, breaking and sharing such a love

as You are, as You bring,
as You have given.

Love should come first –
to become a feeder, a slaker of thirst,

to become an aperture
through which Your light might shine.

O child of God, Meher keeps you
as near to the flame as you can stand.

Climb down

Don't worry, be happy
or, to put it another way –

climb down from the crow's nest,
its queasy, exaggerated susceptibility

to every roll and sway.
Secure yourself below

the water line, go for broke,
all or nothing, ready to drown.

The head is a precarious perch,
a tiny bucket of fear

with a false perspective.
Climb down

into the heart, fearless heart;
rest in the ship's deep, hollow, oak-ribbed hold.

O child of God, worry is a lack –
of heart-sense and faith in God.

My silent partner

Mercy, my spiritual master; compassion,
my steady companion; immediate truth,

my bottom line; love, my silent partner
instructing me, amidst the roaring senses,

the worldly provocation and gyrations,
to be aware of that small, still Presence

that counters every bluster,
every colorful, odious suggestion

indicating I am one hopelessly alone,
utterly lost traveler, without home or safe harbor.

Love, my silent partner, to turn to in faith
and truth and find the way, comforted,

subtly led from this land of shadows
into the bright, perfect Light.

O child of God, listen with all your heart
to the wisdom of your silent partner.

Streets without love

Hold to My damaan, Meher said;
for those times when there's left

not a shred of anything else within reach;
a damaan of straw, one last hope to grasp

where He dare not refuse;
when you need to

unburden your chest of the weighty
function and duty of self;

when you can't possibly weave your way
alone any farther through streets without love;

a damaan with which to dry tears,
clean slates, bind wounds;

to yield a small sheer rectangle –
the fluttering white flag of surrender.

O child of God, hold to His damaan
until you are ready to unhand everything.

Tilting the scales

If you're looking to me for answers,
I've run shy.

If you're looking for questions
I can loan you some

you've never even considered.
Most people view them

as a lack of faith
but I see them as confirmation.

Who would question while not believing
there are answers to be had?

They may be legitimate targets for admonition
but a display of apostasy, they are not.

I feel unbalanced, though.
So many questions and so few answers

tilting the scales, skewing the data,
listing my somber progression

ominously to one side. It tends to
make me go around in circles.

O child of God, when will you stop dealing
in words, intellect and superficial knowledge?

To cull and glean

Jesus performed miracles.
Curious that word performed,

its theatrical connotation,
a mesmerized crowd attracted

and then love let loose to cull and glean
those with ears to hear;

to winnow out those drawn to power,
to avoidance of the necessity

of suffering and surrender.
Only one miracle, claimed my Lord –

to alter the human heart into submission,
the switch from power to love.

O child of God, put this realm behind you
by seeking the unparalleled majesty of love.

Collected poems

How pathetic must sound my poems
to those in the fire! How sad –

my quavering approach to the precipice's edge.
Words of love with no love there, just a discussion,

a hypothesis, no substance or fire.
Not whispering endearments but interrogations;

cold, analytic chatter.
Those in the fire long in sympathy

for my ultimate defeat –
collected poems, accumulated pages

torn and crushed, fed
into the eagerly awaiting flames.

O child of God, don't let words withhold you
from becoming silent ash and dust.

The ruddy marrow

Love is nothing like a tattoo –
facing outward like a bumper sticker,

its splendor or wisdom
a public assertion of affection or opinion

designed for the elucidation
and edification of others.

Love is a tattoo pointing inward,
a stain on the underside of the dermis,

ink in the blood
down to the ruddy marrow,

an indelible, inviolable, privately negotiated
contract with one's true self,

nothing to do with advocacy or influence,
identity or display but a personal,

permanent rejoinder, reminder –
the pearls of a secret adherence

never reaching the gawking,
insensitive eyes and ears of swine.

O child of God, keep counsel with your pillow
and enter into thy closet to pray.

The farthest skies

Wings naturally contract, necessarily,
yet that wavering, faithless bird

invariably predicts and laments each time
a calamitous plummet from the grand heights,

ever astonished to witness,
following panic, its wings unfold anew,

catch the air beneath
and keep itself tremblingly aloft.

Full extension, followed by an essential recouping,
the gathering of vital resistance

used to climb the farthest skies
and yet, perpetually, through lack of faith,

fear and suffering accompany
our fateful, solitary and majestic flight.

O child of God, hold on tightly.
You're just along for the ride.

By blood and flesh

By blood and flesh, our Liberator
was bound every step,

His superbly draped coat thrown
over delicate heartbeat and fragile bones

yet also by invisible fetters,
inviolate parameters

of His task and duty,
His sacred function and mission

from which He could not stray an inch.
A casual moment, a whimsical gesture,

not a frolic, a whit, a whirl,
but every move ordained

and subservient to the purpose
for which He entered the fray.

O child of God, the great freedom comes
with surrendering to Who you really are.

Pitched bottles

I'm running low on ink, pen,
stationary, bottles and cork,

the Milky Way moving above me
like a vast blue sea, tides

and currents sweeping away
my inquiries never to return.

Sitting on a rough beach
I seldom pace anymore,

but often soil my knees with prayer,
wondering increasingly

if the shell of sky and ocean
somehow forms the answer –

me without ears to hear, held up too small
and distant against the eternal,

not a climbing path anywhere
among the flying stars and heaving waves,

these pitched bottles merely
a poor substitute for drowning.

O child of God, facing sea and skyward
distracts you from your inherent solitude.

A brief coupling

Some people think of poetry
as a string of words that rhyme.

It must be, others opine,
musings ingeniously inspired

or stilted profundities, oddly arranged.
Some insist upon evocative phrasing

or words obscure and impenetrable
and yet poetry is not words at all

but a redolence that drifts
through the bars of our cages

or not even that but a dark,
nuanced display at a moment's notice

on bright, open palms, stolen like a breath
from the reader's chest,

a brief coupling alluding to, more or less,
the gasping, thunderous truth in us all;

a hint of the ultimate affinity
for which every heart pines.

O child of God, why ever would you endeavor
to put into words what poetry is?

Keep sharp the axe

It's not like felling a tree, I've gathered,
an accumulation of blows

the more disciplined and precisely delivered,
the sooner the accomplished task.

I am not the wielder of the axe, for example;
I'm more like the tree or both or neither

and when it finally comes down,
I won't be there to mark it.

Yet, it must be attended to, it bars the way
or perhaps the topmost branches

hold the key to my awakening,
the elusive revelation and relationship,

the axe blows merely knocks upon my door,
my best friend wishing me

in the bright green sunlight
to come outside and play.

O child of God, the purpose of conjecture
is to keep sharp the axe.

The root of courage

Cor is the root of courage,
Latin for heart

from which it springs.
Yes, a heart and courage grown faint

but only when we coronate
its pretender, its appropriator,

the Vizier we employ
in heartbreaking irony to meet life's threats,

real and imagined; the very maker
of fear, the saboteur of love,

ever in opposition by dominance,
usurpation of the heart,

the *cor*, the coeur, the core
from which all courage springs.

O child of God, yield your head
to the heart's dominion.

The impedimenta of desire

Lessons in the course of a lifetime are not
(it seems) so much consciousness expanding

as they are encumbrances shed, yet so few
and paltry that little more light shines through

than in the beginning; each lifetime
threatened by smudges of vice,

the impedimenta of desire
to overwhelm the journey's

natural divestiture and unveiling.
Aeons it seems, requires the process,

the gathering up, the breaking off,
littering the landscape, a-tisket, a-tasket,

every broken, mortal, humble basket,
until each core of light triumphs

over the entombed, encrusted alias
of Who, by faith, we really are.

O child of God, hide not your lamp
beneath the bushel but let it shine.

You are here

reads the big X on the lexan-protected
hiking trail map – You are here.

But, the truth is not about
where I am in the woods,

but where I am in the story.
Time, space, perception and being,

as well as components beyond conception
intersect at the ungraspable,

irrevocably fluid point of *now*.
Where I am is who I am,

path and pilgrim one and the same,
as deeply inseparable as I am

from the Companion Who is even now here
on this ineffable path to nowhere.

O child of God, study the map
to find out just where and who you are.

Your only chance

We crave choice having not asked
for birth or death; choosing not the realm

into which we are tossed
and must so inelegantly depart.

Left out of the big choices
we covet the petty ones,

gather them to our breasts,
refuse to share power

real or imagined and rankle
under the yoke of necessity.

Only self chooses, if choices are made,
choosing itself over and over

while all the genuine Masters
point to renunciation and surrender.

O child of God, your only chance at freedom
is the unremitting commitment to become a slave.

Six foot grave

Spiritual conversations should be
constructed of the negative –

neti, neti – until silence triumphs,
reigns deeper than a six foot grave.

Judgments, opinions, philosophies
have nothing to do with Reality,

evolution no truer than
the garden of Eden.

Nothing enters our heads
without ignorance attached to it –

ever fishing in the wrong stream.
This poem, like all the others, has one message –

not this, not this – simply because
I have yet to stumble upon anything that is.

O child of God, the tool you use
to apprehend Reality must be abandoned.

Ruminations on Rumi

When was I less by dying? Rumi asked,
encouraging us over that dark hump

but, one day, apparently we shall dispense
with all considerations of loss and gain.

At the forked road divest ourselves of preference,
stratagems and ruminations.

No true path or every path taken as true,
the art of pleasing God quietly set aside

to please Him by the art of quietly setting it aside.
Encompassed in our empty arms,

witnessed through our wide-open,
awestruck, love-drenched eyes

the agony, rapture, the dispossession and gain,
the anguish, solace, pleasure and pain,

every distinguishable aspect razed, leveled,
hammered and pressed into hearty, holy unleavened bread.

O child of God, surrender involves a loss
only superficially similar, by faith, to death.

The opposite of love

Love asks no questions, You said.
Doubt, apparently, is love's opposite,

a rocky, futile path to truth
avoided by the highest form

of fawn-eyed credulity.
Our impotence exposed, truth found out

when inquiries cease altogether.
Not hatred then, not indifference,

but doubt is the opposite of love,
love a blitheness achieved

only by the death of the lover
asking no questions from the bottom of a grave.

O child of God, whosoever will
lose his life for My sake shall find it.

The sole discordance

God is everything I am not. Apparently.
Everything but little ol' me,

the bubble over the Ocean drop.
Everything not the self made of Self,

asserting its appropriateness
by its very existence. Up against that

ubiquitous voice I have no say
for anything in the world

I wish not to be the way it is
or to resolve and go away

or to not exist at all; I have no say
because what is not me

speaks with the premeditated,
authentic, primeval voice of God.

O child of God, you are the sole
discordance in a chorus of Oneness.

The promise of me

I keep going back
to the elephant in the dark,

seeing deeply the universal tent
bedimmed and the elephant ubiquitous;

not as a revelation
but the truth of ignorance,

getting a whiff of it, seeing
my fingers blindly grope

while the promise of me
standing eagle-eyed in some golden dawn

is just as false. This dark narrowness
cannot be relieved, escaped or removed

without destroying the tent,
the elephant and just who I am.

O child of God, darkness is not answered
by seeing through your fingers.

It takes a death

It takes a death, often
to bring us down to earth,

to the dove's heart a blow,
an arrow bestirring the dust,

a crucifixion of some sort,
whether on rough timbers

or the rotting beams of old bones;
grave dust laden and silhouetting

our common little crucifixes built humbly
upon the rickety bridges of nothingness.

But also revealing the genuinely endearing
human qualities of valor and gallantry –

for how else may God be brave but through us?
Clearing the air long enough to glimpse:

Everyone is continuously reaching for God,
for love, for the above ground truth of who we are.

O child of God, there's nothing to seek;
nothing to find but the hidden One.

Something better besides

To seek the truth
is to covet what God knows.

To seek nothing
is to honor His secret.

To seek nothing is the ultimate faith.
A dearth of trust is truth-seeking,

the self-seeking of reward.
To seek nothing is to abandon

the paradigm of loss and gain,
truth being only what is now.

Nothing else to be known; unstorable,
untranslatable into knowledge.

Grasp at truth? Or hold out simply
your God-issued begging bowl?

O child of God, truth is greater than illusion
but there's still something better besides.

What daredevils learn

No sense in fearing
what can't be controlled.

Each purposeful, fearful moment
arising from our pseudo-autonomy,

our obsessive self-protection.
Fear is the essence of self.

Its absence is love.
Everything but the self is love!

Lose your fearful self and become fear's absence.
Become love; become that Everything.

O child of God, shed the false; become the true.
Shed the self; become Love Itself.

Rainy day

To never die, our selves desire.
Yet, mortality is illusion, as per the Masters,

as are all such objects –
inherently erroneous.

Our one true deficiency
being the blot and blur

of our desiring self.
Its erasure is all we lack

in the trek from nowhere to nowhere.
Our timeless, motionless passage

an entertainment, a false relief
from God's idle, eternal limbo –

a brief distraction
during a rainy day, shut-in afternoon.

O child of God, whimsicality and pretense
run the gamut of all existence.

Original grain

I want to not know
any other way to be.

Cut my alternatives
down to zero, the original grain

good for me, good for me;
truth will out and out of that truth

a worn out humbleness, holiness revealed;
holy however imperfect, impure, impaired.

Dream if you must
of unbridled potential.

I want to not know
any other way to be,

rubbed down to the nub, the original grain
and go with that, go with that, go with that.

O child of God, Meher said God is found
where you are not.

Play dead

I've received the handoff, apparently,
deep in my own territory,

lumbering towards daylight
but they're after me.

It's all a mistake!
I don't want to be here

but there it is
deep in my belly.

A shaky glimpse
of that impossibly distant goal;

lurching forward
until I'm roughly brought down,

one shrill, sharp whistle
blowing the play dead.

O child of God, existence, Meher Baba said,
is a game God began on a whim.

Dipped in the baptistery

Dipped in the baptistery
or the slow pulling river,

a new creature born in Christ *this* day,
every day – a dropped hint, a rough image.

To the death required of every new birth,
the mind by its nature remains impervious.

The door to Life eternal is nailed shut
but it can be glimpsed through the keyhole.

What it takes, apparently, to enter,
is every mental construct,

scheme and worry to be left behind –
becoming pure spirit, finer than smoke,

a cipher, zephyr, light as light
while yet in the flesh,

to sift and strain freely through the open,
keyless aperture into Truth and Immortality.

O child of God, you are not the man you were
nor the man you are yet to become.

Lovely winged words

I'm no angel and this ain't heaven.
Every human endeavor

beginning on this rough stretch –
the ocean's edge of ignorance

where nothing grows; soon swept away
to what surely looks like dissolution and calamity.

These poems of ignorance
scratched into the surface between tides

repeat the only message – all I have to say
to my one potential overhead rescuer: *HELP!*

Angels, perhaps, have their choice
of lovely winged words, singing

God's praises; floating about heaven
but I'm no angel and this ain't heaven.

O child of God, even your impudent, raucous cries,
the angels say, reach God as tunes of humility.

I came across Christ

I came across Christ stripped of scriptural restraints;
uplifted in outstretched, agonized triumph.

I came across Christ as He double-crossed
the stone sepulcher; came across death,

across Truth in a walkabout that led to Jesus in India,
thousands of years from the sophistry,

the accumulated errors, the calcified ruins.
I came across Christ, the palpable flesh and blood

hanged from a cross of the Carpenter's own making,
His silent returning, His timely, masterful, merciful

descent, the ethereal made extant in the milieu
of our latest, chronic human lunacy and despair.

O child of God, follow the ancient thread that runs
from Zoroaster's kushti to the sadra of Meher.

It's your bird

A sailor somewhere taught the bird to curse.
Now there is nothing to be done,

profanity and earthiness
an integral stain on its vocabulary.

It can't be unlearned
though it knows not a single definition.

No changing of feathers now;
no silencing cover up

or wringing it's pretty green neck.
It's your bird. You can't disown it.

But unhitch its tether; stop feeding it.
The best you can, live with it

until the day it undertakes
through an open window

its flight long forgotten and among the heights
renounces its acquired, artificial ability to speak.

O child of God, neither parrot nor songbird
bears even the slightest resemblance to truth.

Boat the oars

Boat the oars and bewildered lie
in your gently creaking casket;

view the flowering stars
without clarity or curiosity.

Shatter your sword. Give up
your one shot at redemption.

Abjure the bindings of every proposal.
Store no provisions.

Abandon all fantasies of rescue,
mercy; pardon and reward.

Invite your own demise without really knowing
what it might be like nor how to go about it,

solely as the next obedient, sequential phase,
your last wisp of a motive being

the release, as best you can,
completely, of fallacy and fear.

O child of God, hope for hopelessness.
Attempt utter passivity.

Portrait

A charcoal portrait which represents me
as much as apparently anything else,

all down on paper in black and white;
stationary lines arc and wriggle,

twist and flow, crafting brows,
hairlines and facial features.

I'm the empty space, I suppose,
sketchy, binary, insinuated;

formed and shaped
by shades of black and gray.

The black is my ignorance –
overwhelming; peripheral; defining.

The white is my emptiness
at center stage, the light's facsimile.

I become visible where there is nothing,
allowing the backdrop to seep through.

Having mislocated myself, I cleave desperately
to the ignorance that appears to define me.

O child of God, why not lose yourself
in the vast benevolence of God?

My shop is not yet sold

Ramjoo came to You hobbling
upon the crutch of propriety

for liberation and wholeness.
You ordered him to anyone and everyone

say before a greeting or conversation,
my shop is not yet sold.

You gave him a choice he could not evade
and when relatives and neighbors knocked,

the floodgates opened upon shame,
ridicule and ostracism.

Such was Your kindness and his deliverance
from putting any solace ahead of You and God –

the same demand You make of me.
I bolt my door and do not answer;

pretend no one is at home.
(My shop is not yet sold).

O child of God, you reach for God
while tenaciously holding to other investments.

The land of Nod

When the umbilical cord is cut –
our original attachment, not just to mother

but also Father, to any other –
the wound is so deep and great,

rarely does it heal over a lifetime.
Wandering the land of Nod

in hope of a poultice,
a concoction of ultimate remedy.

Over the aeons, we have gotten plastered
by every voodoo cure, herb and root,

mustard seed and devil's club;
chased the old wives' tales

around every bend and corner
and come up empty and hurting,

none the wiser and further
impaired deeper in the core

where it all begins and never leaves,
where the world's cataplasm cannot reach.

So the dog chases its tail, the tale of human history,
unable it seems, to turn and face the truth

of our permanently attached oneness
and our hidden-in-plain-view non-existence.

O child of God, you and I are not we but One
means the notion of you must be abandoned.

Bamboo and rope

You were silent without motive
but so many fine repercussions,

one being a palpable demonstration
of love as emanation

independent of articulation;
subtle in its strength; a shared universal,

indwelling presence and recognition.
Words are for the makeshift

bamboo and rope bridging of distances
while silent love reveals the illusion of distance,

an evolving response, a steady permeation
holding together the hope of the world.

O child of God, bite your tongue
even as you write this poem down.

I am not myself

I've taken up the tightrope these last few years,
having so little to lose, life and time precious

but the cheapness of my indulgences
showing through, while that high,

tense wire is the only path to the other side.
To grieve, to judge, to mind, to intervene

is to indulge in Illusion. When the mind fasts,
every sentiment and desire, every concept

is a tempting morsel of entrenchment,
intransience, disobedience –

bread for the mouth, wine for the throat.
High above the abyss, inching my way

towards whatever beckons from the other side,
I forego as best I might self-perpetuation,

the one exception being to pause continually
and remind myself I am not alone; not myself but Self.

O child of God, if you were to bear alone salvation
nothing would be possible under its crush.

Garden-variety meditation

This serpentine interior monologue –
I break it or allow it to break,

each daisy-chain phrase plucked delicately apart
into pleasant, disconnected incoherence;

letting it run ahead, out of earshot, while I
slip back through that well-oiled gate

where no such whisperings
could ever tempt a soul into anything

contrary to God's benevolent oneness.
Let them die mercilessly on the vine then,

those sticky, persistent, overripe seductions
and pray for the garden to become

a realm of pure observation; a quiet, paled,
semi-permanent, edenic place of dwelling.

O child of God, like pearls string together
those artfully concocted manonash moments.

God's brush

Dinosaur bones found today in Texas
proof of time from earth's dawning;

physical evidence like the morning's
egg-stained dishes and a half cup of cold coffee,

historical data corroborating
our perceptions and assumptions –

the past not only once existed
but time is ever flowing into it;

not a contiguous, static flickering
in the same illogical, illusive now.

Do the bones prove our temporality
or is it just another flourish from God's brush?

Another facet of His ever-present, insoluble,
impossibly intricate and arcane, illusory design?

O child of God, is time endless or an infinitesimal
slice of the wink of an eye?

Soon left to the page

A poem indecipherable, a chore to read
though chock-full of evocative images

ever on the brink of making sense,
hints of eloquence shot randomly through.

If the reader has little faith – the poet
viewed as foolish, inexpert, unduly obscure

with nothing important to convey –
the poem is soon left to the page,

a thick, tiresome, insoluble mystery.
If, however, the reader somehow gets a whiff,

is moved to trust, delves deeper,
takes the random eloquence

as further hint and promise of a hidden treasure,
sensing the passion with which the author

originally took up the pen
then the poem may also be taken up,

endured, persevered – solved and resolved,
experienced, cherished and incorporated

to the ultimate triumph of poet and reader,
one step further towards the two becoming One.

O child of God, the poet is distinguishable by how
he says what everyone already knows.

The breaking of the tape

When I cross the line,
I'll rest from my exertions,

find shelter from the harsh weather –
so they tell me. I would fly like the wind

but I'm pulling like the others,
a crudely built, two-wheeled cart –

accumulations that tell the story of my journey.
Pausing repeatedly to sort out the merchandise;

to remind myself of who I am.
Abandon this cart and I would soon

cross the line into a territory
uninhabitable, unimaginable.

Rather than that, I cling for now to my only
home-on-wheels though it veers and bogs,

falsely identifies me,
egregiously hampers my way

toward the breaking of the tape, the rest,
the refuge, the unknown realm and reward.

O child of God, there's nowhere to go; nowhere
to get to; nowhere to run; nowhere to hide.

The silence of which You spoke

It began on a Whim, You say –
Creation merely God's game.

I try to reconcile this with what You also said –
no one suffers in vain. True freedom

(again You say) is the raison d'être
including, presumably, freedom from suffering;

freedom from the whims of God.
There is nothing to add from this

one tiny mouth looking up into the night sky.
Perhaps, this is the silence of which You spoke,

coming to the end of hope,
reasonableness, accommodation;

where love begins, but how, o Lord?
Where do I turn from here?

The earth is round; I am unable to step over its edge
and plummet into Your timeless, infinite point of view.

O child of God, blow out your candle
to experience the true essence of the night.

Nothing doing

When the linear becomes circular,
poles kiss, spark and blend;

you lean so heavily to the left it becomes right;
journey eastward, arrive in the west;

the world turns upside down.
Discovering the one bad apple is you

tainting everything you touch,
you begin assiduously to unhand –

nothing doing – at the same time
attempting fraternization

with the perfection that existed
before the original, disconcerting scratch;

attempt worldly non-participation
while in the thick of it, attending to

the sacred duty of subjugation, abdication
vital to and inclusive of

all the other duties earnestly
entrusted to your care.

O child of God, to serve others might simply be
searching your own pockets for the missing key.

The key

Once you train your will upon freedom,
only the key to the lock has value,

all other objects equally worthless,
crushed and scattered underfoot.

Ignore the ill-fitting, misshapen and static,
props of the inherent slight-of-hand

which do not internally align, similarities
meaningless and obfuscating; the entire range

from noble endeavors to fetid desires –
mere blind alleys, wastes of time.

Freedom whittled down to one tiny,
exactly notched, sharp-pointed instrument.

Once you train your will upon freedom,
only the key to the lock has value.

O child of God, the play of illusion
beguiles you everywhere you turn.

Lifeblood

One day the Friend will just up and walk away.
You'll have no choice but to follow –

by then He'll be your lifeblood. You'll be taken by surprise.
He's indulged you so long; so many lifetimes,

determining one day – enough is enough;
time to unravel the swaddling clothes.

You've led *Him*, your loyal companion,
into and through the darkest, shabbiest places;

the petty, the mean, the absurd, the perverse,
while He's kept a steady eye on you,

offering a Word now and then amidst
your constant bluster and self-justification.

One day the Friend will just up and wander away,
you having reached a certain ripeness

and you'll be forced to leave the familiar,
your loved ones and companions

who will *not* understand nor accompany
you and the Friend into the desert

beneath God's great, scattered handful of stars
to begin the long, solitary except for Him

trek home, *His* way, by *His* authority,
the sovereignty of *His* inviolable divine plan.

O child of God, He has told you from the very first:
I am your one true Friend.

In the silent holy void

Like mewing cats outside the fishmonger's
door, lovers say Your name

knowing not how else to get to the nourishment,
warmth, fresh milk and bloody entrails.

Everything comes true in the end.
No need for disputation – two blind men

arguing over the color of the sky.
There's profound wisdom in knowing

how profoundly ignorant I am;
truth coming near, I must depart

to let it manifest, light the world
except for the dark shape which is me

in the silent holy void where words fade,
lose their power to persuade or be persuaded.

To say how lovely it all is,
is to say too much.

O child of God, seal your lips about
those things of which you know so little.

Our only hope

Everyone is taking sides,
yet everyone is on the same side:

it's our vision versus God's.
Should we not give our tongues

to Him to quell, flesh to subdue,
our thunderous hearts to becalm

amidst this impossible rebellion?
Not in piety and passivity

but as a clear and dutiful course of action,
out of our compassion, such as it is,

out of our ignorance and impairment.
Out of a tenuous devotion to mercurial truth,

to set out along the narrow way, His way,
as best it might be determined, holding out faithfully

for the one great hope – our only hope –
the truth from God's perspective, God's big picture.

O child, keep your opinions to yourself.
Only silence should come from a grave.

No room for why

My monastic cell, narrow as a gate.
No room for why;

discouragement or zeal;
joy or despair; comparisons,

emotions; conviction or doubt;
stripped of everything but one

last dot of self from which to witness;
offer silent praise and prayer.

To be so tiny, my cell
must open to the sky;

have no walls; the whole
round planet for its floor

and contain in its every unfolding moment
the complete history of existence.

Narrow is my monastic cell; only long,
deep and wide enough for God.

O child of God, the scripture says
enter into a closet to pray.

The antonym for compare

There is no antonym for compare
exactly. Not even close. Imagine!

This unremarkable verb
striking at the heart of the mystery.

Oneness ever essentially intact,
apprehended only originally

and left thereafter immaculate
while the self is constructed

of comparisons amidst the aptness,
carving out a niche, divvying up the Oneness.

There is but one antonym for compare
when purely grasped, approximated,

roughly worded beyond the self,
outside the covers of any Thesaurus,

alluded to faithfully, often non-verbally,
by the mystics, one difficult, elusive,

though not quite unattainable antonym
for compare – non-existence.

O child of God, get back to the garden,
to that pristine original, incomparable view.

Speaking of God

Make Me your constant companion,
gestured Lord Meher, speaking of God.

Like an imaginary friend,
I told myself . . . but, no, not imaginary –

beyond imagination and conception.
From Aloneness God created loneliness,

the illusion of separateness, of other,
to be eventually quenched,

so love could run its course
and God could find Himself

though He was never really lost.
God alone is Real, my Lord gestured also.

O my friends! It is you and I,
His playmates, who are imaginary.

O child of God, apparently, everything is love. Love
the verb, love the noun, love the ongoing mystery of God.

Ephemera

Paper products primarily, made for short-term use,
then thrown away – tickets, paper cups,

posters, flyers, tissue, confetti.
We are that, apparently, our bodies,

personalities, our immediate human histories;
utility and sacrifice the purpose

of our very existence,
the execution and fulfillment

of some long-term ineffable
goal of the soul

with no opinions worthy of a listen
from a crushed paper cup

or complaint from a torn ticket stub –
the temporal, the discardable

in the face of the Eternal;
the creature as opposed to Creator.

O child of God, escape to a realm where time
and space, weight and gauge do not exist.

One brushstroke

He Who gifted the most gifted –
every saint, genius and artist who ever lived –

is painting every moment a meticulous portrait
of existence while nearby I stand,

standard issue brush and palette in hand.
What new theme or rectification,

what shade and stroke dare I contribute
to His underlying expertise – even to my own

small portrait and portion of the vast canvas –
when anything at all is a presumption

beyond my ability and limited view?
Surely, my judgment and opinion will only

add to the chaos and conflict of all the other countless
contributions, perspectives, advocacies and interdictions.

Surely, the less the infinitely better –
a humble acknowledgement and yielding

to the autonomy, authority, the vision,
the omniscient artistry of the Master.

O child of God, forgo the temptation to add
even one brushstroke to God's creation.

His dancing body

To appreciate God's imagination
I must stop cherishing my own.

To view His dancing body,
  I must sit still myself

and cease drawing the curtains
upon His performance, cease staging,

for my own benefit, fantastical inner choreography,
  arranged, directed and starring

  my unlimbered, imagined self.
God is dancing eternally before my eyes

  but I am unable to catch a glimpse
for the tall man standing in front of me

  for a better view himself.
No, wait. I'm the standing man

  and the only barrier
  between God and myself

is a hard, green willfulness, a failure
of consent, intention, discipline and nerve.

O child of God, we abandon heaven at a whim
to play yet another casual game of pretend.

Inconsequential

Honoring God just might require you
to become inconsequential – disappear in fact,

or failing that, a mere dust mote
floating upon the light, slanted air.

You might find it your sacred duty
to fold yourself away in a drawer

somewhere or stay mutely perched
upon some high shelf way in the back,

becoming, in only apparent ways,
one of the least, the very least.

The laudable Joshu insisted it is better
to go without even one laudable thing.

O child of God, Meher said nothing matters
(in this wicked old world) but love for God.

Deathbed

Sort of poetry by then, her juxtapositions
sans contexts, tenses, pertinence;

a dark, intuitive truth,
a poetically incoherent beauty

plumbing a deeper level if (loved) one
only knew how to listen, but one never does.

Wrapped up in who she thought she was
and should have been, tried earnestly to be

or not to be, exhausting after a while the listener,
telling her last minute truth from the bed

of a murmuring brook
and really what is there left to say or hear

after a lifetime of chatter and love,
dutiful endeavor, compulsive volatility?

That was her poetry, too, largely incoherent
to everyone around even to herself

and yet, as I have suggested,
strangely brave, beautiful and worthy.

O child of God, how better to greet the mystery
than with humble bewilderment and incoherence?

God's vision

Consider for a moment the fidelity of God's vision –
indiscriminate laws in unyielding self-adherence

intended to convince us every holy moment
we are who we seem to be – a life independent

with a real past and future other than the moment,
other than Him, other than That.

Down to the infinitesimal minutia,
fashioned and nailed

with a luminous, transcendent artistry
so His game of love's hide and seek

might be heartily, earnestly, desperately
engaged in good faith; meeting us

everywhere we turn, as we must
ultimately meet Him everywhere in return,

the adventure, the miraculous excursion worthy
of our ultimate ecstatic triumph and defeat.

O child of God, consider for a moment God's vision,
His wondrously intricate faithfulness and care.

My practice

A salesman keeps knocking
on my door, not easily dissuaded.

My practice is to pretend I'm not at home,
purchasing never again, as I have lifelong,

fading, fraying things that sate and jade,
shatter, wither and pale,

always less than advertised,
ripe for plunder, loss or neglect.

His persistency echoes now
through the near empty house,

like a hearth fire or the grandfather clock
in the parlor, joining its natural

ticks, murmurs, creaks and groans.
At some point, the salesman will go away,

the fire die out, the clock run down.
No one then truly will be at home.

O child of God, truth comes not
from accumulation but gentle subduction.

I can't begin to tell you

A peace symbol on a faded day-glo poster
tacked to the old shed's raw interior wall,

thorns worming through the cracks;
baby food jar lids screwed

to the underside of a shelf
holding rusted bolts, nails, screws,

gaskets and washers
someone once had faith

would one day fasten and secure
something of value, utility

like the bucket hanging high from a winch,
pooled water in the well's bottom,

twisted by the breeze at rope's end.
Peace at last. Peace at last. Peace at last.

I get it wrong implying simple abandonment,
disuse, a quelling, thwarting but not quite

and words are all I have
even as I have lost faith in words.

I can't begin to tell you, nor could you hear,
how misguided I've come to believe

are all our various quests
and human endeavors.

O child of God, you cry out for peace
while unwilling to walk the necessary path.

What is given

Accept only what is given –
I think I've learned that much;

rather than what is coveted
though what is coveted will be given

another day in one form or another.
This is the great circle which binds us

to the center and indicates
only slightly a pathway of escape.

Virtue might become in time a matter
of etiquette, tact, reciprocity, gratitude.

Accept only what is given in the natural flow
of a humble, illumined, obedient life.

O child of God, that which is heaven-sent
leads to lasting blessings and unfathomable peace.

Get lost

Unless you get lost on purpose,
Ryokan by moonlight wrote

you won't get this far –
rugged path through a deep forest

among towering mountains,
a steep glen shielded by mist.

But if I plunge into the thick
of my perplexity, eschew my bearings,

redirect my vigilance, trek the path
unconcerned where it leads, I might just

climb in deeply enough to come upon
an abandoned hut, a patch of woods

where once he hunted mushrooms;
the spring where he drew water;

sit and view the moon left in the window
like a congratulatory note.

O child of God, the world is telling you
to get lost. When will you oblige?

Peeking over the edge

I light a tea candle in my room
before a photograph of the Tomb

adorned with dried Samadhi roses
and assorted other gleaned icons

relevant almost exclusively to me
in a round red shallow, bowl-shaped

votive vase, the flame at once
strong, high, bright;

shadows thrown about the room.
I lower my eyes and gently invite

truth, surrender, Oneness, God
into my prayer chamber.

Much later, I raise my eyes again,
prepare to rise upon my muscles.

The flame is low, meek by then,
barely peeking over the edge,

floating humbly, improbably
in the spent fuel of limpid wax.

My room is dark again; vast,
intimate, evidentially divine.

O child of God, to experience the Everything
allow yourself to be reduced to nothing.

Archery practice

Before the effortless –
pure effort is required, quiet aim.

Arrow in the fingers' cradle,
drawn bow and string;

settled breath and mind, attentiveness,
guidance, a necessary tension,

the brief distortion of a purpose.
Escaping the pinch – letting it fly and float,

precise intentions left behind.
Send it on its way;

beyond the grasp
toward the gathered central mark.

O child of God, before the effortless –
pure effort, quiet aim.

The evidentiary truth

In the forest is a house made of forest –
stone, wood, clay. Nothing in it is false.

Thickly overgrown, scarcely can it be seen.
Things are just as they are –

appropriate, timeless, undiminished.
Only the furnishings change their positions.

People visit but most often
walk through to the back

and out again into the weather,
the wilds – unimpressed.

They have come to the woods
for their dreams; to put down elaborate roots.

They want nothing to do
with the evidentiary truth of this house.

Only a returning few ever discover
the hidden beauty of such an austerity.

O child of God, rest in that sturdy shelter,
beyond any notions of rescue.

The excursion

A dust-shape drifting through drifts of snow
down a worn path to temporary shelter.

Escape by plunging into life –
this is the practice given to me.

Not fanciful ideas of life –
but walking out onto the lake,

the ice thinner the farther I get from shore,
as I glide and slip into next-to-nothing

in this floating world timeless and invulnerable.
When I break through at last, they tell me,

suddenly I will become nothing and everything
at the same propitious moment but right now

the excursion is simply everything,
nothing and enough; more than enough.

O child of God, who is there to hear you
above the wind's icy roar?

A holy partaking

They send me photographs,
friends traveling the world –

colorful glossies; include
a note of their adventures.

No missives may be posted
from the realms I explore.

I just sit. Or tour my small house
and yard. Do routine chores.

Enjoy quiet conversations with old friends.
I work on my flexibility; equanimity.

Read; compose; prepare simple meals.
The beauty of these ordinary happenings

I cannot reciprocally send their way
to fall upon busy, itinerant eyes and ears;

too subtle for photographs and words,
for the established premises, patterns,

constructs and commonality
of human communication.

O child of God, each morsel is a holy partaking
from the table which has been laid before us.

Flatfoot

Feed me something that sticks
to my ribs; fills my belly.

Pour me a cup that'll buckle my knees.
Let me hear shouts of Jesus

among the wooden pews.
I want to flatfoot to a fiddle tune,

boots scraping a raw plank floor.
Daintiness is for tatting doilies.

Utter me verses blunt and thick,
rough as a cob. My house is the one

where my grandfather entered the world,
made of chopped-down timber, daubed mud,

a stone and mortar hearth. It's where I first
look for rudimentary comfort and warmth,

to find the treasure I was promised
lies buried somewhere beneath.

O child of God, there are as many paths to God
as there are souls in the universe.

The avenue to no-self

Take heed, the Buddhists say,
to keep the mirror bright, dust-free.

Or stated in another tradition –
become, as best we might, dust ourselves

at the Master's feet –
self-effacement; mastery in servitude.

Kishizawa Ian was renowned
for his willful nature – a tiger,

self-proclaimed, as a young monk.
As an old abbot – a pussycat;

a callous upon his forehead
from incessant bowing –

his obstinacy turned upon itself
to eliminate his greatest impediment.

O child of God, a dust grain is the Ocean drop,
the avenue to no-self, Oneness, Love Divine.

Stray dog

For lifetimes I've turned up my nose
at the gift God offers –

a stray dog sniffing the hand
of a stranger it dares not trust.

Serving two masters breaks the world in two.
To seek is to ignore what is already here.

This is the moment, every moment,
to receive God's gift – no other.

Whatever I desire is a rejection
of what I am given,

the one true gift exchanged for an impure,
fleeting reward of my own imagination.

O child of God, Meher said,
I am your one true friend.

The lonely truth

That which has brought me here,
I must give up;

that which has served me well,
protected me;

which has grown into my skin,
become part of me, part of my life;

that which I have clutched
so bitterly for comfort and refuge,

which has always understood me
when no one else could,

is now keeping me from the heights
to which I must attain.

That which I thought of always
as my most loyal companion,

I must abandon, to find the lonely truth
of who I am and that which it is not.

O child of God, the lonely truth, it is said,
leads beyond companionship to union.

The formless pitch

When the stars go out at last,
God will fold up the tent,

His performance over for a while.
We can all have a good rest.

The catch is that each star
must burn itself out deliberately,

voluntarily, against all good judgment,
accepting its own inherent emptiness

rather than the roaring flame
of its separate existence.

It will happen – it is foretold;
as one by one the innumerable,

temporal stars give way to the original face of God
made visible again in the formless pitch.

O child of God, you speak of stars while failing
to grasp the immediate at your fingertips.

Salt grain

Today the ocean is rough; yesterday it was serene.
I no longer hope it to be one way or the other.

My shouting above its roar, flailing about in the surf,
my quiet prayers ashore leave no lasting impression.

There is a way of sorts – a footpath through the dunes
that widens upon a rock-solid perch with a panoramic view

where I might sit dispassionately; partake of the salt air,
the siren music, become drenched in its erratic spray –

at a distance – breathing room –
until that distance dissolves

in the salt grain of an ocean drop
joining without boundaries or objections

its mighty eternal, infinite
storm and calm, ebb and flow.

O child of God, the Ocean calls you.
Work to get more than your feet wet.

Adapting the words of Shunryu Suzuki –

God is not something to find.
God is something you are.

The Way is not something to figure out.
The Way is something to express.

Let's sit down here in the cypress shade.
In this quiet dust take up our instruments.

And we will ask no questions;
take no measurements

but learn to play and sing –
not to express ourselves but to express God.

O child of God, Meher said you are looking
for something you have never lost.

Untapped reservoir

When I had nothing better to do,
nothing else going on, I would reach out

to the Lord of the universe. Little ol' me.
And, of course, when troubles arose

I was always right there tugging at His coat.
Just in case it was true.

One day, down a lonely path,
through a flurry of leaves,

I saw Him ahead of me, plainly beckoning,
inviting me to His house for tea.

If you're not too busy, He said.
If you've nothing better to do.

Tears, held back a lifetime,
wet my cheeks, the sleeves of my coat –

cleansing rivers coming from the broken,
untapped reservoir within my chest.

O child of God, wherever fate takes you
never forget the mercy of the Lord of Mercy.

Made of ocean

Maybe I'm made of ocean,
having always considered myself an island,

the probable cause of so much suffering,
assuming this loose but utile

congregation of aggregates
constitutes a trustworthy place to stand –

solid, apart, enduring; ever looking outward
in the wrong direction.

Maybe I'm made of Infinite Ocean,
no room for this tiny dab of me anywhere;

with lonely suffering the sole root and result
of my imaginary, separate existence.

O child of God, Meher spoke of the Ocean of Love.
Take the plunge and drown.

Hitch a ride

Viewing the moon's rise and flight
cater-corner across the backyard,

rearranging the shadows and reflections
as it goes. Only so many more left to catch

this time around, like a giant pearl
rising from the green wood.

Take me with you, I want to shout.
If I could hitch a ride, sit atop its soft light

making its rounds, illuminating, befriending,
without preference or intention;

always up there to fade into, to lift up
with one strong arm and plant me on its back

so we might leisurely patrol together
the heavens with a quiet non-attachment

toward the busy, frightful workings
of this illusory, binding world below.

O child of God, ride the moon that never rises,
never sets, neither waxes nor wanes.

The author of chaos

At the center of attention, I'm the author of chaos –
things ever-shifting outside myself and within –

rise and fall, come and go; strong winds afoot;
east and west never to meet; time marching on.

But when I make it to the periphery,
a hush falls over existence; a timelessness

comes to the ever-changing scene.
Things settle into a pristine order;

beauty rises on the wind; subtleties
become obvious and celebrated.

Moving from the center to the periphery
the center disappears – God has my back.

I'm no longer surrounded;
the past forever behind me,

returned to that sustaining,
mighty arena of the Unborn.

When I lose my grip on the periphery I am told,
I'll go hurtling off into Oneness.

O child of God, the great illusion, Meher said,
is that you have ever been separate from the One.

Yonder

You might have to leave your home
and go yonder; leave your loved ones,

the land of your birth and go yonder;
for the sake of family and friends,

go yonder, yonder, alone,
across the wide meadow;

nothing romantic or remarkable,
just the quiet unfolding of fate

and the winding of the path into the hills
from which comes your strength.

O beloved Lord, you might ask,
or silently require of the impersonal Way –

open Your gate – for nothing else matters
because everything else matters;

because ephemeral beauty, truth and virtue
are beautiful and virtuous and true;

because Love is majestic and Its own validation.
You might have to leave home and go yonder,

yonder, yonder on a singular path
until God and It, the Life and the Way,

are no longer out of grasp
but in your hands and under your feet at last.

O child of God, lonely is the path of Love
and impersonal the Buddha's Way.

That old zen saw

Ride your horse, goes that old zen saw,
along the edge of a sword, observing calmly –

to one side, the outer forms;
to the other, the inner realm.

Ride between, grasping neither, clean
as a whistle, not a hoof print left behind.

Bodhidharma counseled outside –
no engagement, no entanglements,

no arousal or intervention.
Inside – no indulgences, no rejection,

no denial or shying away. Settle down
where there is no settling down –

in the saddle of the horse,
along the sword's edge; ride on,

a part of neither, caught not in the dust-mire
of the outer nor the seductive fantasy of the inner.

O child of God, you are, apparently,
the whole of both and more.

Cul-de-sac

Easier these latter years to be content
with everyday chores, knowing

the mind's once distracting visions
come to naught at best, heartache more;

that flailing away at ourselves redeems not
the future, serving only to entrench

even deeper the recalcitrant self.
All life's conflicts are resolved here –

in the sparrow's wing, the hand on the plow,
the hammer of the bell, the eternally shifting now.

Consuming a simple breakfast,
strolling the April garden, a tune

sung in the quiet dusk – a cul-de-sac,
not a crossroads of judgments, decisions;

regrets and desires, realized or thwarted.
No running out of time here.

Thoroughly encountering the mundane,
the mundane becomes unworldly,

extraordinary, no sacrifice –
enough, enough, more than enough.

O child of God, whatsoever thy hand findeth to do,
rest assured, it has just left the fingertips of God.

The work that must be done

It appears the loneliness
will become almost unbearable.

Sorted out along the way
by unidentifiable voices,

stripped of being the soldier
you always prided yourself on being;

nothing at all dramatic –
just the bleak, quiet, tedious,

bare-boned loneliness
of the immeasurable, unmarked terrain,

once you get down to it –
the work that must be done.

No one to share your trials, triumphs,
failures or whether the mission bears fruit,

not the least recognition given
except from God, perhaps, if He so deigns.

O child of God, your every thought and utterance
binds you to the delusion under which you suffer.

The existence of Existence

Destined are we everyone
someday to be awed and enamored

in our lives at last solely
by the existence of Existence,

crushing and outshining all other
colorful, binding seductions

of this natural spectacle – the frailty
and fraud of our being the human creature.

Returned to that long-veiled, original,
invulnerable point of view,

continuously and only then
shall we marvel in everything

we do and sense – each moment
face to face, toe to toe with the Creator –

marvel at the existence of Existence,
our lives at once profound and ordinary,

meaningless and sublime;
empty, artless and full to the brim.

O child of God, snap your pen in two;
let the ink flow like blood.

Regarding the mystery

This language which I do not speak,
lately comes to me by way

of the great mystery no one comprehends
and so I remain silent mostly – better not

to understand, nor speak, *this* wisdom
than the human, understandable points

held forth daily, apparently far from any truth –
the constant parroting of love and mercy,

courage and virtue without the least authenticity
or reality behind the uttered words.

So perhaps better mere silence, refraining
from complicity, regarding the mystery

and its tenacious beauty, so terrible
and unimaginable – this Word, this God

unutterable on every human tongue,
this purported Oneness,

this homecoming along the inexhaustible,
unfathomable, inexpressible Way.

O child of God, you regret your silence
and then you regret your speech.

For Him also

Time apparently non-existent before God
premiered His kaleidoscopic Creation,

breaking Himself into pieces – near and far,
large and small, lover and Beloved;

space emerging with time like conjoined twins;
color not existing until He broke

the Light of Himself over His own knee;
movement not existing until the fragments

swam to each other, embraced and kissed.
Separating Himself; leaving us

to make our own sense of His strewn
bits, textures, shapes and colors.

For us all apparently to exist and know ourselves
but for Him also, in relation to us,

for how could Love ever Be without a lover
and how could God ever exist without a witness?

O child of God, the One became two,
says the old man, then three, then ten thousand.

This illusory fleck

You might be given a choice one day – art or truth.
Surely, you'll drop the attachment then

to language, inspiration, conceptual thinking;
take a bite out of that red bright, indisputable apple,

a mouth too full to speak. Or in shrieks of laughter,
ankle-deep wade the mountain stream.

Like a holy roller on the pinewood floor,
bewilderment and incoherence your worship,

your life's duty – not from any ecstasy
but from piety, sobriety and humility.

Wave from the flowing bridge; engage
in the marvelous activity of doing nothing

to understand and change this illusory fleck
you, as a person of words, have tenaciously explored

and so patently, obsessively, for yourself
and others, attempted to navigate and explain.

O child of God, if you are ever given the chance –
drop the words; kneel in awestruck silence.

Until purity regains its footing

I keep my body immobile
like the leg of an old pier.

I want the stream to run clear
and if that's not possible,

the opacities to be mere
insubstantial tricks of light,

or barring that, discolorations
of the stream itself, ever-flowing and untainted.

And when the dirt is ruffled from the bottom,
I want my body to remain stationary

until purity regains its footing.
That's what this is – this sitting here

quietly folded – letting the stream of existence
pour unimpeded over whoever it is I am.

O child of God, to no longer know who you are
is a gift in kind from the great Unknowable.

A dark, narrow place

Go into a closet to pray, Jesus said,
not just to thwart a pious display –

but to go to God is to go alone,
into a dark, narrow place –

that being the reason so few venture toward the Divine.
We hug and gabble of brotherhood and spiritual links,

but if you are not laid low,
lonely as the day you were born,

unacceptable to the many,
you have no chance at all

of securing an audience with the One
Who is shy of crowds and flattering strangers.

Strait is the gate, quoting Jesus again,
and narrow (as a grave) is the way.

Best to pare down, pilgrim; get lonely,
odd and disconnected, rather

than dressing yourself in virtue,
hiding among the bowed, religious crowd –

the sure way to speciousness,
death, rejection and return.

O child of God, when you address pilgrims
you must surely always include yourself.

Disassociation

Oneness is attained (apparently)
by disassociation from the illusion of self.

These deftly orbiting aggregates
don't mean the hub of self exists

as more than a not-quite-arbitrarily
selected point in space, a makeshift home

where we might hang our cognizant hats
until we're ready to walk away from it all.

There is only one attachment to break
(which propagates all others) –

Oneness is attained by disassociation!
O pilgrim, honor your name –

quit the symbiotic partnership
that binds you to one spot

and venture forth, toward
whatever there may be beyond.

O child of God, infinity has no center.
To what do you daily tether yourself?

Green pastures

Jesus left the ninety-nine to find the one lost
and maybe that one lost, if its story be told,

was the only one *not* left behind, but truly
found, scooped up in the Savior's arms.

You have to get lost to be found, I think.
You have to lose the flock,

go out on your own two shaky legs
into the dark fields, trading all there evidently is

for all that might be, short of any real evidence.
Thinking maybe of finding your own way if you must,

but not really caring anymore,
just tired to the bone of the painful,

the false and fleeting and at that moment
of utter despair and defeat, maybe

you get lifted up, or you die trying – and perhaps,
you get carried away, led – not back into the fold but safely

released onto those metaphorical green pastures
to fatten you up before your next adventure.

O child of God, to escape the counterfeit,
surround yourself with the Mystery.

Out of earshot

You've been given enough words, said my Lord,
but in truth, I have been long content with words

    measuring my appraised worth against
    distant utterings and their echoes –

sound waves crashing upon an empty shore;
quotations taken always from someone else's book.

I have sought lifelong the living among the dead,
    surrounding myself like a consensus

    with cardboard and paper gravestones
    as I pray so touchingly, beseech so effetely

    for a truth that was never there for me
    or has long since fled.

So very long it has taken me to hear it –
    truth doesn't enter through the ear.

O child of God, seek the truth out of earshot –
    in the cavern of your chest.

The shelter

There's a shelter, rain on the roof,
wind in the trees the only sounds.

And your own breath.
Let the storm outside rage.

Hard to find and keep, this shelter –
a hidden niche in a valley

deep with loneliness, habit and fear;
false assurances, reckless promises;

the urge for artificial light.
In this shelter the new life begins,

a different journey – the outward,
the known discarded – trusting someOne,

someThing other than yourself,
shrugging off the weight of the world

and reaching out a hand
to be led wherever truth may take you.

A small room where you trust
because you no longer care

and give yourself over to the steadfast shelter
of the only permanence you have ever met.

O child of God, Meher Baba said,
take your stand on the truth within.

Paper tiger

At some point, the path becomes self-verifying,
its own guide; with easily discernible boundaries.

At some turn in the road, annihilation
portends freedom, the right thing to do;

the only treasure to give. Every self-assertion
becomes transparent and repugnant;

every question identified as the dodge,
deflection that it is; every guile pathetic,

the crumbling castle, feet of clay;
the paper tiger insufficient in its roar.

At some point, the arrows fail to penetrate
and the clamor of the crowd, the invalidation

of the enchanted, the drunken and oblivious
become palm leaves under donkey hooves,

aiding the pilgrim to wend his the way.
At some arrival, you swing through a door

and though you weave in and out for a time thereafter,
losing your grip and footing, there's no turning back,

no way to remain that which you no longer
seem to be and have lifelong been.

O child of God, the path never gets easier
but dedication brings surety and daring.

The One Who never leaves

O pilgrim! We come into this world,
grow up, grow old and depart, or so it seems.

This existence into which we are tossed
stays and we move on, or so it seems.

But a few have come over the ages to say:
I am the One Who never leaves!

I am the One Who never leaves!
They come to say: I am with you always

and you and I are One. O pilgrim,
we are the One Who never leaves!

Pilgrim is a misnomer – We are the One
Who never goes anywhere. Never fades away.

We are the still river the bridge flows through.
Ceaselessly around *Us*, the stationary One,

illusion arises, flourishes, then is destroyed –
again and again, ephemeral, temporal,

defined by duality, by space and time; ceaselessly
it flows around the One eternal existence which is Us.

Illusion comes and goes, comes and goes –
around the Creator, the Observer,

the pure Consciousness,
the One Who never leaves.

O child of God, maya is the apparently erroneous
notion that you are born, you live and you die.

Perfect servitude

Mastery in servitude, Meher said.
Liberation attained by becoming

the perfect slave – sitting raptly
at the feet of the Master,

the slave's whole being ever attuned
and attentive to the Lord's whim;

personal concerns and desires
revealed to be indulgences and distractions

to be shooed away like bothersome flies.
To sit in meditation is simply

to sit at the Master's feet,
nothing to achieve but emptiness,

perfect servitude, the relinquishment
of a personal will. Daily loss upon loss.

To meditate is to surrender the false
to the true, the fragment to the whole –

to surrender our misshapen, fraudulent identities
which underwrite all the calamities of the world.

O child of God, maya is the ignorance
of Who you really are.

The journey that never was

A kind of exile you are now in
unable to walk the same aisles,

sit in the same pew as others,
hands folded quietly in your lap.

Your eccentricity showing through
the burst seams of your threadbare coat.

You've dropped the things you're supposed to
care about; your interests few. Old friends

(who never really were) have drifted away
while *you* to some measure have left behind

your loved ones, for their sake,
to go searching for the eternal connection.

You follow the flow of an uncharted river
as you push toward oblivion

and wonder when this latest rug
will be pulled out from under your feet.

It doesn't really matter anymore.
It's all a part of the journey that never was.

O child of God, should it be surprising
that the new life is nothing like the old?

The green promise

A wedding in Cana and the water is turned to wine.
Jesus saving the best for last.

An exchange of vows and then transfiguration –
on the tongues of true believers, water is wine.

A double-yoked life then
and a conception: an offspring –

the child you must become, father to the man.
An exchange of vows, a green promise

and a sweet new crush after the ripening
and the best saved for last.

O honored guest, through these daunting times
let us drink to the green promise,

the sweet crush, the saving
of the best for last, the best for last.

O child of God, to reach the Oneness
get drunk enough to obliterate all boundaries.

Our guaranteed return

The world's a nothingness and God's a myth,
Francis said. *You have shown me this.*

You have shown me . . .
setting Francis to roam the nothingness,

singing 'neath that boundless starry dome,
singing words awaiting, awaiting the flood

of the Word of words; Francis lost,
a mote in a dust whorl, left behind

by the Reality to Which the myth alludes.
A billion years to get his heart in tune,

ready to sing the Real song. O Francis,
I am with you. I am with you on the dusty plain,

'neath the spangled bell jar dome, singing,
singing and waiting for the Lord to take us home.

O child of God, let the longing pierce your songs
with the sweetness of our guaranteed return.

Elder beauty

Older now, I see it - the elder beauty,
the younger comeliness

ghostly about faces and bones,
the eyes, particularly. Courage there also –

ah! the beauty of courage –
and patience that has volunteered

in our well-kept gardens. Perseverance, too,
and the consent of loss with so much gain,

continuing into our personal future
and that future's ultimate demise.

Older now, I see the flesh give way
to the ancient, shining soul.

It shone through, Mani said
of Baba's divinity. *It shone through.*

I see it; I see its subtle emanations
in unexpected glimmers –

the elder, ethereal beauty I could glimpse
only rarely in my youth.

O child of God, what a bounty you have received.
And the Beloved is not through with you yet!

Call His name

The darning of a coat,
a pulling on the oars;

the sawing of a casket plank,
a bell's tolling;

a calling bird in the green wood;
its flap of wings across the sky;

the knocking on a door,
the chimes of a clock,

singsong, singsong, say His name –
Meher Meher Meher Meher . . .

sewing us up; sewing ourselves
to His silence, with each stitch

more inseverable, each stroke, toll,
call and flap; chime, each knock

upon heaven's solid, heavy door;
calling to the One inside.

O child of God, call His name
until it sings in your veins.

This empty cup

Enough for me, this empty cup.
With Your own lips

You have drained it of the world's wine
and left a promise –

the distant scent and stain of Your own wine.
Each day I enfold my hands

around its rough clay and murmur a prayer,
lift to my lips its soured nothingness

to taste the exasperatingly faint
intimation of *Your* nothingness.

And setting it down, abandon again
the world's shimmering images,

imaginings and intoxications,
its brief, bitter sweetness.

For me, enough (is enough) this empty cup,
until its clay mouth is crushed again,

its hollowness filled with debris,
buried in the earth's whirling wheel

for yet another stab at Your ethereal lightness,
assured Oneness, Your sobering, holy wine.

O child of God, the world is mad with drink.
Rejoice in your disaffected indifference.

Salvage and salvation

Over a lifetime, in my own way,
I've been moving toward You –

in darkness, by fits and starts, studying warily
the scriptures, claims, promises,

attuning myself to some real
or imagined inner guide.

Here and there at various speeds and coming
now and then to a complete stop,

wondering which bedimmed fork to take,
or why go on with such a lonely, desperate search.

But only very recently, the sun has peeked
over the heaving edge of the world

enough for me to see that I have
ever been trekking the vast deck of a ship

as You return me surely, safely,
irrevocably to home port.

I'm leaning on the rail right now,
taking in the breaking sun, the salt wind

and wondering what I might do, if anything,
to aid in my own salvage and salvation.

O child of God, learn your ship duties;
prepare well for the immeasurable voyage ahead.

A spot of fiction

I glimpsed the truth of the apparent world –
a reflection on the surface of a lake,

a shimmering ostensibility
floating thinly above the dark drowning

and the deep stillness that supports all the seeming.
The self itself a trick of light, moving as the sun moves,

no more when the sun goes under;
a spot of fiction from which to center

the illusory play of light, color and movement
as the sun journeys the inexplicable sky.

Every chance I get, I pay strict heed now
to this dream excursion

and to Your timely reminders to turn away,
turn away at every opportunity

from the apparent, the artificial, the fictitious surface
to leave myself possible and open for That which is beneath.

O child of God, hold out for the Reality
solely because it is Real.

Not quite a poem

To denounce someone, the first thing
given up is humility. Elementary physics and geometry –

I must elevate myself to look down upon others.
Not telling anyone to refrain, mind you –

make your own decisions –
just pointing out the price that is always there.

I crane my neck looking up at the mountain.
From the top, I might see equally in all directions.

Knowing intuitively I have not the strength, the discipline,
the courage, the expertise to complete the climb,

I slip on my backpack and start up the rocky trail.
Better to die on the slopes than back at camp.

So many people in the world,
I'm sure they can do without me

adding my own brand of stridency
to the din of blind opinion.

Whatever you guys decide is fine with me,
knowing it will be the Whim and Will of God.

O child of God, you have paid the price,
lost your humility, writing and reciting this not quite a poem.

Rumi's field

Rumi's field – beyond ideas
of wrong-doing and right-doing –

is not so far away.
I'm running my hand

along the top of its fence. It was never
a great distance to traverse

but a coming to a halt, turning the handle
and swinging wide the gate.

No one to meet me there but myself,
unencumbered of my knothole view.

Ah, to lie down burden-free
in that long grass with the wildflower scent

in the sun-warmed field, upheld
and surrendered like a body on the ocean face

letting the current move me where it will.
It's so near, just over the fence,

and I won't leave without a fight
or find a way through its summoning gate.

O child of God, not far away nor far in the future.
Seek advice from your constant Companion.

Up the pike

Looking over my shoulder,
I can't say I remember

a crossroads or even a fork in the path
with a free choice of which way to go.

This is how it seems to me this far up the pike –
as if the word freedom has never been applicable.

Thus considerably more agreeable
is the premise of my own necessary annihilation

when removed from my shoulders,
its particulars locked into inevitability;

convinced there never was
an autonomous self – an existence apart –

from which to freely choose or reject
my obliterating surrender to the One.

O child of God, the concept of freedom applies
neither to Illusion nor the Infinite-Eternal.

Monk's garden

Somehow it's good to know I haven't a prayer.
Like old Job – no say-so in the winding up,

the unwinding of my own affairs.
God is in the details and I'm merely one,

hoping to serve by a studious abstention.
I weed my monk's garden, encouraged

by the yield of abeyance and abrogation.
The old urgency has deserted my legs and lungs

in mid-stride and the pace, this late
in the game, has slowed considerably;

enough to where it's more comfortable
to take His hand and follow His lead;

relinquish a bit more the irresistible
compulsion and illusion of plotting my own course.

O child of God, settle in as best you might
under the vast foot of the elephant.

A divine opportunity

When the razing began, I thought
the garden walls would go first,

(romantic that I am) – a flood of love
upending my neglected grounds,

enabling a long-hoped-for hidden eden.
But You began with the house, my shelter,

dismantling it down to the bare slab,
me too numb to foresee or care anymore

what subsequent half-structure will take its place,
simply trusting it will be apt.

This ruination holds neither hope nor shame.
Like any other death, of spirit or flesh,

it's merely a naked opportunity for something
to be built beyond the outmoded purpose of the original
structure.

O child of God, approach your undoing
with the God-given composure of faith.

Persistent honesty

The monk's cell is bare except for solitude.
Plenty of that which I have shouldered

outside these walls my whole life –
marked by it, encapsulated, enisled.

Is it everyone, I wonder, or just me?
Much like I wonder if there is not

at the heart of everyone, where the self stands
naked before its own illegitimacy,

an inherent antipathy yoked with a desperate longing
for that which is True; that which is Whole –

the solitude of the monk's cell
and our impenetrable selves

merely the lonely, persistent honesty
of every beating human heart.

O child of God, the self is built
of fallacy, reclusion and alarm.

Estranged hearts

Those latter years of Meherazad seclusions –
the perfect silence You kept, inside and out –

to the point of having the mandali
shoo away the cawing crows.

A manonash silence –
one hundred percent work completed,

Your gift across time and space,
the boundaries of logic, flesh and mind.

And with Your silence,
all the real things given by You,

received by Your lovers,
manifesting years later –

offering more than admonitions,
the unkept precepts, tattered scriptures.

Your silence penetrating where words
are too cumbersome to pass through,

to invade and awaken estranged hearts
from their ancient slumber.

O child of God, be assured your own silence
is heard and shared by the silence of Meher.

The heart's ears

For a taste of Heaven, a sip of the raw proof,
   settle under a spire where they sing

of pearly gates, the breath of flowers,
   the holy fountain, amaranthine bowers,

your heart's ears to hear and follow.
Miss not the chance in your Sunday suit

to scramble up the mountainside,
   lift to your lips the waters of Union

as clearly and truly as might be
brought to this realm by human voices.

And if you cannot yet believe, o seeker,
   tear at the obstructions stopping up

your heart's ears, the sort of
small-minded, literal logic and reasons

that doom the soul again and again
to the ancient rounds of birth and death.

O child of God, listen to both music and silence
with the same transcendent ears of the heart.

The one gauge

Just love Me, my Lord said.
Perhaps His only request.

Love for love's sake – without hope
of gain, advantage or favor.

There is a dearth in my heart of such love.
And fear growing rank.

The best I might give, Lord, is gratitude
which I have come by honestly –

in response to Your kindness.
Gratitude for the life I've led

and for the life You led.
Gratitude for a family and my imperfect love

for all their human beauty.
And gratitude especially for You, Lord,

being indeed my only source of truth,
however ill at times I receive it,

the one gauge in this troubled dreamscape
I trust and cling to, without which

I would have long ago become untethered,
alone, overwhelmed and lost.

O child of God, not knowing what love is,
how can you judge your lack of it?

A journeyman's hands

Francis said as stone into dust –
long to be crushed!

The duty of the lover is to sing
his Beloved's gift of song;

articulate the pain in the distance
between mouth and Ear;

between heart and Heart
solely for the Beloved's

amusement and entertainment.
Sing, o lover! a reminder of the day,

when you'll bear no song,
no mouth and no need of one –

being, at last, the unutterable Truth.
That's the promise Francis clutched

in a journeyman's hands;
sang with wine-bright eyes

through an old man's broken throat –
a gift for his Beloved and for His lovers

gathered near and soon to follow
that bowed, dusty codger into oblivion.

O child of God, begin your apprenticeship as a lover
under that old Aussie ploughman stone mason poet.

Poem of apology

To everyone in this lifetime
whose path I've crossed –

I ask forgiveness:
I have lacked humility.

Not my only sin, of course,
but perhaps the most pernicious,

the root of all others,
for it has kept me

from loving you
the way you should be loved,

the way I dream about,
the way my Lord advocates,

the way that would draw us all
nearer to our divine inheritance.

Take this poem as a timorous,
though heartfelt opportunity

for me to seek your forgiveness,
unable ever to ask you face to face.

O child of God, the one reduced to true humility
is no longer there to be forgiven.

You Who Are

You always are. I'm struck by the beautiful
absurdity of that; its marvelous audacity.

My thoughts, trailing to and fro in time
get lost in a whirling miasma,

my every construct dissipating
at the far reaches of possibility.

But even in holding myself apart,
crying out in my own brief flare,

I take remarkable comfort
in the ill-defined notion that Someone –

You, at least You, (You You You)
always were, always are and always will be.

My heart leaps for You, for Your singularity,
for Your unimaginable existence: You . . . Who Are.

O child of God, when will you stop examining truth
through the blurry loupe of your own intellect?

Swiss army knife

Everyone has been issued a Swiss army knife
but lately I've discovered there's one blade

few people ever use,
deeming it useless or superfluous.

It's the only blade I ever use –
the blade for which I, perhaps incorrectly,

assume the knife was made – the one that probes,
pares down, whittles away; the one that digs,

challenges and yet is also the one that spoon feeds.
Persistent use has kept my blade shiny, honed

while most of the others never trouble
to pry theirs open. This is not a boast ...

or if it is, it's an oddly forlorn, collateral one.
I simply move about most everywhere,

not knowing any other way to live,
out of loneliness, fear, curiosity, discontent,

blade in hand and observe how it interacts
with the world and what it uncovers.

O child of God, the Beloved supplies
each lover uniquely with the tools required.

The death of desire

Desire only to be desireless, my Lord said.
But that's the story of my quest!

Unwittingly, I have lifelong pursued
the death of desire (and failed).

In every stage and phase, every permutation,
I have endeavored by strict indulgence to slay

once and for all that indefatigable dragon
that keeps roaring back from the ashes;

to quench its insatiable voracity;
to quell its constant fire which has solely

fueled my quest, to rest (at last) eternally
in that ice-coated, God-promised peace.

Fashion me a sword, o Lord,
to ultimately slay that dragon,

driving it deeply into the exact
hidden, sweet, deadly spot.

O child of God, love is the absence of desire;
when the pendulous heart finally settles into rest.

Diaphaneity

There's no choice, He said.
I'm all you've got.

Forgo the negotiations –
you've no collateral.

Forgo the calculations.
You're in over your head.

There are no inducements
to any sort of compromise.

It's the falsity of yourself or the truth of no self;
this apparent, ephemeral insubstantiality

or the resolute putting of it to a stop.
Grab hold of Me, He said, or go around

(around and around) trying to stuff
into your empty pockets fistfuls of diaphaneity.

O child of God, the dream can't be grasped.
All you have to hold on to is Meher Baba.

Leading with my chin

As an old man now, I aspire
to be somebody who can take a punch –

not a speed bag's wobbly pummeling,
mind you, but a stolid heavy bag full of grit,

eye-bolted solidly through a ceiling beam
and not in some gymnasium for anyone

to try but maybe a garage or cellar,
collecting dust in the corner but still intact.

Somebody who can take a punch if need be
and absorb the blow from any angle,

any adversary and not be moved
more than an inch or two off dead center,

returning quickly to a perfect plumbness.
I'd be going through life then leading with my chin,

not from haughtiness or spunk
but with poise and a quiet faith,

bearing the blows of whatever
rough-housing opponents may cross my path.

To be somebody who can take a punch,
take a punch, take a punch and not hit back.

O child of God, aspire to the love that allows
an innocent man to turn his cheek for just one more blow.

The ancient discrepancy

The sun rises, it seems, from the heart
spilling onto a sky bright sails of hope,

invariably to founder upon the day's living reefs;
tired old bindings to be sure, but ever-new tendrils

and the spellbound inertia, the snug-enough shroud.
Evident in the distance between

lightning's flare and the thunder's roar,
the ancient discrepancy,

as I hurtle toward yet another failure –
everyday and the lifetime, the ages-old –

the slowly-becoming awareness of how
thoroughly deep go the erected barriers,

an integral part, alas, of the structure itself.
The sun rising every morning from the heart

to shine upon my impotence and light
beyond me the fair, faraway face of my Savior.

O child of God, hopelessness in the New Life
has nothing to do with failure or despair.

Under the tent flap

In darkness, I keep returning
to the elephant's fan and spear,

serpent and rope, column and throne,
each being not only partial and false but, also –

in our singularly karmic, piecemeal journeys –
heartbreakingly valid and vital.

Each to his own under the tent flap
and in that similar captivity,

I am required to assign myself
no greater accuracy or piety

than any other of those rowdy souls groping,
out of necessity, the enigmatic shape before us

and include myself first
among the mere mortals

in their inherent inability to ever coax
the entire creature fully into the light.

O child of God, withhold judgment
of a particular for the sake of the One.

Pumpkin stone

Lord, when will I ripen, ready
to enroll in that course of liberation

filled with wine but drained of blood? When
will I quit this sad rummaging and oscillation,

crack the looking glass and scatter the shards;
settle fixedly (like that famous pumpkin stone)

outside the door of my Lord's charnel house,
(which was once, apparently, a noted tavern)

to long desperately, like Francis before me,
to be crushed into singing dust

by the Master's hand and hammer;
strewn along Love Street (under His feet),

to rise and dance only at His passing by;
to cling lightly then to His skirt and sandals

and be carried inside the great manor,
courtyard and darbar of the Beloved?

Lord, when will I ripen?
When will I be ready?

O child of God, surrender (also like Francis)
your impatience to the whim of His immaculate timing.

The mercy of His court

If you're sure of anything in this world,
o child, be sure you are mistaken.

When you feel yourself hardening
into one position, take the necessary steps

to remove yourself from that easy overlook.
Talk yourself down from the heights

to the dust-view of God –
God being not up in heaven

but in the field doing His spade-and-hoe work,
seeing everything in His omnipresence

at every moment from everywhere.
To draw nearer to that Truth, o child,

and to Him, concede in every judgment,
your ignorance and incapacity;

throw yourself and everyone in your ken
upon the celebrated mercy of His court.

O child of God, the least, proud thought,
Meher says, veils you from Reality.

The whetstone

I sought from my Lord daily relief
from the persistent disquiet and shame;

sought absolution and allowance
for my chronic failures,

my miserable inadequacy,
until one day my Lord said to me:

It was I who hobbled you –
to keep you from straying too far.

I cuffed your wrists to keep your hands
out of mischief and folded in prayer.

I placed the blinders on – to train your vision
in the one direction you need to go.

I plugged your ears to reveal the inner voice.
I built you strange-tongued, odd and solitary

to separate you from the seductive crowd
because you belong to no one else but Me.

O child of God, to properly sharpen the blade,
rough and fine-grained must be the whetstone.

The only game in town

Side with the virtuous; battle the others.
Fight the good fight.

It's all part of the game
and it's the only game in town.

Shake your fist; speak truth to power.
It's all part of the game

and it's the only game in town.
But when you see the game has you in its grasp,

when you see through it, when you give up on it,
when you want desperately out – turn away;

cease your resistance – and your participation.
Turn to the only chance there is

(for you and humankind)
and in your deepest humility and helplessness,

surrender yourself to the one endeavor worth pursuing,
the one freedom, the one treasure worth the quest.

O child of God, this is the game
and it's the only game in town.

Bold experiments

I have read the gestures, the finger-tracings;
heeded the later, lived-in mandali stories

so as not to be led astray nor gamble
upon imaginings, vagaries, the ruses of ego.

Gone by the book and the left-behind road maps.
But when the Friend appears beside me

whispering of alternative avenues
tailored to my peculiar journey, an unheralded route

sewn into the soft fabric of my heart
I am made averse to safe-playing;

willing to risk my likely being led astray
to obey words that have touched

neither lips nor page; words never meant
to be taught nor shared, never to reach

the light of reputable wisdom or discernment;
words that appear from nowhere

to rapidly fade into the mystery
from whence they came.

O child of God, Meher advised his lovers
to take risks and make bold experiments.

Eyes divine

We are all looking through God's eyes
which is to say God is looking through our eyes

if only we could climb back
into our original face before it became

encrusted with the journey's dust.
Everyone we meet is just Who we are

under the dust-caked makeup – spooked ghosts
treading the boards rather valiantly in our assigned roles,

looking up rarely from the issued script,
too obliged, too immersed, too stage-frightened

to look beyond each clay facade or within our own;
nor project ahead to the God-directed,

neatly-tied plot resolutions
and the deep, heavy curtains sliding closed.

O child of God, o stage-struck one, imagine that!
You are destined to see your Self.

Heed Hafiz

My dear, the fault lies in your own
incapacity to understand him. – Hafiz

No, never wrong is the Master,
until His truth touches *my* ears

too unwieldy and unfathomable
for language and meaning to bear.

So I cautiously heed Hafiz,
my faith and allegiance

pledged to the silent Godman
but only tentatively and tangentially

to His words of which I have
no true capacity or authority to comprehend.

O child of God, by what possible measure can you
presume to know what God is talking about?

Divest yourself

All roads lead to Rome, the saying goes,
making it difficult, back then, to get lost, I suppose,

as long as you knew which side of the city you were on.
All paths lead to God, we are similarly told –

not just the broadly tramped swaths of traditional religions
but the narrow, individual windings through the rocky wilds.

There are as many paths to God,
the Sufis say, as there are the souls of men.

The Zen Buddhists put it more succinctly –
comparisons are odious.

To look down upon another's path means only
that you have diverted your eyes from the Goal;

let another soul into your sacred relationship
with the Divine Companion;

assumed a height which you have not attained.
Perhaps, you are looking backwards,

judging your own path –
the bruising episodes, the cowardice,

the sins and betrayals from an authority
and perspective you do not possess –

not from the helplessness and hopelessness
you profess to acknowledge.

O child of God, to reach the Goal, divest yourself
of everything you once thought you knew.

Climb through the ropes

I can almost grasp it – how the sword
must slice itself into pieces.

And blood must be used –
to wipe away the blood.

You are a boxer in the ring
and then the referee between the two

and then an intimate spectator expected
to absorb the blows without wince or cry,

bleeding at the violent end of a leather glove
yet also from a nosebleed seat

just over the county line. Yes, I can almost grasp it,
as it slips through my gloved hands –

I'm being circled in the ring,
unencumbered of any defensive pose,

facing the impossible with a daunted inadequacy,
rushing forward to catch the punishing blows

and offer a bare, bloodied neck
to the melded shards of the original sword.

O child of God, to resolve the soul's intrinsic quandary,
courage and forbearance must climb through the ropes.

Only the witness

The sole witness to our dreams,
we are most often the main character –

until we awaken and see we never
really were a participant; only the witness.

As in this waking dream, the Awakener adds.
When roused from sleep, once and forever, says He,

we shall see, we shall see – we never really were
the participant we think we are;

only the witness to an insubstantiality,
suffering its illusory bindings

yet removed from any real peril,
having never left our very own beds.

Only an intimate witness are we to this waking dream
beyond anyone's choosing, design and control

with only one dreamed-up character a willing participant;
only One, sowing with perfect equanimity

this hardscrabble dreamscape
with seeds of irrepressible truth.

O child of God, auspicious is your dream.
This time you envisioned the Avatar.

To Whom it may concern

I continue my search
without knowing why or how.

If it's truth I'm after, I might find out,
enamored of the answer or not.

If the source is fear, I'm afraid
I'm doomed. But then, I always was. O Lord!

If there's something I can do, help me with it.
If there is nothing I can do, let my efforts

be a lifelong appeal to Whom it may concern –
a wish that something might be done.

Let my search be a running toward rather than away,
my one request being – a divesting of all requests,

coming from the depths of me who I do not know
to the One Whom I beseech and also know not.

O child of God, sometimes the path is merely
the placing of one foot in front of the other.

The ring of truth

Thank You for all You have given me,
and all You have taken away;

for remembering me
and for allowing me to remember You.

Thank You for wisdom's ripening;
for the dust of the grave;

the shards of my poverty; for the rasp
of the world which has sharpened my longing.

Thank You for Your name
and the knowledge of Its significance;

for the soul's dogged progression;
the inevitability of the goal;

for the human joy and affliction,
the revelation and mystification

which leads ultimately to dissolution,
to the unveiling of the indwelling Self and Union.

O child of God, the gratitude you've expressed
for years has begun to bear the ring of truth.

The deep, deep hammer

He's teaching me another language –
the One known as the silent Christ.

I run to spread the news and quickly learn
no one else speaks it; even I don't know

what I'm talking about – the resemblance
to sheer gibberish dispelled only

by a resonance in the deep, deep hammer,
anvil and stirrup of my boxed ears,

the throttled pipes of my throat,
my heart beating under His heel.

A very thin stitching holds my world together.
Ambiguous and elusive –

reaching for a word suddenly unpronounceable;
just as well, for it has lost all sense,

come to a thousand shades of meaning –
one thing this moment, another the next.

I'm being taught a language
where I speak only by listening,

dismantling as we go the definition
of every word I have every uttered.

O child of God, faithfully say your prayers
and with all your heart listen to the silent Christ.

Chronic homesickness

I'll face my fears one day (I'm told),
a steady gaze dispelling them at last,

not to prove myself worthy
nor to please the Lord of Bliss,

not with the intention of becoming
Who I reportedly already am

but merely to settle an outstanding debt.
To offer in obedience and good conscience

the only mite of currency I possess,
returning (at last) what belongs to Him

and in the process becoming empty enough
to be wafted back to the now foreign shore of my origin.

O child of God, for your lonely, chronic
homesickness, surrender is the only cure.

Attempted saints

Nothing more natural than a saint
in rolled-up sleeves guilelessly attending

to the daily chores and prayers
shoulder to shoulder, perhaps,

with the attempted saints
zealously scrubbing their own souls

to emulate the perfect Jesus
and be pleasing in the sight of God.

Last and least, along come the inveterate
devotees who seek in their own way

to escape the wheel of birth and death –
rescue, rejection and renunciation

being the cornerstones of their calculated
austerities, chores, readings and prayers.

O child of God, how might you reconcile
your unremitting efforts with total surrender?

Content with God

God bless the lover who takes
his Beloved for granted;

who no longer seeks because he has found
and once found never again reaches

for that which is always at his fingertips.
Who finds God beside him everywhere –

no more probing, testing out of fear
the false comforts of understanding –

knowledge instead of faith;
some cheap assurance rather than submission.

God bless the lover who shares his path
all along, every moment,

content with God as Companion
not as the Goal of the New Life road,

who is as disinterested in immediate liberation
as he is in his inevitable destiny.

O child of God, the journey is Baba's business;
your business is to be with Him every moment of that journey.

My sons

I glimpsed my sons as fellow sojourners –
souls at least as old and equal to mine

whose karma my blood and house has taken,
a compassion deeper flowering in me

than paternal love; a timeless empathy;
reverence; camaraderie –

a much needed shift in perspective.
Not my sons at all, but His lovers,

not those young-bodied men but ancient souls
with their own evolving karma,

their own ageless relationship with Him.
I can't protect them; never could,

nor guide them along their own inimitable way.
Can't aid them any more than they can aid me

upon our mutual souls' journey.
We are and always have been

in the hands of God – *His* sons,
my brothers, too, of the one true Father.

O child of God, Meher emphasized the connection –
we are not we but one.

The illusion of autonomy

Rather than say, forgive me, Lord,
why not say thank You, thank You?

Not only for the pointed-out errors
but for the standing apart from them,

the by-His-grace opening of the eyes,
mind and heart, at least in retrospect,

to the sins that doom; that once went
undetected and unchallenged;

that once were deemed necessary,
even taken to be virtues.

Thank You for the ripening –
the slow gentle pull of the pure soul

up from the muck of illusion;
the ageless apparent journey

from stone hardness to fruition to dissolution.
And thank You, Lord, thank You,

for being the one witness to my battle,
my only gauge, my helpmate,

my guide, my only companion;
my one source of encouragement.

O child of God, let go of everything
by letting go the illusion of autonomy.

The kiss of the Prince

Every Avatar could be called the Awakener
none having come to teach, words ineffectual

except perhaps as a backdrop.
And all instructions coming down to this:

You can't get *there* from *here*
by any will or effort of your own.

Dormant souls require the kiss of the Prince.
Can't bear otherwise to leave their beds;

tear themselves away from the latest
exploits of their fantastical selves.

Only a perfect surrender bestowed from Perfection
(by perfect grace) can pierce the ancient spell

to awaken from its repose
the latent, dreaming soul.

O child of God, all words and ideas
are mere explorations of the dream.

A kiss

You came to awaken but then held Your tongue,
pursing Your lips instead for a kiss.

Asking first that we clear the heart-room
for such an intimacy and our waking-up,

long love-look into Your eyes.
You came to awaken us, then roughly turned the tables,

asking to be roused from Your ages-old habit
of sleeping on a park bench

under the umbrage of our human, inhospitable hearts.
You came to awaken and what teachings,

what tongue, what tones are required
for a slumberer to awaken Himself?

O child of God, the God you seek resides
in the fleshy chambers of the human heart.

Ropes and rules

A colorful fleck in a kaleidoscope
floating this way and that, eternally

turned in the hands of a child,
uneasily, I examine my position –

explore every fluid arrangement,
jockey for situations deemed favorable;

fancying myself a player successfully
riding the waves, if not holding sway.

Having no power over the child,
I seek now desperately to know somehow

with an accumulated wisdom
the granted ropes and rules of this realm

for the protection of my little fleck and brood,
no power to leave and trust

the turning of the mechanism
to the delight and whim

of that deeply mysterious, omnipotent,
uncontrollable and mischievous child.

O child of God, your autonomy thwarted at every turn,
still you believe your surrender depends upon you.

Red herrings and wild geese

Neti, neti . . . neti, neti –
the process of negation and elimination.

No choice, really, but a seeing through,
an unhanding of anything unimaginable anymore

as valuable or desirable and so life narrows down –
the passion, pain and pleasure of it.

One day (I'm told) we'll see the whole as neti, neti,
nothing of any value to attach ourselves to

having run out of red herrings and wild geese.
Then, we can never go back,

the only choice left in the Oneness being
all or nothing – Truth or illusion, God or self;

not a choice really but a seeing through, an unhanding
of our non-existence and acceptance of God as everything.

O child of God, seek now the pristine view of the dream –
empty and momentary, dependent, signifying nothing.

These earthen fingers

I'll never be allowed to enter the gates.
Saint Peter will ask for identification.

If my photo bears any resemblance, I'll be turned away.
There's no one sitting at the feet of Jesus.

The Father *is* the house of many mansions.
Jesus is the only One home.

Reaching the human stage, I can rise no higher.
Earth was built for worms and human beings.

Shed my sanskaras? I *am* my sanskaras.
Working frantically for the balloon to rise,

I find myself a bag of sand, no way
for these earthen fingers to unknot the rope.

O child of God, you must become a child,
one who has not yet been given a name.

Not one thing

Remove thyself, said Hafiz,
for thou art the veil. Speaking of himself

but telling me also the solution to my dilemma.
Or perhaps telling me there is no solution –

I am my own dilemma, dilemmas not
allowed into the kingdom of heaven.

You can't jump over your own head, Baba said.
No matter how small and low you get

or how high you leap, it's impossible
for you to rise above the mire of yourself.

Not one thing can ever become everything.
And the grievous truth about death (He said)

is that you don't die, but escape
to become yet another barrier to freedom.

O child of God, as a poet you know well enough
the inadequacy of words outside the dream.

The promised skies

If this wordsmith fashioned with iron
the letters of my thousand poems,

they would not balance a single nugget
of truth yet in the buried ore.

I take the words I am given dutifully
but none of their meticulously arranged letters

are key-shaped to fit the locks of my fetters.
Pain exists apparently to keep us

from getting too comfortable on our perch
with joy an intermittent spur to not lose heart entirely –

inarticulate glimpses of the possibilities beyond.
These poems are a part of the chains

forged in this lifetime; part of your chains, too.
Enduring a perch from which I can find

no way to lift my pinioned body
and explore the promised skies.

O child of God, the worth of these poems
may lie in their inability to tell the truth.

Trapeze

This imperfect human love
and its accompanying grief

which my Lord has marked
as hypocritical and self-serving,

is, as my Lord well knows,
all I have, the best part of me

and though it invites suffering
I cannot let it go, knowing

that motive would also be
hypocritical and self-serving.

I grip one bar of the trapeze
while trying to grasp the other

and end up crucified between the two
suspended far above the sawdust

not knowing which way to swing
daring not to let go of either.

O child of God, it is the duality of existence
that makes for every difficulty.

Straw boss

As a spiritual pilgrim, I must go (I am told)
from being an egocentric being

to a being without a center;
dust adrift in a cosmic wind,

settling eventually on Love Street
at the feet of my Lord.

I might have been a straw boss once.
Now I'm being pummeled into dust,

this sack of flesh containing the lot
of my accumulated wisdom.

Any glint among the grains a mere trick of light.
Apparently, I have only just come under the hammer

and it's a long, long journey
from here to nowhere.

O child of God, what matters the length
of a trek you have no choice but to undertake?

Verisimilitude

Similes, metaphors, homonyms,
various other poetic devices resonating

with two, three simultaneous meanings
the more intricately nuanced the merrier,

expressing the ambiguity not only of words
but of life itself and pointing to, paradoxically,

the ultimate Oneness of Truth.
If a poem's every word were to wear

a thousand shades of meaning, the poet would then
only be approaching a sufficient description,

depiction of the whole cloth Truth
(which readers, by the way, could yet only grasp

through the seine of their own private translations),
that unimaginable poem ending up

an enigmatic everything and nothing,
having achieved the verisimilitude of Truth.

O child of God, lament not your fated obsession –
trying to squeeze blood from stone.

A yellow wood

In a yellow wood, came I to a divergence –
the road I take the next leg of my journey,

the other a phantom companion.
O Lord, let it be true that the freedom

and certainty of karma and fate rule the road
rather than my fear and ignorance

determining where I shall end up,
the life I shall encounter along the way.

Praying to God I might set down at last
the staggering baggage of my presumed autonomy

on every more or less traveled road
taken or not taken and accept the long term

remedial grace and benevolence
of a hand-held, divinely-guided tour.

O child of God, you plot your itinerary
knowing not how you have arrived at where you are.

Only the breath

A creature molded of river clay,
how can it not stain everything it touches?

Leave its separative, alien markings
everywhere it goes?

Made of clay. Not just layered in it.
To the core and out the other side.

How could that creature ever flow?
Rise above? Become transparent?

How might the light ever shine through?
Whatever benign shape it's molded into,

will it not always be a creature thick, slow,
cumbersome, pliable and impotent?

Only the breath God gave it – only the breath.
Miraculous, invisible, ancient and holy.

O child of God, God's living breath –
the only redemption for a creature of clay.

Blithe aplomb

Saint Francis took to the hills of Umbria,
radiating sheer joy (all the poor fellow owned).

It came as a reminder. Where had failed
clergy, scripture, pomposity and ritual

and the wilderness cry of the human heart,
prevailed this young man's mute testimony

to stay the brutal stones, feed empty souls,
draw his future sisters and brothers.

Otherwise, who would have followed
through the snow those mad footprints,

were it not for joy and the fire's roar
of his Jesus-love above any frail warmth

or posturing the world could offer?
One drop of the holy wine Francis

handled with such blithe aplomb
and hearts were kindled, souls *reminded*,

keenly felt then their own lack of joy –
a memory lost in their dimly remembered past.

O child of God, to love your Lord
as did Saint Francis, is to please Him.

Soft words

I have come not to teach,
said my Lord, but to awaken.

He began then using a voice
too soft for the human ear.

Speaking not, apparently, to our human selves
but to our God selves, laying down the soft words

which would never harden into law,
scriptures, tenets and dogma;

reaching not our immediate ears
but engaging directly in the timeless,

immaculate soul and Self we always are
but who have not yet heard

the soft-spoken truth of the Christ
above the roaring of this world.

O child of God, shun the spoken word.
Become intimate with silent communion.

That bright red apple

The great sin in the garden
was not disobedience but doubt –

a lack of faith in the perfection
and benevolence of God.

Sparked by a mortal fear
swiftly it flared into pride

and from there broadened
into resentment, envy, greed . . .

until, in head-swimming fashion,
the hapless couple found themselves

outside the fastened gate,
having to wander the earth

under the burden of their own
willful, intrinsic, self-perpetuating sins.

O child of God! Still you forsake Eden
for the lure that bright red apple.

The milkman

Realization at dawn on the morrow,
the Master promised his impatient disciple.

After an excited and restless night,
the disciple overslept. Arrived at the Master's door

to find the milkman was now a Jivanmukta.
You might think this venerable story

points to the patience and constant vigilance
required of the devotee,

earned and achieved through ardent preparation
(obedience, renunciation, prayers and penances).

But, no. That's not it.
The milkman owned none of these virtues

and yet was granted Realization on the spot.
It's all according to the Whim, Meher said.

The Whim knows everything from the beginning
and knows always where it should flow.

O child of God, always one
with the Whim is the Perfect One.

The stone pillow

The stone pillow of Saint Francis,
the sting of snow under his feet,

his empty belly, the tender stigmata –
all he took to be blessings

because they kept him
from going back to sleep.

I have not been a lover of God
but a lover of comfort and conformity.

A stone pillow is so discomfiting!
It will not bend to the contours of my dreams.

Yet there is a certain attractiveness to it,
(within the dark cave of my solitude)

a silent, loyal simplicity and immutability
I must learn to lie down with

until my shape conforms, my dreams cease
and I awaken like Francis to the truth of myself.

O child of God, when you rise from that pillow,
the Mystics say, you will never go back to sleep.

Five

I have not been a lover in this lifetime
but an analyst and a calculator.

Evaluate – accept or reject.
What adds up must be true;

what doesn't add up must not be true.
Only recently have I learned

there are innumerable dimensions
to every simple equation

and innumerable equations
yet to be proven.

A lifetime of effort with nothing to show
but ignorance, ambiguity, partiality and error.

The infinite spaces of all the data
I am not privy to means nothing will ever add up

until I accept the notion that somewhere
beyond me, at every moment, two and two make five.

O child of God, Meher said all existence
amounts to one big zero.

Baby powder

Powder sprinkled on the infant skin
is made of stone, made soothing,

soft and smooth by being crushed;
by being processed and converted.

In soapstone, likewise, the same talc
makes for a yielding, utile medium of art

able to be notched and sculpted
into various forms of divine expression.

Primitive man once aspired
to be an adamant warrior –

aspired to be glorious, god-like, impregnable;
leaving an imprint; making an impression.

The Avatar came along and said
(time and again said) to the human heart –

become dust, soft, crushed, soothing;
become curative, servient, a comfort

and inspiration to the most innocent
and vulnerable among you.

O child of God, you dream of gentleness
while your heart is made of stone.

The trick

When you try and try, said Lao Tzu,
the world is then beyond the winning.

To attempt (or strive)
is one definition of the word try.

To *tax* (or *strain*) is another –
to go through a trial.

The trick, said Lao Tzu, is to act
without trying – strive without distress;

non-doing within non-duality.
Surrender is the ultimate abandonment

of attempt and strain –
an unimaginable state

in which we live without strife,
neither enduring nor causing friction,

illimitable, amenable drops dissolved
in the oceanic whim and will of God.

O child of (that same) God, everything,
says Lao Tzu, is won by those who let it go.

Stone bearer

Often I do not suffer fools lightly –
a great sin because there are

so many fools in the world,
especially those arrogant ones

who do not suffer fools lightly.
It's difficult for me to embrace

my human family because I refuse
to set down the stones I bear in each fist.

Stone bearer, stone *caster*. I chuck
those bruising missiles in thought and word

to relieve the weight of my own burden
but immediately find myself

picking up more, ever on the ready,
never letting it sink in that it is the weight

of those stones that keeps me yoked
and grounded to this dark, dark earth.

O child of God, where did you ever gather the notion
that compassion makes you vulnerable?

Free radical

The fault is mine, I hear myself say
but it isn't quite true.

Better than blaming others
which is even less true but,

contrary to worldly wisdom, the teachings
suggest that to blame is to blaspheme,

adopting the self-centered, heretical conceit
that I am not (nor is anyone else)

entirely under God's authority,
a loose cannon somehow, a free radical.

It is, apparently, the ineffable, inarticulate truth
that all the blame must rest solidly

upon the vast, irreproachable shoulders of God
and the sooner we come to know

and live that truth, the nearer we approach
the illusive fellowship of the new humanity.

O child of God, take your cue from the fallen leaf
and the half farthing sparrow.

Graveyard gates

I have come not to teach, said my Lord.
Liberation, apparently, not something you learn how to do.

With this lifetime of accumulated knowledge,
it's difficult to become a vessel now with a perfectly hollow
ring.

There's an old joke about a drunk
stumbling into an open grave.

I've forgotten the punch line. I've dug my own grave;
settled into the bottom, studying the sky.

I can dig no deeper nor climb back to the surface.
I thought the virtue of patience

referred to the length of the journey.
Now I see it only begins

when the path veers from the highway
and enters through the graveyard gates.

O child of God, how stubbornly you cling
to the only thing you know.

An amazing tale

God woke up; uttered the first Word
(a question, no less!) – Who am I?

Or so I have been taught quite collaterally
by the One Who didn't come for that.

A variation of His entreaty – Come unto Me;
powerful enough to pull all drop souls

from their warm beds and shoo them out
into the inhospitable weather.

A pronouncement that has never lost
over the ages its strength to lure us

from stone to humanity, imploring our souls
through our finger-plugged ears,

our clamped-shut flesh to find out
Who He is and who we really are.

O child of God, the Silent One relates an amazing tale.
Check within to see if it rings true.

Bullock cart

A lame man riding through the dark
in the bed of a bullock cart, a pummeling

with each pothole, road rut;
the destination vague and remote.

No stopping, no turning back.
A perfect One leads the way

telling stories, singing ballads
of the valiant and the persistent.

My Lord gave the lepers comfort, not healing.
The cure was there already, in the process of time,

in the death of diseased bodies and the taking
of new ones. Comfort was His gift.

In the dark, nursing my wounds,
I see clearly now my own eventual cure

somewhere beyond the thumps of time and distance,
assured by the promise and nature of the malady.

As I listen to my Lord's songs,
hold His hand, sup from His spoon,

the old cart shudders, rumbles along, winding its way
towards dawn and those inevitable, far-away gates.

O child of God, Meher says every bump in the road
is a shedding and a shaping of your eventual perfection.

The stirrings of the heart

This pink sunrise reminds me
of a certain iconic coat.

You said You wear both,
on body and sky

and we accept Your Word
with its obvious implausibility,

(no more than the utterings of other
great mystics nor Buddha and Jesus)

attributing our perplexity to the limitations
of language, consciousness and intellectuality

purely because Your awakening prods
and stirrings of the heart

satisfy so deeply our hunger
while remaining yet a mere promise,

an intimation of the inconceivable,
ineffable glory that is our eventual due.

O child of God, truth does not appease
but perplexes the human mind.

To satisfy our thirst

A wayfarer in the wilderness dying of thirst
stumbles upon a cave where monks once lived.

His great hope dashed – finding it deserted,
dust-laden, with empty jugs, parched manuscripts,

roughly sketched maps of doomed, abandoned wells.
My Lord said He has come not to teach

but ... *to satisfy our thirst*. Promising
the wayfarer shall by appointment meet

someone somewhere who will restore him –
in precious, strategic sips of life-giving water,

guide him gently to a higher realm
of deep, icy pools where his thirst

will be satisfied entirely, then forgotten,
becoming ultimately inconceivable.

O child of God, the only value of your imagination
is its aid to the remembrance of your Beloved.

The presence of His absence

Towards the end of my life,
for the most part, it's God and me.

When it's only me, I become unsettled,
plumb my heart, enter into prayer.

I review the articles of my faith
like thumbing through

a well-worn photo album;
imagine, rehearse His presence

until the reappearance and assurance
of the One Who never leaves.

Almost nothing in my purse now,
particularly in His sort of currency.

There's only an either/or proposition:
His presence in my everyday life

or the presence of His absence.
And whether by grace or effort,

this trivial bit of remainder is my only asset
and He the last, lingering object of my enthusiasm.

Have faith, o child of God. One day your very freedom
might be purchased by the dust in your purse.

This inherent buoyancy

Drown in My Ocean, said my Lord.
Perhaps that begins with a lonely,

formidable attempt to swim across it.
Enter the cold bitterness, pushing beyond

the breakers, far from the populated shore.
How soon we lose our bearings!

Weary, no longer able to plumb
the depths or determine a direction,

we find ourselves in a sort of drifting limbo
at the mercy of the Ocean's shove and heave;

not a spit of sand in sight. Drown, yes,
but how to go about it? With this inherent

buoyancy, these lungs involuntarily
gasping every other moment for air.

I'm told I'm made of salt water
but it doesn't feel that way.

It feels like I am a speck of synthetic debris
bobbing forever separately atop it.

O child of God, why mewl endlessly
about a mystery much too deep to fathom?

Bark and bite

The doorbell rings and in a pavlovian reaction
the sleeping dog leaps to the threshold

barking, snarling, poised for combat,
warily assessing the danger of the intrusion.

The ego is an indefatigable usurper
who considers its proper (God-given) role

to be the judge and protector of every approach,
threatening or benevolent.

Whenever the householder's particular sanctuary
is even mildly challenged, a button is pushed,

the alarm sounds, the watchdog leaps into action,
protecting its home and master.

Few, if any, can train their faithful dog
to ignore and betray its natural instincts.

The best that might be negotiated
is the point at which the command

is firmly assumed and established
by the master of both house and dog.

O child of God, humility is the eventual
quelling of the watchdog's bark and bite.

Full flower

To become perfect, said Jesus,
leave all and follow Me

and the young man went away sad
for he had many possessions.

I am saddened also by the great wealth
of fear I refuse to leave behind.

But I do not go away. I trail my Lord
from a safe distance carrying my bundles with me.

Just love Me, says my Lord,
turning to me every now and then.

I don't quite grasp His meaning but I cannot
let Him go without me into the yonder hills.

My will is bent toward Him
(whether I bent it that way or did He)

and I pray my bruising, ironclad resolve
is but a rudimentary form of love, a seed perhaps,

which in some distant lifetime hence
shall come into full flower.

O child of God, how might your Lord be embraced
without dropping everything else you hold dear?

Call me down

Call me Zacchaeus in the sycamore tree,
a small man keeping myself above the crowd,

asking God for a glimpse only
of the One among the multitude,

that striding flesh of love and purity
ever beyond my outstretched hands.

I have attained this reasonable height
by effort and cleverness.

Hidden among the foliage to pray
with as much heart as I can muster –

come by me, Lord, and call me down.
Address me this day or any other

and lead me home along Your route
to bless it beyond my understanding.

O child of God, the ancient path, says Meher,
is a circuitous one, leading back home.

To dwell in eternity

To train our minds upon the truth
we cannot see and do not live,

returning solely, doggedly to it
and to His eternal promise and solace –

this is the heart of our renunciation.
Invulnerable, immortal beings

(not creatures) are we, far removed in reality
from the world's chaos, threat and drama.

This is our meditation,
the venue of our remembrance,

the bread we are daily given,
calling us ceaselessly, silently,

to guide us through our frightening,
obscure dreams into the final (we pray) clarity.

O child of God, the choice we have if any
is to dwell in the world or to dwell in eternity.

The green essence

Chop it down. Fell that tree.
Let the chips fall where they may,

tumbling thunderously around me.
Bring it all down – my elevated, foliated perches,

crow's nests views, my hopes in the high branches,
with Your sharp-bladed axe

cutting to the quick, deeper to the core.
I want to say this even as we both know

it's but useless bluster once it reaches
my vulnerable mouth which has broken

its teeth on a thousand such hopeless cries.
But it starts pure enough, in the dark

heart of the spar, far from the accruements
of time and the journey, ignorance and self.

Truly sincere, holy as the green essence
from which it first emerged.

O child of God, you talk big yet
moan and sigh at the slightest quiver.

On being a human being

When the prospect hits you,
in theory if not in practice,

that no one is responsible for anything
they think, say or do, you grow silent.

Immobile. A preposterous idea at odds with
being a human being, life on the planet earth,

societal structures, religion and morality,
relationships of every stripe. Silent because

it's a notion inexplicable and indefensible.
And wondrous – how human existence

might have evolved from scratch
on precepts that are simply not true,

information incomplete about who
and what we are, every supposition

negated by our fundamental ignorance.
Start off on the wrong foot and whatever

territory you tread will be hostile,
foreign, fearsome and strange.

O child of God, a mystery within a mystery,
approach it with humility and faith.

The blood and body of Christ

Might we liken the Avatar to a fermenting agent?
Yeast added to the dough; to the must;

incrementally altering our nature
and completing thus our destined becoming –

sacred bread and wine; the blood and body of Christ.
Our journeys a transformation rather than a quest,

a rising up from the rough, raw mix into holy bread.
An inevitable organic turning from the murky

skin-and-stem juice and pomace
into clean, lucent, holy wine.

O child of God, your musings and metaphors
could never capture the complexity of the Mystery.

My Revealer

The true lover, Baba said, seals his lips
as I'm tending to do these days

not from fiery longing (alas) but from the fear
that someone overhearing might want me

fitted for a jacket with very long sleeves.
I was a reasonable fellow once

who has turned irrational, making everyone nervous.
I'm nervous, too, and weary, trying to wedge

the pieces of my crumbling world back
into some semblance of order. It's frightening.

With a certain thrill to it, also. A strange, secret freedom.
I sound out my friends with my newfound wisdom.

They are embarrassed for me, nodding politely,
shying away. I get the idea that once

they turn the corner they break into a run. No matter.
One of the earth-shattering truths (or self-delusions)

which has come to me of late is that there is only myself
and my Revealer. I answer to no one else.

O child of God, get wisdom from others only
by observing your reactions to their words and behavior.

The Great Ignorer

Eruch once advised a lover to become the Great Ignorer
and though the suggestion was specific, it is my goal

of late to become such a man – the Great Ignorer.
Does not non-attachment require it?

Being not of the world; turning the other cheek;
loving thy neighbor as thyself – do they not

require a great ignoring of everyone's
(including my own) transgressions and differences?

Perhaps, to ignore our virtues also,
born of karma, a forgetting of self and God's grace

not individual human strength and effort.
Urgently Maya is tugging at my sleeve

every moment offering fear, pleasure, forgetfulness
while someOne within seems to be urging remembrance:

to turn my attention solely toward my Beloved
and to all else become the Great Ignorer.

O child of God, nothing is real but God, said Meher.
And nothing matters but love for God.

Think of Noah

Start your own project, Rumi advised.
As absurd as Noah laboring daily

in the sandy shade of the ship's hulk,
not a drop to show for all his devotion,

his lofty pronouncements and endeavors.
His self-opposition far harder to ignore

than the public's derision, those habitual lapses
of faith and resolve – empty, arid days,

nights of isolation and confusion,
seductive arguments for capitulation and abandonment.

And doubt! Would it not all come down
to a great dusty naught? Start your own project,

Rumi advised, constructed daily –
the ribs of an inward, sturdy vessel

contrary to your own and all apparent
worldly reason, wisdom and evidence.

O child of God, whenever you distrust
your inner God-directed duties, think of Noah.

A beautiful confusion

I've taken up watercolors, by the way.
After all these years in the sculptor's studio.

Foregone the hammer which I have
dearly loved for its weight and authority

and the heavy, productive clinking in my ears.
No more trying to chisel and pound

the amorphous hardness into an image of my choosing
(or as near as I could get to it with these human hands).

I started painting out of habit with the same sort
of bold strokes and then I would fill in the delicate colors.

But of late, through necessity and inner guidance,
I have abandoned all shapes, boundaries and distinctions.

I put the wonderful colors to the delicate paper
and let them run where they will. No strategy.

No aim, no standards now; no communication
beyond myself and my Muse. Just a beautiful confusion.

The colors, whose distinctions are but a trick of light,
blend and bleed into one another,

a crude, necessary attempt at return
to the colorless oneness from which they emerged.

O child of God, you are brushing up
against the blurry edges of the mystery.

Not one crumb

Words fail me. With a deft swipe
I'm tempted to wipe clean this page

like clearing tiles from a board game.
Not one crumb do I know

of the great secrets and mysteries.
Meanwhile I'm being methodically

stripped of fear in a process
far beyond my understanding and abilities,

an ungovernable aspect of my awakening.
My only choice is between love and fear –

that old conflict of heart and head –
to battle strident and self-glorious

my illusory enemies or to fall silently
on my Lord's terrible outstretched sword.

O child of God, words fail you because you
speak of things you know so little about.

The world's damaan

I entered the Samadhi perfectly sane,
though frightened and weary,

emerging mad and drunken,
stumbling downhill to meet

the world which no longer knew me.
My agenda and the agenda of my Lord

are universes apart, yet hidden somehow
beneath the folds of what I deem

myself and existence to be,
with His law (the only Reality) taking precedent.

Coming around again now near the end,
my world from rough handling

shattered in my hands and no glue
nor strategy to piece it back.

Trying to hold the wheel and Meher
asking again and again what is your heading?

What is your heading, your harbor and why not
let the sea take you where it will?

O child of God, truth wrenches and tugs
and still you clutch tightly the world's damaan.

The deeper you plunge

When at last you see the Lord
is not going to give you what you want,

love has an opportunity to emerge.
You can cease the charade.

Those posturings might have helped you once
get nearer to where you are but they must be

left outside like sandals at the Tomb.
Struck dumb by the process the deeper you plunge,

the Creator seems to have taken a shine to you –
apple of His eye, and you are thoroughly humbled

(for a little while), roughly shaken down to your boots.
This Friend Who is the One stealing away your shame

(though you keep grabbing it back),
painstakingly scrubbing away your fear

to reveal the love underneath worth more
than anything you ever dreamed you were wanting.

O child of God, put it into words best you can,
guessing how very far it is from the truth.

Moving through the fair

The carousel whirling full speed
and even now the temptation

is to mount a carved steed and charge!
Wield a pretend sword and 'round and 'round

gallop amidst the scintillating lights,
music, laughter and movement.

To appear to myself and others
to be grandly going somewhere.

There's a carousel also inside my head.
One in my chest, too, with similar temptations.

It's my task to keep myself to myself,
keep the peace, note in passing

everything in this parti-colored world,
this ceaseless reel of thought,

this battleground which is my heart,
wending my way through the glitter

and the sham, confusion and despair
out there and in here; in here and out there.

O child of God, spiritual poise
is moving through the fair unfazed.

The silence of Meher

You began Your ministry at a loss for words
amidst the human misery and longing,

enmity and despair. What words to add
after three thousand years of empty human rhetoric,

the true teachings skewed and obfuscated,
almost never penetrating either hearts or heads?

Best to go back to a clean slate, a new language
older than clay, not intended for mouth nor ear,

straight to the heart, pinning
Your fortunate lovers to the wall,

communicating through the quivering shaft of your arrow.
And not just Your lovers (You say), all of Creation.

And only incrementally have I come to accept, mutely enrapt,
the power and primacy of your wordless awakenings.

O child of God, so many verses you have written
trying to express the silence of Meher.

Pretend game

Meher referred to existence as the divine game –
but not a contest; not a flag to capture.

A pretend game. A masquerade.
And once you find yourself

a mandated participant, the only course left
is to play your role best you can.

The only way, apparently,
to bow out is to make that

holy, hair's-breadth shift of perspective
where every moment you act

not for the moment but for the eternal,
ever aware of the pretense, recognizing

yourself and your fellow players
under the make-up and costumes to be

none other than God playing solitaire,
God the great ubiquitous pretender.

O child of God, follow the clues as best you can
until you are able to see through the charade.

A desert silence

I have been as lost as the world
and in innumerable ways I still am.

The mystery of which I often speak
is only with the borrowed authority

of my Lord, the tenuous authority of my faith.
I am unequal to the world

but my Lord has overcome it,
shown me true things (I pray), inside and out;

leading me from my numerous trepidations
step by step; awakening me even here

in this bewildering wilderness with a desert silence.
O this restless world (!)

is but a dirt-encrusted pearl
spinning in silent space

having fallen from a necklace
torn from around His mighty throat.

O child of God, each day with trust and faith
you piece together His obscure, subjective clues.

The exemplars

Where are the exemplars ? I asked my Lord.
The embodiments of Your teachings?

We are old now. Years and years
of Your tutelage and influence.

In myself and others, I see only
egoism, bewilderment and fear.

My Lord answered by allowing me
to chance upon His lovers at random,

opportune moments – soft words,
small gestures, kindness to others

while yet under the thumb of self,
not for show, not for show, nor gain,

not with calculation but striving silently,
solitary (except for Him), with little or no

reward or recognition their very sincere best
to live the way a faithful child of Meher should.

No long term motive – just the immediate reward
of love burgeoning from the dry husks of aged hearts.

O child of God, the Avatar is the measure
but every other consideration tilts toward leniency.

The truth all along

The road of truth is along a narrow shelf.
Stray to the left you hit stone.

Stray to the right you go over the edge.
Nowhere to stop or turn around.

Very soon you want to be somewhere else,
relinquish the wheel, not from boredom

but from the unrelenting strain of concentration.
But anywhere else is a looming threat,

an idle illusion, an escape from the task at hand.
Any delay is a postponement, not of arrival,

but of the truth all along – truth of the journey,
the route, the mountain, the vehicle,

the hands upon the wheel. Truth of the One
Who has led you to where you are.

O child of God, your duty is to face Reality
as best you might, now and forever.

Before the angels

A church bell at the end of my rope
might better suit. I could tug it

instead of words and we could both listen
to the tolls and the tolls fading.

The world at my windows is growing fainter, too,
little by little not quite there, having run out

of hocus pocus, steam and bluster which is all it ever was.
The same faded repertoire to keep me at the knotted end;

coax me back from the cliff-edge darkness
into heavy traffic or inside the whispers and sighs

of so many naive and incoherent promises.
I have a darkness waiting for me and a depth

(I feel it), a light in the midst and so I repair, repair
with my Beloved into solitude and companionship,

mystery and resolution as the world in its wrong-headed way
keeps showing me how so very little I truly have to lose.

O child of God, lose yourself as best you might
before the angels come to cart you away.

The platypus

I have evolved, similar to the platypus,
according to certain aquatic necessities

in spite of my sedentary, faintly terrene attributes.
It's left me a rather misshapen hodgepodge

wondering at my true nature – if ever I was
or ever should have considered myself a river creature.

This late in the game, I hope to construct
a reed hut somewhere on the bank;

sit and watch the river flow where it will
and be not tempted to dip my hands, wet my feet;

no thought to follow where the river might lead;
no attempt to seek nourishment there, to seek a life.

O child of God, you are not the body or mind (per Meher)
of that illusion-soaked and oddly shaped creature.

Clouds of glory

Baba means father but also babe.
Your sweat-soaked sadra

before being washed was passed around,
the women mandali burying their noses in it

to get a whiff of Your purity.
Someone new to Baba once

picked up the same scent at Meher Abode
on Your bedspread under her bowed head.

Vernix caseosa and roses, she said.
Vernix caseosa and roses.

A dewy new pale pink rose
born into this dusty old world

has put me again onto Your scent,
a newborn granddaughter

trailing perhaps clouds of glory
as You did Your whole long life, every step –

the fragrance of an ancient, inviolable purity,
the wafting, wondrous clouds of an unearthly glory.

O child of God, an old soul in a new body!
By dying and rebirth become yourself a child again.

One minus one

The opposite of something is not nothing.
The opposite of something is everything.

(According to the mystics.)
Roulette is a losing game,

round and round, round and round,
odds stacked heavily in the house's favor.

The only way to win is to walk away,
a feat that has proven near impossible

what with the lure of the jackpot,
the mere exhilaration of the game

and the belief etched in the depths
of every mind that this elaborately staged table

surrounded by its fanatical players
is the only game in town.

O child of God, one minus one, say the mystics,
is not zero. One minus one is God.

The word true

Nothing is true but God, said Meher.
That is – nothing to do with us is true.

True? – such a flimsy word
dependent upon the false for substantiality.

As vague and elusive a concept
as heaven or Union or bliss

all of which become meaningless
beyond the purlieus of this and that.

What is true in the midst of a dream?
Which mist-veiled path leads up the mountain

to a realm of clarity, an awakened state
where truth is no longer claimed or spoken?

Once life and death are put aside
the goal disappears, is vanquished.

The word true becomes no longer utterable –
absorbed, let us imagine, in His great silence.

O child of God, you long ago stopped believing in words.
Now you are losing faith in truth itself.

Ink-stained fingers

There's no puzzle to solve.
The crossword has been filled in from the first

(very faintly, with a soft lead pencil) –
an answer for every clue.

We interpret it, in our mad dash
down and across, as a set of instructions

and with ink-stained fingers
put meaning to it, ignoring the inconsistencies,

the strange syntax, those troubling black gaps,
reading it according to our particular karma –

add the missing, leave out the intolerable.
There's no puzzle to solve. (Thank God!)

We haven't the equipment for it.
And in our blustering headlong interference

we ignore the original clues, miss the underlying solution,
cling to our dark, heavily-edited versions

rather than find the faith to live
without a solution, without answers, without a clue.

O child of God, begin to grasp the truth
by realizing your own profound ignorance.

Face the music

I never know the truth or always know the truth
(either one) and it is only my particular thumb

on the scales that bears false witness;
false also because of what it takes lightly.

My thumb an adoption, an adaptation
according to my individual predominant fears.

The last neti-neti ends in nothing . . . or everything
but, perhaps it doesn't matter what the truth is

out there but what it is in here
when only silence is left, vastness,

stillness and darkness, the guttering flame
at last having gone irrevocably out.

O child of God, dance 'round and 'round
'til you're ready to stop and face the music.

The silent parlance

There seems to be something sacred
in turning my ears around

long before my approach to the inner Path,
listening to the wind

upon the knolls and hollows
of my own interior landscape.

In all humility not traipsing about
learning from others how to live,

answering to others' advice,
but heeding only and putting my sole faith

in that seemingly desultory inner voice,
the faint, unintelligible hints and suggestions

that come wafting across the moor,
often making little sense in the worldly scheme.

Having the great faith that You and I
shall one day converse until time's end,

once I capture and master anew
the lost, silent parlance of my soul.

O child of God, to elude the self,
trek deeper and deeper into the interior.

They also serve

They also serve who only stand and wait,
Milton wrote, comforting himself in his blindness.

Stand and wait, stand and wait.
These days I have lain aside,

for the most part my quest
and comfort myself that somehow

this will serve Him best.
To stand aside and wait for my Lord

to enter and restructure this dark interior
according to His whim and authority,

my former strivings an apparently necessary effort,
the required creation for the impending removal

of this provisional structure and by His hands
its destined replacement, inhabitance and completion.

O child of God, surrender requires patience
and a certain passivity – a strong yielding to His will.

The preliminary beauty

Aren't we beautiful? Aren't we brave?
We try so hard

to please our Lord, to serve Him,
to give of ourselves, to connect with others.

We are not very good at it
but that doesn't weaken our resolve.

My very young granddaughter
is just learning to use her fingers.

Grasping clumsily at objects.
She's not very good at it,

but it's the beauty of her efforts,
the concentration, determination

and my already knowing she will one day
use her hands with such perfect grace

to express her love, to give and receive,
to serve and please her Lord.

O child of God, the more you see the preliminary beauty,
the nearer you are to the viewpoint of God.

My old friend fear

I didn't start out searching for God.
My quest(ion) was – is it possible

to live without fear? Yes,
though apparently only through

the almost impossible task of surrender.
Now my fear has stepped into a better light,

an aura of beauty surrounding its dark shape.
Wasn't it fear that began my search for God?

My old friend fear that has kept me on task,
shooing me relentlessly from each bleak shelter,

chasing me down the path towards the light,
the peace and bliss which is my promised destiny?

O child of God, everything in illusion
is an integral part of your unfolding.

The great assumption

We are the lie no one ever told
who readily becomes the lie

we tell ourselves and others.
We are the great assumption

that never proves true and yet
we can never quite disbelieve,

escape our own lies and the lies of others.
The whole of humanity is whispering lies,

the smartest people in the world, in history,
insisting upon our collective view of truth.

So it all begins with faith and ends in realization,
if it turns out that you and I and the world

and our assumptions about it
are lies to ourselves and others

and Truth is after all what the mystics
have always asserted it to be.

O child of God, you are the living lie,
Meher said, of the truth that is you.

Buddhism in a nutshell

Buddhism in a nutshell (so far as I can tell)
is an arduous inward trek to reach

and remain behind a one way mirror.
Leave completely the phenomenal world.

Go deeper – behind the senses,
past thoughts, emotions and moods.

Deeper still, beyond the makeshift self
(that shameless impostor).

Unattached then, settle
behind the mirror, observe

without urgency the sundry layers
you have plunged through –

the whole of this highly synchronized illusion
inside and out, until destiny shatters

the glass of separation, annihilating
and returning you to the ancient underlying Void.

O child of God, balance on the brink
until you lose your mistaken identity.

Join the tended sparrows

Everything is in God's hands.
So says my faith and what a relief

to feel powerless and ineffectual –
personal culpability abdicated to karma's iron law;

proceeding afresh without the capacity
to botch entirely my soul's journey

or hurt any other except as just another
heedless agent of God's inexorable will.

So let me stop now wrestling with my bindings,
join the tended sparrows in song-praise

among the God-noted leaves, above
the numbered grains and mustard seeds,

even to the corrupting moths and rust.
Let me celebrate these swaddling clothes;

tightly secured as I am until fully accountable/
acceptable to God and my destined ultimate liberty.

O child of God, whatever occurs is perfect
and whatever does not occur never could have been.

Return to Canaan

A pillar of fire and cloud guided Moses
and the chosen ones day and night

on their tramp through the desert –
their return to Canaan. Arranged by God

to keep them from getting lost,
discouraged and distracted.

Meher Baba has replaced the fire and cloud
in our nowadays desert with His own image

and the sound of His name,
to keep us from getting lost,

discouraged and distracted.
Guiding His lovers – those newly gathered,

ragtag expatriates – in a night-and-day beeline
to our predestined, long-promised rendezvous.

O child of God, forty years is but a half-step
in the journey that lies afore and aft.

The bosom of Abraham

It's not about solving the mystery anymore;
locking in the puzzle pieces.

It seems now to be about forbearance
(in lieu of utter acceptance). About giving up.

An attempt to care no longer for myself
for the sake of all the others I do care for

knowing all the while I make my way just as they do –
alone . . . alone except for our mutual Friend.

Towards the end of a life of compulsions,
the one choice that seems open to me

is to disregard the interior prods and pulls
and the exterior promptings that trigger them

and to nestle myself, such as I am,
into the bosom of my particular Abraham.

O child of God, the Friend who is guiding you
is the Friend who is calling you home.

His One perfect response

Any question asked of God
is an implicit demand for an answer.

After a lifetime (to my dismay)
of such implications, I am beginning now

to hear (by His grace) the one answer
which has always been there – His silence;

(wherein only real things are exchanged
and wherein God alone is real).

I took a silent, invisible God
to be distant, unapproachable

while He's been faithfully
answering me all along

in a Voice – because it is so unlike mine –
I've had not the ears to hear.

Now I might grasp a bit more His admonition –
Love doesn't ask. Because Oneness hasn't a tongue.

O child of God, Love is silent, benevolent,
His One and only perfect response.

That promised quenched peace

Once my heart lush green, fresh from sky and earth,
time soon turned a fiery red, flush with hot-blooded desire.

A constant thwarting chilled its ardor, withered it yellow,
a timid fellow burrowing deeper into my chest

where bound in icy veins, it turned a dark bruised blue.
Today before its inevitable ceasing altogether

it beats a weathered gray, slow in its movements,
shedding its tears and quietly turning hoary white.

Perhaps true love will some lifetime hence,
as faith requires, fetch it up clear and colorless,

as incorporeal as the mystery that inhabits it
since first it arose beating, lonely and dim

to endure the mortal assaults of ignorance and illusion;
plucked from its checkered, colorful path to rest

eternally onward in that promised
quenched peace beyond its fleshly ken.

O child of God, what florid poetry you use
to recount the brutal facts and pray for redemption.

God instead

I don't know the particulars
but I'm going to have to leave

this world one day, the only one
I ever remember knowing;

leave behind everyone
and everything I hold dear

because the sea is (after all) cardboard
and the moon is made of paper.

I'm not talking about death's overtaking
but as a clear-eyed, deep-breath resolution.

Because if I and Love are eternal,
my affections and their objects (like myself)

are but pale, irresolvable reflections.
And to reach beyond the facade I must one day

unhand voluntarily their brief, illusory
solace and choose God instead.

O child of God, repeating the mystic promises,
you hover constantly near the edge of the abyss.

Faith in love

Words fail, but one word refuses to go away –
love – which Meher Baba uses to cover all bases

and list under one category the inexplicable.
Love which we know well enough

to desire its taste but not well enough
to drown in – its depths to reveal.

So we are left with faith instead, through it
to learn a new blind, deaf, dumb way to live,

nearer to love, nearer to truth, rooted in the ancient way,
trusting everything we are to His will and whim.

O child of God, faith in Meher Baba
is faith in love.

This time around

Friends of mine tour Europe.
Some attend the Super Bowl.

Others go to Yosemite or the Big Apple,
rock concerts, skydiving, sailing the high seas.

Africa, China, the Middle East.
Fine and wondrous adventures

I will miss out on this time around.
These things are not what I care for.

These things are not what I lack.
This time, when I kick the bucket

I want it to ring hollow,
resounding in the chill air

throughout the somber countryside,
tolling for my Lord and for myself,

for this brief stretch of our adventure as companions
this time around on my arduous trek back to Union.

O child of God, everyone is on their way home
by as many routes as there are wayward souls.

Eternal sweetness

On its outward flight, the honeybee
zigzags its dogged way amidst the garden

scents and colors, collecting in its honey pouch
here and there the makings of sweetness.

But on returning – home to the hive –
there is no waywardness, no lingering in its labor.

Laden, ponderously caked,
full of pollen it makes a beeline

for the dripping honeycomb
and the Queen's golden haven.

Would that I be, Lord, on my way home,
forsaking the world's bright wavering garden,

having foraged all I need of it to enter in
and turn the inner realms into eternal sweetness.

O child of God, how fanciful you are
in depicting your inevitable return to Reality.

Fig leaf

One of the most fortunate (for us)
attributes of God the Omniscient

is He's never disappointed.
We can't let God down.

He didn't build a garden that through
human error went hopelessly awry.

Shame before God is a dishonesty,
a lack of humility, hiding behind a fig leaf,

seeing ourselves as more culpable
than we could ever possibly be.

Humility is a way back to the garden,
recognizing God's sovereignty,

offering God our worst and best.
Humility is the opposite of shame –

it unravels our pretensions –
presenting ourselves to God (and to everyone)

nakedly honest, precisely who we are
not who we wish we were nor hope to become.

O child of God, how haughty you are
to speak so freely of God or humility.

My candled paper lantern

My faith is a chochin lantern
shaped from bamboo and paper

with past impromptu fortifications
of old shoelaces, paper clips,

thumbtacks and Scotch tape.
It's an easy target

for the glib and resourceful.
I rarely bring it out in public

to withstand the buffeting winds
and random crushing blows.

Not that my faith has ever been
doused or shattered by mere words.

It shines for me in such an incommunicable way –
my candled paper lantern

with its bright, fragile, flammable covering.
It shines for me dangling afore,

offering steady, silent comfort and guidance
through this great harrowing darkness of a world.

O child of God, keep your little lantern lit
until you become a six foot blaze yourself.

In hushed gratitude

I had no deep relationship with the mandali –
not like I had with my grandparents,

my mother and father, aunts and uncles
who have now for the most part passed on.

To be a good human being, I've learned,
is a great and difficult thing.

I aspire to be like those I love.
If I ever reach their level,

I might look for loftier souls to emulate.
If I had them with me again

I'd embrace each one in hushed gratitude,
then send their humble souls on their way

so much farther down the road than me,
toward that high, sweet mansion on the hill.

O child of God, the blessings you have received
in this lifetime grow more evident every day.

My worn out boots

My worn out boots are on His porch
but my back is to His door.

I've knocked randomly, rang the bell.
Without an answer I've turned again

toward where I came from
down the shady stone walk

through the trim, thick grass
that leads back to the busy street.

Everything passing out there seems
(momentarily) important – each phase,

crisis, new adventure, each fleeting attachment.
Everything but God at every moment

seems alive and urgent. Everything
but this quiet house set back from the road;

everything but getting a foot inside that door.
My worn out boots are on His welcome mat.

I'm not going anywhere – a blessing
and a curse – as I turn again briefly

to ring and knock, shout and study how
at last I might slip inside.

O child of God, to enter His house
turn forever your back upon the world.

Giving myself up for dead

I got myself lost in the back country,
romping out of the barn on a jet black horse

just as day broke. Rode wild and loose
for a long ways. Lost my bearings.

I've nosed my old horse around ever since
studying every bleached-boned hint of a trail,

every wagon rut, dry gulch
cattle run that might lead home.

At last I stumbled upon
an old ghost of a prospector

who advised me to drop the reins.
Let that tired, hungry horse under me

find its own way back to the stable.
I might not like the route or ride it takes,

but return, the old man said,
by giving myself up for dead;

by dropping all pride and purpose,
false hope, shallow expertise

to surrender completely,
beyond any intent or desire.

O child of God, not a trace of resistance!
Surrender tolerates no dishonesty.

The mercy of God

They sell a child's car seat
with a steering wheel attached

to keep junior busy in the backseat
driving the car along with Dad.

Such is my relationship with God.
I've sought most of my life and failed

to find one truth which would
disprove the obvious, terrifying notion

that I am utterly at the mercy of God.
God *Almighty* has left me no choice,

no influence, power or control.
No saving myself through any efforts,

merit, prayers of my own.
Yes, all the Realized Ones

say God is Love. God is my true Self.
I am firmly lodged under my own thumb.

But that truth is so very far away.
Not much comfort to my unrealized self

with no work to do, no vows to keep,
no power of rescue or the alleviation of pain.

O child of God, becoming helpless and hopeless
is not an attainment but a revelation.

When you look for God

The path seems more like a river now
than a road – I'm being pulled down it.

I haven't the choice even
of opening or shutting my eyes.

God, through the Law, does that.
The river wends where it will,

flowing also through my mind –
torrents of thoughts, emotions, moods

often turgid with the impedimenta of fear.
Attachment is not only about desire,

it's about existence – my existence. In truth,
I am a witness not a participant of my journey.

Thus I am bound and thus I am infinitely free.
Realization of that freedom is my destiny.

My search (which is not mine to claim)
is an unfolding of that destiny –

ever fated to seek and never find God
for I do not exist apart from Him.

O child, when you look for God, Rumi said,
God is in the look of your eyes.

God-sent

If my virtue requires a villain
I can be sure that I'm duping myself,

dabbling in duality with a quality
that belongs to another realm.

True virtue is God-sent, borne
of benevolence, humility and equanimity.

It breaks us down – nearer to dust and ashes.
Virtue that lifts us above others

is a subtle self promotion, an empty grand gesture
that for whatever good it does,

adds to the darkness, the ignorance
and hypocrisy of ourselves and the world.

O child of God, in the depths of a ruse
nothing is ever completely what it seems.

Wondrous to consider

It's wondrous to consider
I might consciously be God right now

if I didn't take so much delight in being
my vain, silly scoundrel of a self.

All the evidence is now in
indicating that to reach Paradise

I will have to leave my front porch.
Routinely, I sift through my verifications

calling it prayer, meditation, study and praise.
It's much safer and easier than to risk the task

of true effacement. Easier to sit tight
in this familiar old rocking chair

than trekking out into that lonely, austere terrain.
Repeatedly, I lament my predicament

and yet time and again – still –
I choose myself over God.

O child, impossibly difficult, Meher Baba said,
to become what you already are.

Of stars and stones

When they plant my stone on the green hillside
nothing earth-shattering will occur –

the ocean and the stars will function as ever before
once my little boat slips under the waves.

Often I listen to the world now as if I'm in a casket.
Listen to my thoughts as if they were wind in the trees.

Listen beyond the palpable noises,
beyond the stream of my thoughts

to the silence underlying every sound, inside and out.
The silence of stars and stones. The silence of the blue sky

behind the clouds. The silence of death.
I listen to – whether real or imagined –

the silence my Lord saved up for a lifetime
and left for me and others to listen to in our loneliness.

O child of God, why not, asked my Lord,
consider yourself already dead?

The perfect me

Forgive me, humanity, I have not been
the human being – the father, son, brother,

husband, partner, friend – I had hoped to be.
Nowhere near, not within a country mile.

What I *am* and have been –
to complete perfection – is the perfect me.

No one could ever come close
to being as perfect a me as me.

Soon enough I'll meet the perfect death,
this version of self ceasing forever to exist

and move on to what is next.
I don't ask forgiveness from God.

I thank God for sharing with me
the opportunity of serving Him

(fitting so aptly into His plan)
by being the unique, imperfect perfect me;

expressing precisely all He wished to be expressed,
attaining all that was required by my particular incarnation.

O child of God, don't worry. Be happy.
Perfection is in the eye of the Beholder.

His silence

Leather on the soles of my tender feet
protecting me from the sharpness of the path

must be abandoned before entering the Samadhi –
for the sake of reverence and humility

and simply because protection is no longer required.
Removed to get me into the right posture and mode

to accept what blessings (by His grace) might flow.
Years later, I stand at the threshold of His Silence.

My desperate yearning to understand must also
be abandoned, its protection no longer valid,

so that I might in reverence and humility
embrace the mystery, utterly at His mercy;

the right posture and mode to receive (by His grace)
whatever blessings He might choose to bestow.

O child of God, rejoice! His silence
is the answer to all your questions.

The everywhere ocean

O how I have paced the quay
longing to leave the shore!

Throw myself into the ocean of Love
to drown there – a returning (I am told)

to my lost, original existence.
But, only lately have I begun to suspect

that I am now (and forever have been)
continuously sunk, fathomlessly deep,

utterly drenched in Love's boundless ocean.
God is Love, said Meher. And God is everywhere.

I swim about daily in the ocean of God
clinging to the thin veil that estranges me,

prevents my experiencing down to the marrow
my original and continuous existence

as an immeasurable drop
in the everywhere ocean of Love.

O child of God, there is no point of departure
for anywhere you might think you need to be.

The ancient song

Let him step to the music which he hears,
said Thoreau. However measured or far away.

Music which leads the soul homeward –
God's drumbeat into chosen ears.

Becoming tricky then, two rhythms
competing in an open field

for the souls of a few lovers
who misstep, lose stride,

turning aside from the wide path
to the winding narrows, able no longer

to keep the world's tempo nor dance to its tune.
A faint song at first, growing inescapable –

when God starts drumming up business
to serve One, abandon all, another wave of lovers

struggling to keep pace, leave in the dust
the world's throng and cadence.

O child of God, there's no hope for you –
enchanted forevermore by the ancient song of Meher.

Ocean shell

Cup this shell to your ear
and listen to the ocean –

its hollow, hushed white noise
somewhere between a silence and a roar.

Shell to ear, ear to heart,
this is the silence Baba left

(with its intimate roar)
to drown out the world's bellow,

its furor and anguish,
sham and shallow glamour;

the mind's incessant stream of self.
Cup this ocean shell to your ear

and leave the populous shore
for the solitude and intangible promise

of the deep high seas, farther out, farther out
towards oblivion and soundless nonexistence.

O child of God, ride the ocean waves
until you lose your boundaries in its briny vastness.

The turn of a knob

I hold my tongue (as You suggested
through the silence of a lifetime)

and meet You in that immeasurable space
where real things are exchanged.

Even in these raw, preliminary stages,
I'm allowed through that door

where at the turn of a knob
I'm greeted by Your silence.

There to listen instead of barter,
quiescent rather than seeking,

immobile instead of on the prowl,
humble instead of scheming –

o Lord, I am the silence I listen to.
You are the silence I listen to.

We mingle there as one –
as I mutely place my hand in Yours.

O child of God, continue with your raucous verses.
Meher's silence contains all sound.

That nonexistent shore

My little soul is not a drop in the bucket
but according to Meher a drop in an ocean

only faintly comparable to a terrestrial ocean –
an ocean without a shore,

without sky above nor floor below.
An ocean if there is only ocean.

And my soul is not on a journey –
no space to move through,

nowhere to go and no time to get there.
I have no fellow beings, no boundaries,

no autonomy, no existence.
And yet here I am – every day just as if

there were days and nights, lives and deaths,
flesh and bone, five senses, mind and knowledge.

Here I am, o Lord, calling to You as if You
had ears and I had a throat and tongue.

O child of God, let your mind twist and swirl
until it's dashed upon the stones of that nonexistent shore.

Nonexistence

Not one thing did I attain, said the Buddha
(per Zen tradition) *by realization.*

When the illusory bubble over the drop soul bursts,
there is (apparently) no change at all – to drop or Ocean.

You have to get rid of I, me, my and mine, said Meher.
That doesn't mean become less selfish.

He's talking about nonexistence.
He's talking about becoming

as nonexistent as the illusion that surrounds us.
God alone is Real, Meher said – which means we are not.

Or to put it another way – *not we but One.*
And when we realize *That*

nothing is different from what it was
because we never really were at all.

O child of God, one great attribute of God
is that He never changes.

Under their trilling

The path of knowledge has petered out
into a thick pine wood ripe with scent and birdsong.

Its remainder does not lie undiscovered up ahead.
It simply goes no farther.

There's no key to God's door
on my considerable chain –

a weight I've accumulated for years.
There's no lock on God's door;

most likely there's no door at all out this far.
What I should do now is toss these keys,

scatter the last of my bread crumbs
for the gathered, guileless birds

and await my Beloved under their trilling –
hand outstretched but no longer for begging,

merely waiting, do or die, for Him
to take my hand and lead me home.

O child of God, leave it – your salvation
has always been entirely up to Him.

Famous blue overcoat

O if I could shed my cleverness like an old coat!
Leave it in the seat of a city bus, say,

groaning on without me
or stuff it in a local thrift store bin.

Where it started out as occasional apparel
donned for style, secrecy, protection,

over time it became an essential part of me,
holding everything together.

It became how I daily get through life.
And now that I want to come clean;

strip down to simple naked faith,
now that I yearn to fall apart,

stubbornly, heavily it clings
(and I to it) concealing the real me

as I wrestle and suffocate
under its weight and cover.

O child of God, Meher is leading you by the hand.
Take solace in the truth of your plight.

Unencumbered of woe

Holding Meher Baba's umbrella,
my long legs, tall frame keep pace

as He strides the rough terrain
of early Meherabad.

We halt in the middle of a field
and after a long silence He turns,

gestures for me to step nearer,
out of the harsh sun into the circle of shade.

I obey and leave beyond its rim myself,
my quest and all such fearsome bindings;

leave behind the rest of the world.
No need for anything else

save His Presence, this shelter
beyond attainment, beyond understanding.

O child of God, to trust Meher
is to become unencumbered of woe.

This dewy morning

A green trail left in the morning dew
where I have walked to the newly turned garden.

No point in asking where the dew
will be later on in the day

nor where it was the crisp cold evening last.
That's all being taken care of by someone else.

I bend to work the hoe in dew-drenched hands,
till the dewy soil, strike with the blade

the occasional dew-like, hidden pebbles.
I anticipate a succulent harvest a few months hence,

fitting myself as best I might into this small patch
of the universal scheme, accepting whatever the price

and stipulations of its brief sustenance and bounty.
Everything else is being taken care of by someone else.

O child of God, surrender is a quiet thing,
begun every sunrise in humble, laboring silence.

Knowledge Itself

Imagine a realm where there's nothing to ponder.
Not a realm of omniscience, mind you,

but of quiescence; a dousing deeply satisfying –
the flame snuffed out; the pendulum

come (at last) to a dead plumb stop.
For years now my Lord has preached in my wilderness

for His lover to become desireless.
I have strung Him along –

answered His quenching wisdom
with all manner of inquiries, ruminations, suppositions.

Cheekily I have begged to be an exception –
to be taught – though He did not come for that.

Strange to discover after a near-lifetime of searching
that my fondest desire, of which I cannot let go,

is to *know* within this tiny, mortal,
bone-hard skull of mine Knowledge Itself

and that this wrong-headed obsession
is keeping me from an unstipulated surrender

that would allow all my doubts to die
peacefully unrequited within my mortal frame.

O child of God, you keep coming back to the same
fundamentals you were told from the very first.

A child of Meher

I heard of a man named Mercy,
those drawn to Him are known as lovers

and ever since that long ago day,
in spite of my distrust, I have inwardly

longed to be wholeheartedly
one of those sisters and brothers.

But how might a man of so little love,
so little mercy align himself honestly

with the lovers of the Lord of Love;
the Father of Mercy? I have remained a beggar

outside the gates; listened to their songs of love,
even composed a few myself of praise and complaint,

expressing my allegiance, my hope for love,
my gratitude for the still-open invitation;

marveling at the path I have taken
since I first heard the mercy of His name.

O child of God, however stubborn your fears,
you could never deny – you are a child of Meher.

Another name for God

My Lord allowed Himself
to be named Father of Mercy,

perhaps to keep us reminded
subliminally that we are ever and utterly

at the mercy of God the Omnipotent.
The religious of us tiptoe

around this terrible truth
by the assumption of a chosen status;

by ritualistic appeasement, petitions and blandishments.
Others seek solace in an existential detachment –

even to the point of atheism – to avoid
any possible threat of judgment,

a comparative sense of inferiority
or simply because they place nothing above

the god of their mind.
God is Love, said my Lord

but it's not our sort of love – attachment,
affection, infatuation; pity and remorse.

Love is simply another name for God –
His unimaginable Oneness.

O child of God, child of the Father, pray that you might
one day know the true meaning of mercy.

A brighter lantern

All talk about the Path and the Goal,
said my Lord, is a lantern carried by a blind man.

Afraid of the darkness and feeling no one
near enough trustworthy (save myself)

to traverse the perilous way, I have begged
time and again for more light! A brighter lantern!

A blind man needs a staff in his hand, said my Lord.
And He has provided me one of a sort,

merely out of compassion – a substitute for sight;
shown the methods of probing with it,

my hitting upon many a brief, comforting revelation
when I have been unable to move forward

any other way, incapable of perceiving Him
always near and ever ready

to provide all the guidance I should ever require.
The lover needs his hand in the God-Man's, He said.

And I am groping blindly now for that hand,
ready to discard at last the false

and temporary solace of the ineffectual lantern,
the rigid, unwieldy staff.

O child of God, it is up to you and your fate to grasp
and yield to His omnipotent authority and shelter.

Some enchanted evening

you may see a stranger, you may
see a stranger across a crowded room . . .

and o how many and often a crowd of strangers
comes between that beautiful One and myself!

Taps on the shoulder, the commandeering of elbows,
various pitches; elaborate dances and wild melees

all the while my trying to keep a steady eye
on the stranger moving silently through the room.

Moving pure and graceful through the room,
parting the crowd effortlessly with each step.

Seeming to come nearer . . . ever nearer.
An irresistible urge to touch His garment;

an effort to tear myself away from the others;
to push through, move beyond;

fly to Him, fly to that preternatural,
healing figure of enchantment.

O child of God, how many and often a crowd
comes between you and your true Self.

Save God

No one loves Me, said my Lord, as I should be loved.
And if I were daring, could I not say the same

for myself among my fellow human beings?
No one knows (save God) my soul and history entirely

and thus a judgment by others (and myself) out of ignorance
is rendered that invariably negates true love.

I love you more than you could ever love yourself,
said my Lord also, speaking from God's perspective.

Loving me utterly because He is in truth one with me.
Out of ignorance is my love lacking –

out of ignorance is my love piecemeal and provisional –
for my Lord, my God; myself and fellow beings.

Ignorance is the chain that binds, the veils limiting
and clouding the expression and return of our own true love.

O child of God, you speak boldly of love
while never having had a real taste of it.

The inner voice

I speak less these days.
I live alone save for the Silent One

Who has no need for words. Perhaps,
some of His more human ways

are rubbing off on me.
I say His name more than ever

but it's silence I prefer –
long stretches of it, as much as I can bear

inside and out, in my mind and throat,
silence more and more

so that I might also give and receive
(more and more) the real things.

O child of God, heed the inner voice
and whatever you do will be a blessing.

Treasured postcards

This may look and read like a poem
but for me it is simply another piece

of evidence to be numbered and filed away
with poems of the past like treasured postcards

sent from my Beloved. Reread over the years
to bolster my faith when I find myself at sea,

alone in the dark, my hand seemingly slipped from His.
Not the art of them nor their elucidations.

No, their very existence is my evidence,
the blessed assurance that my Lord

is with me, responding then, now and always.
This poetry is not mine. I haven't it in me.

These poems are the patient, particular
answers and encouragement He has given me

through the years, leading me onward,
quenching my doubts, quelling my fears.

His prints are all over them – typed out onto a blank screen
but written all the same in His generous flowing hand.

O child of God, trade in your circumstantial evidence
for the conviction of real experience.

Slow of speech

How fearful and sad – Moses,
descending from the mountain

aware he could bring down only
God's words – not (as he had witnessed)

His voice and fire. God's living truth
carved rigidly into stone – fixed, deadly,

visible from a thousand different views.
Slow of speech was Moses, his inarticulacy

even more pronounced and urgent
on the twist of his tongue around

the terrible, majestic truth of the God
he had to leave behind

whose presence below would have
broken all commandments, sealed all promises

and set burning His truth
into the hearts of humanity.

How could he explain? The laws are a method,
a benevolence, a beginning, boundaries along the path

and God is always and already among His people
even though they know Him not.

O child, God conceals Himself in a cloud,
saying, no man sees My face and lives.

Castle in the air

I've built a castle in the air,
rooted precariously in the clouds.

I move through it daily inspecting
inconsistencies, shifts in solidarity

and alignment – yet also marveling each step
at its impracticable beauty and intricate improbability.

It began with a frail hope, then a desperate faith.
Now a feckless audacity keeps me

roaming its uncharted wings,
knowing what an absurd indulgence

my efforts are considered
by almost everyone stuck in the mire below.

Riding the clouds, built upon the wind,
having perhaps not a whit of substance

but, o I have found nothing
on terra firma to outweigh its promise,

its solace and my holy obsession
with its lofty, ethereal beauty.

O child of God, to reside within the mystery,
rise above everything on earth taken to be true.

One gulp

There is no instead; no road not taken.
No opportunity lost nor circumstance forsaken.

We ride a tiger through an evanescent realm
unable to steer, stop, start or climb down.

Best make ourselves cozy as possible
high up there in the catbird seat;

ride the necessary rough and tumble,
become soul witness,

keep silence, suspend judgment
until the tiger turns upon each of us

and all our accoutrements
slip from their perch,

our whole accumulated world
devoured in one gulp.

O child of God, the more you distance yourself
from the game the nearer you are to God.

Hair shirt

Wool gave Sufis their name –
desert ascetics in their harsh prickly robes.

I wear my own hair shirt these days.
O how it pierces, bites and stifles!

Where once they went unnoticed, taken for granted
comes now the stings of my arrogance,

sanctimony and self-satisfaction, my disdainful envy,
the rash flaunting of my cleverness

and my own vaunted exceptionality.
O how now they chafe and bind when in retrospect

I compare my past (and current) sad posturing,
my feeble cloaked disguise

to the mute humility and renunciation
to which I so achingly aspire

and view so unequivocally as the next
fated stretch of the path set before me.

O child of God, self-knowledge is always painful
yet ultimately liberating in its prickly impracticality.

God's blood

One day to the garden shall we return,
each of us experience anew

the wonder and bewilderment
felt Adam and Eve first waking up –

one with God and His creation; no will but His.
Biting into the apple was the great sin

of breaking in two and then into pieces
the faith and unity of I and Thou,

letting into our original allegiance
and relationship the taint of the other.

One day afresh we shall look childlike
upon the world – our wonder restored,

our bewilderment savored at every turn
in this miraculous setting,

knowing God again as the Father
and ourselves as God's blood-

flesh-and-bone brood roaming
shamelessly naked the garden.

O child of God, the breaking of the Oneness
was never real – only heartbreakingly semblant.

God's door

I see now that knowledge is not
the proper tool – a key lacking

the apposite notches to turn
the given tumblers.

With the key of knowledge
I might just as effectively

tap urgently on the jamb
or jingle the whole chain like a bell

hoping God comes forth
to see who stands on His porch.

That which opens God's door
is apparently grace as always

beyond the fingertips of our keyless hands,
induced not by knowledge

but attentiveness, supplication,
longing and obsessive intention.

O child of God, recall Rumi's assertion –
you are knocking on the door from the inside.

The original dust

This metaphor – perhaps it will hold water:
I am a clay jug with a crack in it.

Compulsively, I pour into myself
intoxicants, refreshments, elixirs

but end up always empty and athirst,
my vessel inherently unsuitable

for containment and repletion.
Indeed, this hollowed-out jug

is a barrier to my true function,
my ultimate immersion and satiation.

Nothing on earth (say the mystics)
can permanently plug the crack.

The only cure is abstention – allow myself
to become and remain utterly dry.

Then, will my Beloved come along,
return me by His hammer to the original dust.

O child of God, let your malformed nothingness
be absorbed into His perfect everything.

The emptiness of the dream

When I began my quest,
the world made perfect sense;

the pieces fit together snugly,
clung tightly into place.

Then You came along,
bounding down the open road,

upending the apple cart,
proclaiming a new life –

a great living and breathing Mystery
and I was intrigued enough to follow,

study, query, surmise and conject.
Years later, You have become

the only thing that makes sense.
Not because I've come anywhere near

plumbing Your depths but because
You have shown me the emptiness of the dream.

I look to You now for the unfathomable truth
because everything else in my world

has proven demonstrably false, fleeting,
insubstantial, partial and delusory.

O child of God, it is Maya – ignorance –
that undergirds the Illusion.

The less you milk the dream

As it turns out, the only bargain's end
to uphold is my relationship with the One,

my allegiance bit by bit being switched
from the multifarious, strangely enough

drawing me subtly nearer to the many
in which the One is contained.

Non-attachment (inside and out) is more feasible
as I learn continuously that I hold no sway –

becoming not an attainment but a godsend,
not a method but the truth, an immense

and steadfast comfort the more I dare practice it.
Choices revealed as mere competing compulsions –

effete illusions – the compelling force (as Meher avers)
that drives this individual and collective dream.

It becomes a release that is not an evasion
but an acceptance, an acknowledgement,

the long sought key to the long conjectured
and proposed obedience and surrender.

O child of God, the less you milk the dream
the more true sustenance you receive.

A bee in my bonnet

Ever since I heard of that honey-laden hive,
I've had a bee in my bonnet,

a brain-itch that can't be scratched.
A nagging thought that I must have

forgotten something vital – misplaced a key,
unable to remember where I left it.

Thus, have I been for my life's better part
unable to pay the world my full attention –

reluctant to make its necessary choices.
I don't believe in choices anymore.

I believe in karma and compulsion –
to obey or ignore their urgencies.

The Avatar of the age has come
to guide, instill and accentuate

yet another compulsion – the blood-deep
burning need to know who I really am.

O child of God, follow that bee
back to the honey in the rock.

Nothing of substance

Dust is existence without blood,
wrote the poet Francis.

Most likely the same thought
in a different language

spoken by Francis the saint.
As in dust at His feet –

bloodless . . . without spit, too,
without tears, dried up,

crushed, yet breathing, speaking,
doing, thinking – serving the Lord.

Returned to the dust from which
the servant was fashioned

long before the ropes lower him
to his earthly repose; serving the Lord

as a jar of dust holding nothing
of substance – nothing of substance –

only the God-part, the love-essence,
the elusive, ethereal soul.

O child of God, emptiness is completeness
(say the mystics). Nothing is everything.

Child of God

An identity and a relationship;
a way of addressing myself

in the last couplet; not so bold
as inserting my name

into the body of the poem.
It was chosen for me,

its truth revealed a thousand poems later –
this settled upon child of God

being who I really am – all I really am
and who I must of my own accord

solely become, eschewing all other
false, ephemeral and relative identities –

poet, author, mortal man;
father, grandfather, brother, son;

husband, lover, citizen, friend . . .
pared down to this one identity,

this one naked fundamental –
my relationship with my Creator.

O child of God, pray for the dissolution
of all identities and relationships.

Toward a graveyard silence

Even in a choir these days you can always tell
which throat is mine – it's the one

shot through with an arrow
(like the piercing of a heart)

thick with blood, sounding less and less true,
moving toward a graveyard silence.

I'm tired of singing, of telling, advocating,
arguing. Only my mind still wants to argue.

My hands are done with finger-pointing;
my heart weary of rebuttals.

(To disagree is so . . . disagreeable!)
My eyes want only to read –

read the hearts of others and find them free
of any blame or error on my account.

O child of God, how peaceful it is when your heart
goes for a long, brave ride and your mind takes a backseat.

The heart's tender

Not for the fainthearted, said my Lord – love,
borne of strength and true understanding.

Acts of compassion absent of submission
and faith are tainted by fear,

anger and sanctimony; the false assumption
of duty and authority. The way of love is not

to become tenderhearted
but to become the heart's tender –

where God is met and looked after,
keeping down the head;

not to be pulled aside, bogged down,
intimidated by the sentiments

and enticements (good and evil) of the world.
Keeping one's self to one's Self –

the only authentic relationship, leading to
the birth of peace and the truth of action.

O child of God, the best you can do
for the world is turn inward.

Once the spigot runs dry

Nary an island of truth, apparently,
in this vast sea of illusion

to set a solid foot upon.
Deep in my cups, I drown

in my ignorance and isolation,
cling to sentimentalities, spout

my judgments and objections ...
but once the spigot runs dry, I sober up,

fold up my deficiencies, release
every prejudice I hold like paper lanterns

onto the flowing currents
and settle best I might under the stars

into a quiet receptivity
(which has nothing at all

to do with knowledge or perception)
of a truth so encompassing, so indisputable,

its every tongueless expression and persuasion
leaves no room for any possibility of refutation.

O child of God, the one sweet spot of truth
in the whole universe is stowed away inside your chest.

Horse-hooves knowledge

A lifetime of wandering here and there
among the trees looking for the forest.

A plastic sequin on a cheap gown –
such it is that snags the mind –

spangles not only worthless but pernicious
for they divert us from the real and the true.

At ocean's shore the galloping horse stumbles,
unable to enter deeply where it can neither

stand nor swim or float; rear or whinny –
do anything other than drown

in wild, flaring confusion. We cling
to the shore and the horse that got us there.

Numerous lifetimes it takes to know
we do not know, can never know

anything of the ocean, anything of where
the horse is a foreign, ineffectual creature;

anything but the dust-ridden,
horse-hooves knowledge

that keeps us ever on the scent, ever
following one false trail after another.

O child of God, the mind reigns in duality
but can never leave itself to reach beyond.

Sixty-nine years
(a birthday poem)

Sixty-nine years and I'm no wiser.
I've learned nothing along the way.

Scenes have passed. Some illusions
have been worn through (maybe)

but none concerning the truth.
Sixty-nine years and I've grown no older.

Have not changed a whit
from the day I was born.

Immutable and eternal, nothing
has touched me and nothing ever will.

Truth doesn't come from experience
nor accumulation of knowledge.

There are no lessons to learn.
No growth or maturation to attain.

This much I've learned but this much
has nothing to do with the truth that is me.

O child of God, when will you awaken?
Meher said He did not come to teach.

The madman of Chu

No one seems to know, said Kieh Yu
(the madman of Chu),

how useful it is to be useless.
But You have given some

in this intimate age a hint of that knowledge,
leaving them vertiginous, empty and ruined.

Reducing others to a flood of tears –
mooning over You for weeks

while the world rattles on without them.
Still others allowed a refuge

carved out inwardly, letting the waves break
soundlessly upon the deserted shore.

And there were those sanctified ones
who served You madly,

their every effort made useless
by the surrender of self,

their every dedicated outcome
determined solely by Your will and reign.

O child of God, pray your every poem one day
becomes a useless, holy endeavor.

That clear still center

If I had my way, I'd never come back
to another lifetime of sin and ignorance,

causing pain and harm to myself and others.
But that's no virtue –

not wanting to cause suffering.
It's just another desire – the root of suffering,

the barrier to surrender and non-return.
In the realm of illusion

where might pure virtue be found?
Purity has nothing to do with perfection.

It has to do, apparently, with getting off the wheel
onto that clear still center even as

the rest of the world shakes and gyres,
rattles and quakes, wavers around you.

If I had my way, I'd never come back
but then – it's never been about me having my way.

O child of God, round and round and round you go,
too drunk to find your way off the dance floor.

His child

Go into a closet to pray, advised Jesus.
O if I could lock myself in a closet

and not come out again!
A narrow, soundproof cell,

too dark to use my eyes, nothing in reach
to afford or encourage escape,

everything at last falling away –
cleverness, confidence, obstinacy,

even faith and the last rays of hope.
Cornered and abandoned,

stripped of the extraneous,
down to the raw truth of myself,

nowhere to turn but to my Maker.
No one to be but His child.

There and then, might I be able
to articulate a closing prayer –

one that asks for nothing and receives
whatever it is, (what*ever* it is!) God has to give.

O child of God, it's your worldly involvement
that keeps you from going home.

The sole barrier

Everything is allegorical, metaphorical,
true and not true at the same time

but if you spend too much on the seeming –
its enchantment and beauty,

the aptness of it, its sturm und drang,
its marvelous (self-created) synchronicity,

you'll find yourself once again mired
in the enthralling labyrinths and blind alleys

of the mind, the maze, the path, the dream.
And it's a wondrous dream –

far beyond our ability to fathom it,
with little profit in trying –

save to reach the end of effort.
Just imagine (but not too desperately)

the truth behind it,
the truth of the One

Who conjured up all this seeming . . .
out of nothing. For us, for Himself.

O child of God, you remain (say the mystics)
the sole barrier between semblance and truth.

Piscean

Here's another poem
about the wind-swept sea –

its froth and spray, churn and tumble,
bitter dash upon the shore.

Another poem diving only
deep as I can hold my breath,

gather my fears, buck my buoyancy –
everything below that left unfathomed.

One day, as per my Lord, I'll become Piscean,
crafted and structured to bear the weight

and pressure of the depths.
When that happens, ages hence,

I'll be known for my wide-eyed
oceanic silence, my lack of output –

no fingers to hold a pen or type a letter.
No fleshy mechanism to form a word.

O child of God, when you come to know,
surely you'll have nothing to say.

In God we trust

The sea-knowledge of the onetime fisherman
    drained his faith and sank Peter short

of reaching Jesus as he walked the pitching sea;
    kept the others frightened aboard,

entreating their Savior, yet trusting instead
    a makeshift construct to keep them afloat.

But it was Jesus who lifted Peter from the brine,
subdued the storm and brought the ship to shore.

In God we trust . . . there's no one else –
    save our treacherous selves.

Everything is true and congruent to the whole
except our separateness. The one false thing

(never to be trusted) – our erroneous faith
in ourselves and who we take ourselves to be.

O child of God, the construct of the false self
    is the source of an ocean of suffering.

By candlelight

By candlelight I search my self's
nooks and crannies for the source of darkness.

How deep is myself? It has no end
so long as I'm looking for it,

upheld in the ever deepening maw
by invisible threads always a bit beyond

the tip of my outstretched sword.
Down through the mountain gap,

I've entered now the redemptive ocean
but my walking stick keeps me afloat

and I'm kept on the inside dust-dry
by my impermeable skin.

I've tried silence and cessation as well,
huddled with myself in the expectant dark,

at His infinite mercy but it's no good –
just another phony calculation,

inadequate as every other attempt
to lure the grace that admits no compulsion.

O child of God, that which would deliver you
you have no idea how to do.

The only one in the room

In Your presence (and in their memory)
often they would say

You were the only one in the room.
Even Eruch (or some other) interpreting

your gestures or reading the board
became a disembodied voice

as they beheld You –
the essence of Love and Truth,

the only one in the room.
These latter days when we

are alone together so often,
let it be my meditation

to dwell upon You
until You are once more

the only one in the room,
leaving this illusory life,

myself and all the insistent,
suffering world behind.

O child of God, within and without, Meher said,
present and past, existent or imagined, God alone is real.

Jiminy Cricket

Did you know Jiminy Cricket
is a euphemism for Jesus Christ?

We tend to make God and the Godman
convenient for ourselves – inconsequential,

lest faith becomes too burdensome,
getting in the way of our will and desire.

(Unless, of course, we hit a rough patch
and require His comfort and fortitude).

We make Him small enough to fit in our pocket,
ride upon our shoulders; imagine Him loyal,

wise, the truth He utters (in a comical chirping voice)
a mere suggestion to take or leave

as through the titillating world we wend and weave,
nodding our sculpted wooden heads,

bearing our cumbersome, accumulated lies,
hoping to one day become real, untainted, true and alive!

And to one day find that diffident fellow
who we once were before we lost our way.

O child of God, every memorable story is one
of the soul's search for the Father.

The sum of my parts

I am not a white man
Alabama blue collar (retired)

grandfather father brother son.
I am You. I am You.

I am not a Vedantist Christian Sufi
Buddhist lover of Meher Baba.

Not a novelist poet seeker songwriter.
I am You. I am You.

Not a sinner beseecher intellectual eremite
introvert; not social political communal.

Not myself nor the sum of my parts.
I am You. I am You.

I have yet to realize the truth of Who I am
but my faith is in Your presence and Your Word –

We are not we but one. I am not the living lie.
I am the truth. I am You. I am You.

So now my prayer and daily duty is to ever
turn away, turn away from that which I am not

toward the truth of my Self, the truth of Us.
I am You. I am You.

O child of God, in duality you have an identity.
In Reality there is only the infinite One.

A tongueless bell

From these poems one might guess
I'm getting a bit desperate

but my Beloved skirts and shields me
from desperation while allowing

(apparently) my compulsions to momentously
flower and die; desires to wither by His grace

into a vapid, gray, tin ear sort of indetermination,
empty to me now as a tongueless bell.

My interest no longer vested, turning
my holdings over to loved ones

to make their way through the maze
each according to their own karma.

Just bank-sitting now, paralyzed by indifference
except toward the One who quickens my pulse,

sharpens my ears, whets my thirst. The one
in all the world who rings true. Rings true.

O child of God, the path of renunciation, through His grace,
has been rendered smoother than you could ever have
imagined.

Nom-de-plume

I am the ribbon in the typewriter
(near as to anything else), the lead in the pencil,

ink in the pen, scattered pixels on the screen.
You write these poems. You ask the questions,

provide the answers, make comments and observations.
The boundary between us then is vague,

shallow and negligible, only apparent
as I write it down, sit and wonder

where I'm being led, what will be asked
and said in a verse ironically tagged

with the nom-de-plume of my ignorance. O Beloved!
How You shake me up! Rattle my bones!

O child of God, to write these poems is a breathless dip
into the depthless pool of His mystery.

The king's hand

When the flood of Your words
leaves me speechless and hollow,

my own expressions meaningless
as the complaints of a flag

dealt roughly by the wind,
it's like the story of the king

who allowed his attendants
to seize any one treasure

to be given freely unto them. O Beloved!
Like the faithful servant girl,

let me grasp the king's hand, the source
of these riches and every other,

evident or hidden, honoring the Poet,
His words and wisdom, His prowess and plan.

O child of God, these poems should always
leave you empty of any comparisons.

Good clean fun

You get to a point every now and then
where fun is just another waste of time –

and you don't know how much
you have left (not near enough),

the house odds so utterly against you
only a miracle (call it grace)

could put you ahead of the game, get you
escorted out slightly woozy, flush with cash

and still you would be light years from home.
Good clean fun being one of the few

egalitarian pleasures given to us
on this planet, those who walk away

are deemed to have something inside
gone terribly awry. Or maybe

they just have other business to attend to,
a distant trumpet, dimly familiar, calling them back

to where in truth they might belong,
far from everything they ever once thought fun.

O child of God, you are an eternal being (per Meher).
How could you ever run out of time?

Living precept

Certain ones grown old become lighter,
a foretaste of their flying away.

Shoulders nudged forward by age
as if to accept wings, unhitched

from a long duration of burdens;
footprints shallow in the sandy soil.

Rather than well worn words out of elderly mouths,
an arresting smile, eyes shiny with eloquence.

Not frailty but etherealness – a dearth inside
of leaden opinions, judgment and grudge.

Collect a loose embrace from those
who can no longer be held down.

These are the living precepts,
their bodies atremble with vulnerability

not for death but for a yielding to truth,
the last gasp before an overtaking,

a settled down surrender and a faithful waiting
for a new adventure to begin.

O child of God, may your last breath
place you that much nearer to God.

Incomparable perfection

Since my Beloved told me I am an eternal being,
much of the old urgency has fallen away.

Since I stopped believing in myself,
ceased rattling my karmic chains,

played my hunch on the law of must,
time matters little to me now.

Wherever it is I'm bound, God will get around to it,
my arrival as precisely orchestrated as the flight of stars.

How could it be otherwise under His exacting command?
If I've misjudged my position there will be

an abundance of time to correct the error.
What's a few more centuries plastered on

to the end of my eternity? Or an additional
allotment of comparative binding and suffering

before my fated release into the infinite sea of bliss?
Time is naught when the mind is fixed on the now,

more and more serving the Master every moment
in the lover's body as He once was served in His own.

O child of God, your every thought and occurrence
is an integral element in the incomparable perfection of God.

Suspects at large

Once upon the path, the purity of my motives
seemed of paramount importance, self

strictly monitored and swiftly brought to heel.
These days I see plainly my notions

of a motive afford me too much power
because I have no true center –

beneath this mutable persona
there is only You and has been You all along.

It's Your game within me and without.
I have no purity, no sincerity; no lack of such.

I have nothing on which to hang my hat.
And You, having only a Whim,

have no lack, no cause or motive
to do what You do nor to be Who You are.

O child of God, there are no suspects
at large on which to pin a motive.

You never let go

After I wised up, I told my adult self
I knew not what I was doing –

nine years old tramping down the aisle
to give my life to Jesus. But lately I see

I knew exactly what I was doing,
my untouched heart roughly awakened

and refusing then to settle for anything less.
Very soon I wised up, took back my life

and went my worldly way. It was when I began
to reawaken and search for You

that I knew not what I was doing,
yet reduced by the painful invalidity of the world

to having nothing else worth doing.
And learning later that once You accept

a lamb into the fold You never let go.
It was You who initiated my adult search

for the one Who is within me all along
and for that child, lost but not abandoned,

being now mercifully relieved
of all his worldly wisdom.

O child of God, you have not changed a whit
since that surrender and neither has your Lord.

Felling the yew

The tree in the garden was a yew,
it's red fruit succulent and benign

but the toxicity of the seeds tainted
the ruined couple's blood and their progeny.

The needled limbs of that ancient yew
poison yet the garden breeze;

its roots contaminate the soil,
the wind-and-rain-scattered seeds

seasonally propagate new toxins.
Many a game child has tried their honed axe

upon that lonely tree grown iron-like and huge
but it requires instead an abeyance and a spurning,

a love-soaked immobilization and purity
possessed by no son or daughter of Adam.

It requires a blow by a lightweight,
reborn, new life, post-garden child of God.

O child of God, pray someday your pen name
reflects the accomplished reality of your soul.

Honey and venom

I have been in the world and of the world.
Now grown old I retire to a monk's cell.

No great hardship – the door of my chamber
shutting out the croon and roar, glamour and paste,

honey and venom of the great Illusion.
I see now: No worldly temptations

ever lured me into the streets without
the inner promptings of my tumultuous

heart and mind and (says my Beloved)
the surplus compulsions of the deceived creature

whom I once was and have for ages ever been.
To become purely a child of God, at last,

I must leave myself behind, breaking ages-old habits,
scatter the ashes and debris of my desire,

relinquish bit by bit a lifelong faith
in my illusory lack, my alias and alibi,

recognize and embrace, moment to moment,
(in new-found servitude and trust)

that dimly glimpsed part of me
that is and belongs always to my Beloved.

O child of God, another hit-and-miss attempt
to express the ineffable workings of the path.

The crust of armor

After laying down the sword
the self must unhand its shield,

climb from its crust of armor naked and doomed.
Surrender comes not only when the soldier

finds his cause hopelessly lost
but also unworthy, his rebellion needless,

his allegiances distorted, his submission righteous,
his adversary, in truth, his liberator.

And when the armor is abandoned
(per the mystics) the self proves to be

the armor itself – superfluous, illusory,
enclosing an ancient and ineffectual ghost.

O child of God, surrender is impossible without
the solace and beguilement of the Saviour.

The fisher of men

My search began as if You were a fish eluding a net!
You evaded my every snare.

All the while, the grit of my discontent
became slowly the pearl of my dependency.

O seekers! The Avatar is the fisher of men,
not amenable to being caught Himself,

apparently delighting in the unique challenge
and personal victory of individually

hooking each lover and hauling them,
exhausted and defeated, aboard His ship.

O child of God, it's not the triumph of the seeker
that leads to the Beloved – but his or her's utter defeat.

Meher's silence

I want to know Your language
(having come to the end of mine)

following Your dove-like hands
intent upon telling me the Truth,

but invariably I lose my bearings
amid the flurried sleight-of-hand.

But perhaps Your telling is not for me
to grasp the truth but to let go

of a lifetime I have taken to be true,
its reality in Your hands

proven so patently short of the mark.
Someday (You promise) I'll learn

the gist of Your immaculate fluency
and bow out of the conversation,

there having been said between us
all there ever need be said.

O child of God, so many words you use
to express your desire for Meher's silence.

The original silence

I lived for years with a silence
to which I would not pay heed.

Instead I tried to fill it with words.
It proved to be (only recently) one

not of deficiency, but of satiation –
a brimful cup – yet also the silence

of longing, like the Master's glance
rendering His lover speechless inside and out.

A silent tune to pay a mind to
rather than thought-words or the world's roar.

A silence without the cessation of noise
yet which no sound may penetrate

nor could it ever be dispelled
because it is the original silence

to which we all must return –
where the real things are given and received.

O child of God, enough of words.
Let silence speak for itself.

Signpost

There I am basking in the glow,
sitting unperturbed at Your feet

when a tumult outside the darbar
jerks me up and I hasten out

to confront the insolence and irreverence
of the intruder, the disturber of my peace.

Almost to the door (most times now),
I realize I have left without instruction

or permission Your presence,
turned my back on You; rushing away

to address the issues of my own contentions.
As my sanctimony shrivels, I skulk back,

lay my head at Your feet where I realize
I do not as yet belong in an upright body.

O child of God, anger is a signpost
letting you know you have gone astray.

The delicate efficacy

I speak again of things I know nothing about,
rather than wait until I am awake.

Periodically, my Lord leads me
down this particular garden path.

The frail limbs of my perceptions
are incapable of bearing fruit

but from His immaculate silence
and incomparable explanations,

comes the great notion that it's best
not to rely so much on what He says

(because of the language barrier)
but in Who He undoubtedly is,

taking the irrevocable plunge into utter faith,
where no parables, comparisons or analogies may reach.

O child of God, from Meher's teachings
glean the delicate efficacy of silence.

Homeland

God being infinite and endless,
how might I ever come to a conclusion!

Rather than plucking out all these loose ends
and judging the whole by the particular,

when will I feel sufficiently thwarted,
weary enough to leave my work

for the restful shade of His promise?
When will I ever trust His Word?

Enough to keep quiet,
to actually grasp its meaning

in a tongue foreign to my own –
the lost language of my homeland.

O child of God, there is a cloth spread
with bread and wine under His tender branches.

Soft spot

I've a soft spot in my heart for You.
I hope it's an early indication of ripening;

a gently expanding center of urgency.
Those of us with hardened hearts

are misjudged – our vulnerability
is why we grow the impervious rind,

adhere so firmly to the core,
our hearts remaining evergreen,

credulous, timid and pristine.
A soft spot now inside me,

pliable enough to shape into a haven,
a home, a harbor; soft enough to embrace,

to yield to, flee to without fear
and find my Self there waiting.

O child of God, slowly the fortress
is being overrun by irresistible forces of Love.

All your worldly cares

I've a pendant on a chain
that hovers near my heart,

its necklace strung with beads.
A gift from my Beloved,

I wear it into the world.
When I am quiet enough,

here and there during the day,
I feel its presence upon my skin.

No worries touch me in that faithful condition.
The things of the world carry no weight.

My hope and prayer (along the beaded chain)
is to someday know without a lapse

the wearing of that pendant, a shield
and a haven near my heart and in my mind,

an assurance as I move daily through it
that nothing in the world can touch me.

O child of God, surrender is the gift to Meher
of all your worldly cares.

A wine-soaked heart

God asked Moses if he believed in manna from heaven.
Moses couldn't answer. His once-famished mouth was full.

Jesus asked the disciples if they believed
in water turned to wine. They countered not,

their drunken lips unable to form syllables.
Bhau clamored for a wine-soaked heart

and a truth he could neither do nor say.
Where he ended up is between him and his Beloved.

I sought, apparently, spiritual intoxication.
You left me punch drunk and reeling,

bruised and (a bit fearfully) begging for more.
To say we are on the path is a trick of language.

The path is in our chest, above our chronic stumbling –
unfolding, enfolding, up and down;

twisting, turning, shaking us loose
from our ineffectual pedestrian gait.

O child of God, as a child Jesus was gentle with you.
Meher, to your great fortune, has taken off the gloves.

All or nothing

Slowed by age, my relationship
with the Friend has perked up,

wringing out, at times, from the very
heart and marrow, wine and tears.

I harbor no hope, as this intimacy
steadily grows, for a long life,

knowing, by faith, time is a fantasy.
I'll depart whenever,

at the perfect moment and while my life shall end,
(strictly speaking, by a sort of carefree conviction)

I'll keep hurtling onward without pause or lapse,
my Companion clutched to my breast,

toward the end and the Goal –
wherever the Truth may take us.

O child of God, it is all arranged, all benevolent
or else nothing, nothing, nothing matters at all.

This old vase

Even through the faithless years, I've prayed,
(in the tight spots) above the panic's roar.

These days my prayers are a shared quietude,
a silent acquiescence not so much to God

but to my nature, the innumerable lifetimes
it will take to subdue it. Asking forgiveness,

all the while believing everything is ordained and necessary.
This old vase won't hold water, cracks of fear

and well worn desire, all the habitual reasons
for turning away from the truth of God's existence

to the provisional comforts of my own.
Pure praise, said my Lord, is the best prayer.

But when I can't pluck up the courage,
muster enough sincerity then I'm left with

displaying the raw vitals of myself,
as much as I dare, for both of us to view,

using Meher's example of silence
to ask for nothing and receive my wincing due.

O child of God, live so that
your every breath becomes a prayer.

A gospel fundamental

Raised with Jesus in a fundamental way,
I abandoned later most of my faith,

lured by the usual culprits and intoxications.
It wasn't Jesus through the hard work days,

the fearsome nights I turned to for comfort.
And now that I am retired from hard work,

my Lord allows nothing much
but faith to be stored in my warehouse,

the labels dating back to childhood
when grace flowed neck-deep and freely.

A gospel fundamental enough for a child
(whom He suffered to come unto Him) –

faith and innocence necessities,
not to be discarded at the first rail stop

but clung to and employed, carried firmly
into the heart of a faithless world.

O child of God, Meher said (like Jesus)
you must become, not childish, but childlike.

Myself

I mention myself as if I know who I am.
As if I exist in the way I suppose.

Allude to my identity, which has never
revealed itself as to who I might really be.

I've never fathomed myself to see how deep I go
or grasped myself to see what I am made of.

Instead, I've gone all these years without proof
on the childish assumption that somewhere

under this skull, behind these mortal ears and eyes,
there is a definite, knowable point –

an abiding seat of judgment and resolution which is me,
continually plotting (and lifelong has)

the course of my existence – responsible for who I am,
what I do, what my life has been and will be.

All my life, I have taken myself for granted –
that I exist in the way my mind tells me I exist.

O child of God, to find out who you are
seek an authority above the mind.

The burning grounds

As the fabric unravels, the differences laid bare
between the veils of egoism

and humility's threadbare coat,
I'm painfully aware at every turn

of my habitual (quite human) culpability,
my unforced, everyday defilements of love,

becoming ever more wise to myself and penitent
yet, at each candid moment,

the shame is tinged with joy and relief –
where transgressions once passed unnoticed

each now is being led onto the burning grounds,
returned to the nothingness they are and always were.

O child of God, part of the inducement of surrender
is the abandonment of guilt and remorse.

Brimful quiet

Humility never crosses their minds –
the humble ones, nor envy their hearts,

allowing the world to go its way,
having eschewed complexity

for truth's simple fare.
Traded their wine for water

and drink of it deeply,
upholding soberness and clarity.

Like large stones on the wayside,
they let nothing sway them

or carry them away;
add nothing nor subtract.

And if they are waiting for God,
they do so without clamor or petition,

their threadbare lives brimful quiet,
cherishing the lack, doing without

the things they have long determined
have no substance or worth.

O child of God, speak of the humble ones
with all the humility you can muster.

The chime

The chime is at the mercy of the breeze,
too lightweight to resist the merest ripple,

incapable of sustaining a mute immobility
and thus its music and silence are never its own.

Repeatedly, stirrings of ire and sanctimony
jostle the chime within me, shattering all composure.

Yet, its clang and clamor is not my own!
It comes from a tempestuous source to which I have

for ages been a slave and which I now renounce;
seek to still and soften its influence; diligently

labor to insulate my gossamer susceptibilities
from the harsh winds of Maya and Mind.

O child of God, the source of discordant music
is your cracked and misshapen instrument of self.

Origin and remedy

Siddhartha chose not the path of faith but of inquiry;
a quest not for God but for the cause of human suffering.

It was truth he was after – truth of origin and remedy;
truth with its tacit certitude, whatever it turned out to be.

Centuries later, I followed truth down the Buddha path,
not a thought in the world for God, love or fidelity,

until my Lord took me aside
and said, *I am the Truth you seek;*

the One Who prompts these questions in you.
Now my quest is full-bodied, of heart and head,

faith and inquiry into the truth of Meher Baba
and the ancient path to His holy feet.

O child of God, pray one day your inquiries
become kindling for the roaring fire of conviction.

A sea of grace

Empty your heart of everything
of which you are not certain, said my Lord.

Then, you will find Me there.
True faith, apparently, comes as a last resort,

resounding in the dark alley you've been chased down,
even as you pledged over your shoulder

the undying quality of your faithless love.
It matters little how you got there.

It's all grace from here on out
as you see that it was always grace,

a sea of grace, where you will be swept along
by the tides until you drown.

O child of God, do you really want
the fate of your soul to be left in your own hands?

After the last ki jai

Certain rituals have I adopted
to commune with my Lord

between protracted stretches
where I lose Him as companion –

left in the coil of a rosary,
between the pages of a book;

or after the last ki jai.
Lost somewhere from here to there

as I wend my solitary way.
Certain rituals have I custom made

to bridge the episodic estrangement,
reacquaint myself with His everpresent

solace and mercy; rekindle the hope
of a promised prospective communion

where I shall remain continuously and then eternally
awake and aware within His holy presence.

O child of God, counter your isolation
by embracing your own non-existence.

Rawhide and bones

My mind is at a gallop in a runaway herd of horses,
a stampede through the middle of town

having lured my unhitched steed along with them.
I leap into the saddle, seize the reins,

halt my mount at the edge of town
as the wild herd disappears in a cloud of dust.

One day, You promise, my old horse
will never leave the barn,

(innumerable lifetimes from now)
whittled down to rawhide and bones.

In the meantime my occupation,
my devotion, is to You, the holy part of me,

the true part, working patiently
to rope, break and hobble the feral steed.

O child of God, you are a child also
of Sunday school mornings and Saturday matinees.

Goodwill

My Lord, being perfect, said,
give Me what I don't have –

your imperfections, urging us
to lay them freely at His feet,

not keeping them egregiously with us
nor leaving them for Him to painfully extract.

Still, every personal quirk,
tendency and failing that shapes us

(even as we seek to give them away)
shall (apparently) remain with us to the end.

It's not perfection we shall develop but love –
a universal goodwill, a generosity toward others,

a natural, unforced and spontaneous
flowing from imperfect hearts –

this being but another humble step
on the long road to Realization.

O child of God, to come under the Master's care
is to abandon all rancor and grievance.

If life is a prayer

You stood up for us – even towards the end
when You couldn't walk without help.

Insisted on Eruch reading the prayers
and You arose to participate,

mandali on either side for support,
gesturing for Eruch to go ever faster

because of the strain. *You are
named Ezad the only one worthy of worship.*

If life is a prayer I am nearing my amen.
Early on, as I was making it up, seemingly

without support from You, it never amounted
to more than a periodic, desperate plea.

But over the years, You've shown me how to pray,
(not done with me yet), incrementally

changing the heart of my prayers from I to You,
a metaphor for You becoming more and more

the heart of whoever it is offering my prayer
to Whoever it is Who receives it.

O child of God, the perfect prayer is a silent,
continuous obeisance from the very core.

A short, private prayer

I am what anyone takes Me to be, said Meher Baba.
The Highest of High (Who alone exists)

apparently reflecting and responding
to every soul according

to their existing awareness.
When the atheist declares my Lord

a madman or fraud, he is telling the truth
as per the evidence of his individual perception.

When the sophisticate smiles with condescension;
when the Buddhist nods, agreeably non-committal;

when the Christian, Muslim, Jew shouts blasphemy,
it is of no occasion for dispute or refutation

but instead the moment for a short, private prayer –
thank You, Lord, for revealing Yourself to me.

O child of God, your business is to love Him.
His business is everything else.

This old house

This old house grumbles
in the wee hours of wind and rain;

my body griping, too, lying awake –
cramped muscles, aching back,

the roil of digestion, urgency in the bladder.
Running through the usual worries, my mind,

distraught, complains of a lack of diversion
while my heart aches for refuge and peace.

But there is another part of me awake,
unmolested by all the bother –

the core of me which You have unveiled,
employing these awakenings for communion,

solace and a centering upon You,
the warmth of Your presence flowing

from the hub of my being to hush and settle
all the rancor of the peripheries.

O child of God, the storm didn't wake you.
Your Lord has called you to His court.

Remnants of the Way

Once the Way is lost, Lao Tzu taught,
then comes virtue – birthing innumerable sins,

the far-reaching and the trivial –
pride, disdain, judgment,

envy, division, exclusion . . .
inevitably creating its opposite;

setting up the incessant battle within.
All because we have strayed

from the original mandate; abandoned God
as constant Companion, inner arbiter and guide,

creating instead our own world
from the remnants of the Way,

striving without wisdom, purity or strength
to live by (and constantly failing) our own rules.

O child of God, the Way, the Truth and the Life
is the lost inheritance of each soul.

The sum of existence

Seven times seventy, instructed Jesus.
Because a grudge-bearer like myself

is not really who I am and the trespasser
is not to blame and truth is honored

in the surrender of forgiveness.
The culprit being a provisional, apparently

essential, impostor sorting out and managing
the mind's disparate sensations

but errant in its identification with the body
and mind, creating within each of us

an artificial separation from the sum of existence.
Self-perpetuating, without compunction,

navigating illusion, keeping us rigidly
to the karmic path, but that ill-borne personality,

impermanent and transitional,
is not (as per my Lord) who I am.

I am the Self, a God-infused,
love-instilled, eternal ocean-drop of soul.

O child of God, compare the Oneness of God
to the cramped duality of your inner being.

Ashes and dust

To deny the self is to invest in the concept of self.
To practice non-attachment is to be attached to a practice.

Lovers should instead fasten themselves,
(as per Meher) like dust to the Beloved's damaan –

one attachment to burn away all others;
the self reduced to ashes and dust.

Ashes and dust on His skirt, His feet and sandals,
outside His threshold lying quietly

until He briefly enters or departs,
His lovers then stirred up in His wake,

whirling like dervishes in their insubstantiality.
O lovers, true non-attachment comes

from seizing roughly the hem of His garment
and holding on for dear life.

O child of God, make Meher your world
and He will become your sole attachment.

Wordplay

Perhaps, the promise of eternal bliss
is merely a bright carrot

for those of us stuck in mortal fear,
a vague but appealing image

in our imperfect capacity and experience,
leading us farther along the journey.

The Avatar is limited by language,
flesh and circumstance,

by the inviolate laws of the Game itself
and, within those parameters,

incapable of describing the indescribable,
explaining the inexplicable or delivering precisely

the workings of the One infinite and eternal God.
Meher declared Himself free of all promises

and emphasized He did not come to teach.
What He seems to have done is brought down God

to dwell among us and touch each of our lives
in a host of unfathomable and incommunicable ways.

O child of God, rely not on promise nor wordplay
but on the here and now presence of His divine Love.

Barakoti

Twelve Coats danced for joy
when he stood before his Beloved

yet he would not remove his coats.
Threadbare and ragged, odious with filth,

he had not the faith to part with
that which routinely embraced him,

sheltered and insulated him from the world.
Baba's Presence enlivened the old man

but not enough to let him slip out from under
a lifetime of accumulated concealment and buffer,

shed his superstitions (with their dubious protection)
and grant him the courage to dance naked before his Lord.

O child of God, you know almost nothing about Barakoti;
maybe just enough to use him innocuously as a metaphor.

Know it all

Lying on the beach, eyes closed;
enjoying the heat of the sun,

a soft wind, the roar of the waves.
An old man ambles up.

Wagging his finger, he says,
'You're responsible for this – the sun, the sky,

the sea, the beach have all come out of you'.
I nod and tell him they're probably

looking for him back at the nursing home.
He wanders off down the beach.

I roll over to get some sun on my back
and wake up in my bed in the middle of the night.

O child of God, when you become certain
of just one thing, you will know it all.

In transition

I'm not a pilgrim, apparently.
I'm a jewel encased in stone.

Not in transit, but in attrition
from accoutrements to essence.

There are no way stations, only stages,
the destination under my bulk.

Nowhere to go but to the Lord
Who is everywhere and already with me.

Nothing to do but do as I'm told,
not in words but by circumstance.

My life has only the meaning I give it
and when I reach the truth I apparently am,

my life will have no meaning at all – like God,
which is Who I am and all of this, too.

O child of God, keep trying to put it into words –
the impossible task your Beloved has granted you.

Wallflower peace

I've got this song stuck in my head.
It's got a good beat. I give it a 95.

When will I cease dancing to its tune?
Get caught up instead in the silence of my Lord?

Trade in these irksome gyrations
for the wallflower peace

of obeisance and remembrance;
quit the cotillion irrevocably

for my Lord's chamber.
Have us there a marathon

here-and-now heart to heart,
me folded up securely at His feet,

silent and rapt, enchanted
by His ancient song of love.

O child of God, do not absent yourself
for a moment, advised Hafiz.

God-glimpse

An infinite Being has no place to hide.
No room or reason to sidestep.

Is obvious and Self-evident,
negating the need for a search.

Like a deranged soul racing the asylum grounds
trying to run down his hallucinations,

there is nowhere in infinite illusion
to leave where God is not

nor escape to where God is more
attainable and tangible than He is

at the moment, wherever it is we happen to be.
Only a clear-eyed, unadorned God-glimpse

is the difference between here and there,
perhaps mercifully to be granted at appointed times,

whenever we turn up vigilant and avid,
of the One eternal, all-inclusive Reality.

O child of God, step away from duality by thinking
no longer in terms of movement, time and place.

The remote promise

It doesn't take much to become dust.
I mean, it's not like you start out a hero.

You have not to yield anything of real value.
Not a sacrifice really but the overseeing of a collapse.

It takes obstinacy, mind you, an obsessive vigilance;
persistence through constant failure;

a disheartening familiarity
with your own depthless inadequacy;

faith in the remote promise of a distant victory
constructed upon utter defeat.

But what else is there to do when your Beloved
rouses in you the first inchoate stirrings of humility?

When He speaks of love and you discover your poverty,
your heart aloof and non-comprehending?

What else to do with the shame from a lifetime
of duplicity, mistrust and a dearth of pity?

What else to do when your effort might bring
a brief smile, a nod of the head from your Lord

while you both wait for the one miracle
He promised He has come to perform?

O child of God, what else on God's green earth
has more value than the dust gathered at Meher's feet?

The beast in the parlor

The elephant in the dark is the elephant in the room.
So dominant is its presence, its size and strength,

that we grab on early to a nearby part,
shape ourselves grotesquely around it,

settle as best we might
into our fixed and jostled, adversarial lives.

It's not really there (we've been told by mystics of every stripe).
Done with shadows, suggestion, smoke and mirrors.

But almost no one ever hears nor fathoms what they hear.
The Avatar has come to lead us away –

to disbelieve the beast in the parlor,
the evident and the obvious

and believe instead in Him, abandoning
forever (almost entirely upon faith)

the readily apparent elephant, our twisted response
and the dark house of our enchantment.

O child of God, the truth is explored when the seeker
becomes vastly indifferent to the obvious charade.

Another poem

If you have any complaints, take it up with management.
God welcomes our grievances if we lay them at His feet.

He knows (apparently) even our deepest grief,
our direst travails, somehow will be

of little consequence in the light of Truth.
So it returns to faith. I've run away from faith

all my life, demanding proof but proof is evidently,
in every circumstance, well, circumstantial.

And certitude is the great Illusion.
Funny thing is, after all these years

refusing to embrace faith, faith has begun
to embrace me, obliquely

and at the most unexpected moments,
revealing my hidden prejudices and presumptions,

errors in logic, offering me one or more alternatives
to every shred of damning evidence I uncover.

O child of God, your faith is strongest when the Beloved
gives you another poem to write.

Devoted inquiry

All we have is His name. And mindful remembrance
to draw nearer to Him. And perhaps, devoted inquiry –

not from any acuity we might possess, but perhaps
useful in articulating our latent heart's desire,

a personal extension of God's inquiry – Who am I?
The setting aside of earthly concerns,

the turning and narrowing of our will
from egocentric survival

to a God-centered exploration
of the One Eternal Source and Goal –

the only possible true purpose
(if there is one) of our existence.

O child of God, outside the realm of duality,
inquiry is grace – another gift from God.

Gather your people

The story of Noah and the Ark –
those who believe it are labeled literalists,

often deemed silly, deluded people of faith –
treated much like Noah himself.

But those who mock them,
are they not literalists, also?

Dismissing the story out of hand,
its origin and development

without an attempt to explain
how and why it has survived millenniums,

nor appraise its import and value
concerning our relationship with God.

God and Noah walked stem to stern
inspecting the constructed ark.

God approved of Noah's effort and care,
his obedience, loyalty and rock-ribbed *faith*.

He said, Gather your people aboard.
You are all safe now – whether it rains or not.

O child of God, the value of faith in our lives
goes far beyond the obvious and the literal.

The Sole Doer

'Attribute everything to Me,' said Meher Baba.
'Have the full and firm faith of Baba as the sole doer.'

I look around at God and listen to Him.
I smell, touch and taste God.

I study Him in my head and body;
trace His movements in my heart.

I attempt the faith of experiencing Him
as being everywhere and doing everything,

praying one day by grace to realize
the truth of my faith and disappear

within the everything of God.
A method and meditation divinely sent my way,

seemingly patterned on a sixth plane pilgrim
who we are told sees God everywhere

until he knows Himself to also be God,
the Sole Doer, the One without a second.

O child of God, how to search for your Self
when God alone exists?

The symphony of Existence

When everything is attuned, settled
and still, there can be no music.

Required is an adversarial arrangement,
artfully constructed – the bow across the neck –

a violation of the once quiescent strings;
the air trembling into a carefully shaped emptiness

and music is formed from components
which alone and inert make no sound.

And if everything is infinitely One,
perfect, absolute, attuned and quiescent,

it takes an illusory breach, tension and division
to draw the bow and quiver the strings,

to create the moment to moment performance
of the singular symphony of Existence.

O child of God, have faith in the utter necessity
of every aspect of God's composition.

Of birdsong caliber

If ever this poetry could touch the dulcet chirruping of
birdsong,
each word's import would become superfluous to its charm.

Nonsense syllables would be at its heart,
the gist of a riddle giving everyone a good laugh;

each poem an ornament hung from the neck,
a stud in the lobe of an ear, a beauty that speaks for itself

rather than this old hair shirt cut to fit, dutifully gilding
the dissonance and duplicity of both words and thought.

This birdsong poetry would then take flight
and I would follow, no longer grounded

by my inarticulacy, ignorance and desire.
Truth and beauty would appear together onstage,

in pure harmony singing the story of existence –
a love song without meaning beyond the telling of the tale,

the love that creates and sustains it
and the love of which it is constructed.

O child of God, if ever you are able to write poems
of birdsong caliber, you will have no need for words.

A life edgeways

I've never had much to do with today
(where You say all the action is)

always barreling through to tomorrow
or sifting through yesterday's ashes.

So when have I ever had time
to fit in a life edgeways?

Never had much to do with
where You say the opportunity is,

too unsettled to function easily within it.
You keep calling me back, though, to explore

the here-and-now God and let go of everything else –
even the components of my present moments,

staring at the puzzle before my eyes until I make out
the one Reality You say is hidden among the extraneous;

extricate God and myself from the very idea
of Him and me and just who in the world we really are.

O child of God, when you look for God
(said Rumi), God is in the look of your eyes.

My trembling fingers

I've never come near to humility
but I've admired it from afar.

I was raised neck-deep in it,
a down-to-earth natural position

where the power and grace of God
was an evident firsthand everyday experience

yet my own humility early on gave way
to shame and pride and then a lifelong duplicity.

Baba would sometimes ask (as a test)
a would-be disciple to walk the streets naked.

My mind explores the possibility
but my trembling fingers

can't unfasten and remove my clothing.
It was humility lost long ago in the Garden

(the essence of innocence) and it is shame to this day
that keeps God's children hidden among the leaves.

O child of God, humility is the nakedness
required to learn at last who you really are.

Where is the gamble?

Certitude is not required to start down this path,
just the lifelong lack of a workable alternative.

What's at stake here? A few more years
of inadequacy, fraught with dread and sorrow?

Garbed in the world, I become its infinitesimal center.
I'm not cut out to be a Qutub! –

the ill-shaped cogs and wheels, bolts and gears
screech and grind, sparking in their turn.

Not certitude but a verification comes
in the quiet fluidity of my daily practice.

When I wrap myself in the Beloved's sadra,
I begin to disappear in His eternal Presence

as does also this tainted world to which
I do not (and never once did) belong.

O child of God, if the Beloved does it all
and does it with love, where is the gamble?

The One calling you

Enticed by the promise of annihilation,
dust as the goal instead of paradise,

chances are you never were
much enamored of yourself.

Perhaps some sort of epiphany
has shaken the reasonableness from your bones

or the unexpected purity and sincerity
of the One who offers the barter

has overcome your fear of death.
Ask for nothing, the Master says, and you might

have always believed nothing is what you deserve.
Still, a proposal of renunciation and servitude,

ending with annihilation is an odd enticement.
Maybe you have considered all along

yourself a mistake –
that there needs to be a correction.

You've known it deep down forever
and longed for your lonely light

to be extinguished or outshone –
made extraneous by the eternal light of its Maker.

O child of God, the One calling you
is the One you have been awaiting for ages.

Become the sought

Fool that I am, I have searched for You all these years –
the One Who is everywhere and in everything.

I'm not sure of what I'm seeking
but You've given it a name: Meher Baba.

I suppose I'm nearer the goal after all this time.
I've no way to gauge the distance.

You didn't come to teach
and I've learned nothing of consequence.

Either I am You or Your creature
or somehow both and I'll end up with You

some lifetime or another – or not.
You might never be mine

but just the same I belong to You.
I may be a fool but I'm Your fool,

hoping to die
with Your name on my lips.

O child of God, Meher said stop seeking
and become the sought.

The auspices of Meher

To live my best in this dream life,
I am told by faith (until I awaken)

to trade it in for a different sort of dream,
shrugging off the old, taking up the new

under the aegis of the Perfect Seeker,
unheralded and itinerant

through the heart of the world but not of it.
Guard my tongue, ignore my compulsions;

forsake perceptions; my opinions of no more
consequence than the peeping of a bird.

Drift through the New Life with a Companion divine,
the one true Friend, nurturing that relationship

and fellowship until I awaken my Self
at dream's end to the promised eternal Reality of God.

O child, abandon yourself to the auspices of Meher,
the One and only Truth there is.

God's endless existence

Done 100%, He said;
all that urgent business

fitted into one lifetime.
While on the eternal side of the veil

tranquility ever reigns.
The Avatar has His mission

over the cycles of time, while God
has no unfinished business whatsoever.

Perfect equanimity knows no urgency.
No need for us to grow fearful or impatient

with God's endless existence
and Baba's completed work all plotted out,

unfolding inviolate and precise,
each soul having already arrived on schedule

at the same timeless moment
in the realm of the perfect and eternal.

O child of God, illusion makes possible God's game.
Don't get caught up in its imperatives.

Dust-speck existence

I have been made aware that Your universal work,
done in seclusion long ago, included me,

not as a dust-speck in the cosmos
but as a companion on the new life road.

Those last human years, painfully at prayer,
alone in the bus or in Your room,

fist pounding to keep the connection – with me,
among others in our gross plane lives.

I was long in the body by then, halfway around the world
and in some unfathomable, intimate way, You reached me

through a childhood and adolescent Jesus,
revealing the ruin and insolvency of the world,

retrieving me from my own seclusion and dust-speck existence
to reunite with You, consciously connected,

moving briskly down the road toward freedom
from the bindings of self, body, time, ignorance and fear.

O child of God, everything is happening here and in the
moment.
The Godman knows no boundaries of space or time.

Very much in play

Years ago I decided it would be best
to surrender to my Beloved,

trying ever after to talk my heart into it.
Intractable, quavering, non-committal,

what could I say at this point to sway the jury?
So these days I keep quiet.

It's an unhanding now I know,
a facing up, a sorting out;

a painful, bit by bit, incursion and endeavor,
yielding by inches the sovereign native soil.

It would be best, I long ago decided,
to surrender to Meher Baba and since that day

His wondrous, enigmatic unfolding within me
is still very much in play.

O child of God, you've never had the sole authority
to so radically decide your fate.

The only Way

The Lord of Mercy is wielding His sword,
deflating my pretensions, exposing my duplicity,

pointing out irrefutably what a villain
I am, have been, ever will be.

Behind these whitewashed walls,
my egregious sins are buried in the backyard,

disowned and denied even to myself.
The reflection in His unsheathed sword

reveals myself to me. He allows no turning aside.
And thus I am nearer to His grace and expertise –

the only Way there is to deconstruct this sad contradiction,
get me whittled down to the one worthy purpose

for which and for Whom I was created –
to serve my Lord, a slave of His love.

O child of God, fear not His honest blade
slicing through the bindings of Maya.

The beginning of surrender

I can't do this alone. I'm no warrior.
I'm a lover lost in his own dream; no match

for my ageless opponent of which my Lord
has given me a harrowing and disheartening glimpse.

Thank God, I'm not at that one's mercy (he has none)
but at the mercy of the Father of Mercy.

My orders now are to wrap myself in my Lord's bright flag;
allow my enemy to languish outside the gates.

With this method little valor is required,
yet few lovers take it on until each is shown

the bottomless depravity of the adversary within.
An incomprehensible battle it is

to the death and beyond,
but it's no longer mine to fight.

Such is the beginning of surrender.
Only the Beloved with His divine grace,

His sure swift sword can be the One
to gain the ultimate victory.

O child of God, one of the path's inherent difficulties
is the divided loyalty of the lover.

The idol

How full of virtue is the false self!
How easily it hides among its subtleties,

conjuring up on demand any and all
righteous attributes to further its own cause.

Empathy, benevolence, patience, generosity –
you name it – the false self has it in store.

An impostor to the aspirant as well as to others.
If you don't know yet how low the ego can go

and are not frightened by it, then you remain,
o pilgrim, outside the palace court,

far from the renunciation required,
the urgency and the heart to break free

from the tyranny and manipulation of the idol
which dominates your existence.

O child of God, turning to the Beloved usually
involves an intense disenchantment with one's self.

The next rising phenomenon

Everything comes from nothing and goes back.
From nowhere, anger, for instance, appears

and briefly I claim it. I *am* anger until it fades
and I become whatever next appears.

So it is with all experience. It rises, I identify with it;
it fades and I latch onto the next rising phenomenon.

Even physical existence apparently comes and goes this way –
comes from nothing each moment and each moment returns

creating the illusion of continuity and substance.
And in all of this coming and going,

where is there room for I, me, my and mine?
Everything comes from nothing and goes back.

Attaching myself to this procession of experiences,
I call that me. I am that. That is mine.

If I yell and shake my fist at God,
it is God shaking His fist at Himself,

my raised voice as meaningless and natural as thunder,
my shaking fist a tree branch in a brisk wind.

O child of God, in all of infinite existence
there is no room for the separate self.

Mime and pantomime

I don't have any answers.
I don't have any questions.

You know my words before I speak.
I know nothing of Your language.

To my chatter of fearful irrelevancies,
Your replies only echo

my own inadequate vocabulary.
Yet, even with all this, I swear

I am getting nearer to the Truth.
The Truth of You and Your silent Presence.

I don't know how it works –
this mime and pantomime!

But I beg You, Lord – keep up the conversation.
Let me hear and come to know better than my own

that voice of Yours not formed by a human mouth
and heard only in the broken-open human heart.

O child of God, Meher's silence forms the one Word
you have been ever longing to hear.

The perfect aspect

Meher said, Together we must love God.
But how might my self ever love

when love by its nature is devoid of self?
I pledge only an allegiance – with which I barter

for protection and prosperity;
for favor in His sight;

peace and health in the body
and promises later of heaven, union, bliss.

What sort of love is this?
Yet, apparently we must

love God however poorly –
love being the perfect aspect

of our imperfect selves
and God being not only the one

worthy object of love, but in Truth,
the sole Being to love in all of Existence.

O child, love God and through love
become God.

A tinge of truth

I've called it as I've seen it and though it seems
I've acquired a bit of knowledge along the way,

there's no need to amend my previous assertions
because everything on the path is true

at one point or another and it does not become
false later, merely belayed or transcended.

Meanwhile, the truth of my Self
(the seed from whence this poetry arises)

is inviolable, untouchable and eternal.
These poems concern illusion,

only hinting at the Truth beyond.
All I know of God is a hint, a beauty,

a faint, brief suggestion of That
which is unknowable and indescribable.

O child of God, words fail you again
yet there's a tinge of truth in every poem your write.

Take a hike

Take a hike and don't stop until you are atop
a distant hill, looking down upon everything,

especially yourself, your thoughts and moods.
Go until you get outside of the dream.

Not a far piece really – a hair's breadth away;
a hundred millenniums' distance.

You know you will have arrived when you are
able to view yourself and the world fearlessly

but not at all benumbed or sedated.
All your cleverness will have vanished by then

along with your strategies and worries.
You'll be obliged to come up with nothing.

It will all be done for you. Take a hike
and arrive where you always were,

being the being you truly are,
dreaming the dream from an elevated view

and realize forever you have hiked
and climbed all the way to the journey's end.

O child of God, get the true perspective
by getting just a hair outside yourself.

A bodhisattva effect

It's selfish to desire liberation (however phrased):
union, bliss, realization; to be free from affliction

when it means abandoning in our attainment
our loved ones (as well as the whole of humanity).

Yet, how might an imperfect,
in-the-flesh sufferer offer any assistance

toward liberating others while hopelessly
entangled in the same snare?

The object of liberation is not our human selves,
but the Godly Self within each of us –

the cleaving of the bonds, the clearing of the veils
that bind the true Self to Illusion;

that prevent Truth from knowing Itself as True.
Surely if we are One, with every individual liberation

there is a bodhisattva effect of some sort
beyond the incarnated self, a universal

further shifting of the tides, one day to sweep
every entrapped soul out to sea; to dissolve

(for however long forever is)
the illusory separation of God from God.

O child of God, use imagination and rationalization
to keep you focused on the eventual Reunion.

Walk of life

Do we not all go by God's grace
whatever walk of life we tread?

Grace to counter the dominance of Mind,
Maya's deception, the dishonesty

of an ego without compunction.
These malefic three creating the illusion

within each ordinary human being
of superiority, distinction, enislement

and the resulting blame and disavowal of others.
Jesus, Baba, Saint Francis each embraced lepers

in our shared humanity but also as a symbol
of the disfigurement and adulteration

each of us suffer, must uncover
and accept in ourselves and others.

We've been tricked out of our humility
and prohibited from our righteous service

as the slaves of God we could be, the slaves
to Mercy and Grace and eternal Oneness.

O child of God, the difficult-to-grasp truth is
that we all receive the same beneficent grace of God.

In a motel lobby

Feel heavy these days, though I'm skin and bones,
trudging the path I once raced down.

Not much I care to see with these dimming eyes,
while nearer to death I seem to or pretend to

make out more distinctly Baba's ineffable silence.
Inured now to a mystery that no longer seems a barrier,

merely a depthless realm offering no sure footing.
Innumerable ages I've been wandering,

seeking the door to my own heart
while God, motionless in His infinity,

needless in His oneness, sated in His omniscience,
heartless in His incorporeality is posted forever

on both sides of a door that does not exist.
I wonder what goes on here.

Where there is a search there is a presumed deficiency.
These are just words I write in my ignorance and need.

Something to pass the time –
like reading a dated magazine in a motel lobby.

O child of God, don't lose heart.
You're not alone in your quest to find the Father.

The long remainder

He said in His silence He is always speaking
and His words have come to us

as well as His silent universal work.
Came and became and has become

and always was and is an essential component
of the world's collective and individual karma

whether one knows Him or not.
We don't find our Redeemer after a long search,

then choose to follow Him. Way back,
at time's genesis, He chose us, at the birth

of the soul-flight, the existential diaspora.
Chose us for whatever appointed time we come

into His Godman orbit and embrace,
to take His hand and as always and ever,

be delivered the long remainder
of the illusory journey home.

O child of God, the work of the Avatar is too vast
and timeless for the human mind to grasp.

An immaculate surrender

My virtue splayed before me like a dealt hand,
the subtle grime of conceit on every card I play –

my righteousness as dishonest as my sins.
How might a false self ever prove true?

Redemption, say the mystics,
lies in an immaculate surrender

to the One beyond duality,
beyond the Mind, at One with fate,

attempting not to discern
and extract my true Self

from the torrents of illusory impulses
but by disavowing my existence whole cloth,

all I am compelled to think, say and do
by the inviolate raveling and unraveling of my karma.

O child of God, the truth of you
lies beyond the veils of Illusion.

Until love dawns

At first I trusted everything as real.
Myself, my life, my world. Then I met You

and I soon began to question everything,
finding not one plausible place to stand.

After all these years I've come to know
I must trust by faith everything

as being (real or not) God-ordained,
my human existence, however impermanent,

perfectly suited to fit my soul and God's scheme;
my unrevealed and indefinable self

a divinely structured vessel shaped for God's use
to answer His one question

and unveil Himself to Himself as God.
If I am to trust anything there's nothing else

to trust but God. God is everything.
To trust everything is to trust God.

O child of God, trust in God is the only
feasible approach until love dawns.

The ancient Chandler

God bless the Candlemaker and the candle
lighted within each of our chests. God bless

the projected light and shadow images
flickering upon the curtained screen,

emerging from the tumultuous awakening
of God within us. God bless the candleglow

illuminating each drop soul, defining its boundaries,
disclosing its purity, eventually to reveal

its origin and essence. God bless
the lighting of one candle by another;

the flame of longing and the mingling of light.
God bless the yielding of darkness

and the opening of the gates.
God bless the ancient Chandler,

His duty to perform – the dispelling
of darkness by the light of Love.

O child of God, if you must use words to describe
Meher's Light, then you have not yet begun to burn.

The Source of grace

In my youth I assembled
the great puzzle of the universe,

God being the only left out piece
which was fine with me.

It felt like freedom, yet fear
lurked in the interstices

and I was soon sick with it: afraid
of freedom; afraid of myself.

My universe now long since broken into rubble,
it was grace that led me through;

a life of grace I in no way deserved
nor understood at the time

and yet now I ask for more – instructed
to ask for nothing, I ask God for more –

the grace of being the Source of grace,
forever free and no longer afraid.

O child of God, annihilation in Union
is the only refuge. Your self is made of fear.

Our rendezvous with destiny

Baba on route to the rendezvous in Prague
instructed Elizabeth to pull off the road,

where He paced the shoulder deep within Himself,
urging Elizabeth later to drive faster

upon the rain slickened two lane.
Only in retrospect can we note the calculation –

having to be at a certain spot
at the precisely scheduled moment.

When we have seemingly failed again our Beloved,
sidetracked, distracted, rather than

dwell upon our guilt and discouragement
might we not view our lapse

as God's adjustment to the pace
of our divinely scheduled arrival? –

humbled yet heartened by the faith that we are
doing nothing and God is doing everything,

in total control, down the long winding highway
to our rendezvous with destiny.

O child of God, repent of your shortcomings
but don't overestimate your clout.

The blessedness

Your name was once a plea I made for mercy.
Now it's an anointment and a benediction.

Now it's a speechlessness and a shelter.
Eruch described it as a beholden.

He was talking about the blessedness
of being at Your mercy –

the blessedness of being at Your mercy.
Beholden to You, a relationship

wherein the pardon is mine to receive
and Yours alone to give.

The blessedness of being at Your mercy –
the Father of mercy

in our one and only intimacy
before the two become One.

O child of God, Meher answered your beggary
with the only coin in His purse.

The love of which He spoke

Bent deep in the pretzel-shaped body and mind of Zen,
I was confused when I first read of Meher Baba

and His emphasis on love. What has love,
I wondered, to do with enlightenment?

Soon I was off myself down the path of Love,
finding that the love of which He spoke

was not my kind of love but the God-is-Love-kind.
Groping for an approximate synonym,

I settled for Oneness – something to do with Oneness.
Lately, I've employed a more startling substitute –

Love is another word for annihilation;
for the flames of self-immolation.

Meher Baba's kind of Love is the Love
my intact self will never be able to fully

give or receive, only able to become Love Itself
through obliteration and non-existence.

O child of God, meditate on Love
from the viewpoint of God's aloneness.

God, by definition

I'm idling at a stop sign, free to turn east or west.
God's not in the seat next to me wondering which way I'll go.

God knows. God, by definition, already knows.
How is my own will free if God already knows?

And where might enter in, any idea of personal freedom?
East or west, whichever direction I choose

is and will always be determined by an authority
greater than chance or circumstance, greater than myself.

Determined by the Oneness of God's vision
and the assigned sovereignty of my personal unfolding destiny.

O child of God, the value of your musings
is your subsequent focus upon God the Beloved.

Oneness lost

Adam and Eve bit into the apple
and tasted loneliness – the One become three,

shame and shyness before the Father
and one another as sin began

to bloom in each private darkness.
We are trying yet to be no longer alone,

to be trusted and trust, to be loved and love
while concealing our naked fear.

The purpose of our every move is to get back
to that original paradise, merely a distant

memory now within our blood and bones;
our loneliness an ancient longing

for the Father in the Garden
and the restoration of Oneness lost.

O child of God, let the wine of Meher
remove that bitter taste from your mouth.

The Mystery of mysteries

The Mystery can't be spoken say the Masters,
but it is (apparently) embodied by the Living Word

Who may or may not choose to converse
beyond the pronouncements of His own Presence.

Speaking of the Mystery, I always come to the point
where I don't know the definitions of the words I use,

like having learned a foreign language by rote.
But I'm told it's *my* language, an exile raised

where the duality of words and meanings
are too limited and primitive to explain

or contain the Mystery of mysteries;
Thus, a stranger am I, on a foreign shore

praying to become dumbstruck forever
by a mere whisper of the original Word.

O child of God, incessantly the wordsmith
points out the essential pointlessness of speech.

According to His will

Baba said we could please Him
by having no thoughts, words or deeds

we would not hesitate
to think, say or do in His presence.

A way He has given us, I thought,
to strictly tend to our kindness and virtue.

Years later, I came across Eruch's elucidation.
It's mostly about remembrance, He said –

our making a provisional reality (unto ourselves)
of the ultimate Reality that Baba is

the divine Companion. Remembrance
by feeling we are always in His presence,

mindful of His wishes and seeking
righteously at every moment

to think, speak and act
according to His will.

O child of God, the Godman's teachings
exemplify the Oneness of God.

Your tomblike silence

I've adjusted my theories about You,
at times, but I've held firmly onto them.

Whether they be right or wrong,
I don't know what I'm talking about.

I know You not at all; You know my every sin.
You are ever clothed in the divine mystery;

I am naked and ashamed, afraid
to be in the same room with You,

cooped up in Your tomblike silence.
I keep up this chatter to escape

Your soundless, fearsome intimacy.
When I run out of questions

I'll be totally at Your mercy, just as I am now
but with no words with which to pretend otherwise.

O child of God, the truth you are seeking
will never be on your side.

Lies to myself

When His truth reveals the pattern of lies
I've told myself, the lies my self has told me,

annihilation seems nearer to being the mere
erasing of a mistake, the removal of a rotten plank.

Numerous sins the lies cover and compound
drenching me in unworthiness and dread.

But my Lord tells me ignorance, not evil,
is the cause of sin and dishonesty,

each dispelled by truth – with lies (to myself)
being nearest at hand and the obvious place to start.

Ignorance dispelled. The learning of myself.
Realization of the truth – the truth of karma,

of Oneness, the truth that I am not the sinner
but the immaculate, awakening drop soul of God.

O child of God, Meher said, God is Perfect Honesty
and you are, in Reality, One with God.

The plundering of the apple tree

When God shaped the clay into Adam and Eve,
He knew already of the trespassing to come,

the eating of the forbidden fruit. Violation
of Oneness was the sin in the garden;

Oneness in which there is no personal liability.
His creatures became sinners

by trespassing into individuality; in duality
finding themselves opposed to their Creator.

The truth is they were and we still are
wholly one with God and His divine will

(such as the plundering of the apple tree),
their sin and ours, their guilt and ours,

tied up not in Reality but in the Illusion
of otherness and alienation.

O child of God, there's nothing doing outside
God's will and without the sinner, there is no sin.

The paling of my enclosure

It's hard to get to know another.
We rarely see more than the bars of their cage.

Hard for me to show myself, as I pace and roar,
only dimly aware of my own captivity,

yet ever conscious of my vulnerability,
letting not others near enough

to see between the paling of my enclosure.
What we fear and detest in others

is not the poor ensnared creature within
but the barrier erected to keep others out.

Add to that our own defenses and a double bind exists
that each heart's lament rarely penetrates.

One of the difficulties in breaking from our cage,
even in our staunchest resolve,

is that in our exposure we encounter still
the repellent bars of other cages

which sends us scurrying back
to the safety and sanctimony of our own.

O child of God, the Avatar comes along,
an assortment of keys jangling from His belt.

An obscure remembrance

Comes a point in every sojourn where comparable
is the world to cotton candy laced with razor blades.

Nothing but pain and injury in which to sink our teeth;
our tongues sated but hunger undiminished

by its gossamer, sugary nothingness while every
beautiful and meaningful thing is glimpsed

through the fleeting windows of an outbound train.
On the platform, cherished ones distantly holding

each other in our similarly impotent arms; at the mercy
ever of unassailable flesh, time and schedule.

It's more than a delicate hope
that counters the dream's insistence;

draws the sojourner to the eternal; more than fate –
the yearning of the part for the whole.

It is an obscure remembrance deeper than time;
the briefly beheld and faintly tasted lure

of a love beyond our humanity yet which is
the timeless, hinted at essence of our existence.

O child of God, transcendence is possible
once you lose your taste for sweetness.

Your timid heart

I've been headstrong on this path, I know;
refused to follow, refused to lead;

trekking my way alone if I must.
Envisioning my insights as revelation,

sacrosanct and peculiar to me. Headstrong,
yet all the while, since I fell into Meher's orbit,

I've longed to become heartstrong instead –
like Baba motioning to LePage: Be mighty in My love!

I have come lately to see I lack the equipment –
not like a rabbit wishing to be a bear,

more like a bear wishing to be a lion –
just as futile perhaps but not as far-fetched.

I am to continue pondering then – calculate,
surmise, question and opine; move nearer

to my Lord through my individual, God-given
relationship, attributes and talents, enough,

more than enough, to see me through
this lifetime and into the next.

O child of God, follow your destiny
and leave your timid heart to Meher.

Join the club

So you know not who you are.
Join the club, o weary traveler.

Nor where you are bound.
Cheer up, my long lost friend!

Even God (we are told), when He awoke
this time around could only groggily

ask of Himself – Who am I?
Surely we are meant to learn the answer –

to our question and God's – simultaneously
at the inevitable point of our ultimate culmination.

The answer to the question God asked first;
whispered into the back of everyone's mind,

propelling our search for the answer; the whole driving force
behind our ceaseless desires, behind this infinite, circular,

eternally revolving inner and outer cosmos –
Who am I, o God? Who am I and Who are You?

O child of God, it's more than a question,
deserving of so much more than an answer.

www.ingramcontent.com/pod-product-compliance
Lightning Source LLC
Chambersburg PA
CBHW060238100426
42742CB00011B/1571